WileyPLUS Learning Space

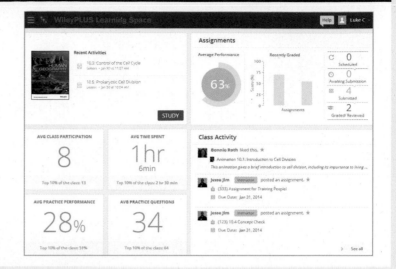

An easy way to help your students learn, collaborate, and grow.

Personalized Experience

Students create their own study guide while they interact with course content and work on learning activities.

Flexible Course Design

Educators can quickly organize learning activities, manage student collaboration, and customize their course—giving them full control over content as well as the amount of interactivity between students.

Clear Path to Action

With visual reports, it's easy for both students and educators to gauge problem areas and act on what's most important.

Instructor Benefits

- Assign activities and add your own materials
- Guide students through what's important in the interactive e-textbook by easily assigning specific content
- Set up and monitor collaborative learning groups
- Assess learner engagement
- Gain immediate insights to help inform teaching

Student Benefits

- Instantly know what you need to work on
- Create a personal study plan
- Assess progress along the way
- Participate in class discussions
- Remember what you have learned because you have made deeper connections to the content

We are dedicated to supporting you from idea to outcome.

WILEY

HUMAN GEOGRAPHY

People, Place, and Culture

SECOND CANADIAN EDITION

Erin H. Fouberg
Northern State University

Catherine J. Nash
Brock University

Alexander B. Murphy
University of Oregon

H. J. de Blij
Michigan State University

WILEY

Library and Archives Canada Cataloguing in Publication
Fouberg, Erin Hogan, author
Human geography: people, place, and culture/Erin H. Fouberg
(Northern State University), Catherine J. Nash (Brock
University), Alexander B. Murphy (University of Oregon),
H.J. de Blij (Michigan State University).—Second Canadian edition.

Issued in print and electronic formats.
Includes bibliographical references and index.
ISBN 978-1-119-02281-7 (bound).—ISBN 978-1-119-04544-1 (loose-leaf)
—ISBN 978-1-119-05072-8 (pdf)

1. Human geography—Textbooks.   I. Nash, Catherine J., 1958-,
author   II. Murphy, Alexander B., 1954-, author   III. De Blij, Harm J., author
IV. Title.

GF41.H893 2015   304.2   C2015-902470-6

Production Credits
VP & Director of Market Solutions: Veronica Visentin
Senior Marketing Manager: Patty Maher
Editorial Manager: Karen Staudinger
Production and Media Specialist: Meaghan MacDonald
Developmental Editor: Gail Brown
Media Editor: Luisa Begani
Editorial Assistant: Maureen Lau
Interior Design: Joanna Vieira
Cover Design: Joanna Vieira
Cover Image: © Tan Yilmaz/Getty Images
Typesetting: Aptara Inc.
Printing and Binding: Courier

Printed and bound in the United States of America
1 2 3 4 5 CC 19 18 17 16 15

John Wiley & Sons Canada, Ltd.
5353 Dundas Street West, Suite 400
Toronto, ON, M9B 6H8 Canada
Visit our website at: www.wiley.ca

PREFACE

Welcome to the second Canadian edition of *Human Geography: People, Place, and Culture*. The goal for this edition was to build on the strengths of the first edition, in light of very helpful and positive feedback from students, professors, and reviewers. A global perspective remains of central and critical importance to our understandings of the intricate and complicated interrelationships between people and places across constantly shifting and multiple scales—the human-environment relationship. In updating the Canadian edition, it was important to ensure that a geographically specific Canadian focus was maintained while positioning that focus within the political, economic, and social global networks. This was achieved in three main ways:

- By using Canadian examples in conjunction with broader international and global illustrations to integrate a sense of the distinctive Canadian geographical circumstances within broader contexts. Most of these examples draw on well-known contemporary and historical events of interest to encourage attentiveness to Canadian histories and geographies.

- By highlighting the research and publications of top Canadian scholars influential in geographical scholarship in the various subdisciplines. These stand side-by-side with references to the leading work in the field, highlighting Canadians' contributions to international research and scholarship.

- By including in each chapter a field note authored by Canadian scholars commenting on how and why they came to do the work they do and a brief discussion of the nature of their research. These are designed to demonstrate the passion and personal commitment scholars bring to their careers and to encourage students to think about their own curiosities and interests.

The perspectives on the processes and impacts of globalization are highly contested but undeniable in both their presence and their influence. Canada occupies a particular (and mobile) place within these processes. Globalization is a set of processes that flow and pulsate across and through country boundaries—processes that have different outcomes in different places and across scales. The second Canadian edition continues to guide students toward an appreciation of the role people play in shaping places and the way that places shape people, while positioning discussions within larger global contexts. The second Canadian edition strives to give students the tools to engage in the complexities of the debates about the political, social, and economic fallout of globalization and to understand the importance of thinking geographically as a way to understand the world.

Most important, perhaps, students today are living in a world that is quite different from what any other generation has experienced; they are living, as geographer Andrew Kirby explains, "not in a world without boundaries or without limits, but simply a world." Today's students engage daily with the world, whether or not they are conscious of that fact. Students are part of the world, and many have a global identity. They need to make sense of themselves not just in their home, college or university, locality, nation, and region, but also beyond their world. Globalization means that people and places across the world are constantly interacting. For good or for ill, each of us is a part of that interaction. Each of us, therefore, must make sense of who we are and what our role is in this globalized world, and we each must think critically about how we can shape our world. With globalization, the way people make places and shape their identities has global, local, and individual implications. What people do today, whether making a pilgrimage to a river or buying a product, happens in a global context.

Hallmark Features

This second Canadian edition integrates text, photos, and illustrations to help students understand the role people play in shaping the world, to provide geographic context to the issues we discuss, to teach students to think geographically and critically, and to explain the complexities of thinking geographically and what that actually means; that is, understanding that "place matters" and that who they are and their possibilities, limitations, and opportunities depend on where they are. For this reason, each chapter begins at the level of the personal, with examples and illustrations that will resonate with most students' experiences in their everyday lives.

The second Canadian edition strives to cultivate a spatial perspective in students as they study a range of issues from political elections and urban shantytowns to gay urban neighbourhoods and farming life. While there are many possible ways to conceptualize the spatial, this edition uses five themes to organize students' thinking—location, region, place, landscape, and movement. Throughout the chapters, one or more of these themes is examined within the context of human-environment relations.

In this new edition, Key Questions continue to be used as the organizing principle for each chapter in the text. The Key Questions are listed after the opening field note of each chapter and serve as the outline for the chapter. At the end of each section, the reader is presented with a summary of Main Points that are the key concepts or ideas discussed in that section and that help to answer the Key Questions for that section. Students may use the Key Questions and the Main Points as a convenient summary of the information and for study purposes. Instructors may use the Key Questions and Main Points to prepare lectures, develop examination questions, or generate class discussion.

Several features of the Canadian edition provide context and help students learn to think geographically. Each chapter in this edition includes one or more Field Notes (including a chapter-opening field note), written by one of the authors, providing context for the particular author's experiences in the field and pulling students into the chapter. Each chapter also includes one or more Guest Field Notes contributed by professionals and researchers in the field. The author field notes serve as models of how to think geographically and the guest field notes detail scholars' commitment to the discipline of geography through their specific research interests. Finally, a series of discussion questions are provided at the end of each chapter to promote discussion and engagement.

The second Canadian edition has several key additions:

- The second Canadian edition of *Human Geography* pays particular attention to incorporating material on the impacts and importance of new technologies and social media on how we understand and experience the geographical. Themes related to this issue are intertwined throughout the text together with pertinent and timely examples. This is particularly important given that this generation of students is thoroughly steeped in the use of digital technologies and understands their spatial interactions through these engagements.

- Each chapter has been updated with new examples drawn from contemporary events from around the globe. This allows for the development of assignments, seminars, and discussions that develop students' abilities to view and understand events and the world from a geographical perspective. Where available and appropriate, updated statistical data, including Canadian census data from 2011, has been included.

- New and relevant visual materials, including images, graphs, charts, maps and other illustrations, have been added to each chapter, enhancing the visual appeal and readability of each chapter and helping to convey the information in a variety of ways that acknowledges distinctive learning styles.

Chapter Organization

This text is organized around the main subdisciplines in geography. The chapter order reflects the desire to introduce students to geographical scholarship through a logical and intuitive structure. The text begins with a discussion in the first two chapters about the processes and debates around the concept of globalization, which provides the wider context for the rest of the book. Chapter 3 introduces the subdiscipline of political geography, providing the pivotal historical background for understanding the current world order, including the political, economic, and social circumstances. We then consider the distribution of human populations over the surface of the earth by examining population geography in Chapter 4 and migration in Chapter 5. The human-environment relationship, the heart of geographical enquiry, is the focus of Chapter 6 as we survey the scholarship on nature, society, and the environment. Chapters 7 and 8 constitute an introduction to the subdisciplines of social and cultural geography, respectively. Chapter 9 focuses on agricultural development and

the emergence of stable human settlements as well as rural life. In Chapter 10, we examine the process of urbanization, a central concern of geographers given that the majority of the world's people live in urban environments. We explore aspects of economic and development geographies in Chapter 11 and make important linkages with those themes of globalization introduced in Chapter 2. In Chapter 12, we examine the important field of transportation geographies, a timely topic given increasing global concerns about pollution, environmental degradation, and the problems of moving people and goods on a variety of scales. Chapter 13 concludes the text with a consideration of the geographies of industrialization and the service sector.

Finally, please note the selective use of Canadian census data in this text. The mandatory long-form questionnaire was replaced with a voluntary national household survey in 2010. As a result, Statistics Canada issued a disclaimer concerning the reliability of certain aspects of the 2011 data and is no longer providing certain previously available data sets (see Chapter 4 for further discussion). For this reason, the text uses 2011 data where appropriate, while continuing to rely on the more detailed, fine-grained data available from the 2006 census.

The Teaching and Learning Package

The second Canadian edition of *Human Geography: People, Place, and Culture* is supported by a comprehensive supplements package that includes an extensive selection of resources.

WileyPLUS Learning Space

The factors that contribute to success—both in college and in life—aren't comprised of intellectual capabilities alone. In fact, there are other traits, strategies, and even daily habits that contribute to the overall picture of success. Studies show that people who can delay instant gratification, work through tasks even if they are not immediately rewarding, and follow through with a plan have the skills that are not only valuable in the classroom, but also in the workplace and their personal lives. A place where students can define their strengths and nurture these skills, *WileyPLUS Learning Space* transforms course content into an online learning community. *WileyPLUS Learning Space* invites students to experience learning activities, work through self-assessment, ask questions and share insights. As they interact with the course content, peers and their instructor, *WileyPLUS Learning Space* creates a personalized study guide for each student.

As research shows, when students collaborate with each other, they make deeper connections to the content. When students work together, they also feel part of a community so that they can grow in areas beyond topics in the course. With *WileyPLUS Learning Space*, students are invested in their learning experience and can use their time efficiently as they develop skills like critical thinking and teamwork.

Through a flexible course design, you can quickly organize learning activities, manage student collaboration, and customize your course—having full control over content as well as the amount of interactivity between students.

WileyPLUS Learning Space lets you:

- Assign activities and add your own materials

- Guide your students through what's important in the interactive e-textbook by easily assigning specific content

- Set up and monitor group learning

- Assess student engagement

- Gain immediate insights to help inform teaching

Defining a clear path to action, the visual reports in *WileyPLUS Learning Space* help both you and your students gauge problem areas and act on what's most important.

With the visual reports, you can:

- See exactly where your students are struggling for early intervention

- Help students see exactly what they don't know to better prepare for exams

- Give students insight into their strengths and weaknesses so that they can succeed in your course

RESOURCES THAT HELP TEACHERS TEACH

On-Location Videos. This rich collection of original and relevant footage was taken during H. J. de Blij's travels. These videos, which are available in *WileyPLUS Learning Space*, cover a wide range of themes and locations.

The *Human Geography: People, Place, and Culture* second Canadian Edition **Instructor Site** (**www.wiley.com/go/foubergcanada**) provides a wealth of resources for instructors to facilitate their teaching and course management and to help enhance their students' learning. The site includes:

- A complete collection of **PowerPoint presentations**. These presentations are intended to enhance lecture presentations and serve as an effective overview and point-form summary of the key concepts of each chapter.

- A comprehensive **Test Bank** with multiple-choice, fill-in, matching, and essay questions. The Test Bank is distributed via the secure instructor website and can be used in all major test application programs.

- A collection of 15 **Clicker Questions** per chapter that can be used with a variety of personal response (or "clicker") systems.

- A comprehensive collection of **additional resources**.

Wiley Faculty Network (WFN). This peer-to-peer network of faculty is ready to support your use of on-line course management tools and discipline-specific software/learning systems in the classroom. The WFN will help you apply innovative classroom techniques, implement software packages, tailor the technology experience to the needs of each individual class, and provide you with virtual training sessions led by faculty for faculty.

RESOURCES THAT HELP STUDENTS LEARN

The easy-to-use and student-focused website (www.wiley.com/go/foubergcanada) provides **Practice Quizzes** to help students check their understanding and prepare for tests. These quizzes provide immediate feedback to true/false, multiple choice, and short-answer questions. **Web Links** are also provided to put useful electronic resources into context.

Acknowledgements

In preparing the second Canadian edition of *Human Geography*, we benefited immensely from the feedback and suggestions of colleagues in geography. We thank them, as well as reviewers of the previous Canadian edition, for their insightful and invaluable feedback.

Mark Troy Burnett, *Mount Royal University*

Robert Dilley, *Lakehead University*

Sean Doherty, *Wilfrid Laurier University*

Michael Fox, *Mount Allison University*

Charles Greenberg, *Capilano University*

Jason Grek-Martin, *Saint Mary's University*

Jutta Gutberlet, *University of Victoria*

Leah Huff, *Mount Allison University*

Michael Imort, *Wilfrid Laurier University*

Jeanne Mikita, *Capilano University*

Heather Nicol, *Trent University*

Daniel H. Olsen, *Brandon University*

Derek Smith, *Carleton University*

Lucy M. Sportza, *University of Guelph*

Rosario Turvey, *Lakehead University*

Jon Unruh, *McGill University*

Francis Yee, *Camosun College*

In the second Canadian edition, a number of our colleagues in geography contributed guest field notes, which added a wonderful dimension to the text. These guest field notes will help students to better appreciate the role of fieldwork in geographic research and we hope they will help to motivate students in their own research. We thank the following contributors.

Sylvia Bawa, *York University*

Sarah de Leeuw, *University of Northern British Columbia*

Victoria Fast, *Brock University*

Christopher Fullerton, *Brock University*

Sutama Ghosh, *Ryerson University*

Nicole Gombay, *University of Canterbury*

Jason Grek-Martin, *Saint Mary's University*

Katie Hemsworth, *Queen's University*

Marilyne Jollineau, *Brock University*

Sean Jowsey, Master Mariner

Heather Maguire, *York University*

Sarah Jane Meharg, *Royal Military College of Canada*

Robert Oliver, *Virginia Polytechnic Institute and State University*

Natalie Oswin, *McGill University*

Valerie Thomas, *Virginia Polytechnic Institute and State University*

Nicole Yantzi, *Laurentian University*

Thank you to the following team at Wiley for their commitment to excellence and their professionalism: Darren Lalonde, Acquisitions Editor; Patty Maher, Marketing Manager; and Gail Brown, Developmental Editor. Thank you also to all those involved in the production of this textbook, in particular copy editor Audrey McClennan, proofreader Laurel Hyatt, and permissions and photo research of MRM Associates. All the writing, producing, and marketing of this book would be wasted without an energetic and dedicated sales staff. We sincerely thank all the publishing representatives for their tireless efforts and energy. Sincerest thanks are also offered to Mark Troy Burnett (Mount Royal University) and Rosario Turvey (Lakehead University) for their contributions to the supplements and ancillaries for this textbook.

I am very grateful to family and friends who supported me in the writing of this textbook. Many thanks to my partner, Cindy Berry, and to my colleagues in the Department of Geography who contributed time and effort to the production of this text. A special thanks to Christopher Fullerton for bringing his expertise to this project and in writing Chapter 9 (Agriculture), Chapter 11 (Development), and a chapter unique to the Canadian edition, Chapter 12 (Transportation). Another special thank you to Marilyne Jollineau, not only for contributing the Guest Field Note for Chapter 1, but for reviewing the section on remote sensing and the appendix on mapping. Finally, this text could not have been completed without the commitment, dedication, and expertise of Heather Maguire, research assistant par excellence.

Catherine Nash
St. Catharines, Ontario

April 2015

ABOUT THE AUTHORS

ERIN H. FOUBERG

Erin Hogan Fouberg grew up in eastern South Dakota. She moved to Washington, D.C. to attend Georgetown University's School of Foreign Service, where she took a class in Human Geography from Harm de Blij. At Georgetown, Erin found her International Relations classes lacking in context and discovered a passion for political geography. She earned her master's and Ph.D. at the University of Nebraska-Lincoln (1997). After graduating, Dr. Fouberg taught for several years at the University of Mary Washington in Fredericksburg, Virginia, where the graduating class of 2001 bestowed on her the Mary Pinschmidt Award, given to the faculty member who made the biggest impact on their lives.

Dr. Fouberg is Professor of Geography and Director of the Honors Program at Northern State University in Aberdeen, South Dakota, where she won the Outstanding Faculty Award in 2011. Her research and publications focus on the governance and sovereignty of American Indian tribes, geography education, and the geography of elections. Professor Fouberg served as Vice President of Publications and Products of the National Council for Geographic Education. Dr. Fouberg co-authors *Understanding World Regional Geography* with William G. Moseley, also published by Wiley. She is active in her community, serving leadership roles on the soccer board, PTA, and fundraising campaigns for children's charities. She enjoys travelling, reading, golfing, and watching athletic and theatre events at Northern State.

CATHERINE J. NASH

Catherine Jean Nash was born into a military (Navy) family and spent the first decade of her life moving from Victoria to Ottawa, Halifax, Montreal, and finally Ottawa again. She began her working life as a lawyer practising municipal law, expropriations, and land development. After eight years in private practice, she returned to university and completed a Masters in Regional and Urban Planning at Queen's University. It was there that Professor Nash took a third-year geography course, Gender and Geography, sparking her interest in the geographical. Professor Nash completed her Ph.D. at Queen's in 2004 and is currently a Professor in the Department of Geography at Brock University in St. Catharines, Ontario. More information about Professor Nash's research and teaching interests can be found at www.brocku.ca/social-sciences/departments-and-centres/geography/faculty/catherine-nash.

ALEXANDER B. MURPHY

Alec Murphy grew up in the western United States, but he spent several of his early years in Europe and Japan. He obtained his undergraduate degree at Yale University, studied law at the Columbia University School of Law, practised law for a short time in Chicago, and then pursued a doctoral degree in geography (Ph.D. University of Chicago, 1987). After graduating, Dr. Murphy joined the faculty of the University of Oregon, where he is now Professor of Geography and holder of the James F. and Shirley K. Rippey Chair in Liberal Arts and Sciences. Professor Murphy is a widely published scholar in the fields of political, cultural, and environmental geography. His work has been supported by the National Science Foundation, the National Endowment for the Humanities, the Rockefeller Foundation, and the Fulbright-Hays foreign fellowship program.

Professor Murphy served as the President of the Association of American Geographers in 2003. He is also Vice President of the American Geographical Society. For 11 years he was one of the editors of *Progress in Human Geography*; he currently co-edits *Eurasian Geography and Economics*. In the late 1990s, he led the effort to add geography to the College Board's Advanced Placement Program. His interests include hiking, skiing, camping, music, and of course exploring the diverse places that make up our planet.

H. J. DE BLIJ

Harm de Blij received his early schooling in Europe, his college education in Africa, and his higher degrees in the United States (Ph.D. Northwestern, 1959). He published more than 30 books and over 100 articles, and received five honorary degrees. Several of his books were translated into foreign languages.

Dr. de Blij held the position of John A. Hannah Professor of Geography at Michigan State University. He also held the George Landegger Chair at Georgetown University's School of Foreign Service, the John Deaver Drinko Chair of Geography at Marshall University, and faculty positions at the Colorado School of Mines and the University of Miami. He was the Geography Editor on ABC-TV's "Good Morning America" program for seven years and later served as Geography Analyst for NBC News. He was for more than 20 years a member of the National Geographic Society's Committee for Research and Exploration and was the founding editor of its scholarly journal, *National Geographic Research*. In recognition of his service, he became an honorary lifetime member of the Society. Professor de Blij was a renaissance man. He was a soccer fan, an avid wine collector, an amateur violinist, and an inveterate traveller.

BRIEF CONTENTS

BRIEF CONTENTS

CONTENTS

HUMAN
GEOGRAPHY
People, Place, and Culture

1 INTRODUCTION TO HUMAN GEOGRAPHY

The Geographical Imagination

IN APRIL 2007, the Canadian Broadcasting Corporation (CBC) launched the *Seven Wonders of Canada* event. The organizers challenged Canadians to nominate their choice for the top Canadian *wonder*. They defined a wonder as either a spectacular physical site or an amazing human creation. Contestants had to demonstrate how their choice reflected an essential Canadian-ness. Submissions were judged on their uniqueness and originality, their historical significance, and their ability to inspire and to provoke emotion and pride in our Canadian places.

The event drew some 25,000 nominations and over one million votes. In on-line voting through the CBC website, six of the top seven wonders were Niagara Falls, the northern lights, the Cabot Trail, Nahanni National Park, the Canadian Rockies, and the Sleeping Giant. The top pick was the Bay of Fundy (**Figure 1.1**), with the highest tides in the world; spectacular marine, animal, and plant life; and distinctive tidal bores, mud flats, and marshes. Human creations were also showcased: the Green Gables House, the Library of Parliament, the Spiral Tunnels of the Canadian Pacific Railway in British Columbia, Château Montebello, and the Canadian National Vimy Memorial.

In formal judging, the final list was an eclectic mix of human-made and physical sites. Taking top spot was the canoe, arguably the quintessential Canadian icon and a truly inspired choice. It speaks of our colonial history of exploration and settlement and our connections with Canada's indigenous peoples and wilderness landscapes. Many of our well-known writers, artists, and politicians—such as Bill Mason, E. Pauline Johnson, and Pierre Elliot Trudeau—sought inspiration, comfort, and solitude by canoeing our lakes and rivers. Today, no summer camp, cottage, or recreational area—from Canada's national parks to the Rideau Canal—is likely to be without a canoe (**Figure 1.2**).

(a)

(b)

(c)

FIGURE 1.1 Wonders of Canada. (a) Bay of Fundy, New Brunswick. (b) Canadian National Vimy Memorial, France. (c) Niagara Falls, Ontario.

The runners-up also reflected Canadians' connections with places of both natural beauty and architectural wonder: the Rockies, Pier 21, Prairie skies, Niagara Falls, the igloo, and Old Quebec City. Even if we have never been to Niagara Falls, for example, it is part of our imagined sense of Canada, giving us a collective sense of connection to well-known places, including those we haven't seen. What it means to be Canadian is, for many of us, deeply attached to these everyday landscapes in which we live, be they urban or rural, natural or human built.

For a human geographer, the *Seven Wonders of Canada* competition illustrates the multiple interests of geographical studies—the political, the social, the economic, and the cultural. Human geography is about the ties that bind us to place and the emotions that drive us apart. It is about how we interact with our environment, how we change it, and how our landscapes have an impact on us. For human geographers, then, the relationship between the human and natural worlds is a constant preoccupation, providing us with never-ending possibilities for exploration and study.

Source: *Seven Wonders of Canada,* www.cbc.ca/sevenwonders.

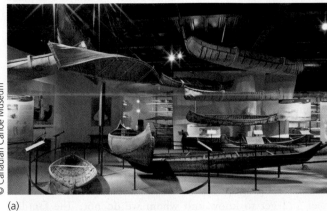
© Canadian Canoe Museum

(a)

© Photo by Fred C. Sears/Library and Archives Canada PA-148593

PA-148593

(b)

Peter Bregg/The Canadian Press

(c)

FIGURE 1.2 The canoe in Canada. The canoe and canoeing are intrinsic to Canada. (a) The Canadian Canoe Museum, Peterborough, Ontario. (b) Innu making canoes near Sheshatshiu, Newfoundland, ca. 1920. (c) Pierre Trudeau paddles a canoe in 1968, in the waters off Baffin Island's Clearwater Fiord.

KEY QUESTIONS FOR CHAPTER 1

1. What is human geography?

2. What are geographic questions?

3. Why do geographers use maps and what do maps tell us?

4. Why are geographers concerned with scale and connectedness?

5. What does it mean to "think geographically" and how do we do it?

1.1 What Is Human Geography?

It's not the land that has made our country what it is . . . it's the way we've shaped it and the things we've built on it, the monumental achievements of engineering and imagination in which we took a wilderness and forged it into a nation.
(Christopher Hume, *Toronto Star*, June 9, 2007)

> **Human-environment** The reciprocal relationship between humans and environment.
>
> **Human geography** One of the two major divisions of geography; the spatial analysis of human population, its cultures, activities, and landscapes.
>
> **Physical geography** One of the two major divisions of geography; the spatial analysis of the structure, processes, and location of the Earth's natural phenomena, such as climate, soil, plants, animals, and topography.

Geographers study **human-environment** relationships. In this context, "environment" refers to both the natural world and the myriad places created or built by humans. The field of **human geography** focuses on how humans create places in the natural or physical world, how we interact with each other in and across different places, and how we make sense of others and ourselves. We are all geographers at heart as we navigate through our everyday lives, creating our own private spaces of "home," perhaps travelling to faraway lands, and carefully negotiating the best route to ensure that we get our chores done.

While the disciplines of human and **physical geography** are closely related areas of study, physical geographers explore the processes and patterns at work in the physical world, while human geographers examine human activities interacting with that physical world. Human geography is also concerned with the processes of change. We examine past activities to see how they affect contemporary places, and we consider how both past and present activities might shape our world, for better or for worse, in the future.

> **Anthropocentric view** A view in which human interests and perspectives are highlighted.

The quotation from Christopher Hume, a *Toronto Star* architecture and urban affairs columnist, at the beginning of this chapter highlights our dynamic impact on the world around us. But in writing about the winners of the Seven Wonders of Canada contest, Hume's focus was the nation-building activities of Canada's colonizing peoples. He did not mention the presence and activities of First Nations peoples in North America. Also, the quotation suggests that human-environment interaction operates in one direction: humans, through their ingenuity, alter their environment for their own benefit. This is an **anthropocentric view**—one in which human interests and perspectives alone are highlighted. Most human geographers take a relational view, arguing that just as human activities constantly change our physical and built environment, so too do the physical and built environments have a profound effect on us as individuals and as a society. The places we grow up, and the places we experience, in positive or negative ways,

influence our sense of self and our norms, values, and beliefs. Our sense of self and our norms and values, in turn, affect how we see others and how we understand the world.

Human geographers use the term **sense of place** to highlight our relationships to the places we build and inhabit. This term suggests that we not only think about a location's physical or material characteristics, but we also consider the sentiments we feel and meanings we hold for particular places. This sense of place underpins our everyday decisions, including where we want to live and work and, perhaps, have a family. Our sense of place is also pivotal when we make our most important decisions, such as whether we consider a place worth dying for if we face the choice of defending that place in a war.

> **Sense of place** State of mind derived through the infusion of a place with meaning and emotion by remembering important events that occurred in that place or by labelling a place with a certain character.

One deceptively simple concept in human geography is the idea that "place matters." Where we are literally affects our life chances—the possibilities for success or failure, health and happiness, life or death. Place has an impact on our ability to access public services, such as health care, or to find employment, afford a house, or breathe less polluted air. Whether we live in Newfoundland or Alberta affects whether we can find a job, what kind of job we will work at every day for many years, and our resulting quality of life. Place determines whom we meet and get to know and whom we do not. The familiar phrase "a place for everything and everything in its place" tells us something about our expectations—about whom we should expect to find in certain places and when people might be seen as "out of place"—which in turn have serious implications for individuals and groups that might be regarded as being in places where they do not belong. In South Africa, for example, between 1948 and 1994, those populations classified as other than "white" experienced diminished rights as citizens and often experienced restrictions in travel, including the places in which they could participate (**Figure 1.3a**). In a different example, women in Ottawa held a "flash feed-in" at a local IKEA in March 2014 to publicly breastfeed their children (**Figure 1.3b**). The *Ontario Human Rights Act* protects the right of mothers to breastfeed in public, although some people may not be comfortable with the practice. Often, whom we expect to see and where we expect to see them depends on our ideas about age, race, ethnicity, gender, and other markers of the self. The geography of our everyday lives is pivotal in influencing who we are and what we might become.

No place on Earth is untouched by people. As people explore, travel, migrate, interact, play, live, and work, they make places. They organize themselves into communities, nations, and broader societal networks, establishing political, economic, religious, linguistic, and cultural systems that enable them to function in space. People adapt to, alter, manipulate, and cope with their physical geographic environment and are, in turn, influenced by their experiences in that environment. No place stands apart from human action, nor is human action undertaken apart from place.

UN Photo

(a)

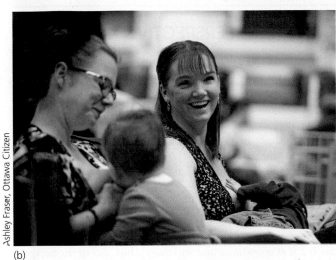

Ashley Fraser, Ottawa Citizen

(b)

FIGURE 1.3 (a) A segregated beach in South Africa, 1982. (b) Breastfeeding in public at IKEA, Ottawa, Ontario.

Clearly, places do not exist in splendid isolation, and human geographers are interested in the interconnections between different places. Throughout human history, advances in communication and transportation technologies have made places and people more interconnected. Only 100 years ago, the fastest modes of transportation were the steamship, the railroad, and the horse and buggy. Today we can cross the globe in record time, with easy access to automobiles, airplanes, and ships. Added to this, the Internet and mobile technologies are changing the ways in which we connect across time and space, through constant connection and instantaneous communication. Increased interconnections between people can now happen through on-line education, e-mail, text messaging, and the development of virtual communities on the Internet, to name but a few. Geographers are increasingly interested not only in the emergence of virtual places on the Internet, but also in how these on-line communities and social activities shape, and are shaped by, our off-line, physical lives.

The interconnections between places are not only about how humans move from one place to another. Aspects of popular culture, such as fashion and architecture, are in some ways making many people and places seem more alike. Despite all these changes, our world still encompasses a multitude of ways in

which people identify themselves and others. Nearly 200 countries, a diversity of religions, thousands of languages, and any number of settlement types, from small villages to enormous cities, come together in different ways around the globe to create a world of endlessly diverse places and people. Understanding and explaining this diversity is the mission of human geography.

One term used frequently to describe the contemporary interconnections between places is *globalization*, a concept discussed in detail in Chapter 2. For now, we can think about globalization as a set of processes that reflect increasing interactions and heightening interdependence among and between places, with diminishing regard for national borders. Globalization also refers to a set of outcomes that result from these processes. These outcomes are unevenly distributed—that is, the processes of globalization are experienced differently in different locations, with different results across the world. For example, the fashion industry encompasses a far-reaching set of global processes that include consumerism, advertising, manufacturing, and shipping. However, the fashion industry experienced by a garment worker in Cambodia (**Figure 1.4**) is significantly different from that experienced by a teenager in Winnipeg, Manitoba.

Discussions about the processes of globalization often focus on the pull between the global—seen as a blanket covering the world—and the local—seen as a continuation of the traditional despite the blanket of globalization. Geographers are well positioned to understand globalization as much more than this. When they describe the outcomes of global-

> **Scale** (1) Representation of a real-world phenomenon at a certain level of reduction or generalization. In cartography, the ratio of map distance to ground distance, indicated on a map as a bar graph, representative fraction, and/or verbal statement. (2) The territorial extent of something. When we refer to scale throughout this book, we are generally using the second of these definitions.

ization as unevenly distributed, they are not only talking about effects and changes at the local level. Geographers use the concept of **scale** to understand the networked interrelationships among individual, local, regional, national, and global. Globalizing processes

© Tang Chhin Sothy/AFP/Getty Images

FIGURE 1.4 Garment workers in Cambodia.

MAIN POINTS 1.1 What Is Human Geography?

- Human geographers study human-environment relations—both the impact we have on the physical and built environment and the interrelated impact the physical and material world has on us, individually and collectively.

- Human geographers are concerned with our sense of place—that is, how we make sense of place and our emotions, sentiments, and attachments to place.

- Human geographers argue that "place matters." Where we are affects our sense of self (individually and also collectively, as a society), determines our ability to access

services such as education and health care, and influences whom we expect to see in which places.

- Places are interconnected in complex ways. One of those ways is through globalization, which can be understood as a set of processes that reflect increasing interactions, deepening relationships, and heightening interdependence among and between places without regard to national borders. It also refers to a set of outcomes that are felt from these global processes—outcomes that are unevenly distributed and differently manifested across the world.

---

occur at the world scale and are visible in such things as the global financial markets or even global environmental change. However, the processes of globalization do not magically appear at the global scale: *what happens at other scales (individual, local, regional, national) helps create the processes of globalization and shape the outcomes of globalization.* To reduce our understanding of the world to a consideration of only the local and the global is to miss all the complex interactions across, and cutting through, a multiplicity of scales. In this book, we study these processes and outcomes of globalization, and we use scale to assess the dynamic effects and impacts on place.

1.2 What Are Geographic Questions?

Geographer Marvin Mikesell defines geography succinctly as the "why of where." Why and how do things come together in certain places to produce particular outcomes? Why are some things found in certain places but not in others? To what extent do things in one place influence those in other places? To these questions, we add "so what?" Why does it matter that things are different across space? What role does a place play in its region and in the world, and what does that mean for people there and elsewhere? Questions such as these are at the core of geographic inquiry—whether human or physical—and they are of critical importance in any effort to make sense of our world.

> **Spatial** Pertaining to space on the Earth's surface; sometimes used as a synonym for geographic.

If the field of geography deals with so many aspects of our world, ranging from people and places to coastlines and climates, what do the various facets of this wide-ranging discipline have in common? The answer lies in a perspective that both human and physical geographers use: the **spatial**. Virtually all geographers are interested in the spatial arrangement of places and phenomena: how they are laid out, organized, and arranged on the Earth, and how they appear in the landscape.

THE SPATIAL PERSPECTIVE

Geography, and being geographically literate, involves much more than memorizing places on a map. In this sense, the disciplines of geography and history have much in common. History is not merely memorizing dates. To understand history is to appreciate how events, circumstances, and ideas came together at particular times to produce certain outcomes. Knowledge of how events have developed over time is critical to understanding who we are and where we are going.

Understanding change over time is critically important, and understanding change across space is equally important. The great German philosopher Immanuel Kant argued that we need to pay scholarly attention not only to particular phenomena (such as economics and sociology), but also to the perspectives of time (history) and space (geography). The disciplines of history and geography have intellectual cores defined by perspective rather than by subject matter.

Human geographers use a **spatial perspective** as they study a multitude of phenomena, ranging from political elections and shantytowns to gay urban neighbourhoods, on-line communities, and folk music. The goal here is for you to develop a spatial perspective on the world around you and the everyday spaces you experience. While there are many possible ways to conceptualize the spatial, we have selected **five themes** derived from the spatial perspective in geography to organize this book.

> **Spatial perspective** Observing variations in geographic phenomena across space.
>
> **Five themes (of geography)** The five themes derived from the spatial perspective of geography: location, region, place, landscape, and movement.

THE FIVE THEMES

Throughout this book, we draw in five major themes or concepts: location, region, place, landscape, and movement. This means that in every discussion about human-environment relations, we will use one or more of these themes. Several of them overlap or have similarities in meaning, and human geographers use the concepts in different combinations as they think about the geographical.

> **Location** The geographical situation of people and things.

Location. To have a spatial perspective is to be thoughtful about or aware of **location**. Thinking about location highlights how the geographical position of people and things on the Earth's surface matters in terms of what happens where, how, and why. A concern with location underlies almost all geographical work, as location helps to establish the context within which events and processes are situated.

> **Location theory** A logical attempt to explain the locational pattern of an economic activity and the manner in which its producing areas are interrelated. The agricultural location theory contained in the von Thünen model in Chapter 9 is a leading example.

Some geographers develop elaborate (often quantitative) models describing the locational properties of particular phenomena—even predicting where things are likely to occur. Such undertakings have fostered an interest in **location theory**, an element of contemporary human geography that seeks answers to a wide range of questions—some of them theoretical, others highly practical—such as, why are villages, towns, and cities spaced or located the way they are? A geographer versed in location theory might make a decision about where a Canadian Tire store or Tim Hortons should be built, based on an assessment of the demographics and median income of the surrounding neighbourhoods, the locations of other shopping areas, and the existing and future road system. Similarly, a geographer could determine the best location for a wildlife refuge, given existing wildlife habitats and migration patterns, human settlement patterns, and road networks.

> **Region** An area on the Earth's surface marked by a degree of formal, functional, or perceptual homogeneity of some phenomenon.

Region. From our spatial perspective, we can determine that phenomena are not evenly distributed on the surface of the Earth. Instead, features tend to be concentrated in particular areas, which we call **regions**, the second concept we will draw on in this text. Novelist James Michener once wrote that whenever he started writing a new book, he first prepared himself by turning to books written by regional geographers about the setting for his story. Understanding the regional geography of a place allows us to make sense of much of the information we have about that place and to digest new information as well.

> **Formal region** A type of region marked by a certain degree of homogeneity in one or more phenomena; also called uniform region or homogeneous region.

In geography, an area characterized by shared physical or cultural attributes constitutes a region. To identify and delimit a region, geographers must establish the criteria that will define it. Those criteria can be physical, cultural, functional, or perceptual. A physical region, such as the Canadian Shield, is defined by a shared physical geographic criterion. When geographers choose one or more physical or cultural criteria to define a region, they are looking for a **formal region**. A formal region has a shared trait—it can be a shared cultural trait or physical trait. In a formal cultural region, people share one or more cultural traits. For example, the region of Europe where the majority of people speak French can be thought of as a French-speaking region. When the scale of analysis shifts, the formal region changes. If we shift scales to the world, the French-speaking formal region expands beyond France into former French colonies of Africa and into the overseas departments that are still associated politically with France.

> **Functional region** A region defined by the particular set of activities or interactions that occur within it.

A **functional region** is defined by a particular set of activities or interactions that occur within it. Places that are part of the same functional region interact to create connections. They also share a political, social, or economic purpose. Functional regions are not necessarily culturally homogeneous. Instead, the people within the region function together politically, socially, or economically. The city of Toronto is a functional region, and the city itself has internal functional regions, such the central business district. Alternatively, the city of Mississauga is nested within the Golden Horseshoe, a larger functional region linked politically, economically, and socially. The name reflects a geographical shape and a consolidated economic region.

> **Perceptual region** A region that exists only as a conceptualization or an idea and not as a physically demarcated entity—for example, the North or the Maritimes.

Regions may be primarily in the minds of people—a product of our imagination (think, for example, about our perceptions of Newfoundland, the North, or the Maritimes). This does not mean the region is not "real." Rather, such a region has less to do with material locations and more to do with how we understand a place. **Perceptual regions** are intellectual constructs designed to help us understand the nature and distribution of phenomena in human geography. As **Figure 1.5** demonstrates, perceptual regions can sometimes take on a comedic character. Geographers

FIGURE 1.5 Perceptual regions of Canada.

FIGURE 1.6 Regional distinctions within Canada. From Robert M. Bone, The Regional Geography of Canada (3rd ed.), Figure 1.2, p. 11.

FIGURE 1.7 Boundaries between First Nations territories in British Columbia. In this presentation, the boundaries are deliberately blended to show the complex territorial relations being negotiated. Retrieved from Government of British Columbia website, www.bced.gov.bc.ca/abed/map.htm.

do not agree entirely on regional properties, but we do concur that we all have impressions and images of various regions and cultures. How people think about regions has influenced everything from daily activity patterns to large-scale international conflict. A perceptual region can include people, their cultural traits (such as dress, food, and religion), economic indicators (such as corporate locations or industrial base), places and their physical traits (such as mountains, plains, or coasts), and built environments (such as windmills, barns, skyscrapers, or beach houses).

Regions, whether formal, functional, or perceptual, are a form of spatial classification. They provide a means by which we can organize humans geographically or handle large amounts of information so we can make sense of it.

In her classic study of the forces of regionalism in Canada, Mildred Schwartz argues that regionalism in the Canadian context is shaped by shared past economic experiences, which have led to unequal development and political and social relationships. Regions in Canada have developed as a result of distinctive settlement patterns, distinctive cultural groups, and the ensuing economic and political regionalization. As **Figure 1.6** illustrates, many of us have a collective sense of Canadian regions that are a blend of these various factors. In thinking about Canada and its regions, we can consider the physical characteristics of regions, such as the Rockies or the Canadian Shield, or the cultural and social history of a place, such as the unique history of the peoples of Quebec or the North. We can also consider economic structures and political identities as well as transportation systems and urban development.

It is important to remember, however, that these political, cultural, physical, and perceptual regions are largely based on British and French colonial settlement patterns and not on an understanding of underlying indigenous populations. Ongoing land claims disputes remind us that First Nations' histories and understandings of the Canadian landscapes may be different from those reflected in our standard textbooks (**Figure 1.7**).

Place. The third theme arising from our spatial perspective is the seemingly simple idea of **place**, which is a key concept in geography. Geographers tend to distinguish the notion of "space" from that of "place," although there are different ways of understanding this distinction. Generally, when we speak of "space" we are referring to a more mathematical or abstract sense of space, such as identifying a location by latitude or longitude or indicating that a city is so many

> **Place** The uniqueness of human experience, including sights, smells, emotions, and experiences of a specific area or location on Earth.

kilometres from another city. When we speak of place, we are usually referencing some uniquely human experience of place—that is, how we experience a place through sights, sounds, and smells; our emotional attachment to place; and the meanings we give to places. All places have uniquely human and/or physical characteristics, and one of the purposes of geography is to study the special character and meaning of places for various individuals and groups of people. While place may be thought of as a bounded area or territory, it may also be a location with no clear boundaries that is part of our collective or imagined memory. We can, therefore, be interested in place as a point on a map, or we can study individual experiences of place in terms of emotions and attachments. People individually and collectively develop a sense of place based on the ways in which places take on meaning and emotion in various ways—we can remember important events that occurred in a place, or we can imbue a place with a certain character. Canadian geographer Edward Relph has argued that our sense of place is "an innate faculty, possessed in some degree by everyone, that connects us to the world" (1997, p. 208).

Some geographers note that we may also be developing a sense of "placelessness" because of the way so many landscapes seem similar or indistinguishable. For example, the layouts of airports, strip malls, food chains, and shopping centres have become largely interchangeable, so that no matter where we are in the world, these spaces may seem exactly the same. Geographer Yi-Fu Tuan coined the term "topophilia" to describe the emotional bond people have to place and to highlight his argument that the loss of the diversity and authenticity of place may lead to forms of alienation. We will explore the intricate relationships between people, place, identity, and social relations more deeply in chapters 7 and 8, on social geography and cultural geography, respectively.

Landscape. Landscape is the fourth core theme related to a spatial perspective. Human geographers generally understand landscapes to be the visible imprint of human activity

> **Landscape** The overall appearance of an area. Most landscapes comprise a combination of natural and human-induced influences.

on the physical environment. It is important to note that the term is also used in different ways by others, such as physical geographers or ecologists. Carl Sauer, formerly a professor at the University of California at Berkeley, is the geographer whose name is most closely identified with this concept (we consider Sauer's work in more detail in Chapter 8). In 1927, Sauer wrote an article, "Recent Developments in Cultural Geography," in which he argued that cultural landscapes comprise the "forms superimposed on the physical landscape" by human activity. We will delve into this more deeply in Chapter 8.

The Tanzanian city of Dar-es-Salaam provides an interesting urban example of a landscape possessing visible imprints of changing occupancy. Arabs from Zanzibar first chose the African site in 1866 as a summer retreat. Next, German colonizers imprinted a new layout and architectural style (wood-beamed Teutonic) when they chose the city as the centre of their East African colonies in 1891. After World War I, when the Germans were ousted, a British administration took over the city and began yet another period of transformation. The British encouraged immigration from their colony in India to Tanzania. The new Asian migrant population created a zone of three- and four-storey apartment houses, which look as if they were transplanted from Mumbai, India (**Figure 1.8**). Then, in the early 1960s, Dar-es-Salaam became the capital of newly independent Tanzania. Thus, the city experienced four stages of cultural dominance in less than one century, and each stage of the sequence remains imprinted in the cultural landscape.

(a)   (b)

© Alexander B. Murphy

FIGURE 1.8 (a) Mumbai, India. Apartment buildings throughout Mumbai (formerly Bombay), India, are typically four storeys with balconies. **(b) Dar-es-Salaam, Tanzania.** This four-storey walk-up stands where single-family African dwellings once stood, reflecting the sequential occupancy of the city.

The cultural landscape can be seen as a kind of book offering clues into each chapter of the cultural practices, values, and priorities of its various occupiers. As geographer Peirce Lewis explained in *Axioms for Reading the Landscape* (1979), "Our human landscape is our unwitting autobiography, reflecting our tastes, our values, our aspirations, and even our fears, in tangible, visible form." Lewis recommends looking for layers of history in cultural landscapes, adding that most major changes in the cultural landscape occur after a major event, such as a war, an invention, or an economic depression.

Movement. The fifth theme drawing on a spatial perspective is **movement**, which refers to the mobility of people, goods, and ideas across the surface of the planet. Movement is an expression of the interconnectedness of places. **Spatial interaction** between places depends on the **distance** (the measured physical space between two places) between places, the **accessibility** (the ease of reaching one location from another) of places, and the transportation and communication **connectivity** (the degree of linkage between locations in a network) among places. Interactions of many kinds shape the human geography of the world, and understanding these interactions is an important aspect of comprehending the global spatial order.

> **Movement** The mobility of people, goods, and ideas across the surface of the planet.
>
> **Spatial interaction** The nature and extent of interconnections and linkages. This depends on the distance between places, the accessibility of places, and the transportation and communication connectivity among places.
>
> **Distance** Measurement of the physical space between two places.
>
> **Accessibility** The degree of ease with which it is possible to reach a certain location from other locations. Accessibility varies from place to place and can be measured.
>
> **Connectivity** The degree of direct linkage between one particular location and other locations in a network.

Transportation has become an important site of geographic inquiry that focuses on the movement of people and goods, the infrastructure to support that movement, and the interconnectedness of transportation systems with other aspects of human geography. Chapter 12 provides a detailed analysis of transportation geography. Moreover, there has been considerable scholarly inquiry into geographies that focus specifically on movement. Scholars interested in the "new mobilities paradigm" suggest that it is helpful to understand geography not as static, but in a constant state of movement and flux. As geographers Tim Cresswell and Peter Merriman state, "geographical knowledge often assumes a stable point of view, a world of places and boundaries and territories rooted in time and bounded in space. A new focus on mobilities in geography allows us to re-centre it in the discipline" (Cresswell & Merriman, 2011: 4). Mobilities research, therefore, asks geographers to think about being "on the move," linking transportation and communication technologies including mobile phones, mobile computing, and Internet-based devices, and considering how these changes are (re)shaping our experiences across time and space.

1.3 Why Do Geographers Use Maps and What Do Maps Tell Us?

Maps are an incredibly powerful geographic tool, and **cartography**, the art and science of making maps, is as old as geography itself. (For details on the cartographic arts, see Appendix A.) Maps have countless purposes—they can be used to wage war, promote political propaganda, solve medical problems, locate shopping centres, guide refugees, and warn of natural hazards. There are many distinctive kinds of mapping that convey incredible amounts of information. In our daily lives, most of us make use of several relatively common types of maps: reference maps, thematic maps, and mental maps help us make sense of the world. New technologies such as remote sensing and the Global Positioning System (GPS) add to our arsenal of technical tools for navigating our physical world.

> **Cartography** The art and science of making maps, including data compilation, layout, and design. Also concerned with the interpretation of mapped patterns.

It is important to bear in mind that all maps simplify the world. A reference map of the world cannot show every place there is. Likewise, a thematic map of hurricane tracks in the Atlantic Ocean cannot pinpoint every hurricane and its precise path for the last 50 years. The very act of mapping—that is, putting pen to paper—erases some places from human memory and brings others into being. This is also illustrated in Figure 1.7, which details indigenous territorial understandings in British Columbia. When they map data, geographers make decisions about what information to include and generalize the information they present on maps. Many of the maps in this book are thematic maps of the world in which shadings show how much or how little of some phenomenon can be found on a part of the

Earth's surface. While these generalized maps help us see broad trends, we cannot see all cases of a given phenomenon. For example, the map of world precipitation (**Figure 1.9**) is a generalized map of mean annual precipitation received around the world. The areas shaded burgundy, dark blue, and vibrant green indicate places that receive the most rain, and those shaded orange receive the least rain on average. Take a pen and trace along the equator on the map. Notice how many of the high-precipitation areas on the map are along the equator. The consistent heating of the equator over the course of the year brings consistent precipitation to the equatorial region. At the scale of the world, we can see general trends in precipitation like this, but it is difficult to see the micro-scale areas of intense precipitation everywhere in the world.

REFERENCE MAPS

> **Reference maps** Maps that show the absolute location of places and geographic features determined by a frame of reference, typically latitude and longitude.
>
> **Absolute location** The position or place of a certain item on the surface of the Earth as expressed in degrees, minutes, and seconds of latitude, 0° to 90° north or south of the equator, and longitude, 0° to 180° east or west of the Prime Meridian passing through Greenwich, England (a suburb of London).

Reference maps focus on accuracy in showing the **absolute locations** of places and geographic features. These maps use a coordinate system that allows you to plot precisely where something is on Earth. Imagine taking an orange, drawing a dot on it with a marker, and then trying to describe the exact location of that dot to someone who is holding another orange so she can mark the same spot on her orange. If you draw and number the same coordinate system on both oranges, the task of drawing the absolute location on each orange is not only doable but also simple. The most frequently used coordinate system is latitude and longitude. For example, the absolute location of Mogadishu, the capital of Somalia, is 2° 04' N and 45° 22' E. Using these coordinates, you can plot the location of Mogadishu on any globe or map that is marked with latitude and longitude.

> **Relative location** The regional position or situation of a place relative to the position of other places. Distance, accessibility, and connectivity affect relative location.

While reference maps show absolute locations, we often want to know where we are in terms of our relationship to other places. **Relative location** describes a place in relation to other human and physical features. Descriptors such as "The city of Ottawa is located at the confluence of the Ottawa, Rideau, and Gatineau rivers" or "Calgary is the hub of the oil, gas, and wheat markets in western Canada" locate a place relative to other features. In eastern Ontario, all roads lead to Ottawa (**Figure 1.10**), and many of the people within that region would define much of their lives relative to Ottawa because of the tight interconnectedness between Ottawa and the eastern Ontario region.

THEMATIC MAPS

> **Thematic maps** Maps that tell stories, typically showing the degree of some attribute or the movement of a geographic phenomenon.
>
> **Spatial distribution** Physical location of geographic phenomena across space.
>
> **Pattern** The design of a spatial distribution (e.g., scattered or concentrated).

Thematic maps tell stories, typically showing the degree of some attribute or the movement of a geographic phenomenon. Although humans have used maps for navigation for thousands of years, it is only in more recent times that we have begun to appreciate how mapping the **spatial distribution** of a phenomenon is the first step to understanding it. By looking at a map that shows how something is distributed across space, we can raise questions about how the arrangement came about, what processes create and sustain the particular **pattern** of the distribution, and what relationships exist between different places and things. Thematic maps portray the social, political, economic, physical, agricultural, and other aspects of a particular place, region, or area. A unique example of thematic mapping is shown in **Figure 1.11**. Using data obtained from the Wikipedia data dump in November 2009, this map has been created to reveal the number of Wikipedia articles tagged to each country. There are approximately 500,000 Wikipedia articles that are about either a place or an event that occurred in a particular location, which include the absolute location coordinates for geotagging. Mapping the tags reveals the extent to which Wikipedia is dominated by U.S. and western European countries. Nearly 90,000 articles are tagged to the United States, for example. This map reveals how information itself is geographical and how the Internet (and Wikipedia in particular) is colonized in particular ways, and calls into question the neutrality of data found on-line.

> **Pandemic** An outbreak of a disease that spreads worldwide.

An excellent example of how the mapping of patterns can lead to valuable discoveries is found in the work of Dr. John Snow. In 1854, Dr. Snow, a noted anesthesiologist in London, England, mapped cases of cholera in London's Soho district. Cholera refers to a set of diseases in which diarrhea and dehydration are the chief symptoms. Up until the early 1800s, cholera had been confined to India, but it began to spread to China, Japan, East Africa, and Mediterranean Europe in the first of several **pandemics**, worldwide outbreaks of the disease. This initial wave had abated by 1823, but by then the very name of cholera was feared throughout the world, for it had killed people everywhere by the thousands. A second cholera pandemic struck North America between 1826 and 1837, and during a third pandemic, England was severely hit and the disease again spread into North America.

When the pandemic that began in 1842 reached England in the 1850s, cholera swept through Soho. In an effort to understand the disease, Dr. Snow mapped London's Soho district, marking all the area's water pumps, where residents obtained their water supply for home use. Dr. Snow marked these pumps with the letter P and also marked with a dot the residence of each person who died from cholera (**Figure 1.12**). Approximately

FIGURE 1.9 Average annual precipitation of the world. A generalized map of the mean annual precipitation received around the world.

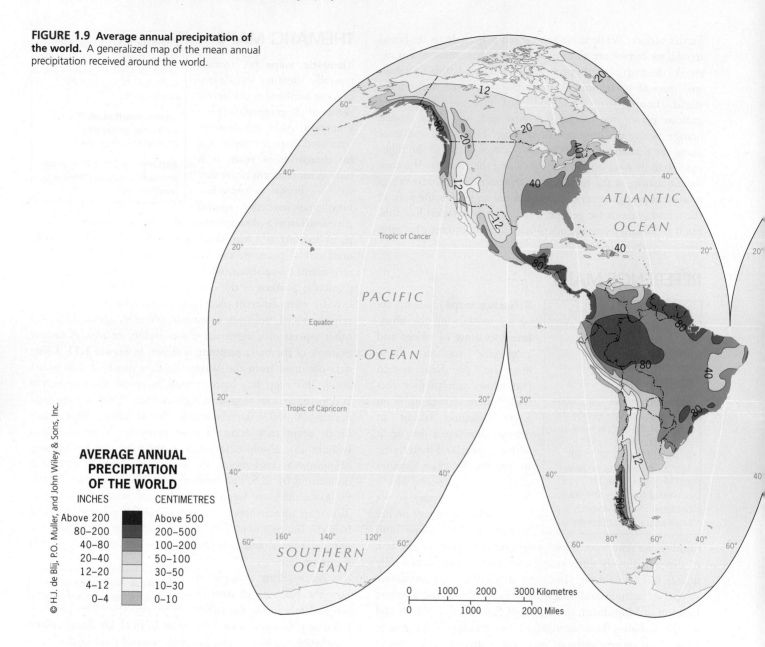

© H.J. de Blij, P.O. Muller, and John Wiley & Sons, Inc.

AVERAGE ANNUAL PRECIPITATION OF THE WORLD

INCHES	CENTIMETRES
Above 200	Above 500
80–200	200–500
40–80	100–200
20–40	50–100
12–20	30–50
4–12	10–30
0–4	0–10

500 deaths occurred in Soho, and as the map took shape, Snow noticed that an especially large number of those deaths clustered around the water pump on Broad Street. Plotting the spatial distribution of the phenomenon made visible certain patterns that had previously been undetected. At Snow's request, city authorities removed the handle from the Broad Street pump, making it impossible to get water from that pump. The result was dramatic: almost immediately the number of reported new cases fell to nearly zero. Snow's theory about the role of water in the spread of cholera was confirmed, partly through the use of a thematic map.

Cholera has not been defeated completely, however, and in some ways the risks have risen in recent years. In the teeming shantytowns of the growing cities of the developing world, and in the refugee camps of Africa and Asia, cholera remains a threat. For example, in the aftermath of the Haitian earthquake in January 2010, damage to water supply systems and deteriorating sanitary conditions led to an outbreak of cholera in that country for the

first time in 100 years. Until the 1990s, major outbreaks remained few and limited (after remaining cholera-free for a half century, Europe had its first reappearance of cholera in Naples in 1972), and most cases were reported in Africa. But an outbreak in the slums of Lima, Peru, in December 1990 became a fast-spreading **epidemic** (regional outbreak of a disease) that, although confined to the Americas, touched every country in the hemisphere, infected more than one million people, and killed over 10,000. In 2006, a cholera outbreak in Angola spread quickly, abruptly ending Angola's civil war. The end of the war allowed people to move around the country more easily, which in turn inadvertently helped spread the disease. Proper hygiene prevents cholera, but contaminated water abounds in many of the tropical world's cities. A cholera vaccine exists, but it is costly and remains effective for only six months. Dr. Snow achieved a victory through the application of geographical reasoning, but the war against cholera is not yet won.

> **Epidemic** Regional outbreak of a disease.

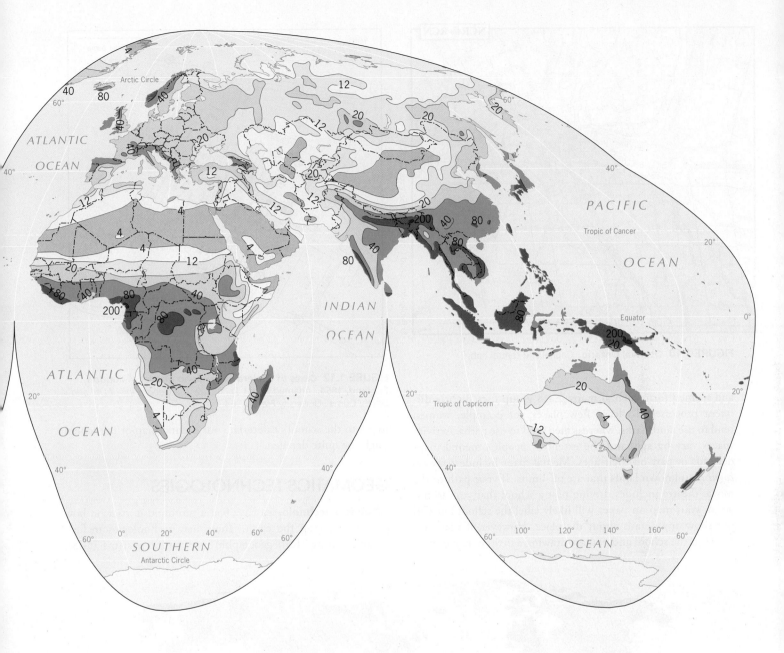

MENTAL MAPS

Mental map Image or picture of the way space is organized as determined by an individual's perception, impression, and knowledge of that space.

While we often think about maps as something we can hold and touch, it is also important to think about how we all carry maps in our minds of places we have been and places we have merely heard of—our internal **mental maps**. Even if you have never been to the Maritimes, for example, you may have studied wall maps and atlases or come across descriptions of the region in books, magazines, newspapers, websites, or television advertisements frequently enough to envision the provinces of the region (Nova Scotia, Prince Edward Island, and New Brunswick) in your mind. If you hear on the news that a hurricane caused damage in Halifax, you use your mental map of the region to make sense of where the hurricane occurred and its impact.

Our mental maps of the places within our **activity spaces** (those places we travel

Activity space The space within which daily activity occurs.

to routinely in our rounds of daily activity) are more accurate and detailed than our maps of places we have never been (**Figure 1.13**). If your friend calls and asks you to meet her at the movie theatre you go to all the time, your mental map will engage automatically. You will envision the hallway, the front door, the walk to your car, the lane to choose in order to be prepared for the left turn you must make, the spot where you will park your car, and your path into the theatre and up to the popcorn stand.

Geographers who study human-environment behaviour have made extensive studies on how people develop their mental maps. The earliest humans, who were nomadic, had incredibly accurate mental maps of where to find food and shelter. Today, people use mental maps to find their way through the intricacies of cities and suburbs. Geographers have also studied how children, people who are blind, new residents to cities, and men

FIGURE 1.10 Ottawa, Ontario. Capital and central hub.

© Public Works and Government Services Canada

FIGURE 1.12 Cases of cholera in the Soho district of London, England, 1854. Adapted from L.D. Stamp, *The Geography of Life and Death,* Cornell University Press, 1964.

and women form mental maps. Each group uses slightly different processes. To learn new places, for example, women tend to use landmarks, whereas men tend to use paths. Activity spaces vary by age, and the extent of people's mental maps depends in part on their ages. Mental maps include *terra incognita*, unknown lands that are off-limits. If your path to the movie theatre includes driving past a school that you do not go to, your map on paper will likely label the school but will not show any details about the place. However, if you have access to the school and you are drawing a mental map of how

to get to the school's cafeteria, your mental map of the school might be quite detailed.

GEOMATICS TECHNOLOGIES

Geomatics technologies have had a profound impact on how geographers map the earth. These new technologies include remote sensing (RS), geographic information systems (GIS),

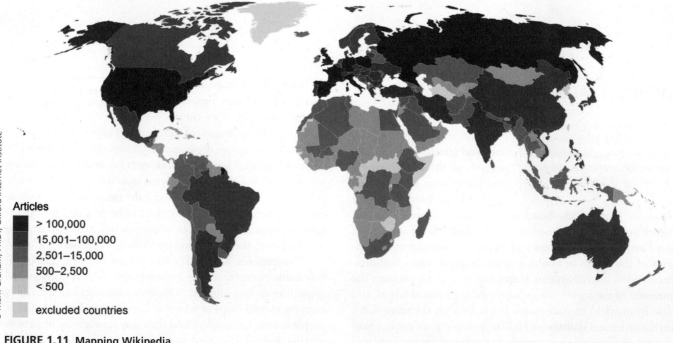

© Mark Graham, Ph.D., Oxford Internet Institute

Articles
> 100,000
15,001–100,000
2,501–15,000
500–2,500
< 500

excluded countries

FIGURE 1.11 Mapping Wikipedia.

FIGURE 1.13 An example of mental mapping.

technology and data storage, increasing accessibility to location-specific data and GPS technology, and the creation of software products tailored to specific geographic uses have all driven incredible advances in **geographic information systems (GIS)** over the last two decades. Geographers use GIS to compare a variety of spatial data by

> **Geographic information system (GIS)** A collection of computer hardware and software that permits spatial data to be collected, recorded, stored, retrieved, manipulated, analyzed, and displayed to the user.

FIGURE 1.14 Remotely sensed image of the Red River flood in Manitoba, 1997. This image was acquired by RADARSAT-1, an earth observation satellite developed in Canada. Since water bodies and wet surfaces produce lower levels of radar backscatter, flooded areas appear in darker tones on this radar image, while dry or upland areas appear in lighter tones. The extent of flooding is also highlighted in blue.

> **Geomatics technologies** Those processes and tools used in the collection and analysis of spatial data, including remote sensing (RS), geographic information systems (GIS), Global Positioning System (GPS), and related forms of earth mapping.
>
> **Remote sensing** A method of collecting data or information through the use of instruments (e.g., satellites) that are physically distant from the area or object of study.

and the Global Positioning System (GPS).

Geographers use **remote sensing** (RS) to monitor the Earth from a distance. Their data are collected by satellites, aircraft, or other technology located some distance away from the place being studied, and the resulting information is available almost instantaneously. After a major weather event, such as the Red River flood in 1997 (**Figures 1.14** and **1.15**) or the devastating mud slide in Washington state in 2014 (**Figure 1.16**), remotely sensed data show us the major areas of impact.

Remote sensing helps geographers understand the physical and human geography of a place, and the Internet ensures that such information is widely available. Google Earth, for example, is an on-line set of remotely sensed images from around the world that are freely accessible to anyone with Internet access. You can think of Google Earth as a quilt of remotely sensed images taken all over the world; the images come from several sources and are sewn together like a patchwork quilt. As a result, the resolution (the measure of the smallest object or the degree of detail that can be resolved by the sensor) of the images differs.

Geographers can incorporate remotely sensed images in a map and study absolute locations over time by plotting the changes depicted in remotely sensed images. Advances in computer

FIGURE 1.15 Airborne remote-sensing image of flood waters surrounding Morris, Manitoba, during the 1997 Red River flood.

(a)

(b)

© DigitalGlobe/Getty Images

© DigitalGlobe/Getty Images

FIGURE 1.16 **Satellite images of the small community of Oso, Washington, devastated by a landslide on March 22, 2014.** (a) Before the landslide, captured July 13, 2013, and (b) after the landslide, captured March 31, 2014.

creating digitized representations of the environment (figures 1.14 and 1.16), combining layers of spatial data, and creating maps on which patterns and processes are superimposed. Geographers also use GIS to analyze data, which can give us new insight into geographic patterns and relationships.

Geographers trained in GIS apply the software technologies in countless fields today. Students who earn undergraduate degrees in geography are employed by software companies, government agencies, and businesses to use GIS to survey wildlife, map soils, analyze natural disasters, follow diseases, assist first responders, plan cities, plot transportation improvements, and track weather systems. For example, a group of geographers working for one GIS company tailors its software to serve branches of the military and the defence intelligence community. The vast amounts of data gathered by the various intelligence agencies can be integrated into a GIS and then analyzed spatially. Geographers working in the defence intelligence community can use GIS to query a large amount of intelligence, interpret spatial data, and make recommendations on issues of security and defence.

> **Global Positioning System (GPS)** Satellite-based system for determining the absolute location of places or geographic features.

The establishment of the satellite-based **Global Positioning System (GPS)** allows us to locate things on the surface of the Earth with extraordinary accuracy. Researchers collect data quickly and easily in the field, and low-priced GPS units are encouraging fishers, hunters, and hikers to use GPS in their hobbies. Many new cars are equipped with GPS units, and dashboard map displays help commuters navigate traffic and travellers find their way. These new geomatics technologies are being used in new and unexpected ways. As Vickie Fast and Dr. Marilyne Jollineau discuss in their *Guest Field Note*, geomatics technologies can offer new information and data useful for cultivating grapes and making wine. As well as improving wine production and taste, these techniques help improve soil and water quality, reduce pesticide and herbicide use, and improve land management practices.

Geographic information science (GISc) is an emerging research field concerned with studying the development and use of geospatial concepts and techniques to examine geographic patterns and processes. Your school may have a program in GISc that draws across disciplines, bringing together the computer scientists who write the programs, the engineers who create sensors that gather data about the Earth, and the geographers who combine layers of data and interpret them to make sense of our world. One more intriguing use of new technologies is the hobby of **geocaching**. Geocachers use their GPS units to play a treasure hunt game all over the world. People find a location for the treasures ("geocaches"), mark the coordinates on their GPS, and post clues on the Internet. If you find the geocache, you sign either an electronic or physical logbook, indicating your success. If you choose to take the treasure, you must leave something of equal or greater value for the next geocacher to find. According to www.geocaching.com, there are now over 2.5 million active geocaches located around the globe. What makes geocaching so much fun is that caches are hidden in such a way that most people would walk right past them. Geocachers are highly creative in hiding their caches, which makes the seeking, aided with GPS technologies, more challenging (**Figure 1.17**).

> **Geocaching** A hunt for a cache, the Global Positioning System (GPS) coordinates of which are posted on the Internet by other geocachers.

© Taplight/Alamy

FIGURE 1.17 **A carefully hidden geocache.**

GUEST FIELD NOTE

The Geography of Wine Production: Using Geomatics Technologies in the Niagara Wine Region

The effect of geographic location on grape production is known as *terroir*: the interaction of soil, geology, weather, climate, microclimate, and vineyard management strategy. The *terroir* is unique for each wine-producing region, which is why the Champagne region in France produces very different wines than the Bordeaux region in France. Champagne is ideally suited for growing Chardonnay, while Bordeaux, 400 kilometres away, is ideally suited for growing Merlot. Even when two different areas produce the same grape variety, the flavours are unique. An expert *sommelier* (a wine steward) can, for example, differentiate between a Chardonnay wine produced from grapes grown in California and one produced from grapes grown in Australia, Spain, or Germany.

In Canada, multiple regions have *terroir* ideally suited for grape production. In British Columbia, the Okanagan Valley and Kelowna have thriving wine regions that have evolved to be tourism destinations. Nova Scotia and other eastern provinces are also beginning to experiment with wine production. Ontario has three distinct wine growing regions: Prince Edward County, Lake Erie North Shore and Pelee Island (the most southern point in Canada), and the Niagara Region.

The Niagara Region, in particular, is one of Canada's leading wine-producing regions. Situated at 43° north latitude, Niagara has a latitude similar to many famous wine-producing regions, including the Napa Valley in California, Bordeaux in France, and Tuscany in Italy. However, in contrast to the many Old World wine regions that have had thousands of years to develop their vineyards and establish best management practices, Canadian vineyards and wineries are relatively young. Historically, Niagara grapes were of the native *Vitis labrusca* variety, which produced poor-quality wines with maximum alcohol content. It wasn't until the early 1980s that viticulturists introduced French *Vitis vinifera* and hybrid varieties associated with premium wines (e.g., Chardonnay, Riesling, Pinot Noir, and Cabernet Franc) to Niagara, despite warnings that they would not survive the harsh winter. Fortunately, the French varieties did unexpectedly well in Niagara's *terroir*, effectively kick-starting the local wine economy.

As geographers, we have the opportunity to use various tools to contribute to the improvement of wine production and quality in the Niagara Region. Given that local winemakers have not had generations to develop vineyard management practices best suited for the production of premium grapes, geomatics technologies—including geographic information systems (GIS), the Global Positioning System (GPS), and remote sensing—can be used to improve methods of managing vineyards. Many vineyard management practices treat fields as though they are uniform when, in actuality, they are varied and complex. **Figure 1.18** illustrates the spatial variation in vine vigour on a standard false-colour satellite image, where red represents areas of high vine vigour and healthy vegetation, and blue-green (known as cyan) represents areas of low vine vigour and possibly unhealthy vegetation. Managers can make better decisions if they understand and manipulate these underlying spatial variations to the advantage of the grape grower. This concept is known as precision viticulture, which is closely related to precision agriculture.

An example of a precision viticulture study is one of our research projects, which sought to understand the spatial variability in soil moisture at Stratus Wines, a 25-hectare vineyard and winery in Niagara-on-the-Lake, Ontario. Using GPS to geolocate sample vines and a time-domain reflectometer to quantify the vineyard's soil moisture at those sample vines, we applied spatial analysis techniques within a GIS environment (including spatial interpolation and spatial autocorrelation) to the data to measure spatial pattern. We identified temporally stable clustered patterns in soil moisture, as shown in **Figure 1.19**. In other words, we determined that the wettest and driest soil moisture zones within vineyards were consistent over time. Combined with other vineyard variables (e.g., vine vigour), farmers can tailor their vineyard management practices (e.g., irrigation and pest/disease control) based on different zones of characteristic performance within their vineyards.

© CNES, licensed by the Alberta Terrestrial Imaging Centre, www.uleth.ca/research/alberta-terrestrial-imaging-centre-atic

FIGURE 1.18 Vineyard spatial variability. SPOT satellite image over Niagara, July 22, 2007.

© Victoria Fast and Marilyne Jollineau

Overall, Canada's grape and wine industry is in a time of rapid development. During this period of growth, integrating geomatics technologies into existing vineyard management practices has the potential to improve what we know about our local vineyards and, in turn, significantly increase vineyard productivity, production efficiency, and profitability over the long term, while minimizing the impact of farm operations on the natural environment.

FIGURE 1.19 Spatial and temporal variability of soil moisture in a Cabernet Franc (CF) vineyard block at Stratus Wines.

Victoria Fast and Dr. Marilyne Jollineau, Department of Geography, Brock University, St. Catharines, Ontario.

MAIN POINTS 1.3 Why Do Geographers Use Maps and What Do Maps Tell Us?

- Maps are incredibly powerful tools that allow us to plot and visualize an array of data for any number of purposes. We use reference and thematic maps that can indicate absolute and relative locations, highlight unforeseen patterns, and provide more generalized information.

- Mental maps chart the internal sense of place that we develop from our actual experiences in places and from the information that we hear about places we perhaps have never been. Not surprisingly, researchers find differences in

how we draw our mental maps depending on age, race, gender, and class.

- Geomatics technologies, including remote sensing, geographical information systems, and the Global Positioning System, are another set of powerful mapping tools with a range of economic, social, and political uses. Use of these technologies can capture the processes of change in places over time, track the movement of people and goods, and aid in providing assistance and information to those in need.

1.4 Why Are Geographers Concerned with Scale and Connectedness?

Geographers study places and patterns at a variety of scales, including local, regional, national, and global. In other words, human geographers work at a variety of scales, from the local to the global and from the level of the individual (body), to the neighbourhood or community, to the town or city, nation (country) or planet, as well as many points in between. Scale has two meanings in geography: it refers to the distance on a map compared to the distance on the Earth; it can also refer to the territorial extent of something. When we refer to scale throughout this book, we are generally using the second of these definitions. As geographers, the scale of

our research or analysis matters because we can make different observations at different scales. We can study a single phenomenon across different scales in order to see how things that are happening at the global scale affect localities and how things that are happening at a local scale affect the globe. Geographers recognize that phenomena, whether human or physical, happen in a context, and that context looks different at different scales.

The scale at which we study a geographic phenomenon tells us what level of detail we can expect to see. We also see different patterns at different scales. For example, when we study the distribution of wealth on a global scale, we see that the countries in western Europe, Canada, the United States, Japan, and Australia are the wealthiest, and the countries of sub-Saharan Africa and Southeast Asia are the poorest (**Figure 1.20**). Does that mean everyone in the United States is wealthy and everyone in Indonesia is poor? Certainly not,

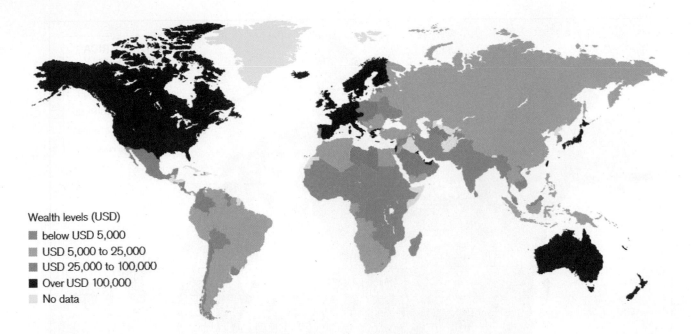

James Davies, Rodrigo Lluberas, and Anthony Shorrocks, Credit Suisse Global Wealth Databook 2014

Wealth levels (USD)

- below USD 5,000
- USD 5,000 to 25,000
- USD 25,000 to 100,000
- Over USD 100,000
- No data

FIGURE 1.20 Global distribution of wealth by country, 2014. This map depicts global wealth per capita, in U.S. dollars, wherein wealth is understood not as income, but rather as the value of physical and financial assets less debts. Source: Credit Suisse, Research Institute, Global Wealth Databook 2014, Figure 2-2, p.19.

but on a global-scale map of states, that is how the data appear.

When you shift scales to North America and examine the data for U.S. states and Canadian provinces, you see that the wealthiest areas are on the coasts and the poorest are in the interior and the extreme northeast and south. The state of Alaska and Canada's Northwest Territories have high gross per capita incomes stemming largely from oil revenues that are shared among the residents (**Figure 1.21**).

Shifting scales to just one city—for example, the Census Metropolitan Area (CMA) of Montreal, Quebec (**Figure 1.22**)—we can see how less than 10 percent of the population in surrounding areas, such as Beaconsfield, is considered low income, whereas there is greater diversity of income within the more central parts of the city, such as near the region of Westmount. Shifting scales again, this time to the individual, if we conducted fieldwork in Saskatoon, Saskatchewan, and interviewed people who live below the poverty line, we would quickly find that each person's experience of poverty and reasons for being in poverty vary—making it difficult to generalize. We might find some trends—such as how women who have children cope with poverty differently from single men, or how illegal immigrants cope differently from legal immigrants—but the details would still vary from person to person.

Because the level of detail and the patterns observed change as the scale changes, geographers must be sensitive to their scale of analysis and must also be wary of researchers who make generalizations about a people or a place at a particular scale without considering other scales of analysis.

Geographers are also interested in how people use scale politically. Local political movements, such as the Zapatistas in southern Mexico, have learned to **rescale** their actions—to involve players at other scales and create a global outcry of support for their position. By taking their political campaign from the individual and local scale to the national scale through their protests against the North American Free Trade Agreement, and then effectively using the Internet to wage a global campaign, the Zapatistas gained attention from the world media, a feat few local political movements achieve.

Rescale Involvement of players at other scales to generate support for a position or an initiative (e.g., use of the Internet to generate interest on a national or global scale for a local position or initiative).

Geographer Victoria Lawson uses the term "jumping scale" to describe rescaling. She compares the ways in which Western countries, multinational corporations, and the World Trade Organization take products and ideas created in Western places and by Western corporations and globalize all rights to profits from them through intellectual property law. Efforts to push European and American views of intellectual property on the globe negate other local and regional views of products and ideas. To the West, rice is a product that can be owned, privatized, and bought and sold. To East Asians, rice is integral to culture; new rice strains and new ideas about growing rice can help build community, not just profit. Lawson explains that taking a single regional view and jumping scale to globalize it legitimates that view and negates other regional and local views. For example, according to the international corporate watchdog organization CorpWatch, there was concern that in the aftermath of the earthquake in Haiti in January 2010, large multinational corporations such as Monsanto would use the disaster to gain a larger foothold in local economies. Peasant farmers, wary because of a long

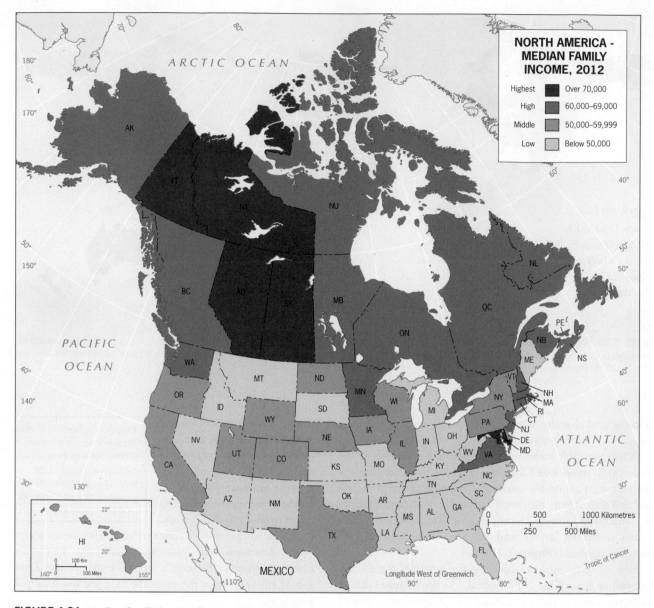

FIGURE 1.21 **Median family income (in U.S. dollars), 2012.** Data from United States Census Bureau and Statistics Canada.

history of international exploitation disguised as aid, burned seeds donated by Monsanto in protest (**Figure 1.23**). Monsanto, a U.S.-based multinational agricultural corporation, has been criticized widely by farming groups for its practice of copyrighting genetically modified seeds; copyrighting seeds reduces or eliminates farmers' ability to harvest seeds and replant the following year, a critical aspect of sustainable farming.

CONNECTEDNESS THROUGH DIFFUSION

> **Diffusion** The spatial spreading or dissemination of a culture element (such as a technological innovation) or some other phenomenon (such as a disease outbreak).

Geographers focus on the "connectedness" of places. By this we mean the ways in which sometimes distant and apparently unrelated places exhibit unexpected linkages. We find these connections through the various processes of **diffusion**. Diffusion occurs

when people, goods, or ideas move across space and across a number of different scales (see Chapter 8). (Remember that movement is one of the five

> **Cultural diffusion** The expansion and adoption of a cultural element from its place of origin to a wider area.

themes organizing this book.) The process by which an idea or innovation spreads from its hearth (source area) to other places is known as **cultural diffusion**. Carl Sauer focused attention on this process in his book *Agricultural Origins and Dispersals*, in which he defined the ancient hearths of agriculture and traced the diffusion of agricultural practices from the hearths. In 1970, Swedish geographer Torsten Hägerstrand published pioneering research on the role of time in the diffusion process. Hägerstrand's research revealed how time, as well as distance, affects individual human behaviour and the diffusion of people and ideas. Sauer and Hägerstrand's fascinating research attracted many geographers to the study of diffusion processes. For example, cultural diffusion has been used to study the historic spread of hearth

Statistics Canada

FIGURE 1.22 **Percentage of population with low income, Montreal, 2010.** Statistics Canada, Thematic Maps 2011 Census.

cultures globally, such as the spread of Roman Catholicism in the Americas during the 16th and 17th centuries. More recent research considers the interrelationship between culture and corporations, studying such phenomena as the "McDonaldization" of the world, in which American culture is diffused internationally through the franchising of McDonald's restaurants on a global scale. Geographers are still using principles of diffusion to model movement and dissemination through GIS and other geographic techniques.

> **Cultural barrier** Prevailing cultural attitude rendering certain innovations, ideas, or practices unacceptable or unadoptable in that particular culture.

Not all people in all spaces and places view the diffusion of new ideas, concepts, or goods as a positive outcome, and **cultural barriers** can work against diffusion. Certain innovations, ideas, or practices may not be acceptable or adoptable in particular cultures because of prevailing attitudes or even taboos. For example, cultural barriers against practices such as the use of contraceptives influence diffusion processes and are highly politicized in some places where the transmission of HIV/AIDS is being fought. Other places may seek to preserve their language, history, and geography from the diffusion of ideas and such cultural artefacts as music, writing, and technology. In Canada, the Province of Quebec considers that legislative and policy initiatives to protect Québécois culture and language are crucial to the province's survival. As **Figure 1.24** illustrates, changing signs to enforce these requirements can be awkward. At the national level, the Canadian Radio-television and Telecommunications Commission has the task of protecting Canadian culture (the television, radio, and telecommunications industries) from foreign (mainly U.S.) domination.

EXPANSION DIFFUSION

Geographers divide diffusion processes into two broad categories: expansion diffusion and relocation diffusion. In the case of **expansion diffusion**, an innovation or idea develops in a hearth, which is an area where cultural traits develop and from which the cultural

> **Expansion diffusion** The spread of an innovation or an idea through a population in an area in such a way that the number of those influenced grows continuously larger, resulting in an expanding area of dissemination.

traits diffuse, and remains strong there while also spreading outward (**Figure 1.25**). For example, we can study the spread of Islam from its hearth on the Arabian Peninsula to Egypt and North Africa, through Southwest Asia, and into West Africa. If we were to draw a series of maps of followers of Islam (Muslims) at 50-year intervals beginning in 620 CE, the area of adoption of Islam would be larger in each successive period.

Alice Speri/AFP/Getty Images

FIGURE 1.23 **Symbolic burning of Monsanto's hybrid corn seed in Haiti.**

FIGURE 1.24 Altered street sign in Quebec. The English word "street" has been changed to "rue," the French word for street.

© Francis Mariani

> **Contagious diffusion** The distance-controlled spreading of an idea, innovation, or some other item through a local population by person-to-person contact—analogous to the communication of a contagious illness.

Expansion diffusion takes three main forms. **Contagious diffusion** is diffusion in which nearly all adjacent individuals and places are affected. A disease can spread in this way, infecting almost everyone in a population (although not everyone may show symptoms of the disease). However, an idea such as a new fashion or new

genre of music may not always spread throughout a contiguous population. **Hierarchical diffusion** is diffusion in which an idea or innovation spreads by passing first among the most connected places or peoples. For example, the spread of Crocs footwear is a case of hierarchical diffusion, in

> **Hierarchical diffusion** A form of diffusion in which an idea or innovation spreads by passing first among the most connected places or peoples. An urban hierarchy is usually involved, encouraging the leapfrogging of innovations over wide areas, with geographic distance a less important influence.

which the main channel of diffusion is some segment of those who are susceptible to (or adopting) what is being diffused. In the case of Crocs, founder Scott Seamans found a clog manufactured by a Canadian company that was created out of the unique croc resin material. Seamans, an avid sailor, put a strap on the back of the clog and added a few holes to allow for drainage. He and two co-founders set up their company in Boulder, Colorado, had the shoes manufactured, and sold them at boat shows in 2002 and 2003. Crocs footwear diffused from boating enthusiasts to gardeners to the American and Canadian public—becoming especially popular among children who adorned their Crocs with Jibbitz, or charms designed for Crocs. The hierarchy of boaters, gardeners, and then the contagious diffusion that followed helps explain the rapid growth of the Crocs brand, whose revenues peaked in 2007 at $800 million, having sold over 30 million pairs of shoes worldwide in that year alone.

A third form of expansion diffusion is **stimulus diffusion**. Not all ideas can be readily and directly adopted by a receiving population; some are simply too vague, too unattainable, too dif-

> **Stimulus diffusion** A form of diffusion in which a cultural adaptation is created as a result of the introduction of a cultural trait from another place.

ferent, or too impractical for immediate adoption. Yet these ideals can still have an impact. They may indirectly promote local experimentation and eventual changes in the ways people do things. For example, the diffusion of mass-produced food items in the late 20th century—pushed by multinational retailers—led to the introduction of the hamburger in India. The Hindu religion in India prohibits consumption of beef, which was a major cultural obstacle to the adoption of the hamburger (**Figure 1.26**). However, retailers experimented and began selling burgers made of vegetable products, an adaptation stimulated by the diffusion of the hamburger, which took on a new form in the cultural context of India.

RELOCATION DIFFUSION

Expansion diffusion spreads across space without requiring people to physically move to become "knowers" of the trait or innovation. Instead, the people stay put and the innovation, idea, trait, or disease does the moving. **Relocation diffusion**, in contrast, involves the actual movement of

> **Relocation diffusion** Sequential diffusion process in which the items being diffused are transmitted by their carrier agents as they evacuate the old areas and relocate to new ones. The most common form of relocation diffusion involves the spreading of innovations by a migrating population.

A. Contagious Diffusion

B. Hierarchial Diffusion

LEGEND

- ● Hearth
- ● Early diffusion
- ● Later diffusion
- ○ Important person or place
- ● No diffusion

FIGURE 1.25 Contagious and hierarchical diffusion.

© E.H. Fouberg, A.B. Murphy, H.J. de Blij, and John Wiley & Sons, Inc.

(a)

(b)

FIGURE 1.26 (a) New Delhi, India, and (b) Vrindavan, India. Hindus believe cows are holy, and evidence of that belief can be seen everywhere in India, from cows roaming the streets to the menu at McDonald's. In 1996, the first McDonald's restaurant opened in New Delhi, India, serving Maharaja Macs and vegetable burgers with cheese. In Indian towns, such as Jodhpur, cows are protected and are seen along the streets.

individuals who have already adopted the idea or innovation, and who carry it to a new, perhaps distant locale, where they proceed to disseminate it.

Relocation diffusion occurs most frequently through migration. When migrants move from their homeland, they take their cultural traits with them. Developing an ethnic neighbourhood in a new country helps immigrants maintain their culture in the midst of an unfamiliar one. If the homeland of the immigrants loses enough of its population, the cultural customs may fade in the hearth while gaining strength in the ethnic neighbourhoods abroad.

MAIN POINTS 1.4 Why Are Geographers Concerned with Scale and Connectedness?

- The scale of geographical research or analysis matters because we can make different observations at different scales. Geographers can study a single phenomenon across different scales or any number of phenomena at a single scale. Often what is happening at the global scale affects localities, and what is happening at a local scale may have global implications.

- Geographers study places and patterns at a variety of scales, usually focusing on the territorial extent of a phenomenon. The scale determines the level of detail we can expect to see. By "jumping scales" or rescaling, we can see how political and social ideas are mobilized at different scales.

- Using scales, we can see how people, goods, or ideas move across space (movement being one of the five themes in this text). A good example of this is the cultural diffusion of cultural artefacts such as music or fashion. Sometimes places try to set up cultural barriers to prevent ideas or goods from coming to a place or as an attempt to preserve local language and culture. Geographers divide diffusion into two broad categories: expansion diffusion (which can take the form of contagious, hierarchical, or stimulus diffusion) and relocation diffusion.

1.5 What Does It Mean to "Think Geographically" and How Do We Do It?

Today's research, thought, and writing in human geography are grounded in a variety of theories and philosophies that can be traced back thousands of years. You might be surprised by the depth and range of research topics explored by geographers.

Human beings are decidedly geographical because where we are matters to us very much. As nomads, early humans covered vast distances in search of shelter and sustenance, and our earliest written records are often pictograms or drawings of where we have come from and, perhaps, where we would like to go.

Geography as a distinct subject taught in what we now consider to be the formal education system evolved in western Europe from the 17th century onward as part of the formation of higher institutions of learning called universities or colleges. By tracing the numerous ways scholars approached their task, we can see how their ideas about what is "geographical" and how we should "do" geography changed over time. New geographical work (and academic work as a whole) often comes about because of critiques of older or established approaches. These critiques create a divergence in perspectives, foci, and methods as scholars shift their thinking about the nature of the geographical. It is important to realize that there is no singular approach or mode of analysis in geographical scholarship and, in fact, there is considerable debate over the usefulness and viability of one set of approaches over another. A history of geographical thought demonstrates how diverse theoretical and philosophical ideas produce different ideas about what we consider geographical knowledge. We must remember that changes in perspective are influenced by the historical context of the era.

The main focus in this text is on contemporary human geography as it developed in the Western world after World War II, although there is some reference to pre-war scholarship. In this section, we get a taste of how geographical scholarship evolved from the age of exploration and "discovery" in western Europe to the present day. We will then consider 20th-century perspectives on the geographical—perspectives such as environmental determinism and possibilism, regional geography, geography as a spatial science, humanistic and behavioural geography, radical and Marxist geographies, and feminist geographies. While adherents of environmental determinism and possibilism have largely fallen by the wayside, geographers today continue to approach geographical questions using any number and combination of these approaches. This generates a diverse and intriguing body of geographical knowledge for study.

THEORIZING THE GEOGRAPHICAL

Most scholars agree that the formal discipline of geography emerged as a result of the participation of adventurer/scholars in the European age of exploration and "discovery" during the 13th and 14th centuries. Western Europeans travelled the globe, mapping and documenting a seemingly limitless array of new "discoveries"—new peoples and places, new species of plants and animals, and new technologies, architecture, and cultures. (It is worth pointing out that these were discoveries for European explorers only, as the indigenous peoples already knew about the places, plants, animals, and cultures around them!) Considerable labour was required to catalogue, classify, and categorize this endless stream of new and often perplexing information. Scholars such as Alexander von Humboldt (1769–1859) and Carl Ritter (1779–1859) are recognized as among the first to look for underlying universal patterns and structures organizing all earthly phenomenon into some coherent whole. Carl Ritter produced a 19-volume work, entitled *Erdkunde*, in which he struggled to organize geographical data into a coherent whole to provide a sense of unity and purpose.

ENVIRONMENTAL DETERMINISM

Drawing on this vast array of new data, 20th-century geographers turned their attention to theorizing about why certain peoples and phenomena appeared in certain places and not in others and displayed particular and collective characteristics and traits. The

notion of **environmental determinism**, which argues that human behaviour, individually and collectively, is strongly affected by—even controlled or determined by—the physical environment, became popular. This philosophy has its roots in the biological and sociological thinking of such scholars as Charles Darwin and Herbert Spencer. Environmental determinists conceptualize human society as a social organism, displaying traits similar to those of a biological organism that responds to its need to expand, develop, and interact with its surrounding environment.

> **Environmental determinism**
> The view that the natural environment has a controlling influence over various aspects of human life, including cultural development.

The idea that there is a strong interconnection between peoples, their social organization, and their territories or environment has a long history. The ancient Greeks, finding that some of the peoples subjugated by their expanding empire were relatively docile while others were rebellious, attributed such differences to variations in climate. Over 2,000 years ago, Aristotle described northern Europeans as "full of spirit . . . but incapable of ruling others" and characterized Asian people (by which he meant inhabitants of modern-day Turkey) as "intelligent and inventive . . . [but] always in a state of subjection and slavery." Aristotle attributed these traits to the respective climates of the regions—the cold north versus the more tropical Mediterranean.

These views resurfaced as recently as the first half of the 20th century in the work of such geographers as Friedrich Ratzel and Ellen Churchill Semple. As Ron Johnston argues, some geographers went to great lengths to suggest that human behaviours and patterns can be directly linked to an environmental cause. An example is found in the *Principles of Human Geography* (1940), by Ellsworth Huntington and S.W. Cushing:

> *The well-known contrast between the energetic peoples of the most progressive parts of the temperate zone and the inert inhabitants of the tropics and even of intermediate regions, such as Persia, is largely due to climate. . . . The people of the cyclonic regions rank so far above those of the other parts of the world that they are the natural leaders.* (p. 453)

Cushing and Huntington suggested that climate is the critical factor in how humans behave. Yet what constitutes an "ideal" climate lies in the eyes of the beholder. For Aristotle, it was the climate of Greece. More recent commentators from western Europe and North America see the climates most suited to progress and productiveness in culture, politics, and technology as (you guessed it) those of western Europe and the northeastern United States. Such perspectives arguably served to legitimize the colonial and imperial aspirations of European rulers in the new lands they came to govern.

Despite the appeal of explanations provided by environmental determinism, many geographers doubted whether such sweeping generalizations about human-environment connections were valid. They recognized exceptions to the environmental determinists' theories (for example, the Maya civilization in the Americas arose in a tropical climate that most assumed was incapable of complex cultures; see **Figure 1.27**) and argued that humanity was capable of much more than merely adapting to and being constructed by the natural environment. Environmental determinist theories that suggest Europe is superior to the rest of

FIGURE 1.27 The Mayan city of Tikal. (a) This model depicts what the ruins of Tikal, a Mayan city in what is now Guatemala, would have looked like during its apogee. (b) The ruins of Tikal shown in 2008. The Maya civilization caused many geographers to question environmental determinists' belief about human-environment connections. The civilization flourished in a tropical climate, which environmental determinists assumed was incapable of complex cultures.

the world because of the climate and location of the region ignore the fact that for thousands of years the most technologically advanced civilizations were found outside Europe—in North Africa, Southwest Asia, Southeast Asia, and East Asia.

Geographers grew increasingly cautious about such speculative notions and began asking new questions about human-environment relationships. They believed that if generalizations were to be made, they ought to arise from detailed, carefully designed research. Everyone agrees that the natural environment affects human activity in some ways, but people are the decision-makers and the modifiers—not just the slaves of environmental forces. People, their cultures, and their technologies shape environments, constantly altering the landscape and affecting environmental systems. For those who think less carefully about the human-environment dynamic, environmental determinism continues to hold an allure, leading to some highly questionable generalizations about the impact of the environment on humans and a multitude of popular books that use environment as the dominant force in explaining complex histories.

POSSIBILISM

> **Possibilism** Geographic viewpoint, a response to environmental determinism that holds that human decision-making, not the environment, is the crucial factor in cultural development. Nonetheless, possibilists view the environment as providing a set of broad constraints that limits the possibilities of human choice.

Reactions to environmental determinism produced critique and counter-argument. An approach known as **possibilism** emerged, espoused by geographers who argued that the natural environment merely serves to limit the range of choices available to a culture. The choices that a society makes depend on what its members need and on what technology is available to them. Geographers increasingly accepted the doctrine of possibilism, and increasingly discredited environmental determinism.

Even possibilism has its limitations, however, because it encourages a line of inquiry that starts with the physical environment and asks what it allows. Human cultures frequently push the boundaries of what is "environmentally possible" through advances in technology, which are the result of their own ideas and ingenuity. In the interconnected, technologically dependent world we live in today, it is possible to do many things that are at odds with the local environment.

REGIONAL GEOGRAPHY

Dissatisfaction with environmental determinism in Europe and North America took some geographers in a new direction, and **regional geography** vied for a central place as the framework for undertaking geographical work. Proponents such as Richard Hartshorne (1899–1992) and Alfred Hettner (1859–1941) argued for a descriptive geography that divided the world into natural regions by identifying phenomena that grouped themselves in distinctive ways in particular areas. Regional geographers argued that places are unique, disputing the idea that universal and generalizable statements could be made. This notion of "areal differentiation," or the distinctiveness of places, narrowed the geographer's task to a systematic but largely descriptive undertaking. Geography, according to Hartshorne in his *The Nature of Geography: A Critical Survey of Current Thought in the Light of the Past* (1939), was

> **Regional geography** The study of a region's unique characteristics, including its natural and human characteristics, in order to understand how areas differ from each other.

> *a science that interprets the realities of areal differentiation as they are found, not only in terms of the differences in certain things from place to place, but also in terms of the total combination of phenomenon in each place, different from those of every other place* (p. 462).

While Hartshorne's approach was dominant in this period, the work of Carl Sauer and the Berkeley school marked a distinct specialization in the study of cultural landscapes (see Chapter 8, as well as the discussion of landscape in section 1.2 earlier in this chapter). Sauer made important contributions through his focus on both the cultural and natural processes at work in human interactions with the environment.

GEOGRAPHY AS A SPATIAL SCIENCE

In the post-war period, many geographers found the regional focus too narrow and descriptive. While it is important to understand a place in detail, description is only the first step in asking questions about why things are the way they are. Regional geography as it was then practised lacked scientific rigour and had little to say about contemporary political, social, and economic issues. In 1953, geographer Frederick Schaefer authored a paper strongly critical of Hartshorne's regional geography. In "Exceptionalism in Geography: A Methodological Examination," Schaefer argued that geography needed to integrate methods from the positivist sciences and concern itself not only with description but also with explanation. Geography, he argued, should be approached as "a science concerned with the formulation of laws concerning the spatial distribution of certain features on the surface of the earth" (p. 227). In other words, geography should concern itself with the search for the laws of location and spatial organization. This was a marked departure from the work of regional geographers, who regarded regions as unique in all respects. This perceived uniqueness made it impossible to develop general, universal, quantitative laws governing spatial organization.

> **Spatial analysis** Quantitative procedures used to understand the spatial arrangement of phenomena and the related patterns of connections and flows.

Schaefer's paper marked the beginning of a new approach to geography called **spatial analysis**. By spatial analysis, we mean those quantitative procedures used to understand the spatial arrangement of phenomena and the related patterns of connections and flows. His appeal for systematic analysis and scientific methods sparked what some call a "quantitative revolution" in geography, as practitioners began testing hypotheses and identifying repeatable and recognizable causal factors governing spatial relations. Scholars both within and outside geography, such as Walter Christaller, developed models predicting certain spatial patterns and regularities—approaches we will consider in Chapter 10. This approach remains popular in a number of subdisciplinary areas today, including urban planning, transportation, and economic geographies.

HUMANISTIC AND BEHAVIOURAL GEOGRAPHY

> **Behavioural geography** An approach that seeks to understand and model human behaviour and the decision-making processes implicated in human relationships with place.

While "quantitative" approaches yielded models and laws of spatial organization, a growing critique in the 1960s argued that these models and laws provided poor descriptions of reality. Some geographers suggested that spatial analysis, with its scientific focus, could not take the unpredictability of human actions into account. These behavioural geographers sought to understand and model human behaviour and the decision-making processes implicated in human relationships with place. This involved thinking about the cultural and social norms and values guiding human decision-making processes. **Behavioural geography** covered a wide range of topics, from human-natural environment interactions to conceptual or mental mapping and time-geography. Much of this work drew on other social sciences, such as sociology and psychology, but many practitioners continued to use the statistical processes developed by spatial analysts for analyzing behavioural data, which made them the target of a wider critique of positivistic approaches.

> **Humanistic geography** An approach that focuses on the human aspects of place, including human emotions, values and desires.

While behavioural geographers were attempting to predict human behaviour using a spatial science approach, another group of geographers developed yet another form of geographical inquiry: humanistic geography. As geographer Nicholas Entrikin notes, this approach rejected what adherents regarded as the "overly objective, narrow, mechanistic and deterministic view" of human beings found in behavioural geography (1976, p. 16). Humanistic geographers argued that geography's main interest should be the human aspects of place, including human emotions, values, and desires. Yi-Fu Tuan defined **humanistic geography** as the study of "people's relations to nature, their geographical behaviour as well as their feelings and ideas in regard to space and place" (1976, p. 266). Geographers turned to phenomenology, existentialism, and hermeneutics as they attempted to understand humans' everyday interactions in place. Canadian geographer Edward Relph (1970) asserted that our ability to know and learn about place is fundamental to human existence and that geographers should investigate how our direct experience of the material world is foundational to all geographical knowledge. Much of the research carried out from this perspective underpins more recent work in cultural and social geography that addresses how people's sense of identity and collective community is bound up with place. We will explore this approach further in Chapter 7.

RADICAL AND MARXIST GEOGRAPHY

Both behavioural and humanistic geographers focused on human choices and experiences in place, albeit from different perspectives. During the social and political upheavals of the 1960s and early 1970s, other geographers looked for more direct ways to engage with the ideological and activist debates beyond the academy. As Richard Peet (1998) argues, the revolutionary and often violent social movement activism in Western countries "made the concerns of the traditional discipline of geography, for all its quantitative update and even humanistic concerns, seem socially and politically irrelevant" (p. 67). Radical and Marxist geographers sought to make the study of geography more useful and relevant, and they pressed the discipline to produce research that contributed to furthering social justice. David Harvey urged geographers to enter the fray, arguing that, as Peet says, "geography can no longer be simply an academic discipline, isolated in its ivory towers." Geographers interested in these pursuits turned to social theory and methodologies based on the work of Karl Marx (1818–1883), Henri Lefebvre (1901–1991), and Raymond Williams (1921–1988), which positioned spatial production and organization at the heart of social justice issues and gave geography a role in working for and reshaping society.

GEOGRAPHY AND IDENTITY

In the 1970s, and in conjunction with the feminist social movements beyond the academy, women in geography increasingly asserted that gender and gender relations had serious but largely overlooked geographical implications (**Figure 1.28**). What it means to be a "woman" or a "man" varies geographically as well as historically. Spaces and places themselves can also be gendered in that some places are seen as more appropriately feminine, such as the home or domestic spaces, and other spaces more properly masculine, such as the public space of work and political engagement. A number of different perspectives have emerged—liberal feminism, socialist feminism, Marxist feminism, lesbian feminism, postmodern/poststructuralist feminism— and a substantial body of research attests to the spatial implications of gender and gender relations. As we shall see in chapters 7 and 8, geographers have also examined how sexualities are constituted and regulated in and through the spatial. Much of this work also emphasizes the importance of race, ethnicity, age, able-bodiedness, and other social and cultural markers of identity in how we experience spaces and understand ourselves in space.

FIGURE 1.28 Feminist protest, 1970.

York University Digital Library, Clara Thomas Archives and Special Collections, Toronto Telegram, ASC04612

POSTMODERNISM AND THE CULTURAL TURN

By the 1980s, broad philosophical shifts were challenging the very foundations of modern thought, including assumptions about the nature of truth and knowledge, the objectivity of the scientific method, and the possibilities of finding universal laws and an underlying coherence at the heart of much of the work in geography. Termed "postmodernism," this complex and highly contested worldview has informed contemporary geographical research across many subdisciplines, from economic and political geographies to social and cultural geographies. It is beyond the scope of this text to explore postmodernist ideas in any great detail, but it is enough to say that geographers have taken up the challenges of postmodern thought in myriad ways, and students of geography will come across this thinking in many subdisciplines, particularly in social and cultural geographies, feminist and queer geographies, and geographies of sexuality.

CONTEMPORARY HUMAN GEOGRAPHY

As this overview suggests, human geographers undertake their studies from a variety of theoretical and conceptual perspectives, producing a wide array of geographical knowledges that are often contradictory and contested. Human geographers focus on an impressive range of topics, which are reflected in the variety of subdisciplines, including population geography and demographics, political geography, social and cultural geography, economic geography, transportation geography, and urban geography. We touch on many of these areas in this text. To appreciate more fully the vast topics researched by human geographers, examine the multitude of occupations filled by human geographers, including location analyst, urban planner, diplomat, remote sensing analyst, geographic information scientist, area specialist, travel consultant, political analyst, intelligence officer, cartographer, educator, soil scientist, transportation planner, park ranger, or environmental consultant. All of these careers and more are open to geographers because each of these fields is grounded in place and is advanced through spatial analysis.

MAIN POINTS 1.5 What Does It Mean to "Think Geographically" and How Do We Do It?

- What we might consider modern geographical research and knowledge began in the 1500s and is largely associated with the age of exploration, when European nations travelled the globe "discovering" (for themselves) new lands and peoples, animals, plants, rocks, and minerals.

- From its earliest beginnings, geography has used a number of different philosophical and theoretical approaches to study human-environment relations. These include environmental determinism, possibilism, regional geography, spatial science, humanistic and behavioural geography, radical and Marxist geography, and feminist, queer, and postmodern/poststructuralist geographies.

- Geographical scholarship today employs a range of philosophical and theoretical perspectives that make the discipline a rich and intriguing area of study.

SUMMARY

Canadian historian Ursula Franklin, in her 1990 CBC Massey Lectures, stated:

> We are living in a very difficult, very interesting time, a time in which a major historical period is coming to a convoluted end. I think we live in a time in which the social and political upheaval is as great or greater than it was in the time of the Reformation (p. 1).

In the last decade alone, we have witnessed the Arab Spring, devastating tsunamis in Thailand and Japan, the financial crisis and Black Monday, the Occupy movement, the legalization of same-sex marriage in Canada, Facebook, Twitter, YouTube, Hurricane Katrina, *An Inconvenient Truth*, the iPhone, the Keystone Pipeline, the earthquake in Haiti, the election of Barack Obama, crowdsourcing, YOLO, the Rob Ford crack scandal, eLearning, the H1N1 virus, and much, much more. There is no doubt that the world is rapidly changing and we need to question these events, and consider their reasons and implications for human-environment relations. New technologies (particularly the Internet and mobile technologies) are changing our social worlds and asking us to reimagine time-space relationships. Social movements are shifting in their organizing practices. Health and health care are increasingly global issues. Education is no longer spatially bound. This is what studying geography is all about.

"For me, geography is a great adventure with a purpose," says Michael Palin, President of the Royal Geographical Society. The adventure takes place in the field. Geographers use a variety of philosophical, theoretical, and conceptual frameworks for thinking through geographical questions, but they have adventures while doing so. Many of today's most pressing issues, including food security, climate change, the causes and consequences of migration, urbanization, gentrification, and environmental degradation benefit from a geographical perspective. Scale, as an organizing principle, together with the five themes of this book—location, place, region, landscape, and movement—focus attention on these events, activities, and human behaviours from a spatial perspective, and help to unpack the complexity of these challenging issues. All of these contribute to the existence of a rich and complex body of geographical thought and knowledge, much of which we highlight in the chapters that follow.

At the same time, employers appreciate the skill sets and knowledge that geography graduates have. Geographers' ability to go out into the world, do fieldwork, think critically and analytically about what they observe, and write carefully about their observations are crucial skills in today's workforce. Government agencies stress the need for analytical thinkers—those who are able to consider the impacts of policy and regulatory changes on populations in particular places and locations—and geographers are well suited for this task. Geography graduates become policy analysts, field researchers, environmental consultants, schoolteachers, GIS specialists, cartographers, demographers, community developers, fundraisers, and urban planners, to name but a few. In other words, there are many exciting, rewarding careers to be had with a degree in geography.

Our study of human geography will analyze people and places and explain how they interact across space and time to create our world. Chapters 2 and 3 lay the basis for our study of human geography by looking at the changing political territorial organization through colonialism, imperialism, and globalization. Chapters 4 and 5 focus on populations and immigration, while chapters 7 and 8 focus on aspects of social organization and how people use culture and identity to make sense of themselves in their world. The remaining chapters examine how people have created a world in which they function economically and how they organize themselves across both rural and urban spaces, as well as how their activities in those realms re-create themselves and their world.

DISCUSSION AND REVIEW QUESTIONS

1. What was the *Seven Wonders of Canada* competition and what does it reveal about the nature of human geography as a field of inquiry? Further, what would you have chosen for the competition and why?

2. While maps are the most familiar and recognizable tool of geography, the concept of "place" is what arguably unifies the field. Discuss this concept of place, paying particular attention to notions of "sense of place," "place matters," and "the globalization of place."

3. "Landscape" is another important theme related to a spatial perspective. What is landscape and with whom is the concept most associated? How does the Tanzanian city of Dar-es-Salaam illustrate the variety of forces involved in landscape practices?

4. Compare and contrast reference maps with thematic maps. Who was Dr. John Snow and how was he able to use mapping in the field of medicine? Can you think of any contemporary examples where various types of mapping might be useful in helping to solve contemporary problems?

5. Human geographers approach their studies from a variety of theoretical and conceptual perspectives, which in turn lead to the production and dissemination of a wide array of geographical knowledge. Compare and contrast two such theoretical and conceptual perspectives, focusing on key individuals, concepts, and outcomes.

GEOGRAPHIC CONCEPTS

absolute location   11
accessibility   10
activity space   13
anthropocentric view   4
behavioural geography   26
cartography   10
connectivity   10
contagious diffusion   22
cultural barrier   21
cultural diffusion   20
diffusion   20
distance   10
environmental determinism   24
epidemic   12
expansion diffusion   21
five themes (of geography)   6
formal region   7
functional region   7
geocaching   16
geographic information systems (GIS)   15
geomatics technologies   15
Global Positioning System (GPS)   16
hierarchical diffusion   22
human geography   4
human-environment   4
humanistic geography   26
landscape   9

location   7
location theory   7
mental map   13
movement   10
pandemic   11
pattern   11
perceptual region   7
physical geography   4
place   8
possibilism   25
reference maps   11
region   7
regional geography   25
relative location   11
relocation diffusion   22
remote sensing   15
rescale   19
scale   5
sense of place   4
spatial   6
spatial analysis   26
spatial distribution   11
spatial interaction   10
spatial perspective   6
stimulus diffusion   22
thematic maps   11

ADDITIONAL RESOURCES ON-LINE

Association of American Geographers: www.aag.org

Canadian Association of Geographers: www.cag-acg.ca

Canadian Geographic magazine: www.cangeo.ca

Canadian Canoe Museum: www.canoemuseum.ca

Royal Canadian Geographical Society: www.rcgs.org

Geocaching: www.geocaching.org

Globalization and Geography: www.lboro.ac.uk/gawc/rb/rb40.html

John Snow and His Work on Cholera: www.ph.ucla.edu/epi/snow.html

The State of Food Insecurity in the World: www.fao.org

World Hunger: www.wfp.org

Google Earth: www.googleearth.com

Indigenous Knowledges: www.nativemaps.org

Humanistic geography scholar Yi-Fu Tuan's website: www.yifutuan.org

Zapatista Revolution: www.zapatistarevolution.com

CHAPTER 2
GLOBALIZATION AND GEOGRAPHIES

Global Consumption

ON APRIL 24, 2013, shortly before 8:00 a.m., 3,639 garment industry workers in Savar, Bangladesh, refused to enter the Rana Plaza factory building because it was unsafe. Rana Plaza housed five factories, a bank, and several shops, and had been deemed too dangerous to enter the previous day due to large cracks in the walls. The factory managers insisted that the building was safe and reopened the next morning. When the garment workers refused to enter the building, the factory managers threatened to withhold their pay for the month and paid gang members to physically force them into the building by hitting them with sticks. Forty-five minutes later, just before 9:00 a.m., the building collapsed, killing at least 1,138 people and injuring more than 2,500 (**Figure 2.1**).

The factories in Rana Plaza manufactured clothing for brands such as Benetton, Bonmarché, The Children's Place, Primark, Walmart, and Canadian-owned Joe Fresh. The images that flooded western media included pictures of heaps of clothing, destined for Canadian, American, and European store shelves (**Figure 2.2**). These pictures bring into sharp focus the unevenness of globalization, and raise difficult questions about cheap clothes and global consumption practices.

Economic geographers study the geographies of consumption, which includes studying consumer choices—how consumers make choices and whether social or political concerns, such as where, how, and at whose cost consumer goods are made, play a role in their purchasing decisions. Increasingly, consumers are demanding "fast fashion"—fashion designs that move from concept to store shelf faster and more cheaply than ever. This means that companies such as Joe Fresh must source out the cheapest possible locations to manufacture clothing. One of these places is Bangladesh because the Canadian government dropped its import duties from Bangladesh in 2003. As a result, imports into Canada from Bangladesh have increased by 618 percent.

FIGURE 2.1 Rana Plaza, Savar, Bangladesh. The building, which housed five garment factories, a bank, and several shops, collapsed on April 24, 2013, killing at least 1,138 people.

© Andrew Biraj/Reuters/Corbis

Jeff Holt/Bloomberg via Getty Images

FIGURE 2.2 Joe Fresh labelled clothes. These were pulled from the rubble after the Rana Plaza building collapsed in Savar, Bangladesh.

According to a 2011 report, a polo shirt made in Bangladesh retails in Canada for $14 but costs the retailer only $5.67 (**Figure 2.3**). Of the remaining $8.33, only $0.12 goes to the worker who made the shirt. In fact, according to the Institute for Global Labour and Human Rights, a standard shift at Rana Plaza was 13 to 14½ hours per day, about 100 hours per week, with just two days off a month. Eighty percent of these workers were young women who earned between $10.56 and $12.48 per week. Poor and unsafe working conditions, little if any regulations, and the constant threat of job loss are a daily reality for those working in the garment industry in Bangladesh.

Changing global economic agreements, improved logistics and supply-chain management, and increased demand for cheap "fast fashion," are among the many important factors to consider when asking questions about the geographies of consumption. The tragic fallout of Western consumer behaviour, as experienced by the workers in Rana Plaza, Bangladesh, stands as a reminder of the local consequences of global practices, and brings to light questions that many Canadians have previously ignored: Where does my shirt come from? Who made it? At what cost?

FACTORY OVERHEAD: **$0.07**

AGENT: **$0.18**

LABOUR: **$0.12**

FACTORY MARGIN: **$0.58**

FREIGHT, INSURANCE AND DUTIES **$1.03**

MATERIALS AND FINISHING: **$3.69**

TOTAL COST TO CONSUMER WITH 60% MARKUP: **$14.00**

TOTAL COST TO A RETAILER: **$5.67**

Lauren Cattermole for Maclean's Magazine

FIGURE 2.3 What does that shirt really cost?

KEY QUESTIONS FOR CHAPTER 2

1. What is globalization, and what are the major debates about globalization?

2. What are the connections between globalization and the geographical?

3. Why do some people or groups oppose or resist globalization?

2.1 What Is Globalization, and What Are the Major Debates about Globalization?

Commodity chain Series of links connecting the many places of production and distribution and resulting in a commodity that is then exchanged on the world market.

As you read this paragraph, take a quick inventory of your possessions and surroundings. Who made your shoes? What about your pants? Does your shirt or blouse have a "Made in Canada" label? Where was your purse or knapsack made? Are you drinking a Tim Horton's coffee or one from Starbucks? Is it organic or fair trade coffee? Do you care? When we stop to think about our daily routines, we realize how tightly our consumption choices connect us to people and

their labour in places all over the globe. If you own a laptop, you could probably map the process of its manufacture down a global **commodity chain**—a complex network of people, labour, and production processes starting with the extraction of raw materials from the earth itself and ending with your purchase of the final product. Once you dispose of that product, either by placing it in the garbage or recycling it, the product continues to travel. It may go to either a landfill site or a recycling depot where it is broken down and its various parts are made available for further consumption (see Figure 2.19). The fruit you eat, the fish you consume, the music you play, your knapsack, your hat, your pens and paper, cell phone, and iPod all circulated through these global commodity chains until you "consumed" them. While these interconnected production circuits provide a wealth of material goods at inexpensive prices, as a knowledgeable "player" in this global "game," you are implicated at a very personal level in its successes and failures, its exploitative and oppressive regimes, and its possibilities for positive change and progress.

Our role as consumers is just one of many ways we may find ourselves drawn into social and political debates that are taking place far beyond our local neighbourhoods or even our own country. In this chapter, we consider the definition of the term "globalization" and introduce the main issues related to globalization processes and outcomes. In particular, we consider the debates about what globalization means, when it began, and whether it is a positive or negative process, or both. Finally, we consider why there is resistance or opposition to globalization. As noted in Chapter 1, questions about globalization, its processes, and outcomes are fundamental to human geographers' consideration of the current organization of place at a variety of scales and to our understanding of location, region, place, landscape, and movement—our spatial perspective.

WHAT IS GLOBALIZATION?

The meaning of the term "globalization" is a hotly contested topic, and any position we take has serious political, social, and economic implications. Scholars disagree about how to define globalization; they argue over when these globalizing processes began and they debate vigorously whether globalization has positive or negative consequences (or both). Some scholars go so far as to argue that there is no such thing as globalization and that, economically at least, the world is no more interconnected now than in previous eras. Steven Firth and Peter McMichael suggest that globalization is more properly understood as an "agenda" or a "project" in which dominant Western countries work to actively create opportunities for themselves to accumulate capital and profit. Others argue that the processes, activities, and outcomes of globalization are so fundamentally different from previous global interactions that we are experiencing radical and decisive economic, social, and political shifts in relations at many scales, including the global.

> **Globalization** "An accelerating set of processes involving flows that encompass ever-greater numbers of the world spaces and that lead to increasing integration and interconnectivity among those spaces." (Ritzer, 2007, p. 1)

Among those who do agree that the world is experiencing something understood as globalization, it remains difficult to reach a consensus about what the term actually means. George Ritzer suggests that various definitions have a number of common elements. Based on those shared attributes, he defines **globalization** as "an accelerating set of processes involving flows that encompass ever-greater numbers of the world spaces and that lead to increasing integration and interconnectivity among those spaces" (2007, p. 1). This text uses Ritzer's definition as the starting point from which to argue that we are experiencing something unique called "globalization," and that its processes and outcomes have spatial consequences.

Two important points spring to mind from Ritzer's definition. First, it refers to "processes" without specifying what those processes might be. While the processes of globalization are often understood as largely economic (that is, the activities of capitalist enterprise), the term "processes" also refers to cultural, political, social, and technological activities and practices. For example, technological processes can accelerate the flow of cultural traits (such as music or fashion) and political ideas into new and increasingly interconnected places (see Chapter 8 for details). Globalization comes about through improved technologies, new and emerging international financial and labour markets, and the growth of global consumer markets with an appetite for an ever-increasing array of goods.

Second, the definition highlights the geographical implications of globalization by focusing on how processes involve flows that, for better or worse, increase interactions, deepen relationships, and heighten interdependence between peoples and places. A geographer's spatial perspective helps in understanding the geographical implications of globalization. We need to consider spatial processes at a variety of intertwined scales, from the local to the global, and to think about how global processes and activities are continually forging links and connections. Canadian geographer Glen Norcliffe emphasizes that the processes and outcomes of globalization are not predictable or orderly and are best understood as chaotic and unruly, with places and people experiencing its effects in highly variable ways. The global shipping lanes illustrated in **Figure 2.4a** help us visualize how trade in various goods creates linkages and connections among and between numerous places—but not everywhere with everyone. As **Figure 2.4b** illustrates, countries such as North Korea, which are isolated both politically and economically, find themselves excluded from these global shipping lanes, as well as from other financial, technological, and social connections. Globalization processes and outcomes are not evenly distributed through time and space. Global interactions pass by some places and include others only tangentially, resulting in both positive and negative implications for those places. A geographical eye helps us consider these different experiences of globalization.

THE BEGINNINGS OF GLOBALIZATION

Scholars disagree about when globalizing processes began. We might argue that we have been living in a globalizing world since the early 14th century, when newly emerging nation states in western Europe, including Spain, Portugal, France, and England, began exploring and colonizing on a global scale. In the early 1400s, the first wave of sailing adventurers and explorers, including Christopher Columbus (Spain) and Vasco da Gama (Portugal), led expeditions to the shores of the Americas and around Africa's Cape of Good Hope to India and beyond—the outer reaches of the known world. In a second wave of exploration in the early 1800s, Spain, Portugal, the Netherlands, Great Britain, and France established colonies around the world, consolidating a global system of trade and commerce (**Figure 2.5**). The colonizing countries' relations with the colonized were largely exploitative. Colonizers organized the administration of their colonies to ensure the most efficient processes for moving raw materials from the interior of the country to the coast for export. By the end of the 1800s, most of the world's territories had been drawn into the capitalist economy.

The *world systems approach* or theory, developed by Immanuel Maurice Wallerstein in the early 1970s, provides one

FIGURE 2.4 (a) Global shipping lanes. This map traces over 3,000 shipping routes used by commercial and government vessels during 2006. The red lines mark the most frequently used shipping lanes.

FIGURE 2.4 (b) Shipping dead zone. This map uses Automatic Identification System (AIS) data to show a shipping "dead zone" around North Korea.

way to understand the organizational structure of these colonial and imperial enterprises. According to this approach, discussed in more detail in Chapter 11, the interaction and exchange resulting from these successive waves of exploration, colonization, and imperialism resulted in the current organization of nation states. In Wallerstein's system, states are classified as *core, periphery,* and *semi-periphery* (**Figure 2.6**). Natural resources, foodstuffs, and labour are redistributed from the periphery to the core through the operation of the world market.

Colonizing countries, mainly in the Western industrialized regions, constitute the core of the world economy because of their ability to dominate commercial, financial, and production activities. Core regions control the major production facilities and technologies, lead in trade and investment, and can maintain and protect their interests through political and military strength. Periphery regions, drawn into the global capitalist economy to varying degrees through colonization and engagement in trade, remain underdeveloped, supplying the core with raw materials, labour, and foodstuffs. Semi-periphery regions are able to make use of the resources of peripheral regions but also find themselves exploited by core regions. Many semi-peripheral countries were once members of the periphery, but through various circumstances they shifted their positioning within the world system. Obviously, the world system has organized itself differently depending on the historical era. Varying perspectives regarding the prospects for countries to move along the peripheral—semi-peripheral—core trajectory are discussed at length in Chapter 11.

Geographers describe how nation-states are connected and interact by relying on metaphors such as the above-mentioned core-periphery model, or North-South and First-Second-Third World. These metaphors are powerful, seeking to describe the spatial organization of nation-states within the global economic order. However, it has been argued that there are somewhere between 5,000 and 6,000 nations that are internationally unrecognized, yet maintain a distinct political culture within the

FIGURE 2.5 **Major global trade routes, 1800s.**

states that claim their territories. The term "Fourth World" was coined in 1974 by Shuswap Chief George Manuel, who defined it as the "indigenous peoples descended from a country's aboriginal population and who today are completely or partly deprived of the right to their own territories and its riches" (1990, p. 40). This definition has been developed and expanded

upon, and today the more precise "internationally unrecognized nations" is used to allow for inclusive discussions about populations that are not bound by citizenship to a specific nation-state, nations without a sovereign state, and religiously defined peoples within the economic world system. For example, Romani people around the world, Maori people in New Zealand, and

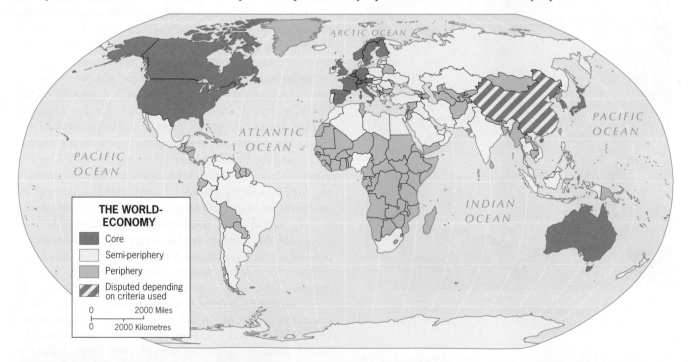

FIGURE 2.6 **The three-tier structure of the world economy.** One representation of core, periphery, and semi-periphery based on a calculation called World-Economy Centrality, derived by sociologist Paul Prew. The authors took into consideration factors not quantified in Prew's data, including membership in the European Union, in moving some countries from the categories Prew's data recommended to other categories. Data from: Paul Prew, "World-Economy Centrality and Carbon Dioxide Emissions: A New Look at the Position in the Capitalist World-System and Environmental Pollution," *American Sociological Association*, 12, 2 (2010) 162–191.

FIGURE 2.7 **Internet visualization map, 2011.** This illustration uses router configurations to document world city-to-city Internet connections. Note how no geographic markers are shown on this map, yet it is still possible to orient yourself.

Courtesy Chris Harrison, Carnegie Melon University, U.S.A.

Aboriginal peoples of Canada would all be understood as part of the Fourth World. The *Guest Field Note* by Sarah de Leeuw illustrates both a view from—and the importance of—Fourth World research.

Sociologist Manuel Castells takes the Fourth World thesis further by extending its applicability to those who are not included in the so-called "information society." According to Castells, intertwined with a new technological reordering brought about by the information age (specifically, Internet access) comes "rising inequality and social exclusion throughout the world" (2000, p. 68). He argues that with the collapse of the USSR in 1991 and thus the end of the three-worlds theory, the First World has failed to reach its potential because a new world has emerged—a world of social exclusion and "black holes of informational capitalism." The Fourth World, therefore, stands as a critique of globalization and the promises of the Internet; those excluded from access to information via new technologies have formed a new global digital divide.

Castells's work is significant to geographers as he reminds us that the Internet itself (and those who do and do not have access) are geographic matters; there is a spatial perspective to this Fourth World of exclusion from the information society—a global digital divide that warrants exploring. One particularly interesting visualization of this spatial perspective is provided by Chris Harrison (**Figure 2.7**). He maps Internet connectivity around the globe based on router configuration. Note how there are no geographic features or country borders shown. Despite this, we can still see the greater connectivity of North America and western Europe, as opposed to places in Africa where there is much less density.

CANADA AND GLOBALIZATION

Canada's history highlights the nature of the shifting relationships initiated by the processes of exploration and colonization that began in the 1400s. As the *Guest Field Note* from Sarah de Leeuw argues, this colonization had a profound effect on the North American indigenous population that is still felt today. The country was colonized by successive waves of Spanish, French, and British explorers, settlers, and adventurers, beginning in the mid-1550s when Basque fishers and whalers explored the sea coasts of Newfoundland and Labrador. The St. Lawrence River became a major inland waterway, opening up the interior of Canada to fur traders and lumber barons shipping raw goods back to European markets. Between 1550 and 1750, Canada developed as a staples economy, exporting its rich resources and importing manufactured goods that were needed to support the growing export trade. Local manufacturing, always modest, developed as an adjunct to the export trade, producing ships, agricultural equipment, and steel machinery for the railway. Because it initially served as an exporter of raw materials, Canada was drawn into the developing world system as a peripheral region. The country's long association with the sea (**Figure 2.8**) as the primary means of moving our exports is reflected in our art and music.

With successive waves of industrialization, Canada was increasingly incorporated into the world economy but with continued dependence on the global core—at that time, the colonial core countries of Europe. As the west was settled, Canada added wheat and mineral resources to its list of exports and by World War II was one of the leading producers of oil and gas. As Harold Innis describes it, Canada developed a distinctive staples-based economy even as it emerged as part of one of the world's three major core regions—North America, Europe, and East Asia. The **staples thesis**, proposed by Innis, argues that Canada's economy developed through the export of "staples" such as fish, lumber, fur, wheat, and minerals back to Europe. However, Canada holds a less dominant position today due to its geographical location and its economic linkages to what is currently one of the world's largest economies, the United States. As Glen Norcliffe argues, Canada may have developed a manufacturing and service base but "the staples economy still looms larger in Canada's hinterland" (2001, p. 18). This makes Canada vulnerable to fluctuations in the global prices for resources and hinders economic development in manufacturing. In its reliance on resource export,

> **Staples thesis** The theory that Canada's economy developed through the export of raw resources to Europe and that, as a result, Canada did not develop a strong manufacturing base, preferring to import finished goods.

(a)

(b)

© Library and Archives, Canada C-32706;

© National Film Board of Canada. Still Photography Division/Library and Archives Canada, R1196-14-7-E

FIGURE 2.8 (a) Whaling. The dangers of traditional whaling are shown in this 19th-century lithograph. **(b) Ship building.** Shipyard workmen and women gathered to witness the launching of a ship from the Burrard yard, Vancouver circa 1944.

Canada has been slower to develop the technologies and processes to refine and manufacture raw materials from those resources, preferring to import finished goods. While a contested perspective, the staples thesis does help explain Canada's seemingly contradictory position as both a member of the global core and a secondary economic player.

Today, Canada's position as a key producer and exporter of oil from the Alberta oil sands is a good example of how our staples-based economy continues to resonate. The third-largest proven crude oil reserve in the world (next to Saudi Arabia and Venezuela), the oil sands produce over 1.9 million barrels per day. On a global scale, Alberta's oil reserves are about 11 percent

GUEST FIELD NOTE

Geographies of a Neocolonial British Columbia

At the age of 12, I stood beside Bill Reid on a long rocky beach stretching the length of the Skidegate Indian Reserve on Haida Gwaii. Bill Reid was an old man on that sunny afternoon in 1986. I was participating in the launch of *Loo Taas*, or *Wave Eater* in English, a 15-foot war canoe Reid carved from a single red cedar tree (**Figure 2.9a**). At the time, I did not understand Reid was one of Canada's most talented artists, dedicated to revitalizing the Haida Nation and culture (**Figure 2.9b**). Instead, I stood beside a man I knew was about the same age as my Opa, had a grand-fatherly-like presence, and was draped in a beautiful button blanket. I remember he had a gentle handshake and a shock of white hair.

Like many British Columbians, or arguably like many Canadians, I knew nothing about the long geographic history of that relatively small space where, for a relatively short moment in the closing years of the 20th century, I stood watching *Loo Taas* break, and then for the first time hungrily eat, waves crashing

on the shore of the Pacific Ocean. In 1986, I did not know that the islands where I lived were once called something other than The Queen Charlotte Islands, a name that referenced both a queen—likely Britain's first Black, African-descent queen—and the ship of Captain George Dixon, the man who surveyed the islands in 1787. I did not know that an Indian reserve was a specific jurisdiction, governed under different policies than the town of Queen Charlotte City where my family and I lived, about 9 kilometres up the highway. And, as I stood and listened to speeches made in a language I did not comprehend, made by men and women I simply thought of as the grandparents of children I went to school with, I had no idea that, not so long ago, many of those elderly people would have been placed in schools where they likely suffered beatings and other violences for speaking in their Haida language, for being Haida.

Given the plethora of my other naiveties, I certainly had no idea that linkages existed between those historic violences and the tragedies like suicide and drug addiction that claimed too many of my young classmates from the Indian reserves on the islands I knew only by an English name. I also had no idea that the ravens and killer whales and beavers and bears that stretched

(a)

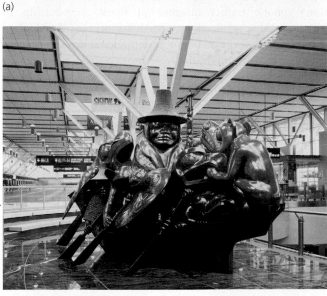

(b)

FIGURE 2.9 (a) The launch of Bill Reid's *Loo Taas (Wave Eater)* in 1986. (b) *The Spirit of Haida Gwaii—The Jade Canoe.* The six-tonne sculpture by Haida artist Bill Reid is on display at Vancouver International Airport. The second and final bronze casting in the collection of the Vancouver International Airport Authority.

out across the button blankets and headdresses that the speakers wore, or that reached skywards in the totem poles dotting the beach behind us, were testaments to a strong, complex, self-determining, and sovereign people. Because I was young, and a product of a school system that taught me Christopher Columbus "discovered" the Americas in 1492, I had no idea what self-determining or sovereign meant. I had certainly never heard words like postcolonial, or neocolonial, and a concept like "edge of empire" would have just made me giggle.

Over the years, I have become fascinated with that moment on a beach in 1986. In a way, what I research today is always in reference to Skidegate Village, Bill Reid, and *Loo Taas*. The work I do involves producing a deeper understanding about

how that moment, the small space in which it unfolded and the people of which it was composed, embodied a history of missionary activity, a production of reserves, the renaming of lands, efforts to transform indigenous peoples, and the sustained work of Haida people to maintain social, cultural, and even geographic sovereignty.

Broadly speaking, I am interested in the relationships between indigenous peoples and people who might best be described as settlers in the province. In some ways, like the memory of Queen Charlotte herself, it must be remembered that non-indigenous peoples are certainly not homogenous but, instead, are complex racialized peoples with varied histories and geographies. Most specifically, then, I am interested in the ways British Columbia's colonial history manifests in certain kinds of geographies, in particular types of power dynamics often shot-through with issues of identity, and in a variety of social naiveties, tensions, and injustices in the province. To this end, I undertake cultural, social, and historic geographic research. This includes, for instance, searching archives in order to find records and documents of indigenous peoples' responses to colonial projects like residential schooling. I also analyze historic and contemporary government policies and laws so as to demonstrate linkages between 19th and 20th century ideas about "savage Indians" and 21st century realities, including unprecedented high rates of child apprehensions from indigenous families. I also write creatively, but always with an emphasis on geographic themes. I think of all these efforts as part of my broader research agenda.

In efforts to demonstrate that British Columbia is not a post-colonial geography—a space, in other words, no longer shaped and reshaped in the present day by myriad and different settler colonial peoples and our polices—I write and produce research linking the past to the present. To this end, some of my work has argued that when Aboriginal patients visit a doctor, they are met with a medical system that does not fully account for a history of residential schooling, living on an Indian reserve, or being governed under the *Indian Act*, each of which have particular impacts on people's health. At other times, and usually in partnership with Aboriginal organizations, my work has focused on feelings of trust—or mistrust—that indigenous peoples may have toward various spaces and peoples with which they interact.

All of these different research projects are connected because, at their base, I am concerned with ameliorating the significant disparities that exist between indigenous and settler colonial peoples in British Columbia and, arguably, around the world. Ultimately, I hope for a future in British Columbia and elsewhere wherein grave naiveties, like mine in 1986, do not dominate understandings about relationships between indigenous and settler peoples in the province. Geographic research can assist in building this future, and undertaking this research from a variety of angles will lead to a richer, more nuanced and complex array of understandings.

Sarah de Leeuw, Northern Medical Program, UNBC, Faculty of Medicine, UBC of total global oil reserves; we export over 1.3 million barrels per day to the United States alone, supplying 7 percent of total U.S. demand. Interestingly, not all of the oil-producing projects in Alberta are fully Canadian owned. In some instances, large transnational corporations are heavily invested. For example, a 2012 analysis of the top 10 producing projects revealed significant foreign investment, including one project with investments by the United States (30 percent), China (9 percent), and Japan (5 percent). Another project had Anglo-Dutch (60 percent) and U.S. (40 percent) investment, with no Canadian interest whatsoever. Alberta oil sands projects accounted for 27.6 percent of Alberta's gross domestic product (GDP) in 2011. These energy-related projects are being touted as "nation-building" activities that position Canada as a strong player in the global marketplace. We must remember, however, that there is another side to Canada's oil-producing activities. The Keystone XL pipeline is a highly contested international project. Canada's oil sands have been criticized for producing "dirty oil" because of the high greenhouse gas emissions resulting from the extraction process (read more on this in Chapter 6). As well, Aboriginal peoples who live in the oil sands regions have reported serious health concerns, damage to the environment, and harm to the animals who live off the land under production.

The world system is constantly reorganizing, and the growing global importance of China, South Korea, Taiwan, and Japan as emergent economic and political centres refocused the global economy on the Pacific Rim in the 1990s. By the end of that decade, Japan had become an economic powerhouse, with major investments in North America and Europe and a host of multinational corporations engaged in automobile manufacturing (Honda, Toyota, Nissan, and Mitsubishi) and electronics production (Fujitsu, Sharp, Sony, and Panasonic) exporting goods around the world. However,

the instability of the world's markets in the fall of 2008 and the subsequent recession had a serious impact on the world's major economies. The GDP of several of the world's major economies declined significantly in the fourth quarter of 2008 and the first quarter of 2009. Several economies, including those of Japan and the United States, began to rebound in 2009, but by early 2010, declines were again apparent in the economies of Japan, the United States, and Greece. Canada weathered the economic storm reasonably well but did experience a modest economic downturn.

The KOF Index of Globalization is one way of measuring globalization by considering not only the economic dimensions of globalization but the social and political dimensions as well. It helps us to understand the extent to which a country fits into these global dimensions and paints a picture of global integration. The index examines a number of factors, including actual flows of trade, foreign direct investment, international phone traffic, information flows, membership in international organizations, participation in the United Nations, and the number of international treaties signed. Among the main trends, the KOF Index noted increasing globalization from the end of the Cold War in 1989 until the economy stalled in 2000–2001—a result of the bursting of the dot-com bubble and the 9/11 terrorist attacks. According to the index, globalization has again slowed considerably since the financial crisis of 2008. In KOF's 2014 index, which uses data from 2011—the year of the Arab Spring, the nuclear disaster in Fukushima, and the Eurozone debt crisis—Ireland ranked first in terms of economic, social, and political globalization, followed by Belgium and the Netherlands. Canada has consistently ranked high and, in 2014, ranked 12th (**Figure 2.10**). Among the least globalized countries are Sudan, Tonga, Myanmar, and Burundi.

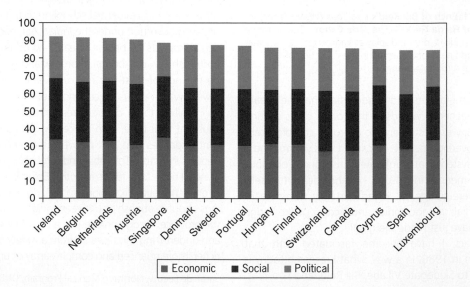

FIGURE 2.10 **KOF Index of Globalization, 2014.** This chart shows the top 15 most globalized countries, based upon social, political, and economic indicators. Data from KOF Swiss Economic Institute press release, April 14, 2014.

China, the world's most populous country (an estimated 1.35 billion in 2014), continues to gain strength in the global economy. Since the death in 1976 of Mao Zedong, leader of the governing Communist Party from 1949, China's government has increasingly drawn the country into the global economic system and encouraged rapid economic growth, particularly in the last 30 years. China joined the World Trade Organization in 2001 and has experienced a marked increase in exports and foreign investment. According to the World Bank, Japan's economy grew by some 5 percent while China's experienced a staggering 261 percent growth between 2000 and 2008. Moreover, the World Bank's International Comparison Project released its 2014 data (comparing world's economies from 2011), reporting that while the United States has had the world's largest economy for more than 140 years, that was likely to end in 2014, when China's economy surpasses it. Much of China's industrial and manufacturing development takes place along the eastern shore, in Beijing and port cities such as Shanghai and the former British Territory of Hong Kong, which are the contact points for international trade. China has experienced rapid urbanization (**Figure 2.11a**). For example, the population of Beijing was estimated at 20 million in 2010, and cities such as Shanghai and Tianjin are centres of economic, social, and cultural development. The impact of intense industrialization and urbanization has led to serious air quality concerns. Images of barely visible skylines, masked pedestrians, and empty streets tell the story of what some are calling an "airpocalypse" (**Figure 2.11b**).

Canada has worked hard to develop an economic relationship with China. In June 2010, China's president Hu Jintao visited Canada as part of efforts on behalf of both countries to establish stronger economic, political, and social ties. As of 2010, China ranks among Canada's largest trading partners, with over $40 billion in trade annually. Of the many industries caught up in Canadian-Chinese relations, shipbuilding has become increasingly significant. This is, in part, due to a tariff change in 2010, where Ottawa eliminated a 25-percent duty on new ship construction in non-NAFTA (North American Free Trade Agreement) countries. Canada's two largest shipping companies, Algoma Central Corporation and Canada Steamship Lines (CSL), have both increased their fleets with new builds from China. Algoma ordered eight new Equinox-class bulk carriers for its fleet and CSL increased its Canadian fleet with four new Trillium Class vessels.

Shipbuilding is not only an important aspect of Canada-China economic relations but also exemplifies the processes of globalization generally when we consider the complicated history of its construction and deployment. For example, *Victorious/John J. Carrick* is a Canadian articulated tug-barge (ATB) unit built at the Penglai Bohai Shipyard in Penglai City, China, in 2009. ATB *Victorious/John J. Carrick* is owned and operated by Toronto-based McAsphalt Marine Transportation Ltd. The Articouple system that connects the tug and barge is Japanese; the NORIS system that provides engine-room monitoring and controls is German; most of the navigational equipment is provided by British-based Sperry Marine; the main engines are from MaK, another German company; the thermal oil heaters on the barge are Swedish; the Collomatic winches are

(a)

(b)

FIGURE 2.11 Urbanization and development in China.
(a) A Starbucks Coffee shop inside the Forbidden City, Beijing. (b) A man wearing a mask looks out over the smog shrouded Forbidden City. Beijing's air quality index regularly tops 300, a rate considered "hazardous."

made in Canada; and the main switchboards and motor control centres use Telemecanique components, relays, overloads, and programmable logic circuits—all made in France. There are at least 10 countries involved in making this Canadian vessel (**Figure 2.12**). Once complete, the ATB was sailed from China to Canada via the Pacific Ocean, through the Panama Canal, before picking up its first load of asphalt in Louisiana. It now regularly sails the Great Lakes–St. Lawrence Seaway system to the east coast of North America, moving asphalt and other oil products between the United States and Canada.

WORLD CITIES

Globalization is having a profound effect on urban areas as cities take up new positions that were not anticipated. Many of the most important processes in global relations occur among and

FIGURE 2.12 *ATB Victorious/John J. Carrick*.

Courtesy of McAsphalt Industries Ltd.

New York, London, and Tokyo are the most important world cities, but after those three, the list and the definition of what makes a world city changes depending on the perspective of the person defining the term. Two Canadian cities, Toronto and Vancouver, are often on the list of world cities, but they usually appear far down that list. For example, on the 2014 Global Power City Index in Chapter 10 (Figure 10.37), Toronto and Vancouver rank 17th and 22nd respectively. Various ranking systems are used to identify world cities, with each system emphasizing different characteristics and giving cities a higher or lower rank based on, for example, their livability and sustainability, their economic or technological functions, and/or their position in relation to other cities. Researchers adopt the system that reflects what they consider the most important criteria for evaluating urban areas.

World cities do not exist merely as players in the global economy; they often continue their role as the capital cities of states. For example, even though London and Paris are only a short distance apart, both function as world cities, in part because of the role they play within their respective states. Each became a magnet for economic and political activity within Great Britain and France, respectively, and then the globe. In each case, the national government concentrated on developing the country's capital city, thereby bolstering that city above other cities in the state, and also encouraged interconnectedness between that city and the rest of the world. World cities, such as London, serve as major financial capitals, transportation links, and centres of tourism and service industries partly because of their geographical location. Such cities usually go to great lengths to ensure they have impressive landscapes with distinctive architecture and historic sites (**Figure 2.13**).

> **World city** Dominant city in terms of its role in the global political economy. Not the world's biggest city in terms of population or industrial output, but rather a centre of strategic control of the world economy.

between cities. In fact, what we now call **world cities** function as the service centres of the world economy, often superceding state borders. These world cities are connected to other cities at the global level, and the forces shaping the world economy pulse across these connections and through the cities.

World cities currently operate within a hierarchy (which we will discuss in detail in Chapter 10). Many geographers agree that

(a)

(b)

© Richard Nowitz/National Geographic Society/Corbis

© Robert Glusic/Getty Images

FIGURE 2.13 World cities. (a) The London Eye, the world's largest cantilevered observation wheel, was completed in 2000. Standing next to it is the London Sea Life Aquarium, formerly the headquarters of the London County Council, which opened in 1922. (b) Toronto's distinctive skyline boasts the iconic CN Tower and the dome of the Rogers Centre, home of the Toronto Blue Jays baseball team.

FREE TRADE ZONES

Free trade zones Areas set aside within countries to make foreign investment and trade easier by reducing or eliminating trade barriers, and providing inexpensive labour and raw materials.

In addition to the emergence of world cities, **free trade zones** (FTZs) have also become increasingly important for the movement of goods and capital on a global scale. FTZs are areas set aside within countries to make foreign investment and trade easier by reducing or eliminating trade barriers, including tariffs and bureaucratic requirements. The zones, which usually emerge in peripheral nations, are labour-intensive manufacturing centres where inexpensive labour and raw materials are brought together to produce clothing, electronics, and other mass-produced consumer goods for transnational corporations. The earliest FTZs were established in the 1920s in Argentina and Uruguay, but the idea spread quickly; as of 2007, over 63 million people were employed in more than 2,700l FTZs in 116 countries. In developing or peripheral nations, the establishment of FTZs is considered central to economic growth because the zones provide an important opportunity for the periphery to connect economically with core countries. For example, 14 FTZs have been set up in Sri Lanka since the 1970s. They employ over 250,000 people, 80 percent of whom are women drawn to these locations by the promise of steady employment (**Figure 2.14**). The garment and textile industries make up the vast majority of manufacturing in Sri Lankan FTZs. Criticism of FTZs comes from a variety of sources and is similar to that expressed in the chapter opener about Bangladesh. Such criticism is frequently levelled by labour unions concerned about the rights and safety of workers who toil in poor conditions for low wages and who often lack job security and basic labour rights.

DEBATING GLOBALIZATION

The world systems approach provided a valuable conceptualization of world economic organization up to World War II. However, most scholars agree that this system began to undergo

FIGURE 2.14 Female workers at a factory in one of Sri Lanka's free trade zones.

fundamental changes in the 1950s. One of the most influential writers describing these changes was Canadian literary critic Marshall McLuhan, whose description of the new world order is captured in the term "global village." McLuhan was reflecting on the rapid and profound impacts new technologies and communications were having on social and cultural life. Human geographers might agree, somewhat tentatively, that global processes, activities, and outcomes are continuing to foster substantial economic, political, and social transformation at myriad scales—a process described by the term "globalization." However, vitriolic disagreement persists over whom these alterations benefit and whether they are generally for better or for worse.

Thomas Friedman, in his book *The World Is Flat*, presents globalization in a positive light, arguing that we are seeing a "flattening" of the world as nations drop barriers to trade and migration. Friedman suggests that the **friction of distance**—the increase in time and cost that usually comes with increasing distance—has been overcome by technological improvements as well as free

Friction of distance The increase in time and cost that usually comes with increasing distance.

Neo-liberalism An ideologically driven set of practices that seek to open and expand capitalist markets, reduce or eliminate government regulation and constraint of the free market, and develop frameworks that enhance global market processes.

trade agreements. This neoliberal political perspective understands globalization as a mainly progressive economic process that, with a few bumps along the way, promotes democracy, prosperity, and peace. Geographer David Harvey defines **neoliberalism** as a political-economic theory that suggests that human well-being will come about by "liberating individual entrepreneurial freedoms and skills" through state protection of "private property rights, free markets and free trade" (2005, p. 2). In this framework, the role of the state is not only to maintain these protections but also to see they become as much a part of the global condition as possible. Proponents of neoliberalism argue that greater participation in the world economy and in democratic politics by individuals, corporations, and states will ensure improved conditions for all. Economist Keith Maskus asserts, "Free trade raises the well-being of all countries by inducing them to specialize their resources in those goods they produce relatively most efficiently" (2004, p. 98-116), resulting in lower production costs. By engaging in global competition through trade, a country can expect to increase its long-term growth rate by gaining access to global technologies and becoming more innovative.

Other observers argue that the neoliberalism currently underpinning the economic and political policies of core countries has resulted in unchecked free market capitalism, which benefits some individuals, corporations, nation-states, and regions over others. This has led to new or continued economic, social, and cultural domination by some of the beneficiary countries, which exploit and marginalize other countries. From this perspective, globalization processes are understood as operating unevenly or generating uneven or inequitable outcomes, creating an ever-widening gap between the "haves" and the "have-nots" in terms of income, access to education, technology and health care, and global environmental justice issues. Scholars largely agree that inequities between people have increased dramatically, and they disagree about whether these inequalities will diminish (as we will see in Chapter 11).

Despite the concerns of critics, globalization is not likely to stop. Even if there were a desire to reverse the processes, there are powerful forces opposed to such a move. Many scholars and grassroots organizations suggest that globalization itself is not the problem but, rather, the way it operates. If globalization in its current form leads to economic exploitation and domination for the benefit of some over others, then perhaps there is a way to redirect or transform global processes so they lead to less inequality and exploitation and greater democratic reform (which is not always viewed positively by all), economic and social development, and prosperity. Numerous grassroots organizations and international governmental and non-governmental organizations (IGOs and INGOs) have proposed reforms to address the inequities stemming from globalizing forces while taking advantage of the benefits of participation and engagement; we will discuss some of these proposals in the final section of this chapter.

Whether in favour of, or opposed to globalization, most people would agree that the process is not a natural evolution in humanity. We need to question whether the overwhelming dominance of capitalism as an economic system makes globalization necessary and unstoppable. According to geographer John O'Loughlin and his colleagues, globalization is "neither an inevitable nor an irreversible set of processes" (2004, p. 4), while Andrew Kirby states that it is "not proceeding according to any particular playbook" (2004, p. 133–158). Globalization is perhaps better understood as an unpredictable and highly selective set of processes and outcomes created by people, be they corporate CEOs, university administrators, readers of blogs, or protesters at a trade meeting. The processes of globalization and the connectedness created through globalization are not limited to state-to-state interaction. Rather, the connection occurs across scales and across networks, regardless of state borders. The focus on human agency, participation, and choice highlights how both scholarship and grassroots protest might be harnessed to work with the possibilities and potentials of globalizing processes to foster more beneficial, universal outcomes.

MAIN POINTS 2.1 What Is Globalization, and What Are the Major Debates about Globalization?

- Globalization, according to George Ritzer, is an accelerating set of processes involving flows that encompass ever-greater numbers of the world spaces and that lead to increasing integration and interconnectivity among those spaces.

- The processes involved are often seen as economic but are also political, cultural, social, and technological. Although globalization is often seen as a global process, it has profound local implications.

- The current world system, in which globalization is a contemporary process, is rooted in some 500 years of colonial and imperial exploration by European countries. In this

- world system, countries are viewed as constituting part of the core, periphery, or semi-periphery.

- Globalization processes have changed the nature and organization of cities, creating what we now call world cities, such as London, New York, and Tokyo. These cities are often centres of finance, information, and administration and are interconnected at the global scale.

- There is considerable debate about the form, definition, characteristics, and outcomes of globalization as well as contestations over how its positive and negative outcomes should be addressed.

2.2 What Are the Connections between Globalization and the Geographical?

The world seems smaller as a result of the explosion in information and communication technologies since World War II. We can send information great distances in the blink of an eye, travel anywhere on the globe relatively quickly, and pluck vast amounts of information out of cyberspace with the click of a mouse. We make intellectual and emotional connections with people and places whether we have actually met them or been

there, creating a complex network of relationships, linkages, and interdependencies. These rapid and unprecedented transformations have provoked some scholars, including Richard O'Brien, to herald "the end of geography," declaring that in economic matters, at least, "geographic location no longer matters" (1992, p. 1). Needless to say, geographers and other social scientists have resisted this somewhat cavalier dismissal of the importance of the geographical. In this section, we consider how geographers, using their spatial perspective, have attempted to conceptualize the geographical operations of globalizing processes and outcomes. Here we consider several different approaches: David Harvey's notion of "time-space compression," the idea of networks, the concept of "placelessness," and the new relations of the global-local captured in the term "glocalization."

TIME-SPACE COMPRESSION

Time-space compression The process by which global markets seem to reorganize the perception of time so as to reduce the constraints of space on their activities; associated with the work of David Harvey.

Globalization arguably transforms time and space in novel and unexpected ways. We know that social life is experienced in material places, so changes in how we comprehend time and space must have an effect on social relations. Sociologist Anthony Giddens argues that globalization brings about time-space "distanciation," which means we experience "the intensification of worldwide social relations" such that local experiences are being shaped by events occurring at great distances and vice versa. Geographer David Harvey links globalization directly to the dynamics of the capitalist market system, suggesting it is responsible for a surge in **time-space compression**: the process by which global markets seem to reorganize the

FIGURE 2.16 *Stadia II.* This work by artist Julie Mehretu captures how individuals might experience globalization's transformation of time and space. (Carnegie Museum of Art, Pittsburgh; Gift of Jeanne Greenberg Rohatyn and Nicolas Rohatyn and A. W. Mellon Acquisition Endowment Fund. By permission.)

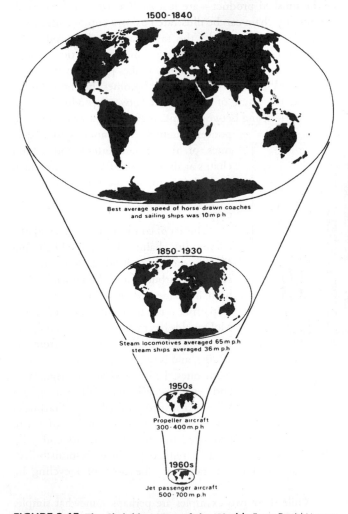

1500-1840

Best average speed of horse drawn coaches and sailing ships was 10 m p h

1850-1930

Steam locomotives averaged 65 m p h steam ships averaged 36 m p h

1950s

Propeller aircraft 300-400 m p h

1960s

Jet passenger aircraft 500-700 m p h

FIGURE 2.15 The Shrinking Map of the World. From David Harvey, *The Condition of Postmodernity*, Oxford and Cambridge, MA: Basil Blackwell, 1989, p. 241, plate 3.1.

perception of time so as to reduce the constraints of space on their activities. In other words, as new technologies such as telephones, telegraph, radio, automobiles, and now the Internet appear to be speeding time up, the barriers of space seem to be removed. Take, for example, Harvey's depiction of the Shrinking Map of the World (**Figure 2.15**). Here, Harvey shows us that in the year 1500, the average speed of horse-drawn carriages and ships was 10 miles per hour. In 1960, the average speed of a jet was 700 miles per hour. Thus, according to Harvey's time-space compression, the world feels 70 times smaller in 1960 than it did in 1500.

These changes have a profound effect on how human beings understand and operate in their world. Artist Julie Mehretu graphically captures how we, as individuals, might be experiencing these changes (**Figure 2.16**). According to the Williams College Museum of Art, her work "combines maps, urban grids, and architectural renderings to articulate complex social and geopolitical structures," and to "[query] what impact an individual can have, and what one person contributes to the construction of a larger narrative."

Time-space compression means that certain places, such as world cities, are more interconnected than ever as a result of their access to communication and transportation networks, while other places are farther removed than ever. A major divide in access to information technology networks is a hallmark of the current world and an example of the uneven outcomes of globalization among peripheral, semi-peripheral, and core regions. In 2004, the United Nations Development Programme's Human Development Report divided the world's states into high income, middle income, and low income (according to gross domestic product) and reported on accessibility to technology according to these classes. At the same time, high-income states had, on average, 507 telephone mainlines, 582 cellular subscribers, and 382.6 Internet users per 1,000 people. Middle-income states had, on average, 111 telephone mainlines, 104 cellular subscribers, and 37.2 Internet users per 1,000 people, while states in the low-income class had an average of 11 telephone mainlines, 15 cellular subscriptions, and 5.9 Internet users per 1,000 people. The uneven access to, and use of, these technologies suggests that those excluded from the technology networks will experience increasing disadvantage and marginalization; as discussed earlier in this chapter, Manuel Castells refers to this lack of access to communication technology as the Fourth World. The quickening pace of change in technology is another hallmark of the globalized world and magnifies the global technological divide. We may be shocked to see how quickly technology has changed and diffused. In 1992, the highest-income states had, on average, only 10 cellular subscribers and 2.5 Internet users per 1,000 people (contrasted with 582 and 382.6, respectively, in 2002). In Canada, governments at the local, provincial, and national levels are concerned with the uneven availability of high-speed Internet access, which has become increasingly important in our ability to access government services and information. As **Figure 2.17** illustrates, there is a vast divide between rural and urban access both in terms of Internet penetration and download speeds. As part of its economic action plan, the federal government implemented *Broadband Canada: Connecting Rural Canadians*, a $225-million investment in providing broadband Internet access to unserved and underserved Canadian areas.

NETWORKS

As our definition of globalization suggests, places are interconnected now in such complex ways that we need to think conceptually across bounded and defined spaces and envision the connections, or networks, between places. Manuel Castells defines a **network** as "a set of interconnected nodes." An increasing multitude of networks—financial, transportation, communication, kinship, corporate, nongovernmental, trade, government, media, education, and dozens of others—exist in the world, enabling globalization to occur and creating a higher degree of interaction and interdependence among people than ever before in human history.

> **Networks** A set of interconnected nodes without a centre, as defined by Manuel Castells.

As we noted earlier, commodity chains—those networks of labour and production processes that begin with the extraction or production of raw materials and end with the delivery of the finished product—are just such a network. One such commodity chain can be illustrated using a cup of coffee from Starbucks. For Starbucks the raw materials for production (paper for cups, coffee, and sugar) come from particular parts of the world, whereas consumption takes place in very different places (**Figure 2.18**). Starbucks becomes the "hub" on the network, the point of connection between production and consumption, and between some of the world's wealthiest and poorest countries. Comparing the revenues of the largest international food chains against the GDP of a country such as Afghanistan, we are reminded of the tremendous power of these transnational corporations.

The act of consumption is the end of a commodity chain; it is also the beginning of the product's afterlife. Corporations such as Starbucks and McDonalds have both implemented recycling programs to help offset waste from cups and packaging. McDonalds has moved away from polystyrene clamshell burger containers (from the 1990s), and is testing paper cups to replace foam ones. Paper cups are biodegradable and easily recyclable, while posing no known threat to public health. Starbucks has responded to criticism about waste produced by consumers of its coffee by adopting what is called "extended producer responsibility" where the corporation takes on the costs of recycling its products.

While these two examples are perhaps somewhat simple, imagine the waste produced through Western consumption of electronics. What happens when you discard or donate your

FIGURE 2.17 Broadband availability in Canada: urban vs. rural, 2012. This chart shows urban (maroon and light blue) vs. rural (taupe and beige) access in terms of percentage of households and download speeds. Urban centres have higher penetration rates, nearing 100% across all download speeds. Rural areas have lower penetration rates and slower download speeds. Data from the Canadian Radio-television and Telecommunications Commission Communications Monitoring Report, 2013.

FIGURE 2.18 **Howard Schultz, chairman, president and CEO of Starbucks Corp., centre, visits a coffee farm in Yunnan province, China, in 2010.** Starbucks signed a Memorandum of Understanding with Pu'er city to collaborate on producing high-quality coffee and responsible growing practices in Yunnan.

electronics, and what are the costs or benefits created by the funds (whether revenue for a charity or profits for a corporation) generated by your purchase? In many world cities in poorer parts of the globe, adults and children work in garbage dumps to recover valuable copper wire and other components of computers and electronics discarded by consumers in the western world (**Figure 2.19**).

While networks have always existed, Castells argues that they have fundamentally changed over the last 20 years. He suggests that globalization has proceeded via information technology networks, albeit unevenly, by "linking up all that, according to dominant interests, has value anywhere in the planet, and discarding anything (people, firms, territories, resources) which has no value or becomes devalued" (2000, p. 5–24). Information technology networks link some places more than others, helping to create the spatial unevenness of globalization as well as the uneven outcomes of globalization. Thinking about connections between places as networks and flows lets us imaginatively conceptualize how places are situated (or excluded) in these communication, financial, social, and political networks. It also helps us understand the struggle of some places to achieve greater inclusion and the desire of others to perhaps remain beyond the reach of these dominant forces. Places such as China and Nepal seek to limit access to the Internet and the wider global flow of information in an attempt to preserve cultural autonomy and distinctiveness.

The ideal network is conceptualized as horizontally structured, with no centre of power. While we know this type of structure encourages frequent interaction among nodes, we also know that power relations within networks mean that flows are uneven and inequitable, with some places experiencing greater access to and advantage within these global networks than others. In this section, we examine two major networks in the world today—media and retail corporations—and the scales at which they operate in the globalized world. Within each type of network, nodes interact on a global scale, but individuals have also created their own local or regional networks, often in response to network operations at the global scale. We will consider both the global and local or regional scales of activity for each type of network.

NETWORKS IN MEDIA

Global diffusion of products and ideas in popular culture depends largely on global media and retail store networks as well as the advertising in which both engage. Today's global media encompass much more than print, radio, and television. They also include spaces of entertainment, such as the New Amsterdam Theatre in Times Square in New York (owned by Disney); songs produced for record labels like RCA, Jive, and BMG (all owned by Bertelsmann); games played on PlayStation (owned by Sony); information about movies from MovieFone and directions to movie theatres from MapQuest (both owned by Time-Warner, as is the New Line Cinema movie you chose to see).

FIGURE 2.19 **China recycling.** Circuit boards in Guiyu, Guangdong Province, 2004.

Vertical integration
Ownership by the same firm of a number of companies that exist along a variety of points on a commodity chain.

Through a series of mergers and consolidations occurring mostly in the post-Cold War era, global media are now largely controlled by six global corporations: Time-Warner, Disney, Bertelsmann, Viacom, News Corporation, and Vivendi Universal. These six media corporations (along with other smaller media corporations) are masters of **vertical integration**. A vertically integrated corporation owns companies and, in this case, media, at a variety of points along the production and consumption nodes of a commodity chain.

Synergy The cross-promotion of vertically integrated goods.

In a 2002 report, Miguel Mendes Pereira stated that media companies compete for three things: content, delivery, and consumers. Through consolidation and mergers, global media companies such as the Walt Disney Corporation (**Figure 2.20**) become vertically integrated in order to gain content (e.g., production companies, radio shows, television programming, films, books) and delivery (e.g., radio and television stations, magazines, movie theatres). Delivery of content also refers to the infrastructure of technology—the proprietary technologies used for creating and sharing digital media. Vertical integration helps media giants attract and maintain customers through **synergy**, or the cross-promotion of vertically integrated goods. For example, within the vertical integration of Disney, you can visit Disney's Hollywood Studios at Walt Disney World, go to a *High School Musical* pep rally, and meet Muppet characters at Muppet*Vision 3D. Then, you can hop over to Disney's Animal Kingdom to catch the *Festival of the Lion King*, based on the Disney theatrical production that was based on the Disney movie *The Lion King*.

Vertical integration of media changes the geography of the flow of ideas globally by limiting the ultimate number of gatekeepers—that is, the people or corporations who control access to information. A gatekeeper can choose not to tell a story and the story will not be heard. We can interpret the consolidation of media as an attempt to limit the number of gatekeepers to the big media conglomerates. Or we can focus on the competition media (e.g., the vast number of cable television channels, radio stations, Internet sources, and magazines) and argue that there are more gatekeepers in the world.

NETWORKS OF RETAIL CORPORATIONS

Horizontal integration
Ownership by the same firm of a number of companies that exist at the same point on a commodity chain.

While major media corporations are vertically integrated, major retail corporations are typically **horizontally integrated**. In a horizontally integrated retail corporation, stores that at first glance appear to be owned by different retail companies in pursuit of different market shares turn out to be owned by the same parent corporation. For example, if you go to the mall to buy a pair of jeans, you can choose to shop at Banana Republic,

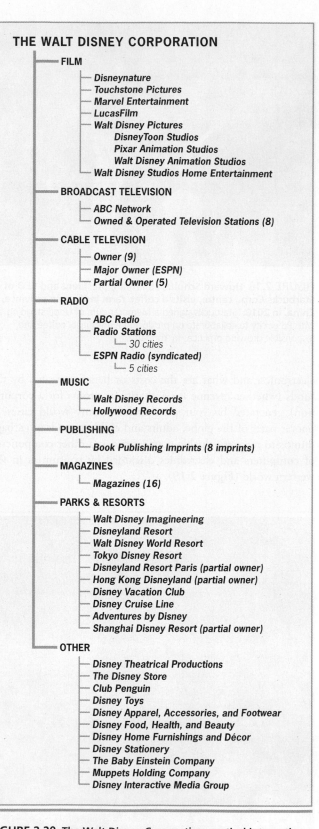

FIGURE 2.20 The Walt Disney Corporation, vertical integration. A list of companies that are part of the Walt Disney Company, based on data collected by the Columbia School of Journalism in 2013. By owning film, television, radio, and publishing, Disney can keep its message intact through vertical integration and synergy. Data from Columbia Journalism Review, Who Owns What, www.cjarchives.org/tools/owners/disney.asp.

The Gap, or Old Navy, but your money will go to one parent company, Gap Inc. If you take a break at the food court to drink Gatorade, eat a bag of Doritos, and buy a Quaker granola bar for later, all your dollars go to PepsiCo. You may look up and wonder when Taco Bell started selling Kentucky Fried Chicken and Pizza Hut pizza. (All three are part of Yum! Brands Inc., which also owns A&W and Long John Silvers. Yum! is a spinoff of PepsiCo.)

Neil Wrigley, Neil Coe, and Andrew Currah have studied the globalization of retail corporations such as Walmart (U.S.), Costco (U.S.), IKEA (Sweden), Metro (Germany), and Carrefour (France). In their comparison of manufacturing and retail corporations, they found that global retailers are more spatially disaggregated, with stores in hundreds or thousands of locations, whereas global manufacturers are more spatially concentrated, especially at production sites. In addition, global retailers engage directly with consumers and have a local presence that manufacturing corporations do not. Consumers who enter local stores interact directly with the global retailer at the local scale. While some individuals view global retail as a positive presence in their area and organize networks to invite stores to their community, others create networks of protest against the building of a global retail store.

By analyzing the global networks of development, global consolidation of media, and the global presence of retail corporations, we see the diversity in global networks, with some increasingly centralized and others increasingly disaggregated. In each case, the global network does not change local places in the same way. People interact with the global network, shaping it, resisting it, embracing it, and responding to globalization in unique ways.

PLACELESSNESS

> **Placelessness** The loss of uniqueness of place in the cultural landscape so that one place looks like the next, as defined by geographer Edward Relph.

Many observers believe globalization is creating a sense of **placelessness**, or a loss of heterogeneity between places. In their view, every place is becoming the same, with the same restaurant franchises, retail stores, books, movies, fashion, automobiles, and architecture. This idea is aptly captured in George Ritzer's term "McDonaldization," which encapsulates what some see as a trend to reduce diversity across cultural boundaries. Ritzer coined the term to describe how notions of efficiency, predictability, and control are embedded in global consumerism. We might be seeing a worrying diminishment in the variety and uniqueness of places and, perhaps, in the "authenticity" (a highly contested notion) of local experience. The images of Vancouver International Airport and the Tokyo International Airport in **Figure 2.21** illustrate this idea of placelessness. In many ways, it is impossible to tell where the airports are based upon their architecture. While this similarity provides comfort for some of us travelling to unfamiliar places, we might also experience a generic blandness obliterating the distinctive nature of places. Globalization is seen as creating a universal placelessness, to the detriment of the local and the specific.

(a)

(b)

FIGURE 2.21 (a) Vancouver International Airport. (b) Tokyo International Airport, Japan.

If we accept that globalization is experienced unevenly and differentially, we must acknowledge that the impacts and reactions at the local level vary as well. In some places, a defensive response to the perceived ills of global capital has resulted in a resurgence of claims to local community ties and territories. This suggests that people's sense of place is distinctly individual and experiential, and that total homogenization of the meaning and sense of place is impossible. It also reasserts the heterogeneity of people in place—an individual's gender, race, class, age, sexuality, and religion, for example, profoundly affect how that individual understands place and his or her position in that place—which in turn highlights how globalizing processes and outcomes are experienced differently by individuals who live and work in the same place.

These varied responses raise a key point about human agency. Just as globalization is not inevitable, neither are the people caught up in these processes powerless or passive. The differences among and between places exist because of local reactions to and engagement with globalization, as well as the complicated intersections of social relations across places and space.

GLOBAL-LOCAL

> **Glocalization** The process by which people in a local place mediate and alter regional, national, and global processes.

The term **glocalization** was coined by geographer Eric Swyngedouw in an attempt to counter the concept of "deterritorialization" (the severance of social, political, and cultural practices from their native places and populations) behind geographical notions of placelessness. Swyngedouw argues that places are both heterogeneous and homogeneous simultaneously, and that despite our sense of people, goods, and money moving rapidly and nimbly from place to place, these activities are in fact deeply materialistic, embedded in place, and grounded, if only for a moment. Put simply, places are both "similar" and "different" at the same time, and while we might think people, goods, and money are moving rapidly, they are actually caught up (unevenly and at different rates) in each place depending on its characteristics. As Peter Dicken argues, cultural, political, and economic processes have a "spatial fixedness" that must be taken into account. The reinsertion of the local and the material is a necessary corrective to the tendency of thinking about globalization as only a set of macro-processes.

Places themselves have a history and a spatial fixity that they bring to bear on globalizing processes of flows, networks, and time-space compression. The history of how a place or region came into the current world system; its relations with other places; its internal infrastructure and location in circulating networks of goods, foodstuffs, and resources; and the resources it has to inject into the system are all significant in *glocal* relations. We must look to the socio-spatial, historical, cultural, and political specificity as part of the larger tale. This perspective helps us focus on the fact that we are experiencing forms of homogeneity and homogenization that, according to Douglas Goodman's examination of consumer culture, "make people more different but in a similar way" (2004, p. 60).

Globalization networks interlink us. The flow of information technology is one way we are interlinked with the globe every day. A person may be overwhelmed by the flow of information and choose to ignore it, but even this person has a global identity. As the flow of information continues, many people feel a need to make sense of the world by identifying with or against other people and places at the local, regional, and global scale. People personalize the flow of information and in so doing feel more or less connected to the globe, altering their local cultural landscapes to reflect their feeling of connectedness.

For example, news of the death of Michael Jackson in June 2009 travelled quickly from global media sources, through social networking sites, and among friends, family, and even strangers. Many felt the need to mourn Jackson's death with others they had never met in a place they had never been. Some wanted to leave a token offering—a note, a candle, CDs, songs, photographs. Memorials to Jackson sprang up in many cities and towns, marking the personal connection many felt because of his music (**Figure 2.22**).

In an incredibly divided world in which the rift between rich and poor is growing at the global scale, what made people

(a)

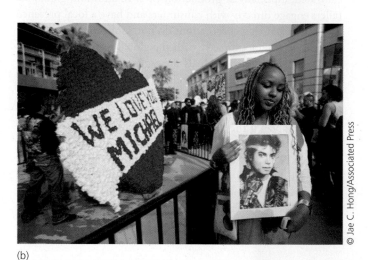

(b)

FIGURE 2.22 Michael Jackson memorials. (a) A Michael Jackson memorial at an HMV store in London, England, in 2009. (b) Basra Arte, from Canada, stands outside Staples Center, in Los Angeles, before a memorial service for Michael Jackson on Tuesday, July 7, 2009.

feel connected to a person who was a distant image and a member of an elite group of people of wealth and privilege? The idea that people around the world are linked and share experiences, such as death, tragedy, and sorrow, draws from Benedict Anderson's concept of the nation as an "imagined community." Anderson argues that a nation "is imagined because the members of even the smallest nation will never know most of their fellow-members, meet them, or even hear of them, yet in the minds of each lives the image of their communion" (1991, p. 224). The desire to personalize or localize a tragedy springs from the hope that all people in the imagined global community feel or experience the loss tangentially.

When a death or a tragedy does happen, how do people choose a local space in which to express a personal and/or global sorrow? Although many academics argue that place and territory are unimportant because things like global superhighways of information transcend place, people continue to recognize territories and create places. In the case of Michael Jackson's death, people created hundreds of spaces of sorrow to mourn the loss of a larger-than-life person whose life was cut short. In the case of the destruction of the World Trade Center on September 11, 2001, people transformed homes, schools, public spaces, and houses of worship into places of reflection by creating human chains, participating in moments of silence, or holding prayer vigils for the victims.

MAIN POINTS 2.2 What Are the Connections between Globalization and the Geographical?

- Global processes and outcomes are geographical in nature. They operate unevenly across a variety of scales and are experienced differently in different places with different results.

- Globalization is constantly reordering relations between places on a variety of scales, creating interdependencies, linkages, and interconnections, although it does not do so the same way each time or for all places.

- Geographers conceptualize the geographical operations of globalizing processes and outcomes using a number of overlapping approaches, including time-space compression, networks, placelessness, and glocalization.

2.3 Why Do Some People or Groups Oppose or Resist Globalization?

Globalization processes and outcomes have not been greeted favourably in all places or by all peoples because of the uneven and inequitable outcomes. The term "anti-globalization" is perhaps a misnomer, as most organizations believe it is unrealistic to seek an end to globalization processes. For groups seeking social justice, the term "alter-globalization" may be more accurate. However, resistance or opposition movements run the gamut from the progressive to the most right-wing and conservative. All take a critical view of globalization, albeit for different reasons, which is not surprising given that globalization itself is seen as complex and contradictory, operating unevenly across time and space.

Those opposing the processes and forces of globalization are often conceptualized as constituting some form of global civil society, itself a globalizing process that struggles to create new political and social forums as it agitates for participatory democracy and social justice on a global scale (**Figure 2.23**).

FIGURE 2.23 Opponents of neoliberal economic policies at the World Social Forum in Porto Alegre, Brazil.

This exemplifies how globalization may take positive as well as negative forms.

Opponents of neoliberal economic policies argue that international organizations such as the World Bank, International Monetary Fund, and World Trade Organization are set up to benefit the countries of the global economic core. Proponents of the dependency theory, outlined in Chapter 11, contend that the countries of the core continue to protect their own economies while forcing the countries of the semi-periphery and periphery to open their economies to foreign direct investment and remove protections on their domestic production. As Keith Maskus suggests, the rules negotiated for the World Trade Organization "inevitably reflect the economic interest of powerful lobbyists" in states such as the United States and the European Union. From this perspective, free trade is not "free" nor is it fair. Rather, it builds up a global economic network that sends most benefits to the core.

In response to the uneven and inequitable distribution of globalization's disadvantages and possibilities, a number of non-governmental organizations (NGOs) have sprung up in the last two decades. These groups, which often originate at the local or regional level, have fostered a web of global development networks in response to what they see as top-down decision-making by hegemonic global organizations dominated by Western interests (e.g., the World Bank and the International Monetary Fund). The development networks serve a counter-hegemonic or resistive function, opposing or challenging the major global decision-makers. The aim of these NGOs is to advocate for the poor, the marginalized, and those directly affected by global development processes, permitting these groups to engage with and oppose the processes they see as unfavourable or negatively affecting their lives. Within these development networks, northern and southern NGOs strive to work together to reach a consensus on how to achieve favourable and more helpful economic development in a particular place.

Visible opposition in the form of public protests has been a part of every major economic and political meeting since the World Trade Organization ministerial conference in Seattle during 1999. In Canada, protestors picketed the Summit of the Americas conference in Quebec City in April 2001—an event marred by what many regard as excessive security and police action (**Figure 2.24a**). The G20 meeting of world leaders in Toronto in 2010 precipitated a repeat of that violence (**Figure 2.24b**), although the global movement has been refining its style and message, using communications technology such as the Internet and cell phones to draw together disparate and loosely associated political and social organizations at the global scale.

This change in approach speaks to a growing global solidarity and is reflected in the formation of the World Social Forum, which since 2001 has been holding counter-summits to the World Economic Forum. These new movements have made certain issues a focus of global concern, especially questions of environmental degradation, justice (specifically human rights), health and security, and the development of a global normative culture.

Resistance to globalization at the extreme right of the political spectrum is driven by concern about the perceived threat to local, traditional cultures and values. The possibility of global governance has given rise to strong nationalist movements and religious fundamentalism.

Global social movements of all political stripes, networked on a local, regional, national, or international scale, have developed practical local approaches for dealing with globalizing processes. We will examine two of these local solutions to development: participatory development and local currencies.

PARTICIPATORY DEVELOPMENT

Participatory development The notion that locals should be engaged in deciding what development means for them and how it should be achieved.	**Participatory development**— the idea that locals should be engaged in deciding what development means for them and how to achieve it—is one

response to top-down decision-making. Stuart Corbridge has studied how the global push for participatory development encouraged the government of India to enact participatory development programs. Corbridge and his colleague Sanjay Kumar describe the goal of participatory development as giving the people who are directly affected by policies and programs a voice in making the policies and programs—that is, to use local networks to shape development for local goals.

Kumar and Corbridge studied a program in India that was meant to get seeds to farmers and create irrigation schemes. The program was successful for many farmers, though not for the poorest farmers because, the geographers discovered, local politics factored into the distribution of poverty-alleviation schemes, and richer farmers and elites in rural areas tended to be most involved with the program. However, Kumar and Corbridge claimed that the poorer farmers' lack of participation was not a reason to abandon the participatory program. They concluded that all participatory development programs have to "operate in an environment that is dominated by better off farmers and particular community groups"; therefore, the definition of success must change because development organizations cannot expect the poorest to "participate in groups that have little meaning for them." Nevertheless, awareness of the local factors that cause inequalities in the benefits of a program means those delivering such programs should work to minimize these problems.

The World Bank, the International Monetary Fund, and even state governments are increasingly embracing the ideal of participatory development and reducing demands for trade liberalization in the periphery and semi-periphery. As Kumar and Corbridge explain, politics will enter participatory development, just as they enter the development networks and the global development organizations. The goal of participatory

© Tom Hanson/The Canadian Press

© Carolyn Kaster/Associated Press

(a)   (b)

FIGURE 2.24 (a) Summit of the Americas Conference in Quebec City, 2001. Thousands of protesters from Canada, the United States, and abroad arrived in Quebec City to speak out against globalization. **(b) Protesters in downtown Toronto during the G20 Summit, June 26, 2010.**

development is worthwhile, even if the short-term results do not mesh with Western concepts of success.

LOCAL CURRENCIES

Uneven development affects not just the periphery but also the core and semi-periphery. Economic downturns are a common occurrence in local places of all regions, and unemployment is frequently the result. As Michael Pacione explains, finding families and neighbours who can help in times of economic hardship may be difficult because globalization results in less connectedness:

> Social trends inherent in global capitalism, including decreasing household size, increasing distance between relatives, and attenuation of neighbouring relations within cities, have served to inhibit the operation of informal relations in which disadvantaged households could exchange goods and services for partial or no payment within the "moral" economy of their own family or neighbourhood. (1997, p. 1179–1199)

Local exchange trading system (LETS) A barter system whereby a local currency is created through which members trade services or goods in a local network separated from the formal economy.

One way people can cope with such downturns, whether in the core, semi-periphery, or periphery, is by establishing a local currency. During the 1980s, the people of the Comox Valley in British Columbia established the first **local exchange trading system (LETS)**. When the two major employers in the area closed, many of the area's 50,000 residents faced severe economic hardship. The community began a local exchange system, LETS, through which members traded services or goods in a local network separated from the formal economy. People who needed services (such as plumbing) would pay others with their own services or goods (such as providing accounting services in exchange for the plumbing call).

LETS systems and other local currency systems are alternatives to global norms of development, serving as a local response to global or regional economic change affecting a community or region (**Figure 2.25**). Because the currency is local and can only be traded locally, it fuels the local economy. The person who spends LETS credits for shoes, for example, can only spend them at the local shoe store, and not at an on-line store or in a catalogue.

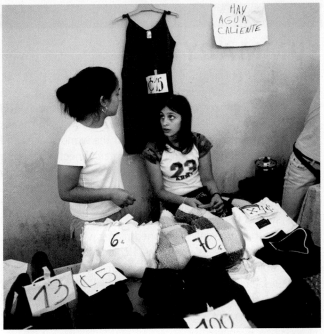

FIGURE 2.25 Bernal, Buenos Aires, Argentina. When the Argentinian economy collapsed in 1999, the number of local currencies in the country proliferated, eventually hovering around 5,000 different currencies and barter clubs. In this suburb of Buenos Aires, girls sold clothing that was priced with "credits" based on values established in their local currency system.

The number of local currencies in use in the world today totals well over 1,000. Many are used in rural areas, but local currency systems have also been successful in cities as diverse as Glasgow, Scotland, and Berkeley, California. In Berkeley, the local currency did not develop as a response to economic hardship but rather as a desire to avoid supporting the global currency system. As well, we are seeing digital currency begin to take hold on the Internet. Bitcoin, a peer-to-peer payment system, was introduced in 2009, and more merchants are beginning to accept it. Bitcoins work without banks, without fees, and are not tied to any particular nation or government. While bitcoins are still not common or universal, they indicate a movement toward anonymous, no-fee currency exchange that transcends geographical borders and boundaries.

MAIN POINTS 2.3 Why Do Some People or Groups Oppose or Resist Globalization?

- There are different perspectives on whether globalization produces positive or negative results. Many argue that globalization benefits the core regions to the detriment of the periphery and the semi-periphery.

- Resistance or oppositional movements develop their own views on what is wrong with globalization and how these difficulties might be fixed.

- Participatory development and local currencies are two examples of distinctive approaches to dealing with the perceived ills of globalization.

SUMMARY

Globalization is a complicated and contested concept. As a starting point, in Ritzer's view, globalization can be understood generally "as an accelerating set of processes involving flows that encompass ever-greater numbers of the world spaces and that lead to increasing integration and interconnectivity among those spaces" (2007, p. 1). Space and places are increasingly connected by improved technologies as more and more locations are drawn into the global capitalist markets. The current world system is the result of some 500 years of exploration and colonialism that unevenly positioned places within that system for different purposes. Canada, as a colonized country, developed a staples economy, supplying resources to an almost insatiable European market. Canada's colonial past established some of the historical factors that partially explain the country's current role as part of a global core region.

Globalization processes operate in chaotic and unruly ways, with uneven and varying impacts. Human geographers have been compelled to imagine new ways of thinking about the geographical in response to these processes and outcomes, and concepts such as "time-space compression," networks, "placelessness," and "glocalization" have emerged as a result.

Those who oppose globalization processes for different reasons have formed a global counter-movement, comprising a loose collection of different groups, which has successfully pushed a number of items onto the global agenda—such as environmental justice, human rights, and health and security.

The spatial perspective of human geographers is particularly useful for coming to grips with the possibilities, limitations, and uncertainties of these globalizing processes.

DISCUSSION AND REVIEW QUESTIONS

1. What is globalization? Think about the place where you live: how has it been affected by and/or how does it affect modern globalization?

2. What is the "staples thesis," and what does it reveal about how Canada has historically been integrated into the processes of globalization?

3. To succeed in the globalized economy requires a variety of corporate strategies. Two such strategies are "vertical" and "horizontal" integration. Explain these strategies and discuss the specific industries where they have proven most successful.

4. Many observers believe globalization is creating a sense of "placelessness." What do they mean by this and based on your experience and where you live, do you agree or disagree?

5. Globalization processes and outcomes have not been favourably viewed in all places or by all peoples. The movement that has arisen to challenge the logic of globalization has been dubbed "alternative globalization." Identify who are the proponents of this movement and discuss their arguments against globalization. What are their ideas for improving globalization?

GEOGRAPHIC CONCEPTS

commodity chain 31
free trade zones 41
friction of distance 41
globalization 32
glocalization 48
horizontal integration 46
local exchange trading system (LETS) 51
neo-liberalism 41

networks 44
participatory development 50
placelessness 47
staples thesis 35
synergy 46
time-space compression 43
vertical integration 46
world city 40

ADDITIONAL RESOURCES ON-LINE

Alberta oil sands ownership: http://business.financialpost.com/2012/10/31/who-owns-the-oil-sands/?__lsa=f60b-dcd2

Media ownership in Canada: www.crtc.gc.ca/ownership/eng/title_org.htm

Media ownership in the U.S., *Columbia Journalism Review*'s Who Owns What website: www.cjrarchives.org/tools/owners

The Global Fund: www.theglobalfund.org/EN

Global Cities Index 2014: www.atkearney.com/research-studies/global-cities-index

Global Cities Initiative: www.brookings.edu/about/projects/global-cities

World Social Forum, 2015: www.uclg.org/en/media/events/world-social-forum-2015

World Trade Organization: www.wto.org

Unionizing Workers in Sri Lankan free trade zones: www.waronwant.org/overseas-work/sweatshops-and-plantations/free-trade-zones-in-sri-lanka

"Made in Bangladesh," *Fifth Estate* original broadcast date Oct. 11, 2013: www.cbc.ca/fifth/episodes/2013-2014/made-in-bangladesh

Canadian Naomi Klein takes aim at transnational corporations: www.naomiklein.org/no-logo

No Logo, on-line documentary: http://topdocumentaryfilms.com/no-logo-brands-globalization-resistance

Meltdown: A Global Tsunami: www.cbc.ca/player/Shows/Shows/Doc+Zone/Meltdown/ID/2064453825/

CHAPTER
3 POLITICAL GEOGRAPHY

Gold, History, and Women in Post-Colonial Ghana

WHEN GHANA GAINED INDEPENDENCE FROM BRITAIN in 1957, it had the arduous task of cobbling together a nation from the amalgamation of different ethnic states that existed independently of each other before being drawn up together in a territorial area assigned to the British in a meeting by European colonizing powers in 1885 in Berlin where they, in simple fashion, shared Africa among themselves. As the first sub-Saharan African country to gain independence from colonial rule, Ghana contributed economically, psychologically, and philosophically to the burgeoning liberation movements that swept through the continent from the late 1950s into the 1960s. Ghana's independence gave hope to other African countries of the possibility of independence from colonialism. Dr. Kwame Nkrumah, who led Ghana to independence, is one of the founding fathers of Pan-Africanism and the African Union.

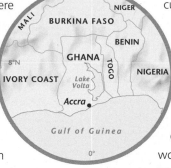

Currently, Ghana characteristically mirrors other post-colonial states in terms of its struggles against economic, cultural, and political imperialism. Understandably, people in post-colonial states are wary of new forms of colonialism and often try to assert autonomy and sovereignty in a variety of ways. Notably, culture serves as an appropriate site for asserting difference; i.e., difference from western and recently departed colonizers. Political geographers are interested in the ways in which political and cultural forces work together within and across national and international boundaries (**Figure 3.1**). They recognize that the political organization of space both shapes, and is shaped by the socio-cultural dimensions and ethnic identities of the people affected by such decisions.

Culture is a controversial site of struggle for women in Ghana, who make up more than half of the country's population. Advocacy for women's individual rights often clash with tenets of a communitarian culture where individual rights are typically suppressed for the common good. In 2007, after 50 years of independence (**Figure 3.2**), Ghana passed a domestic violence bill into law. Women's rights leaders and activists jubilated. It had taken five years to achieve this. Interest groups who feared the bill was influenced by western feminist traditions vehemently opposed it. They claimed that the demands of the bill, and the women's movement for that matter, were not cultural. "Ridiculous!," activists retorted. "Violence is not part of Ghanaian culture." Indeed, the notion of a unitary culture in a country with over 46 different ethnicities is merely romantic. However, "culture" is sometimes used as an excuse to justify oppressive practices against women. The women's movement in Ghana, in campaigning against these practices, is careful not to ignore the ways in which unfavourable neoliberal international development programs also negatively impact women and subsequently reinforce local cultural traditions that disadvantage women. The challenges women's rights activists face in Ghana provide an opportunity for reflecting on a history and lasting legacies of colonialism on women's identity and oppression in the post-colonial state.

—Dr. Sylvia Bawa, York University

FIGURE 3.1 Female leaders from Ghana's Western Region participate in USAID-supported work aimed at strengthening civil reforms.

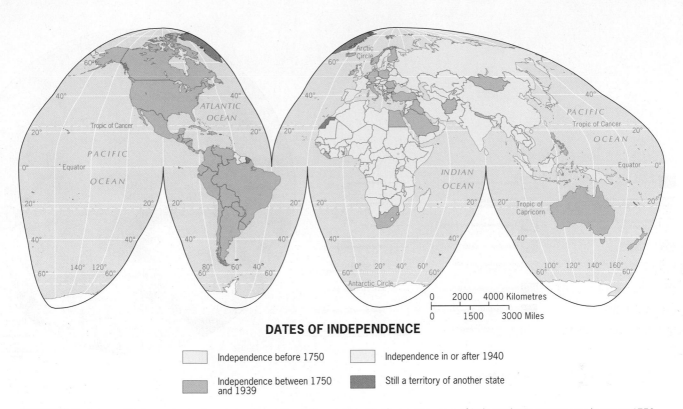

DATES OF INDEPENDENCE

☐ Independence before 1750   ☐ Independence in or after 1940

☐ Independence between 1750 and 1939   ☐ Still a territory of another state

FIGURE 3.2 Dates of independence for states throughout the world. The first major wave of independence movements between 1750 and 1939 occurred mainly in the Americas. The second major wave of independence movements after 1940 occurred mainly in Africa and Asia. South Sudan became the most recently recognized independent state in July 2011, bringing the total number of member states in the United Nations to 193. Data from: United Nations, 2011

KEY QUESTIONS FOR CHAPTER 3

1. How is space organized into states and nations?

2. How did the modern nation-state come into being?

3. How is the governance of states spatially organized?

4. How do geopolitics and critical geopolitics help us understand the world?

5. What are supranational organizations, and what is the future of the state?

3.1 How Is Space Organized into States and Nations?

Politics and place are intertwined. Our lives—where we live, the taxes we pay, the schools we attend, and the places we travel or work—are regulated by various levels of government and state institutions. We come to understand ourselves as people living in bounded places, either imagined or otherwise. We have mental maps of our neighbourhoods, our school districts, and the "city limits." We identify as being from a particular province, and we see ourselves as Canadians living in an identifiable and bounded territory. Political geographers are interested in nations and states, their territories and boundaries, and the

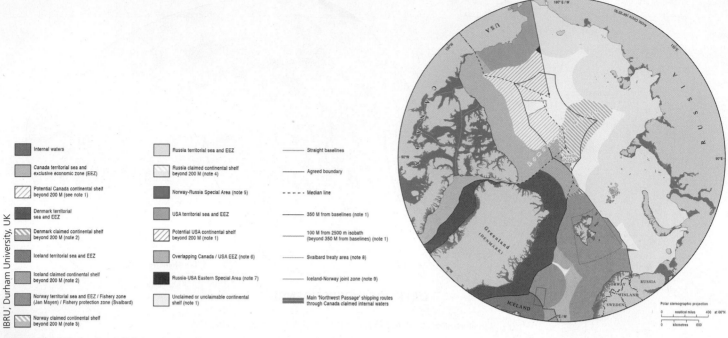

FIGURE 3.3 Territorial claims in the Arctic.

Ideology A set of shared ideas or beliefs that serve to justify the interests of dominant groups. In political geography, often understood as a world view about how societies do and should work.

Political geography A subdivision of human geography focused on the nature and implications of the evolving spatial organization of political governance and formal political practice on the Earth's surface. It is concerned with why political spaces emerge in the places that they do and with how the character of those spaces affects social, political, economic, and environmental understandings and practices.

ideologies of nationalism and sovereignty that constitute the geographies of everyday lives. As Canadians, we should be deeply concerned about the politics of geography and the geography of politics—about Arctic sovereignty (**Figure 3.3**), Afghanistan, offshore drilling in the Beaufort Sea, or the security or permeability of our borders.

In Chapter 1, we noted that human geographers are interested in the geography of human-environmental inter-relations. In this chapter, we focus on the political aspects of these relationships in terms of the themes of location, region, place, landscape, and movement as they relate to the subdiscipline of **political geography**. When we speak about the "political," we generally mean the organization, structure, and administration of a country and its relationships with other countries and its citizens. When a country acts in particular ways, there are distinctive spatial effects. For example, when one country invades another country, boundaries change, people are displaced, and new relationships are formed between people and place: people may be forced to flee their homeland and become "refugees"—a new political and social entity grounded in a different location through forced movement or migration.

THE MODERN STATE

At the global scale, we have a world divided into individual countries or, more properly, states. A **state** is a politically organized entity with a permanent population, a defined territory, and a government. To achieve statehood, an entity must be recognized as such by other states. Article 2 of the United Nations' Charter enshrines the principle that all member states must uphold the territorial integrity of other member states and not interfere in their internal domestic affairs. While states and international relations are an important focus for political geographers, many work at the microscale, studying smaller administrative units such as regions, urban areas, provinces, or electoral districts.

The present-day division of the world into states is the result of endless contests and accommodations within and between human societies. On the conventional political map, a mosaic of colours represents more than 200 countries and territories, a visualization that accentuates the separation of these countries by boundaries (see **Figure 3.4**). The political map is the world map most of us learn first. We look at it, memorize it, and name the countries and perhaps each country's capital. It hangs in the front of our classrooms, is used to organize maps in

State A politically organized entity that is administered by a sovereign government and is recognized by a significant portion of the international community. A state has a defined territory, a permanent population, a government, and is recognized by other states.

our textbooks, and becomes so familiar to us that *we begin to think it is natural.*

Yet we must think carefully about how "natural" these divisions are and consider the implications flowing from such assumptions. As geographer Richard Jackson argues:

> *When school children are repeatedly shown a political map of the world . . . they can easily end up regarding [states] in the same light as the physical features such as rivers, or mountain ranges which sometimes delimit their natural boundaries . . . Far from being natural entities, modern sovereign states are entirely historical artefacts the oldest of which have been in existence in their present shape and alignment only for the past three or four centuries.* (1990, p. 7)

The world map of states is anything but natural. Just as people create places, imparting character to space and shaping culture, people, their actions, and their history make, shape, and refine states and state boundaries.

> **Territoriality** In political geography, a country's or more local community's sense of property and attachment toward its territory, as expressed by its determination to keep it inviolable and strongly defended.

Central to the idea of the state is the concept of **territoriality**, which geographer Robert Sack (1986) defines as "the attempt by an individual or group to affect, influence, or control people, phenomena, and relationships, by delimiting and asserting control over a geographic area." Sack sees human territoriality as a key ingredient in the construction of social and political spaces. He argues that human territoriality takes many different forms, depending on the historical, social, and geographical context. We need, he suggests, a better understanding of the human organization of the planet through a consideration of how and why different territorial strategies are pursued at different times and in different places.

> **Sovereignty** A principle of international relations that holds that final authority over social, economic, and political matters should rest with the legitimate rulers of independent states.

Political geographers study territoriality across scales, cultures, and histories. They examine how people have changed the way territoriality is expressed and how ideas about territoriality vary over space and time. Today, territoriality is tied closely to the concept of **sovereignty**, which refers to a state's right to exercise power and control over people in a particular territory, a right that is recognized in international law. The UN principle requiring the international community of states to recognize an entity as a legitimate state and as being sovereign within its borders stems from the concept of territoriality.

Sometimes states will refuse to recognize other places that claim to be states in their own right. For example, territoriality has led to the heavy contestation of space in the former Yugoslavia. The Republic of Kosovo declared independence on February 17, 2008. By July 2014, some 107 of the 198 member states in the United Nations (including Canada, the United States, Australia, and most of the European Union) recognized Kosovo as a sovereign state. However, many states did not, including Serbia and Russia (**Figure 3.5**). The notion of recognition is a complicated one. A state may be recognized as having a particular territory by its government but may not be recognized if the government is perceived as invalid, for example, when it is the result of an internal military coup. A state government may not be recognized formally but may maintain informal relations with a large number of other states. Under international law, states have the right to defend what they perceive as their **territorial integrity** against incursion from other states, which means they could go to war if invaded by another state. These modern ideas of how state, sovereignty, and territory are intertwined began in mid-17th-century Europe and diffused to the rest of the world.

> **Territorial integrity** The right of a state to defend sovereign territory against incursion from other states.

BOUNDARIES

International boundaries or borders separate individual states. Boundaries may appear on maps as straight lines or may twist and turn to conform to the bends of rivers and the curves of hills and valleys. But a boundary is more than a line and is far more than a fence or wall on the ground. A **boundary** between states is actually a vertical plane that cuts through the rocks below (called the subsoil) and the airspace above, dividing one state territory from another (**Figure 3.6**). Only where the vertical plane intersects the Earth's surface (on land or at sea) does it form the line we see on a map.

> **Boundary** Vertical plane between states that cuts through the rocks below (called the subsoil), and the airspace above the surface, dividing one state territory from another.

Many boundaries on the contemporary world map were established before the extent or significance of subsoil resources was known. A major issue between Iraq and Kuwait, which in part led to Iraq's invasion of Kuwait in 1990, was the oil in the Rumaylah reserve that lies underneath the desert and crosses the boundary between the two states. The Iraqis asserted that the Kuwaitis were drilling too many wells and draining the reserve too quickly; they also alleged that the Kuwaitis were drilling oblique boreholes to penetrate the vertical plane extending downward along the boundary. At the time the Iraq-Kuwait boundary was established, however, no one knew this giant oil reserve lay in the subsoil or that it would help create an international crisis (**Figure 3.7**).

Above the ground, too, the interpretation of boundaries as vertical planes has serious implications. A state's "airspace" is defined by the atmosphere above its land area as marked by its boundaries, as well as by what lies beyond, at higher altitudes. But how high does the airspace extend? Most states insist on controlling the airline traffic over their territories, but states do not yet control the paths of satellite orbits.

FIGURE 3.4 States of the world, 2011.

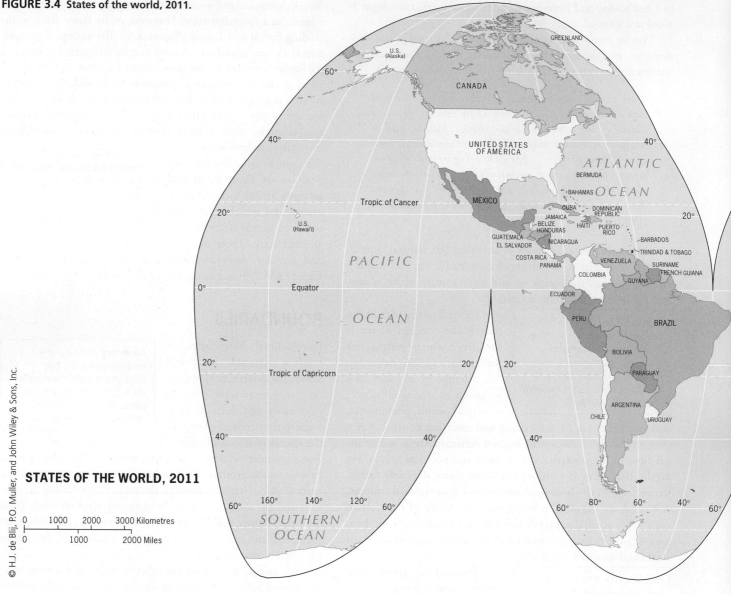

STATES OF THE WORLD, 2011

ESTABLISHING BOUNDARIES

Demarcating and controlling territory is a central function of the state. Clearly, the ability to control the border is a primary concern. A boundary helps define who belongs and who does not, who must stay and who can go. Boundaries affect the movement of people from different places, locations, and regions; by allowing or inhibiting movement they affect life changes, influence the possibilities for work or travel, and, in some cases, determine whether or not one will survive.

Practically speaking, establishing a boundary between two states typically involves four steps. First, states *define* the boundary through a treaty-like legal document in which actual points

in the landscape or points of latitude and longitude are described. Next, cartographers *delimit* the boundary by drawing it on a map. Third, if either or both of the states on each side of the border so desire, they can *demarcate* the boundary by using steel posts, concrete pillars, fences, walls, or some other visible means to mark the boundary on the ground. A good example of unilateral fence building is illustrated in **Figure 3.8**. The border between the United States and Mexico spans over 3,100 kilometres, crossing a vast array of terrain from urban centres to deserts. The barrier comprises a variety of technologies, including steel and wire fencing, floodlighting, surveillance cameras and equipment, and tightly controlled border crossings. By no

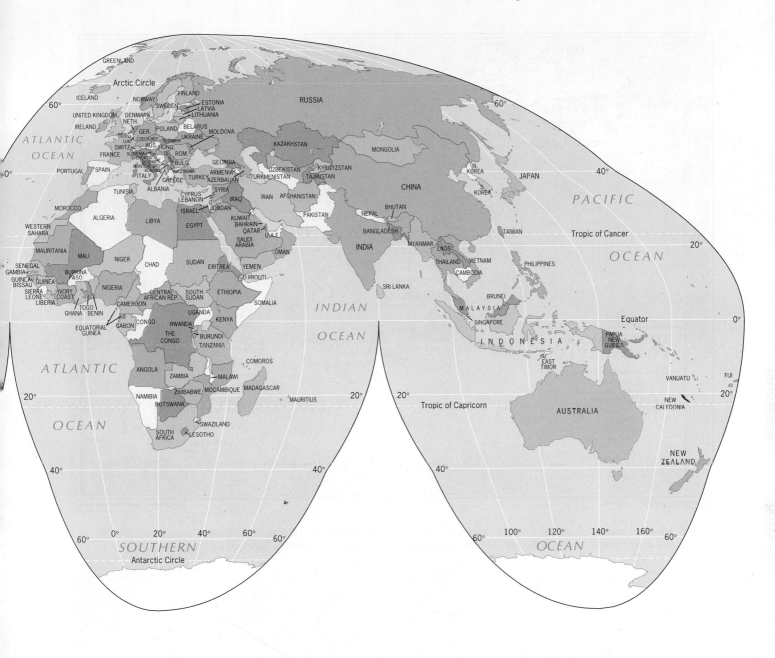

means are all boundaries on the world map demarcated. Demarcating a lengthy boundary is expensive, and it is hardly worth the effort in high mountains, vast deserts, frigid polar lands, or other places with few permanent settlements. The final step is to *administrate* the boundary—to determine how the boundary will be maintained and how goods and people will cross the boundary.

TYPES OF BOUNDARIES

When boundaries are drawn using grid systems such as latitude and longitude or township and range, political geographers refer to them as **geometric boundaries**. In North America, the United States and Canada used a single line of latitude west of the Great Lakes to define their boundary (**Figure 3.9**).

At different times, political geographers and other academics have advocated "natural" boundaries over geometric boundaries because they are visible on the landscape as physical geographic features. **Physical-political boundaries** (also called natural-political boundaries) follow

> **Geometric boundary** Political boundary defined and delimited (and occasionally demarcated) as a straight line or an arc.
>
> **Physical political (natural-political) boundary** Political boundary defined and delimited (and occasionally demarcated) by a prominent physical feature in the natural landscape, such as a river or the crest ridges of a mountain range.

FIGURE 3.5 The former Yugoslavia. The contested geography of the former Yugoslavia, and in particular Kosovo, as discussed, provides a good example of territoriality. Map from the United Nations Department of Peacekeeping Operations Cartographic Section, June 2007.

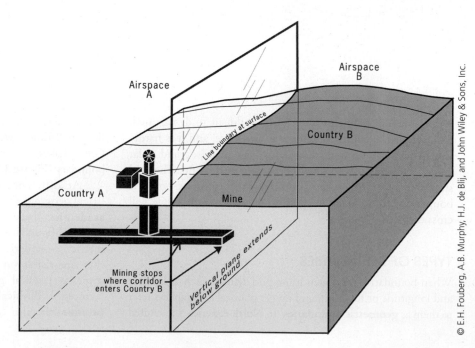

FIGURE 3.6 The vertical plane of a political boundary.

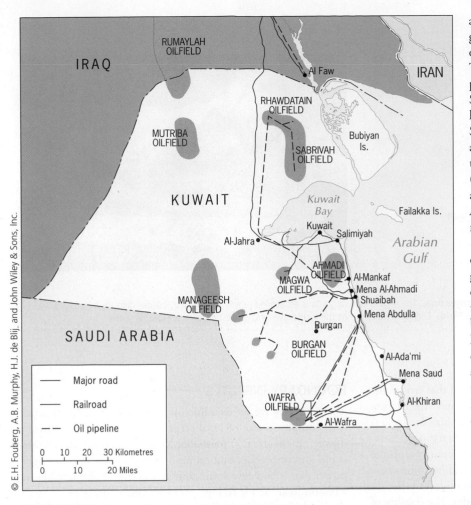

FIGURE 3.7 The international boundary between Iraq and Kuwait. Kuwait's northern boundary was redefined and delimited by a United Nations boundary commission; it was demarcated by a series of concrete pillars 2 kilometres apart.

an agreed-upon feature in the physical geographic landscape, such as the centre point of a river or the crest of a mountain range. The Rio Grande is an important physical-political boundary between the United States and Mexico; an older boundary follows crest lines of the Pyrenees between Spain and France. Lakes sometimes serve as boundaries as well; for example, four of the five Great Lakes of North America (between the United States and Canada) and several of the Great Lakes of East Africa (between Congo and its eastern neighbours) serve as boundaries.

Physical features sometimes make convenient political boundaries, but topographic features are not static. Rivers change course, volcanoes erupt, and, slowly, mountains erode. People perceive physical-political boundaries as more stable, but many states have entered territorial conflicts over physical-political boundaries. For example, Chile and Argentina, which share the world's third-longest international border (5,300 kilometres) have a long history of dispute over their border. A complex series of treaties and agreements has attempted to establish a border between the two countries, long before the geography was fully understood, and date back to the Boundary Treaty of 1881 (**Figure 3.10a**). Recently, one of the disputes has been over 161 kilometres of contested land known as the Southern Patagonian Ice Field (**Figure 3.10b**). This area, which contains the second-largest reserve of potable

FIGURE 3.8 The U.S.-Mexico border wall. The border wall or fence runs along and through hillsides at Border Field State Park along the U.S.-Mexico border across from Playas de Tijuana (left) near San Diego, California.

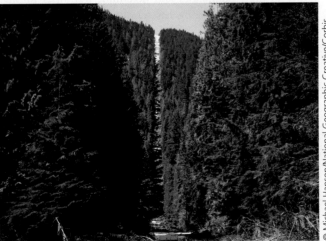

FIGURE 3.9 The 49th parallel, facing west, with the United States (Washington State) on the left and Canada (British Columbia) on the right. The border between the United States and Canada follows the 49th parallel for 2,043 kilometres, from Lake of the Woods (Minnesota/Manitoba) to the Pacific Ocean. A six-metre-wide path is clearcut along this stretch of the border, marked by over 900 survey markers.

(a)

(b)

© Momatiuk-Eastcott/Corbis

FIGURE 3.10 **(a) Border between Chile and Argentina.** The region of Patagonia is embroiled in a long-standing border dispute between Chile and Argentina. **(b) The Southern Patagonian Ice Field.** This ice field contains the world's second-largest reserve of potable water.

water in the world, is part of Patagonia, a region that crosses the Andes. The area was traversed only in 1998 and still has not been completely mapped. The Southern Patagonian Ice Field is the last remaining border issue between the two nations.

Similarly, physical boundaries do not necessarily stop the flow of people or goods across boundaries, leading some states to reinforce physical boundaries with human-built obstacles (as the United States has done on the Rio Grande). The stability of boundaries has more to do with local historical and geographical circumstances than with the character of the boundary itself. As the *Guest Field Note* from Jason Grek Martin suggests, the power to draw boundaries and determine territories through mapping and map-making has serious implications for those living "on the ground."

BOUNDARY DISPUTES

The boundary we see as a line on an atlas map is the product of a complex series of legal steps that begins with a written description of the boundary. Sometimes that legal description is old and imprecise. Sometimes it was dictated by a stronger power that is now less dominant, giving the weaker neighbour a reason to argue for change. At other times, the geography of the borderland has actually changed; the river that marked the boundary may have changed course, or a portion of it could be cut off. Resources lying across a boundary can lead to conflict. In short, states often argue about their boundaries. These boundary disputes take four principal forms: definitional, locational, operational, and allocational.

GUEST FIELD NOTE

Maps and Power in a Canadian Colonial Context

"As much as guns and warships, maps have been the weapons of imperialism." With these words, map historian J. B. Harley (2001, p. 57) seeks to debunk the notion that cartography offers a neutral and objective depiction of the world. Rather than showing the terrain "as it is," maps make arguments about the geographies they represent. They naturalize particular and often quite contested spatial understandings at the expense of competing perspectives. To paraphrase another map historian, maps work by serving interests; by "showing this but not that" (Wood, 1992, pp. 4 and 48).

I have been a cartophile my whole life and spent hours as a child pouring over atlases and drawing elaborate maps of my own. This fascination intensified as an undergraduate student after the insights of Harley and Wood showed me that maps were powerful geopolitical statements, worthy of careful intellectual scrutiny. As Harley suggests, this is especially apparent with maps made in the context of colonialism and imperialism.

George Dawson's geological map of Haida Gwaii (formerly the Queen Charlotte Islands), published in 1880, is a good example. As a field scientist for the Geological Survey of Canada, Dawson was responsible for exploring vast portions of the western territories acquired by Canada from Great Britain in 1870–71. The Survey aimed to provide the scientific knowledge

GUEST FIELD NOTE   Maps and Power in a Canadian Colonial Context *continued*

to help Canada effectively colonize its new acquisitions in the West. Dawson surveyed Haida Gwaii and several other portions of British Columbia's coastline in 1878. His task was to locate, examine, and document the natural amenities of the islands to assist future settlement and resource extraction. Dawson also studied the Haida, the archipelago's native population, to advance an anthropological understanding of their fascinating society. His season's work produced the first detailed report describing the indigenous Haida inhabitants and the abundant resource wealth of the islands. The report was accompanied by an impressive geological map of the islands that significantly improved upon previous maps.

Dawson's map of the archipelago largely erased the Haida from the landscape despite their extensive presence. Their most significant villages were marked and labelled but the vast majority of the mapped terrain bore no trace of human presence. The extensive, intimate and often quite formalized proprietary relations the Haida had with their homeland were not inscribed on Dawson's map, even though he had taken care to document this complex cultural geography in the accompanying report. In place of a cultural landscape, the map presented the islands as an uninhabited geological landscape of colour-coded rock formations and topographic relief. By focusing on underlying geology, Dawson's cartography stripped away the human landscape of the islands, rendering the Haida invisible.

Dawson took the cartographic erasure of the Haida a step further through the renaming of topographical features on the archipelago. In the colonial context, assigning names to places imposed order and signified authority over territory. Published maps formally codified new place names and erased the old. This quest for order and authority was particularly important on Haida Gwaii, which had never been thoroughly surveyed and mapped prior to Dawson's work in 1878. According to the colonial conventions of the day, Dawson had the right to name any previously "unmarked" topographical features that he should happen to "discover" in the course of his surveys. But, this notion of discovery was Eurocentric, given the indigenous Haida population had long since applied their own names to the unmarked landscapes Dawson (re)-named in 1878. While Dawson adopted a few of these existing indigenous names, he assigned a significant number of new names to the islands, headlands, and waterways found along the eastern coastline of the archipelago. Dawson entrenched a colonial tradition begun over a century earlier, when English explorer George Dixon—oblivious to the fact that these islands had already been named *Haida Gwaii* by their indigenous inhabitants—christened them the *Queen Charlotte Islands*.

In place of Haida toponyms, Dawson imposed new place names paying tribute to early European explorers to the region as well as to some of the leading figures in 19th-century science. **Figure 3.11** shows Dawson's cartographic depiction of Juan Perez Sound, a place name created to commemorate the first European explorer to set eyes on the islands in 1774. On the map, the inlets and headlands of Juan Perez Sound are sprinkled

FIGURE 3.11 George Dawson's map showing Juan Perez Sound, Haida Gwaii (known then as the Queen Charlotte Islands). From: George Dawson, "Report on the Queen Charlotte Islands, 1878." In *Report of Progress for 1878–1879*, Geological Survey of Canada, Montreal: Dawson Brothers, 1880, 1B-239B.

with the names of prominent geologists and naturalists: Charles Darwin, Charles Lyell, Roderick Murchison, Thomas Huxley, Abraham Werner, James Hutton, and many others. The symbolism of this naming practice is profound: Dawson inscribed the leading figures of science into the topography of Haida Gwaii, symbolically asserting scientific authority over landscapes that his surveying had just begun to make legible. Dawson's commemoration of Perez made reference to the early exploration of the islands and connected his 1878 survey to a long history of celebrated Pacific exploration. Through his place naming, Dawson was able to symbolically position himself at the intersection of two great imperial traditions—exploration and natural science. Dawson's surveying merged both traditions into an enterprise enhancing his own reputation and symbolizing the power of the Canadian state to assert its authority over even its most remote territorial outposts.

In the process, the Haida presence on these islands was overwritten on Dawson's geological map. A people that had occupied this archipelago since time immemorial were callously mapped out of the landscapes they considered their exclusive home. In their place, an enticing picture of resource abundance and available real estate was inserted, beckoning settlers westward. In the colonial context of late 19th-century Western Canada, Dawson's geological map of Haida Gwaii was not the neutral territorial depiction it purported to be. Rather, it was precisely the kind of weapon of imperialism that Harley describes.

Jason Grek Martin, Assistant Professor, St. Mary's University, Halifax, Nova Scotia

Definitional boundary disputes focus on the legal language of the boundary agreement. For example, a boundary definition may stipulate that the median line of a river will mark the boundary. That would seem clear enough, but the water levels of rivers vary. If the river valley is asymmetrical, the median line will move back and forth between low-water and high-water stages of the stream. This may involve hundreds of metres of movement—not very much, it would seem, but enough to cause serious argument, especially if there are resources in the river. The solution is to refine the definition to suit both parties.

Locational boundary disputes centre on the delimitation and possibly the demarcation of the boundary. The definition is not in dispute, but its interpretation is. Sometimes the language of boundary treaties is vague enough to allow mapmakers to delimit the line in various ways. For example, when the colonial powers defined their empires in Africa and Asia, they specified their international boundaries rather carefully. But internal administrative boundaries often were not strictly defined. When those internal boundaries became the boundaries of independent states, there was plenty of room for argument. In a few instances, locational disputes arise because no definition of the boundary exists at all. An important case involves Saudi Arabia and Yemen, whose potentially oil-rich boundary area is not covered by a treaty.

Operational boundary disputes involve neighbours who differ over the way their border should function. When two adjoining countries agree on how cross-border migration should be controlled, the border functions satisfactorily. However, if one state wants to limit migration while the other does not, a dispute may arise. The United States now requires Canadian citizens to have passports when crossing into the United States. Canada has not imposed a similar requirement on Americans entering Canada. Similarly, efforts to prevent smuggling across borders sometimes lead to operational disputes when one state's efforts are not matched (or are possibly even sabotaged) by its neighbour's. And in areas where nomadic lifeways still prevail, the movement of people and their livestock across international borders can lead to conflict.

Allocational boundary disputes, of the kind described earlier involving Iraq and Kuwait over oil, are becoming more common as the search for resources intensifies. Today, many such disputes involve international boundaries at sea. Oil reserves under the sea floor below coastal waters sometimes lie in areas where exact boundary delimitation may be difficult or subject to debate; the contested terrain in the Arctic described earlier is such an example (Figure 3.3). Another growing area of allocational dispute has to do with water supplies: the Tigris, Nile, Colorado, and other rivers are subject to such disputes. When a river crosses an international boundary, the rights of the upstream and downstream users of the river often come into conflict. The Euphrates-Tigris River Basin (**Figure 3.12**) is a contested region in the Middle East. Turkey, Iraq, and Syria all rely upon the water supply in the basin, and the site has become known as

The World Factbook 2009. Washington, DC: Central Intelligence Agency, 2009

FIGURE 3.12 Euphrates-Tigris River Basin.

a potential "water wars" region. Issues such as dam building, water navigation, and access to fresh water are central to this allocation boundary dispute.

BOUNDARIES, BORDERS, AND FRONTIERS

As we read in Chapter 2, the processes of globalization are leading to an increasingly interconnected world where geography continues to play an important role. As countries around the globe continue to build trade relationships and form agreements that increase interconnectedness and interdependence between places, there has been some question as to whether boundaries and borders still matter; borders might seem more permeable, as people, information, goods, and capital flow around the world. Political geographers, however, assert that in this "borderless world," geography—and the borders and boundaries that shape geography—are more important than ever. In fact, as Julian Minghi (1963) has argued:

> *Because political boundaries form the areal expression of the limits of jurisdiction and power of the system to which they belong, they are perhaps the most palpable political geographic phenomena.* (p. 407)

It is important to begin with some definitions, as it is easy to slip between borders, boundaries, and frontiers, yet they all have different meanings. Professor Anssi Paasi (2009) from the University of Oulu (Finland) provides the following useful

Boundaries Physical or imaginary lines of contact between states, including the social institutions and symbols that exist in social practices and discourses.

Borders Adjacent areas lining boundaries.

Borderlands Transition zones within which a boundary (line) is located.

Frontier Political divisions between states or divisions between settled and uninhabited areas within a state.

definitions. **Boundaries** can be defined as physical or imaginary lines of contact between states, including the institutions and symbols that exist and are reproduced in social practices and discourses. **Borders** are understood as the adjacent areas lining boundaries. **Borderlands** are the transition zones within which a boundary (line) is located. Finally, a **frontier** is a category that usually refers to political divisions (zones) between states or to divisions between settled and uninhabited areas within a state.

Since the 1980s, we have witnessed tremendous changes to the borders and boundaries that shape the modern world, such as the taking down of the Berlin Wall (1989) (**Figure 3.13**), the collapse of the former Soviet Union (1991), the formation of the European Union (1993), the signing of the North American Free Trade Agreement (1993), and the myriad terrorism-related security concerns after 9/11 (2001). All of these examples, and many more, reveal the need to study borders beyond just the geopolitical divisions. Geographers today, working in boundary and border studies, recognize that borders are never natural. They are always socially constructed; they are products of social practice, historical context, and are often the result of conflict.

When borders and boundaries are first and foremost understood as social practices, it is possible to question not just their geopolitical history, but the dynamic processes that create, maintain, and shift them. We can consider the cultural dimensions of borders, including the unique borderlands that emerge around territorial borders, and pose questions about such things as the relationship between borders and the construction of identity; the meaning of borders as both joiners and dividers between spaces; and the complex processes of inclusion and

FIGURE 3.14 Vehicles make their way through U.S. inspections at the Paso del Norte Port of Entry. The Paso del Norte International Bridge connects El Paso, Texas, with Juarez, Mexico. A Mexican teenage boy was shot and killed by U.S. border security in 2010, causing an international outcry about the strict measures the United States uses to control the entry of illegal immigrants at this busy border crossing.

exclusion that are practised through the establishment, maintenance, and even defence of borders. What borders mean to people in their everyday lives, then, becomes the focus of geographers in border and boundary studies. For example, a wall can mean security and safety for some, and oppression and limited freedom for others. A bridge between territories can mean connection and mobility, but it can also mean threat, exclusion, and fear for others (**Figure 3.14**). These contradictions, and many more, are the focus of political geographers as they engage in the study of boundaries, borders, and borderlands.

NATIONS

The popular media and press often use the words "nation," "state," and "country" interchangeably. Political geographers use "state" and "country" interchangeably (often preferring "state"), but the word "nation" is distinct. "State" is a legal term in international law, and the international political community has some agreement about what this term means. "Nation," on the other hand, is a culturally defined term, and few people agree on exactly what it means. Definitions are important as few words are as politically charged as the concept of nation.

The *Dictionary of Human Geography* (4th edition) defines a **nation** as

Nation A tightly knit group of people possessing bonds of language, ethnicity, religion, and other shared cultural attributes. Such homogeneity actually prevails within very few states.

a community of people whose members are bound together by a sense of solidarity rooted in an historic attachment to a homeland and a common culture, and by a sense of consciousness of being define from other nations. (p. 532)

FIGURE 3.13 Taking down the Berlin Wall, 1989.

A nation, then, is a group of people who think of themselves as collectively bound together based on a sense of shared culture and history, and who have some identification with a territory or place—a homeland. This idea encompasses different kinds of culturally and historically defined nations. Nations variously see themselves as sharing a religion, a language, an ethnicity, or a history. The French are often considered to be the classic example of a nation, but the most French-feeling person in France today is the product of a melding of a wide variety of cultural groups over time, including Celts, ancient Romans, Franks, and Goths. If the majority of inhabitants of modern France belong to the French nation, it is because they claim the French nation as an identity—not because the French nation exists as an always existing primordial group. Historically, nations were treated as something we are born into, something natural that changes over time. The widely held view was that all people belong to a nation and always have. Recently, scholars have argued that nations are constructed, that people create nations to give themselves an identity at that scale. Benedict Anderson, one of the most widely read scholars on nationalism today, defines the nation as an "imagined community"—imagined because, even though you will never meet all of the people in your nation and community, you still see yourself as part of a collective.

Because a nation is identified by those who are able to define and control membership, we cannot simply define a nation as the people within a territory. Indeed, rarely does a nation's extent correspond precisely with a state's borders. For example, in the country of Belgium, two nations—the Flemish and the Walloons—exist within the state borders. While some groups who envision themselves as nations do not seek territorial control and autonomy, there are numerous examples of groups seeking independence and the creation of their own territorially defined nation-state—for example, the Kurds of Iraq, Turkey, Syria, and Iran; Tamils in northern Sri Lanka; and the Québécois in the province of Quebec.

MAIN POINTS 3.1 How Is Space Organized into States and Nations?

- Political geographers are interested in nations and states, their territorial organization and boundaries, and nationalist ideologies. Political geographers are also interested in the political organization of space from the global to the local.

- Borders are never natural. They are always socially constructed; they are products of social practice, historical context, and are often the result of conflict.

- A state is not a "natural" organizational structure. It is a particular form of political and social order created by humans. The state is a politically organized territory with a permanent population, a defined territory, and a government.

- It must be recognized as such by the international community in accordance with international law.

- States need to establish boundaries and do so in a number of different ways. Disputes between countries about boundaries take a number of different forms including definitional, locational, operational, and allocational.

- A nation is a group of people who collectively understand themselves as having a shared history and a common culture attached to a particular homeland. Some states are made up of many nations, and many nations do not have their own state.

3.2 How Did the Modern Nation-State Come into Being?

Human beings have organized themselves into groups claiming control over territories for most of known human history. The great kingdoms of China and Japan, the earliest beginnings of human settlement in Mesopotamia some 7,000 years ago, and the long-lost civilizations of the Aztecs and the Incas speak to the territorial complexity of human social and political organization. The dominant modern European idea of the "state" is a relatively recent invention, emerging some 500 years ago out of the peculiar histories and geographies of exploration, colonialism, imperialism, and revolution. Prior to that time, medieval Europe was a hodgepodge of city-states, small kingdoms, duchies, and principalities engaged in seemingly endless petty feuds, minor skirmishes, and multiple wars

over boundaries and territorial control. **Figure 3.15** illustrates the organization of Europe in 1190, which looks considerably different than it does today.

The emergence of the contemporary European state as we know it is intertwined with changing economic relations from the Dark Ages onward. A growing land and sea trade beginning in the 1150s gave rise in many European urban centres to the merchant class—a new grouping distinguishable from the aristocracy on the one hand and landless, labouring classes on the other. As a group, the merchants increasingly used forms of money as a means of exchange as they developed long-distance trade in spices, woods, fabric, and slaves. Trade routes sprang up across the globe, drawing more of the world's territory into these global circuits.

By the early 1300s, competitive rivalries sprang up between the great trading nations of Spain, Portugal, Holland, Britain, and France. These rivalries escalated with the increasing belief in

FIGURE 3.15 Medieval Europe, c. 1190. From: *Historical Atlas*, published by W. & A.K. Johnston Limited, 1911 (colour litho) by English School (20th century).

Mercantilism In a general sense, associated with the promotion of commercialism and trade. More specifically, a protectionist policy of European states during the 16th to the 18th centuries that promoted a state's economic position in the contest with other countries. The acquisition of gold and silver and the maintenance of a favourable trade balance (more exports than imports) were central to the policy.

mercantilism, which began to take hold in the 1500s. Adherents to this belief argued that it was the state's responsibility to directly finance foreign trade by hiring merchants, explorers, and adventurers in order to promote the state's economic interests abroad. Each state sought to accumulate wealth through plunder, colonization, and the protection of home industries and foreign markets. Rivalry and competition intensified in Europe as well as abroad. Powerful royal families struggled for dominance in eastern and southern Europe. Instability was the rule, strife occurred frequently, and repressive governments prevailed. Some states were able to expand and consolidate their control and to raise revenues through increasingly sophisticated means of government control, bureaucratic regulation, and taxation. The ability to collect revenue was central to the formation of the modern state. The ability to raise funds to support state activities remains crucial today to the stability and effectiveness of the modern state.

In 1648, relative peace and stability was achieved in Europe when the **Peace of Westphalia** was negotiated

among the princes of the states making up the Holy Roman Empire, as well as the rulers of a few neighbouring states (**Figure 3.16**). The treaties that constituted this peace concluded the Thirty Years' War, Europe's most destructive internal struggle over religion. These treaties contained new language recognizing the rights of rulers within defined, demarcated territories. The language of the treaties laid the

Peace of Westphalia Peace negotiated in 1648 to end the Thirty Years' War, Europe's most destructive internal struggle over religion. The treaties contained new language recognizing statehood and nationhood, clearly defined borders, and guarantees of security.

FIGURE 3.16 Peace of Westphalia. The treaties that became known as the Peace of Westphalia ended the Thirty Years' War in Europe in 1648. The result was the drawing of new boundaries around European states, including an independent Portugal and Netherlands, and the growth of the Ottoman Empire. From: *Historical Atlas,* published by W. & A.K. Johnston Limited, 1911 (colour litho), English School (20th century).

foundations for a Europe made up of territorially defined states. They originally applied only to the states that were party to the treaty, but they gave rise to a political-territorial order that spread throughout western and central Europe.

The Westphalian treaties set the stage for the emergence of a state system that marked a fundamental change in the relationship between people and territory. In previous eras, societies had largely defined their territories. In the Westphalian system, territories defined societies (for example, the French are the people who live in France). Territory is treated as a fixed element of political identification, and states define exclusive, non-overlapping territories. State rulers are sovereign over their territories and the people who inhabit them.

Well after the Peace of Westphalia, absolutist rulers continued to control most European states. During the later 17th and 18th centuries, however, the development of an increasingly wealthy middle class proved to be the undoing of absolutism in parts of Western Europe. City-based merchants gained wealth and prestige, while the nobility declined. Money and influence were increasingly concentrated in urban areas, and the traditional measure of affluence—land—became less important. Merchants and businessmen demanded political recognition. In the 1780s, a series of upheavals began that would change the sociopolitical face of the continent—most notably the French Revolution of 1789. That revolution, conducted in the name of the French people, ushered in an era in which the foundations for political authority came to be seen as resting with a state's citizenry, not with a hereditary monarch.

THE NATION-STATE

> **Nation-state** Theoretically, a recognized member of the modern state system possessing formal sovereignty and occupied by a people who see themselves as a single, united nation. Most nations and states aspire to this form, but it is realized almost nowhere. Nonetheless, in common parlance, nation-state is used as a synonym for country or state.

A **nation-state** is a politically organized area in which nation and state occupy the same space. That is, people who collectively understand themselves as a nation, bound together by history, identity, and/or culture, occupy a bounded territory governed by a state. Few (if any) states are nation-states. Many states, such as Canada, are made up of groups who consider themselves a different nation—Quebec nationalists and First Nations peoples, for example. Given this reality, the importance of the nation-state concept lies primarily in the idea behind it. States, and the governments that run states, desire a unified nation within their borders to create stability and to replace other politically charged identities that may challenge the state and the government's control of the state.

People began to see the idea of the nation-state as the ultimate form of political-territorial organization, the right

expression of sovereignty, and the best route to stability. The key problem associated with the idea of the nation-state is that it assumes the presence of reasonably well-defined, stable nations living contiguously within discrete territories. Very few places in the world come close to satisfying this requirement. Nonetheless, in Europe during the 18th and 19th centuries, many believed the condition could be achieved.

The quest to form nation-states in the Europe of the 1800s was associated with a rise in **nationalism**. Flint and Taylor (2007) define nation-

> **Nationalism** Both an ideology and a political practice that all nations need their own sovereign government and territory.

alism as an ideology and a political practice that assumes all nations should have their own state—a nation-state—in their own territory—the national homeland. In this sense, nationalism is a relatively recent phenomenon and constitutes a powerful link between politics, place, and culture. It requires that a group of people feel they belong to a nation (a collective imagined community) that corresponds to a particular bounded territory. In Canada, this feeling of collective imagined community is evident every year as thousands of flag-waving Canadians gather on Parliament Hill for Canada Day celebrations.

We can view nationalism from two vantage points: that of the people and that of the state. When *people* in a nation feel a strong sense of nationalism, they have a loyalty to the nation and a belief in the nation. This loyalty to a nation does not necessarily coincide with the borders of the state. A *state* does not have a strong sense of nationalism; rather, the government of a state is nationalistic. In this sense, the government promotes the nation, and because the government is the representative of the state, it seeks to promote a nation that coincides with the borders of the state. In the name of nationalism, a state that contains more than one nation can attempt to build a single national identity out of the divergent people within its borders. In the name of nationalism, a state can also promote a war against another state that threatens its territorial integrity.

In 19th-century Europe, states used nationalism to achieve a variety of goals. In some cases they integrated their population into an ever-more-cohesive national whole (e.g., France, Spain), and in other cases they brought together people with shared cultural characteristics within a single state (e.g., Germany and Italy). Similarly, people who saw themselves as a separate nation within another state or empire launched successful separatist movements and achieved independence (e.g., the Republic of Ireland, Norway, and Poland).

European state leaders used the tool of nationalism to strengthen the state. The modern map of Europe is still fragmented, but much less so than it was in the 1600s (**Figure 3.17**). In the process of creating nation-states in Europe, states absorbed smaller entities into their borders, resolved conflicts by force as well as by negotiation, and defined borders.

To help people within the borders relate to the dominant national ideal, states provide security, goods, and

FIGURE 3.17 European political fragmentation in 1648. A generalized map of the fragmentation of Western Europe in the 1600s.

services to the citizens. They support education, infrastructure, health care, and a military to preserve the state and to create a connection between the people and the state—to build a nation-state. European states even used the colonization of Africa and Asia in the late 1800s and early 1900s to promote nationalism. People could take pride in their state, in their nation, and in its vast colonial empire. People could identify themselves with their French, Dutch, or British nation by contrasting themselves with the people in the colonies—people whom they defined as mystical or savage. By identifying against an "other," the state and the people helped identify the traits of their nation—and in so doing, they worked to build a nation-state.

An important aspect of the building of a nationalist ideology is the development of a discourse of militarism; the role of the military and of civilians who support the military is central to the imagery of the nation-state. The British recruitment posters in **Figure 3.18** exemplify the ways in which governments encourage their citizens to enlist in armies. In Figure 3.18a the poster not only employs a sense of difference in terms of "us versus them," but it also uses gendered representations of the ways in which men (as protectors) and women (as victims in need of protecting) are understood within the nation-state to encourage enlistment. In Figure 3.18b the poster

demonstrates the other side of this gendered narrative as it encourages women to "come into the factories" to do their part in the war effort.

(a) (b)

FIGURE 3.18 (a) British World War I pre-conscription recruitment poster. (b) Specialist war recruitment poster urging women to go to work in factories.

MULTISTATE NATIONS, MULTINATIONAL STATES, AND STATELESS NATIONS

> **Multinational state** A state with more than one nation within its borders.

The sense of belonging to a nation rarely meshes perfectly with state borders. The lack of fit between nation and state creates complications, such as states with more than one nation, nations with more than one state, and nations without a state. Nearly every state in the world is a **multinational state**, a state with more than one nation inside its borders. Millions of people who were citizens of the former state of Yugoslavia never had a strong sense of Yugoslav nationality—instead they identified themselves as Slovenes, Croats, Serbs, Armenians, or members of other nations or ethnic groups within the state or region. Yugoslavia was a state that always had more than one nation, and eventually the state collapsed (see Figure 3.5).

> **Multistate nation** A nation that stretches across borders and across states.

When a nation stretches across borders and across states, it is called a **multistate nation**. Political geographer George White studied the states of Romania and Hungary and their overlapping nations. The territory of Transylvania is currently in the middle of the state of Romania, but for two centuries, Hungary's borders stretched far enough east to incorporate Transylvania into the state of Hungary. The Transylvania region today is populated by Romanians and Hungarians, and both states claim a desire and a right to control the territory. Both states identify places within Transylvania that they see as pivotal to the histories of their nations. The desire to control the territory and to stretch the Hungarian state in order to mesh with what Hungarians see as their nation requires the movement of state borders. In the case of Romania and Hungary, and in similar states where the identity of the nation is tied to a particular territory, White explains that nations will defend their territories as strongly as they defend their "language, religion, or way of life."

> **Stateless nation** A nation that does not have a state.

Another complication that arises from the lack of fit between nations and states is that some nations do not have a state; they are **stateless nations**. The Palestinians are an example of a stateless nation. Palestinian Arabs have gained control of the Gaza Strip and fragments of the Occupied Territories, which may form the foundations of a future state. Well over half of the approximately 8 million Palestinians continue to live in Israel, Jordan, Lebanon, Syria, and other Arab states. The international community does not recognize the Palestinian lands as a state.

A much larger stateless nation is that of the over 27 million Kurds who live in an area called Kurdistan that covers parts of six states (**Figure 3.19**). In the aftermath of the 1991 Gulf War, the United Nations established a Kurdish Security Zone north of the 36th parallel in Iraq, but subsequent events have dashed any Kurdish hopes that this might one day become a state. The Kurds form the largest minority in Turkey, and the city of Diyarbakir is the unofficial Kurdish capital; however,

© H.J. de Blij, P.O. Kuller, and John Wiley & Sons, Inc.

FIGURE 3.19   Kurdish region of the Middle East.

relations between the 10 million Kurds in Turkey and the Turkish government in Ankara have been volatile. Without the consent of Turkey, establishing a truly independent Kurdish state will be difficult.

EUROPEAN COLONIALISM AND THE DIFFUSION OF THE NATION-STATE MODEL

As noted in Chapter 2, Europe exported its concepts of state and sovereignty, and the desire for nation-states, to much of the rest of the world through two waves of colonialism. In the 16th century, Spain and Portugal took advantage of their increasingly well-consolidated internal political order and newfound wealth to expand their influence to increasingly far-flung realms during the first wave of colonialism. Later joined by Britain, France, the Netherlands, and Belgium, the first wave of colonialism established a far-reaching capitalist system. After independence movements in the Americas during the late 1700s and 1800s, a second wave of colonialism began in the late 1800s. This time the major colonizers were Britain, France, the Netherlands, Belgium, Germany, and Italy. Driven by motives ranging from economic profit to the desire to bring Christianity to the rest of the world, colonialism projected European power and a European approach to organizing political space into the non-European world (**Figure 3.20**).

With Europe in control of so much of the world, Europeans laid the ground rules for the emerging international state system, and the modern European concept of the nation-state became the model exported and imposed around the world. European colonial states also established and defined the ground rules of the capitalist world economy, creating a system of economic interdependence that persists today.

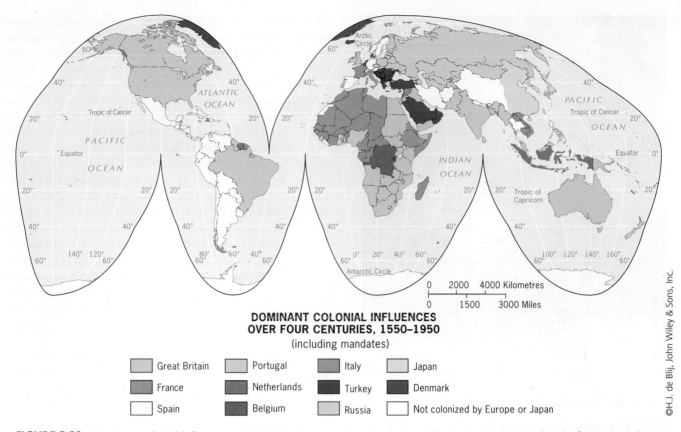

**DOMINANT COLONIAL INFLUENCES
OVER FOUR CENTURIES, 1550–1950**
(including mandates)

Great Britain	Portugal	Italy	Japan
France	Netherlands	Turkey	Denmark
Spain	Belgium	Russia	Not colonized by Europe or Japan

©H.J. de Blij, John Wiley & Sons, Inc.

FIGURE 3.20 Dominant colonial influences, 1550–1950. The map shows the dominant European or Japanese colonial influence in each country over the four centuries.

> **Colonialism** Rule by an autonomous power over a subordinate and alien people and place. Although often established and maintained through political structures, colonialism also creates unequal cultural and economic relations. Because of the magnitude and impact of the European colonial project of the last few centuries, the term is generally understood to refer to that particular colonial endeavour.

During the heyday of **colonialism**, the imperial powers exercised ruthless control over their domains and organized them for maximum economic exploitation. The capacity to install the infrastructure necessary for such efficient profiteering is itself evidence of the power relationships involved: entire populations were regimented in the service of the colonial ruler. Colonizers organized the flows of raw materials for their own benefit, and we can still see the tangible evidence of that organization (i.e., plantations, ports, mines, and railroads) on the cultural landscape.

Although many formerly colonized countries have gained their independence (as noted in the opening field note for this chapter), the political organization of space and the global world economy that arose from colonialism remain. As a result, the economies of these now independent countries are anything but independent. In many cases, raw material flows are as great as they ever were during the colonial era. For example, today in Gabon, Africa, the railroad goes from the interior forest (which is logged for plywood) to the major port and capital city, Libreville. The second largest city, Port Gentil, is located to the south of Libreville, but the two cities are not directly connected by road or railroad. Like Libreville, Port Gentile is export-focused, with global oil corporations responsible for building much of the city and its housing, and employing most of its people (**Figure 3.21**).

CONSTRUCTION OF THE CAPITALIST WORLD ECONOMY

As discussed in Chapter 2, the long-term impacts of colonialism are many and varied and are important to our understanding of the current processes of globalization. One of the most powerful impacts of colonialism was the development of a global order characterized by distinctive differences in economic and political power. The European colonial enterprise gave birth to a globalized economic order in which the European states, and areas dominated by European migrants, emerged as the major centres of economic and political activity. Through colonialism, Europeans extracted wealth from colonies and established the colonized as subservient in the relationship.

Of course, not all Europeans profited equally from colonialism. Enormous poverty persisted within the most powerful European states. Similarly, not all colonizers profited to the same degree. Spain had a large colonial empire in the late

FIGURE 3.21 **Rail and road system, Gabon, Africa.**

17th century, but by then the empire was economically draining Spain. Moreover, Europeans were not the only people to profit from colonialism. During the period of European colonialism (1500–1950), Russia and the United States expanded over land instead of overseas, profiting from the taking of territory and the subjugation of indigenous peoples. Great Britain, the Netherlands, France, the United States, Russia, and Japan all held territory in Asia during this time period. In 2010, Japan apologized to South Korea for its colonization and occupation of that country from 1910 to 1945. In particular, Japan's treatment of women from both Korea and China came under scrutiny; it has been claimed that over 200,000 women were used as "comfort women" for Japan's Imperial Army during this time period. Japan was a regional colonial power, controlling Korea and other parts of East and Southeast Asia as well as Pacific Islands through colonization (**Figure 3.22**). But the concentration of wealth that colonialism brought to Europe, and to parts of the world dominated by European settlers (such as the United States, Canada, and Australia), is at the heart of the highly uneven global distribution of power that is still with us today.

The forces of colonialism played a key role in knitting together the economies of widely separated areas—giving birth to our current global economic order. Immanuel Wallerstein's world systems approach to the global economy, discussed in

COLONIZED ASIA, 1550–1950

Great Britain | France | United States | Netherlands | Japan | Russia

FIGURE 3.22 **Colonized Asia, 1550–1900s.**

Scale Representation of a real-world phenomenon at a certain level of reduction or generalization. In cartography, the ratio of map distance to ground distance; indicated on a map as a bar graph, representative fraction, and/or verbal statement.

Chapter 2, argues that the world economy is a three-tiered structure with a core, periphery, and semi-periphery. Wealth is unevenly distributed in the world economy, as can be seen in statistics on per capita gross national income (GNI) (**Figure 3.23**). For example, Bangladesh's 2009 per capita GNI was only $1,550, whereas Norway's was $55,420. But to truly understand why wealth is distributed unevenly, we cannot simply study each country, its resources, and its production of goods. Rather, we need to understand where countries fit in the world economy through the processes of globalization. That is, we need to see the big picture. To study a single country or even each country individually, we miss the whole. We need to step back and see the whole, as well as the individual elements, studying how one affects the other. This should sound familiar—it is one of the ways geographers think about **scale**.

Not all core countries in the world today were colonial powers. Countries such as Switzerland, Singapore, and Australia have significant global clout even though they were never classic colonial powers, and that clout is tied in significant part to their positions in the global economy. They gained these positions as a result of their access to the networks of production, consumption, and exchange in the wealthiest parts of the world and their ability to take advantage of that access. Canada was once a peripheral country providing raw materials, goods, and resources to markets around the world. Now Canada is considered part of the core, although not as a major economic power. Conversely, China, formerly a peripheral player, is now a major player on the global stage and actively engaged in reworking global political and economic power relations.

But, are economic power and political power one and the same? We would argue, no, they are not, but economic power can certainly bring political power. In the current system, economic power means wealth, and political power refers to the ability to influence others to achieve your goals. Political power is not defined by sovereignty. Each state is sovereign, but not all states have the same ability to influence others or achieve their political goals. Having wealth helps leaders amass political power. For instance, a wealthy country can establish a mighty military. But political influence is not simply a function of hard power; it is also diplomatic. Switzerland's declared neutrality, combined with its economic might, aids the country's diplomatic efforts.

Finally, the idea of meshing the nation and state into a nation-state was not confined to 19th-century Europe or 20th-century Africa. Major players in international relations still see the validity of dividing nations with state borders—of creating nation-states. This remains the case, even in the face of the globalizing processes discussed in Chapter 2 that seem to ignore national boundaries as they weave locations, places, and regions into an ever-more-complex network of economic, political, and social relations. Nevertheless, as we seek solutions to complex political conflicts, we continue to work with the nation-state idea as the social and institutional framework capable of bringing long term peace. People trying to find solutions to the conflicts in the former Yugoslavia and in Israel/Palestine have tried to draw state boundaries around nations—to make nation and state fit. In all of these ways, the European state became the world model and is still shaping the political organization of space in the world.

MAIN POINTS 3.2 How Did the Modern Nation-State Come into Being?

- The nation-state, a politically organized area in which the nation and the state occupy the same territory, is a modern institution.

- The modern nation-state is a product of the historical, cultural, and geographical processes at work in Europe between the 1100s and the present day. The imperial and colonial activities of European states ensured that some form of nation-state government was transported around the world.

- Multistate nations, multinational states, and stateless nations focus our attention on the complicated relationship between the collective sense of being a nation, the territorial affiliations of nations, and the state institutions that govern those territories. We have many examples of multiple nations within the borders of one state or single nations that straddle several states. Finally, we have nations that have no state at all.

- The export of the nation-state model around the globe by colonial and imperial states is the foundation for the current world order. This occurred in part because of the dominance of the capitalist economic system and the legacies of colonial conquest.

- In the world systems approach, developed by Wallerstein (and discussed in Chapter 2), states find themselves organized in a hierarchical relationship as core, peripheral, or semi-peripheral participants in the global economy. This means that some states gain greater benefits than others as a result of their position in the global economy.

- A state's position in the world system can change. Canada was once a peripheral country but is now considered part of the economic core.

FIGURE 3.23 Per capita gross
national income (GNI), 2009.

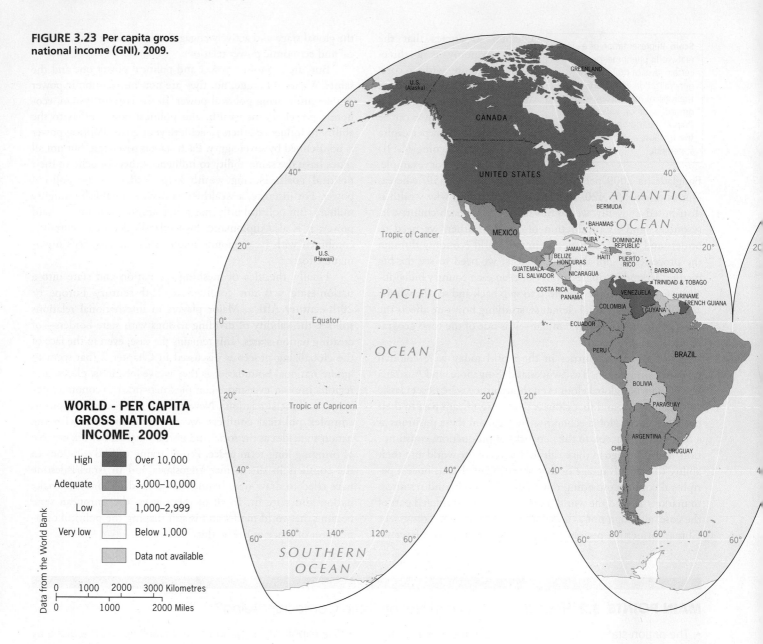

**WORLD - PER CAPITA
GROSS NATIONAL
INCOME, 2009**

High		Over 10,000
Adequate		3,000–10,000
Low		1,000–2,999
Very low		Below 1,000
		Data not available

Data from the World Bank

0   1000   2000   3000 Kilometres

0   1000   2000 Miles

3.3 How Is the Governance of States Spatially Organized?

In the 1950s, political geographer Richard Hartshorne described the forces that unify people within a state as **centripetal** and the forces that divide them as **centrifugal**. According to Hartshorne, a nation's (or a state's) continued existence depends on the balance between centripetal and centrifugal forces. While a useful starting point, most political geographers argue that we cannot take a given event or process and declare it to be centrifugal or centripetal in isolation from the context in which it is situated. An event, such as a war, can pull the state together for a short time and then divide the state over the long term. Timing, scale, interaction, and perspective factor into unification and division in a state at any given point.

Instead of creating a balance sheet of centripetal and centrifugal forces, governments attempt to unify a state by nation-building, by structuring the government in a way that melds the nations within, by defining and defending boundaries, and by expressing control over all of the territory within those boundaries. When we look at how different governments have attempted to unify their states, we are reminded how important geography is. Governance does not take place in a vacuum. The uniqueness of place helps determine whether any possible governmental "solution" solves or exacerbates matters.

> **Centripetal** Forces that tend to unify a country—such as widespread commitment to a national culture, shared ideological objectives, and a common faith.
>
> **Centrifugal** Forces that tend to divide a country—such as internal religious, linguistic, ethnic, or ideological differences.

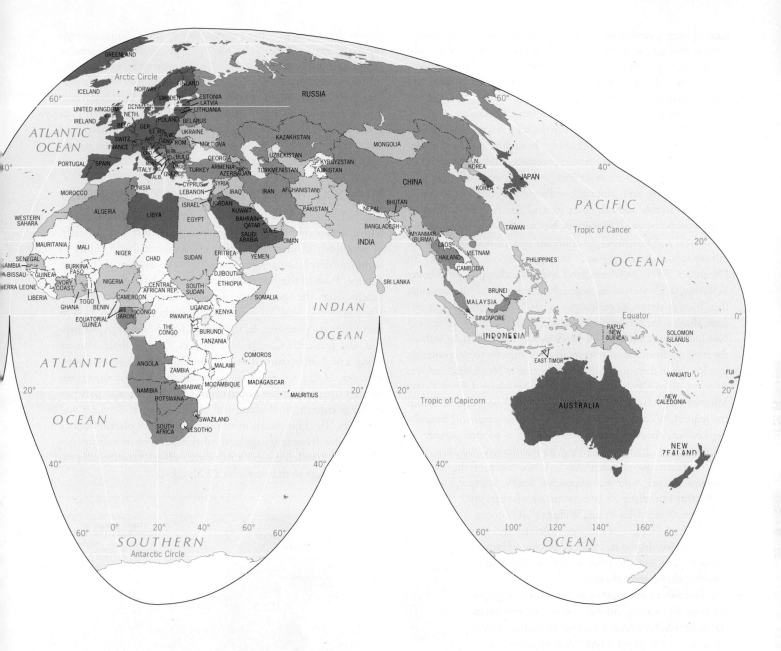

THE STRUCTURE OF GOVERNMENT

One way states promote unification is by choosing a governmental structure that promotes nation-building and quells division within. Two common governmental structures are unitary and federal.

To address multination states, governments, even democratic governments, can and have suppressed dissent by forceful means. Until the end of World War II, most European governments were **unitary** governments: they were highly centralized, with the capital city serving as the focus of power. States made no clear efforts to accommodate minorities or outlying regions where identification with the state was weaker. Europe's nation-states were unitary states, with the culture of the capital city

> **Unitary** (state) A nation-state that has a centralized government and administration that exercises power equally over all parts of the state.

defined as the nation's culture. Any smaller nations within (such as Bretons in France or Basques in Spain) were repressed and suppressed. A unitary government's administrative framework ensures the central government's authority and control over all parts of the state. The French government divided the state into more than 90 *départements*, whose representatives came to Paris not to express regional concerns but to implement governmental decisions back home.

Another way to govern a multinational state is to construct a **federal** system, organizing state territory into regions, substates, provinces, or cantons. In a strong federal system, the regions have a lot of

> **Federal** (state) A political-territorial system wherein a central government represents the various entities within a nation-state where they have common interests—defence, foreign affairs, and the like—yet allows these various entities to retain their own identities and to have their own laws, policies, and customs in certain spheres.

control over government policies and funds; in a weak federal system, they have little control over government policies and funds. Most federal systems are somewhere in between, with governments at the state scale and at the substate scale each having control over certain revenues and certain policy areas. By giving control over certain policies (especially culturally relative policies) to smaller-scale entities, a government can keep the state as a whole together.

Federalism functions differently depending on the context. In Canada, there is a strong central government dealing with issues of national concern such as air transportation, international trade, national security, and criminal law. Provinces, on the other hand, have considerable authority over internal affairs such as taxation, private property, and civil matters. Nevertheless, disputes between the federal and provincial governments over control of resources, infrastructure funding, and immigration are frequent. In December 2004, Newfoundland and Labrador premier Danny Williams (a Conservative) ordered the removal of all Canadian flags from government buildings as a result of a dispute about revenue sharing for offshore oil reserves. With oil prices rising, and Newfoundland's offshore oil fields producing, Williams wanted the royalties from the oil reserves to come directly to the province, in addition to the equalization payments that Newfoundland was receiving from Ottawa as a "have-not" province. Liberal Prime Minister Paul Martin did not agree with him, however, and denied the request. Williams argued, "[The federal government] basically slighted us, they are not treating us as a proper partner in Confederation. It's intolerable and it's insufferable and these flags will be taken down indefinitely." At the time of the dispute, Stephen Harper, who was opposition leader, appeared to agree with him, but when he became prime minister in 2008, he changed his mind. Williams, still furious, began his "ABC" campaign—Anything But Conservative. In the next federal election, Harper's Conservatives lost the three seats they had held in Newfoundland and Labrador.

Federalism attempts to accommodate regional interests by vesting primary power in provinces, states, or other regional units over all matters except those explicitly given to the central government. Choosing a federal system does not always quell nationalist sentiment. After all, the multinational states of the Soviet Union, Yugoslavia, and Czechoslovakia fell apart despite their federalist systems, and the future of Belgium as a single state is increasingly in doubt.

DEVOLUTION

Devolution is the movement of power from the central government to regional governments within the state. Sometimes devolution is achieved by reworking a constitution to establish a federal

Devolution The process whereby regions within a state demand and gain political strength and growing autonomy at the expense of the central government.

system that recognizes the permanency of the regional governments, as Spain has done. In other places, governments devolve power without altering constitutions, almost as an experiment. In the United Kingdom, the Northern Ireland Assembly (a parliamentary body) resulted from devolution; the British government suspended its activities in 2002 but then reinstated it in 2007. Devolutionary forces can surface in all kinds of states, old and young, mature and emergent. These forces arise from several sources: ethnocultural, economic, and spatial.

ETHNOCULTURAL DEVOLUTIONARY MOVEMENTS

Many of Europe's devolutionary movements came from nations within a state that define themselves as ethnically, linguistically, or religiously distinct. The capacity of ethnocultural forces to stimulate devolutionary processes has been evident in Eastern Europe. Parts of the Eastern European map have changed drastically over the past two decades, and two countries—Czechoslovakia and Yugoslavia—succumbed to often violent devolutionary pressures. In the case of Czechoslovakia, the process was peaceful: Czechs and Slovaks divided their country along a new international border. As **Figure 3.24** shows, however, one of the two new states, Slovakia, is not homogeneous: about 11 percent of the population is Hungarian, and that minority is concentrated along the border between Slovakia and Hungary. The Hungarian minority, which faces discriminatory policies involving language and other aspects of its culture, has at times demanded greater autonomy (self-governance) to protect its heritage in the new state of Slovakia.

FIGURE 3.24 Ethnic mosaic of Eastern Europe.

Adapted (in part) with permission from George Huffman, ed., *Europe in the 1990s: A Geographical Analysis*, 6th rev. ed. (New York: Wiley), p. 551

FIGURE 3.25 Europe: Foci of devolutionary pressures, 2014. Devolutionary movements in Europe are found where a nation with a shared history has the political goal of greater autonomy, unification with the rest of their nation, or independence. In 2014 Scotland voted on whether to secede from the United Kingdom, with 55 percent of the people voting against independence.

Compared to the constituent units of the former Yugoslavia, other countries shown in **Figure 3.25** have dealt with devolutionary pressures more peacefully. Among these are Lithuania and, until 2014, Ukraine. The historical geographies of these regions are complex and longstanding, but most recently devolutionary forces came into sharp relief when, in November 2013, Ukraine was on the brink of financial collapse. Ukraine's president, Viktor Yanukovych, had to choose between a deal with the European Union that would be initially "painful" but would bolster integration and trade, or he could take a $15-billion loan from Russia and move the country toward a planned "Eurasian Union" (with Belarus, Kazakhstan, and Russia). Yanukovych chose the Russian loan, and with it, a long history of corruption tied to Russian President Vladimir Putin. Protests erupted in Kiev's Independence Square. Yanukovych eventually fled to Russia, and a coalition government formed out of the opposition. In part, this conflict is about Yanukovych rejecting

FIGURE 3.26 Ukraine.

FIGURE 3.27 Quebec student rally in support of the FLQ (undated).

the EU deal, and drawing the country closer to Russia. There is a stark division between the north and west from the south and east (**Figure 3.26**). Cities that are geographically closest to Europe, such as Lviv, have seen anti-Yanukovych protests, while cities closer to Russia, such as Donesk support Yanokovych and a Russian alliance. The divide in Ukraine between those who wish to rejoin Russia, and those who wish to move toward a European Union relationship is violently polarizing and grounded in longstanding political geographies in the regions.

Elsewhere in the world, ethnocultural fragmentation has produced costly wars. Ethnocultural differences lie at the heart of the decades-long conflict between the Muslim North and the non-Muslim South in Sudan, Africa. Similar forces have given rise to a seemingly endless civil war in Sri Lanka (South Asia), where the Sinhalese (Buddhist) majority was only recently able to suppress revolutionary activities of the Tamil (Hindu) minority. Moreover, devolutionary forces are gaining momentum in places that have long looked stable from the outside. China's far west is a case in point, where Tibetan and Uyghur separatist movements are gaining momentum. The point is that ethnocultural differences are weakening the fabric of many states in today's global political framework. The trend appears to be in the direction of more, rather than fewer, calls for autonomy, or even independence.

In Canada, these ethnocultural devolutionary processes have been seen at critical junctures in Canadian history, particularly in relation to the province of Quebec. Nationalistic sentiments sent Quebec voters to the polls in two referendums, in 1980 and 1995, seeking to gain enough support to secede from Canada. In each case, the "no" side, voting against secession, won the vote (by 59.56 percent in 1980, and by a very narrow margin of 50.58 percent in 1995).

The drive for Quebec's independence takes many forms, with some proposing a form of sovereignty association with Canada and others suggesting full independence as a separate nation-state. Beginning in the 1960s with the so-called Quiet Revolution, more radical and violent calls for Quebec independence emerged in the form of the Front de Libération du Québec (FLQ), an organization responsible for some 200 bombings and the deaths of five people (**Figure 3.27**). On October 5, 1970, the FLQ kidnapped British trade commissioner James R. Cross; five days later they kidnapped, and later murdered, Quebec labour minister Pierre Laporte. The "October Crisis" continued, as Prime Minister Pierre Trudeau invoked the *War Measures Act* and sent the Canadian Army into Quebec to maintain order and protect public figures. The army withdrew on December 28, 1970. Since then, negotiations between the federal government and the province have sought some form of reconciliation. The Meech Lake and Charlottetown accords failed, but on November 27, 2006, the House of Commons passed a motion recognizing that "Québécois form a nation within a united Canada." While devolutionary forces grounded in ethnocultural sentiments are alive and well in Quebec, they are arguably waning at present. During the April 2014 provincial general election, the Parti Québécois, Quebec's independence party, suffered its worst loss since the first election it entered in 1970, winning just 30 seats (25.38 percent of the popular vote) as compared to the Liberal party's 70 seats (41.5 percent of the popular vote). The Parti Québécois, in the space of a few weeks, went from ruling party and front-runner, to a distant second. It was considered a landslide victory for the Liberal Party.

The Inuit in northern Canada have also pressed for some measure of independence from Canada, and the establishment of the territory of Nunavut stands as a recent example of how independence for First Nations peoples can unfold. Nunavut, which means "Our Land" in the Inuktitut dialect of the eastern Arctic Inuit, was established on April 1, 1999, after an agreement was reached with the federal government in September 1992. Parliament passed the Nunavut Land Claims Agreement and the *Nunavut Act* in 1993, establishing Nunavut as a separate territory. Nunavut has its own legislative assembly, with powers equivalent to any other federal territory, and its own Supreme Court. Like the Northwest Territories, Nunavut has a consensus government, which blends the principles of parliamentary democracy with the Aboriginal values of maximum cooperation, effective use of leadership resources, and common accountability.

ECONOMIC DEVOLUTIONARY FORCES

Devolutionary pressures often arise from a combination of sources. In Catalonia, Spain, ethnocultural differences play a significant role, but Catalonians also cite economics; with about 6 percent of Spain's territory and just 17 percent of its population, Catalonia produces some 25 percent of all Spanish exports by value and 40 percent of its industrial exports. Such economic strength lends weight to devolutionary demands based on Catalonian nationalism.

Economic forces play an even more prominent role in Italy and France (Figure 3.25). In Italy, Sardinia's demands for autonomy are deeply rooted in that island's economic circumstances, with accusations of neglect by the government in Rome high on the list of grievances. Italy also faces serious devolutionary forces on its mainland peninsula. One stems from regional disparities between the wealthy north and the poorer Mezzogiorno region to the south, below the Ancona Line (an imaginary border extending from Rome to the Adriatic coast at Ancona). Despite the large subsidies granted to the Mezzogiorno, the development gap between the north, very much a part of the European core, and the south, part of the European periphery, has been widening. Some Italian politicians have exploited widespread impatience with the situation by forming organizations to promote northern interests, including devolution. The most recent of these organizations was the Northern League, which raised the prospect of an independent state called Padania in the part of Italy lying north of the Po River. After a surge of enthusiasm, the Padania campaign faltered. But it did push the Italian government to give more rights to the country's regions, moving it toward a more federal system.

SPATIAL INFLUENCES ON DEVOLUTION

We have seen how political decisions and cultural and economic forces can generate devolutionary processes in states. Devolutionary events have at least one feature in common: they most often occur on the margins of states. Note that every one of the devolution-affected areas shown in Figure 3.25 lies on a coast or on a border. Distance, remoteness, and marginal location are allies of devolution. The regions most likely to seek devolution are those far from the national capital. Many are separated by water, desert, or mountains from the centre of power and adjoin neighbours that may support separatist objectives.

Note also that many islands are subject to devolutionary processes: Corsica (France), Sardinia (Italy), Taiwan (China), Singapore (Malaysia), Zanzibar (Tanzania), Jolo (Philippines), Puerto Rico (United States), Mayotte (Comoros), and East Timor (Indonesia) are notable examples. Some of these islands became independent states, while others were divided during devolution. Insularity clearly has advantages for separatist movements.

Spatial influences can play a significant role in starting and sustaining devolutionary processes. Distance can be compounded by differences in physical geography—a feeling of remoteness can be fuelled when people are isolated in a valley or separated by mountains or a river. Basic physical-geographic and locational factors can thus be key ingredients in the devolutionary process.

MAIN POINTS 3.3 How Is the Governance of States Spatially Organized?

- There are centrifugal and centripetal forces at play in any state. States seek to encourage a sense of unity through nation-building, territorial control, and strong state institutions and governance.

- Multination states can be classified as unitary or federal governments that are distinctive ways of organizing relationships between a central government and its constituent parts.

- While states attempt to create unity and stability, there are often internal pressures calling for the devolution of state power from central governments to a state's regions, provinces, or states. We have many examples of ethnocultural, economic, and spatial devolutionary movements.

3.4 How Do Geopolitics and Critical Geopolitics Help Us Understand the World?

Geopolitics is an area of study that considers the interplay between space, power, and international relations. In political science, for example, scholars tend to focus on governmental institutions, systems, and interactions in international relations. Geopolitics brings the importance of geography to the enquiry with a focus on locational considerations, environmental contexts, territorial perspectives, and spatial assumptions. Geopolitics helps us understand the arrangements and forces that are transforming the map of the world.

CLASSICAL GEOPOLITICS

Geopolitical study has a long history. Classical geopolitics of the late 19th and early 20th centuries generally fit into one of two camps: the German school, which sought to explain why certain states are powerful and how to become powerful, and the British school, which sought to offer strategic advice for states and explain why states interact the way they do. A few scholars tried to bridge the gap, blending the two schools, but for the most part the British school offers classic geostrategic perspectives on the world.

THE GERMAN SCHOOL

Why are certain states powerful, and how do states become powerful? The first political geographer who studied these issues was the German professor Friedrich Ratzel (1844–1904). Influenced by the writings of Charles Darwin, Ratzel postulated that the state resembles a biological organism whose life cycle extends from birth through maturity and, ultimately, decline and death. To prolong its existence, the state requires nourishment, just as an organism needs food. Such nourishment is provided by the acquisition of territories (what Ratzel deemed *lebensraum*) belonging to less-powerful competitors and by the people who live there. If a state is confined within permanent and static boundaries and deprived of overseas domains, Ratzel argued, it will atrophy. Territory is the state's essential, life-giving force. Unfortunately, some of Ratzel's German followers in the 1930s translated his abstract writings into policy recommendations that ultimately led to Nazi expansionism.

THE BRITISH SCHOOL

Not long after the publication of Ratzel's initial ideas, other geographers began studying the physical geographic map of the world with a view to determining where the most strategic places on Earth were located. Prominent among these geographers was Sir Halford J. Mackinder (1861–1947) of Oxford University whose ideas formed the foundation for the British school of classical geopolitics. In 1904, he published an article, "The Geographical Pivot of History," in the Royal Geographical Society's *Geographical Journal*. That article became one of the most intensely debated geographic publications of all time.

Mackinder was concerned with power relationships at a time when Britain had acquired a global empire through its strong navy. To many of his contemporaries, the oceans—the paths to colonies and trade—were the key to world domination, but Mackinder disagreed. He concluded that a land-based power, not a sea power, would ultimately rule the world. His famous article contained a lengthy appraisal of the largest and most populous land mass on Earth—Eurasia (Europe and Asia together). At the heart of Eurasia, he argued, lay an impregnable, resource-rich "pivot area" extending from Eastern Europe to eastern Siberia (**Figure 3.28**). Mackinder issued a warning: if this pivot area became influential in Europe, a great empire could be formed.

Mackinder later renamed his pivot area the heartland, and his warning became known as the **heartland theory**. In his book *Democratic Ideals and Reality* (1919), Mackinder

> **Heartland theory**
> A geopolitical hypothesis, proposed by British geographer Halford Mackinder during the first two decades of the twentieth century, that any political power based in the heart of Eurasia could gain sufficient strength to eventually dominate the world. Mackinder further proposed that since Eastern Europe controlled access to the Eurasian interior, its ruler would command the vast "heartland" to the east.

FIGURE 3.28 The heartland theory. The Pivot Area/Heartland, the Inner Crescent/Rimland, and the World Island described by Halford Mackinder.

(calling Eurasia "the World Island") issued a stronger warning to the winners of World War I, stating:

> *Who rules East Europe commands the Heartland*
>
> *Who rules the Heartland commands the World Island*
>
> *Who rules the World Island commands the World*

When Mackinder proposed his heartland theory, there was little to foretell the rise of a superpower in the heartland. Russia was in disarray, having recently lost a war against Japan (1905), and was facing revolution. Eastern Europe was fractured. Germany, not Russia, was gaining power. But when the Soviet Union emerged and World War II gave Moscow control over much of Eastern Europe, the heartland theory attracted renewed attention.

In 1943, Mackinder wrote a final paper. He was concerned about the power wielded by Joseph Stalin in the Soviet Union and was worried the Soviet Union could exert control over the states of Eastern Europe. He offered strategies for keeping the Soviets in check, including preventing the expansion of the Heartland into the Inner Crescent (Figure 3.28) and creating an alliance around the North Atlantic to join the forces of land and sea powers against the Heartland. Within the next 10 years, the United States began its containment policy (to stop the expansion of the Soviet Union), and the United States, Canada, and Western Europe formed an alliance called the North Atlantic Treaty Organization (NATO).

INFLUENCE OF GEOPOLITICS ON POLITICS

Ratzel and Mackinder are only two of many geographers who influenced international relations. Their writings, grounded in history, current events, and physical geography, sounded logical and influenced many politicians. In some ways, they still do. NATO still exists, and although it has not invited Russia to join the military alliance, it has extended membership to Eastern European states and is working in partnership with former republics of the Soviet Union.

Because of the influence of Ratzel's geopolitical theory on Adolf Hitler and his aspirations for a German homeland, the term "geopolitics" acquired a negative connotation. For some decades after World War II, the term was in such disrepute that few political geographers, even those studying the spatial implications of international power relationships, would identify themselves as students of geopolitics. Time, along with more balanced perspectives, has reinstated geopolitics as an appropriate name for the study of the spatial and territorial dimensions of power relationships past, present, and future.

CRITICAL GEOPOLITICS

Contemporary geographers engaged in geopolitical analysis do much less predicting and prescribing the spatial implications of state actions; instead they focus on revealing and explaining the underlying spatial assumptions and territorial perspectives of politicians guiding state policy. Political geographers Gearoid O'Tuathail and John Agnew refer to the politicians in the most powerful states, the core states, as "intellectuals of statecraft." The basic concept behind today's **critical geopolitics** is that intellectuals of statecraft

Critical geopolitics Process by which geopoliticians deconstruct and focus on explaining the underlying spatial assumptions and territorial perspectives of politicians.

construct ideas about places, and these ideas, in turn, influence and reinforce their political behaviours and policy choices. The ideas also affect how we, the people, process our own notions of places and politics. In other words, critical geopolitics suggests that we need to be conscious of the political power relations driving our understanding of people, ideas, and places. If, for example, we conceptualize a place as "backward" or "primitive," we may then treat that place (and its peoples) in less than respectful ways.

In a number of publications, O'Tuathail has studied American geopolitical reasoning by examining the speeches and statements of U.S. intellectuals of statecraft regarding certain wars, certain places, and certain times. He has highlighted how American intellectuals of statecraft spatialize politics into a world of "us vs. them." By drawing on American cultural logic and certain representations of America, presidents have repeatedly defined an "us" that is pro-democracy, independent, self-sufficient, and free, and a "them" that is in some way against all of these things.

During the Cold War (1945–1991), the United States and its allies were involved in a series of military, political, social, and economic clashes with the Soviet Union and its allies. In 1983, when the Cold War was escalating, then U.S. president Ronald Reagan coined the term "Evil Empire" for the Soviet Union and represented the United States as "the shining city on a hill," an example of the "us versus them" spatialization (**Figure 3.29**).

COLD WAR COUNTRIES

- United States and allies
- Soviet Union and allies
- Other Communist Countries

FIGURE 3.29 Map of the Cold War countries. This map shows the various actors in the Cold War, and illustrates the clash in ideologies of the capitalist West and communist East.

Over the last three presidencies, terrorism has replaced the Soviet Union as the "they." Sounding remarkably similar, Democratic president William J. Clinton and Republican president George W. Bush justified military actions against terrorists. In 1998, President Clinton explained American military action in Sudan and Afghanistan as a response to the terrorist plans, stating that the terrorists "come from diverse places but share a hatred for democracy, a fanatical glorification of violence, and a horrible distortion of their religion, to justify the murder of innocents. They have made the United States their adversary precisely because of what we stand for and what we stand against." Immediately after September 11, 2001, President George W. Bush exclaimed to the world, "They [the terrorists] stand against us because we stand in their way." Statements such as these are rooted in a particular geopolitical perspective on the world—one that divides the globe into opposing political camps. But critical geopolitics seeks to move beyond such differences to explore the spatial ideas and understandings that undergird particular political perspectives and shape policy approaches. The goal of critical geopolitics is to understand the ideological roots and implications of geopolitical reasoning by intellectuals of statecraft as they shape the policies that are pursued and affect what happens on the ground.

GEOPOLITICAL WORLD ORDER

Political geographers study the geopolitical world order—the temporary periods of stability in the way international politics are conducted. For example, during the Cold War, the geopolitical world order was bipolar—the Soviet Union versus the United States and its close allies, including Canada (see Figure 3.29). After a stable geopolitical world order breaks down, the world goes through a transition, eventually settling into a new geopolitical world order.

After the Soviet Union collapsed in 1991, the world entered a transitional period, where a range of world orders was possible. Politicians spoke optimistically about a new world order—one where a standoff of nuclear terror between two superpowers would no longer determine the destinies of states. Supposedly this new geopolitical order would be shaped by forces that connect nations and states—by supranational unions like the European Union (discussed in the next section of this chapter), and by multinational action should any state violate international rules of conduct. The risks of nuclear war would recede, and negotiation would replace confrontation. When Iraq was driven out of Kuwait by a United Nations coalition of states led by the United States in 1991, the framework of a new world order seemed to be taking shape. Russia, which a few years earlier might have led the Soviet Union in support of Iraq, endorsed the United Nations operation. Arab as well as non-Arab forces helped repel the invaders.

Soon, however, doubts and uncertainties began to cloud hopes for a mutually co-operative geopolitical world order. Although states were more closely linked to each other than ever before, national self-interest still acted as a powerful force. For all its faults and changed circumstances, the state continued to

function as a central building block in the new global framework. Nations wanted to become states, and many did—the number of United Nations members increased from 159 in 1990 to 184 by 1993 and 192 by 2006 (**Figure 3.30**); as of July 2014, there were 193 member states. The number and power of economic and social networks that extend across state borders increased. The new world order includes nonstate organizations, such as the World Trade Organization, with political and economic agendas that are not channelled through states—and are often spread across the world.

Some see the new geopolitical world order as one of **unilateralism**, with the United States in a position of hard-power dominance and with U.S. allies following rather

> **Unilateralism** World order in which one state is in a position of dominance with allies following rather than joining the political decision-making process.

than taking part in the political decision-making process. However, in the early 2000s the United States' unabashed unilateralism, its abandonment of traditional diplomatic practices, and its controversial invasion of Iraq significantly undermined its influence in many parts of the globe. Southeast Asian states that had long been oriented toward the United States began to turn away. A significant rift developed between the United States and some European countries, and anti-Americanism surged around the world. Challenges to American unilateralism also came from the processes of globalization, the diffusion of nuclear weapons, the emergence of China and India as global powers, the growth of terrorist groups, and the economic strength of the European Union. Some media outlets are beginning to suggest that China is poised to surpass the United States to become the world's next superpower. Since China introduced market-oriented reforms in 1979, it has experienced tremendous economic growth. Average annual incomes have risen steadily, from less than $1,000 10 years ago to between $6,000 and $8,000 in 2014, when adjusted for purchasing power parity. Simply because of China's size (1.35 billion people, or one-fifth of the world's population), it has become the world's second-largest economy. Economic growth, population size, and a growing military presence (China's defence spending has seen double-digit growth each year since 1989), coupled with the economic downturn in the U.S. since the financial crisis in 2007/2008, have led some to suggest that a new superpower will soon emerge.

Canada, despite its close economic and political ties to the United States, has strongly asserted its independence in international relations. For example, Canada did not join the United States in the Iraq War and continues to maintain open relations with Cuba. Canada is a strong proponent of multilateralism—it attempts to foster co-operation and alliance building when seeking solutions to international conflict. Canada is also known as a peacekeeping nation, heavily involved in sending troops to support United Nations efforts in troubled areas around the globe—though some would argue that Canada's peacekeeping role has been called into question in recent years, given its combative activities in Afghanistan. Canada is often considered a "middle power" in international relations—a

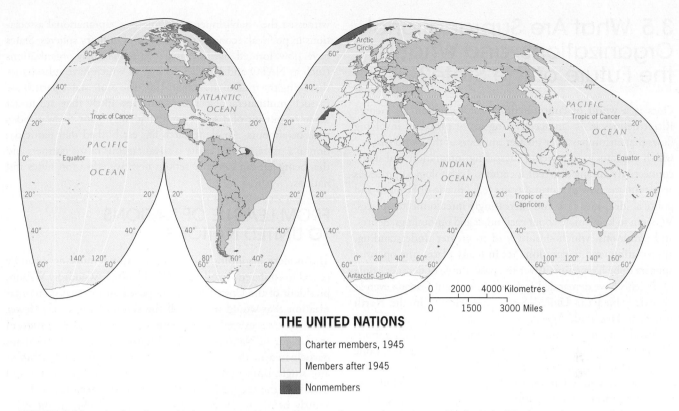

THE UNITED NATIONS

Charter members, 1945

Members after 1945

Nonmembers

FIGURE 3.30 United Nations member states. This map illustrates the countries represented at the United Nations—charter members, members after 1945, and nonmembers. As of July 2014, there were 193 member states. Data from The United Nations.

country that is not among the superpowers but that has sufficient international presence to be an important contributor in world issues.

When geopolitical strategists and intellectuals of statecraft predict future geopolitical orders, they often assume that individual states will continue to be the dominant actors in the international arena. Yet with the traditional powers of the state under increasing strain, other geopolitical arrangements may emerge. A new multi-polar order may arise, with states clustering together as regional forces; or, as we will discuss in Chapter 10, global cities may gain increasing power over issues typically addressed by states. In the final section of this chapter, we consider several other challenges to the state that may influence the next geopolitical order.

MAIN POINTS 3.4 How Do Geopolitics and Critical Geopolitics Help Us Understand the World?

- Classical geopolitics originated in Britain and Germany in the late 1800s. Practitioners were primarily interested in how states came into being and how they expanded and prospered. Halford Mackinder took a global view of the organization and relationships of states based on the idea that control of the Eurasian "pivot area" might lead to global domination.

- Classical geopolitics was very influential. Unfortunately, Hitler used Ratzel's ideas about state expansionism and territorial growth to justify attacking surrounding countries. Mackinder's ideas about a geographical heartland governed Western foreign policy well into the 1970s.

- Contemporary critical geopolitics focuses on the "intellectuals of statecraft" and considers how these individuals create various ideas or conceptualizations about

relationships between states. These ideas then influence how we see, understand, and react to other peoples and states.

- The current geopolitical world order can be understood by examining the historical changes in power relations between states. During the Cold War years (1945–91), the geopolitical world order was bipolar, with the Soviet Union and the United States and its allies developing global spheres of influence.

- Today, the United States is the dominant world power with the ability to act unilaterally. Many argue this has been detrimental to global stability and contributed to a surge of anti-Western sentiment worldwide.

- Canada, as a middle power, is part of the global core.

3.5 What Are Supranational Organizations, and What Is the Future of the State?

Ours is a world of contradictions. Globalization, as George Ritzer defines it, is "an accelerating set of processes involving flows that encompass ever-greater numbers of the world spaces," which suggests we are seeing increasing integration and inter-connectivity among different locations. Technological processes accelerate the flow of cultural traits (e.g., music or fashion) and political ideas into new and increasingly interconnected places. We seem to know more about each other and our feelings, desires, and ambitions, which should lead to greater understanding, appreciation, and integration. Yet in many places, the opposite appears to be happening. Over the past couple of decades, some Québécois have demanded independence from Canada even as Canada joined the United States and Mexico in the North American Free Trade Agreement (NAFTA). At soccer games in Scotland, fans drown out "God Save the Queen" with a thunderous rendition of "Flower of Scotland" (**Figure 3.31**), while in London, Parliament debates Britain's position on the European Monetary Union. At every turn we are reminded of the interconnectedness of nations, states, and regions, yet separatism and calls for autonomy are rampant. In the early years of the 21st century, we appear to be caught between the forces of division and those of unification.

Despite the conflicts arising from these contradictory forces, hardly a country exists today that is not involved in some supra-national organization. A **supranational organization** is an entity composed of three or more states that forge an association and form an administrative structure for mutual benefit and in pursuit of shared goals. The 20th century witnessed the establishment of numerous supranational associations in political, economic, cultural, and military spheres. States have now formed over 60 major supranational organizations (such as NATO and NAFTA), many of which have subsidiaries that bring the total to more than 100. The more states participate in such multilateral associations, the less likely they are to act alone in pursuit of a self-interest that might put them at odds with neighbours. Ample research has established that participation in a supranational entity is advantageous to the partners and that being left out can have serious negative effects on states and nations.

> **Supranational organization**
> A venture involving three or more nation-states involving formal political, economic, and/or cultural co-operation to promote shared objectives. The European Union is one such organization.

FROM LEAGUE OF NATIONS TO UNITED NATIONS

The modern beginnings of the supranational movement can be traced to conferences following World War I. Woodrow Wilson, president of the United States, proposed an international organization that would include all the states of the world (fewer than 75 states existed at that point). This led to the creation of the League of Nations in 1919 (**Figure 3.32**). In all, 63 states participated in the League, although the total membership at any single time never reached that number. Costa Rica and Brazil left the League before 1930; Germany departed in 1933, shortly before the Soviet Union joined in 1934. In the mid-1930s, the League had a major opportunity when Ethiopia's Haile Selassie made a dramatic appeal for help in the face of an invasion by Italy, a member state until 1937. However, the League failed to take action, and in the chaos of the beginning of World War II, the organization collapsed.

Despite its demise, the League of Nations laid the groundwork for the formation of other international organizations. Between World War I and World War II, states created the Permanent Court of International Justice to adjudicate legal issues between states, such as boundary disputes and fishing rights. The

FIGURE 3.31 Scottish independence supporters. "Yes" activists gather in Edinburgh before the referendum on the independence of Scotland in September 2014. The "no" side won, with 55.3 percent of the vote.

FIGURE 3.32 League of Nations. The first assembly of the League of Nations in Geneva, Switzerland, 1920.

League of Nations also initiated international negotiations on maritime boundaries and related aspects of the law of the sea. The conferences organized by the League laid the groundwork for the final resolution on the size of nations' territorial seas decades later.

After World War II, states formed a new organization to foster international security and co-operation: the United Nations (UN). Membership in the UN has grown significantly since its 1945 inception (see Figure 3.30). A handful of states still do not belong to the United Nations, but with the most recent addition in 2014, it now has 193 member states and manages a budget of about U.S. $30 billion, including peacekeeping efforts. The United Nations Security Council, the United Nations General Assembly, and their work are frequently in the news. The United Nations includes numerous other subsidiaries—some more visible than others—such as the Food and Agriculture Organization (FAO), United Nations Educational, Scientific and Cultural Organization (UNESCO), United Nations Children's Fund (UNICEF), and World Health Organization (WHO). Not all UN members participate in every subsidiary, but their work has benefited all humanity.

We can find evidence of the important work of the United Nations in the "world" section of any major newspaper. UN peacekeeping troops have helped maintain stability in some of the most contentious regions of the world (**Figure 3.33**). The UN High Commissioner on Refugees is called upon to aid refugees in crises throughout the world. UN documents on human rights standards, such as the Universal Declaration on Human Rights, the Covenant on Civil and Political Rights, and the Covenant on Economic and Social Rights, set precedents and laid the groundwork for countless human rights groups working in the world today.

By participating in the United Nations, states commit to upholding internationally approved standards of behaviour.

FIGURE 3.33 United Nations peacekeeping operations, 2014. This infographic illustrates the 14 active peacekeeping missions around the globe as of 2014. These missions are made up of a mix of personnel from the military, law enforcement agencies, and volunteers. The graphs show the distribution of personnel on their respective missions. There is no clear definition of "peacekeeping" in the UN Charter, leaving it a somewhat ambiguous, flexible term that can be interpreted differently over time and space.

Many states still violate the standards set out in the United Nations Charter, but such violations can lead to collective action (e.g., economic sanctions or Security Council-supported military action). Scholars of international relations and political geography point to UN actions in South Africa (against apartheid), Iraq (the Gulf War), and North Korea (preventing nuclear proliferation) as examples of the organization's success.

REGIONAL SUPRANATIONAL ORGANIZATIONS

The League of Nations and the United Nations are global manifestations of a phenomenon expressed even more strongly at the regional level. States organize supranational organizations at the regional scale to position themselves more strongly economically, politically, and even militaristically.

Belgium, the Netherlands, and Luxembourg undertook the first major modern experiment in regional economic co-operation. The three countries have much in common culturally and economically. Dutch farm products are sold on Belgian markets, and Belgian industrial goods go to the Netherlands and Luxembourg. During World War II, representatives of the three countries decided to create common tariffs and eliminate import licences and quotas. In 1944, even before the end of the war, the governments of the three states met in London to sign an agreement of co-operation, creating the Benelux (Belgium, the Netherlands, and Luxembourg) region.

Following World War II, U.S. secretary of state George Marshall proposed that the United States finance a European recovery program. A committee representing 16 Western European states, including what was then known as West Germany, presented the United States Congress with a joint program for economic rehabilitation, and Congress approved it. From 1948 to 1952, the United States gave Europe about $12 billion under the Marshall Plan. This investment revived European national economies and also spurred a movement toward co-operation among European states.

THE EUROPEAN UNION

From the European states' involvement in the Marshall Plan came the Organisation for European Economic Co-operation (OEEC), which in turn gave rise to other co-operative organizations. Soon after Europe established the OEEC, France proposed the creation of a European Coal and Steel Community (ECSC), with the goal of lifting the restrictions and obstacles that impeded the flow of coal, iron ore, and steel among the mainland's six primary producers: France, West Germany, Italy, and the three Benelux countries. The six states entered the ECSC, and gradually, through negotiations and agreement, enlarged their sphere of co-operation to include reductions and even eliminations of certain tariffs and a freer flow of labour, capital, and non-steel commodities. This led, in 1958, to the creation of the European Economic Community (EEC).

The success of the EEC induced other countries to apply for membership. Denmark, Ireland, and the United Kingdom joined in 1973; Greece in 1981; and Spain and Portugal in 1986. The organization became known as the European Community (EC) because it began to address issues beyond economics. By the late 1980s, the EC had 12 members: the three giants (Germany, France, and the United Kingdom), the four southern countries (Italy, Spain, Portugal, and Greece), and the five small states (the Netherlands, Belgium, Luxembourg, Denmark, and Ireland). These 12 members initiated a program of co-operation and unification that led to the formal establishment of a European Union (EU) in 1992. In the mid-1990s, Austria, Sweden, and Finland joined the EU, bringing the total number of members to 15. Today there are 28 member countries in the European Union, with 5 "candidate" countries and 3 "potential candidate" countries (**Figure 3.34**).

In the late 1990s, the EU began preparing for the establishment of a single currency—the euro. First, all electronic financial transactions were denominated in euros, and on January 1, 2002, the EU introduced euro coins and notes. Not all EU member states are currently part of the eurozone, but they may join soon as the euro begins to creep into their economies and as the euro gains strength against other global currencies.

The integration of 10 eastern European and Mediterranean island states into the European Union in 2004, and the addition of two more in 2007, are significant developments. Integration is a difficult process and often requires painful adjustments because of the diversity of the European states. For example, agricultural practices and policies have always varied widely. Yet some general policy must govern agriculture throughout the European Union. Individual states have found these adjustments difficult at times, and the EU has had to devise policies to accommodate regional contrasts and delays in implementation. In addition, integration requires significant expenditures. Under the rules of the EU, the richer countries must subsidize (provide financial support to) the poorer ones; therefore, the entry of

eastern European states adds to the financial burden on the wealthier western and northern European members.

Another concern is the loss of traditional state powers. The EU is a patchwork of states with many different ethnic traditions and histories of conflict and competition. Economic success and general well-being tend to submerge such differences, but in the face of difficult economic or social times, divisive forces can, and have, reasserted themselves. Moreover, as the EU grows, it becomes increasingly difficult for individual states to exert significant influence.

A 2013 Pew Research Center Global Attitudes Project suggests that the European Union is the new "sick man" of Europe, with a sharp decline in support from across Europe. The eurozone crisis, which began in early 2009, and which has seen the bail-out of 10 central and eastern European banks, is seen as a key factor in the waning support for European economic integration. Support for the EU has fallen from 60 percent in 2012 to 45 percent in 2013, amid poor economic growth, uncertainty about Greece having to leave the eurozone in 2012, and more recently speculation about Spain leaving the EU in 2014. With continued economic instability, along with high unemployment rates for young people, some are questioning the future of the EU.

HOW DOES SUPRANATIONALISM AFFECT THE STATE?

Supranationalism is a worldwide phenomenon. Other economic associations, such as the North American Free Trade Agreement (NAFTA), the Association of Caribbean States (ACS), the Central American Common Market, the Andean Group, the Southern Common Market (MERCOSUR), the Economic Community of West African States (ECOWAS), the Asia-Pacific Economic Cooperation (APEC), and the Commonwealth of Independent States (CIS), have drawn up treaties to reduce tariffs and import restrictions in order to ease the flow of commerce in their regions. Not all of these alliances are successful, but economic supranationalism is a sign of the times, a grand experiment still in progress.

Yet when we turn back to the European Union, we are looking at a supranational organization that is unlike any other. It is not a state, nor is it simply an organization of states. The European Union is remarkable in that it has taken on a life of its own—with a multi-faceted government structure, three capital cities, and billions of euros flowing through its coffers. The EU is extending its reach into foreign relations, domestic policies, and military policies, with sovereignty over certain issues moving from the states to the organization. In fact, citizens in the Benelux countries (the first members) and in regions where people have been disempowered by their state governments often identify more strongly with the European Union than with their state. With the EU, we may be witnessing a transformation in the political organization of space similar to the development of the modern state system in Europe in the 17th century.

Other major challenges to the state as we know it include the demands for independence from nations within states (discussed earlier), the proliferation of nuclear weapons, economic globalization, and increasing connectedness among people and cultures.

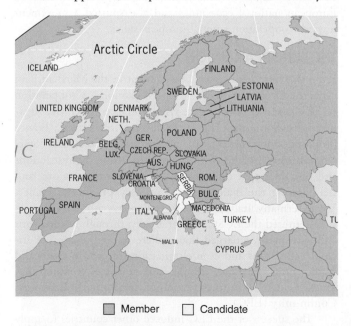

FIGURE 3.34 European Union (EU) as at July 2014. Data from the European Union.

© Bloomberg/Getty Images

FIGURE 3.35 Anti-nuclear protest. Protesters in Seoul, South Korea, demonstrate against North Korea's nuclear test and missile launch in May 2009. North Korea announced that it had conducted a "successful" nuclear test, raising concerns and prompting calls for sanctions against the country and the impeachment of its leader, Kim Jong II.

These and similar developments raise questions about the logic, effectiveness, and even the necessity of the spatial organization of the world into states. Sociologist and urban geographer Manuel Castells became an important figure in articulating the shifting notions of geopolitical space and power in the age of digitization and the rise of the "network society." Castells sees the global shift that privileges information and communication technologies as a challenge to traditional hierarchies of nation-states. He believes power now resides in the "logic of the network" in and around emerging world cities such as New York, London, and Tokyo. According to Castells, it is in the "space of flows" of these global financial centres that the world economic order is structured, controlled, and maintained.

Nuclear weapons give even small states the ability to inflict massive damage on larger and distant adversaries. Combined with missile technology, this may be the most serious danger the world faces. This explains, in part, United Nations efforts to force the dismantling of Iraq's nuclear capacity after the 1991 Gulf War and international concerns about Iran's and North Korea's progress in the nuclear arms arena (**Figure 3.35**). Some states publicize their nuclear weapons programs, and others keep their nuclear abilities a carefully guarded secret. Reports of an enemy's nuclear proliferation have led to military actions in the last 30 years. For example, in 1981, when reports of Iraq's nuclear program reached Israel, the Israelis attacked Iraq. During the apartheid period, South Africa built nuclear weapons; adversaries India and Pakistan both possess nuclear weapons, and Iran may be building itself up as a nuclear power. As nuclear weapons have become smaller, and as "tactical" nuclear arms have been developed, the threat of nuclear weapons sales has to be taken seriously. It is now possible for a hostile state or group to purchase the power with which to threaten the world.

The state still provides the territorial foundations from which producers and consumers operate, and it continues to exert considerable regulatory powers. However, economic globalization makes it more difficult for states to control economic relations. States are responding to this situation in a variety of ways, with some giving up traditional regulatory powers and others seeking to insulate themselves from the international economy. Still others are working to build supranational economic blocs that they hope will help them cope with an increasingly globalized world. The impacts of many of these developments are as yet uncertain, but it is increasingly clear that states now compete with a variety of other forces in the international arena.

Some scholars argue that the state's traditional position is being further eroded by the globalization of social and cultural relations. Networks of interaction are being constructed in ways that do not correspond to the map of states. When unrest breaks out in southern Mexico, for example, activists use the Internet to contact interested people throughout the world. Increased mobility brings individuals from far-flung places into much closer contact than before. Paralleling all this change is the spread of popular culture in ways that make national borders virtually meaningless. Fans from Iceland to Australia listen to Céline Dion; fashions developed in northern Italy are hot items among Japanese tourists visiting Hawai'i; Thai restaurants are found in towns and cities across the United States; Russians hurry home to watch the next episode of soap operas made in Mexico; and movies produced in Hollywood are seen on screens from Mumbai to Santiago.

Another global phenomenon with major implications for a future world order is the role of religion as a force in global affairs. Whether at the local scale, with an individual acting alone, or at the global scale, with an entire network operating, violence by extremists challenges the state. The state's mission to defeat extremism often produces support for the state government in the short term, but the state's inability to defeat extremist attacks may weaken the state in the long term. A wave of international terrorism toward western states began in the 1980s, with events such as the bombing of an airplane in Lockerbie, Scotland, in 1988. Terrorism came to dominate the international scene on September 11, 2001, with the attacks on the World Trade Center and the Pentagon and the downing of Flight 93 in Pennsylvania. However, terrorism is a global phenomenon, and while much media attention focuses on acts of terror in the West, according to the Global Terrorism Index, the first index to systematically rank and compare 158 countries according to the impact of terrorism, it is felt most acutely in the Middle East, Southeast Asia, and parts of Africa (**Figure 3.36**).

Globalization has produced economic, social, and cultural geographies that look less and less like the map of states. At the same time, nationalism continues to be a fundamental social force in the world today. The state system is unlikely to disappear anytime soon, but we are headed for a world in which the spatial distribution of power is more complex than the traditional map of states would suggest. Describing that spatial distribution will be a challenge for geographers for generations to come.

FIGURE 3.36 Global Terrorism Index, 2014.
This index, compiled by the National Consortium
for the Study of Terrorism and Responses to
Terrorism (START) at the University of Maryland,
reveals the global nature of terrorism. Dark
orange countries experience the highest
concentration of acts of terrorism and green
countries report no acts of terrorism. No data
available for countries in grey. Source: Vision
of Humanity, Global Terrorism Index 2014,
www.visionofhumanity.org.

NO IMPACT   HIGHEST IMPACT

visionofhumanity.org

MAIN POINTS 3.5 What Are Supranational Organizations, and What Is the Future of the State?

- The nation-state remains a primary political and social institution for human organization despite globalizing processes
and the emergence of supranational organizations.

- Since World War II, numerous supranational organizations
have come into being. Some are economic, such as the
World Trade Organization, while others have a broader
mandate, such as the United Nations.

- Regional supranational organizations between states are
often designed to promote the economic interests of
member states (e.g., European Economic Community) or

to ensure they will come to each other's aid in the event of
aggression by non-members (e.g., North Atlantic Treaty
Organization [NATO]).

- Scholarship is divided on the state's traditional position given
the emergence of supranational organizations. Some argue
the state's traditional ability to control its own economic and
political direction is being eroded. Others argue that the
mutual aid, co-operation, and increased stability offered by
such alliances will ensure a more peaceful globe. Whether
this will be the result remains to be seen.

SUMMARY

Political geographers are interested in the political aspects of
human-environment relations and how politics at a variety of
scales have spatial implications. The primary unit of interest is
the state, an entity exercising control over people occupying a
bounded territory and recognized by other states. While we
might take the idea of the state for granted, the modern
concept of the state is less than 400 years old and, as an idea
and ideology, was transported around the globe, primarily
through colonialism, imperialism, and globalizing processes. The
state may seem natural and permanent, but it is not. New states
are still being recognized, and existing states are vulnerable to
destructive forces.

We can only understand the current world order—the economic, social, and political relationships—by understanding the
history of the modern nation-state and colonialism and imperialism. European explorers and adventurers travelled the globe,

conquering various locales and dividing up the spoils for the
benefit of their home country. A world systems approach argues
that, in a global economy, there is one global market and a
global division of labour. Further, states in that world economy
are currently organized in a three-tiered structure with a core,
periphery, and semi-periphery. This results in uneven participation in the global economy for the benefit of some over others.
Political geographers have a great deal to contribute to both
understanding and finding solutions for those inequalities.
Canada, despite its colonial beginnings and its continued reliance on resources, is part of the core.

Since World War II, a number of supranational organizations
have emerged and changed the nature of the political and socio-
economic relationships among states at local, regional, and national levels. While some approve of these changes, others do
not. It remains to be seen how future geographies will evolve.

DISCUSSION AND REVIEW QUESTIONS

1. J.B. Harley (2001) observed that "As much as guns and warships, maps have been the weapons of imperialism." What does he mean by this and how does this relate to the specific example of George Dawson's mapping of the Queen Charlotte Islands?

2. "Nation" and "state" are concepts that are often used interchangeably; however, to a political geographer they are not the same. Discuss how these concepts differ. Discuss the concept of a "nation-state."

3. One of the strategies by which states promote unification is by choosing a governmental structure that promotes nation-building and mitigates internal divisions. Two such

structures are "unitary" and "federal." Explain these structures and identify which one most fits Canada. Has Canada's structure been successful?

4. Geopolitics is the branch of political geography that considers the interplay between space, power, and international relations. How has the study of geopolitics changed since its beginnings in late 19th-century Germany and Britain?

5. What is "supranationalism" and why has it become an important political-territorial strategy? Discuss the specific case of the European Union and how it is a historically unique form of supranationalism.

GEOGRAPHIC CONCEPTS

borderlands 65
borders 65
boundaries 65
boundary 57
centrifugal 74
centripetal 74
colonialism 71
critical geopolitics 81
devolution 76
federal 75
frontier 65
geometric boundary 59
heartland theory 80
ideology 56
mercantilism 67
multinational state 70

multistate nation 70
nation 65
nation-state 68
nationalism 68
Peace of Westphalia 67
physical-political boundary 59
political geography 56
scale 73
sovereignty 57
state 56
stateless nation 70
supranational organization 84
territorial integrity 57
territoriality 57
unilateralism 82
unitary 75

ADDITIONAL RESOURCES ON-LINE

Canada's peacekeeping operations: www.canadainternational. gc.ca/prmny-mponu/canada_un-canada_onu/ positions-orientations/peace-paix/peace-operations-paix. aspx?lang=eng

Countries of the world: lcweb2.loc.gov/frd/cs/cshome.html

The European Union: europa.eu/index_en.htm

International refugees: www.refugeesinternational.org

Nationalism: www.nationalismproject.org

Political geography: www.politicalgeography.org

Colonialism: The Story of India, PBS: www.pbs.org/ thestoryofindia

Cuban Missile Crisis: The Other Side of Armageddon: www.bbc. co.uk/bbcfour/documentaries/features/cuban-missile-crisis.shtml

Global Terrorism Index: http://economicsandpeace.org/ research/iep-indices-data/global-terrorism-index

October Crisis: Action: The October Crisis of 1970: www. onf-nfb.gc.ca/eng/collection/film/?id510471

The United Nations in Rwanda: *Shake Hands with the Devil: The Journey of Roméo Dallaire*: www.whitepinepictures. com/all-titles/shake-hands-with-the-devil

The U.S.-Mexico Barrier: Border Stories: A Mosaic Documentary: http://borderstories.org

CHAPTER 4 POPULATION

What's in a Name?

IN NORTH AMERICAN POPULAR CULTURE, we have a long history of naming our generations. These include the "Silent Generation" (those born between 1928 and 1945), so named because these children of the Great Depression and World War II were considered conformist, with strong civic instincts; the "Baby Boomers" (those born between 1946 and 1964), named for the great spike in fertility after World War II; "Generation X" (those born between 1965 and 1980), who are known collectively as savvy, entrepreneurial loners; and most recently the "Millennials" (those born between 1981 and 2003), the first generation of the new millennium. These labels, whether chosen to describe a historic event, rapid social or demographic change, or a major turn in the calendar, are just one of the ways in which we talk about specific populations. Sometimes such labels endure, and sometimes they fall out of fashion. They are important, however, because they provide us with ways of talking about, tracking, and making sense of large swaths of our population.

If you were born between 1981 and 2003, you are considered part of the Millennial Generation (sometimes known as Generation Y, because it follows Generation X). This generation is the largest age grouping in North American history (80 million in the United States, and upwards of 10 million in Canada), and as such, they have become increasingly important to marketers, demographers, and the media. According to Pew Research, generations have personalities, and Millennials are regarded as confident, self-expressive, liberal, upbeat, and open to change. They are more ethnically diverse and less religious, and are becoming the most educated generation in North America. Millennials are known for their connectivity through cellphone and social media use (**Figure 4.1**), their tattoos and piercings (4 in 10 have tattoos, 1 in 4 have piercings in some place other than an earlobe), and their unemployment rates (as of January 2012, 18- to 24-year-olds experienced twice the unemployment rate of the rest of Canada, at 14 percent).

As geographers, we are not only interested in who the Millennials are, but also where they live. A 2014 Nielsen study

(a)

(b)

FIGURE 4.1 Millennial generation. Millenials are known for their active use of technology and social media.

indicates that, in the United States, Millennials are breaking with previous generations' ideals of the white picket fence in the suburbs, preferring instead urban centres. Calling Millennials the "social" generation, the study indicates that Millennials prefer to live in dense, urban areas, where opportunities to be social are just outside their front door. While some reports see this phenomenon as something new, it fits with broader geographic trends in the North American population, which has become markedly less rural, as well as with historic trends of young people moving to urban areas in search of employment during their "highest mobility period of life." The Baby Boomers, for instance, are known for their mass exodus from cities to the suburbs. Cities were often left hollowed-out by this "rise of the suburbs" phenomenon, and the hollowing-out of urban centres readied these spaces for the Millennials, who came in search of affordable housing and employment opportunities. What is different, according to Rolf Pendall of the Urban Institute, is that Millennials are choosing to stay in urban centres. Rather than "settling down" into suburban life, they are embracing the independence and diversity offered by cities on a long-term basis.

Of course, Millennials—as a generation—are still relatively young. However, due to the sheer size of this population, geographers, demographers, marketers, and policy-makers are increasingly interested in studying them, counting them, and documenting the broad trends associated with them over time. These are some of the concepts we consider when we study population geography. In this chapter, we discuss where people live and why they live where they do. We examine the rising world population and contrast it with the aging population in particular regions and countries. Finally, we consider the ramifications of population change, and we question how governments affect population change.

KEY QUESTIONS FOR CHAPTER 4

1. How do we think about populations and how is this "geographical"?
2. Why do populations grow or decline in particular places?
3. How does the geography of health influence population dynamics?
4. How do governments affect population change?

4.1 How Do We Think about Populations and How Is This "Geographical"?

As geographers, we are intensely curious about where people live and why they live where they do. We need to ask questions about how many and what sorts of people inhabit different parts of the world. Where people are born and where they live affect their life chances, who they might meet and get to know, and how they understand who they are and what they might become. Geographers study population to see what patterns might be emerging, or not emerging, in order to understand the meanings that lie behind the presence or absence of areal patterns. We might also ask more troubling questions: Where do people die, when do they die, how, and why? Clearly embedded in these questions are our spatial perspectives—location, region, landscape, place, and movement. Populations have distinctive locations and regions, they create distinctive landscapes and places, and, as we discuss in Chapter 5, populations migrate, relocate, and alter locations as they move from place to place.

Those who study **population geography** are concerned with spatial variations or patterns that are visible for distinctive populations. We call this the study of **demography**—that is, the study of the characteristics of a population, such as race, age, sex, and ethnicity. Population geographers ask questions about the number of men and women in a particular population, or the number of elderly people compared with the number of young. Once they understand the characteristics of a population, population geographers focus on why populations develop certain characteristics and why they distribute themselves across space in particular ways. When they have grasped the characteristics of populations

> **Population geography** The study of why populations have certain characteristics and why they distribute themselves across space in particular ways.
>
> **Demography** The study of the characteristics of a population, such as race, age, sex, and ethnicity.

and their locations, other questions arise: Why are some populations aging more quickly than others? Why might there be significantly more men than women in countries such as China or India? Why do particular ethnic groups seem to favour living and working in certain locales? Why do certain population groups, such as Millennials, prefer urban (or suburban or rural) settings? Population geographers are also concerned with more abstract questions about populations, such as how the term "population" comes to be understood as an object or a "thing," who becomes part of a "population," and how these "populations" are regulated and controlled through state policy and governance.

Before we can begin to work through some of these more detailed questions, we need to compile and understand a few basic facts about the populations we are interested in studying. Population geographers undertake basic calculations about a particular population, such as its density, distribution, and composition. This information provides the starting point for considering the complex spatial organization and movement of populations.

POPULATION DENSITY

> **Population density** A measurement of the number of people per given unit of land.
>
> **Arithmetic population density** The population of a country or region expressed as an average per unit area. The figure is derived by dividing the population of the areal unit by the number of square kilometres or miles that make up the unit.

Demographers report the **population density** of a country as a measure of total population in relation to total land area. They usually calculate density as the number of people located in a particular territorial unit—usually a square kilometre. This is a rather simplistic calculation, as it assumes an even distribution of the population over the total land or territory in question. Clearly, populations are rarely evenly distributed, as people tend to congregate within favourable environments, such as near water or on major transportation routes. In 2014, Canada had a population density of 3.57 people per square kilometre, one of the lowest densities in the world. In the United States, the population density is 32.4 people per square kilometre (more than 9 times higher); France has 118 people per square kilometre (31 times higher); and Bangladesh, the population with the highest density in the world, has 1,087 people per square kilometre (more than 300 times higher than Canada). This density figure is also known as the country's **arithmetic population density**—a simple calculation that divides the population of an area by the total number of square kilometres or miles that make up that area. For example, a region that is 100 square kilometres with 10 people has 1 person for every 10 square kilometres.

No country has an evenly distributed population, and arithmetic population figures do not reflect this unevenness and complexity. For example, Canada's arithmetic population density of 3.57 does not reflect the sparse population in northern Canada or the fact that two out of three Canadians

FIGURE 4.2 North America at night, 2012. In 2012, NASA and the National Oceanic and Atmospheric Administration (NOAA) collaborated to produce satellite images called the "Black Marble," in which the Earth's city lights are visible. Notice how densely populated Canada is along the U.S.-Canada border. In fact, according to Statistics Canada (2011), the most populated areas in Canada are within 210 kilometres of the U.S.-Canada border.

Image courtesy of NASA (www.nasa.gov)

live within 210 kilometres of the Canada-U.S. border (**Figure 4.2**). Moreover, within Canada, we can compare the relative population densities of our provinces and territories, many of which are higher than 3.57 (**Figure 4.3**). This kind of analysis shows us a different picture of Canada than we might otherwise imagine. We often think in terms of sheer size of population, making Ontario (12,851,821 people) and Quebec (7,903,001 people) the largest provinces with the highest population. But when we look at density patterns, Prince Edward Island ranks first, with 24.7 people per square kilometre, and Nova Scotia is second, with 17.4 people per square kilometre.

In other cases, an arithmetic calculation is actually quite misleading. Egypt, with a population of 78.6 million in 2008, has a seemingly moderate arithmetic population density of 78 people per square kilometre However, Egypt's territory of just over 1 million square kilometres is mostly desert, and the vast majority of the population is crowded into the valley and delta of the Nile River. An estimated 98 percent of all Egyptians live on just 3 percent of the country's land, so the arithmetic population density figure is meaningless (**Figure 4.4**).

PHYSIOLOGIC POPULATION DENSITY

Given that populations are unevenly dispersed within a territory, with most people residing in places that are more hospitable to human life, a superior index of population density relates the total population of a country or region to the area of arable (farmable) land it contains. The **physiologic population**

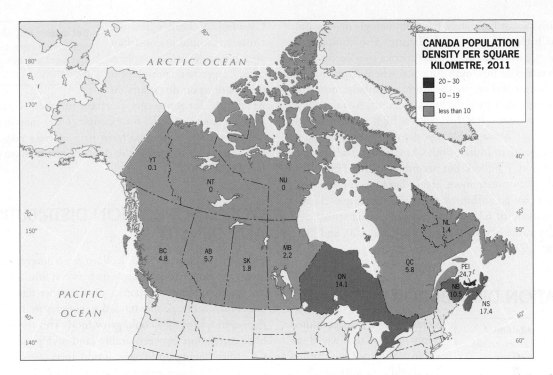

FIGURE 4.3 Population density in Canada (/km²). The map, using data from the 2011 Census, shows the comparative population density of Canadian provinces and territories.

Physiologic population density
The number of people per unit area of arable land.

density, defined as the number of people per unit area of agriculturally productive land, gives us a much better sense of how people are distributed. When we measure the entire population of Egypt relative to the arable land in the country, the resulting physiologic density figure for 2008 is 2,616 people per square kilometre—a density well illustrated by Figure 4.4. This number is far more reflective of Egypt's population pressure, which continues to rise rapidly despite Egypt's efforts to expand its irrigated farmlands.

Appendix B, at the end of this book, provides complete data on both arithmetic and physiologic population densities using 2010 figures, calculated using a land area measure in square kilometres. Some of the data stand out markedly (**Figure 4.5**). Mountainous Switzerland's high physiologic density should be expected: it is 10 times as high as its arithmetic density, indicating that much of the country is uninhabitable. But note the

Columbia University and Centro Internacional de Agricultura Tropical (CIAT), 2005. Gridded Population of the World Version 3 (GPWv3). Palisades, NY: NASA Socioeconomic Data and Applications Center (SEDAC), CIESIN, Columbia University, http://sedac.ciesin.columbia.edu/gpw.

FIGURE 4.4 Population density of Egypt, 2010. The population of Egypt is situated mainly along the valley and delta of the River Nile.

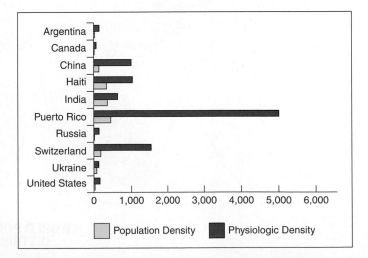

FIGURE 4.5 Comparing arithmetic and physiologic density rates. Drawing from the data in Appendix B, this chart compares the physiologic and arithmetic density rates of certain countries.

Ukraine, with its vast farmlands, has a physiologic density only 1.7 times as high as its arithmetic density. Also compare the high physiologic densities in Central America (see Puerto Rico) to the moderate data for South America, where Argentina has one of the lowest indices in the world. Similarly, note that India's physiologic density is the lowest in South Asia despite its huge population (and is less than twice as high as its arithmetic density), whereas China's physiologic density in 2010 was some 50 percent higher than India's. Both China and India have populations well over 1 billion, but according to the physiologic density, India has much more arable land per person than China. Canada has an arithmetic population density of 3 and a physiologic density of 67. Contrast this to Russia with 8 and 138 respectively, the United States with 32 and 160, and Haiti with 340 and 1,030.

POPULATION DISTRIBUTION

Population distribution
Description of locations on the Earth's surface where populations live.

People are not distributed evenly across the world or within a country. One-third of the world's population lives in China and India. Yet both countries have large expanses of land where people are absent or sparsely distributed (the Himalayas in India and a vast interior desert in China). In addition to studying population densities, geographers study **population distribution**, which describes where on the Earth's surface individuals or groups (depending on the scale) live. For example, Canada's population distribution shows Canadians live close to the

Canada-U.S. border and are clustered around major urban areas (Figure 4.2). Geographers often represent population distributions on **dot maps**, in which one dot represents a certain number of people or objects. At the local scale, for example, a dot map of population can show each individual farm in a sparsely populated rural area. At the global scale, the data are much more generalized (see **Figure 4.6**).

Dot maps Maps where one dot represents a certain number of a phenomenon, such as a population.

WORLD POPULATION DISTRIBUTION AND DENSITY

From the beginning, people have been unevenly distributed across the globe. Today, contrasts between bustling cities on the one hand and empty expanses on the other have only intensified. Historically, people tended to congregate in those parts of the world where they could grow food. This meant there was a high correlation between arable land and population density. Cities first sprang up in agricultural areas (see Chapter 9), and for most of human existence, people have lived closest to the most agriculturally productive areas. Recent advances in agricultural technology and in transportation of agricultural goods have begun to change this pattern.

In Figure 4.6, where each dot on the map represents 100,000 people, three major clusters of population jump out: East Asia, South Asia, and Europe. The three largest population clusters are on the Eurasian (Europe and Asia combined) land mass. The fourth largest is in North America.

@ H.J. de Blij, P.O. Muller, and John Wiley & Sons, Inc.

WORLD POPULATION DISTRIBUTION
One dot represents 100,000 people

FIGURE 4.6 World population distribution.

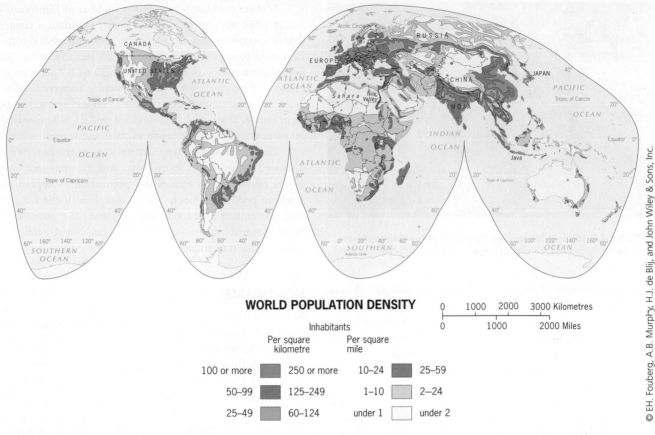

WORLD POPULATION DENSITY

Inhabitants

Per square kilometre		Per square mile	
100 or more	250 or more	10–24	25–59
50–99	125–249	1–10	2–24
25–49	60–124	under 1	under 2

0   1000   2000   3000 Kilometres
0   1000   2000 Miles

FIGURE 4.7 World population density.

EAST ASIA

Although Figure 4.6, the world population distribution map, requires no colour contrasts, **Figure 4.7** depicts world population density through shading: the darker the colour, the larger the number of people per unit area. The most extensive area of dark shading lies in East Asia, primarily in China but also in Korea and Japan. Almost one-quarter of the world's population is concentrated here—over 1.3 billion people in China alone. In addition to high population density in China's large cities, ribbons of high population density extend into the interior along the Yangtze and Yellow River valleys. Farmers along China's major river valleys produce crops of wheat and rice to feed not only themselves but also the population of major Chinese cities such as Shanghai and Beijing.

By the end of 2013, smog and air pollution reached a critical point in China, causing airports and traffic to be shut down, and schools to be closed. While many believed that these pollution levels were connected to population, there was little scientific evidence to support these assumptions. Recently, scientists have begun measuring the relationship between population density and pollution rates. Using satellite images, NASA scientists measured air pollution's dependence on population in China, the United States, Europe, and India. By measuring nitrogen dioxide (NO_2), produced from the burning of fossil fuels, researchers were able to connect population density to levels of air pollution. Variances in geography, per capita

emissions, and industrial development mean that this relationship is not the same everywhere (**Figure 4.8**).

SOUTH ASIA

The second major global population concentration is also in Asia and is similar in many ways to that of East Asia. At the heart of this cluster of more than 1.5 billion people lies India.

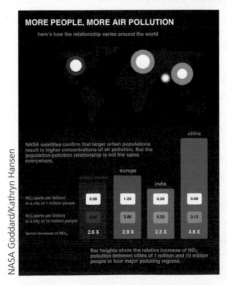

FIGURE 4.8 More people, more air pollution. This map and chart produced by NASA provide an overview of the organization's 2013 study of the relationship between air pollution and population density. Geographic features, industrial development, and per capita emissions are some of the contributing factors to these regional differences.

Dennis Walton/Getty Images

FIGURE 4.9 Hindu pilgrims take holy bath in the Ganges River. The Ganges delta is one of the most densely populated regions in the world.

The concentration extends into Pakistan and Bangladesh and onto the island of Sri Lanka. Here, people again cluster in major cities, on the coasts, and along rivers, such as the Ganges and Indus (**Figure 4.9**). The Ganges delta, for example, has a population density of more than 200 people per square kilometre, making it one of the most densely populated regions in the world.

Two physical barriers create the boundaries of the South Asia population cluster: the Himalayan Mountains to the north, and the desert west of the Indus River Valley in Pakistan. This is a confined region with a rapidly growing population. As in East Asia, the overwhelming majority of the people are farmers, but in South Asia the pressure on the land is even greater. Over large parts of Bangladesh, the rural population density is between 1,153 and 1,922 people per square kilometre. By comparison, in 2006, the population of Alberta was just under 3 million people, and the rural population density was well under 12 people per square kilometre.

EUROPE

A band of dense population extends from Ireland and Great Britain into Russia, encompassing large parts of Germany, Poland, Ukraine, and Belarus and including the Netherlands and Belgium, parts of France, and northern Italy. This European cluster contains over 715 million inhabitants, less than half the population of the South Asia cluster. A comparison of the population density and physical maps indicates that in Europe, terrain and environment are not as closely related to population distribution as they are in East and South Asia. For example, note the population density "protrusion" into Russia in Figure 4.7. Unlike the Asian protrusions, which reflect fertile river valleys, the European extension reflects the orientation of Europe's coalfields. If you look closely at the physical map, you will note that comparatively dense population occurs even in rugged, mountainous country, such as the boundary zone between Poland and its neighbours to the south. A much greater correspondence exists between coastal and river lowlands and high population density in Asia than in Europe generally.

Another contrast is seen in the number of Europeans who live in cities and towns. The European population cluster includes numerous cities and towns that emerged during the Industrial Revolution. In Germany, 88 percent of the people live in urban places; in the United Kingdom, 89 percent; and in France, 74 percent. With so many people concentrated in the cities, the rural countryside is more open and sparsely populated in Europe than it is in East and South Asia, where only about 30 percent of the people reside in cities and towns.

The three major population concentrations we have discussed—East Asia, South Asia, and Europe—account for over 4 billion of the total world population of approximately 7 billion people. Nowhere else on the globe is there a population cluster half as great as any of these. The populations of South America, Africa, and Australia combined barely exceed the population of India alone.

NORTH AMERICA

North America has one densely populated region, stretching through the urban areas of the East Coast from Washington, D.C., in the south to Boston, Massachusetts, in the north. On Figure 4.7, the cities in this region agglomerate into one large urban area that includes Washington, D.C., Baltimore, Philadelphia, New York City, and Boston. Urban geographers use the term **megalopolis** to refer to such huge urban agglomerations. The cities of this megalopolis account for more than 20 percent of the U.S. population (see the "Black Marble" image, Figure 4.2). In Canada, as of 2011, roughly 81 percent of the population lives in urban areas.

> **Megalopolis** Large, coalescing supercities that are forming in diverse parts of the world; the term was formerly used specifically with an uppercase "M" to refer to locations such as the Boston–Washington multi-metropolitan corridor on the northeastern seaboard of the United States.

If you examine the global scale map in Figure 4.7, you will notice the dense population concentration of a megalopolis that includes the Canadian cities of Toronto, Ottawa, Montreal, and Quebec City. Known as the Windsor–Quebec City Corridor, it is the most densely populated region of Canada, with a population of more than 18 million (2011 figures). This corridor is known for its heavy industrialization, its economic and political infrastructure, and, because of its population density, its traffic congestion (**Figure 4.10**). Adding these Canadian cities to the population of the Boston–Washington megalopolis creates a population cluster that is about one-quarter the size of Europe's population cluster. If you have lived or travelled in a megalopolis, you can think about the traffic there and comprehend what dense population means. However, the total population of the megalopolis is 2.8 percent that of the East Asian population cluster, and the 10,194 people per square kilometre density of New York City does not rival the density in world cities like Mumbai, India, with a population density of 22,922 per square kilometre, or Jakarta, Indonesia, with a population density of 14,464 per square kilometre.

FIGURE 4.10 Toronto traffic. Traffic crawls along Highway 401 in Toronto, the major highway linking the Windsor–Quebec City corridor. Vancouver, Toronto, and Montreal are three of the 10 worst cities for traffic congestion in North America.

POPULATION COMPOSITION

> **Population composition**
> Structure of a population in terms of age, sex, and other characteristics, such as marital status and education.

Maps showing distribution and density of populations tell us about the number and organization of people in a country or region, but they do not reveal the characteristics of those populations, such as the number of men and women, or their ages. These aspects of population, the **population composition**, are

important because, for example, a populous country where half the population is very young faces different issues than a populous country where a large proportion of the population is elderly.

A population's "composition" refers to the structure of that population in terms of age, sex, and other characteristics, such as marital status and education. One of the most common tools used by demographers and geographers are

> **Population pyramids** A tool used to visually represent the age and sex composition of a population, in which the percentage of each age group (generally divided in five-year increments) is represented by a horizontal bar, the length of which indicates its relationship to the total population. The males in each age group are represented to the left of the centre line of each horizontal bar; the females in each age group are represented to the right of the centre line.

population pyramids, which are used to visually illustrate a population's age and sex distribution, key indicators of population composition. A population pyramid displays the percentages of each age group (normally five-year groups called "cohorts") in the total population by a horizontal bar whose length represents that cohort's share of the total population. Males in the group are to the left of the centre line, females to the right.

A population pyramid can instantly convey the demographic situation in a population or country. As **Figure 4.11** demonstrates, in the poorer countries, where birth and death rates generally remain high, the pyramid resembles an evergreen tree, with wide branches at the base and short ones near the top. The youngest age groups have the largest share of the population; in the composite pyramids in Figure 4.11, the three groups up to age 14 account for more than 30 percent of the population. Older people, in the three highest age groups, represent only about 4 percent of the total. Slight variations of this pyramidal shape mark the population structure of such countries as Niger and Guatemala. From the 15-to-19 age group on, each group is smaller than the one below it.

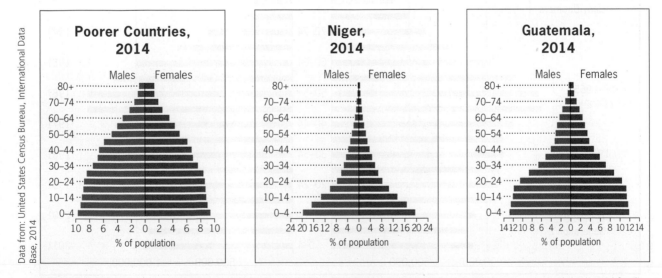

FIGURE 4.11 Age-sex population pyramids for countries with high population growth rates. Countries with high total fertility rates, high infant mortality rates, and low life expectancies will have population pyramids with wide bases and narrow tops.

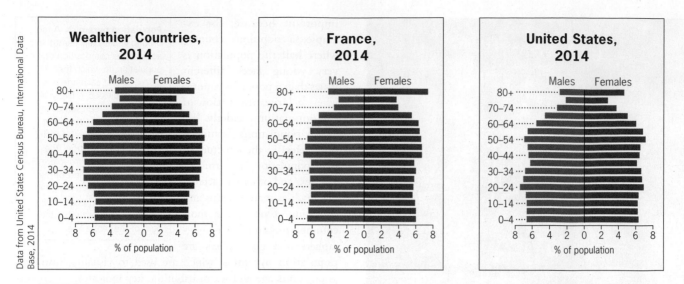

FIGURE 4.12 **Age-sex population pyramids for countries with low population growth rates.** Countries with lower total fertility rates and longer life expectancies have population pyramids shaped more uniformly throughout.

In countries with greater economic wealth, the pyramid shapes change. Families become smaller, children fewer. A composite population pyramid for wealthier countries in 2014 (**Figure 4.12**) looks like a slightly lopsided vase, with the largest components of the population in the middle. The middle-age bulge is moving upward, reflecting the aging of the population and the declining total fertility rate (TFR). Overall, wealthier countries fit into this pyramid mode, including Italy, France, and the United States.

The Canadian population pyramid (**Figure 4.13**) demonstrates that the Canadian population is aging, given that the base of the pyramid is smaller than the middle. In 2006, the median age in Canada was 38.8 years, the highest it has ever

been. Statistics Canada projects that by the year 2056, this median age will reach 46.9 years. The largest population group is between 35 and 54 years of age. **Figure 4.14** illustrates Canada's aging population in more detail over time, showing how, since 1921, the median age has gone up and the number of babies born has gone down. While net international migration has been the main driver of population growth in Canada since the 1990s, it has not affected the overall structure of our aging population.

It is important to remember that Canada's population is diverse and that these overall trends do not necessarily reflect the population composition of various groups within Canada. For example, as **Figure 4.15** reveals, the median age

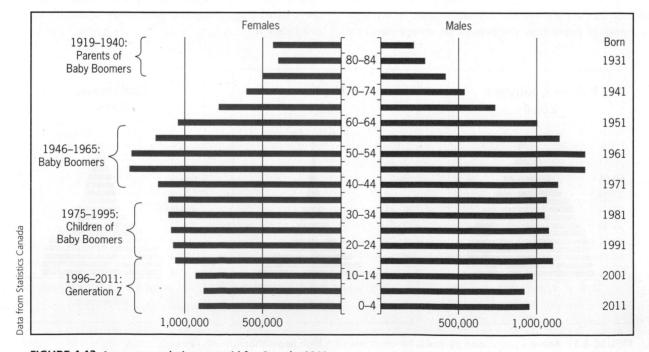

FIGURE 4.13 Age-sex population pyramid for Canada, 2011.

FIGURE 4.14 **Median age and number of children in Canada, 1921–2006.** The light blue line indicates the median age, which has gone up; the dark blue line indicates the average number of children per woman, which has declined.

of those Canadians who claim Aboriginal identity is significantly lower than those of non-Aboriginal identity. Data from Statistics Canada in 2011 reveal a median age for the Aboriginal population, Canada-wide, of 26.7, approximately 13 years younger than the Canadian average of 40.2 years. This difference is due, in part, to a higher birth rate in the Aboriginal population. The data show us that Canada's Aboriginal population is young; Aboriginal children aged 14 and under make up 28 percent of the total Aboriginal population and 7 percent of all children in Canada. Non-Aboriginal children aged 14 and under represent 16.5 percent of the total non-Aboriginal population. Canada's

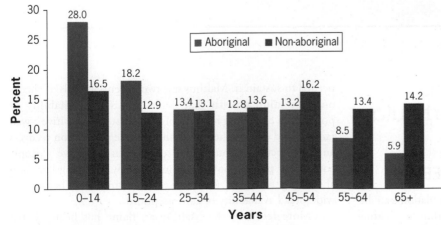

FIGURE 4.15 **Median age for population reporting Aboriginal identity and non-Aboriginal population in Canada, 2011, percent.** Median age is the point at which exactly half of the population is older and the other half is younger. Data from Statistics Canada 2011 National Household Survey.

Aboriginal population is nevertheless aging, albeit more slowly than the rest of Canada, in part due to increased life expectancy and declining birth rates.

RELIABILITY OF POPULATION DATA

A **census** is an official enumeration of a population, completed periodically, that usually provides demographic information about a population. In Canada, a

> **Census** A periodic and official count of a country's population.

census is taken every five years, and Canadian citizens, landed immigrants, refugee claimants, and those holding a work or student permit are legally bound to complete the census questionnaire. The reliability of population data varies from country to country depending on the technologies available, the skill of the data collector, and the mobility and visibility of the population. In the North American context, various groups protest the practice of trying to count every single person in a country. Many advocates for the homeless, minorities, and others insist the census practices result in a serious undercount of these disadvantaged populations. In 2006 and 2009, for example, the City of Toronto came under fire for its attempt to count its homeless population. While not an official Government of Canada census, the program, which used "point in time" methodology and visual identification, was criticized for its lack of verifiable or accurate data, leading to the underestimation of the actual number of homeless. Many homeless people who opt to "couch-surf" are not visible on the street and are therefore not counted during data collection. This is important, particularly because federal and provincial funding is often tied to population data. If the population of a disadvantaged group is undercounted, it translates into a loss of dollars for agencies that rely on different levels of government funding to pay for social services to that group. Advocates are concerned that people who are already members of a disadvantaged group suffer further as a result of census undercounts.

Being undercounted also translates into less government representation when the number of seats for an electoral district is allocated based on census data. Prosperous countries such as Canada and the United States often experience problems conducting an accurate census. For example, there has been a great deal of controversy over issues such as "race" and "ethnic origin" in terms of collecting census data. Greater difficulties must be overcome in less well-off countries, where the cost, organization, and reporting of a census exceed what many countries can afford or handle.

In the summer of 2010, a massive controversy erupted in Canada over the Conservative government's decision to scrap the long-form questionnaire for the 2011 census, replacing it with a voluntary national household survey. The mandatory long-form questionnaire has been used by governments, businesses, educators, and social service agencies to provide services and funding to a vast array of Canadians. As well, academics, including geographers, rely upon this data to analyze population trends and movements over time. Critics of the government's decision to replace the mandatory questionnaire with a voluntary one argue that voluntary surveys are not as statistically rigorous as mandatory ones, and that many groups will be underrepresented in the new voluntary program. The head of Statistics Canada, Munir Sheikh, tendered his resignation over the issue, claiming that the voluntary survey is no replacement for the mandatory long-form questionnaire. When Statistics Canada began releasing data from its 2011 census, the following disclaimer was included in its material:

> We have never previously conducted a survey on the scale of the voluntary National Household Survey, nor are we aware of any other country that has. The new methodology has been introduced relatively rapidly with limited testing. We are confident that the National Household Survey will produce useable and useful data that will meet the needs of

many users. It will not, however, provide a level of quality that would have been achieved through a mandatory long-form census.

With these strong words of caution from the agency in charge of the compilation and analysis of the census, experts have warned that results will contain biases, that the new methodology renders historical comparisons inaccurate, and that these problems will "muddy" other StatsCan surveys.

Several agencies collect data on world population. The United Nations records official statistics that national governments assemble and report. The World Bank and the Population Reference Bureau also gather and generate data and report on the population of the world and of individual countries. If you compare the population data reported by each of these sources, you will find inconsistencies. Data on population, growth rates, food availability, health conditions, and incomes are often informed estimates rather than actual counts. It is important to always think carefully about the source and veracity of the statistics you are using.

MAIN POINTS 4.1 How Do We Think about Populations and How Is This "Geographical"?

- Population geographers use demographic information about age and sex to highlight characteristics of various populations and to point out the patterns of spatial variations that become visible for certain populations. Geographers use mapping techniques and population pyramids to make patterns visible.

- Once certain patterns become visible, geographers are interested in understanding how and why a population has a particular composition or set of characteristics—why are there a certain number of men and women, and what are the reasons for various attributes such as age, income, health, ethnicity, and education levels?

- As geographers, we want to understand why populations are located where they are. Who lives in what places and why? Why is the world's population distributed in four main regions? How does a particular population order its landscape and why? How do people and groups move from place to place and why?

- Population data is often difficult to gather, and different sources may have different data. How data is collected, what is included, and what is overlooked can have a serious effect on the quality of life of particular populations in certain places.

4.2 Why Do Populations Grow or Decline in Particular Places?

THE POPULATION GROWTH DEBATE

The concern over the burgeoning world population can be traced back to 1798, when British economist Thomas Malthus published An Essay on the Principle of Population. Malthus reasoned that food supplies grew linearly, adding acreage and crops incrementally by year, whereas population grew exponentially, compounding on the year before. This suggested that the world's population was increasing faster than the food supplies

needed to sustain it. Malthus saw two potential kinds of checks on population growth that could stall the inevitability of population exceeding food supply. The first was "positive": war, famine, and disease check growth until the population recovers and the cycle continues. The second was "negative": people could keep population growth in check by marrying later and abstaining from sex (Malthus was writing long before the widespread availability of contraception).

More recently, the Malthusian flame has been carried forward by Paul Ehrlich, whose book *The Population Bomb*, published in 1968, had a profound impact on how countries perceived population growth over the next 50 years. Ehrlich, Bing professor of population studies at Stanford University, warned that the world's population was increasing too quickly and outpacing food production, which he predicted would lead to mass starvation in the 1970s and 1980s. Ehrlich described what he foresaw as the increasingly dire state of the environment and food security, arguing that the natural world was being strained beyond capacity by growing populations. An advocate of population control, Ehrlich's predictions were deemed by some to be alarmist, with critics suggesting he was wrong or misguided. According to these critics, what Ehrlich did not foresee were three major global efforts to control populations: governments and non-governmental organizations committing to controlling reproduction rates; agricultural advances, including the "green revolution" and the spread of new technology; and the intensification of global trade, which enabled developing countries to export food in exchange for seeds, machinery, and fertilizers.

On the other side of the debate, some scholars, including Danish economist Ester Boserup, who published *The Conditions of Agricultural Growth: The Economics of Agrarian Change under Population Pressure* in 1965, argue that it is not food supply that determines population, but, rather, society's capacity to develop new technologies and farming techniques that ensures the production of enough food supplies to meet the needs of growing populations. These arguments resonate with the recent arguments about Ehrlich detailed above. Technological advancements have indeed been a major factor in sustaining food levels to meet the demands of a growing population. For example, Malthusians such as Paul and William Paddock, authors of *Famine 1975!*, argued that mass global famine was inevitable, and that India in particular was "foredoomed." However, the efforts of Professor Monkombu Sambasivan Swaminathan, who adapted Nobel Peace Prize winner Norman Borlaug's work, ensured that the green revolution took place in India through a series of technological and agrarian advances that changed the country's ability to produce food. As a result, India declined all foreign food aid by 1975, and is now an emerging global power. It is important to remember, though, that India's forced sterilization programs must also be taken into account when considering the food production/population debate (see discussion below).

Moreover, Malthus assumed food production is confined spatially—what people can eat within a country depends on what is grown in that country. We now know this assumption does not hold true; countries are not closed systems. Malthus did not foresee how globalization would aid the exchange of agricultural goods across the world. As discussed in Chapter 3, mercantilism, colonialism, and capitalism brought interaction among the Americas, Europe, Africa, Asia, and the Pacific. Through global interaction, new agricultural methods developed, and commodities and livestock diffused across oceans. In the 1700s, farmers in Ireland grew dependent on the potato, a South American crop that was well suited to their country's rocky soils. Today, wealthier countries that lack arable land, such as Norway, can import the majority of their foodstuffs, circumventing the limitations of their lands.

Modern food production has grown exponentially as the acreage under cultivation expands, mechanization of agricultural

production spreads, improved strains of seed are developed, and more fertilizers are used. In the 21st century, bioengineering continues to bring new hybrids, genetically modified organisms (GMOs), and countless herbicides and pesticides that enable exponential growth in food production. Conversely, these changes also raise concerns about food safety, the possible risks of GMOs, and the potential dangers of pesticide use to humans and the environment.

Debates about food and our ability to feed ourselves continue and are intimately bound up in our relationship with the environment (see Chapter 6 for more on human-environment relations). In November 2010 the *Globe and Mail* ran a series of articles examining food production in Canada, contextualizing the subject in terms of globalization, food safety, and environmental and climate concerns, among other issues. With headlines proclaiming that Canada's reputation as a world agricultural "superpower" was slipping away, the newspaper reported that while we export over $30 billion in agricultural products annually, we are losing our position on the world's markets due to increased competition globally. Canada's share of the global wheat market has shrunk from 23 percent to 19 percent, and its overall export position has dropped from third to ninth. While Canada's economic investment in agriculture has increased to $8 billion annually, we continue to struggle in a competitive global environment. The Canadian Federation of Agriculture is attempting to address these issues by developing a national food strategy driven by consumer groups, producers, and government representatives.

POPULATION CHANGE AT WORLD, REGIONAL, NATIONAL, AND LOCAL SCALES

Analysis of population change requires attention to scale. While we can consider population growth and decline at different scales, we must be mindful that what happens at

> **Rate of natural increase (RNI)**
> An indicator of population change, calculated by subtracting the crude death rate from the crude birth rate.

one scale can be affected by what is happening at other scales and in other places at the same time. Therefore, we usually begin by considering population change within a defined territory or unit of a country or other administrative unit, such as a province or city. One basic indicator of population change is the **rate of natural increase (RNI)** in a country's population. The RNI is calculated by subtracting the deaths from births for the total population over a particular period of time, usually one year. For example, Canada's RNI in 2011/2012 was 0.4 percent, calculated by subtracting the crude death rate (0.7 percent) from the crude birth rate (1.1 percent).

This is a relatively simple statistic to calculate and comprehend; however, calculating the natural increase misses two other key components in a country's population: immigration, which along with births adds to the total population; and emigration (outmigration), which along with deaths subtracts from the total population. Using these four components, we can calculate demographic change within a territory.

POPULATION CHANGE AT THE WORLD SCALE

World population growth is mapped in **Figure 4.16**. Most of the world's population growth is expected to be in Africa, Asia, and Central and South America. This measure of population growth does not, however, take into account emigration and immigration, which we will discuss in Chapter 5. Other maps and tables of population growth may take into account emigration and immigration. Statistics for each population trait can be calculated globally, by region, by country, or even for smaller locales. When studying population data across scales, we must constantly remind ourselves of exactly what is being calculated and for where. Otherwise, many of the statistics we read will seem contradictory.

> **Total fertility rate (TFR)** The average number of births per woman of childbearing age, usually considered between 15 and 49 years of age.

For example, there has been increasing concern about **total fertility rates (TFRs)** in a number of countries around the world. How can the worldwide population continue to increase when so many countries are experiencing low TFRs and population decline? Despite declining population growth rates and even negative growth rates (growth rates below 0.0) in a number of the world's countries, the global population continues to rise. The worldwide TFR was 2.45 in 2013, which is above the replacement level of 2.33 (replacement level is the TFR needed to maintain a population.) The Population Reference Bureau estimates global population will rise to over 9.3 billion by 2050. This is because the low TFRs and low population growth rates enumerated in this chapter are dwarfed by continued additions to the population in countries where growth rates are still relatively high, such as India, Indonesia, Bangladesh, Pakistan, and Nigeria.

Two thousand years ago, the world's population was an estimated 250 million. More than 16 centuries passed before this total had doubled to 500 million, the estimated population in 1650. Just 170 years later, in 1820 (when Malthus was still writing), the population had doubled again, to 1 billion. Barely more than a century later, in 1930, it reached 2 billion. The

> **Doubling time** The time required for a population to double in size.
>
> **Population explosion** The rapid growth of the world's human population during the past century, attended by ever-shorter doubling times and accelerating rates of increase.

doubling time had declined to 100 years and was dropping fast; the **population explosion** was in full gear. Only 45 years elapsed before the next doubling, to 4 billion (1975). During the mid-1980s, when the rate declined to 1.8 percent, the doubling slowed to 39 years. Today, world population is expected to double in 54 years.

For demographers and population geographers studying global population growth today, the concept of doubling time is losing much of its punch. With populations declining in many places, fears of global population doubling quickly are subsiding. Many indicators, including the slowing of the doubling time, suggest that the explosive population growth of the 20th century will be followed by a marked and accelerating slowdown during

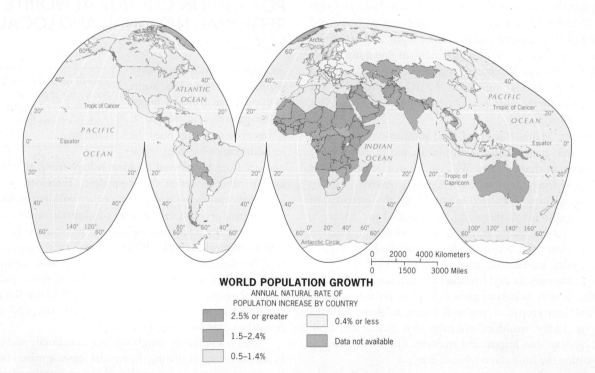

WORLD POPULATION GROWTH
ANNUAL NATURAL RATE OF
POPULATION INCREASE BY COUNTRY

- 2.5% or greater
- 1.5–2.4%
- 0.5–1.4%
- 0.4% or less
- Data not available

FIGURE 4.16 World Population Growth, 2012. Annual natural rate of population increase by country. Population growth rates in Subsaharan Africa remain relatively high, and population growth rates in Europe and Russia remain relatively low. *Data from:* Population Reference Bureau, 2012.

the 21st century. The global growth rate is now down to 1.4 percent or slightly lower. But the world's population is about 6.7 billion today, which yields an annual increase in world population that still exceeds 80 million people. Although this is an improvement over the 90 million annual increase the world experienced in the late 1980s, the population growth rate will have to come down well below 1.0 percent to significantly slow global population growth.

POPULATION CHANGE AT THE REGIONAL AND NATIONAL SCALES

The world map of population growth rates by country (Figure 4.16) confirms the wide range of RNIs in different geographic regions. These variations have existed as long as records have been kept and are the result of countries and regions going through stages of expansion and decline at different times. In the mid-20th century, the population of what was then the Soviet Union was growing vigorously. Thirty years ago, India's population was growing at nearly 3 percent, more than most African countries; then India's growth rate fell below that of sub-Saharan Africa. Today, Africa's RNI remains higher than India's (2.4 percent to 1.7 percent), but sub-Saharan Africa faces the impact of the AIDS epidemic, which is killing millions and orphaning children, reducing life expectancies, and curtailing growth rates.

The map also reveals continuing high growth rates in Muslim countries of north Africa and Southwest Asia. Saudi Arabia has one of the highest growth rates in the world, but some smaller countries in this region are seeing an even faster increase. During the second half of the 20th century, countries in this region saw their growth rates increase even as those in most of the rest of the world declined. More recently, several fast-growing populations—for example, those of Iran and Morocco—have shown significant declines. Demographers point to the correlation between high growth rates and the low standing of women: where cultural traditions restrict educational and professional opportunities for women, and men dominate as a matter of custom, rates of natural increase tend to be high.

South Asia is the most important geographic region in terms of the population growth rate. The region includes the country that appears destined to overtake China as the world's most populous: India. Only one country in this region has a growth rate lower than the world average: Sri Lanka. But Sri Lanka's total population is only 20.4 million, whereas the fast-growing countries of Pakistan and Bangladesh have a combined population exceeding 326 million. India, as Figure 4.16 shows, is still growing above the world average. The situation in East Asia, the world's most populous region, is different. China's official RNI has fallen below 1.0 percent (0.6 in 2008), and Japan's population is no longer growing. Southeast Asia's natural growth rates remain higher, but this region's total population is much lower than that of either East or South Asia; key countries, such as Indonesia, Thailand, and Vietnam, have declining growth rates.

South America's natural population growth rates were alarmingly high just a generation ago but are now experiencing significant reductions. The region as a whole is still growing at 1.5 percent, but Brazil's population growth, for example, has declined from 2.9 percent in the mid-1960s to 1.4 percent today. The populations of Argentina, Chile, and Uruguay are growing at rates well below the world average.

As Figure 4.16 shows, the slowest-growing countries—including those with declining rates of natural population increase—lie in the economically wealthier areas of the world extending from the United States and Canada to Europe and Japan. In the Southern Hemisphere, Australia, New Zealand, and Uruguay are in this category too. Wealth is not the only reason for negative population growth rates. Russia's population is declining because of social dislocation in the wake of the collapse of the Soviet Union; deteriorating health conditions, high rates of alcoholism and drug use, and economic problems combine to shorten life expectancies (especially among males) and to lower birth rates (in recent years, Russia's economy has improved, but its birth rate remains low). Similar problems afflict Ukraine and Kazakhstan, two of Russia's neighbours, which also show slow or negative growth.

No single factor can explain these variations. Economic prosperity and social dislocation reduce natural population growth rates. Economic well-being, associated with urbanization, higher levels of education, later marriage, family planning, and other factors, lowers population growth. Using Appendix B, compare the indices for natural population increase and the percentage of the population that is urbanized; in general, the higher the population's level of urbanization, the lower its natural increase. Cultural traditions also influence rates of population growth. Religion, for example, has a powerful impact on family planning and thus on growth rates, not only in Islamic countries but also in traditional Christian societies (note the growth rate in the Roman Catholic Philippines) and in Hindu-dominated communities (such as India).

POPULATION CHANGE AT THE LOCAL SCALE

The information provided in Figure 4.16 is based on country-wide statistics. Significant demographic variations also occur within countries. In India, for example, some states record population growth rates far above the national average; these states lie mostly in the east of the country (**Figure 4.17**). Other states, in the west and southwest region, are growing much more slowly. India is a federation of 28 states and 7 union territories, and the individual states differ greatly both culturally and politically.

After becoming independent in 1947, India began a population-planning program in the 1950s, long before the modern era's fear of worldwide overpopulation and a global population bomb spread. In the 1960s, when census numbers

FIGURE 4.17 **Population growth rates in India.**

sterilization. The policy granted a shotgun licence in exchange for the sterilization of two people, and a revolver licence in exchange for the sterilization of five people. Abuse began almost immediately, with wealthy landowners sterilizing their labourers in exchange for gun licences. Before the "guns for sterilization" policy, districts in Uttar Pradesh encouraged sterilization by providing access to housing and extra food for people who agreed to be sterilized.

Today, the Indian government continues to push for population control and sterilization is still practised, sometimes with tragic consequences (**Figure 4.18**). Posters urging people to have small families are everywhere, and the government supports a network of family-planning clinics even in the remotest villages. The southern states continue to report the lowest growth rates, correlating with higher wealth and education levels in these states. The eastern and northern states, the poorer regions of India, continue to report the highest growth rates. In countries such as China and India, where there is a preference for male children, there has been a startling increase in the infanticide and abortion of female children. The result is populations with a far greater number of men than women.

revealed extreme growth rates in parts of the country, the Indian government encouraged states to join the national population planning program. As in any federation, the will of the federal government cannot be forcibly imposed upon the states; however, when it became evident that early population planning that was not national in scope was not working, a federal effort was implemented.

Despite the federal effort, rapid population growth continued, especially in the eastern states. Social problems arose in some of the states where governments pursued the campaign vigorously. During the 1970s, the Indian government began a policy of forced sterilization of any man with three or more children. The State of Maharashtra sterilized 3.7 million people before public opposition led to rioting, and the government abandoned the program. Other states also engaged in compulsory sterilization programs, with heavy social and political costs—eventually, 22.5 million people were sterilized.

The horrors of the forced sterilization program of the 1970s are haunting India again. In 2004, three districts in the State of Uttar Pradesh (India's most populous state, with over 170 million people) instituted a policy of exchanging gun licences for

FIGURE 4.18 **A patient recovering after a botched sterilization surgery.** In November 2014 in the Indian state of Chhattisgarh, 11 women died and dozens took ill after doctors allegedly performed botched sterilization surgeries using rusty equipment in a dirty operating room during a state-run mass sterilization "camp."

POPULATION CHANGE IN CANADA

As **Figure 4.19** illustrates, the Canadian population has grown steadily since the mid-1850s. According to Statistics Canada, this growth can be divided into three distinct phases. The first,

FIGURE 4.19 Canadian population growth, 1851 to 2051. From Statistics Canada, "Figure 1: Population of Canada, 1851 to 2051," *Canadian Demographics at a Glance, 2007.*

from 1851 to 1900, was a period of slow growth. There was little natural growth during this time because high fertility rates were offset by very high mortality rates. The second phase, from 1901 to 1945, which included World War I and II, was defined by accelerated growth, due mostly to immigration and the settlement of western Canada. The third phase, from 1946 to the present, is characterized by an even faster pace of growth due to both the baby boom and strong immigration. Canada's population increased from 12.3 million in 1946 to approximately 35 million in 2014.

Yet, as we have learned, population growth comprises both the rate of natural increase (the difference between total births and total deaths) and migration patterns (people entering and leaving Canada). **Figure 4.20** illustrates the overall trend in these two areas. In the 1990s, for instance, natural increase was the main driver of population growth. However, due to lower fertility rates, an aging population, and migratory changes, this is no longer the case. In 2006, migratory increases accounted for two-thirds of the population growth, whereas natural increases accounted for one-third. Statistics Canada projects that by 2030, total deaths will outnumber total births in Canada, which will mean that migration increases will be the sole driver of population growth.

These statistics speak to population at the national scale, but we are also interested in population growth and changes on the local scale. **Figure 4.21** breaks down population growth by province and territory. (Note that this includes population growth from both migratory and natural increases.) Since 2001, population growth has increased in every province and territory except Prince Edward Island (where it remains unchanged), Newfoundland and Labrador, and Saskatchewan. Statistics Canada attributes growth rates in most regions to international immigration patterns, inter-province migration, or both. Two-thirds of the overall growth since 2001 has taken place in Alberta and Ontario. The territories all report significant population growth since 2001. For the most part, the Atlantic region's population remains steady, virtually unchanged between 2001 and 2006. Quebec reported its second-highest growth rate since the end of the baby boom, growing three times faster than it did in the previous reporting period of 1996–2001. This is due to increased international migration to the province, along with less movement out of Quebec to other provinces and territories. The territories all reported growth in the 2001–2006 cycle, which can be attributed to improvement in migration exchanges with other provinces, as well as the region's higher Aboriginal populations, which tend to have a higher fertility rate (**Figure 4.22**).

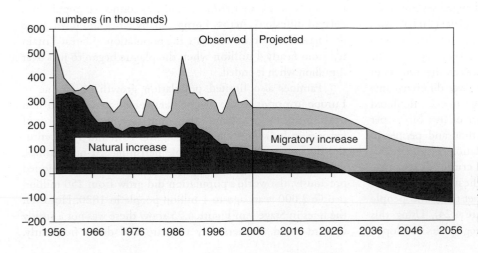

FIGURE 4.20 Canadian population growth: Migratory and natural increase, 1956–2056. From Statistics Canada, "Figure 3: Migratory and natural increase of the Canadian population, 1956 to 2056," *Canadian Demographics at a Glance, 2007.*

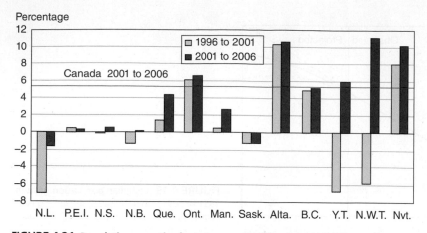

FIGURE 4.21 Population growth of provinces and territories, 1996–2001 and 2001–2006. From Statistics Canada, "Figure 4: Population growth of provinces and territories, 1996 to 2001 and 2001 to 2006," *Population and Dwelling Counts, 2006 Census.*

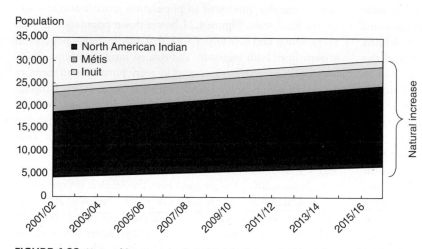

FIGURE 4.22 Natural increase in the Aboriginal populations of Canada, 2001/2002 to 2016/2017. From Statistics Canada, "Figure 4: Population growth of provinces and territories, 1996 to 2001 and 2001 to 2006," *Population and Dwelling Counts, 2006 Census.*

THE DEMOGRAPHIC TRANSITION

The high population growth rates now occurring in many poorer countries are not necessarily permanent. In Europe, for example, the rate of population growth changed several times in the last three centuries. Demographers used data on baptisms and funerals from churches in Great Britain to study changes in birth and death rates of the population. They expected the RNI of the population—the difference between the number of births and the number of deaths—to vary over different time periods. To test this hypothesis, demographers calculated the **crude birth rate (CBR)**, the number of live births per year per thousand people in the population (**Figure 4.23**), and the **crude death rate (CDR)**, the number of deaths per year per thousand people (see **Figure 4.24**). Using this data, demographers developed

> **Crude birth rate (CBR)** The number of live births yearly per thousand people in a population.
>
> **Crude death rate (CDR)** The number of deaths yearly per thousand people in a population.

> **Demographic transition** Multistage model based on Western Europe's experience of changes in population growth exhibited by countries undergoing industrialization. High birth rates and death rates are followed by plunging death rates, producing a huge net population gain; this is followed by the convergence of birth rates and death rates at a low overall level.

a **demographic transition** model reflecting the changes in population growth experienced in Great Britain and elsewhere between 1400 and today. They developed a five-stage model, shown in **Figure 4.25**, to illustrate the process. The model is based on the kind of shift that Great Britain experienced and can be used to compare the transition in other places. Some locations have already undergone a similar shift in their population growth, while others are in the process of doing so.

The initial low-growth phase of the model (Stage 1) is marked by high birth rates and equally high death rates, which seems a common experience for most human populations. In this phase, epidemics and plagues keep the death rates high among all sectors of the population—in some cases so high that they exceed birth rates. For Great Britain and the rest of Europe, death rates exceeded birth rates during the bubonic plague (the Black Death) of the 1300s, which hit in waves beginning in Crimea on the Black Sea. The plague was diffused through trade to Sicily and other Mediterranean islands, largely because of the travel of rats (which hosted the vector—the flea—that spread the plague) north from the Mediterranean (**Figure 4.26**).

Once the plague hit a region, it was likely to return within a few years, bringing another wave of human suffering. Estimates of plague deaths vary between one-quarter and one-half of the population, with the highest death rates recorded in the west (where trade among regions was the greatest) and the lowest in the east (where cooler climates and less-connected populations delayed diffusion). Across Europe, many cities and towns were decimated. Historians estimate the population of Great Britain fell from nearly 4 million when the plague began to just over 2 million when it ended.

Famines also limited population growth. A famine in Europe just prior to the plague likely facilitated the diffusion of the disease by weakening the population health. Records of famines in India and China during the 18th and 19th centuries document millions of people perishing. At other times, destructive wars wiped out population gains. As mentioned previously, the world's population did grow from 250 million people 2,000 years ago to 1 billion people in 1820. However, the lines in Stage 1 of Figure 4.25 show there was not a steady upward trend. Rather, they turn up and down frequently,

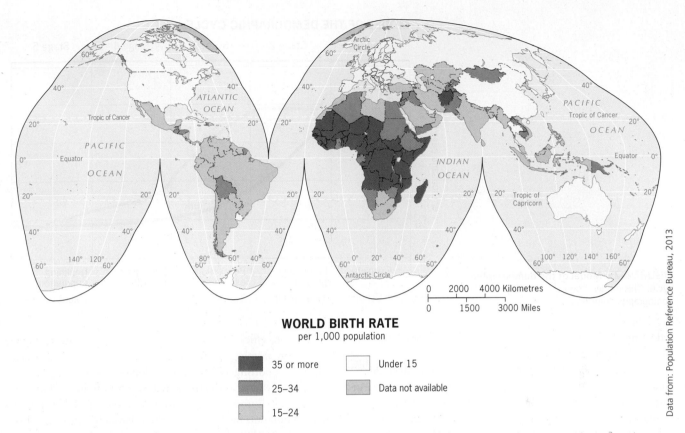

WORLD BIRTH RATE
per 1,000 population

- 35 or more
- 25–34
- 15–24
- Under 15
- Data not available

Data from: Population Reference Bureau, 2013

FIGURE 4.23 Crude birth rate: Number of births in a year per 1,000 people. A fairly distinct north–south pattern is evident, as northern countries have lower crude birth rates than southern countries. The global south has a few clear outliers with low crude birth rates, notably Australia, New Zealand, Chile, and Uruguay.

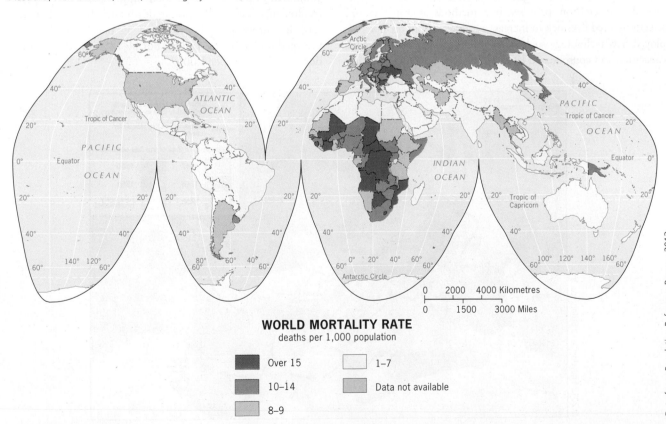

WORLD MORTALITY RATE
deaths per 1,000 population

- Over 15
- 10–14
- 8–9
- 1–7
- Data not available

Data from: Population Reference Bureau, 2013

FIGURE 4.24 Crude death rate: Number of deaths in a year per 1,000 people. The death rate has declined globally as countries have transitioned into the third stage of the demographic transition and beyond. A few countries in the global north have relatively high death rates, including Russia and a number of eastern European countries.

MODEL OF THE DEMOGRAPHIC CYCLE

FIGURE 4.25 Model of the demographic cycle. This model shows the five stages of the demographic transition.

reflecting the impacts of disease, crop failures, and wars, as well as changing farming practices and technologies.

Stage 2 starts at the beginning of the Industrial Revolution, which ushered in a period of accelerating population growth in Europe. Before workers could move from farms to factories, a revolution in agriculture had to occur, and during the 18th century the Second Agricultural Revolution did take place (the first, which occurred thousands of years earlier, is described in Chapter 9). During the Second Agricultural Revolution, farmers improved seed selection, practised new methods of crop rotation, selectively bred livestock to increase production and quality, employed new technology such as the seed drill, expanded storage capacities, and consolidated landholdings for greater efficiencies.

With more efficient farming methods, the number of people needed in farming decreased and the food supply increased, thereby supporting a higher population overall.

In the 1800s, as the Industrial Revolution diffused through continental Europe, other advances also helped lower death rates. Sanitation facilities made the towns and cities safer from epidemics, and medical practices improved. Disease prevention through vaccination introduced a new era in public health. The combined improvements in food supply and medical practice resulted in a drastic reduction in death rates. Before 1750, death rates in Europe probably averaged 35 per 1,000 (birth rates averaged under 40 per 1,000), but by 1850 the death rate was down to about 16 per 1,000.

FIGURE 4.26 The spread of the Black Death. Reprinted with permission from *Encyclopædia Britannica*.

In Stage 3, birth rates fell at a slower rate and the death rate declined, leading to a population explosion. The increase in the rate of population growth in Europe spurred waves of migration. Millions of people left the squalid, crowded, industrial cities and poor rural regions to emigrate to other parts of the world. They were not the first to make this journey. Adventurers, explorers, merchants, and colonists had gone before them. In a major wave of colonization from 1500 through the 1700s, European migrants decimated native populations by conquest, slavery, and the introduction of diseases against which the local people had no natural immunity.

When a second wave of European colonization began in Africa and Asia during the late 1800s, the Europeans brought with them their newfound methods of sanitation and medical techniques, and these had the opposite effect. By the mid-1900s, declining death rates in Africa, India, and South America brought rapid population increases to these regions. At this point, new alarms and cautions of worldwide overpopulation rang out.

These alarms subsided for populations in Europe and North America when population growth rates began to decline in the first half of the 1900s (Stage 3) as a result of a significant decline in birth rates. Populations continued to grow, but at a much slower rate. Many countries in Latin America and Asia experienced falling birth rates later in the 20th century, which helped slow the global population growth rate.

Why have birth rates declined? Throughout the 1900s, lower birth rates appeared first in countries with greater urbanization, wealth, and medical advances. As more and more people moved to cities, both the economics and the culture of large families changed. Children, who were valued as workers on the family farm, became a drain on family finances in urban areas. At the same time, new employment opportunities—especially for women—were often not compatible with the level of care women were expected to provide to large families. Hence, women often delayed marriage and childbearing. Medical advances lowered infant and child mortality rates, lessening the sense that many children were necessary to sustain a family. In recent history, the diffusion of contraceptives, access to safe abortions, and conscious decisions by many women to have fewer children or to start having children later in life have all lowered birth rates within a country.

In some parts of the world, countries are now experiencing exceptionally low total fertility rates (Stages 4 and 5). Low birth rates along with low death rates put these countries in a position of negligible, or even negative, population growth. Birth rates are lowest in countries where women are the most educated and most involved in the labour force. For example, in Canada, half of the women between the ages of 25 and 44 have a post-secondary degree, compared to only 40 percent of men in the same age range. In 2013, Canada's TFR was 1.59, one of the lowest in the world. As we discuss in Chapter 5, countries such as Canada look to immigration to maintain their population.

FUTURE POPULATION GROWTH

It is unwise to assume that the demographic cycles of all countries will follow the sequence that occurred in industrializing Europe or to believe that the still-significant population growth currently taking place in Bangladesh, Mexico, and numerous other countries will simply subside. The classic description of the demographic transition model indicates that the transition took approximately 100 years and is attributed to improved socio-economic conditions, which in turn improved child survival rates and fertility preferences. However, in some developing countries this transition has occurred much more rapidly than it did in developed countries. For instance, in Bangladesh, the transition took place within a span of 10 years, and birth rates have fallen without the simultaneous improvements to socio-economic conditions. Nonetheless, many agencies monitoring global population suggest that most, if not all, countries' populations will stop growing at some point during the 21st century, reaching a so-called **stationary population level (SPL)**. If this happens, the world's population would stabilize, and the major problem would become the aging

> **Stationary population level (SPL)** The level at which a national population ceases to grow.

of the population in some countries. In 2004, the United Nations predicted that world population would stabilize at 9 billion in 300 years.

Such predictions require frequent revision, however, and anticipated dates for population stabilization are often moved back. Only a few years ago, the United Nations predicted world population would stabilize at 10 billion in 200 years. In 2013, the United Nations changed its prediction again, indicating that the world population will reach 9.6 billion by 2050, with more than half this growth occurring in Africa. The United Nations changed its predictions based on lower fertility rates in many countries. All agencies reporting population predictions have to revise their predictions periodically. In the late 1980s, for example, the World Bank predicted that the United States would reach SPL in 2035, with 276 million inhabitants. Brazil's population would stabilize at 353 million in 2070, Mexico's at 254 million in 2075, and China's at 1.4 billion in 2090. India, destined to become the world's most populous country, would reach SPL at 1.6 billion in 2150.

Today these figures are unrealistic. China's population passed the 1.2 billion mark in 1994, and India's reached 1 billion in 1998. If we were to project an optimistic decline in growth rates for both countries, China's population would "stabilize" at 1.5 billion in 2070 and India's at 1.8 billion in the same year. But population increase is a cyclical phenomenon, and overall declines mask lags and spurts as well as regional disparities. This population explosion, according to the UN's Intergovernmental Panel on Climate Change (IPCC), will have "severe impacts on land use and on the demands for energy, fresh water, food and housing." The IPCC calls for any global climate-change strategies to take into account this massive population growth.

MAIN POINTS 4.2 Why Do Populations Grow or Decline in Particular Places?

- Geographers are interested in where and why populations grow and decline. In considering population change, geographers work at a number of scales (global, regional, national, and local) and recognize that what is occurring at one scale can be influenced by activities and events at other scales.

- At the global scale, we can see that the TFR is declining in some countries and remaining stable or increasing in others. By considering statistics on population change at the regional and national scale, we can get a much better

sense of where growth and decline are occurring. The example of India shows us that internal political, social, and technological changes can influence TFR at the local level.

- The demographic transition model reflects the changing demographic patterns noted in Great Britain and much of Europe from the 18th century to the present day. It demonstrates how technological and social changes impact population growth and decline. However, it would be unwise to presume that all countries will follow this model.

4.3 How Does the Geography of Health Influence Population Dynamics?

Understanding the nature of a country's population requires much more than simply knowing the total population or the growth rate, densities, distribution, and composition. Also of significance is the welfare of the country's people across regions, ethnicities, or social classes. Among the most important influences on population dynamics are geographical factors. Location—that is, where one lives and works—influences access to health care, availability of clean water and good sanitation, prevalence of diseases, and quality of housing, nutrition, and education. It is important to consider how different groups, from the elderly to the disabled, experience their everyday geographies. For example, the *Guest Field Note* by Nicole Yantzi illustrates how geography affects and is experienced by those with chronic illnesses and disabilities.

INFANT MORTALITY

> **Infant mortality rate (IMR)** A figure that describes the number of babies that die within the first year of their lives in a given population.

One of the leading measures of the condition of a country's population is the **infant mortality rate (IMR)**. Infant mortality records the death of babies during the first year of life. Child mortality records death between ages one and five. Infant mortality is usually given as the number of deaths per thousand for every thousand live births.

Infant and child mortality reflect the overall health of a society. High infant mortality has a variety of causes, the physical health of the mother being a key factor. In societies where most women bear a large number of babies, women also tend to be inadequately nourished, exhausted from overwork, suffering from disease, and poorly educated. Demographers report that many children die because their parents do not know how to cope with the routine childhood problem of diarrhea. This condition, together with malnutrition, is the leading killer of children throughout the world. Poor sanitation is also a threat to infants and children. Estimates are that more than one-fifth of the world's population lacks ready access to clean drinking water or hygienic human waste disposal facilities.

GUEST FIELD NOTE

Measuring Accessibility

Sibley (1995, p. x) states that the role of human geography is to interrogate "the assumptions of inclusion and exclusion which are implicit in the design of places and spaces". As a person who uses a walker, I have experienced the daily challenges of negotiating inaccessible spaces and how this makes me feel. My overall research goal is to take this personal experience and Sibley's challenge and go beyond examining, questioning, and critiquing, and work toward improving the accessibility and inclusiveness of the spaces that children with disabilities must negotiate.

This work involves developing tools to measure the accessibility and inclusiveness of indoor and outdoor school environments for children who use mobility aids such as crutches, walkers, and wheelchairs. My research is based on the premise that the organization and design of spaces conveys messages of belonging or not belonging to people with disabilities. Although people and organizations do not intentionally make design and spatial organization decisions to exclude people with disabilities, these decisions still convey messages of belonging or not belonging. This is clearly shown by research findings based on a tool that measures the accessibility and suitability of school playgrounds. Although important physical, intellectual, and emotional skills are learned on the playground, data collection and analysis provides evidence that many children cannot get into,

S. Wendorf and L. Stevens

FIGURE 4.27 **Typical organization and design of school playgrounds.**

A. Rose

FIGURE 4.28 **Typical organization and design of a stage.**

move around, or play in these spaces. **Figure 4.27** provides an example of a "typical" elementary school playground in which there are often large plastic or perimeter borders with no breaks, soft surfaces such as sand, and very few, if any, play opportunities. In one Ontario school board I found that almost 60 percent of the playgrounds had this type of large perimeter border that would prevent a child with a mobility aid from entering the playground. This definitely conveys a message to a child, even if unintentional, that they do not belong in this space.

The School Accessibility Tool (SAT) © was developed by a colleague and I to examine the accessibility of interior school spaces. Development of this tool required careful consideration of how children are expected to move around their classroom and school on a daily basis. The accessibility of a variety of school spaces including classrooms, washrooms, libraries, and music rooms is assessed. The tool can compare schools, determine which spaces in a school are particularly problematic, and even identify the specific barriers.

This body of work has been expanded to include community play spaces. Since 2008, I have been working with a neighbourhood association, municipal officials, accessibility advisory group, children's service providers, and local children and their families to revitalize Ridgecrest Playground in Sudbury, Ontario. The Ridgecrest Accessible Neighbourhood Association has accessibility as one of its core values. Along with the local health unit I am now conducting interviews and residential questionnaires with children, youth, and adults to explore the expected and unexpected health outcomes of having this type of play and gathering space in a local neighbourhood. The physical and social health benefits are highlighted in a statement by the local councillor in a news release in which she states that "[T]he accessible amenities will mean children of all abilities can play together in a safe and fun venue, which will give them a sense of belonging."

All the research discussed above required going beyond the walls of the university, and seeking out feedback from health and educational professionals, and parents and children in the community. The SAT was revised several times based on

discussions with school therapists, school board staff, and most importantly students who use mobility aids. After using the SAT to examine the accessibility of 18 schools, we conducted a focus group with students with disabilities to ensure that the tool represented their experiences in navigating school spaces. When we asked the students what school space was the most difficult to manage, the unanimous response was the stage. They said that the stage is where students' accomplishments and contributions are recognized. We discovered that the majority of the students had been unable to participate in plays, ceremonies, and ultimately graduation because most of the stages had stair access (see **Figure 4.28**). Our study found that fewer than 20 percent of stages were deemed accessible in one school board. Our discussion with the students resulted in revising the SAT to ensure that it reflected the importance of the stage.

In order to fulfill my research goal of improving the accessibility and inclusiveness of the spaces used by children and their families, it is essential that the research findings are shared with individuals responsible for funding and developing policies to promote accessibility, and also individuals who have daily interactions with children with disabilities. While this step can be very time consuming and challenging, it is an important part of the research process.

Students associate the word "field" in research with images of trekking through the bush, or travelling to another country to collect data. This field note shows that the field can be a school or playground in your local community. Often research is a collaborative process, and involves organizations, service providers, and individuals in the community. The research that I conduct certainly benefits from including these diverse experiences and understandings in all parts of the process.

Dr. Nicole Yantzi, School of Environment, Laurentian University. Photos were taken by research assistants S. Wendorf, L. Stevens, and A. Rose as part of various research projects led by Dr. Yantzi.

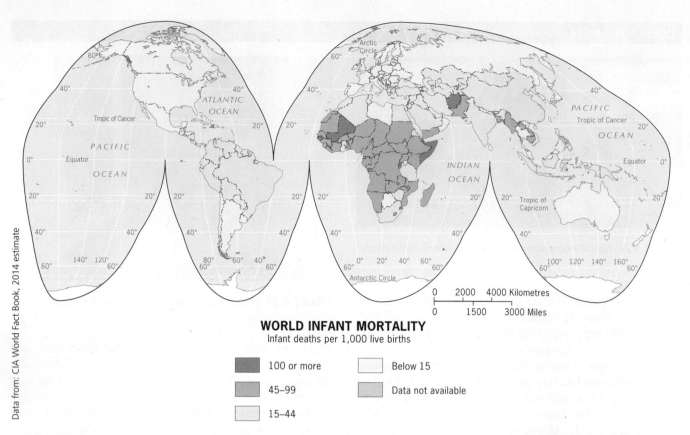

Data from: CIA World Fact Book, 2014 estimate

WORLD INFANT MORTALITY
Infant deaths per 1,000 live births

- 100 or more
- 45–99
- 15–44
- Below 15
- Data not available

FIGURE 4.29 Infant mortality rate, 2008. This map shows infant mortality patterns at five levels ranging from 100 or more per thousand (one death for every eight live births) to fewer than 15.

The map plotting infant mortality rates at the global scale (see **Figure 4.29**) reveals high rates in many poorer countries. Infant mortality patterns are mapped at five levels, ranging from 100 or more per thousand (one death for every eight live births) to fewer than 15. Compare this map to that of the overall crude death rate in Figure 4.24, and the role of infant mortality in societies with high death rates is evident.

The lowest infant mortality rate among larger populations has long been reported by Japan, with 3.0 deaths per thousand live births in a country of over 128 million people. Some less-populated countries show even lower IMRs. Singapore has over 4.5 million people and an incredibly low IMR of fewer than 3.0, and Sweden's nearly 9 million people record an IMR of 2.8. Note how much lower these are than the rates in some of the countries in Africa and East Asia.

Canada's IMR has remained relatively constant in recent years (**Table 4.1**). In 2009, the infant mortality rate was 5.0 deaths per thousand live births. However, in 2010 the CBC reported that in Manitoba, which already has a high IMR, the Aboriginal IMR is more than twice the Canadian average. Researchers suggest that this is due to several factors, including Aboriginal people's location in rural areas, their inadequate access to health care services, and their lack of effective use of these facilities due to language and cultural barriers. Overall, however, infant mortality rates are declining in Canada.

In 2008, 22 countries reported an IMR of 100 or more, and several had rates of 125 or higher—that is, one or more

TABLE 4.1	Canadian Infant Mortality Rates (Both Sexes), by Province and Territory, 2007–2011				
	2007	**2008**	**2009**	**2010**	**2011**
Canada	5.1	5.1	4.9	5.0	4.8
Newfoundland and Labrador	7.5	5.1	6.3	5.3	6.3
Prince Edward Island	5.0	2.0	3.4	3.6	4.2
Nova Scotia	3.3	3.5	3.4	4.6	4.9
New Brunswick	4.3	3.2	5.8	3.4	3.5
Quebec	4.5	4.3	4.4	5.0	4.3
Ontario	5.2	5.3	5.0	5.0	4.6
Manitoba	7.3	6.5	6.3	6.7	7.7
Saskatchewan	5.8	6.2	6.7	5.9	6.7
Alberta	6.0	6.2	5.5	5.9	5.3
British Columbia	4.0	3.7	3.6	3.8	3.8
Yukon	8.5	5.4	7.8	5.2	0.0
Northwest Territories	4.1	9.7	15.5	1.4	7.2
Nunavut	15.1	16.1	14.8	14.5	26.3

The infant mortality rate is calculated as the number of deaths of children less than one year of age per 1,000 live births in the same year. Data from Statistics Canada.

deaths among every eight newborns. Sierra Leone and Afghanistan had the highest IMR: 165. Dreadful as these figures are, they are a substantial improvement over the situation

20 years ago. Globally, infant mortality has been declining, even in the poverty-stricken regions of the world.

Each of these observations about infant mortality rates considers what is happening in an entire country. The IMR varies within countries and provides a lens through which we can see variations in access to health care and health education within a country. The statistic typically varies by region, ethnicity, social class, or other criteria. South Africa's IMR is 48 per thousand, an average of all the people within the country's borders. Using the demographic terminology employed by South Africa, the IMR for South African whites is near the European average; for black Africans it is nearer the African average; and for the Coloured and Asian populations it lies between these two figures. The reported average for South Africa does not tell us about ethnic and class differences within the country.

CHILD MORTALITY

Child mortality rate (CMR)
A figure that describes the number of children who die between the first and fifth years of their lives in a given population.

Infants who survive their first year of life still do not have a long life expectancy in the poorer areas of the world. The **child mortality rate (CMR)**, which records the deaths of children between the ages of one and five, remains staggeringly high in much of Africa and Asia, notably in the protein-deficient tropical and subtropical zones. Kwashiorkor (also known as protein malnutrition), a malady resulting from a lack of protein early in life, afflicts millions of children; marasmus, a condition that results from inadequate protein and insufficient calories, causes the deaths of millions more. In some countries, more than one in five children still die between their first and fifth birthdays, a terrible record in the 21st century. In Canada, the most recent statistics available indicate a CMR that is dropping over time. In 1990, the CMR was 8.0 per thousand live births. In 2011, it was 4.8 per thousand live births. The leading cause of child mortality in Canada is accidents.

The Canadian International Development Agency (CIDA) argues that, at the global scale, child mortality rates can be lowered by providing better access to health care, nutrition, and basic medical treatment. As a result, CIDA plays a leadership role internationally through its Children and Youth Strategy, working to promote immunization, micronutrient supplementation, HIV/AIDS prevention and treatment, and malaria control around the world.

LIFE EXPECTANCY

Another indicator of a society's well-being is provided by calculating the **life expectancy** of its members at birth—the number of years, on average, someone may expect to remain alive. **Figure 4.30** shows the average life expectancies of populations by country and thus

Life expectancy A figure indicating how long, on average, a person may be expected to live. Normally expressed in the context of a particular state.

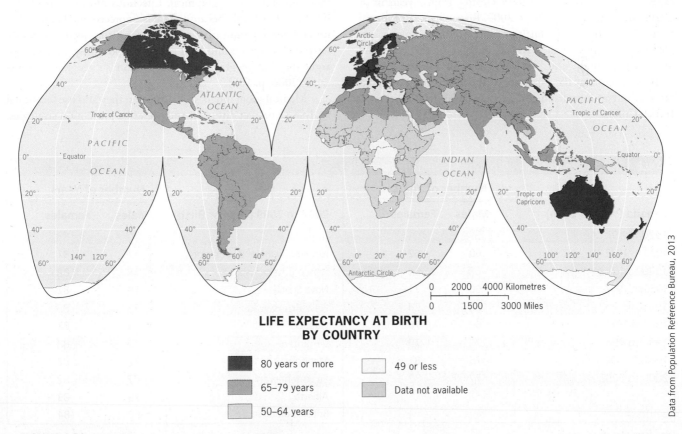

LIFE EXPECTANCY AT BIRTH BY COUNTRY

- 80 years or more
- 65–79 years
- 50–64 years
- 49 or less
- Data not available

FIGURE 4.30 Life expectancy at birth in years, 2013.

Data from Population Reference Bureau, 2013

does not take into account gender differences. In fact, women outlive men by about four years in Europe and East Asia, three years in sub-Saharan Africa, six years in North America, and seven years in South America. In Russia today, the difference is approximately 14 years.

The map does reveal huge regional contrasts. At the start of the century, global average life expectancy was 68 for women and 64 for men. Not only are these levels now exceeded in the wealthy countries of the Western world, but great progress has also been made in East Asia, where Japan's life expectancies are the highest in the world. With its low infant and child mortality rates and low fertility rates, Japan's life expectancy is predicted to rise to 106 by the year 2300. By contrast, the spread of AIDS in sub-Saharan Africa over the past two decades has lowered life expectancies in some countries below 40, a level not seen for centuries. As a result, these countries have the world's lowest life expectancies.

Life expectancies can change in relatively short order. In the former Soviet Union, and especially in Russia, the life expectancies of males dropped precipitously following the collapse of communism, from 68 to 62 years. Today, males in Russia can expect to live only 58 years; female life expectancy also declined, but only slightly, from 74 to 72.

In Canada, life expectancies have risen steadily over the past 100 years. As **Table 4.2** shows, men born in 1920 had a life expectancy of 59, while for females the figure was 61. For people born in 2007, these figures changed to 79 and 83, respectively. It is noteworthy that the gap between men's and women's life expectancy in Canada seems to be closing; from 7 years in the 1970s and 1980s to 4.7 years in 2007. Researchers attribute this to men's focus on health, nutrition, and avoiding smoking, coupled with less stress as men are less likely to be the sole breadwinner in a family unit. Table 4.2 also shows that location matters in terms of life expectancy. The lowest life expectancy rates are in Newfoundland and Labrador, and the highest are in British Columbia.

Life expectancy figures do not mean everyone lives to a certain age. The figure is an average that takes into account the children who die young and the people who survive well beyond the average. The dramatically lower life expectancy figures for the world's poorer countries primarily reflect high infant mortality. A person who has survived childhood may live long past the recorded life expectancy. The low life expectancy figures for countries where malnourishment is common remind us again how difficult life is for children in poorer parts of the world.

GEOGRAPHY'S INFLUENCE ON HEALTH AND WELL-BEING

Health and well-being are closely related to location and environment. People who live in Iceland, where mosquitoes are rare, do not need to worry about contracting malaria unless they travel to parts of the tropics where malaria is prevalent. People who live in close proximity to animals, including livestock, run a greater risk of catching certain diseases than do people who live in cities. When an outbreak of disease occurs on a global scale—for example, H5N1 avian influenza in East Asia, or severe acute respiratory syndrome (SARS)—its source and diffusion are studied by specialists in medical geography, who can reveal the complexity of such outbreaks (**Figure 4.31**). For example, Canadian researchers Roger Keil and S. Harris Ali studied the outbreak of SARS and point to its spread through globalized metropolitan areas, including Toronto. The lessons, they contend, are geographical. Infectious diseases spread rapidly at a global scale because there is unprecedented connectivity between communities and bioregions that were previously separated by oceans and land masses. Importantly, Keil and Ali argue that "the geography of globalization is a geography of disease" (2006, p. 108).

Medical geographers study diseases; they also use locational analysis to predict diffusion and prescribe prevention strategies.

TABLE 4.2 Life Expectancy at Birth, by Sex and Province						
	Number of Years				**Number of Years**	
Canada (Year of Birth)	**Males**	**Females**	**2007 to 2009 (Year of Birth)**	**Males**	**Females**	
1920 to 1922	59	61	Canada	79	83	
1930 to 1932	60	62	Newfoundland and Labrador	77	81	
1940 to 1942	63	66	Prince Edward Island	78	83	
1950 to 1952	66	71	Nova Scotia	78	82	
1960 to 1962	68	74	New Brunswick	78	83	
1970 to 1972	69	76	Quebec	79	83	
1980 to 1982	72	79	Ontario	79	84	
1990 to 1992	75	81	Manitoba	77	82	
2000 to 2002	77	82	Saskatchewan	77	82	
			Alberta	79	83	
			British Columbia	80	84	

Data from Statistics Canada.

England: 6
Ireland: 1
Switzerland: 1
Germany: 6
France: 5
Sweden: 3
Spain: 1
Italy: 3

China: 1512
Hong Kong: 1358
Mongolia: 3
Japan: 4
Taiwan: 29
Australia: 1

Canada: 132
USA: 220

Romania: 1
Kuwait: 1
Brazil: 2
South Africa: 1

India: 1
Thailand: 7
Viet Nam: 63
Singapore: 177
Philippines: 1
Malaysia: 5
Indonesia: 1

*Due to differences in the case definitions being used at a national level, probable cases are reported by all countries except the United States, which is reporting suspect cases under investigation.

SARS: Cumulative Number of Reported Probable* Cases

Total number of cases: 3547 as of April 19, 2003

Country: number of reported cases
■ No Local Transmission
■ Local Transmission

Canadian Environmental Health Atlas

FIGURE 4.31 SARS: Cumulative number of reported cases, 2003.

A medical geographer can answer questions such as: Where is avian flu most likely to diffuse, and according to what timeline, if an outbreak occurs in New York City? If a country receives enough funding to build 25 clinics for people in rural areas, where should these clinics be located to enable the maximum number of patients to reach them? These questions, and their answers, become critical during moments of international crisis. For instance, in the aftermath of the earthquake in Haiti in 2010, the international community paid a great deal of attention to the possibility of disease outbreaks, which could be devastating in the already-precarious circumstances following an earthquake. In late October 2010, approximately 10 months after the earthquake struck, media began to report on an outbreak of cholera in Haiti. How quickly the disease could spread was an immediate concern, particularly in the densely populated camps erected in the capital city of Port-au-Prince. Poor sanitation, the build-up of garbage, lack of fresh water, and widespread poverty were all contributing factors that raised the alarm for aid workers, medical staff, officials, and international agencies working in the region.

Diseases can be grouped into categories to make it easier to understand the risks they pose. About 65 percent of all diseases are known as **infectious diseases**, resulting from an invasion of parasites and their multiplication in the body. Malaria is an infectious disease.

Infectious diseases Diseases that are spread by bacteria, viruses, or parasites. Infectious diseases diffuse directly or indirectly from human to human.

Chronic or degenerative diseases Generally, long-lasting afflictions that are now more common because of higher life expectancies.

The remainder can be divided into **chronic or degenerative diseases**—the maladies of longevity and old age such as heart disease—and **genetic or inherited diseases** we can trace to the chromosomes and genes that define our makeup. Sickle-cell anemia, hemophilia, and lactose intolerance are genetic diseases. These can be of special geographic interest because they tend to appear in certain areas and in particular populations, suggesting the need for specific, local treatment.

Three geographic terms are used to describe the spatial extent of a disease. A disease is **endemic** when it prevails over a small area. A disease is **epidemic** when it spreads over a large region. A **pandemic** disease is global in scope.

Genetic or inherited diseases Diseases caused by variation or mutation of a gene or group of genes in a human.

Endemic When a disease prevails throughout a particular locality or region.

Epidemic Regional outbreak of a disease.

Pandemic An outbreak of a disease that spreads worldwide.

INFECTIOUS DISEASES

Infectious diseases continue to sicken and kill millions of people annually. Malaria, an old tropical disease, still takes more than a million lives annually and infects about 300 million people. HIV/AIDS, an affliction that erupted in Africa only about 30 years ago, has killed about 25 million people since that time. These two maladies illustrate two kinds of infectious disease: vectored and non-vectored.

A vectored infectious disease, such as malaria, is transmitted by an intermediary vector—in the case of malaria, a mosquito.

A mosquito stings an already-infected person or animal, called a host, and sucks up some blood carrying the parasites. These then reproduce and multiply in the mosquito's body and reach its saliva. The next time that mosquito stings someone, some of the parasites are injected into that person's bloodstream. Now that person develops malaria as the parasites multiply in his or her body, and he or she becomes a host.

Mosquitoes are especially effective vectors of infectious diseases ranging from yellow fever (another historic illness) to dengue fever (a newer disease that is spreading quickly). But mosquitoes are only one kind of vector. Fleas, flies, worms, snails, and other vectors transmit such terrible diseases as sleeping sickness, river blindness, guinea worm, elephantiasis, and numerous others. Tropical climates, where biological activity is most intense, are the worst-afflicted areas of the world, but infectious diseases are a global phenomenon.

No disease in human history has taken more lives than malaria, and the battle against this scourge still is not won. On the day you read this, about 3,000 people will die from malaria, the great majority of them in Africa and most of them children. What these numbers do not tell you is that an estimated 3 to 5 million people live lives that are shortened and weakened by malaria infection. If you do not die from malaria as a youngster, you are likely to be incapacitated by it or will struggle with exhaustion arising from chronically severe anemia throughout your life.

Non-vectored infectious diseases, such as influenza, are transmitted by direct contact between host and victim. A kiss, a handshake, or even the slightest brush of physical contact can transmit influenza, a cold, or some other familiar malady. Standing close to another person means that you could breathe in tiny moisture particles in exhaled air that can transmit the disease to you. HIV/AIDS is a non-vectored infectious disease that is transmitted primarily through sexual contact and secondarily through needles shared in intravenous drug use.

As mentioned earlier in this section, the world is experiencing new waves of influenza: H1N1 or "swine flu" in 2009, H5N1 or "avian flu" in 2006 and 2007, SARS in 2003, and MERS (Middle East Respiratory Syndrome) in 2012–2014. Geographers have discussed these diseases in terms of their global scale, noting the incidence of pandemics, which spread quickly around the world. They are diseases of global cities.

CHRONIC AND GENETIC DISEASES

Chronic diseases (also called degenerative diseases) are the afflictions of middle and old age, reflecting higher life expectancies. Heart disease, cancers, and strokes rank as the leading diseases in this category, but pneumonia, diabetes, and liver diseases also take their toll. In Canada 100 years ago, tuberculosis, pneumonia, diarrheal diseases, and heart diseases (in that order) were the chief killers. Today, cancer and heart disease head the list, with cerebrovascular diseases (including strokes) next, and accidents also high on the list (**Table 4.3**). In the early 1900s, tuberculosis and pneumonia caused 20 percent of all deaths; today they cause fewer than 5 percent.

TABLE 4.3 Leading Causes of Death in Canada, 2011			
	Rank	Number	Percent
Total, all causes of death	...	242,074	100.0
Malignant neoplasms [cancers]	1	72,476	29.9
Diseases of the heart	2	47,627	19.7
Cerebrovascular diseases (stroke)	3	13,283	5.5
Chronic lower respiratory diseases	4	11,184	4.6
Accidents (unintentional injuries)	5	10,716	4.4
Diabetes mellitus (diabetes)	6	7,194	3.0
Alzheimer's disease	7	6,356	2.6
Influenza and pneumonia	8	5,728	2.4
Intentional self-harm (suicide)	9	3,728	1.5
Nephritis, nephrotic syndrome and nephrosis (kidney disease)	10	3,294	1.4

Data from Statistics Canada.

The battles against cancer and heart disease are far from won. Recent decades have brought new lifestyles, new pressures, new consumption patterns, and exposure to new chemicals, and we do not know how these will affect our health. In order to distribute adequate food supplies to populations in huge urban areas, we add various kinds of preservatives to foods without knowing exactly how they will affect our health in the long run. We substitute artificial flavouring for sugar and other calorie-rich substances, but some of those substitutes have been proven to be dangerous. Despite all the sugar substitutes, obesity plagues a significant percentage of the Western population, bringing with it heart disease and diabetes. Even treating drinking water with chemicals is a recent development in the scheme of global population change, and we do not know its long-term effects. Future chronic diseases may come from practices we take for granted as normal now.

Genetic diseases are of particular interest to medical geographers because they tend to be transferred from one generation to the next and display clustering that raises questions about environment and long-term adaptation. Prominent among these are metabolic diseases, in which the body is unable to process all elements of the diet. Enzymes play a key role in these diseases. If the body fails to produce enough (or any) of a particular enzyme used in digestion, the result can be serious metabolic malfunction. For example, some people suffer from a malady called primary lactose intolerance: they do not have an adequate supply of one enzyme, or a set of enzymes, needed to break down lactose, a sugar in milk.

AIDS

Low life expectancies in some parts of the world are caused by the ravages of diseases such as **AIDS (acquired immune deficiency syndrome)**, which

AIDS (acquired immune deficiency syndrome) Immune system disease caused by the human immunodeficiency virus (HIV), which over a period of years weakens the capacity of the immune system to fight off infection. Weight loss and weakness set in, and other afflictions such as cancer or pneumonia may hasten an infected person's death.

was identified in Africa in the early 1980s. AIDS took hold in Africa years, perhaps decades, earlier, but its rapid diffusion worldwide began in the 1980s, when it became one of the greatest health catastrophes of the past century. Nowhere has its impact been greater than in Africa itself.

Medical geographers estimate that in 1980, about 200,000 people were infected with HIV (the human immunodeficiency virus, which causes AIDS), all of them Africans. By 2013, according to the United Nations AIDS Program, the number of people infected worldwide exceeded 35.3 million, with 69 percent (23.5 million) of all cases in sub-Saharan Africa. The infection rate has slowed, and some regions are experiencing a downturn, but eastern Europe and central Asia have recently seen a surge in HIV infection.

AIDS is a debilitating disease that weakens the body and reduces its capacity to combat other infections. It is spread through bodily contact that involves the exchange of bodily fluids such as blood or semen. Sexual activity and needles shared among drug users can transmit the virus, but so can blood transfusions. Over a period of years, a person's immune system is impaired, weight loss and weakness set in, and other afflictions, such as cancer or pneumonia, may hasten an infected person's death.

Over the past two decades, the AIDS pandemic has reached virtually all parts of the world, but its full dimensions are unknown. People carrying the HIV virus do not immediately display visible symptoms of the disease; they may carry it for years without being aware of it, and during that period they can unwittingly transmit it to others. In its earliest stages, a blood test is needed to confirm the presence of HIV, but millions go untested. Add to this the social stigma many people attach to this malady, and it is evident that official statistics on AIDS lag far behind the real numbers.

That is true not only in Africa but in other parts of the world as well; both India and China, for example, long denied that AIDS was a serious health threat to their populations. Now China is reporting at least 650,000 cases, and the number in India may well exceed 5 million. Canada reported its first known case of AIDS in 1982, and the Public Health Agency of Canada estimates that 65,000 Canadians are now infected with HIV, an increase of 14 percent since 2005. In Central and South America there are some 2 million cases, but the worst-afflicted geographic realm after Africa is Southeast Asia, with as many as 6 million people affected.

Nowhere is AIDS having the impact it has had on sub-Saharan Africa. In 2011, an estimated 23.5 million people living with HIV resided in sub-Saharan Africa, representing 69 percent of global HIV infections. This includes 23.4 percent of people in Botswana aged 15 to 49; 23.3 percent of the same age group in Lesotho; 26 percent of those in Swaziland; and 17.3 percent of those in South Africa. These are the official data; medical geographers estimate that 20 to 25 percent of the entire population of several tropical African countries is infected. The United Nations AIDS Program reports that more than 1.8 million new HIV infections were reported in sub-Saharan Africa in 2011, down from 2.4 million in 2001—a 25 percent decline in

new infection reporting. Geographer Peter Gould, in his book *The Slow Plague* (1993), calls Africa a "continent in catastrophe," and the demographic statistics support his viewpoint. However, life expectancy rates are improving. In Botswana the life expectancy rate has risen from 34 in 2007 to 47 in 2012; in Swaziland it has risen to 49 in 2012 from 34 in 2007; and in Zimbabwe it has improved from 36 in 2007 to 58 in 2012.

In a continent already ravaged by other diseases, AIDS is the leading cause of death. It is reshaping the population structure of the countries hardest hit by the disease. Demographers look at the projected population pyramids for countries with high rates of infection and see population chimneys, reflecting the major impact AIDS has on the younger population in the country and its future generations (**Figure 4.32**).

Geographers are engaging in fieldwork to understand the human toll of AIDS locally and within families. Geographer Elsbeth Robson, who has studied the impact of AIDS in hard-hit Zimbabwe, found that global processes, such as the diffusion of AIDS and reductions in spending on health care (often mandated by structural adjustment programs), "shape young people's home lives and structure their wider experiences." In sub-Saharan Africa, the number of children

Data from United States Census Bureau, 2005

FIGURE 4.32 Effect of AIDS on the population pyramid for South Africa, predicted 2035. The estimated population of South Africa, male and female, with AIDS and without AIDS.

orphaned when parents die from AIDS is growing rapidly. In 2004, UNICEF reported that between 2001 and 2003, the number of global AIDS orphans (children who have lost a parent to AIDS) rose from 11.5 million to 15 million. As of 2013, this number has reached 17.8 million, and is expected to rise to 25 million by 2015. Approximately 15.1 million, or 85 percent of these children, live in sub-Saharan Africa. As Robson notes in her *Guest Field Note*, in addition to the rising number of AIDS orphans, many young children, especially girls, are taken out of school to serve as caregivers for their relatives with AIDS. In her interviews with young caregivers, she discovered that "more children are becoming young caregivers as households struggle to cope with income and labour losses through illness and mortality."

There are, however, some positives to report. The Global Fund, an organization dedicated to fighting AIDS, tuberculosis, and malaria around the world, reports that new HIV infections have declined steadily over the last decade. In 2013, the world registered 2.3 million new HIV cases, a 33-percent decline from 2001 levels. But these declines are not felt equally around the world. Uganda, once Africa's most afflicted country, has slowed the spread of AIDS through an intensive, government-sponsored campaign of public education and action—notably the distribution of condoms in even the remotest part of the country. In the world's wealthier countries, remedies have been developed that can stave off the effects of AIDS for many years. But African countries cannot afford such luxuries. United Nations calculations suggest that more than $50 billion needs to be spent globally by 2015 to slow AIDS and treat the infected; in 2013, only about $16.8 billion was spent. The impact of AIDS will be felt in African economies and in African demographics for generations to come. HIV/AIDS will constrain African economic development (see Chapter 11) and require world intervention to overcome.

Canadians continue to be involved in the fight against AIDS in Africa. Notably, the Stephen Lewis Foundation, since 2003, has been supporting community-based initiatives in Africa to fight the spread of the disease. The foundation has funded more than 300 projects in 15 countries, providing education, counselling, prevention information, medical care, and community support. On March 7, 2006, on the eve of International Women's Day, Lewis launched the Grandmothers to Grandmothers campaign, which seeks to raise awareness and support in Canada for Africa's grandmothers, who are caring for children orphaned by AIDS. To date, there are over 240 Grandmothers to Grandmothers groups in Canada that have, collectively, raised over $10 million.

GUEST FIELD NOTE

Marich Village, Kenya

This drawing (**Figure 4.33**) was done by a Pokot boy in a remote primary school in northwestern Kenya. He agreed to take part in fieldwork on young carers in sub-Saharan Africa. Early interviews in Zimbabwe highlighted young carers' invisibility—you can't tell who are young carers just by looking at them. Indeed, invisibility is a characteristic of many aspects of the social impacts of HIV/AIDS. This young person drew himself working in the fields and taking care of cattle. The reasons why African young people help with farming and herding are many, but for young caregivers, assisting their sick family members in this way is especially important.

Elsbeth Robson, Keele University, Staffordshire, UK

FIGURE 4.33 Young carers. A young boy depicts himself working in the fields and taking care of cattle.

Elsbeth Robson

MAIN POINTS 4.3 How Does the Geography of Health Influence Population Dynamics?

- Populations are influenced by their geography. Where we live influences many aspects of our quality of life including the type of government we have; our access to health care; the availability of clean water and good sanitation; the prevalence of disease; and the quality of housing, nutrition, and education. All of these affect population composition and dynamics and our individual lives.

- Measures of infant mortality rates, child mortality rates, and life expectancy for particular populations tell us a great deal about the overall health and strength of that population. Location clearly matters, as poorer countries

with fewer health services, a lack of good nutrition, and a high rate of disease suffer high death rates across the population.

- Diseases such as AIDS and malaria not only contribute to high death rates for both children and adults but also have serious social and cultural implications. Adults may be less able to work due to ill health, and may be unable to provide for their families or give adequate care to their children. Children may be orphaned at an early age and may leave school to take up the role of caregiver and provider to the sick and young in their families.

4.4 How Do Governments Affect Population Change?

Over the past century, many of the world's governments have instituted policies designed to influence the overall growth rate of, or ethnic ratios within, their country's population. Certain policies directly affect the birth rate by implementing laws and programs ranging from subsidized abortions to forced sterilization (**Figure 4.34**). Others influence family size through taxation or

Shaughn Butts/Edmonton Journal/The Canadian Press

FIGURE 4.34 Leilani Muir. Leilani Muir is a survivor of Alberta's *Sexual Sterilization Act*. Alberta promoted the forced surgical sterilization of "mental defectives" from 1928 until 1972 (British Columbia's similar policy was continued until 1973). Muir is shown here in 1996 at a news conference after the Alberta government was ordered to pay her $740,780 in compensation.

subvention. These policies fall into three groups: expansive, eugenic, and restrictive.

The former Soviet Union, and China under Mao Zedong, led other communist societies in expansive population policies, which encourage large families and raise the RNI. Ideological, anti-capitalist motives drove those policies, which have now been abandoned. Today, some countries are again pursuing **expansive population policies**, largely because their populations are aging and population growth is declining. The aging population in Europe has moved some countries to institute policies (such as tax incentives and other fiscal measures) that encourage families to have more children.

> **Expansive population policies**
> Government policies that encourage large families and raise the rate of population growth.

Birth rates in Russia plummeted after the 1991 collapse of the Soviet Union. Russia's TFR in 1980 was 2.04; in 2008 it was 1.4, according to the World Bank. Prime Minister Vladimir Putin calls the demographic crisis Russia's greatest current problem. The Russian government offers cash subsidies of $10,000 to women who give birth to a second or third child.

In response to concerns over Russia's aging population, the government of Ulyanovsk province has held a National Day of Conception each September 12 since 2005. In 2007, government and businesses in Ulyanovsk offered people the afternoon off to encourage them to participate. The government planned to award a free car to the proud parents of one of the children born nine months later, on June 12—Russia's National Day. On June 12, 2008, 87 children were born in Ulyanovsk, about four times the average daily birth rate in the province. Russia experienced an increase in TFR in the first half of 2008, but the ability to sustain a high TFR will depend on many factors, including alleviating social problems, stabilizing incomes, and continued government support.

In the past, some governments engaged in **eugenic population policies**, which were designed to favour one racial or cultural sector of the population over others. Nazi Germany was a drastic example of

> **Eugenic population policies**
> Government policies designed to favour one racial or cultural sector over others.

eugenic policies, but other countries have also pursued eugenic strategies, though in more subtle ways. Until the time of the civil rights movement in the 1960s, some observers accused the United States of pursuing social policies tinged with eugenics that worked against the interests of African Americans. Some argue that Japan's nearly homogeneous culture is the result of deliberately eugenic social policies. Eugenic population policies can be practised covertly through discriminatory taxation, biased allocation of resources, and other forms of favouritism.

> **Restrictive population policies** Government policies designed to reduce the rate of natural increase.
>
> **One-child policy** A program established by the Chinese government in 1979 to slow population growth in China. Under the policy, families having more than one child were penalized financially and denied educational opportunities and housing privileges.

Today, the majority of the world's governments seek to reduce the rate of natural increase through various forms of **restrictive population policies**, ranging from toleration of officially unapproved means of birth control to outright prohibition of large families. China's **one-child policy**, instituted after the end of the Maoist period in the 1970s, drastically reduced China's growth rate from one of the world's fastest to one of the developing world's slowest. Under the one-child policy, families having more than one child were penalized financially and denied educational opportunities and housing privileges.

Population growth rates in China fell quickly under the one-child policy. In the 1970s, China's growth rate was 3 percent; in the mid-1980s it was 1.2 percent; today, China's growth rate is 0.7 percent. The main goal of the one-child policy was achieved, but the policy also had several unintended consequences, including an increased abortion rate, an increase in female infanticide, and a high rate of orphaned girls (many of whom were adopted in the United States and Canada).

During the 1990s, under pressure to improve its human rights records, and also realizing its population was quickly becoming gender- and age-imbalanced (**Figure 4.35**), China relaxed its one-child policy. Several caveats allow families to have more than one child. For example, if you live in a rural area and your first child is a girl, you can have a second child, and if both parents of the child are only children, they can have a second child. With these changes, the National Bureau of Statistics of China estimates that the population growth rate in China will climb again over the next 10 years.

The Canadian government attempted to encourage population growth by introducing a "baby bonus" following World War II. Since that time, various provincial initiatives, most recently in Newfoundland and Labrador, have sought to increase birth rates through various incentives. Debates about the effectiveness of such policies are ongoing, and Quebec has been deeply embroiled in these debates. Quebecers historically had big families, thanks to the province's large Roman Catholic population, but Quebec has struggled in the latter half of the 1900s and early 2000s with declining birth rates. In response, the province has taken several pro-natal policy measures. For example, in 1988 Quebec introduced the Allowance for Newborn Children, which paid families up to $8,000 for the birth of a child. Another policy is the subsidized childcare program, which encourages young working couples to have children without having to incur the high costs of daycare. The result of such policies has been positive; birth rates continue to rise annually, and in 2007 the provincial birth rate of 1.65 children per woman exceeded the national average of 1.59. However, these policies are not without criticism. As Queen's University professor Catherine Krull outlines, some feminists see these policies as marginalizing women by objectifying them as simple demographics. Moreover, the $5-a-day daycare policy cannot meet the growing demand, so Quebec's public daycares have some of the longest waiting lists in the country.

LIMITATIONS

Population policies do not operate independently of circumstances that can influence population growth and decline. In the 1980s, for example, the government of Sweden adopted family-friendly policies designed to promote gender equality and boost fertility rates. The programs focused on alleviating much of the cost of having and raising children. Couples who work and have small children receive cash payments, tax incentives, job leaves, and work flexibility that last up to eight years after the birth of a child. The policies led to a mini–baby boom by the early 1990s. When the Swedish economy slowed shortly thereafter, however, so did the birth rate. The children born in 1991 made up a class of 130,000 students in the Swedish education system. But the children born three years later, in 1994, made up a class of only 75,000 students. The government had to build new classrooms for the temporary population boom but then had

FIGURE 4.35 Population pyramids, China: 2010 and 2050.

excess capacity when the boom subsided. Sweden's population policies have helped to produce an RNI that is a little higher than that in many other European countries, but these policies can achieve only so much. With a TFR still well below 2, the Swedish government continues to consider new ways to support families and promote birth rates. One imaginative, but not evidently successful, approach was suggested by a spokeswoman for the Christian Democrat Party, who urged Swedish television to show racier programming at night in hopes of producing a higher birth rate!

MAIN POINTS 4.4 How Do Governments Affect Population Change?

- Governments are often heavily involved in implementing laws and policies designed to influence population change and composition. These can take the form of either incentives or prohibitions to dictate the number of children permitted in a family.

- Approaches to the regulation of population composition include tax incentives, the "baby bonus," state-operated daycare, family planning clinics, and parental leave.

- Governments may also impose limits on the number of children permitted through sterilization programs, family planning, and restrictions on access to education.

- Population regulation is also socially and culturally influenced. In particular, religious beliefs about family, the role of women, and the nature of procreation play a substantial role in government and community decision-making.

SUMMARY

Population geographers are keenly interested in the demographic and locational aspects of populations. They examine population density, distribution, and composition at a variety of scales from the local to the national, regional, and global. Global population density, distribution, and composition tell us a great deal about the health and stability of particular places. The location of a population or group clearly has an impact on that population's health, survival rate, life expectancy, and quality of life.

In the late 1700s, Thomas Malthus sounded the alarm about the rapidly growing population in Great Britain. He feared a massive famine would soon "check" the growing population, bringing widespread suffering. Although the famine in Great Britain did not take place as he predicted, the rapidly growing worldwide population made many others follow Malthus's lead, issuing similar warnings about the population explosion over the next two centuries.

The growth rate of the world population has certainly slowed, but human suffering is not over yet. Dozens of countries still face high death rates. Even in countries where the death rate is low, slowed population growth is often a result of deplorable sanitary and medical conditions, which cause high infant and child mortality; diseases such as AIDS, which ravage the population and orphan the young; or famines, which governments deny and global organizations cannot ameliorate.

Population pyramids illustrate that as wealthier countries worry about supporting their aging populations, poorer countries have problems of their own. A high birth rate in a poor country does not necessarily mean overpopulation. Some of the highest population densities in the world are found in wealthy countries. Even poor countries that have lowered their birth rates and their death rates are constantly negotiating what is morally acceptable to their people and their cultures. Governments worldwide are actively engaged in policies and practices designed to regulate populations in particular ways. There is often considerable disagreement over what policies and approaches should be implemented and for what purpose.

Geography offers much to the study of population. Through geography we can see differences in population problems across space, observe how what happens at one scale affects what goes on at other scales, and learn how different cultures and countries approach population questions.

DISCUSSION AND REVIEW QUESTIONS

1. In an historical context, Europe was known as a region of high population that resulted in mass emigration to the New World. However, the situation today is vastly different. Describe the situation today, its causes, and the impacts it will have on European society. What are specific European countries doing to address the challenges they face?

2. Since the first settlements of the Neolithic, people have been unevenly distributed across the globe. Referring to figures 4.6 and 4.7 discuss the where and why of this distribution. For instance, why is the world's population distributed in four main regions?

3. How has population historically changed in Canada? Referencing any of the demographer's tools (e.g., fertility, mortality rates, population pyramid, demographic transition) discuss the current population situation in Canada.

4. Since the first official cases and recognition of HIV/AIDS in the early 1980s, medical geographers have been involved in fighting the disease. Explain the social and demographic effects of this disease and discuss the contributions of medical geographers.

5. Governments have instituted a variety of policies to directly influence their country's demographics. These policies have varied from the controversial to the benign and have invariably been influenced by social ideology. Discuss some of these policies and, by focusing on specific examples, assess their demographic and social impacts.

GEOGRAPHIC CONCEPTS

ADDITIONAL RESOURCES ON-LINE

Population Growth in the World: www.prb.org

Global AIDS Crisis: www.unaids.org

United Nations Population Fund: www.unfpa.org

Stephen Lewis Foundation: www.stephenlewisfoundation.org

Alberta Sexual Sterilization Act: www.eugenicsarchive.ca

About population transition in Italy: www.learner.org/resources/series85.html#program_descriptions (Click on Video On Demand for "Population Transition in Italy")

Grandmothers to Grandmothers Campaign: www.grandmotherscampaign.org

2010 World Population and Housing Census Program (United Nations): http://unstats.un.org/unsd/demographic/sources/census/2010_PHC/default.htm

CHAPTER
5 MIGRATION

Mobility for a Reason

IN EARLY AUGUST 2010, Canadian newspapers began reporting that MV *Sun Sea*, a ship carrying nearly 500 Sri Lankan refugees, was expected to arrive on the shores of British Columbia within a few days. The ensuing press coverage was conflicting; editorials in Canada's national newspapers, *The Globe and Mail* and the *National Post*, expressed varying positions on who these refugees were and what Canada's response should be. As I read through the barrage of press coverage, I was struck by the loaded language used in these articles. The men, women, and children aboard MV *Sun Sea* were sometimes "migrants," sometimes "refugees," sometimes "terrorists," among other descriptors. This news coverage revealed that the arrival of nearly 500 migrants on Canadian shores calls into question how we understand citizenship, belonging, immigration, the role of the nation-state, border security, and refugees, to name but a few. It also illustrates what geographer Tim Cresswell calls the "brute materialities" of mobility. Mobility and its regulation have very real effects on the racialized, classed, and gendered bodies of those who often risk their lives to immigrate to countries such as Canada. In 2013, Canada Border Services Agency produced a report documenting the ordeal of the Sri Lankan refugees. It described their travel to Bangkok through Singapore and Malaysia, with agents who bribed border officials, before enduring a "horrific" voyage to Canada. For between $20,000 and $35,000 each, the refugees were packed onto a cramped ship, given scant rations of food and water, and abused by the ship's crew. After surviving

(a)

(b)

FIGURE 5.1 "Boat migrants" from Fujian, China. (a) Migrants arrive by boat in Nootka Sound, B.C., August 3,1999. (b) Chinese migrants attend an immigration hearing on August 20, 1999.

this voyage, as of March 2013, only 80 passengers had been accepted as refugees; 82 had their claims rejected, 26 were ordered deported, and other claims were still under review.

Across the world, hundreds of thousands of migrants and refugees have left their homelands on foot or by boat, plane, train, or car for opportunities in other places. Immigrants are sometimes welcomed and sometimes turned away. The Sri Lankans on MV *Sun Sea* are only a recent example of the controversies surrounding migrants in Canada. In another instance, during the summer of 1999, some 600 men, women, and children from Fujian, China, arrived off the coast of British Columbia in four dilapidated boats (**Figure 5.1**). Newspaper and press reports made much of their desperate plight, noting the "boat migrants" had paid human smugglers their life savings for the chance of a new life in Canada. As geographer Alison Mountz notes, their arrival sparked intense debate in Canada about the sovereignty of Canada as a "nation state, manifest in the perception of its ability to police its borders." After spending several years in detention, only 24 individuals received refugee status. Most were deported back to China. While it is difficult to calculate the number of undocumented migrants in Canada, estimates place that number between 50,000 and 250,000. It is important to remember, though, that these numbers are relative. The estimated number of illegal immigrants in the United States is 13 million.

When we think about mobility—the socially produced movements that make up our everyday lives—we often assume it is universal and always positive. In other words, we assume mobility is inherently good and is something to which we all have equal access. As geographers who are concerned with the world around us, though, we must engage with and ask questions about the increased movement of goods, people, information,

and capital at the global, national, regional, and local scales. Who gets to move and who doesn't? How and why do people move? To where are they moving? How are people's movements blocked or impeded? What does it mean to be forced to move? When we begin to ask these questions, it becomes apparent that mobility is a complex issue. Sometimes people have to migrate to avoid persecution or to find work. Sometimes people are not allowed to move and are forced underground.

Mobility is tightly regulated and controlled. Think of the Mexico–United States Barrier (see Chapter 3) or the vast security measures that you have to pass through to enter the United States for a holiday or a shopping trip. We carefully construct "secure" borders using surveillance technologies, walls, fences, border patrols, customs procedures, and so forth. We must also consider the plethora of statutes and legal regulations enacted to manage the movement of immigrants and refugees. In Canada, the primary statute is the *Immigration and Refugee Protection Act* S.C. 2001, c. 27. In the aftermath of the arrival of the Sri Lankan migrants in August 2010, the minority Conservative government introduced a controversial new bill entitled *Preventing Human Smugglers from Abusing Canada's Immigration System Act*, aimed at deterring human smuggling and illegal immigration into Canada. However, the proposed act was harshly criticized by opposition parties—critics claimed that it criminalizes the victims of smugglers—and it was not passed into law. Various international treaties are in place to address trafficking in persons and related conduct, including the *United Nations Convention Against Transnational Organized Crime and the Protocols Thereto*. Both nationally and internationally, governments are working to develop strategies for managing and controlling human smuggling.

KEY QUESTIONS FOR CHAPTER 5

1. What is migration?

2. Why do people migrate?

3. Where do people migrate?

4. How do governments affect migration?

5.1 What Is Migration?

Migration is about human movement, and movement is one of the five themes this book uses to illustrate how we might employ a spatial or geographical perspective in order to better understand

different issues and problems. Movement changes people. It changes how they see themselves and their place in the world. Movement changes places—both the places that people leave and the places in which they settle. Humans bring their own ideas and feelings to their new homes, altering the landscape and building a sense of place and community. Human movement speeds the diffusion of ideas and innovations, intensifies spatial interaction, and transforms regions.

In this chapter, we consider what we mean by "immigration" and we examine various types of migration. We also need to understand why migrants choose to leave a particular place and go to another—the "push" and "pull" aspects of immigration. Some migration is "voluntary"—that is, people migrate to find employment or to be with family. Others are forced to migrate due to war or political or social persecution. As well, government policies shape human migration, so it is important to consider why government immigration policies might change. In our analysis of human migration, we examine the nature and meaning of migration flows and consider why people migrate, where they migrate, and how people, places, and landscapes change as a result.

We cannot understand questions about immigration without considering the processes of globalization, discussed in Chapter 2. Today, we are experiencing increasing integration and interconnectivity among people and places, brought about, in part, by the greater mobility of individuals and groups across state borders, continents, and hemispheres. Globalizing processes seem to be breaking down state borders and challenging the ability of the nation-state to regulate the flows of people and materials, as illustrated in the opening field note. As we discussed in Chapter 3, states are concerned with borders and boundaries and with preserving sovereignty (or control) over what happens within their borders, including who enters into and leaves their territory. Despite the increasing mobility some people might experience through the processes of globalization, states continue to enforce laws that determine who may enter and who may remain within a country's borders. As noted in Chapter 4, in places such as Canada, where the total fertility rate is falling below replacement levels, setting appropriate immigration targets and ensuring we have people with the skills needed in the Canadian workplace is of paramount importance. A properly functioning immigration policy and practice is central to the economic and social well-being of all Canadians.

Migration is about movement, and the movement of humans takes several forms. Mobility ranges from local to global, from daily movements to once-in-a-lifetime relocations. Mobility has increased markedly for some people in some places over the past decades. Those experiencing greater mobility are able to broaden their perspectives, which perhaps encourages further mobility. People are on the move for numerous reasons—fleeing famine and war, seeking greater economic opportunities, moving closer to relatives, or striving for a better education.

FORMS OF MOVEMENT AND MIGRATION

There are a variety of ways in which people move from place to place. For example, the traditional nomadic practices of the world's indigenous peoples are dwindling, but they have been a matter of survival, culture, and tradition—and remain so for nomadic peoples who can still be found in parts of Asia, South and Central America, and Africa. Westerners often envision

nomadism as an aimless wandering across steppe and desert by small groups of rootless roamers, people who claim no

> **Nomadism** Movement among a definite set of places—often cyclic movement.

territory and do not behave territorially. In reality, nomads need to know their territory well in order to find water, food, and shelter in their cyclic movements. Nomadic movement takes place along long-familiar routes followed time and again. The nomads and their animals visit water sources and pastures that have served their ancestors for centuries. Weather conditions may affect the timing of their travel, but barring obstacles such as fenced international borders or the privatization of long-used open country, nomads engage in cyclic movement.

Nomadic people can pose a series of problems for government regulation because they do not fit into the categories of migration outlined below. For example, Roma people, sometimes called gypsies, are a heterogeneous ethnic group that travels through Europe, western Asia, and Latin America. In August 2010, France expelled over 700 Roma people who had set up camps in the country, invoking a policy that required them to have a work permit to prove they could support themselves (**Figure 5.2**). Most were sent to Romania and Bulgaria. France has faced international scrutiny for its dealings with the Roma people; its policies have been called both xenophobic and racist.

When movement results in permanent relocation across significant distances, we call it **migration**. The process of migration involves the long-term

> **Migration** A change in residence intended to be permanent.

relocation of an individual, household, or larger group to a new locale outside the community of origin—movement that is about leaving home for a significant duration, if not permanently. Clearly, this can occur at a variety of scales. We can migrate to a new neighbourhood in the town we grew up in or we can relocate to another country in pursuit of a career or new opportunities.

FIGURE 5.2 France expels Roma people. French police officers escort Roma people to the check-in desk for their departure flights at Roissy Charles de Gaulle Airport, near Paris, August 20, 2010. The French government has come under heavy criticism from human rights groups, who have referred to the expulsions as "disgraceful."

© Michel Euler/The Canadian Press

International migration
Human movement involving movement across international boundaries.

Diaspora From the Greek "to disperse," a term describing forceful or voluntary dispersal of a people from their homeland to a new place. Originally denoting the dispersal of Jews, it is increasingly applied to other population dispersals such as the involuntary relocation of Black peoples during the slave trade or Chinese peoples outside of Mainland China, Taiwan, and Hong Kong.

International migration, or transnational migration, is movement across a country's borders. When people leave their home country, they are classified as emigrants (those who migrate out) of the home country. The term used to describe the migration away from an ancestral homeland by a group of people sharing an ethnic background is **diaspora**. Examples of diasporas include the Irish exiled by the British from their homelands and, perhaps the most well-known example, the Jewish diaspora, when the Israelites were expelled from Israel, Jordan, and parts of Lebanon, beginning in the eighth century BC.

When the same migrants enter a new country, they are classified as immigrants (those who migrate in) to the new country—

Emigration The act of leaving one location or place for another, from the perspective of the beginning location.

Immigration The act of migrating into a new country or area, from the perspective of the destination.

how we are defined depends on where we are. As we discussed in Chapter 4, **emigration** subtracts from the total population of a country, and **immigration** adds to the total population of a country. The United Nations defines international migrants as "persons born in a country other than that in which they live." According to the United Nations, there were approximately 232 million international migrants in the world in 2014—a number that has increased significantly since 1990, when there were 154 million international migrants. Since 2000, migrant stock has grown by about

4.6 million migrants annually; however, since 2010 and the global economic crisis, this number has fallen to 3.6 million. As **Figure 5.3** illustrates, some regions have a much greater migrant population than others. As a percentage of total population, Qatar has the highest percentage of international migrants, at 87 percent, followed by United Arab Emirates (70 percent) and Kuwait (69 percent). In Canada, 21 percent of the total population is composed of international migrants—approximately 7.2 million people.

It is important to remember that international migration is nothing new. During the last major phase of globalization in the late 1800s, the percentage of the world's population that migrated was slightly higher than it is today. There are some important differences, however, between migration today and in the 1800s. Historically, it was very difficult to migrate from one country to another logistically, but once you arrived at your destination, there were relatively few regulatory and/or legal barriers. Today, the opposite is true. While it may be easier to move around the globe with improved transportation and communication technologies, the legal and regulatory frameworks make it much more difficult to settle in a new country than it has been in the past.

Countries also experience **internal migration**—migration that occurs within a single country's borders. Mapping internal migration routes reveals well-defined patterns that change over time. Internal migration varies according to the mobility of the population, which can fluctuate over a country's territory. In mobile societies, internal migration over long distances is common. In less mobile societies than Canada, the pattern of

Internal migration Human movement within a nation-state, such as ongoing westward and southward movements in Canada.

internal migration is often from rural to urban. In Canada, the flow of internal migration is not as simple as rural to urban, although rural to urban migration has been a characteristic of Canada's internal migration for some time. During difficult

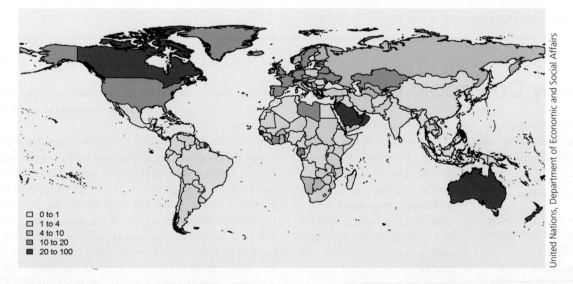

FIGURE 5.3 Migrant stock as a percentage of total population, 2010. This map shows international migrants as a percentage of total population. Countries represented as dark green have the highest concentration of international migrants, at 20 percent or greater. From United Nations, Department of Economic and Social Affairs, Population Division, 2009.

economic times, different regions in Canada experience declining economic conditions, and individuals migrate internally to other parts of the country, often seeking work. For example, after the 1992 cod moratorium, Newfoundland and Labrador experienced 10 years of population decline. While urban centres maintained relatively stable populations, smaller towns and villages—especially those developed around the fishery—experienced losses of up to 18 percent of the total population. Because the population loss was significant and sustained over a long period of time, the province has faced considerable social and economic challenges. However, recent Statistics Canada data reveal that Atlantic Canada has begun to experience a net gain of interprovincial migrants for the first time since 1982/1983. Newfoundland and Labrador, for instance, experienced four consecutive periods of net gains between 2008/2009 and 2011/2012, suggesting that a new pattern might be arising for the province, although it experienced a population decline once again in 2012/2013, as illustrated in **Figure 5.4**.

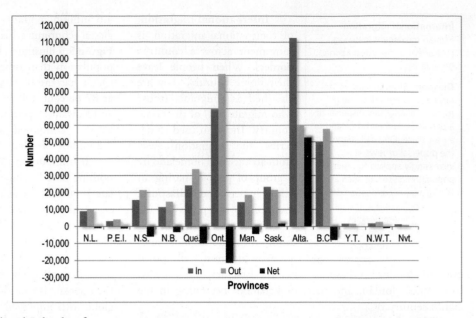

FIGURE 5.4 Canada interprovincial migration by province and territory, 2012/2013. Source: Statistics Canada, Annual Demographic Estimates: Canada, Provinces and Territories. Interprovincial Migration by Province and Territory, 2012/2013, Chart 1.5. Accessed at www.statcan.gc.ca/pub/91-215-x/2013002/ct005-eng.htm.

MAIN POINTS 5.1 What Is Migration?

- Migration is a form of human movement, which can take many forms depending on the nature and permanence of that movement.

- Migration can be international or transnational, meaning the individual crosses a country's borders.

- An emigrant is defined as a person who leaves a place to settle elsewhere, while an immigrant is someone who comes from elsewhere to settle in a place.

- Migration can also be examined on a more local scale. Geographers study population movement within a country's boundaries, such as movement between provinces. They study the movement of people from rural to urban areas or from urban to suburban areas. Finally, they consider movement between neighbourhoods in the same region, city, or town.

5.2 Why Do People Migrate?

Migration can be the result of a voluntary action, a conscious decision to move from one place to the next. It can also be the result of involuntary action, a forced movement imposed

> **Voluntary migration**
> Movement in which people relocate in response to perceived opportunity, not because they are forced to move.
>
> **Forced migration** Human migration flows in which the movers have no choice but to relocate.

by one group of people on another group of people. **Voluntary migration** occurs after a migrant weighs options and choices (even if desperately or not so rationally), and can be analyzed and understood as a series of options or choices that result in movement. **Forced migration**

involves the imposition of authority or power, producing involuntary movement that cannot be understood based on theories of choice.

The distinction between voluntary and forced migration is not always clear-cut. The enormous European migration to North America during the 19th and early 20th centuries is often cited as a prime example of voluntary migration. However, some European migration can be construed as forced. The British treatment of the Irish during their colonial rule over Ireland can be seen as political persecution—a cause for forced migration. During British colonialism in Ireland, the British took control of nearly all the Irish Catholic lands and discouraged the operation of the Catholic Church in Ireland. Until 1829, the British enforced penal laws preventing Irish Catholics from buying land, voting, or carrying weapons. The mass exodus of migrants from Ireland to North America in the mid-1800s can be seen as forced, both because of the British treatment of the Irish and because of the potato famine, but it can also be seen as voluntary in that the Irish chose to go to North America. What is clear is that the notion of "choice" in examples such as this is subject to much debate and controversy.

At the scale of an individual region or country, we can question whether a decision to migrate is forced or voluntary. At the scale of the household, the decision to migrate is all the more complex. For certain members of a migrating household, the move may be under duress, while for others the move may be a preferred choice. The neutral title "migrant" veils the complexities of decision-making at the household scale, including distinctions based on such things as gender or age. At the household scale, geographers consider power relationships, divisions of labour, and gender identities as they attempt to understand migration flows. Here, decisions are made, in geographer Victoria Lawson's terms, in a "cooperative conflict bargaining process." Who has a say in this process and how much of a say each individual has depends on gendered power relationships and responsibilities in the household.

Studies of gender and migration find that, in many regions, men are more mobile than women, and men migrate farther than women. Generally, men have more choices of employment than women, and women earn less than men in the jobs they find at the destination. One study of migration in Mexican households found that strongly patriarchal households shield young women from migration, sending young men out to work. Mexican households without a strong patriarchy send young, unmarried women to the city or another country to gain employment. Geographer Gerry Pratt, in her study of Filipina domestic workers in Vancouver, found that despite their educational credentials, a segregated labour market ensured narrowed occupational possibilities based on assumptions about women's "natural" abilities as caregivers regardless of their level of education.

Geographers cannot easily describe migration flows in terms of men and women or forced and voluntary. Ultimately, the decision or directive to migrate happens to an individual migrant within a household, place, country, region, and world, each of which has its own dynamics. The key difference between voluntary and forced migration, however, is that voluntary migrants have an option (at the very least—where to go or what to do once there); forced migrants do not.

VOLUNTARY MIGRATION

Why do people choose to migrate? Researchers have been intrigued by this question for more than a century. Studies of voluntary migration flows indicate that the intensity of a migration flow varies with such factors as similarities between the source (place of origin) and the destination, the effectiveness of the flow of information from the destination back to the source, and the physical distance between the source and the destination.

Over a century ago, British demographer Ernst Ravenstein sought an answer to the question of why people voluntarily migrate. He studied internal migration in England, and on the basis of his data he proposed several **laws of migration**, many of which are still relevant today, including the following five:

> **Laws of migration** Laws developed by British demographer Ernst Ravenstein that predict the flow of migrants.

1. Every migration flow generates a return or counter-migration.

2. The majority of migrants move a short distance.

3. Migrants who move longer distances tend to choose big-city destinations.

4. Urban residents are less migratory than inhabitants of rural areas.

5. Families are less likely to make international moves than young adults.

Ravenstein also posited an inverse relationship between the volume of migration and the distance between source and destination; that is, the number of migrants to a destination declines as the distance they must travel increases. Ravenstein's ideas were an early articulation of the **gravity model**, which predicts interaction between places based on their population size and the distance between them. The gravity model assumes any form of spatial interaction (such as migration) is directly related to the populations and inversely related to the distance between them—an assumption that had more meaning in an age before airplane travel and the Internet.

> **Gravity model** A mathematical prediction of the interaction of places, the interaction being a function of population size of the respective places and the distance between them.

GUEST WORKERS

Sometimes movement is voluntary but temporary. Many countries in the world seek immigrants to come and work for limited periods of time. For example, after World War II, European countries needed to rebuild their economies and found themselves in need of labourers. Two flows of migration into Western European countries began. The first flow of migrants comprised labourers from poorer European countries, who migrated to European countries that were experiencing solid economic growth. The second flow of **migrant labour** came from outside Europe, as millions of foreign workers emigrated from such North African countries as Algeria, Egypt, Libya, and Sudan. In addition, a large number of migrants came to Germany from Turkey, and many migrants from the Caribbean region, India, and Africa came to the United Kingdom.

> **Migrant labour** A common type of periodic movement involving tens of millions of workers worldwide who cross international borders in search of employment and, in many instances, become immigrants.

> **Guest worker** Legal immigrant who has a work visa, usually short term.

Western European governments called the labour migrants **guest workers**. Guest workers are legal (documented) migrants who have work visas, usually short term, although destination governments will often extend the visas if certain sectors of the economy still need labourers. The international flow of guest workers changes the ethnic, linguistic, and religious mosaic of the places they go, regardless of whether their stay is short or long term. The laws allowing guest workers into Europe assumed the workers were temporary: they would fill the void left by those who died during World War II and would eventually return to their home countries. Instead, the guest workers often stayed—both because they wanted to and because they were needed. Two to three generations of Turks have now been born in Germany, making them far more than "guests." The German government, which for decades defined German citizens as those of German descent, only recently allowed Turks to become German citizens.

> **Remittances** Money migrants send back to family and friends in their home countries, often in cash, forming an important part of the economy in many poorer countries.

In many countries around the world, millions of guest workers live and work far from their home country and send **remittances** back to their families. Guest workers are often employed as agricultural labourers or in service industries (e.g., hotels, restaurants, tourist attractions). The home states of these workers are fully aware that their citizens have visas and are working abroad; in fact, the economies of many poorer countries in the Caribbean, Africa, Central and South America, and Eurasia depend in part on remittances sent to their citizens. Haitian immigrants living in the United States, Canada, and the Caribbean, for example, sent home nearly $21 billion in remittances in 2012, a figure equivalent to one fifth of Haiti's gross domestic product and far outpacing the value of Haitian exports. The 2001 census in Haiti estimates that one in five households in Haiti receives remittances from abroad. In 2007, Mexican immigrants sent $24 billion in remittances home, up from $23 billion the year before. In 2010, at the global scale, estimates indicate that approximately $440 billion in remittances are sent around the world. The actual amount, including unrecorded flows through formal and informal channels, is believed to be significantly larger. The top recipient countries of remittances in 2010 were India, China, Mexico, the Philippines, and France.

Home governments work with destination countries and with international labour organizations to protect the rights of the guest workers. However, despite the legal status of guest workers, and despite the efforts of governments and international organizations to protect them, many employers abuse them with impunity because guest workers are often unaware of their rights. Long hours and low pay are common, but guest workers continue to work because the money is better than they would ordinarily receive and because they are supporting families at home.

In Canada, seasonal agricultural workers are granted admission to enter Canada to fill labour shortages in the agricultural

Patti Gower/The Globe and Mail/The Canadian Press

FIGURE 5.5 Migrant farm workers, near Simcoe, Ontario. These workers toil for long hours for minimum wage. Under CSAWP, workers' flights to and from their home country are paid for, as is their accommodation. All other expenses, including food, must be paid for by the workers. Still, their remittances go a long way toward supporting their families.

sector during peak periods, mainly in southern Ontario and central British Columbia (**Figure 5.5**). The Canadian Seasonal Agricultural Worker Program (CSAWP) is run jointly by the Canadian government, under the *Immigration and Refugee Protection Act,* with the governments of Mexico and participating Caribbean states. According to the North-South Institute, in 2004 there were 10,777 seasonal workers from Mexico and 8,110 from various Caribbean states working in Canada's agricultural industries. In 2012, there were 29,025 temporary foreign workers in Canada under the CSAWP initiative. CSAWP is not without controversy and criticism, mostly focused on the working conditions: seasonal agricultural workers labour 60 to 70 hours a week for minimum wage—conditions that most Canadians will not accept. It is also precarious work, with workers reliant on their employers for transportation, housing, and regular payment of wages. In November 2010, the CBC reported on a small group of Mexican agricultural workers in Simcoe, Ontario, who were stranded when their employer left the country without paying their wages. Owed thousands of dollars, the Mexicans were awaiting support from the Mexican consulate to fly them home. This case makes evident the extent to which guest workers rely on their employers for fair and equitable employment standards. It also shows how easily their situations can become dire when employers do not live up to their agreements.

FORCED MIGRATION

The largest and most devastating forced migration in the history of humanity was the Atlantic slave trade, which carried tens of millions of Africans from their homes to South America, the Caribbean, and North America, with huge loss of life. The number of Africans sold into slavery will never be known (estimates range from 12 million to 30 million). As **Figure 5.6** shows, a considerable majority of Africans forced across the

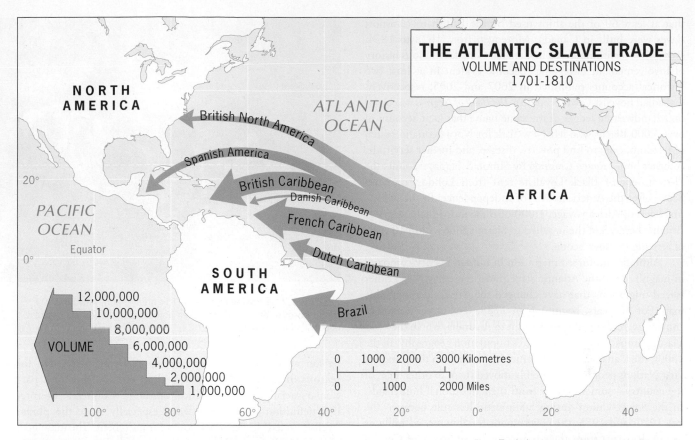

FIGURE 5.6 The Atlantic slave trade. Adapted with permission from Philip D. Curtin, *The Atlantic Slave Trade* (University of Wisconsin Press, 1969), p. 57; and Donald K. Fellows, *Geography* (John Wiley & Sons, Inc., 1967), p. 121.

Atlantic went to the Caribbean, Spanish Central America, and Brazil, a Portuguese colony until 1822. In North America, the destination was more often coastal Middle America (especially Maryland and Virginia) rather than the Deep South.

The Atlantic slave trade began during the 16th century, when Africans were first brought to the Caribbean. In the early decades of the 17th century, they were brought in small numbers to plantations developing in coastal eastern North America. Plantation economies, from the southeastern United States to Brazil, helped drive the slave trade. Plantation work, both planting and harvesting, was labour-intensive, and plantation owners realized their wealth through the exploitation of slave labour. Of all crops produced on plantations in the Americas and Caribbean during the 1700s, sugar was the most important economically, followed by coffee and fruit. The wealth promised by plantation agriculture created a demand for slaves by plantation owners, who paid European shippers for slaves. The shippers, in turn, paid African raiders.

The terror and destruction of slave raiding afflicted large areas of Africa. Much of West Africa, from Liberia to Nigeria and inland to the margins of the Sahara, was exploited. So many Africans were taken to Bahia, in Brazil, from the area that is now Benin that significant elements of the local culture remained intact in the transition. Today there are strong ties between Bahia and Benin, and cultural exchanges are growing stronger. The entire Equatorial African coastal region was victimized as

well, and Portuguese slave traders raided freely in the Portuguese domains of Angola and Mozambique. Arab slave raiders were active in East Africa and the Horn, penetrating Equatorial Africa and often co-operating with the Europeans. Zanzibar, off the coast of mainland Tanzania, was long a major slave market.

We know proportionately where slaves were ultimately relocated, but we can never gauge the full impact of this horrific period. In *A Colonizer's Model of the World*, geographer James Blaut discusses the loss to African civilizations that occurred when significant populations were enslaved. The Atlantic slave trade also changed the Caribbean, where on many islands the vast majority of people are of African-Caribbean descent, and few, if any, indigenous peoples remain. In combination, the slave trade inflicted incalculable damage on African societies and communities, and changed the cultural and ethnic geography of Brazil, Central America, and the United States.

Canada's role in the history of slavery is most often connected to the Underground Railroad, which in the mid-1800s was a series of secret routes and safe houses used to help Black slaves escape to Canada, where slavery had been abolished. Estimates indicate that between 30,000 and 100,000 American slaves came secretly to Canada from 1840 to 1860, settling mostly in a triangle between Toronto, Niagara Falls, and Windsor, Ontario. However, Canada played an important role in the Atlantic slave trade as a colony of both France and Britain, two of the world's largest traffickers of slaves. Research has shown that at least 60 of the ships used by the British to transport slaves were built in Canada. Moreover, from 1628 to 1834, slavery was institutionalized in Canada. Canada's dubious history of involvement in slavery has become evident in at least two historical accounts published in 2007 and 2005, respectively. Canadian novelist Lawrence Hill's *The Book of Negroes* was based on a handwritten ledger of the same name that kept account of over 3,000 Blacks who left New York for Nova Scotia in search of freedom, only to find poverty, disease, and further servitude. Another book, *Rough Crossings* by Simon Schama, recounts the ill-treatment of Black Loyalists sent from London to Nova Scotia after the American War of Independence. In the world's first back-to-Africa voyage, 1,000 of these individuals, angry at Britain's betrayal of them, sailed to Sierra Leone within 10 years of arriving in Nova Scotia.

Although no forced migration in human history compares in magnitude to the Atlantic slave trade, there have been other forced migrations that have changed the world's demographic map. For 50 years, beginning in 1788, tens of thousands of convicts were shipped from Britain to Australia, where they had a lasting impact on the continent's population geography. In the 1800s, the Canadian government took lands from thousands of First Nations peoples and forcibly moved them to other areas of the country—sometimes far from their traditional homelands. In the Soviet Union during Stalin's ruthless rule between the late 1920s and 1953, the government forcibly moved millions of non-Russians from their homes to remote parts of Central Asia and Siberia for political reasons. Forced migration still happens today, often in the form of counter-migration, where governments return migrants caught entering their countries illegally. As noted in the opening field note, Canada deported most of the 600 Chinese "boat immigrants" who landed illegally on the west coast in the summer of 1999.

REFUGEES

Over the last decade or so, television, radio, and print media have documented the thousands upon thousands of people fleeing a crisis in their home region or country by walking. They put their few earthly possessions and their babies on their backs and walk. They walk to another town. They walk beyond their country's border. They walk to a refugee camp without adequate food, water, or amenities. International agencies attempt desperate relief efforts while disease spreads, dooming infants and children, and emaciating adults. For example, when the former Yugoslavia, composed of a federation of six republics, began to disintegrate in 1991, more than 2.3 million people fled their homelands for other nations such as Germany, Hungary, Austria, and Sweden, leading to the largest refugee crisis in Europe since World War II (**Figure 5.7**).

The world's refugee population has grown steadily since the 1951 establishment of the United Nations' *Convention Relating to the Status of Refugees*, an international law specifying who are **refugees** and what legal rights they have. The convention defines a refugee as "a

> **Refugees** People who have fled their country because of political persecution and seek asylum in another country.

FIGURE 5.7 Yugoslav refugees. This photograph, taken in 1999, shows Kosovar refugees fleeing their homeland in the former Yugoslav Republic of Macedonia.

person who has a well-founded fear of being persecuted for reasons of race, religion, nationality, membership of a particular social group, or political opinion." Countries interpret this definition in different ways, especially since the phrase "well-founded" leaves much room for judgment. The main goal of the 1951 Refugee Convention was to help European refugees following the end of World War II. The United Nations High Commissioner for Refugees (UNHCR) helped to repatriate (return to their homeland) most of the refugees from World War II.

In 1970, the United Nations reported 2.9 million persons were refugees; the majority were Palestinian Arabs dislocated by the creation of the state of Israel and the armed conflicts that followed. In 1980, the refugee total had nearly tripled, to over 8 million. In 2013, the UNHCR reported 11.7 million refugees (not counting Palestinian refugees in Jordan and Syria) forced from their homes and across country borders. While there are approximately 16.7 million refugees worldwide in 2013, this is lower than it has been historically. Refugee numbers peaked in the early 1990s, with people trying to escape wars in the former Yugoslavia and Afghanistan. At that time, there were 20 million refugees worldwide.

The UNHCR is the agency that monitors the refugee problem and is the key organization supporting refugees. It organizes and funds international relief efforts and negotiates with governments and regimes on behalf of refugees. But UNHCR is not alone in tracking this global problem; other agencies often contradict UNHCR data, arguing that the situation, especially for **internally displaced persons** (called **IDPs** or internal refugees) is even worse than the United Nations suggests. The United Nations and international law distinguish between refugees, who have crossed one or more

> **Internally displaced persons (IDPs)** People who have been displaced within their own countries and who do not cross international borders as they flee.

international borders during their move and encamped in a country other than their own, and IDPs, who abandon their homes but remain in their own countries (such as the victims of Hurricane Katrina). IDPs tend to remain undercounted, if not almost invisible. In 2013, UNHCR estimated that 33.3 million people (in addition to the 16.7 million official refugees) were IDPs.

Because the status of a refugee is internationally defined and recognized and comes with legal rights, the UNHCR and

> **Asylum** Shelter and protection in one state for refugees from another state.

nation-states distinguish between people who are refugees and those migrants who may be just as poor or desperate but who do not qualify for refugee status. When a refugee meets the official criteria, he or she becomes eligible for assistance, including possible **asylum** (the right to protection in the first country in which the refugee arrives), to which other migrants are not entitled. Such assistance can extend over decades and become the very basis for a way of life, as has happened in the Middle East. In Jordan, Palestinian refugees have become so integrated into the host country's national life that they are regarded as permanent refugees; in Lebanon, however, Palestinians wait in refugee camps for resettlement and still qualify as temporary refugees. In 2013, UNHCR reported 1.2 million asylum seekers.

The United Nations helps ensure that refugees and IDPs are not forcibly returned to a homeland where persecution continues. Once the violence subsides and the conditions improve, the UNHCR helps

> **Repatriation** The process of returning a refugee or group of refugees to their home country, usually with the assistance of a government or a non-governmental organization.
>
> **Genocide** The deliberate and systematic destruction, in whole or in part, of an ethnic, racial, religious, or national group.

return refugees to their homelands, a process called **repatriation**. In the 1990s, hostilities broke out between the Hutu and Tutsi ethnic groups in Rwanda that led to the **genocide** of hundreds of thousands of people and a disastrous exodus of more than 2 million refugees, who fled to neighbouring Democratic Republic of Congo (then called Zaire), Tanzania, and Uganda. The Tutsi-Hutu strife in Rwanda spread to neighbouring Burundi and dislocated tens of thousands there. After the civil war in Rwanda in 1996, the UNHCR and the World Health Organization watched and helped as 500,000 Rwandans returned from nearby nations, including the Democratic Republic of Congo and Uganda (**Figure 5.8**).

PUSH AND PULL FACTORS INFLUENCING MIGRATION

Although Ravenstein's gravity model gives us a guide to expected migration, migration is clearly not as simple as a mathematical equation. When a person, family, or group of people makes a voluntary decision to migrate, push and pull factors come into play. **Push factors** are the conditions and perceptions that help

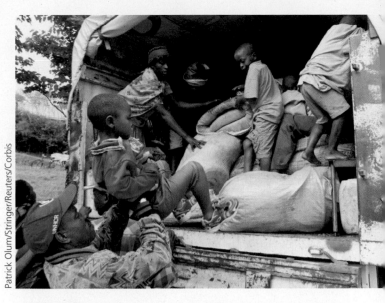

FIGURE 5.8 Rwandans return home. A UNHCR official helps a Rwandan child board a truck at Nakivale refugee camp in western Uganda, January 19, 2004, as a first group of 242 Rwandan refugees, mostly children born after the 1994 genocide, began returning home.

the migrant decide to leave a place. **Pull factors** are the circumstances that effectively attract the migrant to certain locales from other places—the decision about where to go. Migrants' decisions to emigrate from their home country and migrate to a new country

> **Push factors** Negative conditions and perceptions that induce people to leave their abode and migrate to a new locale.
>
> **Pull factors** Positive conditions and perceptions that effectively attract people to new locales from other areas.

are the result of a combination of push and pull factors, and these factors play out differently depending on the circumstance and scale of the migration. Because migrants are likely to be more familiar with their place of residence (source) than with the locale to which they are moving (destination), they will likely perceive push factors more accurately than pull factors. Push factors include individual considerations such as work or retirement conditions, cost of living, personal safety and security, and, for many, environmental catastrophes or even issues such as weather and climate. Pull factors tend to be more vague and may depend solely on perceptions based on things heard and read rather than on personal experiences in the destination place. For example, often migrants move on the basis of excessively positive images and expectations regarding their destinations.

Many migration streams that appear on maps as long, unbroken routes in fact consist of a series of stages, a phenomenon known as **step migration**. A peasant family in rural Brazil, for example, is likely to move first to a village, then to a nearby town, later to a city, and finally to a metropolis such as São Paulo or Rio de Janeiro. At each stage, a new set of pull factors comes into play.

> **Step migration** Migration to a distant destination that occurs in stages; for example, from farm to nearby village and later to town and city.

Not all migrants from one place follow the same steps. For example, when 1,000 people leave a village and migrate to a town in a given year, most, if not all, of them may dream of making it to—and in—the "big city." But perhaps only 500 people actually move from town to city, and of these, only, say, 200 eventually reach the metropolis that impelled them to move in the first place. Along the way, the majority are captured by **intervening opportunity**. In Canada, for example, many migrants from Atlantic Canada make their way westward by way of Montreal and Toronto. While many continue their journey, others find an intervening opportunity in these cities and do not carry on to their original destination. In other cases, intervening obstacles, such as high transportation costs, can dissuade migrants from journeying beyond a particular location.

> **Intervening opportunity** The presence of a nearer opportunity that greatly diminishes the attractiveness of sites farther away.

OTHER FACTORS INFLUENCING MIGRATION

Whether people are forced to migrate or choose to move, there are various factors that shape their possibilities and experiences of mobility. What specific factors prompt people to pull up stakes and leave the familiar for the uncertain? What specific factors help migrants choose a destination? Research has shown that typically a combination of factors, not just one, leads to a decision that it is time to move and a particular decision about where to go. Any single factor can be either a push for the migrant to leave the home country or a pull to the new country, and which factor matters most depends on the migrant and the circumstances surrounding the decision to migrate.

LEGAL STATUS

Migrants can arrive in a country with the consent of the host country (i.e., legally) or without that consent (illegally). All countries establish rules to determine who is allowed to migrate to their country and under what circumstances. If you have a work visa from another country, you are legally allowed to live in the country and work there for the time allotted on the visa (usually a period of months or years). Having a visa makes you a legal migrant because you have your documents, your visa, to show your legal right to be in the place. If you do not have a visa, you are an illegal, or undocumented, migrant in the country. Undocumented or illegal migrants choose very different options for finding their way into the country than legal migrants do, simply because they do not want to be caught for fear of **deportation** (being sent back home).

> **Deportation** The act of a government sending a migrant out of its country and back to the migrant's home country.

ECONOMIC CONDITIONS

Poverty has driven countless millions from their homelands and continues to do so. Perceived opportunities in places such as Western Europe and North America prompt numerous migrants, both legal and illegal, to cross the Atlantic, the Mediterranean, the Caribbean, and the Rio Grande in search of a better life. The reduced economic status of migrants in their host countries can lead to exploitation by employers and others. The United Nations' *Convention on the Protection of the Rights of All Migrant Workers and Members of Their Families* recognizes the precarious position of migrant workers—their need for work and their desire to not be deported. The convention establishes standards of treatment for migrant workers. Although only 47 states have signed on to the convention, its statements on human trafficking and the right of migrant workers to equal wages have some influence on non-signatories' migration policies. Although migrant workers are essential to the economies of southern Ontario and central British Columbia, Canada is not a signatory, nor is any other migrant-receiving state in Western Europe or North America.

CULTURAL FACTORS

Gender, ethnicity, race, and other cultural characteristics are all factors influencing the decision to migrate. The power relationships already embedded in society enable the flow of migrants around the world for the benefit of some and to the detriment of others. Employers who hire migrant workers often have perceptions of what kinds of migrants would best work for them.

Women in the Middle East hire Southeast Asian women to work as domestic servants, housekeepers, and nannies. Geographer Paul Boyle points out that by hiring women from abroad, the female head of the household establishes a relationship in which the employee's "ethnicity and citizenship status differentiates them from their female employer and this influences the power relationships that underpin the working arrangements." In their study of placement agencies that help people hire domestic workers, Stiell and England found that certain ethnicities were portrayed according to a scripted stereotype. For instance, workers from the Caribbean went from being portrayed as "docile, jolly and good with children" to being depicted as "difficult, aggressive and selfish"; women from the Philippines are in demand now as they are being portrayed as "'naturally' docile, subservient, hard-working, good natured, domesticated, and willing to endure long hours of housework and child-care with little complaint."

Race is also a factor in the hiring of migrant workers. For example, carpet companies in Dalton, Georgia (the carpet capital of the world), began hiring Mexican workers after the 1986 passage of the *Immigration Reform and Control Act* (IRCA) because they saw them as hard workers who were loyal to one company. Issues of race and migrant status in hiring can spill over into neighbourhoods, as they have recently in Raleigh, North Carolina, where in the last 10 years conflicts over available affordable housing have arisen between the African Americans who have lived in the neighbourhoods for years and Mexican migrants who have recently moved in.

As well, people who fear that their culture and traditions will not survive a major political transition, and who are able to migrate to places they perceive as safer, will often do so. When British India was partitioned into a mainly Hindu India and an almost exclusively Muslim Pakistan, millions of Muslim residents of India migrated across the border to the new Islamic state, and millions of Hindus migrated from what became Muslim Pakistan to secular India. Similarly, in the 1990s, after decades of Soviet obstruction, more than 2 million Jews left the former Soviet Union for Israel and other destinations. And turbulent political conditions in South Africa during the mid-1990s impelled many whites to emigrate to Australia, Europe, and North America.

POLITICAL CIRCUMSTANCES AND ARMED CONFLICT

Throughout history, oppressive regimes have engendered migration streams. Desperate migrants fled Vietnam by the hundreds of thousands after the communists took control of the country in 1975. In 1972, Uganda's dictator, Idi Amin, expelled 50,000 Asians and Ugandans of Asian descent from the country. The Cuban communist dictatorship expelled more than 125,000 Cubans in 1980 in the "Mariel Boatlift."

Politically driven migration flows are marked by both escape as well as expulsion. The dreadful conflict that engulfed the former Yugoslavia during the 1990s drove as many as 3 million people from their homes, mostly into Western Europe. Many people became permanent emigrants, unable to return home. As mentioned earlier, during the mid-1990s a civil war engulfed Rwanda in Equatorial Africa, pitting militant Hutus against the minority Tutsis and "moderate" Hutus. The carnage claimed an estimated 800,000 to 1 million lives and produced huge migration flows into neighbouring Democratic Republic of Congo (then called Zaire), Uganda, and Tanzania (see Figure 5.8). More than 2 million Rwandans fled their homeland. Canadian Roméo Dallaire, who was commander of the United Nations Assistance Mission for Rwanda in 1994, has become well known for speaking out against the atrocities that took place in that country. His book *Shake Hands With the Devil: The Failure of Humanity in Rwanda* won the Governor General's Literary Award for Non-Fiction in 2004 and was turned into a feature film in 2007 (**Figure 5.9**).

ENVIRONMENTAL CONDITIONS

A major example of migration induced by environmental conditions is the movement of hundreds of thousands of Irish citizens from Ireland to North America during the 1840s. The potato blight destroyed the potato crop, creating famine. The famine was exacerbated by a set of political conditions for which the British government has recently apologized—a reminder that environmental conditions rarely operate in a social vacuum. This migration with an environmental component permanently altered the demographics of both Ireland (the source) and the northeastern region of the United States (the chief destination).

Some environmental crises, such as volcanic eruptions, bring long-term environmental changes to the landscape, making return migration difficult, if not impossible. For example, the Caribbean island of Montserrat had a small population of about 10,000 prior to a volcanic eruption that began in 1995. The volcano has been active since then, prompting a migration flow

Printed by permission of Random House Canada

FIGURE 5.9 Peacekeepers in conflicts. Roméo Dallaire's book, published on the 10th anniversary of the date that UN peacekeepers landed in Rwanda, chronicles his experiences as leader of the UN mission, having witnessed the slaughter of 800,000 Rwandans in 100 days.

(**Figure 5.10**). Over 7,000 people have migrated off the island. The remaining 3,000 migrated to the northern coast of the island, where the effects of the volcano are less serious; however, the soils are thin, the land is rocky, and making a living is difficult.

Jason Dittmer

FIGURE 5.10 Montserrat. This photo shows the damage caused by the 1995 eruption of the Soufrière Hills volcano on the Caribbean island of Montserrat. Many Montserratians fled to the United States when the capital city, Plymouth, was destroyed, and they were given "temporary protected" immigration status. In 2005, the U.S. government told Montserratian refugees to leave—not because the volcanic crisis was over but because the U.S. government expected the crisis to last at least 10 more years, so the Montserratians no longer qualified as "temporary" refugees.

TECHNOLOGICAL ADVANCES

For some migrants, emigration is no longer the difficult and hazardous journey it used to be. Although most migrants still move by simple and even difficult means, some use modern forms of transportation and communication, the availability of which can itself encourage migration.

Gone is the time when would-be emigrants waited months, or even years, for information about distant places. News today travels faster than ever, including news of job opportunities and ways to reach desired destinations. The Internet, television, radio, and cellphones stimulate the migration of millions of people by relaying information about their relatives, opportunities, and already established communities in destination lands. Advances in communication technology strengthen the role of **kinship links** as push or pull factors. When deciding where to go, a migrant is often pulled to places where family and friends have already found success. Thus, Turks quickly heard about Germany's need for immigrant labour. Algerians knew where the most favourable destinations were in

> **Kinship links** Types of push or pull factors that influence a migrant's decision to go where family or friends have already found success.

France. Haitians knew that a "Little Haiti" had sprung up in the Miami area.

When migrants move along and through kinship links, they create what geographers call **chain migration**. Chain migration occurs when the migrant chooses a destination and writes, calls, or communicates through others to tell family and friends at home about the new place. The migrant may help create a positive perception of the destination for family and friends, and may promise help with migration by providing housing and assistance obtaining a job. Reassuring family and friends that a new community has been formed, a place where they can feel at home, encourages further migration along the same chain. Chains of migration built upon each other create **immigration waves**—swells in migration from one source to the same destination.

> **Chain migration** Pattern of migration that develops when migrants move along and through kinship links (i.e., one migrant settles in a place and then writes, calls, or communicates through others to describe this place to family and friends, who in turn migrate there).
>
> **Immigration wave** Phenomenon whereby different patterns of chain migration build on one another to create a swell in migration from one origin to the same destination.

MAIN POINTS 5.2 Why Do People Migrate?

- Migration may be voluntary or forced. Sometimes people choose to leave their home for economic or social reasons, including better employment opportunities or reunion with family members. In other circumstances, individuals are forced to leave due to war, intimidation, or brute force, as in the case of slavery.

- Migrants can be guest workers, refugees, or internally displaced persons.

- In the case of voluntary migration, Ernst Ravenstein developed laws of migration some 100 years ago that are still relevant today. His work marks an early formulation of the gravity model, which predicts interactions between places based on population size and distance.

- Push and pull factors, including legal status, economic conditions, cultural factors, political circumstances, armed conflict and civil war, environmental conditions, and technological advances, are useful to consider when analyzing the migration choices made by different groups.

- Migrants tend to move along migration chains that are linked to kinship and that may build to create immigration waves from one place to another. The location and composition (age, gender, and ethnicity) of these waves change over time and have an impact not only on the point of departure but on the place of relocation as well.

5.3 Where Do People Migrate?

It is tempting to reduce the flow of migration to simple economics—a chance for a job in another place trumps the lack of a job at home. However, migration is much more complicated. As we have discussed, migration depends on various push and pull factors, ranging from persecution in civil war to environmental disaster, from disempowerment in the home to discrimination in the country. Each migration flow is

helped or hampered by existing networks and governmental actions.

In this section, we examine where people migrate—that is, what destinations they choose. At the global, regional, and national scales, we can see several major migration flows over the past 500 years, flows where hundreds of thousands of people migrated along the same general path. We will focus on the "where," on the destinations in these major migration flows. A large movement of migrants changes places—both the place the migrants leave and the destination. As we discuss migration flows at the global, regional, and national scales, remember that these flows give only an overview of migration. At the local and household scales, each individual or family migration requires life-altering decisions, and those decisions foster global change.

GLOBAL MIGRATION FLOWS

In 2013, the United Nations Population Division estimated there were some 232 million international migrants, about 3.2 percent of the world's total population. Before 1500, long-distance global-scale migration occurred haphazardly, typically in pursuit of spices, fame, or exploration. To put exploration in perspective, we need to remember that a complete map of the world's continents did not exist until the early 1800s. European explorers, who included surveyors and cartographers, played a major role in finally mapping the world. On the heels of exploration came European colonization—a physical process whereby the colonizing country takes over another place, putting its own government in charge and either moving its own people into the place or bringing in indentured outsiders to gain control of the people and the land. From the 1500s to the 1800s, Europeans colonized the Americas, the coasts of Africa, and parts of Asia. Then they colonized interior Africa and Asia, starting in the late 1800s and continuing into the 1900s. Between 1846 and 1939, some 59 million people travelled from Europe to North America, Australia, South Africa, and New Zealand.

The past five centuries have witnessed human migration on an unprecedented scale, much of it generated by European colonization. Among the greatest human migrations in recent centuries was the flow from Europe to the Americas. Emigration from Europe (routes 1 and 2 in **Figure 5.11**) began slowly. Before the 1830s, perhaps 2.75 million Europeans left to settle overseas. The British went to North America, Australia, New Zealand, and South Africa (3). From Spain and Portugal, many hundreds of thousands of Europeans emigrated to Central and South America. Early European colonial settlements grew, even in coastal areas of present-day Angola, Kenya, and Indonesia. The rate of European emigration increased sharply between 1835 and 1935, with perhaps as many as 75 million people departing for colonies in Africa and Asia and for economic opportunities in the Americas. Although millions of Europeans eventually returned to their homelands, the net outflow from Europe was enormous, as evidenced by the sheer number of Canadians and Americans who identify themselves as being of European ancestry. As already discussed, the Americas were the destination of another mass of immigrants: African slaves (4). Although this is mapped as just one of the eight major migrations, its immense and lasting impact on both sides of the Atlantic sets it apart from all the others.

Even as the Atlantic slave trade was in progress, the European impact was generating other major migrations as well. The British, who took control of South Asia, transported tens of thousands of "indentured" workers from present-day

© H. J. de Blij, P. O. Muller, and John Wiley & Sons, Inc.

HUMAN MIGRATIONS IN MODERN TIMES

— European emigration

— Migrations by other peoples (tied to European intervention)

FIGURE 5.11 Major routes of human migration between 1500 and 1950. The major flows of global migration include movements from Europe to North America (marked 1 on the map), from southern Europe to South and Central America (2), from Britain and Ireland to Africa and Australia (3), from Africa to the Americas during the period of slavery (4), and from India to eastern Africa, Southeast Asia, and Caribbean America (5).

India, Pakistan, and Sri Lanka to East and South Africa (see route 5 on Figure 5.11). Today, people of Indian ancestry form substantial minorities in South Africa, Kenya, and Tanzania, and, until their forced migration from Uganda, in that country as well. Their disproportionate share of commerce and wealth is now a major source of ethnic friction. Long before the British arrived in India, Hindu influences radiated into Southeast Asia, reaching the Indonesian islands of Java and Bali. Later, the British renewed the Indian migration stream, bringing South Asians to the Malay Peninsula (including Singapore) and to their Pacific holdings, including Fiji. The British were also instrumental in relocating Asians, mainly from India, to such Caribbean countries as Trinidad and Tobago and Guyana (shown by the trans-Pacific stream on Figure 5.11). The Dutch brought many Javanese from what is today Indonesia to their former dependency of Suriname along the same route.

An example of global migration flows involving Canada can be seen with the British Home Children program. Between 1869 and 1930, an estimated 150,000 British children between the ages of 4 and 18 were sent to Canada and other British colonies during the child emigration movement in Britain. Of this total, an estimated 100,000 were sent to Canada (**Figure 5.12**). In the mid-1800s, British philanthropist Annie McPherson saw opportunity for impoverished British children, who were being exploited in urban industrial factories, to find a better life overseas. She began setting up distribution homes in Canada where these British Home Children, as they became known, could be fed and educated in exchange for work as indentured labourers on Canadian farms or as domestic servants until they reached the age of 18. However, critics reported child abuse, exploitation, and displacement as a result of the program. Because it was a forced emigration program, children were often told, falsely, that their parents were dead, or that great prosperity awaited them in Canada. Once in Canada, they were frequently mistreated, ill cared for, not educated, and forced to stay in their placement homes in spite of poor conditions.

The program shrank in the 1930s, due to the economic hardships brought about by the Great Depression, and was officially ended in the 1960s. During an official inquiry in the 1990s, the scope of the tragedy was revealed. The British prime minister, Gordon Brown, issued an official apology in 2010 and set up a compensation fund for families torn apart by the program. Likewise, in 2009, the Australian prime minister, Kevin Rudd, issued a formal apology to the children subjected to the forced migration scheme to that country; his government set up a travel fund to help surviving participants locate their families. Canadian immigration minister Jason Kenney, in response to these apologies, stated that there was "no need for Canada to apologize for abuse and exploitation" of British Home Children in Canada (*Toronto Star*, 2009).

Many of these migration patterns persist even as new forms emerge. A larger number of countries are affected by the acceleration of migration. Countries accepting migrants do so from a much larger number of places. Countries such as Canada are becoming more diverse, particularly in urban areas. As well, countries accept diverse types of migrants—labourers, refugees, and family sponsorships—and have seen a substantial increase in the number of women migrants. Immigration is also becoming an increasingly politicized process, with states experiencing serious internal division over the role of immigrants in the nation's future.

REGIONAL MIGRATION FLOWS

The huge flows of migrants mapped in Figure 5.11 were unprecedented and have few rivals in terms of sheer numbers today. Although some global migration flows already discussed were forced and some were voluntary, each occurred across an ocean. Migration also occurs at a *regional scale*, with migrants going to a neighbouring country to take advantage of short-term economic opportunities, to reconnect with their cultural group across borders, or to flee political conflict or war.

European colonialism helped establish islands of development throughout the world. Islands of development are places within a region or country where most foreign investment goes, where the vast majority of paying jobs are located, and where infrastructure is concentrated. **Islands of development** are often coastal cities because their establishment was based on access to trade. An example of such a phenomenon is found in **Figure 5.13**, which shows the islands of development in sub-Saharan Africa.

> **Island of development** Place built up by a government or corporation to attract foreign investment and that has relatively high concentrations of paying jobs and infrastructure.

To understand migration flows from one poor country to another, it is not sufficient to analyze the flow at the global scale. We need to understand where the region fits into the picture of global interaction, and see how different locations within the region fit into interaction patterns at both the global and regional scales. For example, within the region of West Africa, the

FIGURE 5.12 British home children at the landing stage in Saint John, New Brunswick. In this undated photograph, British immigrant children from Dr. Barnardo's Homes, who were sent to Canada as part of the British Home Children program, await placement in Canadian homes as indentured labourers and domestic servants.

Isaac Erb/Library and Archives Canada/PA-041785

FIGURE 5.13 Islands of development in sub-Saharan Africa. Adapted with permission from Peter J. Taylor and Colin Flint, *Political Geography: World-Economy, Nation-State and Locality,* 5th Edition (Upper Saddle River, NJ: Pearson Education, 2007), p. 96. Reprinted by permission of Pearson Education, Inc. Upper Saddle River, NJ.

Legend:

● Major "islands of development"

- - ▶ "Labour in"

——▶ "Commodities out"

After *Taylor and Flint*

oil-producing areas of Nigeria are islands of development. In the mid-1970s, poor people in Togo, Benin, Ghana, and the northern regions of Nigeria, perceiving that economic life was better in coastal Nigeria, migrated to the coast for short-term jobs while the oil economy was good. The migrants, usually young men, worked as much as they could and sent almost all of the money they earned home as remittances to support their families. They worked until the oil economy took a fall in the early 1980s. At that point the Nigerian government decided the foreign workers were no longer needed and forcibly pushed out 2 million of them.

Global economic processes and the lasting effects of European colonialism certainly played a role in this West African migration flow. If we study such a flow only at the global scale, we see migrants moving from one poor country to another poor country. But if we use both the global and regional scales to study this flow, we understand regional economic influences and the pull of islands of development in Nigeria.

RECONNECTION OF CULTURAL GROUPS WITHIN REGIONS

Regional migration flows also centre on reconnecting cultural groups across borders. A migration stream with enormous consequences is the flow of Jewish immigrants to Israel. At the turn of the 20th century, fewer than 50,000 Jewish residents lived in

what was then Palestine. From 1919 to 1948, Great Britain held control over Palestine, and Britain encouraged Jews (whose ancestors had fled more than a thousand years earlier from the Middle East to Europe) to return to the region. As many as 750,000 Jews resided in Palestine in 1948, when the United Nations intervened to partition the area and establish the independent state of Israel (the original boundaries of the new state are shown in orange in **Figure 5.14**). After the land was divided between the newly created state of Israel and the state of Palestine, another migration stream began—600,000 Palestinian Arabs fled or were pushed out of Israeli territories. Many sought refuge in neighbouring Jordan, Egypt, Syria, and elsewhere. Israel's Law of Return gives residence and Israeli citizenship to Jews from anywhere in the world. This has resulted in significant numbers of Ethiopian Jews (Falashas) residing in Israel, as well as an obscure tribe from northeast India.

Through a series of wars, Israel expanded its area of territorial control (Figure 5.14) and actively built settlements for new Jewish immigrants in Palestinian territories. Jewish immigrants from the Eurasian region continue to migrate to Israel. Following the collapse of the Soviet Union in the early 1990s, thousands of Jews who had been unable to practise their religion in the Soviet Union migrated to Israel. Today, Israel's population of 8.1 million (including about 1.6 million Arab citizens) continues to grow through immigration as well as substantial natural increase.

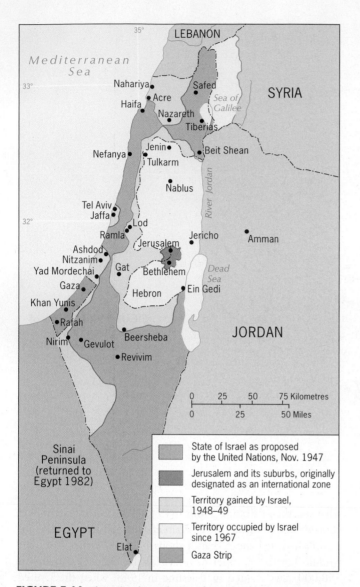

FIGURE 5.14 Changing boundaries of Israel. Adapted with permission from M. Gilbert, *Atlas of the Arab-Israeli Conflict* (New York: Macmillan, 1974), p. 38.

Map legend:
- State of Israel as proposed by the United Nations, Nov. 1947
- Jerusalem and its suburbs, originally designated as an international zone
- Territory gained by Israel, 1948–49
- Territory occupied by Israel since 1967
- Gaza Strip

CONFLICT AND WAR

Regional migration flows are often the result of conflict and war. At the end of World War II, as many as 15 million Germans migrated westward from their homes in Eastern Europe, either voluntarily or because they were forced to leave. Before the East German government built the Berlin Wall, and the Iron Curtain was lowered, several million Germans fled Soviet-controlled East Germany into what was then West Germany. And millions of migrants left Europe altogether to go to the United States (1.8 million), Canada (1.1 million), Australia (1 million), Israel (750,000), Argentina (750,000), Brazil (500,000), Venezuela (500,000), and other countries. As many as 8 million Europeans emigrated from Europe in this postwar stream.

We can see regional migration flows in the North American context in the example of Cuba. Even before Cuba became a communist state, thousands of Cuban citizens applied annually for residency in the United States after Fidel Castro came to power in 1959. During the 1960s, while the Cuban government was establishing the Communist Party of Cuba and formalizing a communist state, Cuban immigration to the United States swelled. The U.S. government formalized the flow as the Cuban Airlift, an authorized movement of persons desiring to escape from a communist government. The vast majority of Cuban immigrants arrived and remained in the greater Miami area. They developed a core of Hispanic culture in southern Florida, and in 1973, Dade County, Florida, declared itself bicultural and bilingual. In 1980, another massive, organized exodus of Cubans occurred, the Mariel Boatlift, bringing more than 125,000 Cubans to U.S. shores; the migrants qualified for refugee status under U.S. regulations. The Cuban influx persisted throughout the 1980s, and in 1994, over 30,000 Cubans fled for the United States. By that point the Soviet Union had collapsed, and the Soviet Union's financial support for the Cuban government had dwindled. The 1994 exodus pushed diplomats in both the United States and Cuba to come to an agreement on Cuban migration, called the "wet foot, dry foot policy." The Cuban government agreed to patrol its seas more closely for boats attempting to leave, and to impose no reprisals on those caught and returned by patrolling U.S. Coast Guard fleets. However, the general rule is that once Cubans reach American soil and are out of American waters, they are allowed to remain in the United States.

NATIONAL MIGRATION FLOWS

National migration flows can also be thought of as internal migration flows. Different countries, with distinctive social, historical, and cultural traditions, have very different internal migration patterns. We outlined the recent internal migration patterns in Canada earlier in this chapter. Another example comes from Russia, which experienced a major internal migration from the heartland of the Russian state (near Moscow and St. Petersburg) east as far as the shores of the Pacific. This eastward migration significantly altered the cultural mosaic of Eurasia, and understanding this migration flow helps us understand the modern map of Eurasia. During the czarist (1800s–1910s) and communist (1920s–1980s) periods, Russian and Soviet rulers tried to occupy and consolidate the country's far eastern frontier, moving industries eastward, building railroads and feeder lines, and establishing Vladivostok on the Pacific coast as one of the world's best-equipped naval bases. As Russia and then the Soviet Union expanded outward and to the east, the country incorporated numerous ethnic minorities into its population. During the communist period, the Soviet government also employed a policy of Russification, which sought to assimilate all the people in the Soviet territory into the Russian culture. One way the Soviets pushed this policy was by encouraging people of Russian heritage to move out of Moscow and St. Petersburg and fill in the country. By 1980, as many as 30 million Russians had moved out toward the borders. After the collapse of the Soviet Union in 1991, some people moved back to their original homelands, but the map will long carry the impact of Russia's eastward expansion.

REGIONS OF DISLOCATION

The refugee situation changes frequently as some refugees return home, conditions permitting, and as new streams of refugees suddenly form. Yet we can make certain generalizations about the overall geography of refugees. In the early 21st century, sub-Saharan Africa had the largest number of refugees in the world as well as the greatest potential for new refugee flows. The second-ranking geographic realm in terms of refugee numbers was Southwest Asia and North Africa, a realm that includes the Middle East, Iraq, and Afghanistan. South Asia, as a result of Pakistan's proximity to Afghanistan, ranked third. The vast majority of the world's refugees come from relatively poor countries and travel to neighbouring countries that are equally poor. The impact of refugee flows is certainly felt most in the poorest countries of the world. (**Figure 5.15**).

AFRICA

Africa's people are severely afflicted by dislocation—and not just in terms of the 8 million "official" refugees accounted for by international relief agencies. Many millions more are internally displaced persons. Of all regions in the world, sub-Saharan Africa experiences the greatest impact from migration because the majority of the world's migration flows involve refugees, and the majority of refugees are in sub-Saharan Africa. Add to that the extreme poverty and devastation of disease in many parts of the region, and each day is a humanitarian crisis somewhere in sub-Saharan Africa.

For example, Sudan, which has been in a civil war for two decades, is the site of one of the worst refugee crises in Africa today. The country's borders, drawn by European colonialism, forced together a largely Arab and Muslim population in the north, and a mostly Black African and Christian or animist (i.e., followers of a traditional religion) population in the south. (Christianity was brought to regions by Western missionaries, while Islam was introduced by North African traders.) The war between north and south Sudan has caused immense damage—over 2.2 million people have died in the fighting or have starved as a result of the war. More than 5 million people have been displaced, with over 1.6 million in neighbouring Uganda alone. Both sides in the Sudanese civil war have interfered with the efforts of international agencies to help the refugees.

This long-lasting refugee crisis in Sudan helps us understand the complexity of political conflict and migration flows in sub-Saharan Africa. The multi-ethnic and religious conflicts occurring in and around Darfur demonstrate that conflict can be generated for numerous reasons, including ethnic tension, religious division, and political manoeuvring. Actors at the regional and global scale strive to deal with the human suffering in the Sudan. On the global scale, the United Nations Security Council met in Kenya in 2004 to try to find a solution and eventually passed a resolution condemning the Sudanese government and threatening punitive damages against the government for its actions in Darfur. Conflict continues to permeate the region and has worsened since 2011, when South Sudan won independence in a referendum. A 2014 UN report stated that the number of South Sudanese fleeing for other countries, including Sudan, Ethiopia, Kenya, and Uganda, could reach 715,000 by the end of 2014. Civil war, famine, and a cholera epidemic have worsened the situation for refugees in South Sudan. Refugees are flowing both ways across the Sudan–South Sudan border, however, with more than 200,000 refugees from Sudan, fleeing the war in Darfur to the newly formed South Sudan as of February 2014. Hostilities continue in the region, with resulting hardship to local peoples.

NORTH AFRICA AND SOUTHWEST ASIA

The geographic region known as North Africa and Southwest Asia extends from Morocco in the west to Afghanistan in the east and contains some of the world's longest-lasting and most deeply entrenched refugee problems. A particularly significant problem centres on Israel and the displaced Arab populations that surround it. Decades of United Nations subventions have more or less stabilized this situation, but many refugees are still in motion or in temporary camps.

The Gulf War of 1991 and the war in Iraq have generated millions of refugees in the region in the last 20 years. In 1991, in the aftermath of the Gulf War, a significant percentage of the Kurdish population of northern Iraq, threatened by the Iraqi government, abandoned villages and towns and streamed across the Turkish and Iranian borders. This migration involved as many as 2.5 million people. International pressure led to the creation of a secure zone for Kurds in northern Iraq, with the hope that displaced Kurds in Turkey and Iran would return, but this effort was only partially successful. Many Kurds remain refugees in Turkey as well as Iran. The war in Iraq has generated upwards of 2 million refugees, most of whom are living in neighbouring Syria and Jordan.

The Soviet invasion of Afghanistan at the end of 1979 generated a double migration stream that carried millions westward into Iran and eastward into Pakistan. At the height of the exodus, it was estimated that some 2.5 million Afghans were living in camps in Iran, and an additional 3.7 million were gathered in tent camps in Pakistan's northwestern province and in southern Baluchistan. The Soviet invasion seemed destined to succeed quickly, but the Russian generals underestimated the strength of Afghan opposition, and the Soviets eventually withdrew. A power struggle among Afghan factions ensued and generated substantial internal instability and turmoil. As a result, most of the more than 6 million Afghani refugees in Iran and Pakistan—about one-quarter of the country's population—stayed where they were.

In 1996, the Taliban, an Islamic fundamentalist movement that began in northwest Pakistan, emerged in Afghanistan and took control of most of the country, imposing strict Islamic rule and suppressing the factional conflicts that had prevailed since the Soviet withdrawal. Although several hundred thousand refugees moved back to Afghanistan from Pakistan, the harsh

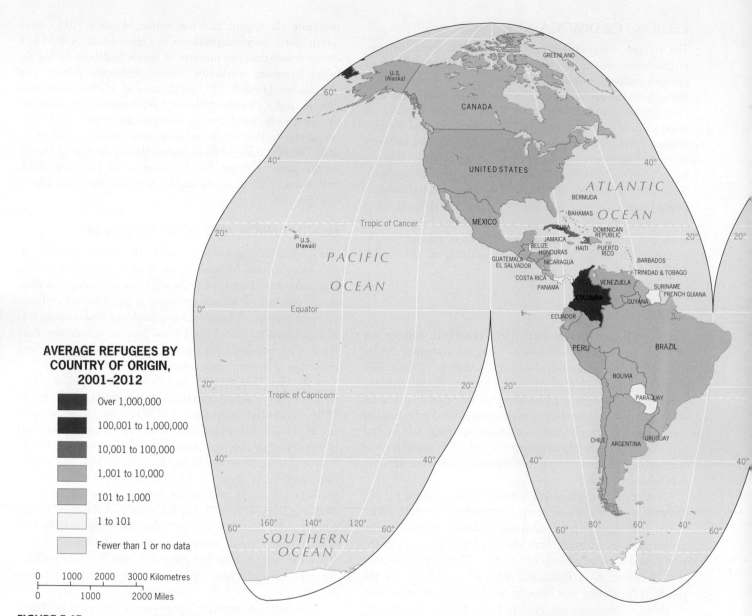

AVERAGE REFUGEES BY COUNTRY OF ORIGIN, 2001–2012

- Over 1,000,000
- 100,001 to 1,000,000
- 10,001 to 100,000
- 1,001 to 10,000
- 101 to 1,000
- 1 to 101
- Fewer than 1 or no data

0   1000   2000   3000 Kilometres
0   1000   2000 Miles

FIGURE 5.15 Average number of refugees by country of origin from 2001 to 2012. This map highlights the home countries of the world's refugees. Afghanistan and Iraq had the highest average number of refugees between 2001 and 2012. The war in Afghanistan generated more than twice as many refugees as the war in Iraq. Civil war in Sudan and continuing strife in Somalia also caused millions to leave their home countries and be classified as refugees. The data are reported through 2012; so, refugees generated by civil war in Syria are not as evident as the protests against Assad and ensuing full scale civil war began in 2011. Data from: World Bank, 2014.

Taliban rule created a counter-migration and led to further movement of some 2.5 million refugees into neighbouring Iran. After September 11, 2001, Western military action to stem global violence drove tens of thousands of Afghan refugees to seek safety in Pakistan and Iran despite efforts by both countries to close their borders, intensifying a refugee crisis that is now nearly a quarter-century old.

SOUTH ASIA

In terms of refugee numbers, South Asia is the third-ranking geographic realm, mainly because of Pakistan's role in accommodating Afghanistan's forced emigrants. The other major refugee problem in South Asia stems from the civil war in Sri Lanka. This conflict, arising from demands by minority Tamils for an independent state on the Sinhalese-dominated and -controlled island, has cost tens of thousands of lives and has severely damaged the economy. The United Nations reports about 200,000 people are now internally displaced. Canada has accepted both refugees and immigrants from all over the world, and as we discussed in Chapter 4, new immigrants have a profound effect on the demographic composition of our cities, both large and small. As the *Guest Field Note* by Sutama Ghosh suggests, immigration patterns in cities such as Toronto contribute to the emergence of new and distinctive neighbourhoods.

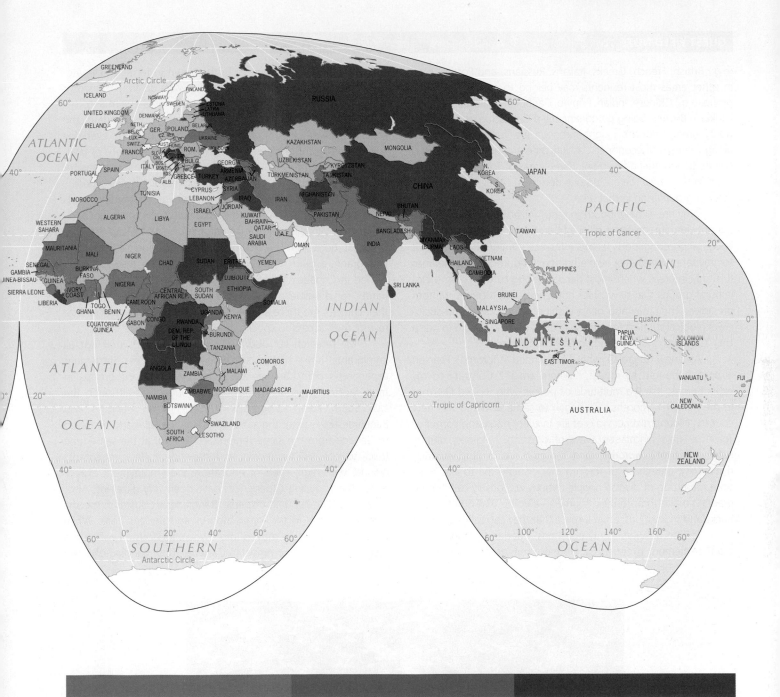

GUEST FIELD NOTE

Living in Toronto, Studying Immigrant Lives

With the exception of the First Nations, Canada is a country of immigrants, with thousands of people arriving in search of a new life and a better future. According to the 2006 Census, about 20 percent of the population was born outside the country.

Often, however, until one actually lives in Canada for a while, one does not realize that all of Canada is not the same. In the urban context, some cities are "richer" than others, socio-culturally, economically, and politically. Toronto, Montreal, and

Vancouver, for instance, are more diverse than many other Canadian cities. One reason for this is that, traditionally, these cities have served as immigrant gateways. Almost 70 percent of immigrants who arrived between 2001 and 2006 settled in Toronto (40 percent), Montreal (15 percent), and Vancouver (14 percent). As a result, whereas in a large city like Toronto it is easy to find someone who is from your own ethnic background, in a smaller town like Elora (in southern Ontario), you may find your family is the only one that looks different or has a lifestyle that is distinct from the general population.

Socio-cultural, economic, and political differences are common within Canadian cities as well. For example, whereas some neighbourhoods of Toronto have more Caucasian immigrants (e.g., British, French, Greeks, Italians, Russians, and Portuguese), in other areas most residents may belong to a visible minority group (e.g., Chinese, Indian, Filipino, Caribbean, Pakistani, and Sri Lankan). Beyond being predominantly a Caucasian or visible minority area, Toronto's neighbourhoods are further segregated along the axes of economic class (income and employment) and culture (language and religion). Some areas of Toronto, however, are mixed; that is, there is no one dominant racial, economic, or cultural group living in that area.

Why are all neighbourhoods not mixed? Why don't visible minority immigrants live in all neighbourhoods? A variety of exogenous and endogenous factors influence immigrant households to gravitate toward their own ethnic neighbourhoods. Sometimes it is only in areas where most people belong to their own sociocultural groups that newcomer households are received without prejudice. They may also get a cushion of economic and sociopsychological support from these people until they begin to grasp the "Canadian system" and find a job or a home.

As a new Canadian, when I first landed at Toronto's Pearson airport, I thought to myself, "Where am I"? Contrary to my expectations, I saw a multitude of people who looked like me! In the next few months, as I began to settle down in this new country, I found distinct ways of life in every nook and corner of Toronto—new languages, ways of dressing, religions, dietary habits, festivals, histories, and struggles. It is the vibrancy, dynamicity, and chaos of Toronto that inspired me to ask: How do a multitude of diverse people (whom we loosely call "immigrants") make Toronto their "home"—a home that is not just of bricks and mortar, but rather a space that they can call their own?

To find answers to my questions, I began to study immigrant settlement experiences. How do immigrants survive in a country that is so different from their own in terms of climate, society, and culture? In which specific ways do they transform the city into their own spaces? I found that it is essential to explore the everyday lives of households. Understanding the atomic, everyday life situations is important because everyday lives of immigrant families are laden with complex webs of challenges and triumphs, be it while searching for suitable shelter and employment, or attempting to express and retain specific elements of their culture. Moreover, this understanding leads the researcher to question and evaluate some of the larger societal forces. What factors cause immigrants to earn less than the Canadian born? Is it the lack of Canadian experience? How can immigrants acquire Canadian experience when they have just landed in Canada? What are the specific reasons that make it harder for a visible minority household to find a residence of their choice? Are there any discrete discriminatory practices that restrict their access to specific parts of the city?

My research corroborated previous findings that not all immigrants have similar settlement experiences. Settlement experiences differ between and within immigrant groups in multi-faceted ways. In my research I found that although the two South Asian subgroups studied—Indian Bengalis and Bangladeshis—speak the same language (Bangla) and migrated to Canada from the same region (South Asia) at the same time (mid- to late 1990s), mostly as independent class immigrants (young, with high levels of education and employment experience), their housing experiences have been very different. Also, whereas Indian Bengalis disperse, Bangladeshis cluster in specific neighbourhoods in the inner suburbs and the city core. While many Indian Bengalis moved into ownership housing within the first five years of their arrival in Canada, most Bangladeshis live

Simon Hayter/Toronto Star

FIGURE 5.16 Regent Park, Toronto. Just east of downtown Toronto, Regent Park, one of Canada's oldest social-housing projects, has been home to many immigrant groups. Seen here in 2005, a 12-year, $1-billion redevelopment project is underway.

in private rental housing that is unaffordable, inadequate, and unsuitable. Some were already in social housing and many were on the waiting list for it.

Despite these problems, however, within a decade of their arrival in Canada, Bangladeshis have successfully transformed three areas of Toronto into their own spaces: the Victoria Park area, also known as "Little Bangladesh"; Regent Park, a social-housing complex immediately east of downtown Toronto, built in the 1940s and 1950s (**Figure 5.16**); and the Markham Road and Eglinton Avenue area in Scarborough. All three areas contain several Bangladeshi retail stores and services, including grocery and clothing stores, beauty parlours, photographic studios, entertainment stores, remittance centres, and immigration consultants. In addition, the main offices of two Bengali newspapers and community agencies serving Bangladeshi-Canadians are also located here. Several mosques are located in the immediate vicinity. This relatively high level of institutional completeness has also played an important role in attracting more Bangladeshi newcomers to these neighbourhoods, thus increasing their residential concentration in these areas.

What my research broadly reflects is that immigrants are not just "economic bodies" (earning wages and paying taxes). They are in fact, the "life of the party," filling our cities with vibrant colours and cultures. What should we do today to make their lives easier, particularly when they first arrive?

Sutama Ghosh, Department of Geography, Ryerson University

SOUTHEAST ASIA

Southeast Asia is a reminder that refugee problems can change quickly. Indochina was the scene of one of the 20th century's most desperate refugee crises—the stream of between 1 and 2 million people who fled Vietnam in the aftermath of the long war that ended in 1975. In the early 1990s, Cambodia produced an exodus of 300,000 refugees escaping from their country's seemingly endless cycle of violence, and ending up in refugee camps on the Thailand side of the border. Today, the largest refugee camps in this realm are internal refugees in Myanmar (formerly Burma), victims of the 2004 tsunami, the 2008 cyclone, and the repressive rule of the generals who are seeking to subjugate the country's minorities.

EUROPE

In the 1990s, the collapse of Yugoslavia and its associated conflicts created the largest refugee crisis in Europe since the end of World War II. In 1995, the UNHCR reported the staggering total of 6,056,600 refugees, a number that some observers felt was inflated by the Europeans' unusually liberal interpretations of the United Nations rules for refugee recognition. Nevertheless, even after the cessation of armed conflict and the implementation of a peace agreement known as the Dayton Accords, the UNHCR still reports as many as 1.6 million internal refugees in the area—people dislocated and unable to return to their homes.

This section has focused on the "where" of migration, on where refugees, IDPs, and others move on a global, regional, and national scale. It is important to remember that where people move is partly contingent on countries' immigration policies. As a result of these global, regional, and national trends, scholars argue there are three main issues shaping immigration policy for countries such as Canada. The first is what Janice Stein (1993) calls the "global economic divide." The current division in the world is based on age. Core countries such as Canada and European states have an aging population, while peripheral countries have youthful populations. Core countries are increasingly looking to immigration to supply young, skilled workers for the labour market. Second, there is a growing demographic inequality in terms of wealth, quality of life, and access to technologies. This has the potential to increase tensions between the more well-off core and the increasingly poor periphery. Finally, we are seeing more barriers to immigration based on security concerns. With the tightening of borders, immigration policy is seen as a security issue that will severely restrict, perhaps unfairly, who gains admission to core countries such as Canada.

MAIN POINTS 5.3 Where Do People Migrate?

- The world has experienced major immigration flows over the last century. Prior to 1500, migration was haphazard, and preliminary population movement was based on colonial settlement patterns.

- In the last five centuries, major immigration flows occurred from southern Europe to North America; from Britain and Ireland to North America; from Africa to the Americas due to slavery; and from India to eastern Africa, Southeast Asia, and Caribbean America.

- We can consider immigration on global, regional, and national scales as well as on more local scales. Many people immigrate for employment opportunities, to reconnect with cultural groups, and because of conflict and war. Many countries have witnessed internal migration for distinctive historical, social, and cultural reasons.

- Refugees are found in every corner of the globe and represent a serious humanitarian issue for all countries.

5.4 How Do Governments Affect Migration?

The control of immigration, legal and illegal; the granting of asylum to refugees; and the fate of cross-border refugees, permanent and temporary, are sensitive issues in countries around the world. Efforts to regulate, organize, and sometimes limit immigration have been a concern of states for millennia. In the 14th century, China built the Great Wall (**Figure 5.17a**) in part as a defensive measure but also as a barrier to emigration (by Chinese trying to escape the control of the Chinese authorities) and immigration (mainly by Mongol "barbarians" from the northern plains). The Berlin Wall (**Figure 5.17b**), the Korean DMZ (demilitarized zone), the fences along the Rio Grande, and the new wall being constructed by Israel are all evidence of the desire of governments to control the movement of people across their borders.

POST-SEPTEMBER 11

Since September 11, 2001, government immigration policies in the United States and Canada, and around the world, have incorporated new security concerns. The U.S. response to the September 11 attacks is a good example of how international immigration policy can be transformed. Prior to that date, the U.S. border patrol was concerned primarily with drug trafficking and human smuggling. Immediately after September 11, the George W. Bush administration cracked down on asylum seekers. The U.S. government marked 33 countries as places where al-Qaeda or other terrorist groups operate, and the government automatically detained anyone from one of these 33 countries who entered the United States seeking asylum.

U.S. government policies also affect illegal immigrants. The United States can detain any illegal immigrant, even if the person has no known ties to terrorist organizations. Similarly, the fence that the government is building along the United States–Mexico border is a response in part to the concern that terrorists will use Mexico as a staging ground to enter the United States illegally and commit terrorist attacks.

People and organizations opposed to the post-September 11 policies counter that raising fences and detaining people will not combat terrorism; rather, it will intensify hatred of the U.S. government, thus promoting terrorism. Organizations such as Human Rights First, Amnesty International, and the Migration Policy Institute claim that the new government crackdowns have violated civil liberties and have done nothing to make Americans safer. Others opposed to the new border regulations argue the crackdown has only slowed traffic and the flow of business and tourism, and has utterly failed to slow illegal immigration, which is increasing along the U.S.–Mexico border. These and other concerns about migration will continue to shape security policy in North America, Europe, and beyond in the decades to come.

MANAGING AND CONTROLLING BORDERS

According to Eric Weiner (2007) at National Public Radio in the United States, "In years past, it was difficult to travel from one country to another, yet relatively easy to clear any regulatory hurdles once you arrived. The reverse is true today. Modern technology makes it easy to travel, but migration is now highly regulated in most parts of the world." This high regulation of migration is due in large part to governmental legal and regulatory frameworks that seek to control who enters and leaves nation-states, especially since the attacks on

(a)　　　　　　　　　　　　　　　　　　　　　(b)

Eddie Granlund/Naturbild/Corbis

Owen Franken/Corbis

FIGURE 5.17 Barriers to immigration. (a) The Great Wall of China, undated, and (b) the Berlin Wall.

September 11, 2001. For example, Canadians were previously able to fly or drive to the United States without a passport. Now, all Canadians over the age of 16 must have a passport to enter the United States.

There are various tools that governments use to control and affect migration. While some of these are more visible—such as the building of walls, the patrolling of borders, and the use of a variety of surveillance technologies—others are built into the legislative and judicial systems of governance. In the opening field note, for example, we discussed Canada's *Immigration and Refugee Protection Act* and the proposed bill to prosecute human smugglers. Along with legal statutes, procedures such as visa applications, or the U.S. "green card" process, control who can work in a particular country, and for how long.

Most of the laws and regulations that come to mind seem to focus on controlling those who are permitted to enter a given country. Yet there are many countries where the exit process is tightly controlled as well. In 2009, the London *Telegraph* published an article about migrant workers in the Kingdom of Saudi Arabia. According to Saudi law, migrant workers must surrender their travel papers, passports, and exit documents to their employer upon arrival in the country. This means that, while it is possible to enter the Kingdom for work, it can be very difficult to leave without their employer's permission. With over 7 million migrant workers, accounting for nearly 28 percent of the Kingdom's population, Saudi Arabia's treatment of its migrant workers has come under international scrutiny.

The Canadian government manages its temporary migrant workforce through the Temporary Foreign Worker Program (TFWP), which is facilitated by Employment and Social Development Canada and by Citizenship and Immigration Canada. In recent years the TFWP has expanded significantly, making it easier for Canadian employers to hire foreign workers to fill labour shortages. While the expansion of this program has allowed migrant worker populations in Canada to increase, the program has also come under a great deal of scrutiny from labour and human rights groups. For example, the Alberta Federation of Labour has called for the program to ensure the provision of better working conditions and has even called for an end to the program in its current form, to be replaced by a program that enables foreign migrant workers to apply for permanent residency. The federation states this would better protect foreign workers' rights. In 2013, investigative reports revealed that in Alberta, temporary foreign workers were paid up to 15 percent less than Canadians doing the same work, suggesting that businesses were using the TWFP not only to fill labour gaps, but also to underpay those workers and drive down wages for many jobs, including nurse aides, food service workers, and heavy equipment operators, among others. This practice was banned as part of a set of comprehensive reforms in June 2014.

WAVES OF IMMIGRATION IN CANADA

Governments have a tremendous impact on immigration through the passage of laws and policies setting out who may immigrate to Canada and for what reasons. Canada is a nation of immigrants, from the arrival of Aboriginal populations some 30,000 years ago to the current influx of immigrants from around the world. In 2008, some 300,000 immigrants came to Canada. Who we are and what we might become depends on the composition of the Canadian population, which is increasingly made up of immigrants from diverse places. Understanding the history of Canadian immigration policy will put us in a better position to direct our future.

Canada was settled through waves of immigration, beginning with the Aboriginal peoples and continuing with the establishment of the French colony of Port Royal in the Annapolis Valley on the Bay of Fundy in 1604. The permanent settlement of Quebec City, established in 1608, became the capital of New France, which by 1759 had a population of 65,000 people. The British were also establishing colonies in parts of Newfoundland and Labrador as well as the Hudson's Bay area. France and Britain fought a series of wars during the 17th and 18th centuries that ultimately resulted in France ceding control of its North American colonies to the British under the Treaty of Paris in 1763.

Throughout the 1800s, British control of the colonies ensured a steady influx of British settlers, supplemented by British Loyalists fleeing the American Revolution. Some 100 years of immigration substantially changed the demographic base from French-speaking to English-speaking peoples, with a mixture of English, Irish, Scottish, and Welsh. By the mid-1800s, the number of immigrants from these places diminished to the point that the newly formed Canadian government looked farther afield for immigrants to populate the Prairies and British Columbia, in part to shore up Canadian claims to these territories against U.S. interest (**Figure 5.18**).

From the late 1870s to the early 1950s, the Canadian government worked to encourage Central Europeans to immigrate to western Canada, causing a demographic shift and new regional differentiation. While Quebec and Ontario were dominated by the French and British, respectively, the Prairies and British Columbia were settled by Ukrainians, Hungarians, Doukhobors, and peoples from Scandinavia and Tsarist Russia, giving western Canada its distinctive cultural roots.

Europeans remained the "preferred nationality" in government policy on immigration until the passage of the *Immigration Act* in 1967. This act refined Canada's system for processing those considered to be refugees and developed two distinct streams of immigrants: family members, who could be sponsored; and those assessed on a point system that analyzed skills and education. This new process was designed, in part, to ensure Canada could attract certain types of skilled workers during labour shortages.

This policy change ushered in a new era that encouraged immigration from all countries, substantially changing Canada's demographic composition over the next 40 years. Prior to 1961, 90 percent of Canadian immigrants came from Europe. By 2001, that figure had declined to less than 20 percent. Over that same period, immigration from Asia increased from just 3 percent before 1961 to over 58 percent in 2001. Between 1991 and

Library and Archives Canada/C-063484

FIGURE 5.18 Passage to Canada, 1870s to 1880s. Posters in Britain and Europe promoting immigration to Canada offered assisted passages and promised free land, good wages, and free schools.

Ernest Brown/Boorne & May/Library and Archives Canada/C-006686B)

FIGURE 5.19 Chinese railway workers, 1884.

2001, most Asian immigrants came from China, India, Hong Kong, and Sri Lanka. As a result, Canada now has a much more diverse society that includes non-European languages and non-Christian religions. Additionally, in 1996, immigrants made up 17.4 percent of Canada's population. By 2001, that figure had risen to nearly 20 percent. This demographic shift has led to growing debate and conflict over what it means to be "Canadian." We saw in Chapter 3 that states strive to foster an internal sense of unity around a shared sense of history and culture. This has become increasingly difficult to achieve in Canada given the country's shifting demographic composition.

As we will discuss in more detail in Chapter 10, most immigrants to Canada gravitate to large cities. Between 1991 and 1995, 93.5 percent of all immigrants located in an urban area; of those, 77 percent located in one of four major metropolitan areas—Toronto, Vancouver, Montreal, and Calgary. Immigrants can have a profound impact on the social, political, and cultural aspects of place at a variety of scales. The social and ethnocultural organization of these cities' neighbourhoods has changed substantially, and this increased diversity has contributed to the vibrancy and economic health of these cities. Nevertheless, some scholars argue that we are also seeing increasing social polarization, segregation, and shifts in the patterns of suburbanization that are not necessarily positive. City administrators, planners, and social service providers are facing new and distinctive challenges in the development of Canada's largest cities.

One group meriting particular attention is the Chinese, who have a long history of immigration to Canada, first appearing in substantial numbers in the 1850s as part of the Fraser River gold rush. However, it was the building of the Canadian Pacific Railway, linking British Columbia and eastern Canada in the 1870s, that spurred Chinese immigration (**Figure 5.19**). With the completion of the railway, the Canadian government sought to stifle Chinese immigration, and from 1885 to the 1920s it imposed an increasingly harsh levy or "head tax" on Chinese immigrants. In 1923 the Canadian government passed the *Chinese Exclusion Act*, banning all Chinese immigration except for special circumstances. The act remained in place until 1947 (when it was repealed) and caused significant hardship for the mainly male immigrants who were already here, as they were unable to marry or raise a family. With the passage of the *Immigration Act* in 1967, Chinese immigration increased considerably. In June 2006, Prime Minister Stephen Harper made a formal apology for the injustices of the "head tax" and offered compensation to the families of those affected.

MULTICULTURALISM AS GOVERNMENT POLICY—THE CASE OF CANADA

As a matter of government policy and cultural tradition, Canada has always been a multicultural nation given its settler history. *The Dictionary of Human Geography* defines "multiculturalism" as "the belief that different ethnic or cultural groups have the right to remain distinct rather than assimilating into 'mainstream' norms" (p. 528). The fact that multiculturalism is government policy impacts immigration flows. In this section, we consider some of the ways in which multiculturalism policy is intertwined with immigration.

Geographer Audrey Kobayashi suggests that the multicultural nature of Canada occurred in three broadly defined stages. In the first demographic stage, Canada became increasingly ethno-culturally diverse, although there was no official policy in place encouraging that diversity. While the French and then the English initially settled Canada, the drive to settle the Prairies broke the English/French domination with an influx of Ukrainians, Poles, Germans, Slavs, and Russians in the late 1800s and early 1900s. After World War II, Canada experienced increases in immigration from Eastern and Central Europe, and immigration policy was committed to notions of assimilation, which ensured the continuing predominance of white, European, and Christian peoples. The *Immigration Act* in 1967 paved the way for an increase in numbers of other ethnic groups beyond Europe and increasingly from Africa, China, India, and South America.

The second, or "symbolic," stage occurred when the Canadian government put in place policies that recognized and promoted multiculturalism without a firm commitment to legislate it as an official government objective. It is largely acknowledged that this shift in policy came out of the report from the Royal Commission on Bilingualism and Biculturalism (1963), which acknowledged the bicultural character of the country but argued Canada also needed to take into account other ethnic groups' contributions to Canadian society and to undertake measures to safeguard their contributions. By 1971, largely due to the commission's recommendations, the Canadian government announced a new official policy of multiculturalism within a bilingual framework. Multiculturalism granted official recognition of the diverse cultures of a plural society and encouraged immigrants to retain their linguistic and ethnic cultures rather than assimilating into the dominant culture. In order to protect the right to retain distinctive cultural traits, the Canadian Human Rights Commission was created in 1978. These rights were further protected with the passage of section 15 of the Charter of Rights and Freedoms in 1982.

The third and final stage is "structural multiculturalism," in which formal government legislation is passed to address core issues such as equality of opportunity, cultural diversity, and protection from discrimination. The *Multiculturalism Act* of 1988 provided a strong legal base by consolidating existing policies and practices and providing a more detailed statement on multiculturalism. Many argue that there are a number of benefits to Canada from promoting multiculturalism. Not only does it make Canada a more interesting place; it also enhances Canada's international image and influence by ensuring demographic links to almost every other country in the world.

However, not everyone is convinced that multiculturalism is a useful or successful policy. For example, Neil Bissoondath, in his book *Selling Illusions: The Cult of Multiculturalism in Canada*, argues that multiculturalism promotes "ghettoization" by encouraging immigrants to remain separate and apart from the dominant culture, and it discourages newcomers from thinking of themselves as Canadians. This arguably detracts from national unity and tends to emphasize people's differences rather than their similarities.

All this is to say that ensuring immigrants are welcome and contributing members of Canadian society is a complicated business. While "multiculturalism" as formal government policy has been successful in terms of ensuring reasonably harmonious relations between "old-timers" and "newcomers," whether it remains the best approach is under reassessment. Nevertheless, Canada will continue to become increasingly diverse given current immigration policy.

MAIN POINTS 5.4 How Do Governments Affect Migration?

- The events of September 11, 2001, have singularly shaped immigration policy around the world.

- Governments influence immigration patterns in both informal and formal ways. In Canada, informal government policies in the late 1800s encouraged immigration from a wide range of European countries through advertisements and incentives. More formally, new Canadian legislation in 1967 opened the door to immigration from all countries in the world and substantially changed Canada's demographic composition.

- Multiculturalism, the official policy of the Canadian government, promotes cultural diversity, distinctiveness, and accommodation of difference. Not everyone agrees that multiculturalism is a successful approach to immigration.

- Historical events may force countries to re-evaluate government policies. The attacks of September 11, 2001, meant that many countries, including Canada, tightened their immigration requirements in ways that limited or excluded certain groups. In other cases, countries seek to exclude migrants by building physical barriers.

SUMMARY

In the last 500 years, humans have travelled the globe, mapped it, connected it through colonization and imperialism, and migrated from one part of the globe to another. Migration can occur as a result of a conscious decision, resulting in a voluntary migration flow, or it can occur under duress, resulting in forced migration. Both kinds of migration have left an indelible mark on the world and on its cultural landscapes. When we consider migration, we can do so at a number of scales, from the national to the regional and the global. Governments attempt to strike a balance between the need for migrant labour, the desire to help people in desperate circumstances, and the desire to stem the tide of migration. Immigration policy, in whatever form it takes, can have a profound effect on the internal composition of a country's population.

Canada is, of course, a country of immigrants. Recent immigration and multiculturalism policy means Canada accepts immigrants from all over the globe, substantially enriching its human resources. Yet increasing diversity has the potential to be problematic as people seek some common ground in their understanding of what it means to be a "Canadian." Canada relies on immigrants to ensure stable population growth given our declining rate of natural increase and our aging population.

As the world's population mushrooms, the volume of migrants will expand. In an increasingly open and interconnected world, neither physical barriers nor politically motivated legislation will stem tides that are as old as human history. Migrations will also further complicate an already complex global cultural pattern, raising questions about identity, race, ethnicity, language, and religion, topics we turn to in upcoming chapters.

DISCUSSION AND REVIEW QUESTIONS

1. What does the case of MV *Sun Sea* reveal about the issue of migration for both Canada and the world? What do you feel is an appropriate response to the questions posed by this event?

2. As a key part of studying and understanding migration, human geographers focus on determining who migrants are. Discuss and assess the typology constructed to understand the migrant experience. What, if any, is your personal experience with migration?

3. The Atlantic slave trade is arguably one of the most devastating and pernicious cases of forced migration in human history. It profoundly altered the human geographies of Africa, the Caribbean, North America, and South

America. Discuss its history and the geographic impacts. What was Canada's role in the history of slavery?

4. Canada has often been described as a "multicultural" nation. What does this mean and how is it related to the history of the country? What, if any, criticisms are there of Canada's multicultural policy?

5. Reread the *Guest Field Note* "Living in Toronto." Have you ever thought about your own or your family's migratory experience? When did your ancestors move to Canada? What were the "push" or "pull" factors that brought them to the country? Where did they first arrive and how have they moved since? Has it been mainly a positive or a negative experience?

GEOGRAPHIC CONCEPTS

asylum   133
chain migration   136
deportation   134
diaspora   127
emigration   127
forced migration   128
genocide   133
gravity model   129
guest worker   130
immigration   127
immigration wave   136
internal migration   127
internally displaced persons (IDPs)   132
international migration   127
intervening opportunity   134

island of development   138
kinship links   136
laws of migration   129
migrant labour   129
migration   126
nomadism   126
pull factors   133
push factors   133
refugees   132
remittances   130
repatriation   133
step migration   133
voluntary migration   128

ADDITIONAL RESOURCES ON-LINE

About foreign policy and international development issues (North-South Institute): www.nsi-ins.ca

United Nations High Commissioner for Refugees: www.unhcr.org

About internally displaced persons: www.internal-displacement.org

International Organization for Migration: www.iom.int/jahia/Jahia/lang/en/pid/1

About migration and identity: www.learner.org/resources/series85.html#program_descriptions (Click on Video On Demand for "A Migrant's Heart")

About migration and geographic mobility within the United States: www.census.gov/population/www/socdemo/migrate.html

About Canada's Temporary Foreign Worker Program: www.esdc.gc.ca/eng/jobs/foreign_workers/index.shtml

The film *El Contrato*, about Mexican migrant workers on an Ontario farm: www.nfb.ca/film/el_contrato

CHAPTER 6
HUMAN-ENVIRONMENT RELATIONS

Space Race to Mars

WHAT DO YOU THINK ABOUT when you hear the word "environment"? Many people imagine the world around us; perhaps our home, neighbourhood, or city, our country, or even the planet constitute what we understand our environment to be. We can picture our environment as fragile when, for example, we hear of the changing climate's potential to melt Arctic sea ice or of the Ebola outbreak in western Africa. At other times, we think of the environment as incredibly powerful, as when an earthquake and tsunami devastated Japan in 2011, or when the volcanic events at Eyjafjallajökull in Iceland in 2010 caused a massive disruption of air traffic. Now, however, some people are beginning to think of the environment as something different—as something out of this world.

On August 6, 2012, NASA's *Curiosity* rover landed on Mars. Before long, *Curiosity* was transmitting images to Earth of an environment yet to be explored and colonized. Yet, although our first glimpses of Mars were new, the landscape does not look all that unfamiliar (**Figure 6.1**). And as we gazed at these images, one thing became clear: the environment was suddenly bigger than Earth. The space race to Mars is on, and the end goal is to establish a permanent human settlement.

As the world's population surpasses 7 billion people with no signs of slowing down, and as we face increased concerns about food security and access to fresh water and clean air, it seems reasonable that we might begin to consider seeking out new environments to inhabit in order to sustain human life. And at the same time that we begin to ask questions about sustainable development on this planet, we are witnessing remarkable achievements in outer space. *Curiosity* sent back stunning images of a land yet to be explored, and many people around the world watched Canadian astronaut Chris Hadfield tweet, record and send music videos, and host live chats from space (**Figure 6.2**), demonstrating a marked improvement to communication networks in space. These experiences make space, as an environment for human inhabitants, feel not so far away.

As a result, despite the inhospitable conditions on Mars, it nevertheless has become the hope for humanity. Mars One, a non-profit Dutch organization, has developed a plan for a one-way trip to Mars; the first crew of four leaves Earth in 2024. After that, crews of four will be dispatched every two years. More than 200,000 people applied to set up the first human colony on Mars, and as of 2014, the organizers had invited 700 applicants for an interview, including 75 Canadians. The explorers will spend the rest of their lives on the red planet, building the colony (**Figure 6.3**).

For many, the idea of taking a one-way trip to Mars to establish a human colony seems far-fetched. However, others are willing

NASA/JPL-Caltech/MSSS

FIGURE 6.1 Panoramic view from *Curiosity* Mars rover.

FIGURE 6.2 Canadian astronaut Chris Hadfield hosts a live chat from space with students at Chris Hadfield Elementary School, Milton, Ontario, January 17, 2013.

to expand their understanding of human-environment relations to include environments beyond Earth. These endeavours in

FIGURE 6.3 An artist's rendition of the Mars One colony.

space also raise questions about our relationship with planet Earth. Why, instead of striving for sustainable development or understanding ourselves as inherently connected to and part of this planet, do we treat it as something we are separate from, a resource to be used up, at which point we can move on? As candidates for the Mars One expedition provide doctor's certificates and complete interviews, it seems that such questions will need answers sooner than we might ever have imagined.

KEY QUESTIONS FOR CHAPTER 6

1. How do geographers think about the concept of "nature"?

2. What impact do humans have on the environment?

3. How are humans responding to environmental change?

6.1 How Do Geographers Think about the Concept of "Nature"?

In Chapter 1, we defined the discipline of geography as the study of human-environmental relations. In this definition, the term "environment" includes both the natural world and the built environment (and is almost always limited to the environment of Earth). In this chapter, we will consider the concept of "nature" as it has been taken up by geographers and as something we consider separately from the built environment. Although the centrality of the environment to our very existence may fade into the background as we go about our daily business, we are sharply reminded of its significance when we suffer through hurricanes, experience smog or high ultraviolet

exposure, or pay higher prices for food or fuel. Conversely, we are becoming increasingly aware that our individual daily activities, from driving our cars to recycling to the temperature we set in our homes, have an impact on our environment.

As geographers, we are interested in how human-nature relations can be considered in light of our five major themes—location, region, place, landscape, and movement. In this chapter, we begin by examining geographical approaches to thinking about or conceptualizing human-environment interrelationships. Although these are often framed as "binary" relationships—that is, as an interconnection between two things (humans and nature)—we will soon see that the complexity of the human-nature relationship evades straightforward binary descriptions. We then consider the impacts human beings are having on the natural world. In the third and final section, we explore the approaches humans are employing to address such challenges as climate change, species extinction, diminishing air quality, and resource depletion.

Cultural and literary critic Raymond Williams argues that "[the word] nature is perhaps the most complex word in the [English] language" (1988, p. 221). We may use the term "nature" in a number of different ways. For example, we may mean the nature of an object, its inherent and unchanging characteristics—as in the phrase "it is just the nature of things." We may be talking about a physical world untouched by humankind, such as the "wilderness"; or we may be thinking about a natural world that may or may not include human beings. Clearly, these are overlapping ideas, and we cannot usually think of one conceptualization without thinking of the others. Our conceptualization of nature determines our relationship to nature, how we see our place in nature, and how we think we should interact with the natural world.

Many human populations regard human beings and our society or culture as separate from the natural world—they believe we are somehow standing outside or beyond nature. In this conceptualization, nature tends to be a place we look out at or step into, a place we go to for recreation and leisure, relaxation and rest. Nature is portrayed as an undisturbed landscape waiting to be discovered (and possibly developed) by humans. We often see nature as something to be conquered and overcome, brought under the control of humans for their own purposes. Television reality shows such as *Survivorman* and *Mantracker* portray humans battling the forces of nature (**Figure 6.4**). A common element of these ways of thinking is their organization of ideas about nature and humanity as a set of binaries or a set of opposing concepts: nature-culture, nature-society, nature-human. In each of these, we see reflected the idea that humans and human social relations (society and culture) are outside nature.

We might question whether understanding nature as something separate from humankind fairly represents our relationship. Some argue that the current conceptualization of

FIGURE 6.4 Survivorman. Canadian Les Stroud, a filmmaker and survival expert, uses his skills and knowledge to survive in the wilderness, battling nature for days at a time with little food or water.

nature as distinct from society emerged during the Western Age of Enlightenment (17th and 18th centuries). In the late 18th and early 19th centuries, rapid urbanization and industrialization in Western societies radically altered human landscapes, making the distinction between human society (urban) and undeveloped "nature" (the rural) quite stark. As we examined in the chapters on globalization and political geography (chapters 2 and 3, respectively), this was also the age of imperial and colonial exploration by countries such as France, Spain, Britain, Belgium, and Portugal. Colonial enterprises sought to map a vastly expanding world teeming with an unimaginable array of plants, animals, and sea creatures that had previously been unknown to Europeans. It is not surprising that Western nations saw themselves as discoverers of vast new natural resources for human use. Geographers and scientists "discovered" and studied a "nature" that was seen as remote and removed from human society and culture. This perception is distinct from views of nature held by many of the world's Aboriginal populations or by such religions as Buddhism and Taoism, which regard human existence as fully enmeshed in and inseparable from the natural world.

How we view our relationship with nature affects how we use or treat the natural world. If the dominant view is

> **Anthropocentric view** A view in which human interests and perspectives are highlighted.

that nature is a resource for human use, we will think about nature only in the context of its usefulness for humans—an **anthropocentric view**. On the other hand, if we see ourselves as intrinsically bound up with nature, or if we believe that nature is valuable in its own right and not merely as determined by its usefulness to humans, we may see our interaction with the natural world in a different light.

Recent geographical scholarship questions whether the nature-human binary is the best or most accurate way to understand our relationship with nature. Perhaps there are other, more useful, ways to think about these connections given our current concerns about climate change and resource depletion. In this section, we first consider three different ways geographers have thought about our relationship with nature—Marxist-based scholarship, research in cultural geography, and the political ecology approach. Then we consider the history of environmentalism and environmental movements and their ideas about the human-nature relationship.

Many geographers, for instance, are increasingly concerned with **sustainability**, which is defined in *A Dictionary of Human Geography*, (Castree et al., 2013) as, "the property of a system or process that allows for both its use and long-term regeneration." A focus on sustainability asks us to consider

> **Sustainability** Defined by Castree et al., 2013, as "the property of a system or process that allows for both its use and long-term regeneration."

the extent to which human activities, such as industrialization, lead to the potentially irreversible reduction of non-renewable (e.g., fossil fuels, crude oil, coal) and formerly renewable (fish stocks, forests, biodiversity) resources.

MARXIST GEOGRAPHY AND THE PRODUCTION OF NATURE

Geographer Neil Smith, in his book *Uneven Development* (1984), draws on the work of Karl Marx to think about how changes in the world economy brought about by the advent of a new economic system, capitalism, fundamentally altered how we conceive of nature. Capitalism is a relatively new system for organizing the exchange of goods and services that developed during the age of Western exploration, imperialism, and colonialism in the 17th and 18th centuries (see Chapter 3). During that period, urbanization, rapid population growth, and new technologies transformed the organization of human societies around the globe. In core countries, dominant social, economic, and political relations shifted from small rural and agricultural communities to rapidly expanding cities operating within an increasingly global trading system. A new form of government also developed—the democratically constituted nation-state.

Karl Marx (1818–1883) lived during the height of the Industrial Revolution in Europe, a time of dramatic political and economic upheaval and unprecedented social change. He eyed these massive changes with some anxiety and spent his life writing about their implications for humankind. One concept central to his thinking is the idea that human beings increasingly used new technologies to transform nature into something else—mills transformed wood into lumber and furniture, or water into power; plants were modified to produce larger and better crops; and raw materials were extracted to make various metals. Marx argued that through this human manipulation of nature, humans were not only producing something new but were "producing nature" as well. By this he means that humans, in their interactions with nature, produce a new kind of nature. For example, human use of plants and animals led to their domestication in fields and in fenced yards. We began planting crops in tidy rows for human harvest, differentiating miscellaneous plants from "crops" that could be eaten or used for other human needs. We began evaluating forests and rocks with an eye to their resource value, changing our view of them as an object in their own right to a commodity whose value is measured in its worth for human consumption. Setting aside land as a hunting reserve transformed animals into "game"—a truly human-centred way of understanding living creatures. In one example, U.S. television personality Melissa Bachman posted an image of herself and a dead lion on Twitter, tweeting "An incredible day hunting in South Africa! Stalked inside 60-yards on this beautiful male lion … what a hunt!" In the controversy that ensued, critics argued against killing animals for sport as opposed to food and accused Bachman of profiting from the hunt through her reality TV show. Her defenders suggested that "sustained hunts" are a form of conservancy.

As geographer Noel Castree argues, there are three important reasons to think about how humans "produce nature" through their technological and intellectual efforts. First, if we understand that we produce nature, we force ourselves to think about how humans interact and change nature—that is, we can examine how our production of nature changes historically and geographically. For example, hunter-gatherer societies clearly used nature in a different manner than industrial societies do. Second, recognizing that humans produce nature ensures we realize that nature is not unchanging and static but constantly interwoven into human activity. We can consider how, in the process of transforming nature for our own use, we alter the very foundation of the natural world and our relationship to it. Finally, thinking about the production of nature requires that we focus on how we manipulate nature into something to be sold—a commodity—for profit (**Figure 6.5**).

FIGURE 6.5 *Food, Inc.* In his documentary *Food, Inc.*, filmmaker Robert Kenner examines corporations' control of the food industry. This control illustrates one way in which we manipulate and commodify nature.

CULTURAL GEOGRAPHY AND THE CONCEPT OF NATURE

In contrast to Marxist thinkers, cultural geographers argue that what we understand as "nature" comes as much from the human imagination as it does from technological intervention. How we envision nature, and the meanings we give it, affect how we come to use nature and regard our place in it. The subdiscipline of landscape studies has directed considerable attention to the implications of how humans "see" landscapes. As geographers point out, the term "landscape" can mean both the actual world we inhabit and a representational quality we might find in landscape paintings or other art forms. When we look at paintings of landscapes, we see the world through an artist's eye and get a

National Gallery, London

FIGURE 6.6 Mr. and Mrs. Andrews, 1748. Cultural geographers often use Thomas Gainsborough's painting as an example of how landscapes provide a way of seeing the relationship between nature and culture.

sense of how nature is represented or understood by that artist. How the artist represents nature—the colours used, the items included or excluded, the positioning and organizing of trees, people, and buildings—can tell us a great deal about "ways of seeing" nature-human relationships in different cultures and in different historical periods.

In their book *Iconography of Landscape* (1988), geographers Stephen Daniels and Denis Cosgrove argue that we all have our own way of seeing landscape, both individually and collectively as a society. We can argue that the representation of nature in paintings, art, or writing is not a neutral process, as it is influenced by the social norms of the time. One example that cultural geographers have used to illustrate how landscapes draw together nature and culture is a painting, *Mr. and Mrs. Andrews,* by 18th-century artist Thomas Gainsborough (**Figure 6.6**). In this painting, the landowners are seated on the left, and nature appears on the right as a wide-open vista, ready for exploitation. Nature, at the time this painting was produced, was seen as proprietary, and the fact that those who worked the land were not depicted is a commentary of the class relations of the time. When European explorers saw landscapes as literally "empty" (with no indigenous peoples), or as "undeveloped" or "vacant," they could only understand what they saw through the particular cultural lens of that historical era. It follows that whatever the "real" world of nature is, it is also something mediated through human expectations, experiences, and representations. This has serious implications for how we view or think about the world around us. How we understand landscapes influences, for example, which places we assume are important enough to be protected in national parks or designated World Heritage sites, and which are the proper locations for ATV (all-terrain vehicle) trails or human development. All of this suggests that there might be no common or typical way of understanding landscapes and nature. It also suggests, perhaps to our benefit that how we see nature might change and, in turn, prompt a reassessment of humankind's place in it. The

approaches of both Marxist and cultural geographers challenge us to reconsider how we think about human-environment relations.

POLITICAL ECOLOGY AND ENVIRONMENTAL CHANGE

The third method geographers have used to think about our relationship with nature, the political ecology approach, emerged in geographical scholarship in the 1970s and 1980s. This approach suggests the connection between nature and society is better understood if we focus on political and social relations under capitalism. The perspective has been particularly useful in development studies, which examine the positioning of peripheral and semi-peripheral countries within the processes of globalization (see Chapter 11) and the various forms of environmental degradation that seem to occur as these countries are increasingly caught up in the global capitalist economy.

Economic development is clearly linked to environmental change, and, as we will see in Chapter 11, many argue that the benefits of development are captured by core countries while developing countries inequitably bear the costs in the form of environmental degradation and deteriorating social and cultural relations. For example, in the late 1980s, geographers Harold Brookfield and Piers Blaikie argued that ecological problems, such as environmental degradation, actually reflect social and political problems rather than lack of technical or managerial expertise. Brookfield and Blaikie suggested that problems such as soil erosion in Nepal could be explained as environmental mismanagement or overpopulation. Subsequent scholarship developed a more formal political ecology approach, arguing that we might need to take a broader view and look at how globalization has changed social relations at the local level in ways that alter how a community farms or accesses resources. We might also consider how new government regulations, such as taxes or levies, could influence how local communities operate. This approach asserts that to properly understand environmental problems, one needs to take a multiscalar approach that is sensitive to broader historical, political, and social circumstances.

A political ecology approach helps us focus on human-nature relations and on the transformation in social relations among and between social groups based on class, race, gender, or ethnicity within a wider capitalist economic system. Political ecologists focus on questions of property rights, resource control, traditional land management techniques, and labour and production, all central concerns when considering the changing human-nature relationship in peripheral and semi-peripheral countries.

ENVIRONMENTALISM

How we think about or understand our relationship with nature is reflected in the history of the environmental movement in both Canada and the United States. Environmentalism is both an ideology and an activity; that is, it is a particular perspective or set of beliefs about human-environment relations that promotes a set of actions designed to effect change. Put simply, how we understand our relationship with nature has influenced the distinctive perspectives of environmental activism over the last 200 years.

During the age of imperialism, colonialism, and global exploration, the dominant world view was that of manifest destiny—that humans are destined to expand over territory. Sociologist Charles Harper argues that the idea of manifest destiny provided the moral and economic rationale for human exploitation of nature. Such a position, Harper notes, assumes that "nature has no intrinsic value, that human welfare depends on the exploitation and development of nature and that human inventiveness and technology can transcend any resource problem." Such a perspective clearly provided support for the European conquest and exploitation of the resources and peoples of its colonies and continues to provide a rationale for those who support the continued free-market commodification and use of the natural world. Moreover, as we saw in the opening field note, this perspective is providing some motivation for the plans to colonize Mars.

Despite the prominence of this widely held view, concern about environmental degradation and the abuse of nature began to surface in the early 1800s. In Europe, the rapid urbanization occurring as a result of the Industrial Revolution alarmed civic leaders, women's organizations, religious groups, and social planners, who believed the overcrowded and dirty tenement housing and slums of the working poor were unhealthy for children and adults alike. Humans' need for access to the countryside, sunshine, and fresh air became an increasing preoccupation for many.

NORTH AMERICAN ENVIRONMENTALISM

In North America, deforestation, desertification, soil erosion, and the extermination of creatures such as carrier pigeons and the buffalo increased worries about human impacts on nature and paved the way for the first wave of environmentalists. Writers such as Henry David Thoreau, Ralph Waldo Emerson, and James Fenimore Cooper, and politicians including Theodore Roosevelt, argued for the "scientific management" of natural resources and their conservation. Clear divisions emerged between such individuals as John Muir, who founded the Sierra Club in 1892 and who favoured wilderness preservation, and Gifford Pinchot, a member of the American forestry service who argued that natural resources should be used for human benefits but in a responsible way.

Conservationism, the view that humans are part of nature and in destroying our resources we are undermining our own ability to survive, advocates the conservation of resources for future use. Conservationism argues for the "wise use" approach to nature, in which human interactions, such as controlled hunting and fishing, are encouraged. This is in contrast to **preservationism**, which argues for the preservation of wildlife for its own sake and allows only minimal human use. Preservationists understand nature as having intrinsic value in the world (value that is not based on human use). Whereas preservationists were once understood as naïve and simplistic in their views, today preservationism is considered to be a complex set of intertwined ideas about the ecological and aesthetic values of nature. For example, we have come to understand the importance of ecosystems as storehouses of genetic and environmental data and of ecosystem services as intrinsic to the overall health and functioning of the environment, in addition to their value as places of wonder and beauty. For many, it is vital to preserve these ecosystems so as not to disrupt the delicate balance of nature.

In the early environmental movement, the tensions between conservationism and preservationism became evident. Canadian responses to environmental issues were legislative and reflected the view that the natural world was there to provide respite and relief to humans wishing to escape their urban environments. For example, the *Dominion Forest Reserves and Parks Act* of 1913 stated that forests "shall be maintained and made use of as public parks and pleasure grounds for the benefit, advantage, and enjoyment of the people of Canada," clearly a conservationist view of nature. The first national park in Canada was established when Sir John A. Macdonald's government passed the *Rocky Mountains Park Act* in 1887, designating some 674 square kilometres as a protected area that came to be known as Banff National Park. Increasing concern in both the United States and Canada over the hunting of migratory birds led to the passage of the *Migratory Birds Act* in 1911. This law sought to protect migratory birds and their habitats from hunting and trafficking. It is important to note that while the act protects the birds themselves, it does not protect the land or water resources they use. Canada's Dominion Parks Branch, the world's first national park service, was also established in 1911. (Now known as Parks Canada, it is under the purview of Environment Canada.) The Dominion Parks Branch saw to the creation and management of national parks and wildlife areas. The *National Parks Act*, passed in 1930, includes a clause that "dedicates" the parks to the people of Canada. These early legislative interventions demonstrate the desire to preserve certain natural areas largely for the benefit of human beings and, potentially, for the future use of those resources. Today, Canada has 36 national parks and 6 national park reserves—areas designated to be national parks once Aboriginal land claims have been settled. The goal is to have a system of national parks that represents Canada's distinct natural regions (**Figure 6.7**).

Canada's provincial governments also have a long history of creating and maintaining park lands for public use. One of the earliest and largest provincial parks is Ontario's Algonquin Park, created in 1893 as a wildlife and timber preserve, which covers some 7,630 square kilometres. In 2014, Ontario had 334 parks and 295 conservation reserves, 5 regulated dedicated protected areas, 4 non-regulated dedicated protected areas, and 11 wilderness areas. Other provinces have followed suit, although each province has developed its own distinctive

> **Conservationism** A human-centred view of nature that advocates for conservation of resources for future human use.
>
> **Preservationism** A view asserting that nature should be preserved for its own sake, rather than for human use.

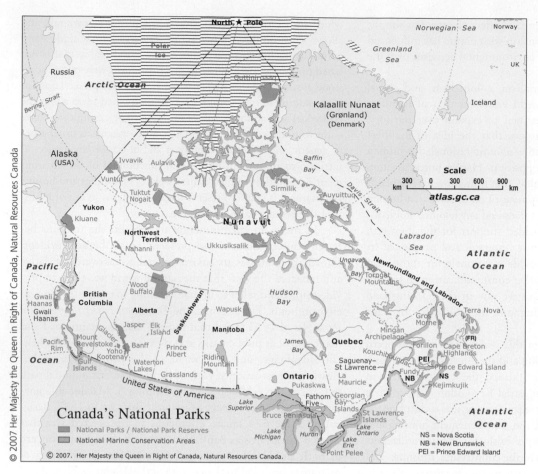

Canada's National Parks

- ▮ National Parks / National Park Reserves
- ▮ National Marine Conservation Areas

© 2007. Her Majesty the Queen in Right of Canada, Natural Resources Canada.

NS = Nova Scotia
NB = New Brunswick
PEI = Prince Edward Island

Scale
300 0 300 600 900
km   km
atlas.gc.ca

FIGURE 6.7 Canada's national parks and marine conservation areas, 2007. Canada has 36 national parks and 6 national park reserves (areas set aside to become national parks once Aboriginal land claims have been settled), as well as 4 national marine conservation areas (which take in the seabed, the water, and any species it contains—outlined by the dotted line on the map), spread across the 10 provinces and 3 territories.

classification system. For example, British Columbia has 14 designations that include marine parks, provincial heritage sites, and ecological reserves. Saskatchewan has created 34 provincial parks, 130 recreational areas, 8 historic sites, and 24 protected areas—each designation reflecting a specific natural or historic feature with a range of recreational and educational purposes. The distinctive modes of designation, protection, preservation, and use of various types of landscapes reflect the range of philosophies behind such designations, from the aspiration to preserve untouched wilderness areas to the wish to generate income from recreational uses that will support the costs of the parks system.

The second phase of the North American environmental movement began in the 1950s and 1960s, and focused on air and water quality and human health issues arising from pollution and from chemical and toxic waste. In the previous phase, environmental activism took the form of government policies and direct intervention. In the second phase, new forms of environmental activism were largely directed by grassroots organizations struggling to address local environmental problems. A series of influential books, including Rachel Carson's *Silent Spring* and Paul Ehrlich's *The Population Bomb,* and Garrett Hardin's article "The Tragedy of the Commons," drew public attention to environmental problems. Several high-profile environmental disasters, such as toxic waste in the Love

Canal neighbourhood (Niagara Falls, New York), environmental degradation in Burlington Bay (Hamilton, Ontario), and the Sydney Tar Ponds (Sydney, Nova Scotia), as well as oil spills off the coast of California in the late 1960s, spurred growing concern for the well-being of both humans and nature. The first Earth Day was celebrated in 1970, organized by American senator Gaylord Nelson. It was attended by 20 million people, and organizers were shocked by the event's success. Greenpeace, now a well-known international environmental organization, was established in Vancouver, B.C., in 1971 to protest American underground nuclear testing at Amchitka Island, off the Alaskan coast, which is home to endangered wildlife (**Figure 6.8**).

The burgeoning environmental movement was made up of activists and organizations using many different approaches to highlight environmental concerns and crises. Some were conservationist in approach, seeking to ensure resources were maintained for future generations; others were strictly preservationist in their attempts to preserve nature for nature's sake; still others walked a fine line between these two perspectives. Collectively, the organizations were referred to as the "environmental lobby." Some groups acted locally, protesting local actions by companies causing pollution or demanding the cleanup of toxic sites. Others lobbied for legislative and policy changes, demanded funding for scientific research, and worked

Choice/Alamy

FIGURE 6.8 **Greenpeace MV** *Arctic Sunrise* **in Leith, Edinburgh, 2007.** Established in Vancouver, B.C., in 1971, Greenpeace is now a well-known international environmental organization.

to raise environmental awareness. It is important to note that at this stage, as well, governments in Canada and the United States continued to take an active role in addressing environmental issues. For example, Canada's federal government established Environment Canada, a federal department, in 1971, and the United States government set up the Environmental Protection Agency in 1970. Over the last several decades, environmental activism and governmental initiatives have expanded to include broader concerns such as global ecological issues, biodiversity, and climate change.

Grassroots activism on environmental issues experienced a resurgence in the late 1980s and early 1990s, particularly in relation to environmental justice, with activists arguing that environmental issues could not be considered separately from questions of race, class, and gender. For example, Blue Planet Project, an organization founded by Canadian Maude Barlow, explicitly considers access to fresh water a woman's issue, given that women around the world, particularly in the peripheral and semi-peripheral countries, struggle to provide fresh water to their families for washing clothes, bathing, domestic cleaning, and human consumption (**Figure 6.9**). Scholars and activists also claim that environmentally undesirable projects, such as garbage dumps, toxic waste sites, nuclear waste facilities, or oil exploration or drilling sites, are often unfairly located near poor or disadvantaged groups that have little ability to protest or engage in community activism. Environmentalism tied to global climate change has increased in visibility, with projects such as Al Gore's 2006 film *An Inconvenient Truth* capturing international interest. In Canada, grassroots environmentalism continues to be intertwined with social justice concerns. The Idle No More movement, for example, began in 2012 when Aboriginal peoples in Canada, along with their non-Aboriginal supporters, initiated protests against the omnibus bill, Bill C-45, proposed by the federal government of Prime Minister Stephen Harper. This legislation, Idle No

More activists argued, eroded indigenous peoples' treaty rights, and threatened the rights of all Canadians. According to their mission statement, "Idle No More calls on all people to join in a revolution which honors and fulfils Indigenous sovereignty which protects the land and water." While Bill C 45 passed, the Idle No More movement continues to lobby and raise awareness of environmental issues through a campaign of teach-ins, social media, and rallies. Today's environmental movement is complicated, made up of local grassroots organizations, national non-governmental and governmental organizations, and international organizations and movements focused on global issues.

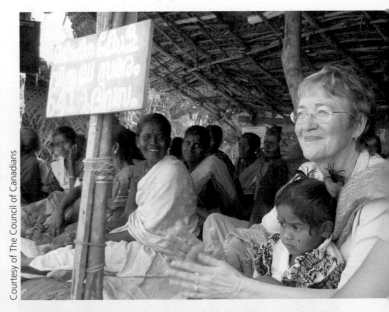

Courtesy of The Council of Canadians

FIGURE 6.9 **Maude Barlow.** Maude Barlow, founder of Blue Planet Project, attends the People's World Water Forum in New Delhi, January 12–14, 2004.

GLOBAL ENVIRONMENTALISM

As mentioned, environmental activism has also gone global, with alliances of nation-states, United Nations organizations, non-governmental organizations (NGOs), and international non-governmental organizations (INGOs). Global organizations with distinct but interrelated concerns are forming alliances too. For example, groups working for women's rights or workers' rights are joining with environmentalists and student groups to link concerns about globalization, environmental degradation, and the exploitation of workers, particularly women and the poor. The World Trade Organization (WTO) protests in Seattle, Washington, in 1999 brought together diverse groups for a common goal. In more recent WTO protests, such as the D5 demonstrations in 2009 in Portland, Oregon, placards read "TEAMSTERS AND TURTLES, TOGETHER AT LAST" and "... TOGETHER STILL" (**Figure 6.10**).

There is no doubt that global environmental issues are a growing concern. Disappearing tropical rainforests, loss of soil, desertification, access to clean water, air pollution, and the development of renewable energy sources to replace non-renewables have become central issues. The United Nations has sponsored a series of environmental conferences—first the UN Conference on the Human Environment in Stockholm, Sweden, in 1972, followed by the UN Conference on Environment and Development (UNCED) (dubbed the "Earth Summit") in Rio de Janeiro in 1992. While no treaties emerged from these conferences, delegates did attain a broad consensus about pollution, biodiversity, and global warming. According to the *Guardian*, since the 1992 summit, global emissions have risen 48 percent, 300 million hectares of forest have been cleared, and the world's population has increased by more than 1.5 billion. In 2012, more than 190 nations met at the Rio+120 Earth Summit—a follow-up to the 1992 Earth Summit—with the aim of setting global sustainable development goals. The meeting produced a document, *The Future We Want*, which attempted to set clear measures for the implementation of sustainable development Environmental justice advocates, however, criticized the document for lacking in

detail and ambition. Overall, and despite considerable disagreement, there seems to be a consensus emerging on the need for sustainable development and environmental protection at the global level. We will revisit this discussion in more detail in the final section of the chapter.

ANTI-ENVIRONMENTALISM

In the 1980s and 1990s, corporations and businesses began organizing against the environmental lobby, usually presenting arguments that supported free market activity and the right of owners to use private property as they wished. When protestors attempted to sabotage the Trans-Alaska Pipeline, the corporation spent thousands of dollars to locate the protestors, even using eavesdropping technologies and surveillance to track them down. Interestingly, while corporations fought government regulation of environmental issues in their industries, they also began public relations campaigns and "green" advertising campaigns to capture the new green consumer.

More recently, scholars have pointed to the formation of a so-called wise use movement, made up predominantly of lumber and mining industries, that work to counter initiatives of the environmental movement. Wise use groups resemble grassroots organizations but are financed by industry and argue against environmentalists' claims—for example, that climate change is a problem and that fish stocks are declining. These groups also argue against environmental regulation because it infringes on private property rights and free enterprise; they claim that tough environmental regulations threaten jobs and makes it more expensive to do business. They insist that by putting some stocks of certain resources, such as oil and natural gas, off-limits by designating parks or wildlife preserves, countries like Canada and the United States will be unable to develop their resources to their own advantage.

Regardless of one's position, the process of thinking through environmental issues and finding information and perspectives that might responsibly guide future decision-making has become increasingly complicated.

Bette Lee

FIGURE 6.10 D5 Demonstrations, 2009. On December 5, 2009, protestors in Portland, Oregon, participated in the global days of action against the World Trade Organization. This protest became known as the "D5 Demonstrations."

MAIN POINTS 6.1 How Do Geographers Think about the Concept of "Nature"?

- Geographers study human-environmental relations. The term "environment" encompasses both the natural world (or "nature") and the built environment. "Nature" is a complicated concept, and how we understand the term influences our relationship to it.

- Human societies have conceptualized "nature" and their relationship with it differently in different historical periods and geographical locations. In core countries, views of human-environment relations are generally structured around a set of binaries or opposing concepts: nature-culture, nature-society, nature-human.

- Geographers use three main conceptual approaches (although there are others) to think about the human-environment

relationship: Marxism, the notion of cultural landscapes, and political ecology.

- The history of the environmental movement in North America demonstrates that activists and grassroots movements, as well as governments and their agencies, take different approaches to the environment, falling along a continuum between preservationism and conservationism.

- The global environmental movement demonstrates the interconnectedness of the environment at the global level while maintaining a focus on specific local concerns.

6.2 What Impact Do Humans Have on the Environment?

While we tend to think of serious human impacts on the environment as a modern event, humans have had an effect on their environment for all of their history. In search of food, they set fires to kill herds of reindeer and bison. They hunted entire species of large mammals to extinction. Polynesians, for example, reduced the forest cover to brush and, as a result of their penchant for wearing bird-feather robes, exterminated more than 80 percent of the regional bird species by the time the first Europeans arrived. Similarly, European fashions over the last 800 years have had a disastrous impact on African species ranging from snakes, crocodiles, and birds to leopards and elephants.

In this section, we consider the impact humans have on the environment by considering such human activities as consumption and energy use and their effects on ecosystems—the biological community of plants and animals that live in a particular region and interact with each other and their environment,

including water, atmosphere, and land. We begin, however, with a discussion of the Columbian Exchange—a process arising from exploration and colonization (discussed in Chapter 3) that continues today.

THE COLUMBIAN EXCHANGE

The age of exploration, which began in the 1400s, had profound environmental impacts. European explorers travelled the world, bringing their technologies, cultures, norms, and beliefs to previously unknown peoples and places. These travellers also carried home a staggering array of seemingly exotic and unknown plants, animals, and peoples. The historian Alfred Crosby, in his book *The Columbian Exchange*, argues that the voyage of Christopher Columbus to the Americas in 1492 launched a large-scale exchange of plants, animals, cultures, ideas, and diseases that had a profound effect on agriculture, the environment, and culture in both the Old World of Europe and the New World of the Americas. As **Figure 6.11** indicates, the global circulation and exchange of plants, animals, and illnesses was incredible.

FIGURE 6.11 The Columbian Exchange. A partial list of the plants, animals, and diseases travelling between the Old World and the New World.

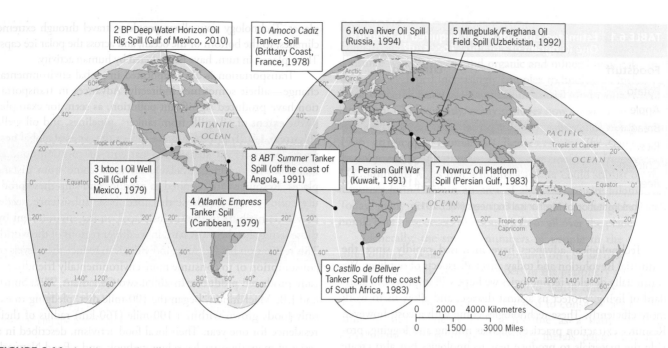

FIGURE 6.14 The biggest oil spills. This map shows the largest known oil spills in history, up to 2010. The *Exxon Valdez*, perhaps one of the most famous spills in history, is small compared to the Transocean Deepwater Horizon spill in 2010 (second largest), and the intentional dumping of oil by Saddam Hussein in 1991 (largest).

the coming decades to meet the growing demand. In developing countries in particular, the need for more energy leads to the development of new sources of fossil fuel. This may help explain why, according to the United States Energy Information Administration, global oil production increased from 45.89 million barrels per day in 1970 to 84.8 million barrels per day in 2012. Canada ranks sixth in the world in oil production, at 4.07 million barrels per day in 2013. In terms of global oil consumption, the United States ranked first in 2013, consuming 19.00 million barrels per day, followed by China with 10.3 million barrels per day, and Japan with 4.5 million barrels per day. Canada consumes 2.4 million barrels per day (**Figure 6.15**).

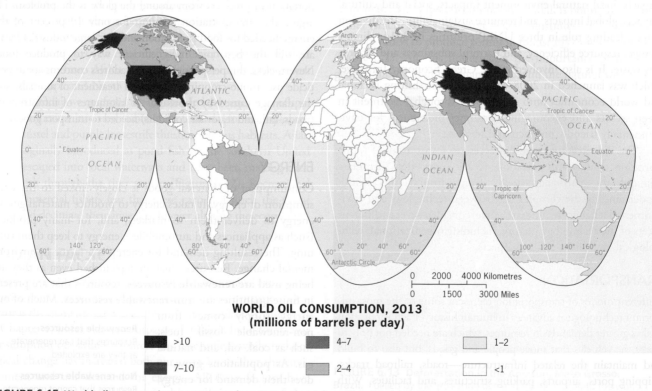

WORLD OIL CONSUMPTION, 2013
(millions of barrels per day)

■ >10	■ 4–7	□ 1–2
■ 7–10	■ 2–4	□ <1

FIGURE 6.15 World oil consumption, 2013. Data from U.S. Energy Information Administration.

Oil is a finite resource. That means there is no question that the world's oil supply will run out someday. The question is *when* it will run out. Because geologists continue to discover new reserves, and because the extraction of fossil fuels is becoming ever more efficient, it is difficult to predict exactly how much longer oil will remain a viable energy source. Many scientists suggest that the current level of oil consumption can be sustained for up to 100 years, although some argue for much shorter or much longer time frames. Despite the range of opinion, the majority of scientists believe that we will have to be developing alternative energy sources by the middle of this century. When we consider that oil could become an increasingly scarce commodity, the importance of finding alternative energy sources is apparent. Adding further urgency are the pollution problems associated with the burning of fossil fuels and the geopolitical tensions that arise from global dependence on a resource concentrated in one part of the world. Moreover, the risk of environmental damage from oil drilling and shipping highlights the need for alternate energy sources that would have less of an environmental impact. The oil spill caused when the *Exxon Valdez* ran aground off the coast of Alaska in 1989, and the explosion and subsequent leaking of the BP's Transocean Deepwater Horizon oil well in the Gulf of Mexico in 2010, graphically illustrate the environmental dangers of reliance on oil (**Figure 6.16**).

New technologies, including fracking, are beginning to revolutionize the oil and gas mining industries, but these procedures are not without controversy. Fracking, or hydraulic fracturing, is a process by which gas and oil are recovered from shale rock by directing a high-pressure mixture of water, sand, and chemicals into rock, allowing the gas and oil to flow out the head of the well (**Figure 6.17**). The practice, however, has prompted environmental concerns about the huge amounts of water needed at the fracking site, the potentially carcinogenic chemicals that might contaminate groundwater, and the growing evidence that fracking can lead to earthquakes. In late 2013 SWN Resources began seismic imaging to test the shale beds of New Brunswick, which has the thickest shale gas reservoir in North America. Demonstrators have been protesting in Rexton, NB, raising environmental concerns, and local First Nations communities have staged protests in support of these demonstrations, citing rulings by the Supreme Court of Canada and lower courts that state local governments have a duty to consult Aboriginal peoples when development is being considered on their lands (both reserve and non-reserve traditional lands) (**Figure 6.18**).

Moving away from a dependence on oil carries with it some clear positives, but it could lead to wrenching socio-economic adjustments as well. Nuclear power is a possible alternative non-renewable energy source, but the long-term radioactivity

FIGURE 6.17 **Fracking.** This illustration shows how the process known as "fracking" works.

Gwen Shockey/Science Source

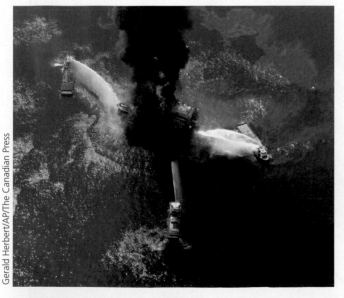

FIGURE 6.16 **BP's Transocean Deepwater Horizon rig burns in the Gulf of Mexico, April 20, 2010.** The explosion of the Transocean Deepwater Horizon rig resulted in the deaths of 11 people and the largest oil spill in U.S. history. Scientists are still assessing the environmental impact of the disaster.

Gerald Herbert/AP/The Canadian Press

FIGURE 6.18 **Fracking protesters.** Protesters take to the streets in Halifax, Nova Scotia in 2013 protesting the potential fracking practices in New Brunswick.

Andrew Vaughan/The Canadian Press

associated with this form of energy production, and the potential for accidents, have limited its expanded use.

The effects of a shift away from oil will certainly be felt to some degree in the industrial and post-industrial countries, where considerable retooling of the economic infrastructure will be necessary. Oil-producing countries will face the greatest adjustments, however. More than half of the world's oil supply is found in the Middle Eastern countries of Saudi Arabia, Iraq, Kuwait, the United Arab Emirates (UAE), and Iran. In each of these countries, the extraction and export of oil accounts for at least 75 percent of total revenue and 90 percent of export-generated income.

ALTERATION OF ECOSYSTEMS

Human alteration of the environment continues in many forms today. For the first time in history, however, the combined impact of humanity's destructive and exploitative actions is capable of producing environmental changes on a global scale. While we have always had an impact on our environment, over the last 500 years both the rate and scale at which humans modify the Earth have increased dramatically. During the last half-century, humans transformed every place on Earth, either directly or indirectly. Our patterns of consumption, technological and transportation advances, and energy consumption have generated environmental stress on our water supply, social and atmospheric quality, and biodiversity.

The natural environment is modified by human activity in many obvious and some less obvious ways. Among the more obvious actions causing **environmental stress** (obvious because they take place around human habitats) are clear-cutting forests and emitting pollutants into the atmosphere. Less obvious actions include burying toxic wastes that foul groundwater supplies, dumping vast amounts of garbage into the oceans, and using pesticides in farming. All these activities have an impact on the environment and raise a number of concerns about the future of water supplies, the state of the atmosphere, and our impact on the terrain.

> **Environmental stress** The threat to environmental security by human activity such as atmospheric and groundwater pollution, deforestation, oil spills, and ocean dumping.

WATER

Water, the essence of life, is a renewable resource. But the available supply of fresh water is not distributed evenly across the globe. The world distribution of precipitation reveals the largest totals recorded in equatorial and tropical areas of Southeast Asia, South Asia, central and coastal West Africa, and Central and South America. That distribution is sustained through the hydrologic cycle, which brings rain and snow from the oceans to the landmasses (**Figure 6.19**). The volume of precipitation in the world as a whole is enormous; spread

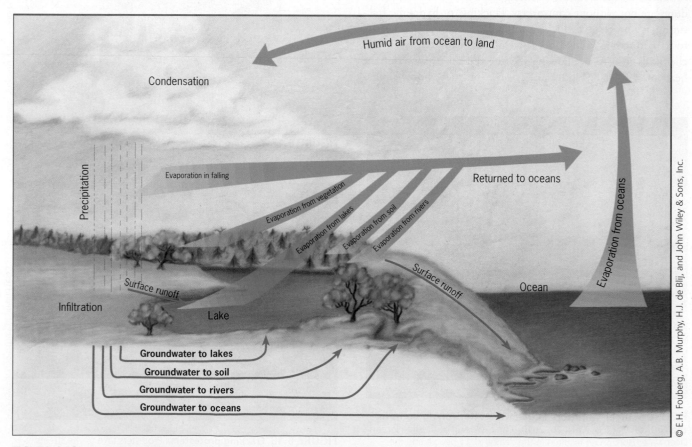

FIGURE 6.19 The hydrologic cycle. The hydrologic cycle carries moisture from the oceans and other bodies of water over the land, where precipitation, runoff, and evapotranspiration sustain the system.

Aquifers Subterranean, porous, water-holding rocks that provide millions of wells with steady flows of water.

out evenly, it would cover the land area of the planet with about 83 centimetres of water each year. Much of that water is lost through runoff and evaporation, but enough of it seeps downward into porous, water-holding rocks called **aquifers** to provide millions of wells with steady flows.

Despite such favourable data, the supply of water is anything but plentiful, and access to fresh water has become a global concern. Chronic water shortages afflict tens of millions of farmers in Africa and hundreds of thousands of city dwellers in southern California. Water rationing has been imposed in rainy south Florida and in Spain, which borders the Mediterranean Sea. In Canada, a severe drought in the 1930s had devastating effects on the Prairies for nearly a decade, turning once fertile land into a "dust bowl." At the same time as the Great Depression, when poverty and unemployment ravaged much of the world, precipitation on the Canadian prairies averaged 40 percent below normal amounts, leading to massive crop failures, grasshopper swarms, dust storms, and the wholesale destruction of livestock herds due to starvation.

H.E. Miguel D'Escoto Brockmann, former president of the United Nations General Assembly, has declared access to fresh water a basic human right, and efforts are underway to revise the UN Declaration of Human Rights to reflect this change. Using "rights" language to claim humans have a "right" to water requires us to think about how we conceptualize nature. As we discussed earlier in this chapter, humans often understand themselves as separate from nature and therefore see themselves as having dominion over it. From a Marxist perspective, nature is often "produced" or commodified within a capitalist system. For example, when companies such as Nestlé bottle water for sale, they are privatizing nature for profit. Canadian Maude Barlow (Figure 6.9), founder of the Blue Planet Project, works with international activist organizations to protect water from the threat of privatization, whether that takes the form of the privatization of water utilities or the bottling of previously accessible water to be sold as a traded commodity. Blue Planet Project's research shows that over 1 billion people worldwide do not have access to clean water (**Figure 6.20**), and 1 million children die each year from diseases attributed to lack of fresh water. These statistics are supported by the World Health Organization and UNICEF. In her fight against the increasing commodification of water, Barlow argues that water should be considered a "commons," a shared natural resource.

As human populations have expanded, people have increasingly settled in arid regions. One of the great ecological disasters of the 20th century occurred in Kazakhstan and Uzbekistan, whose common boundary runs through the Aral

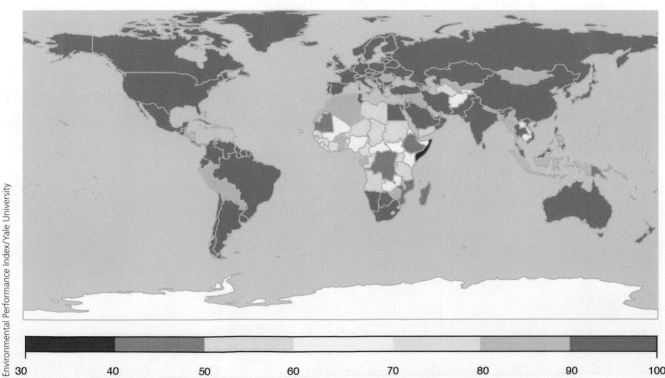

Environmental Performance Index/Yale University

30	40	50	60	70	80	90	100

FIGURE 6.20 Global access to clean drinking water, 2011. The map shows the percentage of each country's population with access to clean drinking water.

Sea. Streams that fed this large body of water were diverted to irrigate the surrounding desert (mainly for commercial cotton production). Heavy use of chemical pesticides ruined the groundwater, causing a health crisis that some observers describe as an "ecological Chernobyl" (a reference to the 1986 nuclear reactor meltdown in the Ukraine that closed down an area within a radius of 30 kilometres around the damaged reactor). Then the Aral Sea began to dry up. In 1960, the Aral Sea was the world's fourth-largest lake; by 2011 it was one-tenth of its original size (**Figure 6.21**). Philip Micklin and Nikolay Aladin, in a 2008 *Scientific American* article, describe a process of what they call "reckless starvation," which siphoned off the Aral's water supply for crop irrigation. The environmental and economic ramifications are vast: fish species declined from 32 varieties in the lake to 6, and 60,000 commercial fishermen lost their jobs when the fisheries closed. Inland waterways have shut down, and toxins, both airborne and ground-based, have become a serious problem for humans and nature alike. The average lifespan for a local resident has dropped from 65 to 61 years of age.

THE ATMOSPHERE

The Earth's **atmosphere** is a thin layer of air lying directly above the lands and oceans. We depend on the atmosphere for our survival: we breathe its oxygen; it shields us from the destructive rays of the sun; it moderates temperatures; and it carries moisture from the oceans over the land, sustaining crops and forests and replenishing soils and wells. The atmosphere has a truly amazing capacity to cleanse itself. In 1883, the Indonesian volcano Krakatau

Atmosphere Blanket of gases surrounding the Earth and located some 600 kilometres above the Earth's surface.

erupted catastrophically, throwing 10 cubic kilometres of rock and ash into the atmosphere. Total darkness prevailed in the area for nearly three days, and dust from the explosion encircled the Earth and created vividly coloured sunsets for years afterward. However, the atmosphere eventually cleared and all traces of the eruption disappeared. In 1980, the eruption of Mount St. Helens in the northwestern United States caused a similar, though much smaller, globe-encircling cloud of volcanic dust in the upper atmosphere. Thirty years later, in 2010, Eyjafjallajökull erupted in Iceland, disrupting air traffic for days. Again, the atmosphere soon cleansed itself.

Human pollution of the atmosphere will likely result in longer-lasting and possibly permanent damage. While the atmosphere can disperse even the densest smoke and most acrid chemical gases, some waste may be producing irreversible change. The nature of the change is still being debated, but two centuries of industrial expansion have caused an enormous increase in global atmospheric pollution, and the rapid industrialization of countries like China, India, and Brazil is compounding the problem. Although global concern and action to limit atmospheric pollution are much in evidence, the problem remains.

Climate Change. Climate change and its effects are an increasing concern around the globe. The United Nations Framework Convention on Climate Change, an international treaty developed during the UN's Conference on Environment and Development in Rio de Janeiro in June 1992, defined climate change as:

a change of climate which is attributed directly or indirectly to human activity that alters the composition of the global atmosphere and which is in addition to natural climate variability observed over comparable time periods. (Article 1).

© E.H. Fouberg, A.B. Murphy, H.J. De Blij, and John Wiley & Sons, Inc.

A Aral Sea, mid-1960s   **B** Aral Sea, early 2000s   **C** Aral Sea, 2014

FIGURE 6.21 The dying Aral Sea. Affected by climatic cycles and afflicted by human interference, the Aral Sea, on the border of Kazakhstan and Uzbekistan, is dying. In a quarter of a century, it lost three-quarters of its surface area and more than 90 percent of its volume.

This definition acknowledges that climate change may occur naturally but that the changes we are interested in are those attributable to human activity. More recent definitions take a more scientific perspective, suggesting that climate change is "a statistically significant variation in either the mean state of the climate or in its variability, persisting for an extended period (typically decades or longer)" (Houghton, 2001). This shifts the focus from an assessment of the activities that alter the composition of the global atmosphere to the process of documenting change.

The United Nations Intergovernmental Panel on Climate Change (IPCC), an intergovernmental body that reviews research on climate change data, argues that there are major negative changes occurring in three areas: global average surface temperature, global average sea level, and Northern Hemisphere snow cover for March–April (IPCC, 2007). Despite natural variation over the short term, the long-term data demonstrate that we are experiencing negative changes in the global climate that have serious local consequences. For example, countries such as the Maldives, made up of a chain of some 1,200 islands and coral reefs off the coast of India, could disappear if sea levels continue to rise. President Nasheed, in an effort to publicize his country's plight, held a cabinet meeting underwater in October 2009 prior to the Climate Change Conference held in Copenhagen in December 2009 (**Figure 6.22**).

Most scientists argue that tropospheric pollution (pollution in the lowest layer of the atmosphere), particularly the release of "greenhouse" gases, causes the Earth to retain more heat (hence the term "greenhouse"). Greenhouse gases include methane, ozone, nitrous oxide, and carbon dioxide. The full effect

Global warming Theory that the Earth is gradually warming as a result of an enhanced greenhouse effect in the Earth's atmosphere caused by ever-increasing amounts of carbon dioxide and other gases produced by various human activities.

of this heating will not be felt until well into the 21st century. Estimates of **global warming** differ: in the early 2000s, computer models still predicted a warming of 2.78°C to 3.78°C over the next 50 years. This might be enough to melt some glacial ice and raise sea levels as much as 15 centimetres. Indeed, this is already happening, as evidenced by the disappearance of two uninhabited islands in the Pacific atoll state of Kiribati. Changes in climate involve changes in the hydrologic cycle, which affect patterns of precipitation. These changes can, in turn, affect where certain types of vegetation grow, which can alter everything from agricultural patterns to the location of animal habitats. One of the most obvious impacts of climate change is the melting of glaciers and ice packs (**Figure 6.23**).

Although there is some debate about how much the Earth will warm, there is no question that growing populations and increased human activity, ranging from the burning of tropical forests to pollution by industry and automobiles, are having an unprecedented impact on the atmosphere. The amounts of key "greenhouse" gases in the atmosphere have been increasing at a rate of about 2 percent per decade. Automobiles, steel mills, refineries, and chemical plants account for a large part of this increase. **Figure 6.24** shows that core countries are the largest producers of carbon dioxide (CO_2) emissions, with China, the United States,

(a)

(b)

U.S. Geological Survey, Department of the Interior/Unknown photographer, courtesy of GNP Archives

U.S. Geological Survey, Department of the Interior/Karen Holzer

FIGURE 6.23 Grinnell Glacier, Glacier National Park, Montana. Grinnell Glacier has retreated substantially between (a) 1940 and (b) 2006.

Mohammed Seeneen/AP/The Canadian Press

FIGURE 6.22 Underwater cabinet myeetings. To draw attention to rising sea levels, which they fear will ultimately cover their island nation, the cabinet of the Maldives government held a meeting underwater in 2009.

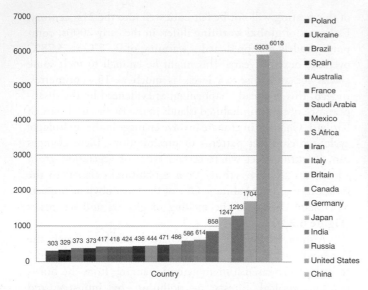

FIGURE 6.24 Carbon dioxide emissions by country (in million metric tonnes), 2009. In 2009, China and the United States had significantly more carbon dioxide emissions than the next highest emitters. Data from Ecosystem Marketplace.

© Design Pics Inc/Alamy

FIGURE 6.25 Cattle farming. Beef cattle are a major source of methane gas, one of the greenhouse gases causing global warming.

Russia, India, and Japan leading the way. We can also see the difference in carbon dioxide production between high-income and low-income nations.

The United Nations Environment Programme (UNEP) argues that in order to understand climate change, we need an emissions inventory that identifies and quantifies a country's sources of greenhouse gases. Questions of accuracy are a concern, although we can have some confidence about emissions calculations from energy and industrial processes (bearing in mind problems with self-reporting). However, agricultural emissions, of such gases as methane and nitrous oxide, are difficult to calculate because they arise from biological processes that are variable. Feed lots—large penned areas where beef cattle are reared for slaughter—are major producers of methane gas (**Figure 6.25**).

Without doubt there will be consequences from greenhouse gas emissions and the resulting global warming; all that remains uncertain is exactly what those consequences will be. In the face of these concerns, international action around climate change is gaining momentum.

> **Acid rain** An environmental peril in which acidified rainwater severely damages plant and animal life; caused by the oxides of sulphur and nitrogen that are released into the atmosphere when coal, oil, and natural gas are burned, especially in major manufacturing zones.

Acid Rain. A by-product of the enormous volume of pollutants spewed into the atmosphere is **acid rain**. Acid rain forms when sulphur dioxide and nitrogen oxides are released into the atmosphere by the burning of fossil fuels. These pollutants combine with water vapour in the air to form dilute solutions of sulphuric and nitric acids, which are washed out of the atmosphere by rain or other types of precipitation, such as fog and snow. Although acid rain usually consists of relatively mild acids, they can be caustic enough to harm certain natural ecosystems. Acid rain is causing acidification of lakes and streams (which, in turn, kills fish that are unable to adapt to the change in acidity of the water), stunted growth of forests, and loss of crops in affected areas.

In cities, acid rain accelerates the corrosion of buildings and monuments. Sudbury, Ontario, is a case study for the effects of acid rain. Sudbury boasts large deposits of ore, most prominently nickel and copper. The smelting process, which turns the ore into metal, releases high levels of sulphur into the atmosphere, which combines with water vapour to make acid rain. As a result, Sudbury became infamous for its destroyed vegetation and wildlife, and more than 7,000 lakes in the area were deemed contaminated due to acid rain. However, scientists and activists, who demanded that emissions be cleaned up and controlled, played a key role in the revitalization of the Sudbury region. Between 1980 and 1997, two of the main smelting companies, Inco and Falconbridge, drastically reduced their emissions, by 75 percent and 56 percent, respectively. The ecosystem is slowly responding to the environmental changes, and the area's flora and fauna are showing signs of recovery. In addition to smelters, emissions from cars, trucks, airplanes, and ships also contribute to the production of acid rain (see Chapter 12).

The geography of acid rain is most closely associated with patterns of industrial concentration and middle- to long-distance wind flows. The highest emissions from coal and oil burning are linked to regions with large concentrations of heavy manufacturing, such as are found in Western and Eastern Europe, the United States, and eastern China. As these industrial areas began to experience increasingly severe air pollution in the second half of the 20th century, many countries (including the

Stephen Amiaga (www.amiaga.com)

Markley Boyer/The Mannahatta Project/Wildlife Conservation Society

FIGURE 6.26 The Mannahatta Project. The Mannahatta Project at the Wildlife Conservation Society provides a fascinating exploration of what Manhattan Island would have looked like circa 1609. The project traces 55 different ecological communities, including a deciduous forest, bears, wolves, fish, and birds.

United States in 1970) enacted legislation establishing minimum standards for clean air. The United States and Western Europe saw positive results as industry complied with legislated emission reductions. In Canada, acid rain from U.S. industrial regions near the border damaged forests and acidified lakes, although some recovery came faster than scientists had predicted. This evidence encouraged other countries to impose stricter controls on factory emissions.

THE LAND

Over the centuries, human population growth has increased pressure on the land surface. More land is cleared and placed under cultivation, rivers are dammed, and cities expand. The effects are seen almost everywhere and are so extensive that it is often difficult to picture what an area might be like in the absence of humans. Yet when we do try to imagine a world without human intervention, the results can be startling (**Figure 6.26**). The most significant examples of human impact on the Earth's land surface are deforestation, soil erosion, waste disposal, and loss of biodiversity.

Deforestation.   From the tropical Amazon Basin to high-latitude North America and Eurasia, humans have cut down forests and whittled away woodlands. The world's forests, especially those of lower and middle latitudes, play a critical role in the **oxygen cycle**. In that cycle, atmospheric oxygen

> **Oxygen cycle** Cycle in which natural processes and human activity consume atmospheric oxygen and produce carbon dioxide, and the Earth's forests and other flora, through photosynthesis, consume carbon dioxide and produce oxygen.

is consumed by natural processes as well as by human activities. Forests counteract this loss through photosynthesis and related processes, which release oxygen into the atmosphere. The destruction of vast tracts of forest—known as **deforestation**—alarms ecologists and others, who warn of unforeseeable and incalculable consequences for the affected areas but also for the planet as a whole. As Valerie Thomas indicates in her *Guest Field Note*, geographers are engaged in research focusing on deforestation and climate change, particularly as it applies to Canadian forests.

> **Deforestation** The clearing and destruction of forests to harvest wood for consumption, clear land for agricultural uses, and make way for expanding settlement frontiers.

In the early 1980s, the Food and Agriculture Organization (FAO) of the United Nations undertook a study of the rate at which forests were being depleted. This analysis showed that 44 percent of the tropical rainforest had already been affected by cutting and that more than 1 percent was being logged every year. In 1990, the FAO predicted that if this rate of cutting were to continue, the entire equatorial rainforest would be gone in less than 90 years. The most recent FAO study, from 2010, shows that the rate of deforestation may be decreasing. Since 2000, approximately 13 million hectares of forest were converted to other uses or lost through natural causes each year, compared to 16 million hectares per year in the 1990s.

While there has been much international focus on clear-cutting of rainforests in Central and South America, Canada has experienced its share of conflict over clear-cutting rights and practices. In 1993, the B.C. government revisited a previous decision on logging in Clayoquot Sound and deemed two-thirds of the old-growth forest available for logging. In the largest act of peaceful civil disobedience in Canadian history, over 12,000 protestors worked with Greenpeace and the Sierra Club to resist plans to clear-cut. Clayoquot Sound was declared a World Biosphere Reserve by UNESCO in 2000.

GUEST FIELD NOTE

Studying the Changes to Canada's Boreal Forests

My work involves the use of remote sensing to study the boreal forest. I was led to this research through my concerns about deforestation and climate change. The boreal forest, which spans the circumpolar region and covers about half of Canada's landmass, contains more carbon stored in vegetation and soil than any other forest ecosystem, including the tropics. This makes it a significant contributor to the global carbon cycle and to global climate. Unfortunately, the vast size and complexity of the boreal forest makes it difficult to study and monitor. My goal is to help improve our ability to predict the impacts of human activities on boreal ecosystem health and function. Remote sensing has facilitated this objective because it allows me to obtain repeated measurements over Canada's boreal landscape, which aids me in characterizing changes over time (**Figure 6.27**).

I use two cutting-edge remote sensing technologies for my research. The first, light detection and ranging (lidar), uses laser pulses to penetrate the forest canopy from above. This gives us very detailed information about the ground surface below the canopy (**Figure 6.28a**). Using geographic information systems (GIS), we can develop high-resolution digital elevation models that show small stream features, hills, valleys, objects on the surface, and other useful information about the terrain.

Lidar data also give us information about the size, shape, and spatial arrangement of trees (**Figure 6.28b**). This

(a)

(b)

FIGURE 6.28 Light detection and ranging (LIDAR). (a) Lidar data showing the ground surface (light brown) and vegetation (green). (b) Lidar side profile of a forest canopy. The mature natural canopy (left) is approximately twice as tall as the young plantation canopy (right). The gap in the middle is a road.

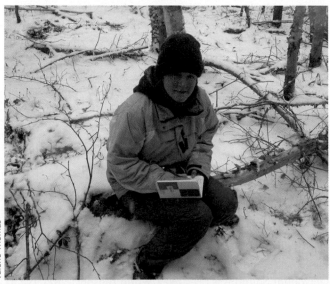

FIGURE 6.27 Writing field notes in a mixed wood forest, Northern Ontario.

enables us to quantify and map variables related to forest structure, including tree height, basal area, stem density, biomass, crown closure, and crown shape. Among other things, we use forest structural information for forest inventories and to obtain estimates of the amount of carbon stored in the vegetation.

The second technology I use in my research is hyperspectral remote sensing, which produces a series of images that show how much sunlight is reflected off the top of the forest canopy at different wavelengths (**Figure 6.29**). We know from previous research that leaves contain different amounts of pigments, chlorophyll, and nutrients under changing environmental conditions. We refer to this as a leaf's biochemistry. Subtle differences in leaf biochemistry will affect the way sunlight reflects off the canopy at different wavelengths, and hyperspectral sensors are capable of detecting these variations. Differences in leaf biochemistry, especially in the amounts of chlorophyll and nitrogen present, are closely related to vegetation health and can control a leaf's ability to photosynthesize (or, in other words, a leaf's ability to extract carbon from the atmosphere). This is all part of a tree's function, or physiology.

By combining the structural information (i.e., heights of trees) derived from lidar data with the physiological information (i.e., amount of stored carbon) derived from hyperspectral data, we can construct a more complete model of forest ecosystem structure and function than is possible with either technology alone. This will help us to develop better models of the forest carbon cycle at local, regional, and national scales. Ultimately, the long-term research goal is to use these technologies to monitor global carbon exchange and integrate them into climate models so that we can generate more accurate predictions of future climate conditions.

Valerie Thomas, Department of Forest Resources and Environmental Conservation, Virginia Polytechnic Institute and State University

FIGURE 6.29 Hyperspectral remote sensing. Hyperspectral image of a boreal mixed wood forest in Northern Ontario. This is a false colour image, where red/pink indicates healthy closed canopies of trembling aspen, and blue indicates open canopies with low chlorophyll (black spruce). The depth indicates reflectance from blue to near infrared wavelengths along the edge of the image.

Soil Erosion.

The loss of potentially productive soil to erosion is described as a "quiet crisis" of global proportions. Ecologists Lester Brown and Edward Wolf point out that the increasing rate of soil loss over the past generation is not the result of a decline in the skills of farmers but, rather, of the pressures on farmers to produce more—an explanation grounded in the political ecology approach. In an integrated world food economy, the pressures on land resources are not confined to particular countries; they permeate the entire world.

> **Soil erosion** The wearing away of the land surface by wind and moving water.

Soil erosion is caused by a variety of factors, but two of the main causes are livestock grazing in areas where they destroy the natural vegetation, and farmers ploughing lands too dry to sustain farming, followed by wind erosion. Why has soil erosion increased so much? Part of the answer lies in population pressure: world population has now surpassed 7 billion. Associated with population growth is the cultivation of ever-steeper slopes, with hastily constructed terraces or without any terraces at all (**Figure 6.30**). As the pressure on land increases, farmers are less able to leave part of their soil fallow (unused) so it can recover its nutrients. Altogether, 99.7 percent of all human food is grown in soil (the rest is grown in water), and annual soil erosion shrinks the cropland available for agriculture. Globally, about 10 million hectares of cropland are lost to soil erosion each year.

Soil is a renewable resource because with proper care it can recover. International cooperation in food distribution, education of farmers and governments, and worldwide dissemination of soil conservation methods are three interrelated solutions that are urgently needed to solve this "quiet crisis."

Waste Disposal.

If anything has grown faster than population itself, it is the waste generated by households, communities, and industries—much of it a matter of bulk, some of it a source of danger. The United States, the world's largest consumer of resources, is also the largest producer of **solid waste**, debris, and garbage discarded by urban populations, industries, mines, and farms. According to current estimates, the United States produces about 1.98 kilograms of solid waste per person per day, which adds up to well over 251 million metric tonnes per year. But the United States is not alone. Other high-technology economies with a high ratio of disposable materials (containers, packaging) face the same problems. Canada, for instance, produces more than 30 million tonnes of solid waste per year, or 1.7 kilograms per person per day.

> **Solid waste** Non-liquid, non-soluble materials ranging from municipal garbage to sewage sludge, agricultural refuse, and mining residues.

FIGURE 6.30 Guangxi-Zhuang, China. Overuse of land in this area of China is leading to the collapse of formerly sound terracing systems.

A growing subsection of the waste problem is e-waste, made up of obsolete electronic goods, such as computers, which often contain hazardous materials: for example, chemicals from discarded electronics leach into the ground or enter the atmosphere. According to the United Nations, the world produced 54 million tonnes of e-waste in 2013, and this number is expected to grow by 33% by 2017. Disposal of e-waste is a global issue, as recycling programs in North America and Europe, filled to capacity domestically, turn to international dump sites in countries like Ghana, Nigeria, Pakistan, India, and China, which often have lax worker and environmental protection laws. As well, it is significantly cheaper for North American and European countries to ship recycling offshore than to manage it domestically. The result is that people working for very little money process tens of thousands of tonnes of e-waste each year, recovering valuable constituent materials of electronic items, including copper, iron, gold, and silicon.

Disposal of waste (not just e-waste) more generally is a major worldwide problem. For example, in Hagersville, Ontario, a huge pile of discarded tires burned for 17 days in 1990. There were an estimated 12 to 14 million tires in the pile, and over 4,000 homes had to be evacuated, as such fires produce a huge amount of toxic smoke. The aftermath of the fire was devastating for nature and humans alike, as toxic chemicals leached into the air and groundwater. Millions of dollars were spent on the environmental cleanup. Years later, firefighters reported developing rare, aggressive forms of cancer that the Workplace Safety and Insurance Board attributed to the fire. Demands for tougher regulations were not addressed until September 1, 2009, when Ontario enacted the Used Tires Stewardship Program.

Finding locations for waste disposal is no longer easy. In poorer countries, waste is thrown onto open dumps, where vermin multiply, decomposition sends methane gas into the air, and rain and waste liquids carry contaminants into the groundwater. In countries that can afford it, such open dumps have been replaced by **sanitary landfills**, where waste is placed in a specially prepared excavation that has a floor of materials to treat seeping liquids. Operators cover each load with soil as it is compacted and deposited in the fill.

> **Sanitary landfills** Disposal sites for non-hazardous solid waste that is spread in layers and compacted to the smallest practical volume. The sites are typically designed with floors made of materials to treat seeping liquids and are covered by soil as the wastes are compacted and deposited in the landfill.

The United States, the European Union, and Japan export solid (including hazardous) wastes to countries in Africa, Central and South America, and East Asia (**Figure 6.31**). While these countries are paid for accepting the waste, they do not always have the capacity to treat it properly, so the waste is often dumped in open landfills, where it creates the very hazards that the exporters want to avoid. In the late 1980s, the richer countries' practice of "managing" waste by exporting it became a controversial

© Allan Ivy/Alamy

FIGURE 6.31 Shipbreaking in Chittagong, Bangladesh. Bangladeshi workers dismantle old ships, including oil tankers, and salvage everything from the steel sides to the doorknobs and toilets. The workers have no safety protection and no labour regulations, and are paid very little.

issue, and in 1989 a treaty was drawn up to control it. The treaty did not prohibit the exporting of hazardous waste, which is what many poorer countries had desired, although it did place some restrictions on trade in hazardous materials.

It is useful to differentiate between two types of hazardous waste: **toxic wastes**, which are dangerous because they may contain chemicals, infectious materials, and the like; and **radioactive wastes**, which are of two types: low-level radioactive wastes, which give off small amounts of radiation and are produced by industry, hospitals, research facilities, and nuclear power plants; and high-level radioactive wastes, which emit strong radiation and are produced by nuclear power plants and nuclear weapons factories. In the United States, low-level radioactive wastes have for many years been disposed of in steel drums placed in six special government-run landfills, three of which are now closed. High-level radioactive waste is extremely dangerous. No satisfactory means of disposal or place for storage of this waste has been found, although many ideas have been suggested, including deep shafts in the bedrock, chambers dug in salt deposits (salt effectively blocks radiation), ice chambers in Antarctica, sediments beneath the ocean floor, and volcanically active mid-ocean trenches. None of these is a completely safe solution.

> **Toxic waste** Hazardous waste containing chemicals and infectious materials.
>
> **Radioactive waste** Hazardous waste emitting radiation from nuclear power plants, nuclear weapons factories, and nuclear equipment in hospitals and industry.

Biodiversity The total variety of plant and animal species in a particular place as well as the diversity of all aspects of life found on Earth from genes to ecosystems.

Biodiversity. Another significant change due to human impact is the accelerating loss of **biodiversity**. An abbreviation of "biological diversity," biodiversity refers to the diversity of all aspects of life found on the Earth. Although the term is commonly used when referring to the diversity of species, it encompasses the entire range of biological diversity, from the genetic variability within individuals of a species to the diversity of ecosystems on the planet.

How many species are there? Estimates range from 10 million to 100 million, although only 1.75 million species have been identified. New species, particularly new species of insects, are being discovered regularly. Yet species are also becoming extinct at a rapid rate. We cannot say exactly how quickly extinctions are occurring, though, because we do not know how many species there are. Although extinction is a natural process, humans have dramatically increased rates of extinction, particularly over the last few hundred years. UNEP's Global Biodiversity Assessment estimates that 8 percent of plants, 5 percent of fish, 11 percent of birds, and 18 percent of the world's mammal species are currently threatened.

Where is biodiversity most threatened? If a species with a small range, a high degree of scarcity, and a small geographic concentration has its habitat threatened, extinction can follow. Because most species have small ranges, change in a small area can be unexpectedly devastating. A 2005 report by Stuart Pimm and Clinton Jenkins in *Scientific American* explained that "clearing a forest, draining a wetland, damming a river or dynamiting a coral reef to kill its fish can more readily eliminate species with small ranges than more widespread species."

Human impacts on biodiversity have increased over time. The domestication of animals, followed by the agricultural domestication of plant life, caused significant changes in our relationship with other species. Large vertebrates have always been particularly hard hit by human activities. Many birds and mammals have been hunted not only for food but also for their skin, feathers, and so forth. During the 18th and 19th centuries, beaver populations in North America were drastically reduced as the beavers were trapped and skinned for their pelts; many bird species were hunted for their feathers, which were sold to decorate fashionable hats. Elephants and walruses continue to be hunted for their ivory tusks. From historical records we know that over 650 species of plants and over 480 animal species have become extinct in just the last 400 years. These represent only the documented extinctions. The actual number of extinctions that occurred during this period is almost certainly much higher.

MAIN POINTS 6.2 What Impact Do Humans Have on the Environment?

- Human beings have had an impact on their environment for all of their existence. Humans have brought animals to the brink of extinction in hunter-gatherer societies, and through technologies such as irrigation and genetic engineering they have fundamentally altered both landscapes and life forms.

- Human patterns of consumption vary between the core, periphery, and semi-periphery. The type and severity of environmental impacts vary geographically. Technologies, modes of transportation, and energy use all have a serious impact on ecosystems and the resources we rely on, including water, the atmosphere, and the land. Increasingly, we are seeing tensions between nation-states as they compete for access to the world's resources while at the same time balancing the need to protect shared resources such as the Great Lakes and St. Lawrence Seaway.

- Negative environmental impacts are unevenly distributed around the globe, with peripheral and semi-peripheral countries often bearing the larger human and environmental costs.

6.3 How Are Humans Responding to Environmental Change?

In this final section, we consider the global responses to the environmental problems discussed in this chapter. It is important to note, however, that local and regional initiatives are also significant, from our individual consumer choices and our responsibility to recycle to the actions of all levels of government regarding waste disposal, air pollution, and energy consumption. A major challenge in addressing environmental problems is that they do not occur within a single jurisdiction; designing policy responses is complicated by the fact that the political map does not reflect the geography of environmental issues. The problem is particularly acute when environmental problems cross international boundaries, for there are few international policy-making bodies with significant authority over multinational environmental spaces. Moreover, those that do exist—the European Union, for example—often have limited authority and must heed the concerns of member states. Those concerns, in turn, may not coincide with the interests of the

(a)

(b)

AP Photo/MTI, Gyoergy Varga

Tamas Kovacs/epa/Corbis

FIGURE 6.32 Hungary's toxic sludge flood. Over one million cubic metres of poisonous chemical sludge from an alumina factory near Ajka, Hungary, flooded three villages, killing nine people and injuring over a hundred in October 2010. (a) An aerial view of the broken dike of the reservoir containing the red chemical waste, October 5, 2010. A village in the path of the toxic sludge is visible in the background. (b) Residents attempt to clean up in the aftermath of the toxic sludge flood.

environment. Within democracies, politicians with an eye to the next election may hesitate to tackle long-term problems that require short-term sacrifices. Most authoritarian regimes have an even worse record, as was seen in the policies of the Soviet-dominated governments of Eastern Europe during the communist era. More recently, in October 2010, chemical waste from an alumina plant in Hungary broke through the retaining wall of a reservoir, flooding into the streets and houses of neighbouring towns and villages (**Figure 6.32**).

The United Nations Framework Convention on Climate Change currently guides international governmental activity on environmental issues and continues to play a crucial role in international efforts to curb climate change. This treaty was drafted at the United Nations Conference on Environment and Development (UNCED), held in Rio de Janeiro in June 1992. Delegates to UNCED gave the Global Environment Facility (GEF)—a joint project of the United Nations and the World Bank—significant authority over environmental action on a global scale. The GEF funds projects related to six issues: loss of biodiversity, climate change, protection of international waters, depletion of the ozone layer, land degradation, and persistent organic pollutants. Delegates to UNCED believed that significant progress could be made through these funded projects, along with bilateral (that is, government-to-government) aid.

These actions hold the promise of a more coherent approach to environmental problem solving than is possible when decisions are made on a state-by-state basis. Yet even though the GEF is charged with protecting key elements of the global environment, it still functions in a state-based world, and individual states continue to influence decisions. As **Figure 6.33** illustrates, the major forested regions in sub-Saharan Africa straddle a number of nation-states. Clearly, the effectiveness of the GEF in protecting distinct regions is often limited by state boundaries and individual state interests. Nevertheless, the GEF serves an important role, providing financial resources to four major international conventions (agreements) on the environment:

the Convention on Biological Diversity, the UN Framework Convention on Climate Change, the UN Convention to Combat Desertification, and the Stockholm Convention on Persistent Organic Pollutants.

A few global environmental issues are so pressing that efforts have been made to create guidelines for action, which take the form of international conventions or treaties. The most prominent examples are in the areas of global climate change, biological diversity, and protection of the ozone layer.

GLOBAL CLIMATE CHANGE

Beginning in the late 1980s, growing concern about climate change led to a series of intergovernmental conferences on the nature and extent of human impacts on Earth's climate. The second of these conferences, which took place in Geneva in 1990, was sponsored by the World Meteorological Organization, UNEP, and other international organizations, and brought together representatives from 137 states and the European Community. The delegates concluded that there was enough evidence of human impacts on climate to justify a treaty on climate change. The final declaration, adopted after hard bargaining, did not specify any international targets for reducing emissions. Instead, it proclaimed climate change as a "common concern of humankind," while noting that "common but differentiated responsibilities" existed between the industrialized core and the less industrialized periphery.

In December 1990, the United Nations General Assembly approved the start of treaty negotiations. A draft convention, prepared and submitted to UNCED delegates for consideration, called on the developed countries to take measures to reduce their emissions to 1990 levels by the year 2000 and to provide technical and financial support for emission-reduction efforts in the developing countries. The convention was signed by 154 states and the European Community at UNCED in Rio de Janeiro.

FIGURE 6.33 Major regions and forest zones in sub-Saharan Africa. Major forest regions in sub-Saharan Africa cross state boundaries, but planning regions are contained within those boundaries. Source: International Bank for Reconstruction and Development/The World Bank: N.P. Sharma, S. Rietbergen, C.R. Heimo, and J. Patel, "A Strategy for the Forest Sector in Sub-Saharan Africa," World Bank Technical Paper No. 251, Africa Technical Department Series, 1994. Adapted with permission.

For several years after UNCED, various committees met to discuss matters relating to the convention. By 1995, mounting concerns about the nature of long-term commitments under the convention led the participants in these discussions to call for a revised treaty that would cover the post-2000 period. They appointed a group to draft an agreement to be considered at a 1997 meeting in Kyoto, Japan. After 10 days of tough negotiations, delegates reached an agreement that required compromises from practically every participating country. The new agreement, known as the Kyoto Protocol, set a target period of 2008–12, by which time the United States, the European Union, and Japan were to cut their greenhouse gas emissions by 7, 8, and 6 percent, respectively, below 1990 levels (see Figure 6.24 for 2009 emissions by country). However, the new agreement did not obligate less-developed countries to adhere to specific reduction goals; instead it called for those countries to implement their own voluntary emission-reduction plans, with financial assistance from industrialized countries.

Neither the United States nor China, the world's two largest emitters of carbon dioxide, signed the Kyoto Protocol, which then expired in 2012. The Doha climate conference, held in 2012 in Doha, Qatar, is one of the most recent global climate

conferences. The main aim of the Doha conference was to set the stage for the 2015 global climate deal. Prior to Doha, only developed nations had legal obligations to reduce emissions, but for the Doha conference, the structure of global climate negotiations was divided between working groups for developed *and* developing nations. Under this new system, all countries—developed and developing alike—would make legal commitments in 2015. For instance, in 2014 the average emission per capita in China was 7.2 tonnes and increasing, whereas Europe's was 7.5 tonnes and decreasing. Having both developing and developed nations making legal commitments to reduce emissions enables all nations to work together under what is called the Durban Platform.

In September 2014, European think-tank Germanwatch and Climate Action Network Europe released its 2014 Climate Change Performance Index. Of the 61 countries measured, Canada ranked 58th, a reflection of its lack of effort to reduce emissions and implement climate change policies. This ranking places Canada among the worst of all industrialized nations, trailed only by Iran, Kazakhstan, and Saudi Arabia. Canada continues to receive international criticism for its lack of response to the social, environmental, political, and economic

(a)   (b)

FIGURE 6.34 **Alberta oil sands (Athabasca tar sands).** (a) Excavation of the tar sands. (b) Oil floats on the surface of a tailings pond which holds waste water from tar sands processing.

impacts of climate change. It was the first country to pull out of the Kyoto Protocol, and Prime Minister Harper's statement commending the Australian government when it repealed that country's carbon tax sent shockwaves around the world.

Another reason for Canada's sullied international reputation is the activity at the Alberta oil sands (**Figure 6.34**). The oil sands, located in northeastern Alberta, are the second-largest proven reserve of crude oil in the world; only Saudi Arabia has a larger reserve. The bitumen (heavy crude oil) deposits are located across 141,000 kilometres of boreal forest and peat bogs. Economically, the oil sands are crucial to Alberta's economy, providing plentiful job opportunities in the Fort McMurray area. As well, in fiscal year 2009–10 the Alberta government collected over $3 billion in royalties. In 2009, companies working in the oil sands produced approximately 170 billion barrels of oil; 1.4 million barrels per day were exported to the United States, accounting for 15 percent of U.S. crude oil imports.

Despite the economic advantages, the Alberta oil sands development has been heavily criticized for the environmental impacts that result from processing practices in the region. Activist groups express concern about clear-cutting of the boreal forest, pollution in the Athabasca river, and toxins in the air and water that threaten birds, fish, and other wildlife. At the same time, according to Greenpeace Canada, human social and health concerns have become an issue. Local First Nations groups have reported high incidences of rare cancers and auto-immune diseases, and in 2014, University of Manitoba researchers linked pollution in the oil sands to elevated cancer rates in Fort Chipewyan on the Athabasca River. At the same time, the high cost of living in the area, along with lack of housing due to the massive influx of workers, have put pressures on long-time residents. After she flew over the area, activist Maude Barlow referred to the tar sands as "Mordor"—a reference to the blackened landscape of Middle-earth in *Lord of the Rings*. Canadian filmmaker James Cameron called the oil sands a "black eye" for Canada's international image.

More recently, two pipelines destined to carry oil from Alberta to international markets have caused controversy.

Keystone XL is a proposed 1,897-kilometre pipeline that would take an average of 830,000 barrels of crude oil per day from Alberta to refineries in Nebraska, Iowa, and Texas. Currently stalled by political battles in both the United States and Canada, Keystone XL has drawn criticism mainly because of its potential for oil spills along the route and its contribution in terms of climate change. Environmental groups, seeking to slow down or stop the production of fossil fuels, see interrupting the crude oil infrastructure as a viable, if not easy, target. The second pipeline, Northern Gateway, which was approved for construction in June 2014, is a 1,177-kilometre twin pipeline that will carry diluted bitumen from Alberta to the town of Kitimat on the coast of British Columbia. From there, the oil will be shipped overseas by oil tankers. Residents of Kitimat, including local Aboriginal groups, voted against having the pipeline run through their town, citing the pipeline company's lack of consultation with, and consideration for, local residents. As well, environmental groups, fearing the potentially disastrous consequences of oil spills on land and in the ocean, have consistently protested its development. Kitimat is not far from the Alaskan shores where the *Exxon Valdez* disaster took place more than two decades ago, and residents are aware that oil from that wreck continues to be found along the Alaskan shoreline.

Canada has a direct and pressing stake in the impacts of climate change, particularly in the Canadian Arctic. In September 2010, the CBC reported that because the waters of the Northwest Passage are free of ice to a greater extent and for a longer period than they have been historically (**Figure 6.35**), the amount of ship traffic is up considerably. The Canadian Border Services Agency reports that by September 2010, 18 ships had cleared customs in Inuvik, NWT, up from only seven in 2009. The Northwest Passage is a shortcut from northern Europe to Alaska and Asia, and as shipping increases, so do concerns about Arctic sovereignty and rights to natural resources beneath the surface of the Arctic Ocean (see Chapter 3 for a map and detailed discussion of interested parties). Moreover, climate change has increased concerns about the future of Arctic wildlife. For instance, polar bears may be at risk because they

FIGURE 6.35 Open waters of the Northwest Passage. In 1969 the S.S. Manhattan became the first commercial ship to cross the Northwest Passage. With the ice cover changing, interest in the area as a viable shipping route has increased.

rely on the sea ice for hunting and breeding. With warmer temperatures, polar bears face shorter hunting seasons and poor den conditions, among other difficulties.

BIOLOGICAL DIVERSITY

International concern arising from the loss of plant and animal species led to calls for a global convention regarding biodiversity as early as 1981. By the beginning of the 1990s, a group working under the auspices of the UNEP reached agreement on the wording of the convention, and it was submitted to UNCED for approval. The Convention on Biological Diversity came into effect in late 1993; by 2001, 168 countries had signed it. The convention calls for the establishment of a system of protected areas and for a coordinated set of national and international regulations on activities that can have significant negative impacts on biodiversity. It also provides funding for developing countries that are trying to meet the terms of the convention.

The biodiversity convention is a step forward as it both affirms the vital significance of preserving biological diversity and provides a framework for cooperation to achieve that end. However, the agreement has proved difficult to implement. There is an ongoing struggle to find a balance between the need of poorer countries to promote local economic development and the need to preserve biodiversity. Also, there has been controversy over how countries will share the costs of conservation programs, which has led to heated debates over ratification of the convention in some countries. Nevertheless, this convention, along with a host of voluntary efforts, has helped focus attention on biodiversity and has promoted the expansion of protected areas. Whether those areas will succeed in providing long-term species protection is an open question.

One approach to environmental protection is biodiversity conservation, which usually takes the form of national parks, World Heritage sites, and Biosphere Reserves. UNESCO's Biosphere Reserves aim to balance the demands of sustainable economic growth, social development, and environmental protection. Biosphere Reserves bring together business partners, different levels of government, researchers, and local residents'

groups, all working to foster socio-culturally and ecologically sustainable economic and human development; contribute to the conservation of landscapes, ecosystems, and biodiversity; and provide support for research, monitoring, education, and information exchange related to local, national, and global conservation and land management. As of 2014, there are 16 Biosphere Reserves in Canada. Protecting areas by using these sorts of designations is seen as the best way to ensure environmental preservation and species survival. The number of such designations has increased substantially in recent years, predominantly in tropical peripheral and semi-peripheral countries. The logic is that biodiversity can only be protected by setting aside vast territories beyond the reach of human development or use. Usually the protecting party is the state, which takes ownership of, or establishes regulatory control over, land that may be used or occupied by others. This raises questions about who is responsible for environmental protection, how resources are monitored and controlled, and how environmental benefits and costs are distributed. Indigenous peoples may find their access to and use of traditional grazing and pasture lands curtailed, or certain areas may become open for tourism and recreation in ways that threaten indigenous ways of life. Regulatory schemes also tend to overlook the impact that indigenous communities had on what is portrayed as a pristine wilderness area. Clearly, a more inclusionary and participatory process that recognizes the linkages between local communities and their habitat may be better able to foster conservation and include these communities in ongoing stewardship. As we noted earlier, in the Canadian context, the federal government has designated areas as national park "reserves" until such time as Aboriginal land claims issues can be settled, a process that may prove to be more inclusionary.

PROTECTION OF THE OZONE LAYER

When found in the troposphere (the layer of atmosphere from 0 to 16 kilometres above the Earth's surface), ozone (O_3) gas is a harmful pollutant associated with the creation of smog (**Figure 6.36**). However, a naturally occurring **ozone layer** in the upper levels of the stratosphere (at an altitude of 30 to 45 kilometres) is of vital importance as it protects the Earth from the sun's harmful ultraviolet rays. In 1985, a group of British scientists working in Antarctica discovered that the thickness of the ozone layer

> **Ozone layer** The layer in the upper atmosphere, located between 30 and 45 kilometres above the Earth's surface, where stratospheric ozone is most densely concentrated. The ozone layer acts as a filter for the sun's harmful ultraviolet rays.
>
> **Chlorofluorocarbons (CFCs)** Synthetic organic compounds first created in the 1950s and used primarily as refrigerants and as propellants. The role of CFCs in the destruction of the ozone layer led to the signing of an international agreement (the Montreal Protocol).

above the South Pole had been dramatically reduced, from 300 Dobson units (DUs) in the 1960s to almost 200 DUs by 1985. (A Dobson unit measures ozone from the Earth's surface.) Studies revealed that the main culprits in ozone depletion were a group of human-made gases known as **chlorofluorocarbons (CFCs)**.

David G. McIntyre/epa/ © Corbis

FIGURE 6.36 Beijing, China. Smog covers the traffic on a motorway in the central business districts of Beijing just a few months before the opening of the 2008 Olympics in Beijing. In 2007, the World Health Organization deemed smog and air pollution in China to be the world's deadliest, killing approximately 656,000 people each year. It was not until the Beijing Olympics in 2008, however, that the pollution levels became an international issue.

These gases, which had only been used in industrial applications, mainly as refrigerants, fire extinguishers, and in aerosol cans, since the 1950s, were thought to be completely harmless to humans. However, the strength of the scientific evidence pointing to their contribution to the rapid reduction of the ozone layer led to an unusually swift and united international response.

In 1985, the **Vienna Convention for the Protection of the Ozone Layer** set out a framework for efforts to protect the ozone layer. Two years later, in September 1987, 105 countries and the European Community defined and agreed on specific targets and timetables for phasing out production and consumption of CFCs when they signed the **Montreal Protocol**. The original agreement called for a 50 percent reduction in the production and consumption of CFCs by 1999. At a meeting in London in 1990, scientific data showing that ozone depletion would continue for many years after CFCs were phased out encouraged the signatories of the Montreal Protocol to agree to halt CFC production entirely by the year 2000. Finally, at a meeting in Copenhagen in 1992, the timetable for CFC phaseout was accelerated; participants agreed to eliminate CFC production by 1996 and speed up plans to phase out other ozone-depleting chemicals, such as halons, hydrochlorofluorocarbons, carbon tetrachloride, methyl chloroform, and methyl bromide. This response is an encouraging example of international cooperation in the face of a significant, albeit clearly defined, problem. Unfortunately, CFCs last for a long time in the atmosphere, which means their effects will be felt for years to come.

As the study of environmental change moves forward, one of the most important lessons we have learned is that global environmental systems are interconnected at numerous temporal and spatial scales. For example, release of CFCs in Japan contributed to the hole in the Earth's ozone layer centred over Antarctica. Industrial production in the Netherlands and Germany contributes to acid rain in Scandinavia. Water drawn from the Rio Grande for irrigation in northern New Mexico affects the amount and quality of water in the river as it flows along the Texas–Mexico border. Human actions, the activities we undertake individually and collectively, are increasingly important factors in all sorts of global environmental changes. To address these changes, we must consider the complex relationship between humans and the environment.

ALTERNATIVE ENERGY

Since the United Nations-sponsored Framework Convention on Climate Change (FCCC) was developed at UNCED in 1992, a number of countries have established implementation programs that encourage the development of "clean" renewable energy technologies and increased energy efficiency in buildings, transportation, and manufacturing.

The European Union (EU) has mandated that a percentage of the funds it provides for regional development be used for renewable energy projects and increased energy efficiency. In 1994 alone, the EU provided 175 million euros (U.S. $159 million) for the development of renewable energy sources in the member

Vienna Convention for the Protection of the Ozone Layer The first international convention aimed at addressing the issue of ozone depletion. Held in 1985, the Vienna Convention was the predecessor to the Montreal Protocol.

Montreal Protocol An international agreement signed in 1987 by 105 countries and the European Community (now European Union). The protocol called for a reduction in the production and consumption of chlorofluorocarbons (CFCs) of 50 percent by 2000. Subsequent meetings in London (1990) and Copenhagen (1992) accelerated the timing of CFC phase-out, and a complete worldwide ban has been in effect since 1996.

FIGURE 6.37 Wolfe Island wind farm. This wind farm, located near Kingston, ON, is home to 93 wind turbines, generating approximately 503 GWh of power.

states, and the amount of EU money going toward renewable energy programs has increased since then. In one case, in 1997, the EU provided 43 million euros (U.S. $39.1 million) for the construction of three wind energy parks in Navarra, a state in northern Spain. The wind energy parks in Navarra and other regions of Spain generated 9,120 GWh (gigawatt hours) of electricity in 2002, creating 695 million euros in income.

These wind energy parks not only help the EU meet its obligations under the FCCC, they also help Navarra achieve a goal of self-sufficiency in energy. Navarra's wind energy parks now provide over 50 percent of the region's electric energy needs. More has changed in Navarra than its energy situation. The wind energy parks, located in the Guerinda Mountains, 30 kilometres southeast of the city of Pamplona, have altered the local landscape and economy in ways that will shape the character of Navarra as a place well into the 21st century.

Renewable energy sources, such as water, sun, and wind, are viable alternatives to fossil fuels, although they are often more expensive to harness and are not without environmental impacts. Wind farms provide a viable, renewable alternative to oil and gas but face resistance from local residents who are concerned about their environmental, health, and aesthetic impact. The adverse effect on birds and waterfowl is well documented. Canada has more than 70 wind farms, producing over 2,550 MW of electricity, and there are approximately 50 more contracted or under construction. Ontario has the largest wind energy capacity in the country, with 702 MW (**Figure 6.37**). Canada is also working to harness the power of the tides; in January 2008 the Nova Scotia government announced that the Fundy tidal power demonstration project would go ahead, setting up a $10-million research facility that would test the ability of underwater turbines to convert tidal energy into electricity.

Damming rivers for hydroelectric power alters freshwater systems and the surrounding environment. The Three Gorges Dam (TGD) in China is the largest hydroelectric project in the world, measuring over 2 kilometres long and 185 metres high, and costing upwards of U.S. $50 billion (**Figure 6.38**). Construction began in 1994 and was completed in 2012. TGD serves three main purposes—flood control, power generation, and navigation—and is considered to be a great success technologically, economically, and socially. Now fully operational, TGD produces 22.5 gigawatts of power (approximately 11 percent of China's total hydropower capacity), which is the equivalent

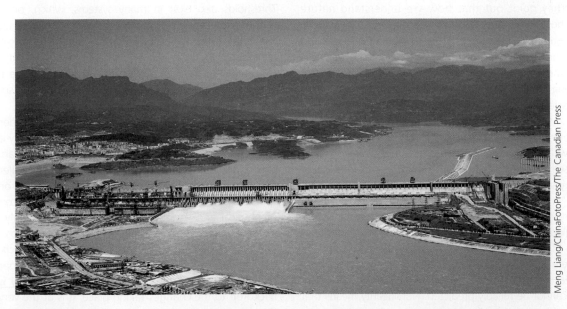

FIGURE 6.38 Three Gorges Dam, China. The Three Gorges Dam spans the Yangtze River in the Hubei and Sichuan provinces of China.

of 16 nuclear power stations. However, the project is not without controversy. Conservative estimates indicate that more than 1.3 million people have been displaced, and fertile agricultural land, cultural landmarks, 13 cities, 140 towns, and 1,300 villages are now underwater. Moreover, while many people have benefited from an improved standard of living, others have struggled with integration strategies that aim to bring farmers into urban environments.

Technology is only one part of the human response to environmental change. The extent and rapidity of that change have led to numerous policies aimed at protecting the environment or reversing the negative impacts of pollution. These policies range from local ordinances that restrict urban development in environmentally sensitive areas to global accords on topics such as biodiversity and climate change. Organizations such as the United Nations Environment Programme, the Intergovernmental Panel on Climate Change, and a broad array of NGOs, activist groups, and citizens' organizations are all working to effect change by developing policy, building social awareness, and encouraging culture shifts. The 2010 United Nations Conference on Climate Change, discussed earlier in this section, is just one of the ways in which governments and NGOs work together to respond to concerns about climate change.

MAIN POINTS 6.3 How Are Humans Responding to Environmental Change?

- The framework currently guiding international governmental activity on environmental issues evolved from the United Nations Conference on Environment and Development (UNCED), held in Rio de Janeiro in June 1992. UNCED produced the United Nations Framework Convention on Climate Change.

- The most prominent issues being addressed at the international policy level include global climate change, biological diversity, and protection of the ozone layer.

- A number of countries are establishing implementation programs that encourage the development of "clean" renewable energy technologies and increased energy efficiency in buildings, transportation, and manufacturing.

SUMMARY

Geographers are actively engaged in studying human-environment relations. They point out that how we understand nature influences how we understand our relationship to it. Various approaches to understanding nature, including Marxist and cultural perspectives, have informed environmental movements and government policy over the last 150 years. In the present day, environmental activism takes many forms and operates across a variety of scales from small local-food movements to global activism addressing genetically modified foods and questions of environmental justice.

What will the future be like? The opening field note suggests that some see the future taking place somewhere beyond Planet Earth. Many would agree with geographer Robert Kates, who foresees a "warmer, more crowded, more connected but more diverse world." As we consider this prospect, we must acknowledge that global environmental changes illustrate the limits of our knowledge of the Earth. Many of today's global environmental changes were not anticipated. Moreover, many global changes are nonlinear, and some are "chaotic" in the sense that future conditions cannot be reliably predicted. Nonlinearity means that small actions in certain situations may result in large impacts and

may be more important than larger actions in causing change. Thresholds also exist in many systems, which, once crossed, cannot be re-crossed; in other words, some changes are irreversible. This occurs, for example, when the habitat for a species is diminished to the point where the species quickly dies off. Unfortunately, we may not be able to identify these thresholds until we pass them. This leaves open the possibility of "surprises"— unanticipated responses by physical systems.

The complexity and urgency of the environmental challenge will tax the energies of the scientific and policy communities for some time to come. Geography must be an essential part of any serious effort to grapple with these challenges. The major changes that are taking place have different origins and spatial expressions, and each results from a unique combination of physical and social processes. We cannot simply focus on system dynamics and generalized causal relationships. We must also consider emerging patterns of environmental change and how different actions have different impacts on the operation of general processes from place to place. Geography is not the backdrop to the changes taking place; it is at the very heart of the changes themselves.

DISCUSSION AND REVIEW QUESTIONS

1. According to the cultural critic Raymond Williams, "nature is perhaps the most complex word in the [English] language." In this chapter we considered three different ways geographers have approached the meaning of nature and our relationship with it. What are these three ways and how does each help our understanding of nature?

2. How we think about or understand our evolving relationship with nature is reflected in the history of the environmental movement in both Canada and the United States. The environmental movement has taken many forms, from groups espousing preservationism or conservationism to corporate and individual initiatives in local communities. What sorts of environmentalism have you noted and what are their major characteristics?

3. How is remote sensing used to study the changes to Canada's boreal forests?

4. It is evident that modern humans and the biosphere face many environmental problems and challenges and that these are interrelated. For example, climate change can be linked to the loss of biodiversity, or water pollution and soil erosion can be linked to deforestation. Can you think of examples in the Canadian context where these linkages are obvious? (Two examples could be development of the oil sands and water pollution or increased cancers in Aboriginal populations.)

5. Despite the numerous environmental problems and challenges, people across the planet have made serious efforts to act and change the unsustainable path. Discuss these efforts, focusing on the various scales at which action is taking place. Do you think these efforts will succeed or are we doomed to the self-imposed catastrophic alteration of the biosphere?

GEOGRAPHIC CONCEPTS

ADDITIONAL RESOURCES ON-LINE

Canadian Biosphere Reserves Association: www.biospherecanada.ca/en/

Edward Burtynsky's photographs of the human-environment relationship: www.edwardburtynsky.com

Intergovernmental Panel on Climate Change reports: www.ipcc.ch/publications_and_data/publications_and_data_reports.shtml

United Nations Environment Programme: www.unep.org

The Welikia Project: Beyond Mannahatta: https://welikia.org/

Center for Political Ecology: www.centerforpoliticalecology.org

National Film Board of Canada: *Manufactured Landscapes*: www.onf-nfb.gc.ca/eng/collection/film/?id553006

The Cove: www.thecovemovie.com

Planet Earth: www.bbc.co.uk/programmes/b006mywy

The Nature of Things: www.cbc.ca/natureofthings

CHAPTER

7 SOCIAL GEOGRAPHIES—IDENTITIES AND PLACE

Building Walls

IF YOU ARE TRAVELLING ON THE Indonesian island of Bali, you are likely to come across brick-making facilities where boys and women build bricks by hand in the hot sun. Young boys scoop wet mud from a quarry by a creek into their wheelbarrows and pour the mud into wooden forms. Once the bricks begin to dry and harden in the sun, someone turns the bricks repeatedly to prevent them from cracking.

The woman in **Figure 7.1** works 10 hours a day, 6 days a week, turning, stacking, and restacking bricks to prevent them from cracking. For her work she earns about 45 cents

FIGURE 7.1 Bedugul, Indonesia. This woman working at a brick-making facility in the village of Bedugul on the Indonesian island of Bali makes about 45 cents (U.S.) per hour and works 10 hours a day, 6 days a week.

(U.S.) per hour. In Bali, women and boys make bricks. In North America and Europe, the vast majority of brick-makers are men, who are aided by machines (one company estimated that 98 percent of its factory employees are men). What makes brick-making a job for women and boys in Bali and a job for men and robots in other places in the world? Does being a brick-maker mean different things in each of these places?

Throughout the world, different cultures and societies have different ideas about what jobs are appropriate for men and what jobs are appropriate for women. Geographers, especially those who study gender, realize people have created divisions of labour that are "gendered," meaning that some jobs are seen as properly men's jobs and other jobs as properly women's jobs. In many societies in poorer countries, families see young women as financial supporters of their families. Thus, many women migrate from rural areas and travel to cities or central industrial locales (such as export production zones, or EPZs) to work and earn a wage that is then sent home to support the schooling of their brothers and their younger sisters (until these girls are also old enough to leave home and work). These financial transactions are called "remittances." We discussed the importance of these remittances in Chapter 5 on migration. In Indonesia and in neighbouring Malaysia and the Philippines, many women temporarily migrate to the Middle East to work as domestics (cooking, cleaning, and providing childcare) in order to send money home to support the family. In North America, rarely does an oldest daughter leave her family in a rural region and migrate to the city to labour in a factory so she can pay for her younger brothers' schooling.

In this chapter, we consider how place and identity are intertwined. That is, we consider how social categories of identity, constructed around ideas about gender, race, ethnicity, and sexuality, vary across and between places, and we look at the implications of this for everyday life.

KEY QUESTIONS FOR CHAPTER 7

1. What is social geography?

2. What is "identity" and how is identity constructed?

3. What is the connection between identity and place?

4. How does geography reflect and shape power relationships among groups of people?

7.1 What Is Social Geography?

Geographers are interested in how our social lives and the places we live, work, and play—our social geographies—are intertwined. Every day we interact with any number of people across a variety of places. We talk to the members of our household, we nod to strangers and say "good morning," we exchange pleasantries with co-workers, and we mix with others at baseball games or the opera. These are examples of social "relations"—that is, the interactions and relationships we have with others around us. In this chapter, we focus on the shifting relationships between the spatial and the social with a particular focus on the specific social categories of gender, race, class, ethnicity, and sexuality. These social categories or identities are the ones we are asked to identify with in a variety of social situations, from answering questionnaires and census forms to applying for housing, opening a bank account, or joining a gym.

While these examples speak to our individual experiences, social geographers also consider how these individual identities come to be understood collectively as constituting a distinct social group, such as the "elderly," "teenagers," or the "working class." Understanding how collective identities come into being and are understood is important because of the social and political implications of collective identity formation. For example, since the end of the Second World War, a number of new political and social movements have emerged based on contested understandings of various categories of identity—the Aboriginal rights movements, the black civil rights movement, the gay rights movement, and the women's rights movement. In many cases, aggressive and sometimes violent political activism has resulted in fundamental changes in social relations between members of different social groups.

Social geographers argue that the nature of these identities, and the form of social relations between individuals and groups, are intertwined with the places in which these social processes take place. As we argued in Chapter 1, "place matters," and the geographies of our everyday lives and social relations are often caught up in power relationships that we must be attentive to when we consider how social categories are positioned in hierarchical arrangements. For example, the wealthy class may have better access to certain services than those in other classes, which is clearly linked to the spatial. Groups such as the "the elderly" experience social spaces differently than, say, certain youth groups, such as "skateboarders," who may find themselves deliberately excluded from some spaces, such as parks, through city bylaws and ordinances.

This chapter begins with a discussion of how we define the object of study for social geography—that is, what do we mean by "the social" and social relations? We then consider what we mean by the term "identity," and we reflect on how identity is constructed by examining the categories of "gender" and "race." After that we turn our attention to the interconnections between the construction of identity categories and the spatial, drawing on examples from ethnic and sexual minority groups. We conclude with a consideration of how the geographical both reflects and shapes power relations between and among various social groups.

Social geography, in the Anglo-American tradition, is defined as "a concern with the ways in which social relations, social identities, and social inequalities are produced in their spatial variation and the role of space in constructing them" (Smith et al., 2009).

It is important to note the considerable interconnection between the knowledges, methodologies, and approaches of social and cultural geographers (Chapter 8), reflected in the interwoven intellectual history of each subdiscipline. Debates about how to delimit the fields of social and cultural geography are numerous, and there are no strict definitions for either subdiscipline. Nevertheless, and for the purposes of this text, contemporary social geography is concerned with social life, social relations, and the construction of subjectivities and identities. Cultural geography, discussed in Chapter 8, concerns itself, in its simplest form, with a study of the shared traits, norms, and values of a particular group, which become visible in particular places or landscapes. Such a perspective has been seriously challenged, however, by those who argue that "culture" cannot be understood as an "object" or a "subject field" that can be easily studied. If, for example, we understand culture as a form of knowledge production, then we need to understand how certain sets of norms and values become dominant and visible in the landscape, while others are overlooked or rendered

FIGURE 7.2 Executive of the Political Equality League, 1916. While Canadian women didn't get the vote until 1919, at the provincial level they were able to vote as early as 1914, thanks to the work of activists including Manitoban Nellie McClung. Organizations such as the Political Equality League, pictured here, were instrumental in gaining the right to vote through efforts that took the form of pamphleteering, petitioning, and holding public events to raise awareness and bring about social change.

from that of the body (and how it is understood in social relations) to that of the household and the street, across urban, suburban, and rural landscapes, or across regions, nations, and continents. Relations among and between individuals and groups depend upon the meanings given to social identities or categories such as race, class, gender, age, ethnicity, and sexuality. How these identities are understood depends on society's cultural, historical, and geographical circumstances. For example, women as a social group in Canadian society were not considered mature or intelligent enough to vote in federal elections until 1919, and even then the right to vote was not extended to women of Asian descent until the late 1940s or to Aboriginal women (as defined by the *Indian Act*) until 1960 (**Figure 7.2**).

invisible. In Chapter 7, therefore, we study both the cultural and social aspects of everyday life that constitute social identities and relations in particular places. In Chapter 8, we focus on the cultural landscapes that are both constituted through and are in play in the formation of particular social identities and relations.

Social geographers are concerned with the nature of social life and social relations, for the individual and for collective groups, from a spatial perspective. What we might study as "social relations" can cut across a variety of scales,

Contemporary social geography as a distinct area of study emerged during the tumultuous events of the 1960s and 1970s, when newly formed groups began to collectively agitate for social change through the formation of political and social movements (**Figure 7.3**). The civil rights movements, the gay liberation movement, and the women's liberation movement brought together individuals who understood themselves as having common bonds based on particular understandings of the social categories of race, sexual orientation, gender, and ethnicity. These sorts of movements are now regarded as engaging in an ideologically based "identity politics," which some scholars call a "politics of difference." Such groups struggle to make visible historical forms of oppression and marginalization, and seek to foster social changes that will ameliorate these difficulties. During this period, these groups held public demonstrations calling for social change and for social justice to eradicate perceived inequalities and injustices based on these social categories (**Figure 7.4**). Geographical research drew attention to structural inequalities, including unequal access to resources such as affordable housing, health care, and public education. Geographers also

(a)

(b)

FIGURE 7.3 Campaigns for social change. (a) Wages for Housework Campaign grew out of feminist political activism in the 1970s. (b) Canadian musician and activist Buffy Sainte-Marie sings at a benefit concert on Piapot Reserve north of Regina on September 8, 1975. Sainte-Marie was awarded a lifetime contribution award at the Canadian Aboriginal Music Awards in November 2008 for her 40-year commitment to peace and the North American Aboriginal rights movement.

FIGURE 7.4 International Women's Day march, Toronto, 1979.

began to engage in a more activist practice, promoting a radical agenda to agitate for social change.

In the 1980s and 1990s, social geographers shifted away from a consideration of these structural inequalities and began thinking about how social categories themselves came into being. Until that time, social categories such as "race" or "class" were taken for granted or assumed to be "natural" or biologically unchanging attributes. Social geographers now argue that social categories such as age, race, class, or sex are **social constructions**, meaning that such categories are unstable and culturally specific. In other words, the social categories structuring social life and relations are not essentialist, biologically based, and "natural" categories but come into being through human perceptions and activities, which generate certain understandings or knowledges about the nature of different kinds of people (including an understanding that groupings of people should be perceived as "different" to begin with).

For example, the concept of "teenager" as an identity, and as a collective and distinctive

group of individuals in core countries, has a fairly recent history, developing in the 1950s. Prior to World War II, no such social category existed, and the line between childhood and adulthood was more crisply drawn. With the development of the idea of the "teenager" as a distinctive identity, we see a host of assumptions about what such as person is like (for example, moody, irresponsible, spontaneous, in transition), which affects how such individuals are perceived and, more important, treated. Similarly, for Millenials (**Figure 7.5**)—another distinctive group—there are assumptions and perceptions based on these assumptions. Such perceptions can also indicate how a person in that category is supposed to act, behave, or feel.

How social categories of identity are constructed and lived depends on a person's location or place. How individuals are understood as "men" or "women," how they are expected to act and behave, and what they are deemed capable of may vary by region and be influenced by the particular assumptions and expectations in place. This makes the geographer's spatial perspective uniquely important in understanding people and place. From our discussion above and the opening field note, we can see that social identities affect how we operate in social relations. When people migrate between regions and across continents, they bring with them their understandings of social categories and relations that may be different from those in the place they settle. As we discussed in Chapter 5 on migration, tensions and disagreements may erupt when social groups with differing cultural and social understandings come into contact with each other. The nature of a place may change with the influx or emigration of different social groups. As social geographers, we are concerned with understanding social life, social relationships, and place in these interactions.

> **Social construction** A perspective that argues that there are not essentialist, biologically based, and "natural" social categories of identity, but, rather, that human perceptions and activities generate particular knowledges about particular groups of individuals. These knowledges may vary historically, culturally, and geographically.

FIGURE 7.5 Geography of Youth. Using images and questions, the Geography of Youth website (www.geographyofyouth.org) tells stories about how Millennials experience public space in different places around the globe. See the *Guest Field Note.*

GUEST FIELD NOTE

The Geography of Youth

"Oftentimes in the media, Millennials are portrayed as being self-centered and overly picky about our careers—which is off-handedly attributed to our being coddled or spoiled."

—Morrigan McCarthy and Alan Winslow

In 2011, Morrigan McCarthy and Alan Winslow, two New York-based freelance photographers aged 30 and 28 respectively, set out on bicycles to meet, interview, and photograph as many Millennials (those born between 1980 and 1995) as they could. McCarthy and Winslow are known as "Restless Collective," a multimedia collective specializing in storytelling through photography. Funded by a Kickstarter campaign, they travelled from Alaska to Argentina, and then through Europe to Morocco, meeting as many young people as they could. They asked 12 questions of those whom they met, and captured them through their camera lenses, with the express purpose of allowing Millennials to speak for themselves. The result, The Geography of Youth project, includes a travelling art exhibit and an on-line repository where people can now upload their own images and answer the same 12 questions that were asked during their bicycle tour (Figure 7.5).

In an interview with *Cut* magazine, McCarthy and Winslow say, "We had friends going to war and friends moving back home with their parents. We pretty quickly set to work designing *The Geography of Youth* with the intention of asking questions about our generation and what unites us on a global scale. There's a lot of static out there about Millennials, and we wanted to allow members of our generation to speak for themselves."

Across a range of spatial scales, from kitchens to public squares, the Geography of Youth project documented young people's lives in different parts of the globe, seeking out similarities and differences, but always careful to note that how Millennials experience the world depends on where they are.

In the past 10 years, geographers have become more attuned to these specific experiences of children and young people, arguing that, until recently, these demographics have been ignored within the discipline. Early research by geographers Holloway and Valentine (2000) suggested three areas for research into the ways that children and youth experience the spaces in which they live:

- *Importance of place* explores how the social construction of children and youth varies across time and space.
- *Everyday spaces* explores how young people negotiate the spaces in which they live their everyday lives, including home, work, school, playgrounds, etc.
- *Spatial discourses* examines what it means to be "young" in a variety of spaces (urban or rural, for example) and how this constructs a particular understanding of the home, work, school.

More recent geographical scholarship has argued that the focus on children's geographies has marginalized the experiences of teenagers and young people. While there is no easy way to delineate "youth" and "children" as distinct categories, it is important to do so, because youth see themselves as separate from children, which means that their experiences should be studied separately.

Today, geographers studying youth geographies, like the photographers behind the Geography of Youth project, seek out young people's experiences in public space. Some of the questions they ask are: How do youth experience public space differently from other age groups? How do discourses about how to behave in public discipline young people to act in particular ways? What kinds of restrictions are placed on young people in public spaces, and why does this matter? Young people's movement through the spaces of our everyday lives are regulated by public policy, discourse, and even media representations; geographies of youth seek to unpack, reveal, and make sense of these experiences.

Heather Maguire, York University

MAIN POINTS 7.1 What Is Social Geography?

- Social geographers are concerned with social relations and identities—how they are produced, and the role of space in constructing those identities and relations.

- Social geographers examine how structural inequality is visible in the built environment. Access to resources such as affordable housing, public education, and health care may differ depending on social categories such as gender, age, race, sexual orientation, ability, and class.

- Social geographers also examine how social categories such as age, race, class, and sexual orientation are socially constructed and vary depending on the historical period and geographic location.

7.2 What Is "Identity" and How Is Identity Constructed?

Identity Defined by geographer Gillian Rose as "how we make sense of ourselves"; how people see themselves at different scales.

Geographer Gillian Rose defines **identity** as "how we make sense of ourselves." How do each of us define ourselves? We construct our own identities through experiences, emotions, and connections that position us within the various social categories available in certain places. That is, if we come to understand ourselves as a "woman," we also come to understand what is expected of us if we fall into that social category. A social identity is a snapshot—an image of who we are able to be at that moment. However, if these categories are socially constructed, identity is fluid, constantly changing, shifting, and becoming. What it means to be a "man" or a "woman" varies depending on cultural and historical circumstances (**Figure 7.6**). Place and space are integral to our identities because our experiences happen in places, and perceptions of place help us make sense of who we are.

In addition to defining ourselves within the categories available to us, we define others and others define us. One of the most powerful ways to construct an identity is by **identifying against** someone else. To identify against, we first define the "other," and then we define ourselves as "not the other." We understand who we are by understanding who we are not. Edward Said wrote thoughtfully about how Europeans, over time, constructed an identity for the region that is now more commonly called the Middle East and Asia, and how Europeans defined the region as the "Orient"—a place populated with strange peoples who displayed mysterious thinking and astonishing traditions. Geographer James Blaut wrote eloquently about how Europeans, during the time of European exploration and colonialism, defined Africans and the Aboriginal people of the Americas as "savage" and also as "mystical." Through these definitions of the "other," Europeans defined themselves as "not mystical" or "not savages" and therefore as "civilized." These ideas about the identities of others still influence our vernacular speech today, through phrases such as "the civilized world" or "before civilization."

Identifying against Constructing an identity by first defining the "other" and then defining ourselves as "not the other."

(a)

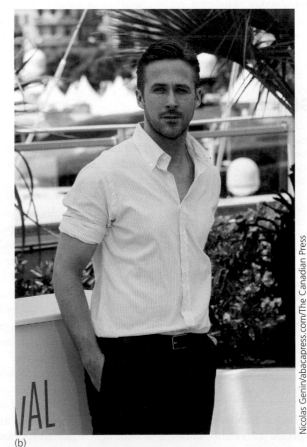

(b)

©Arte & Immagini srl/Corbis

Nicolas Genin/abacapress.com/The Canadian Press

FIGURE 7.6 (a) Louis XIV of France, the Sun King; and (b) Canadian actor, Ryan Gosling. What it meant to be a "man" at the turn of the 18th century is very different from how we understand the role today and must also be understood in the context of race and class. Louis XIV, whose portrait was painted in 1701, wears tights and high heels and has long coiffed hair. Compare this image with a more contemporary example of masculinity, Ryan Gosling.

Phrases such as these invariably mean someone is defining the "other" and, in the process, is defining themselves as superior.

> **Intersectionality** The complex connections and relationships between various social categories, such as race; class, gender, and sexuality.

As we noted in the introduction, there are various contemporary social categories that are central to how we understand ourselves and others in today's world. These include the social categories of race, gender, ethnicity, and sexuality (as well as a host of others, such as affiliation with a religious group). In thinking about these social categories, we need to apply the notion of **intersectionality**, which refers to the complex connections and relationships that exist between these various social categories and that have a material effect on social relations. How we understand ourselves and others depends on the intersection of race, class, gender, and age, among other factors. For example, an elderly white woman sitting in a public park might be viewed very differently than a group of young men of colour standing around in the same location. As well, our social positioning will change over the course of our lifetime as we age and become understood as "middle-aged" or "elderly," or as we perhaps become more wealthy or more poor (class). In thinking about why this might be, we begin by considering the processes of identity construction through a specific analysis of gender and race, We then examine the intersections between identity and place through a discussion of ethnicity and sexuality. Our concluding discussion considers the concept of power relationships through the lenses of gender and ethnicity.

GENDER AND PLACE

> **Gender** Social differences between men and women, rather than the anatomical, biological differences between the sexes. Notions of gender differences—that is, what is considered "feminine" or "masculine"—vary greatly over time and space.
>
> **Sex/gender/sexuality matrix** The expectation that a person is only one of two biological sexes (male or female); that the proper gender characteristics (masculinity or femininity) will be exhibited by that body; and that the normative sexuality is hetero-sexuality.

Feminist geographers Mona Domosh and Joni Seager define **gender** as "a culture's assumptions about the differences between men and women: their 'characters,' the roles they play in society, what they represent." When we think of men and women, we usually begin by identifying individuals by biological sex—those physical features associated with male or female, such as genitals, genetic characteristics, and hormones. The term "gender" is used to describe those socially constructed characteristics expected of bodies identified by biological features as either male or female. Male bodies are expected to exhibit so-called masculine characteristics, and female bodies are expected to demonstrate feminine characteristics. Further, men and women are expected to be heterosexual. Taken together, this reflects the **sex/gender/sexuality matrix**. That is, we expect biologically male bodies to exhibit properly masculine traits and to be heterosexual. The term "heteronormativity" is used to indicate the assumption that heterosexuality is the normative sexuality, thereby excluding other forms of sexual expression (see the *Guest Field Note* by Natalie Oswin later this chapter). Feminist geographers and other scholars argue that gender roles based on biological sexual difference vary historically, geographically, and culturally. In various societies and in different places, there are ongoing and shifting notions about what men and women are like, what they are capable of, and the nature of the relations between them. This suggests that what it means to be a man or a woman is not fixed but is unstable and capable of change.

For example, the opening field note to this chapter described how brick-making is still done by hand by boys and women in Bali, demonstrating how expected or normative gender roles can vary based on social expectations found in particular places. The industry is not technologically sophisticated, and bricks are made one by one. Even beyond brick-making facilities, most of the factory jobs in Indonesia and in poorer countries in the world go to women instead of men. Factory managers in these areas often hire women over men because they see women as an expendable, docile labour pool. Researcher Peter Hancock (2000, p. 18) studied gender relations and women's work in factories in Indonesia and reported, "Research in different global contexts suggests that factory managers employ young women because they are more easily exploited, less likely to strike or form membership organizations, are comparatively free from family responsibilities, and more adept at doing repetitive and delicate tasks associated with assembly line work."

In Canada, until recently, women were thought to be incapable of working in a large number of occupations based on gendered assumptions about intellect, aptitude, and physical strength, but there has been a marked shift in the gendered nature of employment in the last few years. A 2012 Statistics Canada study illustrates this shift, showing a dramatic increase in the number of women in the paid workforce (**Figure 7.7**). In 1976, 41.9 percent of women held paid positions, compared to 72.7 percent of men. By 2012, the gap had closed significantly, with 57.9 percent of women and 65.8 percent of men participating in the paid workforce. Women now comprise the majority of post-secondary graduates. Moreover, women are increasingly working in "non-traditional" sectors such as medicine and law. **Figure 7.8** shows the breakdown by sex across occupational areas. While there has been an increase in the overall number of women in the paid workforce, this chart shows the extent to which occupations are still gendered—that is, they are occupations that seem more appropriate for either men or women. For example, over half of all women occupy positions in one of two categories: business, finance, and administration or sales and service. Men tend to hold positions in trades or transport, as equipment operators, or in sales and service or management occupations. Significantly, in Canada today more men than women still occupy positions in the natural and applied sciences, trades, management, and manufacturing. Many would argue that this disparity reflects continuing barriers to

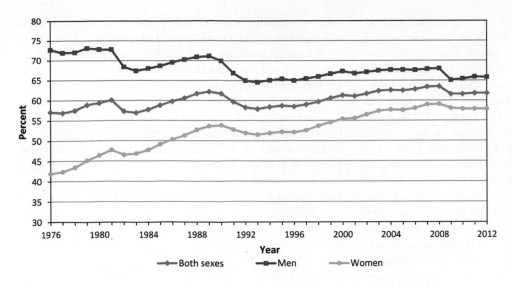

FIGURE 7.7 Labour force participation rates, men and women, 1976 to 2012 (percent). Source: Statistics Canada. *Table 282-0002—Labour force survey estimates (LFS), by sex and detailed age group, annual (persons unless otherwise noted),* CANSIM (database), www4 hrsdc.gc.ca/.3ndic.1t.4r@-eng. jsp?iid=13.

women being accepted into these occupations, rather than any so-called natural difference between men and women.

Statistics Canada data do show an increase in the number of women working in non-traditional jobs, with "non-traditional" defined as sectors previously occupied by a small percentage of women. **Figure 7.9** shows the increase in these sectors based on census data from 1996 and 2006. Professions such as sales, marketing, and advertising; physical sciences; architecture; engineering; and firefighting and policing have all experienced a significant increase in the number of women. All this is to suggest that our assumptions about individual capabilities and

proficiencies based on gendered ideas are socially constructed and that individuals identified as women may do very different things depending on where they live, social expectations, and historical circumstances.

"RACE" AND PLACE

What we mean by the term "race" is not easily defined. As Jamie Winders argues, race has been "conflated with biology and treated as a 'natural' category that predicts intellectual capacity, work ethic, and physical prowess." While we can certainly see

FIGURE 7.8 Percentage distribution of males and females aged 15 and over across major occupational groups, 2011. Source: Statistics Canada, *National Household Survey, 2011,* Figure 3 Distribution of the Employed Population by Major Occupational Groups, Men and Women Aged 15 years and Over, May 2011; www12.statcan.gc.ca/ nhsenm/2011/as-sa/99-012-x/2011002/c-g/c-g03-eng.cfm.

FIGURE 7.9 Non-traditional occupations in which women increased their share of employment between 1996 and 2006. Source: Statistics Canada, *Education Matters: Insights on Education, Learning and Training in Canada,* 81-004-XIE2010001, vol. 7 no. 1, April 2010; www.statcan.gc.ca/bsolc/olc-cel/olc-cel?catno=81-004-X&lang=eng.

differences among people based on outward markers such as skin colour, Castree et al. argue that "race is a collection of ideas and practices through which people have been categorized." We see such categorization in action around us all the time—when we fill out census forms, product warranty information, surveys, medical forms, and application forms that ask us to "check" the box next to our "race" (see **Figure 7.10**). It is important to remember that Caucasian or "white" is also a "race" or a "racialized" identity that is often unremarked. Once indi-

> **Race** A categorization of humans based on skin colour and other physical characteristics. While there are biological differences, racial categories are regarded as social and political constructions because they are based on ideas that some biological differences (especially skin colour) are more important than others (e.g., height), even though the latter might have more significance in terms of human activity. With its roots in 16th-century England, the term is closely associated with European colonialism because of the impact of that development on global understandings of racial differences.

viduals are understood to belong to one "race" or "another," there are material consequences that shape how they are perceived (for example, in terms of intelligence and capabilities) and their life chances.

Most contemporary geographers argue that **race** is a socially constructed identity and a perfect example of how identities are constituted through the geographical. We can see the inscription of "race" geographically in the spatial organization of groups across various landscapes and regions. Race is a useful analytical category as it

asks us to consider how and why certain groups of people come to be understood in a certain way, and it focuses our attention on the spatial implications of racialization. Classic research by Kay Anderson demonstrates how Canadian nationalist discourses constructed the "Chinese" in Vancouver in a certain way over 100 years ago, as reflected in spatial forms such as Vancouver's Chinatown. Legacies of various forms of racialization are visible in many cities in Canada, and elsewhere, in the examples of a "Chinatown" or a "Little Italy"—locations that are now promoted as demonstrating a commitment to multiculturalism and as commodified landscapes of tourism and commerce (see Chapter 8).

Where did society get the idea that humans fall into different racialized social categories? Throughout history, societies in different parts of the world have drawn distinctions among peoples based on their physical characteristics, but many modern assumptions about race grew out of

> **Racism** Frequently referred to as a system or attitude toward visible differences in individuals, racism is an ideology of difference that ascribes (predominantly negative) significance and meaning to culturally, socially, and politically constructed ideas based on phenotypical features.

the period of European exploration and colonialism discussed in Chapter 3. Benedict Anderson argues that differences in socio-economic classes fuelled the concept of superiority attached to race—what we call **racism**. Anderson notes that even before exploration and colonialism, wealthy Europeans defined themselves as superior to those living elsewhere. During exploration and colonialism, the non-wealthy in colonizing countries defined themselves as superior to the people in the countries they colonized.

Anderson (1991, p. 150) explains:

Colonial racism was a major element in that conception of "Empire" which attempted to weld dynastic legitimacy and national community. It did so by generalizing a principle of innate, inherited superiority on which its own domestic position was (however shakily) based to the vastness of the overseas possessions, covertly (or not so covertly) conveying the idea that if, say, English lords were naturally superior to other Englishmen, no matter: these other Englishmen were no less superior to the subjected natives.

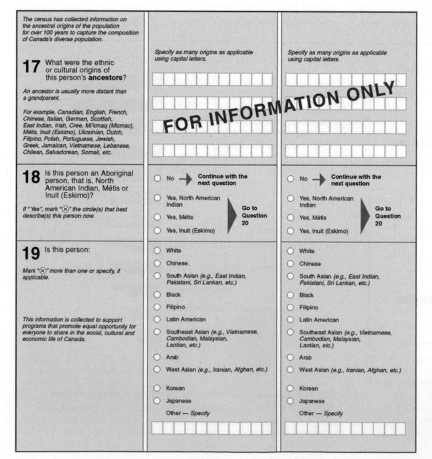

FIGURE 7.10 Canadian census form, 2006. This figure shows part of the 2006 long-form census, which asked questions about identity and ethnicity. In Canada, explicit references to racial origin were included in census forms from 1901 to 1941. All references to "race" were dropped by 1951, and since that time the focus has been upon "ethnic origin." Scholars Boyd, Goldmann, and White (2000) argue that Canada's erratic enumeration practices around race reflect shifting conceptualizations of "race" and race relations in Canadian society. Source: Statistics Canada, Question #19, 2006 Canadian census long form; www.statcan. gc.ca/imdb-bmdi/instrument/3901_Q2_V3-eng.pdf.

The stories the commoners heard about the "barbaric" and "savage" "others" fostered feelings of superiority. One of the easiest ways to define the "other" is through skin colour because it is visible. In building our own identities, an easy way to determine who we are identifying against is by the colour of our skin.

What society typically calls "race" is in fact a combination of physical attributes in a population. Differences in skin colour, eye colour, and hair colour are variations within the human race. The differences likely result from a long history of adaptation to different environments. Sunlight stimulates the production of melanin, which protects skin from damaging ultraviolet rays; the more melanin is present, the darker the skin will be. Many believe that this helps to explain why, over millennia, humans living in lower latitudes—from tropical Africa through southern India to Australia—came to have darker skins. Another (not incompatible) theory holds that the production of vitamin D (a vitamin necessary to live a healthy life) is stimulated by the penetration of ultraviolet rays. Over millennia, natural selection in areas with shorter days in winter and more indirect sun angles (the higher latitudes) favoured those with the least amount of pigmentation, those who most easily absorb ultraviolet rays and in turn produce more vitamin D.

Whatever may be said about the link between environment and the development of particular physical characteristics, it is important to recognize that skin colour is not a reliable indicator of genetic closeness. The indigenous peoples of southern India, New Guinea, and Australia, for example, are about as dark-skinned as native Africans, but native Africans, southern Indians, and Aboriginal Australians are not closely related genetically. There is no biological basis for dividing the human species into four or five groups based on skin colour. Instead, racial categories are the result of how particular cultures have viewed skin colour.

The racial distinctions in place today are drawn from categories of skin colour that are rooted in the cultural history, power relationships, and politics of a place over the past few centuries. Scholarship has demonstrated how historical racialisations of groups as "different" and inferior supported widespread practices of slavery, apartheid, colonialism, imperialism and segregation. Geographer Benjamin Forest (2002, p. 246–247) gives us a global overview of racial distinctions:

In Britain, the term "black" refers not only to Afro-Caribbeans and Africans, but also to individuals from the Indian subcontinent. In Russia, the term "black" is used to describe "Caucasians," that is, people such as Chechens from the Caucasus region. In many parts of Latin America, particularly Brazil, "racial" classification is really a kind of class placement, in which members of the wealthy upper class are generally considered as "white," members of the middle class as mixed race or Mestizo, and members of the lower class as "black." Indeed, because racial classifications are based on class standing and physical appearance rather than ancestry, "the designation of one's racial identity need not be the same as that of the parents, and siblings are often classified differently than one another."

In each of these cases, and in countless others, people have constructed racial categories to justify power, economic exploitation, and social oppression.

RACE IN CANADA

While we may choose to belong to a particular community, culture, or religion, race is an identity that is more often assigned. Benjamin Forest explains that, "in many respects, racial identity is not a self-consciously constructed collection of characteristics, but a condition which is imposed by a set of external social and historical constraints." For example, until 1971 the Canadian government hired enumerators to complete census questionnaires. Up to and including 1941, the census included questions that referred specifically to race. Therefore, these enumerators, working within predetermined census guidelines, assigned racial categories to respondents. The next census, in 1951, referred not to race but to ethnic origin. Scholars Boyd, Goldmann, and White (2000) marked this watershed moment, noting that the move away from the use of the term "race" was due to a combination of factors, including the sensitization of the Western world after World War II in light of the horrors of Nazi termination policies, and the nation-building project in Canada, which was quickly becoming more diverse due to the massive increase in immigration during the post-war era.

The 2006 long-form census questionnaire (Figure 7.10) asks respondents to report their ancestral ethnic origin ("ancestral" meaning more distant than a grandparent) as well as their own identity. These statistics reveal a country whose population is increasing in ethnic, cultural, linguistic, and religious diversity (**Figure 7.11**). The 1901 census revealed 25 ethnic origins, with Aboriginal, French, and English comprising the vast majority. In 2012, the National Household Survey, which replaced the mandatory long-form census, told a much

David Cooper/Toronto Star via Getty Images

FIGURE 7.11 Visible minorities in Canada. South Asians march in the annual Khalsa Day parade in Toronto. Statistics Canada reported in 2010 that visible minorities in Canada will double by 2031.

FIGURE 7.12 Diversity in Canada, 1996 to 2006, and 2017 projections. This bar graph represents the Canadian population, in millions, from 1996 to 2017 (projections). Responses to the "ethnic origin" question on the Canadian census questionnaire reveal an increasingly diverse population, with over 200 different ethnic backgrounds reported. Source: Citizenship and Immigration Canada, *Annual Report on the Operation of the Canadian Multiculturalism Act 2007–2008*; www.cic. gc.ca/english/resources/publications/ multi-report2008/part1.asp. Reproduced with the permission of the Minister of Public Works and Government Services Canada, 2011.

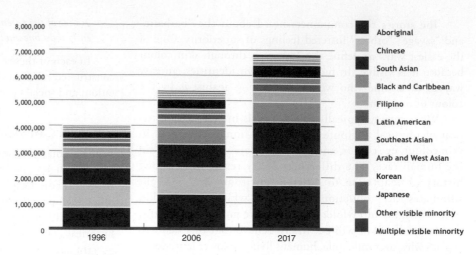

different story; more than 260 different ethnic origins were reported. As **Figure 7.12** shows, predictions for the year 2017 show this diversity to be increasing. As well, the number of people reporting multiple ethnic origins is increasing. The 2011 census data indicated that 42.1 percent of Canadians have more than one ethnic origin.

Additionally, beginning in 1981 and due to increased demand for this information, Statistics Canada began collecting and producing census-based reports addressing another socially constructed category: "visible minorities." While the census questionnaire itself does not ask respondents to identify as a visible minority, Statistics Canada uses the identification information (see Figure 7.10) to make determinations about visible minority status. This status is based on *Employment Equity Act* guidelines that define visible minority persons as "persons, other than Aboriginal peoples, who are non-Caucasian in race or non-white in colour." Since the first year this data was aggregated, there has been a steady increase in the number of persons of visible minority status in Canada. As **Figure 7.13** indicates, in 1981 there were 1.1 million visible minority persons in Canada; the number increased to 1.6 million in the next census, 1986. From 1986 to 1991, the number of visible minority persons almost doubled, to 2.5 million. And over these 10 years the *proportion* of visible minority persons almost doubled—from 4.7 percent of Canada's population in 1981 to 9.4 percent in 1991. In 1996, the visible minority population was 3.2 million, constituting 11.2 percent of Canada's population. The growth in the visible minority population continued in 2001, when it was 3.9 million or 13.4 percent of Canada's population. In 2006, it reached over 5 million and constituted 16.2 percent of the total population of Canada (Figure 7.13).

The statistics in **Table 7.1** reveal a country that is becoming increasingly diverse and multicultural. Canada's visible minority population now accounts for over 19 percent of the total population, and by all accounts this figure will continue to grow. The 2011 census estimated that there were more

than 6.2 million visible minority individuals in Canada (Table 7.1). This population increased from 5.1 million in 2006, with much of this growth attributed to increased immigration from non-European countries. Consequently, the proportion of new immigrants to Canada who are visible minorities has increased. Prior to 1971, 12.4 percent of immigrants were of visible minorities; in 2011, this figure had increased to 78 percent.

RESIDENTIAL ORGANIZATION IN CANADIAN CITIES

As we will discuss in Chapter 10, visible minorities have a strong presence in Canadian urban centres. According to the 2011 census, over 95 percent of visible minorities live in Canadian

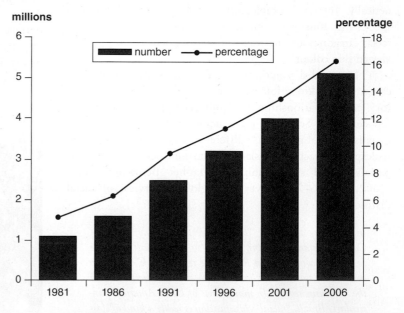

FIGURE 7.13 Number and percentage of visible minority persons in Canada, 1981 to 2006. The absolute number, and the percentage, of visible minority people in Canada has been steadily rising over the past 25 years. Source: Statistics Canada, *Ethnic Origin and Visible Minorities, 2006 Census*, 97-562-XWE2006001, April 2008; www. statcan.gc.ca/bsolc/olc-cel/olc-cel?lang=eng&catno=97-562-X2006001.

TABLE 7.1	Visible Minority Population and Top Three Visible Minority Groups, Selected Census Metropolitan Areas, Canada, 2011			
	Total Population	**Visible Minority Population**		**Top Three Visible Minority Groups**
	Number	**Number**	**Percentage**	
Canada	**32,852,325**	**6,264,755**	**19.1**	**South Asian, Chinese, Black**
Toronto	5,521,235	2,596,420	47.0	South Asian, Chinese, Black
Montréal	3,752,475	762,325	20.3	Black, Arab, Latin American
Vancouver	2,280,695	1,030,335	45.2	Chinese, South Asian, Filipino
Ottawa-Gatineau	1,215,735	234,015	19.2	Black, Arab, Chinese
Calgary	1,199,125	337,420	28.1	South Asian, Chinese, Filipino
Edmonton	1,139,585	254,990	22.4	South Asian, Chinese, Filipino
Winnipeg	714,635	140,770	19.7	Filipino, South Asian, Black
Hamilton	708,175	101,600	14.3	South Asian, Black, Chinese

Source: Statistics Canada, *National Household Survey, 2011,* Table 2 Visible minority population and top three visible minority groups, selected census metropolitan areas, Canada, 2011; www12.statcan.gc.ca/nhs-enm/2011/as-sa/99-010-x/2011001/tbl/tbl2-eng.cfm

cities, as compared to just over 69 percent of Canada's population as a whole. Table 7.1 shows that the major concentrations of this population were in census metropolitan areas (CMAs). The CMAs of Toronto, Montreal, and Vancouver alone were home to 7 out of 10 visible minority persons. In comparison, just over one-third (35.2 percent) of the total population lives in these three CMAs. Geographers Harald Bauder and Bob Sharpe (2002) argue that while these statistics reveal an increasingly diverse and multicultural environment, they simultaneously "produce landscapes of fragmentation and ethnic separation." While the spirit of multiculturalism abounds, the geographic reality is potentially one of segmentation and division.

Africville, Halifax.   One historic example of the "racial separation" in Canadian cities is Africville, a community that was located in Halifax, Nova Scotia. Africville was settled by Black Loyalists who came to Canada after the American Revolutionary War in order to escape slavery and accept the promise of free land. In 1849 the first church congregation was established, and the first elementary school was built in 1883. Although technically part of Halifax, Africville was, by all accounts, a segregated community almost entirely comprised of African Nova Scotians. As a community, Africville struggled to survive, divided by a railway and encroached upon by sewage disposal pits, slaughterhouses, and the open garbage dumps of Halifax. The schools were closed in 1953 as children were moved to racially integrated schools. In the early 1960s, through a process of urban renewal, the city of Halifax decided to demolish Africville to make way for a bridge and the industrial development of the Bedford Basin. **Figure 7.14** shows Africville prior to the demolition.

The demolition of Africville is an example of what scholars Linda Peake and Brian Ray (2001) call practices of "racialized geography" through the "erasure of people of colour from places, memory and the map." Although Africville was a vibrant cultural community, it seemed at the same time to be a "slum" neighbourhood. Urban planners, seeking to solve the urban issues of poverty, crime, and racial tension, opted to flatten the community, erasing it from the Canadian landscape entirely. In February 2010, the government of Nova Scotia

FIGURE 7.14 Africville, Nova Scotia, ca. 1965. Bird's eye view of Africville, showing its location on Bedford Basin, with the north end Halifax and the Narrows in the background. Within two years of this photo being taken, the town of Africville, which was part of Halifax, was completely demolished. All its residents were evicted and relocated.

Bob Brooks/Nova Scotia Archives, 1989-468 vol. 16

issued an official apology to the former residents of Africville and their descendants for the eviction and demolition of the community.

Residential segregation by race/ethnicity has a long history in Canada and can be traced back to the expulsion of Acadians from the Maritimes in 1756 and to the creation of reserves for First Nations peoples, among many other examples. Geographers Bauder and Sharpe (2002), studying census data from 1986, 1991, and 1996, have explored the extent to which residential segregation occurs in Canada's "gateway" cities of Toronto, Montreal, and Vancouver. They conclude that Canada distinguishes itself from the United States in terms of immigrant experiences of residential segregation. Arguably, Canadian visible minority immigrants are not nearly as ghettoized, nor are they as isolated in their communities. While data indicate that visible minorities overwhelmingly settle in major urban centres, it is important to remember that the experiences of immigrants are varied and diverse; different levels of racism, historical circumstances, cultural networks, local attitudes, political environments, and economic forces all contribute to unique experiences for new visible minority immigrants. Bauder and Sharpe suggest that Canada's immigration and multiculturalism policies, which stress the importance of adapting to Canadian society while at the same time respecting cultural differences, have resulted in relatively positive immigrant experiences that are neither ghettoizing nor assimilating.

Kensington Market, Toronto.
New immigrants to a city often move into areas occupied by older immigrants, in a process called **succession**. To demonstrate how succession works, we will focus on a historic district of Toronto called Kensington Market. Kensington Market, designated a National Historic Site of Canada in 2006, is a vibrant and diverse Toronto neighbourhood. Bounded by College Street, Spadina Avenue, Dundas Street West, and Bathurst Street, Kensington is well known for its small shops, densely packed housing, and ethnically diverse population. But Kensington has gone through many waves of settlement (**Figure 7.15**) before becoming what it is today. The land that is now Kensington was originally inhabited by members of the Mississauga First Nation until the first wave of immigrants—European settlers arriving in the late 1700s—took possession as part of a massive land sale treaty. In the early 1900s, a large Jewish population settled in Toronto and grew rapidly from 3,000 in the early 1900s to over 45,000 in 1931. Eighty percent of this Toronto Jewish population settled in Kensington. Jewish merchants set up small shops selling imported European goods, and they offered tailoring services and other services out of the main floors of their homes and out of horse-drawn carts. Schools, synagogues, a medical dispensary, and other

> **Succession** Process by which new immigrants to a city move to and dominate or take over areas or neighbourhoods occupied by older immigrant groups.

John Boyd/Library and Archives Canada/PA-084814

FIGURE 7.15 Jewish immigrants in Kensington Market, 1922.

services soon became part of the local landscape as the neighbourhood grew.

In the 1940s, a growing Black community resided in the region, with many working for the railroads located nearby. Some Black organizations worked to build alliances with Jewish groups to strengthen unions and collaborate on social causes. By the 1950s, most of the Jewish population had left Kensington to more affluent neighbourhoods in the suburbs. They were succeeded by other immigrants, likely due to the area's affordable housing and a European sensibility in the marketplace. Immigrants from the Azores arrived in the 1950s, escaping political unrest in Portugal. They painted the house facades in bright colours, decorated their front yards, and continued the Jewish tradition of operating stores out of the first floors of their homes. Restaurants, cafés, and Tivoli Billiards Hall became local landmarks of the Portuguese community.

In the 1960s and 1970s, immigrants from other regions of the world came to Toronto and settled in Kensington, including people from the Caribbean, Southeast Asia, and parts of North Africa. The Vietnam War brought political refugees from the United States into the region, and the adjacent Chinatown led to an increase in Chinese in the neighbourhood. Kensington became increasingly diverse as new immigrant groups found a place there, drawn to its unique feel and culture. The landscape reflected this diversity, with many ethnic restaurants and food shops appearing on the street. The businesses on the street were built to serve the growing immigrant communities.

Today, as people walk down Augusta Avenue, they can see the process of succession is still going on (**Figure 7.16**). The neighbourhood resists much of the gentrification that has taken place in Toronto, maintaining its sensibility as a marketplace. People still tend to live and work in Kensington, which helps keep its unique feel. More affordable rents, the availability of local goods and services, and a vibrant, diverse population continue to draw new immigrants to the area. The Portuguese community maintains a strong presence, but so too do Chinese, North African, and Caribbean communities, as well as representatives from many other groups.

(a)

(b)

FIGURE 7.16 Kensington street view: Baldwin Street, looking west (a) Then and (b) now.

IDENTITIES ACROSS SCALES

The way we make sense of ourselves in this globalized world is complex. We have different identities at different scales: individual, local, regional, national, and global. At the individual scale, we may see ourselves as a son or daughter, a brother or sister, a golfer, or a student. At the local scale, we may see ourselves as members of a community, leaders of a campus organization, or residents of a neighbourhood. At the regional scale, we may see ourselves as Martimers, Albertans, Torontonians, or newcomers from another region of the world. At the national scale (**Figure 7.17**), we may see ourselves as Canadian, as college students, or as members of a national political party. At the global scale, we may see ourselves as Western, as educated, as relatively wealthy, or as free. We can understand ourselves as all or some of these social categories at the same time.

One of the most powerful foci of identity in the modern world is the state. State nationalism has been such a powerful force that in many contexts people think of themselves first and foremost as a member of their state, whether that means they are French, Japanese, or Canadian. Nationalist identities are a product of the modern state system and a form of identity we discussed in Chapter 3. But nationalist identities coexist with all sorts of other identities that divide humanity—identities that can trump state nationalism in certain contexts and certain scales of interaction.

Geographers have frequently conveyed the idea of an individual's various identities by describing the identities as nested, one inside the other; the appropriate identity is revealed at the appropriate scale or in the appropriate situation. In this context, each large geographic territory has its own corresponding set of identities. Today, however, geographers are more likely to visualize identities as fluid and intertwined, rather than neatly nested, using the notion of intersectionality discussed earlier. Identities affect each other in and across scales, and the ways places and peoples interact across scales simultaneously affect identities within and across scales.

FIGURE 7.17 Unity rally, Montreal, 1995. On October 27, 1995, an estimated 100,000 Canadians rallied in downtown Montreal just days before a referendum vote that was asking Quebeckers whether they wished to secede from Canada. The referendum was a time of great upheaval across the country and around the world, as people across scales, including sovereigntists, federalists, nationalists, First Nations, and many other identity groups, expressed diverse opinions and concerns about the potential of Quebec secession. The "no" campaign won by a narrow margin of 50.58 percent.

MAIN POINTS 7.2 What Is "Identity" and How Is Identity Constructed?

- Social categories of identity are socially constructed and are differently constructed depending on the place, culture, and historical period. In core countries, the most common social categories of identity are "race," ethnicity, class, gender, sexuality, age, and able-bodiedness, although many other social categories are also important.

- Gender is defined as a culture's assumptions and expectations about the differences between men and women. This includes expectations about "proper" feminine and masculine characteristics, interests, capabilities, and relations between the sexes. Those expectations and relations can vary over time and geographical location.

- Race is a socially constructed category. People are "racialized"— that is, assigned to a racial category—based on arbitrary

physical characteristics. There is no biological basis for the various "races."

- Race has been a category in Canada's national census since its inception. The Canadian population is becoming increasingly diverse, and a growing proportion of the total population is made up of visible minorities. This may lead to certain forms of spatial segregation, but in Canada, immigration and multiculturalism policies tend to reduce this effect.

- How we understand ourselves varies across scales. One aspect of identity may be more relevant in some locations and circumstances than others. For example, nationalistic feelings of pride in being "Canadian" may overshadow gender, race, and age during an event like the Olympics.

7.3 What Is the Connection between Identity and Place?

Sense of place State of mind derived when we infuse a place with meaning and emotion by remembering important events that occurred in that place or by labelling a place with a certain character.

The processes of constructing identities and identifying ourselves against others, like any other social or cultural processes, are rooted in places. When we are constituted within particular social categories of identity, we often infuse places with meanings associated with those social categories by attaching memories and experiences to the place. This process of infusing a place with meaning and feeling is what geographer Gillian Rose (1995) and countless other geographers refer to as "developing a **sense of place**." Our sense of place is fluid; it changes as the place changes and as we change.

What is of particular interest to geographers is how people define themselves through places. Our sense of place becomes part of our identity, and our identity affects the ways we define and experience place. Rose explains:

One way in which identity is connected to a particular place is by a feeling that you belong to that place. It's a place in which you feel comfortable, or at home, because part of how you define yourself is symbolized by certain qualities of that place. The geographer Relph, for example, has even gone so far as to claim that "to be human is to live in a world that is filled with significant places: to be human is to have to know your place."

The uniqueness of a place can become a part of who we are. Certain landscapes can feel like "home"—the smell, sight, and sound of the ocean; the wide-open sky of the

prairie; the vastness of a mountainous terrain. Our emotions are deeply attached to and constituted in place, which means we can feel homesick for a place or distinctly out of place in unfamiliar locales. In this section, we use the examples of "ethnicity" and "sexuality" to illustrate the interconnectedness between place and identity. From there, we consider the ways in which our understandings of these connections are being challenged by examining the social geographies of virtual life on the Internet.

ETHNICITY AND PLACE

The word "ethnic" comes from the ancient Greek word ethnos, meaning "people" or "nation." As with understandings of "race," there is no agreed-on definition of "ethnicity." Most scholars understand ethnicity as another form of social classification arising out of social and cultural processes that classify people based on perceived characteristics. Cultural theorist Stuart Hall (1995) explains that "where people share not only a culture but an ethnos, their belongingness or binding into group and place, and their sense of cultural identity, are very strongly defined." Hall explains that ethnic identity is "historically constructed" and is often considered natural because it implies ancient relations among a people over time. The idea of **ethnicity** as an identity stems from the notion that people become closely bounded, even related, in a certain place over time. This is one of the ways we see the intersections between social and cultural geography: individuals with a shared sense of norms, values, and beliefs (in other words, a "culture") become a social group with a set of identities that are constituted through, and become

Ethnicity Affiliation or identity within a group of people bound by common ancestry and culture.

embedded in, visible and distinctive landscapes. Ethnicity offers a good example of how identities affect places and how places affect identities.

The definition of ethnicity may sound simple, but the concept of ethnicity is not. In the United States, for example, a group of people may define their ethnicity as Swiss American. Switzerland is a state in Europe. The people in Switzerland speak four major languages and other minor ones. The strongest identities in Switzerland are most often at the level of the canton—a small geographically defined area that distinguishes cultural groups within the state. So which Swiss are Swiss Americans? The way Swiss Americans see Switzerland as part of who they are may not exist in Switzerland proper (**Figure 7.18**). Ethnicity sways and shifts across scales, across places, and across time. A map showing all recognizable ethnic areas would look like a three-dimensional jigsaw puzzle, with thousands of often-overlapping pieces—some no larger than a neighbourhood, others as large as entire countries.

FIGURE 7.19 Pysanka in Vegreville, Alberta. The Pysanka, or Easter egg, stands as a monument to the diverse ethnicities of Vegreville, Alberta. The dedication message is written in four languages: English, Ukrainian, French, and German. In English it reads: "This Pysanka (Easter Egg) symbolizes the harmony, vitality and culture of the community and is dedicated as a tribute to the One Hundredth Anniversary of the Royal Canadian Mounted Police who brought peace and security to the largest multi-cultural settlement in all of Canada."

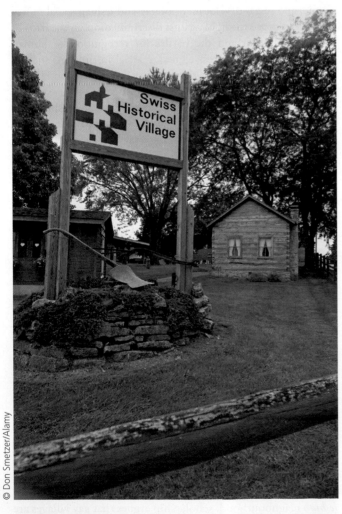

FIGURE 7.18 New Glarus, Wisconsin. The town of New Glarus was established by immigrants from Switzerland in 1845. The Swiss-American town takes pride in its history and culture.

Ethnic identity is greatly affected by scale and place. For example, the Prairie provinces of Alberta, Saskatchewan, and Manitoba are home to a substantial Ukrainian population (**Figure 7.19**). At the time of the first phase of immigration to Canada in the 1890s, Ukrainian territory was divided into two regions: the vast majority ("Greater Ukraine"), containing some 25 million people, was part of the Russian Empire; Western Ukraine, home to approximately 4 million people, was part of the Austro-Hungarian Empire. Those under the rule of the Russian Empire experienced severe repression of the Ukrainian identity, to the point where even the Ukrainian language was banned. In both regions, oppressive regimes led to a poverty-stricken population whose members were divided among themselves. Between 1891 and 1914, an estimated 170,000 Ukrainians immigrated to Canada's western provinces, drawn by the promise of virtually free land. These immigrants, mostly from the Austro-Hungarian region, were searching for a better life and greater prosperity and settled first in and around Edmonton, with the support of the Canadian government, which was seeking to develop the harsh prairie lands. However, concerns about immigrant resistance to Canadian culture led the government, in 1896, to encourage small settlement "pockets" across the Prairie provinces. This first phase of immigration was followed by three more: approximately 68,000 people immigrated between 1922 and 1939; 37,000 arrived between 1946 and 1961; and an ongoing wave began in 1991 with the fall of the former Soviet Union. While there is a complex, rich history behind each wave of immigration, the scale and place of both the Ukrainian territory and the Canadian Prairies shaped the identities of the populations.

Historical accounts of Ukrainian immigration to Canada show how different groups redeveloped their identities based on their experiences in this new land, while at the same time recognizing the regional scales of both their European past and Canadian present.

Cultural groups often invoke ethnicity when race cannot explain differences or antagonisms between groups. Just as "racial conflicts" are rooted in perceptions of distinctiveness based on differences in economics, power, language, religion, lifestyle, or historical experience, so too are "ethnic conflicts." A conflict is often called ethnic when a racial distinction cannot easily be made. For example, an observer may not be able to use physical appearance or skin colour to distinguish between ethnic groups in many of the conflicts around the world. The adversaries in recent conflicts in Northern Ireland, Spain, the former Yugoslavia, Sri Lanka, Ivory Coast, or Rwanda cannot be identified racially, so the parties in the conflicts use "ethnicity" to identify themselves and others.

Ethnicity is also invoked when a distinct cultural group is clustered in one area. Thus, the term "ethnicity" is often used to refer to a small, cohesive, culturally linked group of people who stand apart from the surrounding culture (often as a result of migration). As with other aspects of culture, ethnicity is a dynamic phenomenon that must be understood in terms of the geographic context and scales in which it is situated.

SEXUALITY AND PLACE

> **Gendered** In terms of a place, whether the place is designed for, or claimed by, men or women.
>
> **Heteronormative** A term used to describe a belief system that assumes heterosexuality to be the norm and includes assumptions about biologically based male and female, and normative gendered behaviours of "masculine" and "feminine." Other forms of sexuality, gender, and embodied physicality are excluded or marginalized.

Part of the social relations of a place are the embedded assumptions about ethnicity, gender, and sexuality; assumptions about what certain groups "should" and "should not" do socially, economically, politically, even domestically. Geographers who study social categories of identities, such as gender, ethnicity, race, and sexuality, realize that when people make places, they do so in the context of surrounding social relationships. We can, for example, create places that are **gendered**—places designed for or understood as the appropriate or "normal" location for women or for men. A building can be constructed with the goal of creating gendered spaces within it, or a building can become gendered by the way people use it and interact within it.

Sexuality is part of humanity. Just as gender roles are socially and culturally constructed, so too are our ideas of what is "normal" sexual conduct and practice. In their installment on "Sexuality and Space" in *Geography in America at the Dawn of the 21st Century*, geographers Elder, Knopp, and Nast argue that most social science, across disciplines, is written in a **heteronormative** way. This means that, in the minds of the academics who write articles and do research, the default subject is heterosexual, white, middle-class, and male. These geographers, and many others, are working to find out how the contexts of local cultures and the flow of global culture and politics affect the sexual identities of people.

Geographers' initial forays into the study of sexuality focused largely on the same kinds of questions posed by those who first took up the study of race, gender, and ethnicity: where do people with shared identity cluster? What do they do to create a space for themselves? What kinds of problems do they have? For example, early studies examined gay neighbourhoods in San Francisco, London, and Toronto, focusing on how gay men and lesbians created urban neighbourhoods as their own and what that place meant to their identities, the formation of community, and political and social activism. Gay villages now exist in many medium and large cities in North America and Europe. Studies have also focused on the role of gay pride parades in creating communities, and the nature of the political struggle for access to other parades (such as St. Patrick's Day parades in some cities). Other studies in urban geography examine the role gays and lesbians play in the gentrification of neighbourhoods in city centres.

Gay villages played an important role in the political, economic, and social development of gay and lesbian social movements that drove the fight against discrimination on the basis of sexual orientation and the battles for recognition of human rights and for equal access to major social institutions such as marriage, health benefits, the military, and adoption. In the 1970s and 1980s, urban gay spaces provided individuals with a sense of belonging and community. Many gays and lesbians left smaller towns and rural areas for the "big city" in order to find support and acceptance. That is not to say that gays and lesbians are not found in rural areas. Rather, it suggests that at a particular historical and cultural moment, many gays and lesbians found urban life a better location for understanding their identity and social reality. In recent years, scholarship has demonstrated the increasing mobility of gays and lesbians not only globally, in terms of tourism and migration to more sympathetic countries, but also movement from urban to suburban areas and even more rural locations.

With the HIV/AIDS pandemic of the 1980s, gay villages became the base from which political activists fought discrimination against those with HIV/AIDS and called for the provision of funding and services that would combat the disease and provide needed community support. Government funding for community and social services helped develop gay and lesbian community centres, hospice facilities, and outreach programs for all those affected by HIV/AIDS—and further marked a particular neighbourhood as gay and lesbian. In the first decade of the 21st century, gay villages have been recognized as important indicators of a city's diversity and cosmopolitan nature; they are seen as important assets for attracting well-educated workers to fill jobs in the service sector and tourism. While gay villages are often represented as a gay and *lesbian* neighbourhood, scholarship argues that gay villages are largely dominated by white, male, middle-class values and norms. While lesbians often make use of commercial and residential locations in gay villages, lesbian concentrations in places such as Montreal or New York are separate from gay male enclaves and are more nebulous and unstable.

More recent studies on gay and lesbian neighbourhoods question their purpose and goal in the context of current neo-liberal politics. Previous studies assumed that gay and lesbian neighbourhoods were built in opposition to the dominant culture, but according to geographer Natalie Oswin (2008), newer studies see gay and lesbian neighbourhoods as "extending the norm, not transgressing or challenging it." In other words, residents of gay villages tend to aspire to middle-class, monogamous, and heterosexual norms rather than pressing for more radical challenges to heteronormative gender and sexuality. In a 2006 study, geographer Catherine Jean Nash looked at Toronto's gay village, the historical debate over the meaning of homosexual identity, and how that played out in the Toronto neighbourhood. Her research demonstrated that homosexual "identity" and its association with certain urban spaces changed as the gay village developed.

In 2000, the U.S. Census Bureau counted the number of same-sex households in the United States. These data, by census tract (a small area in cities and larger area in rural America), made it possible for Gary Gates and Jason Ost to publish *The Gay & Lesbian Atlas*. Their detailed maps of major cities in the United States show concentrations of same-sex households in certain neighbourhoods of cities, such as Adams Morgan and Dupont Circle in Washington, D.C., and the West Village and Chelsea in Manhattan (**Figure 7.20**). Taking the census data by county, we can see a pattern of same-sex households in the United States, with concentrations in cities with well-established gay and lesbian neighbourhoods. We can also see the presence of same-sex households throughout the country, even in states where same-sex unions are not legally recognized.

The 2011 Canadian census provides similar information. Beginning with the 2006 census, and reflecting the legalization of same-sex marriage in July 2005, Statistics Canada now includes statistics on same-sex marriages in addition to same-sex households. The 2011 figures show 64,575 same-sex couples, up 42.4 percent from 2006. Of these couples, 21,015 were same-sex married couples and 43,560 were same-sex common-law couples. The number of same-sex married couples nearly tripled between 2006 and 2011, reflecting the first five-year period for which same-sex marriage has been legal across the country. The number of same-sex common-law couples rose 15.0 percent, slightly higher than the 13.8 percent increase for opposite-sex common-law couples.

As in the United States, many same-sex couples in Canada reside in urban centres, for the reasons mentioned above. In 2011, 45.6 percent of all same-sex couples in Canada lived in Toronto, Montreal, or Vancouver, compared to 33.4 percent of opposite-sex couples. This is slightly lower than in 2006 when 50.0 percent of same-sex couples lived in these three CMAs. Same-sex couples in Canada were more likely to be male (54.5 percent) than female (45.5 percent) in 2011. This was the case for both married and common-law couples. Moreover, 9.4 percent had children under the age of 24 living in the home (compared to 47.2 percent of opposite-sex couples).

SAME SEX HOUSEHOLDS IN NEW YORK, 2009

Very high
High
Moderate
Low

0 — 5 Miles
0 — 5 Kilometres

BRONX
MANHATTAN
QUEENS
BROOKLYN
STATEN ISLAND
ATLANTIC OCEAN

FIGURE 7.20 Same-sex households in New York, 2009. Census data were used to show the concentrations of same-sex households in New York, by census tract. Data from U.S. Census Bureau, 2010.

GUEST FIELD NOTE

Queer Time, Global City Space: The Case of Post-Colonial Singapore

The Southeast Asian island of Singapore emerged from a long period of British colonial rule to become an independent city-state in 1965. Since then, its socio-economic development has been nothing short of extraordinary and Singapore has gained recognition as a leading "global city." Maintaining this status in a changing global environment, however, has required a drastic economic reorientation in recent years as state-led development plans have fostered a shift to a post-industrial, knowledge-based economy. As part of these efforts, the Singapore government has taken on board the now-common contention among urban policy advisors that the creative, highly-skilled workers, or "talent," that drive this sort of new economy are attracted to places with "buzz." Phenomenal changes to the urban landscape have been effected as a result. These include infrastructural investments in universities and arts centres, the development of "lifestyle quarters," leisure areas and green spaces, and much more. Further, this new phase in Singapore's global city project has also entailed a remarkable liberalization of the polity, for its government has also taken on board the idea put forward by Richard Florida (2002) in particular that urban buzz is fostered best where there is a certain degree of societal openness.

One of the most striking examples of this liberalization has been the change in the Singapore government's stance on homosexuality. Through the 1990s, police raids on gay bars and surveillance of known cruising areas were not uncommon; representations of homosexuality in the public sphere were tightly controlled through strict censorship restrictions of literature, film, and theatre; and attempts by a gay and lesbian advocacy organization to register as an official society were flatly denied. But since the early 2000s, local gay and lesbian film and theatre productions have been produced with limited censorship, gay and lesbian bars and saunas have been allowed to operate without interference, and a large LGBT gathering that organizers have named Pink Dot has taken place in a public park annually since 2009 (**Figure 7.21**). Indeed, so much has changed that Singapore has come to be popularly known as Asia's "new gay capital." Nonetheless, legislative and policy changes to counter pervasive heterosexual bias have proven stubbornly out of reach. Most significantly, a 2007 lobbying effort to repeal Section 377A of the Penal Code, a colonial-era statute that criminalizes "gross indecency" between men, was dismissed.

My research is animated by this impasse. I ask why, in this apparently "queer" time in Singapore's history, it is still an officially "straight" space. More specifically, since the Singapore government has asserted time and again that it will not enfranchise gays and lesbians because "the family is the basic building block of our society" (Lee, 2007), I seek to advance a critical response to this illiberal sexual politics by asking how and why certain family and sexual norms have been cemented in the urban/national landscape of Singapore. As many critical social and cultural geographers have argued, landscapes are not natural. Rather, they naturalize. Specifically, "the hegemonic role of landscapes . . . relies on their naturalization of ideological systems, made possible because of their dominance in everyday lives and their very tangible and visible materiality, making that which is socially constructed appear to be the natural order of things" (Winchester, Dunn and Kong, 2003, p. 66). So I explore how

©iStockphoto.com/DeanWong

FIGURE 7.21 Supporting gay and lesbian rights in Singapore.
Thousands gather for the Pink Dot rally in Singapore, June 28, 2014.

heteronormativity—the societal privileging of heterosexuality that makes heterosexual identification and heterosexual relationships seem normal—is a socially constructed rather than natural fact of Singapore's landscape. From the contemporary debates over homosexuality in Singapore, my research reaches into the colonial and postcolonial archives to examine how a narrow notion of family (as heterosexual, nuclear, middle- to upper-class, and naturalized) has become a key unit of governance and has led to the advancement of exclusionary discourses and practices of citizenship in the city-state.

Though today the vast majority of households in Singapore are composed of single families, one need not go too far back into the historical record to find a different social formation. Throughout most of its colonial period, Singapore's population was overwhelmingly composed of single male migrant labourers. In the 1920s, however, the colonial administration began to find that its practice of relying on transient labourers was more costly than would be the reproduction of the population in situ. Steps were taken to facilitate this shift including the prioritization of infant and maternal health, the reconfiguration of

immigration policies in order to balance the sex ratio and encourage family formation and reunification, the founding of the family planning association, and so on. Then, in the early post-colonial period, efforts to "upgrade" the family were a central part of the considerable social engineering efforts that the government undertook as it sought to prime Singapore's take-off for modernization. Through a dizzy anti-natalist and then pro-natalist initiatives, the regulation of migration flows, housing policy and practice, and much more, the Singapore state has crafted a specific notion of family to suit its developmental aims.

Thus, while contemporary debates in Singapore have pitted homosexuality against a "normal" heterosexuality, I demonstrate that the heterosexual family's privileged place in the city-state is the product of much work. I advance a queer critique that seeks to render strange the dominant narrative of naturally heteronormative Singapore in the hope that new conversations might be fostered and more democratic forms of sexual citizenship envisaged.

Natalie Oswin, Department of Geography, McGill University

VIRTUAL LIFE

Through our exploration of the connections between identity and place, we have thus far explored two key areas: ethnicity and sexuality. Our discussions of the spaces in which social relations take place have been confined to the material spaces that we move through as we experience different aspects of our identities. This includes thinking across scales—from national scales, to local, and even down to the level of our bodies. However, recent scholarship in social geography recognizes that, for many people in the Global North, much of our social life happens on-line. The proliferation of information and communication technologies (ICTs), together with smartphones and new media, has provided opportunities for new kinds of social relations to take place. On platforms like Facebook, Twitter, and Instagram (**Figure 7.22**), we share our stories, blog about our interests, connect with like-minded people, and perform our identities in particular ways. We telecommute for work and have Skype or Google Hangouts conversations with people far away. Text messaging allows us instantaneous and constant communication across space and time. To some, the speed and ease of connection in virtual spaces has called into question the importance of geography, with some going so far as to declare that geography is dead. When an e-mail can be sent from New York and arrive in Tokyo within moments, the distance between these two global cities seems insignificant, and the "friction of distance" we discussed in Chapter 2 (Figure 2.15) is decreased. At the same time, we name these virtual spaces, sometimes with allusions to more tangible places—the Twitterverse, the blogosphere, cyberspace—all of which points to a merging of digital and "real" spaces.

Early days of the Internet were filled with competing discourses about what happens to our identities in cyberspace. To some, the faceless, nameless world of on-line social life was liberating; no longer defined by our "wetware," we were free to be whoever we wanted to be in cyberspace. While in "real" life, gender, ethnicity, age, and sexuality—all parts of our identity—both shaped and were shaped by the physical world in which we lived, these categories fell away in utopian visions of digital, disembodied life on-line. At the other end of the spectrum, critics argued that so much of our "real" selves was available on-line as we built our social networks and shared photographs, job histories, and myriad personal details in very public on-line forums, that our very identities could be stolen. Rather than freeing us, the social world of the Internet was liable to be used for our increased surveillance, monitoring, and control. Both of these narratives are problematic, though, because both are technologically deterministic; they suggest that technology causes social change. Social geographers, seeking a more sophisticated and nuanced approach, argue that we must consider how technology and society are co-constitutive; they shape each other. Geographer Mike Crang (2011, p. 402) calls this "a layering of socio-technical forms of life, where new media adds to older media, where social action domesticates new technologies, makes them useful and develops them."

From Crang's perspective, the social geography of life on-line reflects a complex socio-technical relationship that neither causes nor is caused by technological change. This geography is uneven, and location remains significant. Life on-line with a high-speed Internet connection is experienced much differently in Winnipeg than it is in Nairobi, for instance. As Crang (2011, p. 401) argues, "The infrastructures, capacities (both hard, like

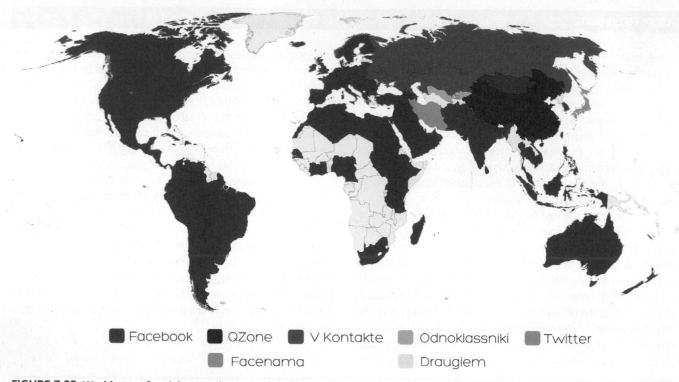

FIGURE 7.22 **World map of social networks, December 2014.** This map shows how Facebook is the dominant social media platform in 130 of 137 countries where data is available. Source: Vincenzo Cosenza, data by Alexa, license: CC-BY-NC, http://vincos.it/world-map-of-social-networks.

fiber cables, and soft, like skills) and thus the scope of possibilities are (still) geographically uneven at all scales from global, to national, to regional, to urban, by age, by class, by ethnicity." In Chapter 2, we examined Chris Harrison's Internet visualization map (Figure 2.7), which illustrated the varied and uneven connections around the globe. At the same time, we must understand that there is more than one digital divide; it is not simply that some countries have faster, more reliable Internet access. Divides also exist between urban and rural connections, between ages, between genders, and between social classes.

> **Analytics** The systematic, computational analysis of large amounts of data.

Researchers are also examining what kinds of social experiences happen on-line, with the aim of understanding the nuances of self-expression in digital environments. Using **analytics**, the systematic, computational analysis of large amounts of data, researchers are able to identify trends in on-line participation, from who has access and what kind of access they have, to key words and conversations. For

example, Morningside Analytics tracks data that analyzes who people are talking to on-line, and what they are talking about. According to their research, people's social geographies are quite narrow and focused in the on-line public sphere. In one study, they tracked two groups of users on Twitter: those who are auto enthusiasts and those who care about ecological issues. In **Figure 7.23**, each dot represents a Twitter account, sized according to number of followers. Larger dots mean more followers. When Twitter users follow the same sets of interests, their dots are closer together, and similar Web surfing habits are grouped by colour. What this image illustrates, by mapping the social geographies of Twitter followers and Internet searches, is that these two groups—who share similar interests in that both are concerned with fuel costs, transportation networks and infrastructure, and pollution—are not really talking to each other. Instead, they remain in separate areas of the Internet, talking to like-minded individuals. The potential for encounter, for meeting someone with a different viewpoint, is slim.

FIGURE 7.23 **Auto enthusiasts and eco enthusiasts on Twitter.**

Auto enthusiasts   Eco enthusiasts   Both groups

While the virtual public sphere seems to be somewhat polarized, there remains the potential for new kinds of social relations to take place, for people to explore aspects of their identity in seemingly anonymous on-line spaces. The Internet and new media provide opportunities for people to explore aspects of their gender and sexuality, for example, through on-line forums, discussion boards, chats, and virtual play areas. Research in the 1990s saw the potential for virtual life to disrupt the hierarchies of gender, ethnicity, and sexuality, with people able to perform their identity in different ways and see the self as "multiple" (Turkle, 1995). More recent research, however, resists such a positive view, arguing that people on-line continue to privilege their off-line identity and supporting information over their on-line presence. Moreover, the sheer lack of anonymity on the Internet, particularly when using social media, renders people and all their social networks so visible that there seems little opportunity for "safe" explorations of multiple or fluid selves.

These are questions that are still very much up for debate. The socio-technical world of the Internet has challenged our notions of space, place, and identity, and will continue to do so. Social geographers seek to gain an understanding of notions of identity in cyberspace, and also examine how social interactions take place when stretched out over digital landscapes. They question the ways in which ICTs disrupt and alter the rhythms of daily urban life. This includes considering the ways in which the rapid growth of the information economy creates new forms of urban life, reconfiguring the spaces and activities in urban centres to support the intensification brought about by digital technologies and their social uses. We must remember that this kind of rapid change is not experienced evenly in all places by all people; there are winners and losers, those who stand to benefit and those who do not. These are important threads in social geography that will continue to be studied.

MAIN POINTS 7.3 What Is the Connection between Identity and Place?

- Social identities are constituted in place. Identities are connected to particular places through the memories and experiences attached to those places. We develop a sense of place by inscribing a set of meanings into that place, which can be comfortable or frightening, soothing or worrisome. A sense of place is fluid and changes as places change and as we change.

- Groups of people who share a culture, an ethnos, and a sense of cultural identity are said to share an ethnicity that is often tightly bound to place over a certain period of time. Ethnic identities are historically constructed in that understandings of that identity develop over time, making it appear natural and unchanging.

- Sexuality and related practices are socially constructed, which means that what is considered "normal" sexual conduct and practice can vary historically, geographically,

and culturally. Geographers are interested in the connections between sexuality and place, and have paid particular attention to the formation of gay villages in major cities in North America and Europe.

- With the legalization of same-sex marriage in Canada in 2005, Statistics Canada began to collect information on same-sex couples in the 2006 census. Not surprisingly, given the connections between urban life and gay and lesbian identity, most married same-sex couples live in one of Canada's three largest cities: Toronto, Montreal, and Vancouver.

- Virtual life on the Internet has challenged our understanding of the relationship between space, place, and identity. The intensification of social networking sites and ICTs has brought about new possibilities for performing identity, while at the same time increasing surveillance, monitoring, and control.

7.4 How Does Geography Reflect and Shape Power Relationships among Groups of People?

Social geographers are interested in how different social categories of identity are part of the processes organizing social groups across places and landscapes, often in uneven and inequitable ways. Certain social groups may have difficulty accessing social services, may be relegated to substandard schools, or may be poorly served by public transit, making it difficult to travel to and from work. The fact that some social groups have better

services and nicer accommodation indicates that some people have more "power" than others.

Power relationships (assumptions about, and structures that determine, who is in control and who has power over others) organize the social relations between various social categories of identities in ways that privilege some social groups over others. The nature of those relations depends on the geographical context in which they are situated. Power relationships also affect social and cultural landscapes, determining what is seen and what is not. Simply put, members of the dominant or hegemonic social groups are able to ensure that their idea of what should be visible in the landscape prevails.

Massey and Jess (1995) explain that landscapes reflect or render visible a human imprint on place, but only the imprint of the dominant group—so what we see reflects power relationships. They argue:

> The identities of both places and cultures, then, have to be made. And they may be made in different, even conflicting ways. And in all this, power will be central: the power to win the contest over how the place should be seen, what meaning to give it; the power, in other words, to construct the dominant imaginative geography, the identities of place and culture.

Power relationships do much more than shape the social and cultural landscapes. They can also subjugate entire groups of people, enabling society to enforce ideas about the ways people should behave or where people should be welcomed or turned away. In this way they alter the distribution of peoples. Policies created by governments can limit the access of certain peoples. For example, the Jim Crow laws in the United States separated "black" spaces from "white" spaces, right down to public drinking fountains. Even without government support, people create places where they limit the access of other peoples. In Canada, there is a long history of anti-Semitism dating back to the beginning of the 20th century. By the 1930s, anti-Semitic behaviours were becoming mainstream. In 1937, St. Andrews Golf Club in Toronto posted a notice stating: "After Sunday, June 20, this course will be restricted to Gentiles only. Please do not question this policy." Even after the *Racial Discrimination Act* was passed in 1944, anti-Semitic practices continued. McGill University restricted Jewish enrolment to 10 percent, for example, and the University of Toronto required higher averages for Jewish students. Toronto's Granite Club and the Royal Canadian Yacht Club restricted access as well, although in private clubs these rules were unwritten or tacit, and so there is no history of when they changed.

In another example, Catholics and Protestants in Belfast, Northern Ireland, have defined certain neighbourhoods that exclude the "other" by painting murals, hanging bunting, and painting curbs (**Figure 7.24**). In major cities in Canada, local governments do not create or enforce laws that define certain spaces as belonging to members of a certain group, but the people themselves create spaces, much as the people of Belfast do, using graffiti, murals, and building colours (**Figure 7.25**).

SHIFTING POWER RELATIONSHIPS AMONG ETHNIC GROUPS

The presence of ethnic groups can be seen in the cultural landscapes of places. Many locales are home to more than one ethnic group, and the result is a unique cultural landscape that reveals how power relationships factor into the ways ethnicities are constructed, revised, and solidified; where ethnic groups live; and who is subjugating whom.

In Canada, the visibility of ethnic neighbourhoods is one of the central ways in which we experience urban space. We understand the relation between ethnicity and space through such neighbourhoods as Fisgard Street's Chinatown in Victoria, Toronto's South Asian community on Gerrard Street East and Little Italy on St. Clair West, the Haitian community in Montreal, and African Canadians in Dartmouth, Nova Scotia, just to name a few (Figure 7.25). Research that explores these urban ethnic landscapes in Canada

AP/Wide World Photos

FIGURE 7.24 Belfast, Northern Ireland. Signs of the conflict in Northern Ireland mark the cultural landscape throughout Belfast. In the Ballymurphy area of Belfast, where Catholics are the majority population, a woman and her children walk past a mural in support of the Irish Republican Army. The mural features images of women who lost their lives in the conflict, including Maureen Meehan, who was shot by the British Army, and Anne Parker, who died when the bomb she planned to detonate exploded prematurely.

shows the shifting relations in these spaces, often tied to immigration policy and practices, socio-economic factors, and cultural practices. For example, researchers have shown how immigration patterns affect urban spaces and neighbourhoods. Prior to World War II, most of the source countries for immigration into Canada were European; however, this has slowly changed, and many of the sources countries are now in Asia, Africa, the Caribbean, and South America. As a result, according to Statistics Canada, minority neighbourhoods, defined as census tracts with over 30 percent of their population from a single visible minority group, increased in number from 6 to 254 between 1981 and 2001.

Los Angeles, California, provides a good example of the operation of power relations around notions of ethnicity and race at varying scales. Over the last four decades, the greatest migration flow into California and the southwestern United States has come from Latin America and the Caribbean, especially Mexico. In the 2000 census, the city of Los Angeles had nearly 3.7 million people. Over 46 percent of them were Hispanic, over 11 percent were black or African American, and 10 percent were Asian (using census categories for race and ethnicity). The Hispanic population in the city grew from 39 percent of the population in 1990 to 46 percent by 2000.

Southeastern Los Angeles County is today "home to one of the largest and highest concentrations of Latinos in Southern

(a)

(b)

Gunter Marx Photography/Corbis

Richard Lautens/Toronto Star

FIGURE 7.25 Ethnicity and space. Our urban landscapes reflect the ethnic composition of neighbourhoods, as illustrated by (a) Chinatown on Fisgard Street in Victoria, and (b) Little India on Gerrard Street East in Toronto.

California," according to a study by geographer James Curtis (2004). Four decades ago, this area of Los Angeles was populated by working-class whites, who were segregated from the African American and Hispanic populations by discriminatory policies and practices. Until the 1960s, southeastern Los Angeles was home to corporations such as General Motors, Bethlehem Steel, and Weiser Lock. During the 1970s and 1980s, the corporations began to close as the process of deindustrialization (see Chapter 11) fundamentally changed where and how goods were produced. As plants closed and white labourers left the neighbourhoods, the Hispanic population migrated into southeastern Los Angeles. A housing crunch followed in the 1980s as more and more Hispanic migrants headed to the area. With a cheap labour supply now readily available in the region again, companies returned to southeastern Los Angeles, this time focusing on smaller-scale production of textiles, pharmaceuticals, furniture, and toys. In addition, the region attracted industrial toxic-waste disposal and petrochemical refining facilities.

> **Barrioization** Defined by geographer James Curtis as the dramatic increase in Hispanic population in a given neighbourhood, referring to barrio, the Spanish word for "neighbourhood."

In his study of the region, Curtis records the changes to the cultural landscape. He calls the change in neighbourhoods, in which the Hispanic population jumped from 4 percent in 1960 to over 90 percent in 2000, a process of **barrioization** (referring to barrio, the Spanish word for "neighbourhood"). With the ethnic succession of the neighbourhood from white to Hispanic, the cultural landscape changed to reflect the culture of the new population. The structure of the streets and the layout of the housing remained largely the same, giving the Hispanic population access to designated parks, schools, libraries, and community centres built by the previous residents and rarely found in other barrios in southern California. However, the buildings, signage, and landscape changed as "traditional Hispanic housescape elements, including the placement of fences and yard shrines as well as the use of bright house colors," diffused through

the neighbourhood. Curtis explains that these elements were added to existing structures, houses, and buildings originally built by the white working class of southeastern Los Angeles.

The influx of new ethnic groups into a region, the replacement of one ethnic group by another within neighbourhoods, changes to the cultural landscape, the persistence of myths such as the belief that Asians are a "model minority," and an economic downturn can create a great deal of volatility in a city. On April 29–30, 1992, the city of Los Angeles became engulfed in one of the worst incidents of civil unrest in United States history. During the two days of rioting, 43 people died, 2,383 people were injured, and 16,291 people were arrested. Property damage was estimated at approximately $1 billion, and over 22,700 law enforcement personnel were deployed to quell the unrest. According to the media, the main catalyst for the mass upheaval was the announcement of a "not guilty" verdict in the trial of four white Los Angeles police officers accused of using excessive force in the videotaped arrest of Rodney King, a black motorist. To the general public, the Los Angeles riots became yet another symbol of the sorry state of race relations between blacks and whites in the United States. Yet a geographic perspective on the Los Angeles riots suggests they were more than a snap response to a single event; they were localized reactions not only to police brutality, but also to sweeping economic, political, and ethnic changes unfolding at regional and even global scales.

The riots took place in South Central Los Angeles. Like southeastern Los Angeles, described above, the South Central area was once a thriving industrial region with dependable, unionized jobs employing the resident population. In the 1960s, however, the population of South Central Los Angeles was working-class African American, and the population of southeastern Los Angeles was working-class white. After 1970, South Central Los Angeles experienced a substantial decrease in the availability of high-paying, unionized manufacturing jobs when plants closed and relocated outside the city and even outside the country. The people of South Central Los Angeles lost over 70,000 manufacturing jobs between 1978 and 1982 alone.

Geographer James Johnson and his colleagues (1992) explored the impact of economic loss on the ethnic and social geography of South Central Los Angeles. They found that the population of the area was over 90 percent African American in 1970, but by 1990 the population was evenly split between African Americans and Hispanics. This change in population composition was accompanied by a steady influx of Korean residents and small-business owners who were trying to find a niche in the rapidly changing urban area (**Figure 7.26**). Johnson and his colleagues argued that the Los Angeles riots were more than a spontaneous reaction to a verdict. They were rooted in the growing despair and frustration of different ethnic groups competing for a decreasing number of jobs in an environment of declining housing conditions and scarce public resources. Their work shows the importance of looking beyond the immediate catalysts of particular news events to the local, national, and global geographical contexts in which they unfold.

JUST WHO COUNTS?

The statistics governments collect and report reflect the power relationships involved in defining what is valued and what is not. As we mentioned above in the discussion about census information on same-sex relationships, until 2001, no census data

FIGURE 7.26 The changing ethnic composition of South Central Los Angeles, 1960–1980. Adapted with permission from J.H. Johnson Jr., C.K. Jones, W.C. Farrell Jr., and M.L. Oliver, "The Los Angeles Rebellion: A Retrospective in View," *Economic Development Quarterly*, 6, no. 4 (1992), pp. 356–72.

THE CHANGING ETHNIC COMPOSITION
OF SOUTH CENTRAL LOS ANGELES
1960-1980

White   Asian
Black   Hispanic
Mixed   ----- Community Boundary

was collected on same-sex relationships, thereby erasing the lived realities of same-sex couples from all analyses of "families." Looking further back in history, women in Canada attained the right to vote in 1919. However, they were not considered "persons" under Canadian law, so while they could vote and hold office, they could not be senators. That changed in 1929, when the Justice Committee of the Privy Council (JCPC) in England overturned the decision of the Supreme Court of Canada and declared Canadian women "persons." It was not until 1960 that First Nations peoples were allowed to vote in federal elections without giving up their status under the *Indian Act*. This example shows how voting rights can be tied to assimilation politics; prior to 1960, only those First Nations peoples willing to give up their identity were allowed to vote.

When the United States and other state governments began to calculate the value of goods and services produced within state borders, they did so with the assumption that the work of the household was reserved for women and that this work did not contribute to the productivity of the state's economy. In Canada, as **Figure 7.27** shows, household work adds up to a substantial amount of time. In 2005, women were doing an average of 4.3 hours of unpaid domestic work per day, while men were doing approximately 2.5 hours per day. The most commonly used statistic on productivity, the gross national income or GNI (i.e., the monetary worth of what is produced within a country, plus income received from investments outside the country), includes neither the unpaid labour of women in the household nor, usually, the work done by rural women in less-developed countries.

Scholars estimate that if women's productivity in the household alone were given a dollar value (for example, by calculating what it would cost to hire people to perform these tasks), the world's total annual GNI (that is, the gross national

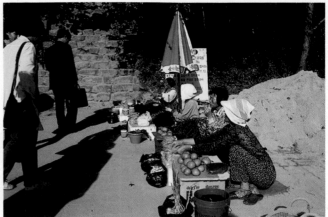

FIGURE 7.28 Informal economy, South Korea. These women sat near one of the ancient temples in southern Korea, selling the modest output from their own market gardens. This activity is one part of the informal economy, the "uncounted" economy, in which women play a large role.

income for all countries combined) would grow by about one-third. In poorer countries, women produce more than half of all the food; they also build homes, dig wells, plant and harvest crops, make clothes, and do many other things that are not recorded in official statistics because they are not seen as being economically productive (**Figure 7.28**).

Despite these conditions, the number of women in the "official" labour force is rising. In 1990, the United Nations estimated that there were 828 million women in the labour force. All but one geographic region showed increases between 1970 and 1990: in the wealthier countries of the world, from 35 to 39 percent of the labour force; in Central and South America, from 24 to 29 percent. In East and Southeast Asia the figure rose very slightly, to 40 and 35 percent, respectively. In sub-Saharan Africa, the percentage of women in the labour force actually declined from 39 percent in 1970 to 37 percent in the 1990s. These statistics reveal that in stagnating or declining economies, women are often the first to suffer from job contraction.

Even though women are in the official labour force in greater proportions than ever before, they continue to be paid less and have less access to food and education than men in nearly all cultures and places around the world. In 2014 there were approximately 786 million illiterate adults in the world, two-thirds of them women. Also, women account for 70 percent of the world's poorest citizens.

According to a 2010 study by the Food and Agriculture Organization (FAO) of the United Nations, women on average compose 43 percent of the agricultural labour force in developing countries; this figure ranges from around 20 percent in Latin America to 50 percent in parts of Africa and Asia, but it exceeds 60 percent in only a few countries. Although the number of women working in industries in these areas is comparatively small, it is rising. The increase has been slowed by the global economic downturn of the early 2000s, as well as by mechanization, which leads to job reductions and hence to layoffs of women workers. In the maquiladoras of northern

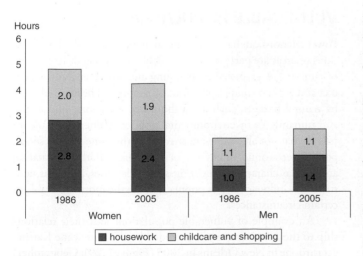

Hours

FIGURE 7.27 Average time women and men spend per day on unpaid domestic work, 1986 and 2005. In 2005, women were spending slightly less time doing unpaid work (including housework and childcare/shopping) than they were in 1986 (down from 4.8 hours per day to 4.3), while men were doing slightly more (up from 2.1 to 2.5 hours per day). Source: Statistics Canada, *Matter of Fact*, 89-630-XWE2008001, September 2008; www.statcan.gc.ca/bsolc/olc-cel/olc-cel?lang=eng&catno=89-630-X.

FIGURE 7.29 Racial characteristics of areas flooded by Hurricane Katrina in New Orleans. African Americans were 67 percent of the total population of New Orleans, but 75 percent of the population in the flooded areas. From Seirup, L. 2006. Racial Characteristics of Areas Flooded by Hurricane Katrina in New Orleans. Socioeconomic Data and Applications Center (SEDAC), Center for International Earth Science Information Network (CIESIN), Columbia University; http://sedac.ciesin.columbia.edu.

Mexico, for example, many women workers lost their jobs when labour markets contracted between 2001 and 2002.

As the foregoing discussion has highlighted, many women engage in "informal" economic activity—that is, private, often home-based activity such as tailoring, brewing beer, preparing food, and making soap. Women who seek to advance beyond subsistence but cannot enter the formal economic sector often turn to such work. In the migrant slums on the fringes of many cities, informal economic activity is the mainstay of the community. As with subsistence farming, however, it is difficult to assess the number of women involved, their productivity, or their contribution to the overall economy.

Statistics showing how much women produce and how little their work is valued are undoubtedly interesting. Yet the work of geographers who study gender goes far beyond the accumulation of such data. Over the last two decades, geographers have asked why society talks about women and their roles in certain ways, and how these ideas, heard and represented throughout our lives, affect the things we say, the ways we frame questions, and the answers we derive. For example, Ann Oberhauser and her co-authors (2003) explained that people in core countries tend to think that women are employed in the textile and jewellery-making fields in poorer countries because the women in these regions are "more docile, submissive, and tradition bound" than women in the core. A geographer studying gender asks where these ideas about women come from and how

the ideas themselves bind women to certain jobs and certain positions in society—key elements in making places what they are.

VULNERABLE POPULATIONS

Power relations can have a fundamental impact on which populations or areas are particularly vulnerable to disease, death, injury, or famine. Geographers use mapping and spatial analysis to predict and explain what populations or people will be affected most by natural hazards, such as earthquakes, volcanoes, hurricanes, and tsunamis, or by environmental policies. Vulnerability theory tells us that not all people are affected in the same way by social, political, economic, or environmental change. Rather, the nature and spatial character of existing social identities, relations, and structures influence which populations are the most vulnerable in certain circumstances.

An example of vulnerable populations and their relationship to their environment is provided by the Hurricane Katrina catastrophe in New Orleans in 2005 (**Figure 7.29**). Geographers Curtis, Mills, and Leitner (2007) studied the events of Katrina, paying close attention to the vulnerability of the urban poor and racial/ethnic minorities. They argue that:

vulnerability can be expressed geographically in terms of site (proximity of a neighborhood to the hazard) and situation (the social context of that neighborhood). During Katrina, the site of many indigent neighborhoods made them vulnerable to flooding due to their proximity to a flooding source (such as a levee break), and the elevation of their homes.

This study explores how the intersection of class (poverty) and race/ethnicity increased the vulnerability of particular groups to the flooding, which led to greater morbidity. Poor, non-white people, they argue, were less likely to leave, more likely to have existing health conditions, and more likely to lack the economic and social resources to rebound after the disaster.

Geographer Joseph Oppong recognizes that the spatial analysis of a disease can reveal what populations are most vulnerable in a country. In North America and Europe, HIV/AIDS is much more prevalent among homosexual and bisexual men than among heterosexual men and women. In sub-Saharan Africa, however, women have much higher rates of HIV/AIDS than men. Oppong explains that "AIDS as a global problem has unique local expressions that reflect the spatial distribution and social networks of vulnerable social groups."

According to Oppong, in most of sub-Saharan Africa, HIV/AIDS rates are highest for women in urban areas and for women who are sex workers. In Ghana, HIV/AIDS rates were lower for women in the urban area of Accra. Oppong postulates that this is because women in Accra have greater access to health care than women in rural areas. Women in rural areas who were not treated for malaria had higher incidences of HIV/AIDS, according to his research. Oppong also found that women in polygamous relationships in the Muslim part of northern Ghana had lower HIV/AIDS rates. Oppong offers two theories as to why these Muslim women had lower HIV/AIDS rates: first, Muslims have a cultural practice of avoiding sexual promiscuity; second, Muslims in Ghana practise male circumcision, which helps lower the rate of HIV/AIDS transmission. Social and cultural practices in a particular place have an impact on which social groups are more and less vulnerable in particular locations.

ABORIGINAL WOMEN IN CANADA

In 2010, the Native Women's Association of Canada issued a report, *Sisters in Spirit Research Report*, to express growing concern about the vulnerability, disappearances, and murders of Aboriginal women and girls in Canada (**Figure 7.30**). Study results show that there is a disproportionate number of Aboriginal women and girls murdered in Canada. Between 2000 and 2008, 153 murders of Aboriginal women were reported, accounting for 10 percent of the total number of women murdered in Canada during that time period, even though Aboriginal females make up only 3 percent of the population. Well over 100 women and girls are missing. Two-thirds of the cases being tracked in the Sisters in Spirit database are from British Columbia, Alberta, Saskatchewan, and Manitoba. More than half the cases involve women under the age of 31, and the vast majority of disappearances (70 percent) and murders (60 percent) took place in urban centres. In 2014, an RCMP report updated these figures, indicating that over the past 30 years, 1,181 Aboriginal women have been reported missing or murdered; this vastly exceeded previous estimates. Of those

FIGURE 7.30 Candlelight vigil for missing or murdered Aboriginal women. On October 4, 2009, a candlelight vigil was held on Parliament Hill in Ottawa on behalf of missing Aboriginal women.

Fred Chartrand/The Canadian Press

1,181 reported cases, 1,017 are homicide victims and 164 are considered missing. And of the total reported cases of murdered and missing indigenous women, 225 remain unresolved.

The report addresses three interconnected questions: What are the circumstances, root causes, and trends leading to violence against Aboriginal women in Canada? How many Aboriginal women and girls have gone missing or have been found murdered in Canada? And how has this violence led to such disturbingly high numbers of missing and murdered Aboriginal women and girls in Canada without action by authorities? Findings reveal that Aboriginals are the group most at risk in Canada for violence against women, and that this violence is largely tied to systemic, gendered forms of racism that are the result of colonialism. Thus the violence is both racialized and sexualized. According to Statistics Canada's General Social Survey (2004), Aboriginal women are three and a half times as likely to experience violence as non-Aboriginal women, and Aboriginal women are three times more likely than non-Aboriginal women to experience spousal and sexual assaults. It is important to note that community-based studies reveal statistics much higher than those of government surveys.

The Sisters in Spirit report connects these high levels of violence, disappearance, and murder to a combination of social, cultural, geographic, political, and economic factors, including the impacts of assimilation policies, residential schools, lack of education, geographic location, poverty, and the "Sixties Scoop," in which an astonishing number of Aboriginal children were adopted out of their own cultures. Moreover, as discussed above, the power of numbers and the idea of "who counts?" prevails here. The discrepancies between government surveys and community-based research are vast, as disappearances go unreported and uninvestigated by authorities, or police departments do not ascertain the Aboriginal identity of individuals who are murdered or missing.

In 2014, the murder of a 15-year-old Aboriginal girl in Manitoba prompted renewed calls for a national inquiry into what many regard as a systemic and collective problem of national importance. Nevertheless, Canadian Prime Minister Stephen Harper argued against an inquiry into missing or murdered Aboriginal women, stating: "We should not view this as sociological phenomenon . . . We should view it as crime. It is crime against innocent people, and it needs to be addressed as such." Such a position denies the existence of what seems to be a vulnerable population—a social group that finds itself more at risk for abduction and murder than the general population.

DOWRY DEATHS IN INDIA

> **Dowry death** In the context of arranged marriages in India, the death of a bride arising from a dispute over the price (the dowry) to be paid by the family of the bride to the father of the groom.

On a 2004 episode of The Oprah Winfrey Show, the talk-show host interviewed journalist Lisa Ling about her travels through India and her reports on dowry deaths in India. The Chicago audience looked stunned when it learned that thousands of girls in India are still forced into arranged marriages and that, in extreme cases, disputes over the price (the dowry) to be paid by the bride's family to the groom's father have led to the bride being brutally punished (often burned) or killed for her family's failure to fulfill the marriage agreement. Only a small fraction of India's girls are involved in **dowry deaths**, but the practice is not declining. According to the Indian government, the number of dowry deaths in 1985 was 999; in 1987, 1,786 women died at the hands of vengeful husbands or in-laws; in 1989, 2,436 perished; in 2001, more than 7,000 women died; and in 2006, it was reported that 7,618 women were the victims of dowry deaths. These figures report only confirmed dowry deaths; many

more are believed to occur but are reported as kitchen accidents or other fatal domestic incidents.

The power relationships that place women below men in India cannot be legislated away. Government entities in India (federal as well as state) have set up legal aid offices to help women who fear dowry death and seek assistance. In 1984, the national legislature passed the *Family Courts Act*, creating a network of "family courts" to hear domestic cases, including dowry disputes. But the judges tend to be older males, and their chief objective, according to women's support groups, is to hold the family together—that is, to force the threatened or battered woman back into the household. Hindu culture attaches great importance to the family structure, and the family courts tend to adhere to this principle.

Unfortunately, not all women in India (or in many other places around the world) feel empowered to stand up to injustices committed against women, nor do they have education, paying jobs, and cell phones that would give them alternatives. Despite the laws against dowry deaths, women remain disempowered in much of Indian society. Some women, when they are pregnant, undergo ultrasound and amniocentesis to determine the gender of their baby and elect to have an abortion when the fetus is a girl. Girls who are born are often victims of infanticide because many parents extend little social value to girls and dread the cost of the dowry they will have to pay when their daughter is married. In all of these cases, moving issues to the global scale has the potential to draw attention to the social ills. Yet for the social ills to be cured, power in social relationships must shift at the family, local, regional, and national scales.

MAIN POINTS 7.4 How Does Geography Reflect and Shape Power Relationships among Groups of People?

- Social identities are connected to place, but power relations privilege some groups over others. These power relations affect the built environment, determining what is seen and what is not seen. Dominant social groups are able to ensure that their views about what should be visible prevail.

- Power relationships in the built environment can also regulate how people behave in places, who has access to places, and who is included and excluded in certain places.

- How governments gather statistics can ensure that what people do and where they do it is either visible or invisible. By

not counting same-sex couples, for example, their presence in certain places can be overlooked. By collecting data on the work that women do in the home, women's unpaid contribution to the productivity of a country can be measured.

- Studies of the locations of vulnerable populations demonstrate that some people are located in better serviced or safer areas than others, as demonstrated by the locational analysis of populations affected by Hurricane Katrina. For other populations, such as Aboriginal women in Canadian cities, many places may be unsafe or dangerous.

SUMMARY

Today, when we imagine our social geographies—the spaces and places of our everyday lives—it is difficult to discern where the boundaries are. New technologies, including mobile phones and the Internet, have brought our work home and our homes to work. We live our social lives on Facebook, Twitter, and Instagram as much as we do in our living rooms and classrooms. That the very notion of social space is being challenged makes it an exciting time to be a social geographer, because there are such opportunities to explore the fluid and ever-changing notions of identity in our complex world. Post-industrial life brings with it differences in how and where we work, study, live, and play.

Now is the time to interrogate those shifts and think about what it means to be gendered, racialized, classed, and sexualized in particular ways across time and space. Social geographers are also asking questions beyond the traditional boundaries of race/class/gender/ethnicity that we explored in this chapter. They are now looking extensively at the politics of difference related to such issues as age/youth (introduced early in this chapter), able-bodiedness, mental health, homelessness, and rural poverty.

Identity is a powerful concept. The way we make sense of ourselves is a personal journey that is mediated and influenced by the political, social, and cultural contexts in which we live and work. Group identities such as gender, ethnicity, race, and sexuality are constructed by self-realization and by identifying against and across scales. When learning about new places and different people, humans are often tempted to put those places and people into boxes, myths, or stereotypes that make them easily

digestible. Power relations order social categories and make some categories more powerful than others, and dominant social groups have the ability to ensure that their views of what the built environment should look like prevail. Geographers are interested in how identities are socially constructed and what role place plays in the construction, maintenance, and enforcement of identities.

Geographers, especially those who spend time in the field, recognize that how people shape and create places varies across time and space. Concurrently, time, space, and place shape people, both individually and in groups. James Curtis ably described the work of a geographer who studies places: "But like the popular images and stereotypical portrayals of all places—whether positive or negative, historical or contemporary—these mask a reality on the ground that is decidedly more complex and dynamic, from both the economic and social perspectives." What Curtis says about places is true about people as well. What we may think to be positive identities, such as the myths of "Orientalism" or of the "model minority," and what we know are negative social ills, such as racism and dowry deaths, are all decidedly more complex and dynamic than they first seem.

DISCUSSION AND REVIEW QUESTIONS

1. What does the author's experience in the brick-making facility on the island of Bali, Indonesia, reveal about the geography of gender and the division of labour?

2. What is identity and how is our understanding of it enhanced by the incorporation of geographic concepts? What is intersectionality and how does it further our understanding of identity?

3. Discuss the gendered nature of employment in Canada.

4. What does it mean when geographers argue that "places are gendered"? What does the study of Canadian and American gay villages reveal about sexuality and space and the gendering of place?

GEOGRAPHIC CONCEPTS

analytics   204
barrioization   207
dowry deaths   212
ethnicity   198
gender   190
gendered   200
heteronormative   200
identifying against   189

identity   189
intersectionality   190
race   192
racism   192
sense of place   198
sex/gender/sexuality matrix   190
social construction   187
succession   196

ADDITIONAL RESOURCES ON-LINE

The Gay and Lesbian Atlas: www.urban.org/pubs/gayatlas

Racial and ethnic residential segregation in the United States, 1980–2000: www.census.gov/hhes/www/housing/resseg/papertoc.html

Ethnicity and the city: "Boston: Ethnic Mosaic": www.learner.org/series/powerofplace/page24.html

Ethnic fragmentation in Canada: "Vancouver: Hong Kong East" and "Montreal: An Island of French": www.learner.org/series/powerofplace/page25.html

Geography of Youth project: www.geographyofyouth.org

CHAPTER 8

LOCAL CULTURE, POPULAR CULTURE, AND CULTURAL LANDSCAPES

Preserving Culture

SIGNS WITH the Tata Group's logo are everywhere in the landscape of Hyderabad in India (**Figure 8.1**): on a Tata corporate building across the street from a block of flats; "Tata" emblazoned on the grills of trucks throughout the city; Tata satellite dishes bringing television into homes; Tata International consulting buildings in the high-tech district of the city.

Tata Group is an Indian multinational conglomerate with interests in communication and information technology, engineering, energy, consumer products, and chemicals. Its headquarters are in Mumbai, India. According to a local resident, "Tata is a family name. The Tata family are members of the Parsi religion, and they own many businesses throughout India and the world." The Parsi are an ethnic group and a religion. They are followers of the Zoroastrian religion and came to India from Persia (present-day Iran).

According to Indian folklore, the Parsi were looking for a place of refuge as they fled from Iran. They sent word to a Hindu ruler in western India that they wanted to settle there. The Hindu ruler sent the Parsi a bowl full of milk to symbolize that they should not come to India—that the western states were already full. Legend has it that the Parsi leader placed a gold ring in the bowl of milk and returned it—symbolizing they would bring wealth to the region without displacing the people. Around 1,500 years ago, the Parsi settled in western India, primarily in the city of Mumbai (formerly known as Bombay).

India is overwhelmingly Hindu (85 percent), but the followers of the Parsi religion, who make up 0.0032 percent of the Indian population (fewer than 40,000 Parsi in the Indian population of 1.25 billion people), control a large share of the Indian economy. The Tata Group recorded revenues of U.S.$103.27 billion in 2013–14, while the entire gross national income (GNI) of India for the same time frame was around $6.7 trillion. In addition to the Tata Group, the Godrej Group, which produces soap, appliances, and office equipment, and the Wadia Company, which produces textiles and owns an airline, are companies established and run by Parsi families in India.

The financial success of the Parsi in India cannot be ascribed to a single cause. Their tight-knit community and maintenance of cultural practices that keep the Parsi together and culturally separate from the dominant Hindu culture were definitely factors in the Parsi success. These same traits now threaten to

FIGURE 8.1 Tata sign in Hyderabad.

destroy the Parsi culture, and their numbers are beginning to dwindle.

A local culture such as the Parsi is maintained through the preservation of cultural traits and cultural practices. Today, however, one core cultural practice among the Parsi threatens the existence of the culture itself. According to an edict set down by Parsi religious leaders in 1918, the Parsi religion recognizes only the children who are born of two Parsi parents. Although some Parsi do accept children born to a Parsi father and non-Parsi mother as members of the community, children born of Parsi women married to non-Parsi (called "outsiders" by the Parsi) are not accepted as community members.

This is significant today because the Parsi have a very high literacy rate in India—98 percent—and many Parsi women are highly educated, have good jobs, and choose either not to marry, to have children late (thus reducing fertility rates), or to marry outside the Parsi community. In addition, thousands of Parsi women and men have migrated to the United States and Europe over the past few decades. One Parsi high priest sees the historical lack of intermarriage as a major reason the Parsi were able to maintain their culture and religion in a world surrounded by Hindu followers. Parsi in India today question whether to count the women married to "outsiders," and the children born to them, as members of the community. If they do not count these women and children, the Parsi population in India has declined over the last 30 years from 100,000 to 40,000.

As we discussed in Chapter 2, in an era of globalization, popular culture has diffused around the world—embraced by some and rejected by others, yet nonetheless infiltrating every corner of the globe. Local cultures continue to exist, but they face constant pressure from larger cultural groups and from the enveloping popular culture. In the face of these pressures, some members of local cultures have clung more tightly to their customs, some have let go, and others have forged a balance between the two. In this chapter, we explore what we mean by the notion of "culture" and how and why "culture" is geographical.

KEY QUESTIONS FOR CHAPTER 8

1. What do we mean by the term "culture" and how is it geographical?

2. What are local and popular cultures?

3. How are local cultures sustained?

4. How is culture diffused?

5. How is culture reflected in the landscape?

8.1 What Do We Mean by the Term "Culture" and How Is It Geographical?

When we look across our backyards or down our streets, when we glance in the windows of businesses or wander different neighbourhoods, we see the symbols and traditions of different ethnic and racial groups, religions, and cultures. Streetscapes come alive with unexpected architectural features, unfamiliar and intriguing street art, distinctive fashions, unknown languages, and the tantalizing smells of foods yet to be sampled. As we noted in Chapter 1, these characteristics, among others, contribute to our "sense of place." Distinctive cultural traditions, norms, and values are interwoven into place and have an impact on those of us who live in or experience those places. As geographers, we are interested in how certain values, norms, and ideas become embedded in the landscape. How is it that one group's architecture, lifestyle, or behaviours become what is expected or acceptable in the world around us and others do not? This question asks us to consider notions of power relations and domination, as well as ideas about social justice and our ability to see ourselves reflected in the built environment around us.

According to cultural theorist Raymond Williams, culture is both "ordinary" and a "whole way of life." A **culture** is a set of shared belief systems, norms, and values practised by a particular group of people. Although this definition of culture sounds simple, the concept is actually quite complex. A group of people who share common beliefs can be recognized as a culture in one of two ways: (1) the people call themselves a culture; or (2) other people (including academics) label them a culture. Some geographers perceive culture as a "way of life" and are intrigued with how certain aspects of that

> **Culture** A set of shared belief systems, norms, and values practised by a particular group of people. According to cultural theorist Raymond Williams, culture is both "ordinary" and a "whole way of life."

way of life become visible in building styles, music, food, religion, and landscapes. Clearly, not everyone in a particular group may adhere completely to a culture's dominant values, beliefs, and norms. As geographers, we understand that a particular set of ideas becomes the most prominent within a particular culture. While it is important to understand and study dominant belief systems, we also need to be attentive to those belief systems that are marginal or less visible.

While we can focus on particular forms of literature, dance, or art as being characteristic of a particular group, such as the painting styles of 18th-century Quebec artists or the music of 19th-century Japan, we can also consider the particular shared beliefs, norms, and values of a cross-section or particular grouping of peoples, such as "working class" culture, "skater" culture, or "corporate" culture. Shared beliefs, norms, and values also change over time as they are challenged or come into contact with other cultures. Sometimes the cultural changes can seem momentous, as was the case with the radical movements of the 1960s (**Figure 8.2**), or change can be incremental and subtle, exemplified by the increasing secularization of public life, such as that experienced in Quebec during the Quiet Revolution. Shared beliefs can be based on long-standing traditions, such as religious teachings or community traditions or they can emerge spontaneously in a particular historical and geographical moment, such as the influential emergence of the grunge music scene in Seattle in the late 1980s.

Culture is geographical. Different cultures are present in different places, and culture both shapes and is shaped by the places in which it emerges. As noted in Chapter 1, by taking a spatial perspective, geographers can consider the intimate and important connections between humans and their environment. This can be seen at the global scale when we look at the difference in landscapes between countries such as Australia and the Philippines, for example, or within countries, such as the distinctive landscapes of Newfoundland and Quebec. We can also note distinctive cultural artefacts in rural, suburban, and urban areas and sometimes between inner-city neighbourhoods

and outer areas. Using the five geographical themes—location, region, place, landscape, and movement—we can sharpen our spatial perspective to think about how we locate culture, how culture has an impact on place and landscapes, and how cultural traits, values, and characteristics diffuse across space.

Geographers bring particular spatial insights to questions of culture and place, but they have approached the question of connections between culture and landscapes in different ways. Contemporary cultural geography developed in the early 1920s with the work of Carl Sauer and his colleagues and students at the University of California at Berkeley—the so-called Berkeley School of cultural geography. Sauer used the term **cultural landscape** to refer to how a natural landscape, itself always changing (through physical processes such as erosion), is altered by cultural groups in distinctive ways. Sauer's work highlights the human–environment relationship at the heart of the geographical endeavour. In his *Morphology of Landscape,* Sauer (1925, p. 1) argued that

> *Culture is the agent, the natural area is the medium, the cultural landscape the result [of cultivation]. Under the influence of a given culture, itself changing through time, the landscape undergoes development, passing through phases, and probably reaching ultimately the end of its cycle of development. With the introduction of a different— that is, an alien—culture [or way of life], a rejuvenation of the cultural landscape sets in, or a new landscape is superimposed on remnants of an older one.*

This rather deterministic view of culture was influential in the study of geography, particularly in North America, well into the 1970s. Sauer's model of the relationship between landscape and culture has been critiqued as taking a "super-organic" perspective. In Sauer's work, "culture" is viewed as an overarching or structural agent seemingly creating or determining a cultural landscape that is constantly changing in response to the influence of these cultural forces. Using this approach, geographers studied the historical transformation of place—how rural landscapes were altered by new farming practices and techniques, or how the distribution or organization of villages, towns, and cities changed. This geographical research on cultural landscape was largely descriptive and documented the dominant features that made the landscapes of different groups distinctive—including the study of specific architectural features in barns and housing, or the construction of places of worship and cemeteries of different cultural groups.

The super-organic approach to culture was tested by social upheavals of the 1960s in North America and Europe. Civil unrest and public protest were the hallmarks of the Black civil rights movement, the American Indian movement, the women's movement, the gay and lesbian movement, anti-Vietnam War demonstrations, and the student and worker demonstrations in North America and Europe (most notably France). Any notion of "culture" as an overarching, unified, and universal or collectively

> **Cultural landscape** The visible imprint of human activity and culture on the landscape. The layers of buildings, forms, and artefacts sequentially imprinted on the landscape by the activities of various human occupants.

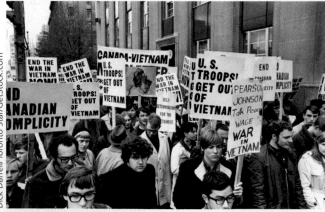

FIGURE 8.2 Canadians protest the war in Vietnam. Around the globe, the 1960s were known as a time of social upheaval, protest, and the emergence of a "counterculture." The civil rights movement, feminism, gay and lesbian rights movement, anti-war demonstrations, and "flower power," among other movements, came to the forefront during this period.

Dick Darrell/Toronto Star/GetStock.com

shared set of values and norms seemed unsupportable given the diverse groups arguing for recognition and inclusion in the social fabric. A descriptive geography, interested in documenting the mark of human activities in the landscape, was not at all helpful in explaining or understanding the deeply felt and sometimes violent social and political unrest of the period.

Geographers were intrigued by these rapid and transformative social and political events, and researchers struggled to understand them using a number of different intellectual approaches. In the 1970s and 1980s, geographers such as David Harvey found Marxist notions of class relations and structural inequalities within capitalism useful in understanding the struggles against poverty and exclusion. Marxists were (and still are) interested in the capitalist mode of production and how it influences human-nature relations, and space itself. More specifically, they argued that capitalism had created social inequalities that provided for material wealth for a few, to the exclusion of many. These scholars recognized that spaces are built and used in particular ways, often to reflect cultural tastes of those in positions of power and authority. For example, gentrification can be understood as the appropriation of rundown urban spaces, which had been occupied by people living in poverty, for the exclusive use of affluent people, thereby forcing those in poverty out of those spaces. Geographer Neil Smith pushed Marxist cultural geography further in his study of the gentrification process in inner-city neighbourhoods, suggesting that urban land prices and speculation were driving the process rather than cultural preference. In other words, the ambition of the wealthy to become wealthier shapes the appropriation of urban (and rural) space. Later in this chapter, we consider the process of commodification—the transformation of ideas, spaces, and other things into goods that can be bought and sold—in relation to the spaces in which we live. Marxist cultural geographers are very interested in this process, and in considering not only how spaces are commodified in particular ways, but also what the impact of these processes are on the lived experiences of various groups of people. Marxists argue that we must examine the social structures out of which spaces are produced or made, in order to change the world for the better.

In what is known as the "cultural turn" in geography, many geographers began to recognize that class was not the only important social division that distinguished different factions and that, as we discussed in Chapter 7, social divisions along the lines of race, gender, age, and sexual orientation also affect life chances and experiences, often inequitably. This recognition called into question the idea that there was such a thing as a "culture" shared by all individuals in a particular place or region. The idea that culture was something stable, fixed, and whole was questioned, as scholars worked to unpack the experiences, behaviours, and identities that were shared by some cultural groups but not others. Geographer Don Mitchell went so far as to argue that "there is no such thing as culture" (1995, p. 102) in terms of an object or area of study distinct from economics or politics. Political systems and economic traditions or ways of doing business are clearly influenced by cultural norms and practices, and vice versa—that is, cultural ideas about consumption and the role of government are influenced by political and economic institutions.

Geographers seeking theories to unpack this new conceptualization of culture as something that is fluid, always changing, and often contradictory drew on the postmodernist and poststructuralist frameworks briefly outlined in Chapter 1. These geographers argued that we need to focus on meanings, power relations, and symbols in order to make sense of cultural landscapes. Whose meanings and symbols come to dominate the landscape? Who has the power to ensure their beliefs and values are built into the world around them? Moving away from analyses of the structures that shape and inform culture, these so-called new cultural geographers began to draw upon literary theory, focusing on how ideas, knowledge, beliefs, and social practices are produced and maintained in the realm of everyday life. **Discourse**—the representative codes and conventions of language that produce culturally specific meanings—became an important tool for cultural geographers seeking to make sense of the world. Using discourse, geographers could "read" the landscape as text and express how particular ways of being become "normal." For some, skyscrapers, highways, and industry represent a landscape that reflects economic development and prosperity. For others, these same landscapes reflect the power of one group (business people or capitalists, for example) to take control of space in particular ways and create landscapes that reflect certain values. Geographers using poststructural frameworks could unpack the meanings embedded in the built environment, recognizing that those meanings are changeable, and that landscapes or the built environment are reflections of power relations. For example, the Pruitt-Igoe Housing Development in St. Louis, Missouri, was built as a "solution" to what some saw as the "problem" of poor, mostly black people in the city. It was designed by George Hellmuth and Minoru Yamasaki in 1951 and fully opened in 1956. Considered at the time to be the "epitome of modern architecture," Pruitt-Igoe was held up as an example of rational, orderly, efficient management of a poverty-stricken population. However, within 20 years the development stood in ruins, considered by many to be a disastrous example of attempting to use technological means to solve social and cultural problems. The entire complex was razed between 1972 and 1976 (**Figure 8.3**).

> **Discourse** The representative codes and conventions of language that produce culturally specific meanings.

Some cultural geographers are interested in the subtle and minute ways that oppression, marginalization, and exclusion are built into landscapes, limiting or narrowing life choices for some and privileging possibilities for others. For example, if the billboards, advertisements, and images in your neighbourhood contain only images of a particular ethnic or racial group, of which you are not a member, your sense of belonging in that neighbourhood might be undermined. If people who build streets, walkways, and buildings presume everyone can walk, then individuals with limited mobility or who use a wheelchair are "excluded by design." Geographers use a number of different perspectives to consider questions of social difference and exclusion. For example, feminist geographers, geographers engaged in critical race studies, and geographers of sexualities and queer geographies are all concerned

Bettman/Corbis

(a)

Bettman/Corbis

(b)

FIGURE 8.3 Pruitt-Igoe Housing Development, St. Louis, Missouri. (a) The Pruitt-Igoe Housing Development in 1971. (b) In 1972, the first building was demolished, and within four years the entire development was razed.

with spatial exclusion and marginalization on the basis of gender, race, and sexuality, respectively. The landscapes we see are the result of contestations and conflict in which the more dominant group is able to successfully mark spaces with its own beliefs and values (**Figure 8.4**). As the *Guest Field Note* by Sarah Jane Meharg shows, some societies have gone to great lengths to destroy other people's cultural places and practices, forcefully dispersing unwelcome groups, and deliberately and systematically destroying an entire people.

Contemporary cultural geography also considers popular culture as well as what some might see as elite or "high-brow" culture, represented by literature, traditional music, opera, theatre, and high art. Yet all cultural forms, including fashion, mainstream movies, domestic life, and street and folk art, are reasonable objects for geographical enquiry. The everyday lives of individual people, and their engagement in the production and consumption of culture, in whatever form, help illuminate broad social, political, and economic processes at work in forging and transforming the built environment and social relations.

dbimages/Alamy

FIGURE 8.4 Montreal's Gay Village. Our built environments can also be marked as alternative spaces. Located on Sainte-Catherine Street East, Montreal's Gay Village is one of North America's largest gay villages.

GUEST FIELD NOTE

Identicide: The Destruction of Place during Armed Conflict

I embarked upon the study of cultural geography, armed with an educational background in landscape architecture and war studies. These two areas of study may seem unrelated, even counterintuitive, to the casual observer, yet my aim was to link the two and focus on post-conflict reconstruction—a term that has gained relevance since the U.S. invasion of Iraq in 2003.

Post-conflict reconstruction—the rebuilding of conflict-affected environments—requires research and expertise in designing

places for people (landscape architecture) and the study of strategic warfare and its destructive acts (war studies). Through cultural geography, I was able to uniquely bridge theories of the "creation of place" and the "destruction of place" in a doctoral dissertation focused upon post-conflict reconstruction. At the time, there were few research projects that examined the destruction of the relationship between people and their places during war, or the tactical methods used to mete out this type of destruction. It was a worthy area of inquiry to pursue, and I was mentored by scholars in heritage studies, art history, and genocide studies throughout this process. Thankfully, I was surrounded by some multidisciplinary thinkers who were not interested in traditional uni-disciplinary projects, but, rather, who

GUEST FIELD NOTE Identicide: The Destruction of Place during Armed Conflict *continued*

encouraged me to connect ideas so I could inductively develop my theory of warfare: identicide.

Although my entry into the study of cultural geography was from an eclectic perspective, it allowed me to see and understand the phenomenon of war in a way that permitted further insight into the nexus of culture and geography. Since graduating, I have been able to continue researching and publishing on the intentional destruction of symbolic places during armed conflict, and have spoken to NATO, the United Nations, the European Union, and the U.S. Army, among other groups, regarding identicide and why culture matters in war and peace.

We are strongly connected to our places, because it is in place that routinized and ritualized daily practices construct our identities. By identity, we mean the characteristics shared by individuals and groups. Identity is space-bound: it stems from the specific places that we create, and it contributes to the particular experience of our lives in such cultural landscapes. This particularity of place reinforces ethnicities, cultures, and identities. Places, with their defining material elements, become a part of the mythology of cultures and are building blocks of identity. As we act upon our places, they, too, act upon us. When they change, we change; when we change, our places seem to shift and alter with our new awareness. We are interconnected, and have a relationship, with our places that informs who we are, what we do, and what we think.

So what happens when the bond between people and their places is destroyed? I have considered this question for many years, and it is an important one for cultural geographers. Significant places are destroyed in many ways, whether through new land developments in North America, industrial practices in rural India, or natural disasters such as Hurricane Katrina. Yet none is more potent or traumatic for people than the intentional destruction of their meaningful places during contemporary armed conflict—a phenomenon that I call "identicide."

By identicide, I mean a strategy of warfare that deliberately targets and destroys cultural landscapes through a variety of means in order to contribute to eventual acculturation, removal, and/or total destruction of a particular identity group. Identicide is the killing of identity. Some societies have gone to great lengths to destroy other people's cultural places and practices, forcefully dispersing unwelcome groups, and deliberately and systematically destroying an entire people. Identicide is the precursor to genocide, but does not necessarily lead to genocide. Strategies to destroy places and cultural practices are a means to rid an area of a marginalized or openly contested group. Typically, this is achieved through the manipulation and control of symbols and the territorialization of the collective space in which they are embedded.

Identicide kills the relatedness between people and place and attempts to eliminate the bond underpinning individual, community, and national identity. These tactics are some of the most effective war tools and have been used in recent conflicts, such as those in Bosnia-Herzegovina. During the intense armed conflict in Bosnia-Herzegovina in 1993, the famous Bridge of Mostar was intentionally destroyed in order to sever the two sides of Mostar—one Croat Christian/Catholic and the other Bosnian Muslim (**Figure 8.5**). Although the lines of ethnic and religious division were not so clear-cut as the river that divided them, the destruction of the bridge caused local, national, and international outrage, because of the bridge's cultural significance and lack of legitimate military utility. The bridge's destruction is a noteworthy example of identicide because the intention of the perpetrators was to sever the bond between the people of Mostar and their beloved Stari Most, the Old Bridge, hence creating a homogeneous culture, rather than allowing the ethnically diverse culture to exist.

Identicide has existed throughout recorded history: the forced Christianization of early pagan symbolic sites in Ireland is one example, as is the changing of Maori place names to the

Nigel Chandler/Sygma/Corbis

(a)

©iStockphoto.com/santirf

(b)

FIGURE 8.5 The Stari Most, Old Bridge, in Mostar, Bosnia-Herzegovina. (a) The destroyed bridge in February 1994. (b) The bridge was rebuilt and reopened in July 2004. The United Nations declared the new bridge a World Heritage Site in 2005, describing it as "a symbol of reconciliation, international co-operation and of the coexistence of diverse cultural, ethnic and religious communities."

GUEST FIELD NOTE   Identicide: The Destruction of Place during Armed Conflict *continued*

lexicon of the colonists in New Zealand. Identicide takes many forms, but serves a single function: to lead to the decimation of a people, their places, and practices. In my experience, when people learn about identicide, they almost always have had a personal experience related to it. Identicide is a concept that allows people to better understand their relationships with place, and the bonds that can be affected when places are intentionally destroyed.

Sarah Jane Meharg, Royal Military College of Canada

MAIN POINTS 8.1 What Do We Mean by the Term "Culture" and How Is It Geographical?

- A culture is a complex and dynamic set of shared belief systems, norms, and values practised by a particular group of people who define themselves or are defined by others as constituting a cultural group.

- The work of Carl Sauer and geographers of the Berkeley School is one strand of contemporary cultural geography that focuses on how human interaction with natural landscapes created distinctive cultural landscapes.

- Other contemporary strands in cultural geography are concerned with social difference and the built environment and with questions of inequality, social justice, exclusion, and marginalization. Geographers in these areas examine how various markers of difference, including gender, sexual orientation, race, ethnicity, age, and disability, are important in considering how cultural landscapes are created and understood.

- Culture is geographical: dominant cultural beliefs, norms, and values are reflected in cultural landscapes. At the same time, cultural landscapes influence the ideas, beliefs, and values of those who experience them in distinctive and not always predictable ways.

8.2 What Are Local and Popular Cultures?

> **Folk culture** Cultural traits such as dress modes, dwellings, traditions, and institutions of usually small, traditional communities.
>
> **Cultural trait** A single element of normal practice in a culture, such as the wearing of a turban.
>
> **Popular culture** Cultural traits such as dress, diet, and music that identify and are part of today's changeable urban-based, media-influenced Western societies.

Academics who accept that there is something called "culture" that can be discerned and studied have traditionally identified cultural groups as either folk cultures or as part of popular culture. **Folk culture** is understood as incorporating a homogeneous population, and as being typically rural with cohesive cultural traits. (A **cultural trait** is a single element of normal practice in a culture, such as the wearing of a turban.) By contrast, **popular culture** is understood as pervasive, as incorporating heterogeneous populations, and as typically urban with rapidly changing cultural traits. Contemporary academic work tends to reject this polarity of folk and popular cultures in favour of understanding folk and popular cultures as points on a continuum.

Further, folk culture can be a somewhat limiting concept as it requires us to create a list of traits (e.g., religious beliefs, musical styles, fashion) and to look for cultures that display that list of traits. This methodology of defining folk cultures leaves much to be desired. Based on this example, are the Amish a folk culture? Are the Navajo a folk culture? Arguably, it is how the people define themselves that matters more.

A **local culture** is a group of people in a particular place who understand that they share experiences, customs, and traits,

> **Local culture** Group of people in a particular place who see themselves as a collective or a community; who share experiences, customs, and traits; and who work to preserve those traits and customs in order to claim uniqueness and to distinguish themselves from others.

and who work to preserve those traits and customs in order to distinguish themselves from others. It is important to bear in mind that just because a certain set of cultural beliefs, values, and norms are dominant in a definable location, this does not mean that everyone in that location is included in these dominant cultural systems. Some may be marginalized based on such things as race, gender, or class. Individuals in a cultural place or region may hold different ideas, may contest certain aspects of local culture, or may adhere to some aspects of the dominant culture while rejecting others. While understanding the dominant culture is important, being attentive to these distinctions is also important.

When we consider local culture instead of folk culture, we are interested in different questions. For example, do the Amish have a group identity? What cultural traits do they understand themselves as sharing? How do the Amish navigate popular culture and defend their local customs? Why do Canadians in Alberta understand themselves as having a different culture from those individuals from central Canada or the Maritimes? Why is it that certain North American holidays, such as St. Patrick's Day, transcend ethnicity and are celebrated as a part of popular culture, even as organizers of a St. Patrick's Day parade prohibit certain groups, such as those identifying as gay or lesbian as well as Irish, from participating?

> **Material culture** The art, housing, clothing, sports, dances, foods, and other similar items constructed or created by a group of people.
>
> **Nonmaterial culture** The beliefs, practices, aesthetics, and values of a group of people.

Some local cultures rely primarily on religion to maintain their belief systems; others rely on community celebrations or family structures; and still others rely on a lack of interaction with other cultures. Local cultures are constantly redefining or refining themselves based on interactions with other cultures (local and popular) and diffusion of cultural traits (local and popular). Local cultures also affect places by establishing neighbourhoods, by building places of worship or community centres to celebrate important days, and by expressing their material and nonmaterial cultures in certain places. The **material culture** of a group of people includes the things they construct, such as art, houses, clothing, sports, dance, and foods. **Nonmaterial culture** includes the beliefs, practices, aesthetics (that is, what they see as attractive), and values. What members of a local culture produce in their material culture reflects and reinforces the beliefs and values of their nonmaterial culture. It is vital to note how people in local cultures accept, reject, or alter diffusing cultural traits, depending on what works for them.

In contrast to local cultures, which are found in relatively small areas, popular culture is understood as ubiquitous and is practised by a heterogeneous group of people from any and all local cultures, anywhere in the world. Popular culture encompasses, among other things, architecture, music, dance, clothing, food preference, religious practices, and aesthetic values. The main paths of diffusion of popular culture are the transportation, marketing, and communication networks that interlink vast parts of the world (see Chapter 2 for further discussion of these networks). When we examine popular culture, we see that some forms of cultural expression appear everywhere, but it is the study of local culture that lets us see how communities, groups, and individuals in particular places take up or reject popular culture. Local culture shows us how those global cultural networks, largely dominated by core countries, touch ground differently in different places, and how popular culture is filtered through local traditions and customs (**Figure 8.6**).

For example, fashions diffuse incredibly quickly today. When Catherine Middleton, Duchess of Cambridge, graced Westminster Abbey in a lace wedding gown designed by Sarah Burton for the House of Alexander McQueen at an estimated cost of $65,000, dress designers around the world interpreted or copied the gown within hours (**Figure 8.7**). Fewer than 10 hours after the wedding aired at 5:30 a.m. Eastern Time, dress designers at Kleinfeld Bridal Salon in New York had replicated Middleton's dress. The salon started selling it for $3,500 within 48 hours.

Kin Cheung/AP/The Canadian Press

FIGURE 8.6 McDonald's in Hong Kong, 2006. McDonald's operates in more than 119 countries on six continents. Its ubiquity has not come without criticism; sociologist George Ritzer termed the chain's cultural dominance at the global level "McDonaldization." However, while all locations serve menu staples like the Big Mac, they also offer menu items adapted from local cultures to suit local tastes. In this image, McDonald's employees in Hong Kong hold up the toasted shrimp rice burger.

Samir Hussein/Wire Image/Getty Images

FIGURE 8.7 Diffusion of fashion. Catherine Middleton, Duchess of Cambridge, enters London's Westminster Abbey on her wedding day. Her wedding gown, designed by Sarah Burton of the House of Alexander McQueen, was replicated and on sale by retailers within a few days.

> **Hierarchical diffusion** A form of diffusion in which an idea or innovation spreads by passing first among the most connected places or peoples. An urban hierarchy is usually involved, encouraging the leapfrogging of innovations over wide areas, with geographic distance a less important influence.
>
> **Hearth** The area where an idea or cultural trait originates.

In popular culture, fashion trends spread rapidly through the interconnected world in a classic case of **hierarchical diffusion** (discussed in Chapter 1). The hierarchy in this case is the fashion world. Key cities such as Milan, Paris, and New York are the **hearth** (the point of origin) or the cases of first diffusion. The next tier of places includes the major fashion houses in world cities. Finally, the suburban mall receives the innovation. Hierarchical diffusion can also occur through a hierarchy of people. In this case, the designer is the hearth; the models are the next tier; and celebrities, editors and writers of major magazines, and subscribers to fashion magazines follow in close order. Finally, anyone walking through a shopping mall can become a "knower" in the diffusion of this innovation.

Local and popular cultures are not seen as two ends of a continuum; rather, they both operate across multiple scales, affecting people and places in different ways. For example, people from Hutterite or Mennonite communities, dressed in the distinctive clothing of their culture, often visit the ultimate in popular culture: a major international department store such as Walmart. While retaining their local culture, they accept some aspects of the popular culture on sale in the store. Moving the other way, traditions based on centuries-old customs of local cultures, such as painting henna on one's hands or practising Kabbalah beliefs, are carried to the global culture by a popular culture icon or by corporations (such as the media industry) that work to construct popular culture (**Figure 8.8**).

Valerie Macon/AFP/Getty Images

FIGURE 8.8 Diffusion of culture. In 2013, while on tour in Auckland, New Zealand, singer Rihanna received a traditional Maori tattoo on her hand and wrist, using a chisel and mallet. Controversy ensued, with some arguing that celebrities receiving Maori tattoos remove the "real" meaning of the tattoo thereby appropriating traditional culture and transforming it into a fashion statement. Maori typically receive moko, pe'a or malu tattoos to signify respect for their culture and status and entry into adulthood. Within weeks, Rihanna covered up her Maori tattoo with a henna-inspired tattoo, aiming for something "decorative, feminine and sexy."

MAIN POINTS 8.2 What Are Local and Popular Cultures?

- Local culture involves a group of people in a particular place who understand themselves as a collective or a community; who share experiences, customs, and traits; and who work to preserve those traits and customs in order to claim uniqueness and distinguish themselves from others.

- Popular culture is dominant, ubiquitous, and able to change rapidly, diffusing new ideas across vast distances. It is practised by a heterogeneous group of people from any and all local cultures, anywhere in the world, and encompasses, among other things, music, dance, clothing, food preference, religious practices, and aesthetic values.

- Geographically, we tend to see local cultures as occupying distinctive and discernible places, locations, and regions. Yet these local cultures are embedded in and influenced by wider popular culture trends that are taken up, rejected, or transformed in local contexts.

- Culture, either local or popular, is not monolithic or universal. Although a certain set of beliefs, norms, and practices may come to dominate, individuals within the cultural group may have their own ideas that are excluded or rejected. Geographers are interested in the ways in which certain cultural ideas come to dominate and others are actively excluded or simply ignored.

- Cultural geographers are interested in both local and popular cultures that operate within a web of customs and cultures diffused and interlinked across a variety of scales.

- Both local and popular cultures operate within a web of innumerable customs and cultures that are diffused and interlinked at a variety of scales. Distinctive cultural traits and forms circulate through a complex web of political and economic forces that shape and limit their practices. Popular culture is diffused through global communications and transportation networks that intricately link certain parts of the world and distance others. At the same time, local cultures work to preserve their uniqueness even as they are enmeshed in the wider popular culture.

8.3 How Are Local Cultures Sustained?

Local cultures often work hard to preserve and maintain their distinctive features in spite of the pervasive influence of cultural beliefs and norms that may emerge both within and beyond the place or region. A good example is the province of Quebec, which has actively worked for several centuries to preserve its language, music, art, and religious traditions. At the national level, the Canadian Radio-television and Telecommunications Commission (CRTC) works to ensure that Canadian actors, artists, writers, film and television producers, and musicians are given adequate representation within Canadian cultural industries.

Assimilation The process through which people lose originally differentiating traits, such as dress, speech particularities, or mannerisms, when they come into contact with another society or culture. Often used to describe immigrant adaptation to new places of residence.

The drive to preserve certain cultural ideas and eradicate others has a lengthy history in the Canadian context. For example, during the 1800s and into the 1900s, the Canadian government had an official policy of **assimilation** of indigenous peoples. It wanted to integrate the country's First Nations peoples into the dominant culture, making them "Canadians" rather than "Indians." The United States, Australia, the Soviet Union, and other colonial powers adopted similar policies toward indigenous peoples, using schools, churches, and government agents to discourage native or indigenous practices. In Canada, the federal government forced tribal members to settle in one place, usually on reserves, and to farm rather than hunt or fish on traditional hunting grounds. Residential schools, managed by religious organizations including the Anglican and Roman Catholic churches, were designed to separate First Nations children from their families and to teach them the English language as the first step in assimilating them (**Figure 8.9**). Missionary school teachers punished tribal members for using their native language.

FIGURE 8.9 Indian residential schools of Canada. It is estimated that about 150,000 Aboriginal, Inuit, and Métis children were removed from their communities and forced to attend residential schools.

Today, several churches and governments have apologized for assimilationist policies. In 2008, the governments of Australia and Canada each officially apologized to their indigenous populations (Aboriginals in Australia and First Nations and Inuit in Canada). On September 19, 2007, the Indian Residential Schools Settlement Agreement came into effect in Canada; it is the largest class action settlement in the country's history. The measures put in place through this agreement include the Common Experience Payment, a $1.9-billion fund from which compensation will be paid to every eligible former residential school student; the Truth and Reconciliation Commission, which gave former students and their families the opportunity to share their experiences, educate non-natives, and raise awareness of the effects of residential schools; the Independent Assessment Process, established to assist those who suffered sexual and physical abuse and other wrongful acts that led to serious psychological injury; Commemoration, to pay tribute to, honour, and remember students from residential schools and their common experiences; and the Aboriginal Healing Foundation, which will provide healing programs and initiatives.

As these examples demonstrate, people attempting to maintain a local culture might

Custom A practice routinely followed by a group of people.

face tremendous difficulties, including removal from their traditional landscape and a complete dislocation from the language and customs particular to a place. Local cultures are sustained by **customs**, which are practices that a group of people routinely follows. People have customs regarding all parts of their lives, from eating and drinking to dancing and sports. These customs may change in small ways over time, but they must be maintained despite the onslaught of popular culture if the local culture is to survive. Members of local cultures, whether rural or urban, often find they are trying to keep their customs for themselves, to prevent others from appropriating their customs for economic benefit. Anthropologists and geographers have studied how others use local cultural knowledge, customs, and even names. For example, First Nations peoples and their non-Aboriginal supporters have long resisted the appropriation of their names and images in sports teams. Teams such as the Washington Redskins, Kansas City Chiefs, Atlanta Braves, and Cleveland Indians (**Figure 8.10**) all use names and images derived from indigenous peoples. These appropriations of names and likenesses by sports teams feed into racially motivated discourses that normalize an understanding of indigenous peoples as violent and savage. We discuss this process of appropriation and commodification later in this chapter.

Researcher Simon Harrison recognizes that local cultural groups purposefully, and often fervently, define themselves as unique, creating boundaries around their culture and distinguishing themselves from other local cultures. In the age of globalization, where popular culture changes quickly and diffuses rapidly, Harrison finds that local cultures typically have two goals: keeping other cultures out and keeping their own culture in so as to avoid "contamination and extinction." Harrison uses

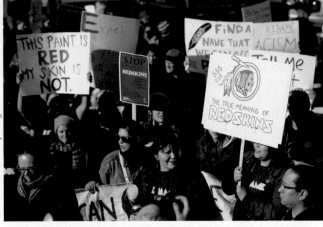

Hannah Foslien/Getty Images

FIGURE 8.10 **Protesters march before a Washington Redskins game, November 2, 2014.** Opponents of the Redskins name believe it's a slur against Native American culture and they want the team to change it.

Suzy Thompson/CPI/The Canadian Press

FIGURE 8.11 **Hutterite women.** A group of Hutterite women near Strathmore, Alberta.

the example of the Notting Hill carnival in London to show how Londoners from the West Indies (the Caribbean) claimed the festival as their own, in conjunction with an increasing sense of collective West Indies culture. The festival did not begin as a Caribbean celebration, but as people from the West Indies shared experiences of "unemployment, police harassment and poor housing conditions" during the 1970s, they began to define themselves as a local culture and redefined the festival as a West Indian celebration.

RURAL LOCAL CULTURES

Members of local cultures in rural areas often have an easier time maintaining their cultures because they are more isolated. By living together in a rural area, members of a local culture can more easily keep external influences on the outside. It is no accident that we find Anabaptist groups, such as the Hutterites, the Amish, and the Mennonites, living in rural areas of South Dakota, Pennsylvania, Virginia, Saskatchewan, Alberta, and other jurisdictions. During the Protestant Reformation in Europe, Anabaptists broke from both the Catholic Church and the new Protestant churches. Followers of the new religion were called Anabaptists (which means "baptized again") because of their belief in the importance of adult baptism, even if they had already been baptized as infants.

Anabaptists broke from the state as well as the church; they embraced pacifism and soon suffered persecution. In response, Anabaptists migrated east to Moravia and Austria, and then to Russia and the Ukraine, continually moving to rural areas to live apart and avoid persecution. A group of Anabaptists called the Hutterites, named for leader Jacob Hutter, eventually migrated to North America in the second half of the 1800s.

The popular media portrays Old Order Anabaptist groups in stereotypical ways, suggesting all groups are the same, but major differences exist between Old Order Amish, Mennonites, Hutterites, and Brethren. The Hutterites are the only Anabaptist

group that lives communally (**Figure 8.11**). Rather than living with immediate family on a farmstead, Hutterites live in colonies of about 100 people, with individuals ranging in age from infant to elderly. There are 461 colonies in North America, with more than half located in Manitoba and Alberta (**Figure 8.12**). In their book *On the Backroad to Heaven*, Donald Kraybill and Carl Bowman explain that the linchpin of each colony is the Hutterite religion. Members of the colony join together every night for a 30-minute service, as well as attending services on Sundays. The most prominent position in a colony is held by the minister, who speaks in archaic German, reading sermons written in the 16th century.

Unlike the Amish, Hutterites readily accept technologies that help them in their agricultural pursuits. However, they do not accept technologies such as televisions, cameras, and cell phones, which encourage individualistic behaviours or undermine the Hutterite religion. Colonies assign separate jobs and tasks to men and women, which reinforces a patriarchal social structure. Kraybill and Bowman explain that marriages happen across colonies, and women move to their husband's colony after marrying. As a result, a single colony is usually composed of only one or two surnames. Moving to their husband's colony perpetuates women's weak political position in the society. Women are expected to rear many children, averaging five or six currently, but the colony as a whole is responsible for raising and disciplining the children.

Hutterite colonies specialize in diversified agriculture, raising feed, food, and livestock on landholdings as big as 10,000 acres. Hutterite men often barter with neighbouring farmers to fix machinery, trade goods, and lend help. Aside from shopping, it is uncommon for most people in the colony to interact with outsiders. The minister serves as liaison with the outside world, and he works with lawyers and bankers to keep the colony corporation operating smoothly and profitably. The most economically successful colonies have created agricultural products, such as animal feed or stainless steel

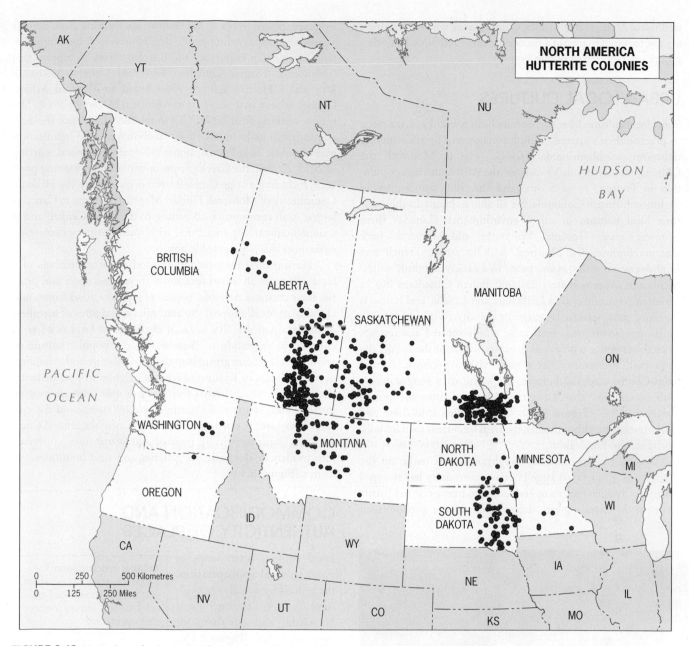

FIGURE 8.12 Hutterite colonies in North America. Alberta and Manitoba are home to the largest number of Hutterite colonies, although there are groups throughout the four western provinces and five U.S. states. Data from: www.hutterites.org.

animal feeders, that they produce in their shops and sell to other farmers. Some colonies have also invested hundreds of thousands of dollars in computerized milking systems for their dairy operations or computerized systems for feeding and raising hogs.

Geographer Dawn Bowen has traced the migration of Mennonites, finding their desire to farm in rural areas led them to the northern reaches of Alberta, where they turned forest-lands into farmlands, and to Bolivia to find a place where they could farm, establish their own schools, and practise their religion without pervasive pressures from the popular culture. Rurality can make it much easier for local cultures to keep their culture intact by separating them from other local cultures and

from popular culture. Rurality also enables local cultures to define their own space; to create a place, a town, that reflects their values; and to practise their customs unfettered in that place.

When a local culture discontinues its major economic activity, it faces the challenge of maintaining the customs that depended on the economic activity and, in turn, sustaining its culture. In the modern world, when a local culture decides to re-engage in a traditional economic activity or other cultural custom, it must navigate the limitations and perceptions imposed by different governments and cultures on a variety of scales. In Canada, for example, we often see conflicts between Aboriginal groups, the local community, and the provincial and federal governments over hunting, fishing, and trapping in traditional Aboriginal territories. Conflicts arise when Aboriginals are not required to obtain a licence for these activities, but other groups are required to obtain licences.

URBAN LOCAL CULTURES

Some local cultures have successfully built a world apart, a place to practise their customs, within a major city by constructing tight-knit neighbourhoods. Hasidic Jews in Montreal; the Chinese community in Vancouver; the Afro-Canadian population in Preston, Nova Scotia; and the Sikh community in Richmond, British Columbia, are all able to maintain their distinct local cultures in urban environments. Canada's three "gateway" cities—Toronto, Vancouver, and Montreal—have vibrant communities. Montreal, with its strong French and English communities, is also home to a variety of ethnic neighbourhoods. Approximately 250,000 Italian Canadians live in Montreal, concentrated in Little Italy and LaSalle, and Italian is the third-most-spoken language in the city. While Montreal's Italian neighbourhoods tend to be family-centred and less apt to establish cultural points of interest outside of the home, the city's Irish community has a more visible presence. Pointe-Saint-Charles and Griffintown are home to a long-standing Irish community that arrived in Montreal after the potato famine in 1847 (**Figure 8.13**). Upon settling into these two working-class neighbourhoods, the Irish built their own schools, churches, and hospitals.

Several smaller minority neighbourhoods make up the diversity of Montreal. A large Haitian community has emerged since the 1990s; in fact, most Haitians who immigrate to Canada settle in Montreal, given that French is the predominant language spoken in Haiti. While most are working class, there is a growing number who operate small businesses, including restaurants, Haitian importers, and travel agencies, to support this community. Former Canadian Governor General Michaëlle Jean was a Haitian refugee who settled in Thetford Mines, Quebec (about two hours from Montreal by car) in 1968. She is now working with UNESCO to rebuild Haiti since the devastating earthquake in 2010 and was chosen to lead Organisation internationale de la Francophonie as Secretary-General, starting in 2015. As well, the Greek community maintains a strong presence, including a large Greek festival organized by the Hellenic Community of Montreal. Finally, Montreal is home to Canada's largest Arab community, according to the 2011 Census, and it too maintains strong social ties, with small businesses emerging to support this demographic group.

Having their own neighbourhood enables members of a local culture in an urban area to set themselves apart and practise their customs. Schools, houses of worship, food stores, and clothing stores all support the aesthetics and desires of members of the local culture. The greatest challenge to local cultures in cities is the migration of members of the popular culture or another local culture group into their neighbourhood. Members of local cultures in Toronto's Parkdale neighbourhood are being challenged by young artists and professionals, who are moving into the area. Rents and housing costs are rising, and the cultural landscape is starting to reflect the neighbourhood's new residents, with artistically painted old warehouses converted into residences alongside art galleries and new boutiques and bistros (**Figure 8.14**).

COMMODIFICATION AND AUTHENTICITY OF PLACES

Local cultures often work to avoid **cultural appropriation**, the process by which other cultures adopt customs and knowledge and use them for their own benefit (**Figure 8.15**).

> **Cultural appropriation** The process by which cultures adopt customs and knowledge from other cultures and use them for their own benefit.

In our globalizing world, as Simon Harrison explains, cultural appropriation is a major concern for local cultures because aspects of cultural knowledge, such as natural pharmaceuticals or musical expression, are being privatized by people outside the local culture and used to accumulate wealth or prestige. This is another reason why local cultures might work to keep their customs and knowledge to themselves.

Geographers see both of these processes—cultural preservation and appropriation—happening within local cultures around the world: local cultures desire to keep popular culture out, keep their culture intact, and maintain control over customs and knowledge. Geographers also recognize that through these actions, places become increasingly important. By defining a place (such as a town or neighbourhood) or a space for a short amount of time (such as an annual festival) as quintessentially representing the local culture's values, members of that local culture reinforce their culture and their beliefs. In the

Graham Hughes/The Montreal Gazette

FIGURE 8.13 Ancient Order of Hibernians, Pointe-Saint-Charles, Montreal, 2009. Members of the Ancient Order of Hibernians arrive at St. Gabriel's Church in Pointe-Saint-Charles, which was the starting point of the march to the Black Rock to commemorate the Irish immigrants who died of typhus in Montreal after fleeing the potato famine in 1847.

(a)

©G. Brown

(b)

FIGURE 8.14 Gladstone Hotel, Parkdale, (a) circa 1950s and (b) 2011. Built in 1889, the Gladstone Hotel is the oldest continuously operating hotel in Toronto. Located on Queen Street West in the Parkdale neighbourhood, the hotel's rich history—from its heyday in the early 1900s, through its decline in the 1970s, to its current restoration and renaissance as an arts/culture destination and boutique hotel—follows the ebbs and flows of the Parkdale neighbourhood.

> **Commodification** The process through which something is given monetary value. Commodification occurs when a good or an idea that previously was not regarded as an object to be bought and sold is turned into something that has a particular price and that can be traded in a market economy.

process, a local culture can re-establish customs, recreate entire towns, or establish urban neighbourhoods.

The process by which something that was not previously regarded as an object to be bought or sold (e.g., a name, a good, an idea, or even a person) becomes an object that can be bought, sold, and traded in the world market is called **commodification.** One need look no further than eBay to see commodification. Newspapers frequently report on bizarre objects, such as a cough drop belonging to former California governor Arnold Schwarzenegger or a person's vote for a London mayoral election, being commodified in Internet space.

Commodification affects local cultures in numerous ways. First, material culture, such as jewellery, clothing, food, and games, can be commodified by members of the culture or by non-members. Similarly, nonmaterial culture, including religion, language, and beliefs, can be commodified, often by non-members selling local spiritual and herbal cures for ailments. Local cultures may be commodified as a whole, as when tour buses take tourists to "observe" the Amish culture of Lancaster, Pennsylvania, or when hikers trek with "traditional" Nepalese guides on spiritual journeys through the Himalayas. The inukshuk, a traditional Inuit marker of location and direction, has been appropriated by others and can be found in urban gardens and at the side of highways—literally "out of place" in the landscape. Most notably, it was used as the logo for the Vancouver 2010 Winter Olympics (**Figure 8.16**). Maintaining nonmaterial and material culture while recognizing that culture is not static or fixed is complicated and is a major concern for many groups, from the local neighbourhood to the nation-state.

When aspects of a culture are commodified and detached from the culture in which they had significance, the question of **authenticity** follows. Usually

> **Authenticity** In the context of local cultures or customs, the accuracy with which a single stereotypical or typecast image or experience conveys an otherwise dynamic and complex local culture or its customs.

FIGURE 8.15 Victoria's Secret model Karlie Kloss poses in a traditional Native American-style headdress at its annual fashion show in New York in 2012. People from around the world were quick to express their outrage, arguing this cultural appropriation was offensive. Kloss tweeted an apology, and Victoria's Secret issued a formal apology, promising to remove the outfit from its forthcoming televised event.

Jennifer Mackenzie/Alamy

FIGURE 8.16 Commodification of cultural symbols. The commodification of cultural forms, specifically the appropriation of the inukshuk for the Games' logo, became one of the most blogged-about critiques of the 2010 Olympic Games held in Vancouver.

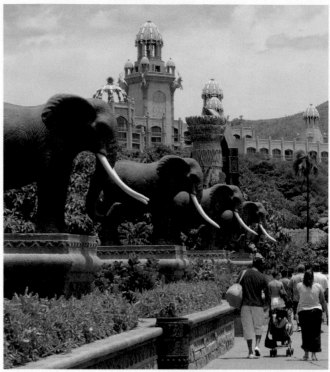

©iStockphoto.com/millerpd

FIGURE 8.17 Sun City, South Africa. The Lost City theme park in Sun City evokes the mystical images of Africa described in a legend.

one image or experience is typecast as the "authentic" image or experience of that culture (e.g., the igloo for the Inuit, or a horse-drawn buggy for the Mennonites), and it is that image or experience that the tourist or buyer desires. However, local cultures are dynamic, and places and people change over time. An "authentic" local culture cannot be conveyed by a single experience or image, nor can it be represented by an object from a bygone time. Rather, a local culture is complex, multi-dimensional, and constantly changing. To gain a sense of that culture, people need to experience its complexity directly, in real time.

The complicated question of authenticity is raised when we examine how certain places are put on display for consumption by others. During the process of colonization, Europeans tagged the cultures they encountered as either savage or mystical. "Authentic" tourist destinations are designed to exploit the mystical or the imagined in local cultures. For example, a South African theme park, the Lost City (built on the site of the Sun City resort), capitalizes on mystical images of Africa described in a legend, thereby "freezing" the continent in a time that never existed (**Figure 8.17**).

In Canada, similar "living museums" have been created to represent and reflect our early history and provide an "authentic" Canadian historical experience. For example, Sainte-Marie Among the Hurons, near Midland, Ontario, preserves the history of a French Jesuit mission that existed on that site in the 17th century. Tourists can experience Canadian pioneer life (e.g., blacksmithing, cooking, family and community life); learn about the introduction of Christianity to First Nations peoples; and walk through a longhouse, among other architectural recreations. Another example is Louisbourg, Nova Scotia (**Figure 8.18**). Operated as a National Historic Site by Parks Canada, Louisbourg is the largest reconstructed 18th-century fortified French town in North America. The fortress of Louisbourg recreates for its visitors stories of a soldier's life, tales

of operating the seaport, building techniques, and religious life, among other things. Both Louisbourg and Sainte-Marie Among the Hurons offer their visitors "authentic" historical experiences, but it is important to remember that a very linear, tidy history is told through these sites.

The commodification of local customs freezes them in place and time for consumption, where claims of "authenticity" abound. The search for "authentic" local cultures implies an effort to identify peoples who are untouched by change or

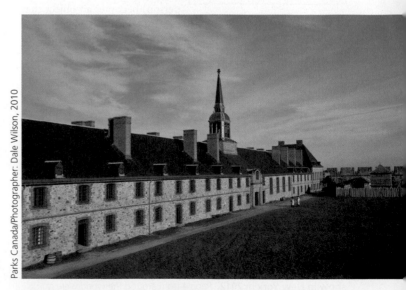

Parks Canada/Photographer: Dale Wilson, 2010

FIGURE 8.18 Fortress of Louisbourg, Nova Scotia. This National Historic Site provides visitors with an "authentic" soldier's experience at the 18th-century fortified French town.

external influence. However, all local cultures (rural and urban) are dynamic, and all have been touched by external influences throughout their existence. The search for an "authentic" local culture merely perpetuates myths about these cultures, whose members are constantly renegotiating their place in this world and making sense of who they are in the midst of the popular culture onslaught.

> **Tourism commodification**
> A process by which "local customs, rituals, festivals and ethnic arts become tourist attractions, performed for tourist consumption and produced for market-based instrumental activities" (Gotham, 2002, p. 1737).

Geographers have become increasingly interested in the interplay between commodification and authenticity, especially in terms of increased mobility and tourism. **Tourism commodification** is a process by which "local customs, rituals, festivals and ethnic arts become tourist attractions, performed for tourist consumption and produced for market-based instrumental activities" (Gotham, 2002, p. 1737). This form of commodification is understood as a relationship, albeit uneven, between the global tourism industry and local cultures and places, and it is often propelled by Western media through such television shows as *Survivor*, *The Bachelor*, and *The Bachelorette*. These shows send groups of North American people to exotic locations to win money or love, and the locations themselves become part of the narrative. For example, in the summer of 2014, *The Bachelor* spinoff *Bachelor In Paradise*, a reality TV show dating game, was filmed at an exotic beachfront location called Casa Palapa in Tulum, Mexico. Contestants visited

FIGURE 8.19 The Tulum Ruins. Crowds of tourists visit the Tulum Ruins in Mexico.

the Tulum Ruins (**Figure 8.19**)—a historic Mayan port—and swam in an ancient cenote (sinkhole), among other activities. In this example, the place itself becomes an "exotic other"—and a perfect backdrop for falling in love. Not only are these images of an ancient place consumed by reality TV audiences, but fans of the show seek out that location for their own romantic holidays, further transforming Tulum into a marketplace for love and romance. Tourism, for many countries, brings tremendous economic benefit to local regions and countries. However, the commodification of local landscapes and cultures for the express benefit of Western audiences and tourists is not without cost. Cultural geographers work to explore this unevenness.

MAIN POINTS 8.3 How Are Local Cultures Sustained?

- Local cultures often work hard to preserve and maintain their distinctive features from the influence of cultural beliefs and norms that may emerge both within and beyond the place or region.

- Local cultures can work to preserve culture and prevent cultural appropriation through legislative and policy protection, boundary control, and the practice of local customs.

- Local cultures can experience the process of commodification, by which something (e.g., a name, a good, an idea, a

place, or even a person) that was not previously regarded as a sellable item becomes an object that can be bought, sold, and traded in the world market.

- When aspects of a culture are commodified and detached from the culture in which they had significance, the question of authenticity is raised. Often a commodity freezes a particular culture in time and does not reflect accurately the complexity of the culture being represented.

8.4 How Is Culture Diffused?

DIFFUSION OF POPULAR CULTURE

Over the past century, the time it takes for people, innovations, and ideas to diffuse around the world has changed dramatically. As discussed in Chapter 9, early agricultural innovations that originated in a number of distinctive hearths (Figure 9.3) transformed groups of hunter-gatherers into agrarian societies and

took nearly 10,000 years to diffuse globally. In more recent times, the diffusion of developments such as the printing press or the technologies of the Industrial Revolution was measured in decades or centuries. During the 1900s, the pace of diffusion shrank to months, weeks, days, and in some cases even hours. Simultaneously, the spatial extent of diffusion has expanded, so that more and more parts of the Earth's surface are affected by ideas and innovations from faraway places. For example, as of 2014, the social networking site Facebook had over 1.28 billion monthly active users, including 19 million Canadians, and was adding many new members each day. With that many subscribers and various forms of instant communication, news can travel quickly through the Facebook network.

In the past few decades, major world cities have become much closer to each other as a result of modern technologies, including airplanes, high-speed trains, expressways, telephones and fax machines, wireless connections, and e-mail. Conversely, places that lack transportation and communications technologies are now more removed from interconnected places than ever. All of the new technologies create the infrastructure through which innovations diffuse. Because the technologies link some places more closely than others, ideas diffuse through interconnected places rapidly rather than diffusing at constant rates across similar distances. It is important to remember as well that while the Internet might seem to be ubiquitous in Canada, where approximately 82 percent of the population has Internet access, this is not true of the world. As of 2014, only 38 percent of the world's population had access to the Internet, far less than half.

HEARTHS OF POPULAR CULTURE

As we saw in the section on local culture, even local customs practised for centuries in one place can be swept up into popular culture. How does a custom, idea, song, or object become part of popular culture? It is relatively easy to follow the communications, transportation, and marketing networks that account for the diffusion of popular culture, but how do we find the hearths of popular culture, and how do certain places establish themselves as the hearths of popular culture?

All aspects of popular culture—music, sports, television, and dance—have a hearth, a place of origin. Typically, a hearth begins with contagious diffusion: developers of an idea or innovation may find they have followers who dress as they do or listen to the music they play. A multitude of Canadian singers and musical groups (e.g., Tragically Hip, Bedouin Soundclash, Alexisonfire, Moist) began as college bands or in college towns. They played a few sets in a campus bar or at a campus party and gained followers. The groups then started to play at bars and campuses in nearby college towns and soon began selling self-made compact discs at their concerts.

Bands that begin on college campuses or in college towns and build from their base typically follow the path of building a hearth for their sound's diffusion first through contagious diffusion and then through hierarchical diffusion. The Tragically Hip was formed in 1983 by musicians who had gone to school and university together in Kingston, Ontario, and who created and perfected their sound in that town during the mid- to late 1980s (**Figure 8.20**). The Tragically Hip spent its early days playing small venues throughout Ontario, carving out a niche for themselves against the tide of American bands. The band's unique sound and contagious diffusion caught the attention of record producers, and they were signed by MCA in 1987, although they didn't gain the attention of critics until 1989, with their album *Up to Here*. Hierarchical diffusion of the band soon followed. College charts were attracted to the Hip's unique sound,

FIGURE 8.20 Tragically Hip, Hamilton Place, 2009. A Canadian band, the Hip has had much success in Canada but has not actively sought a greater international following, choosing instead to live and work in the Kingston, Ontario, area.

and they began extensive club and concert tours. The group has achieved much success in Canada, releasing 12 studio albums, 2 live albums, and 46 singles, and winning many national awards. While the Hip has been heavily promoted in the United States, the group has never really sought "breakthrough" success there. Their distinct Canadian sound and references to Canadian places and stories remain central to their music. For example, they have written songs about Group of Seven affiliate painter Tom Thomson, explorer Jacques Cartier, Toronto Maple Leaf Bill Barilko, and the wrongful conviction of David Milgaard.

The landscape of music production, distribution, and consumption has changed drastically due to processes of digitization and the proliferation of the Internet, particularly social networking platforms like Facebook and Twitter. While contagious and hierarchical diffusion continue to be important aspects of the development of popular culture hearths, digital hearths are becoming increasingly significant. Real-time streaming of live concerts over the Internet is beginning to occur. In 2009, for example, a Phish concert was streamed live from an iPhone, and fans at the show were tweeting updates constantly to those at home. YouTube has been crucial to the diffusion of music, as bands that lack the resources to tour, or who choose not to tour for environmental reasons, are able to promote their music by posting videos on the service. The importance of social media, where users can be "friends" with bands, or become "fans," cannot be downplayed.

MANUFACTURING A HEARTH

In the examples discussed so far, there is the suggestion that hearths appear organically or "naturally" and that cultural artefacts, such as music or fashion, are diffused through various networks in perhaps a haphazard or uncontrolled way. But in the current age, the media, marketing agencies, and many others are actively engaged in the manufacture of hearths and the diffusion of cultural artefacts, suggesting that cultural diffusion is

Noam Galai/Getty Images

FIGURE 8.21 MTV's global reach. A billboard advertising MTV's EMA (Europe Music Awards) in Times Square reflects the network's global reach and influence.

a much more guided and directed state of affairs than we might think. In this age of powerful social networking and varied digital possibilities, whether a college band "makes it" depends greatly on the choices and actions of record producers and music media corporate giants. Corporations such as Viacom, the parent company of MTV, generate and produce popular culture, pushing innovations through the communications infrastructure that links it with the rest of the world (**Figure 8.21**). Geographer Clayton Rosati studied the infrastructure of MTV and its role in the production of popular culture and geographies of popular culture. In his study, he found that MTV produces popular culture by opening globalized spaces to local culture, thereby globalizing the local. Rosati explained that "MTV's incorporation of rap music and Hip Hop expressive forms into its production since 1997" helped produce music celebrities and opened the MTV space to "artists and forms that were often formerly relegated to street corners, block parties and mix tapes—broadening the unification of popular aspirations with the machinery of the industrial production of culture."

A 2001 documentary produced by PBS, *The Merchants of Cool*, looked at the roles corporations and marketing agencies play in creating popular culture. By conducting focus groups with teenagers (the main demographic for innovations in popular culture), by amassing enormous databases of what teenagers do and like, by sending "cool hunters" ("cool" kids) out to talk with other "cool" kids about what is "cool," and by rummaging through teenagers' bedrooms (which, Rosati noted, is what MTV does when casting its reality shows), MTV and marketing companies create what is cool and new in popular culture. *Merchants of Cool* producers interviewed Sharon Lee, one of the founding partners of Look-Look, a research company specializing in youth culture, who explained how trends in popular culture are spread from the hearth:

> Actually it's a triangle. At the top of the triangle there's the innovator, which is like 2 to 3 percent of the population. Underneath them is the trend-setter, which we would say is about 17 percent. And what they do is they pick up on ideas that the innovators are doing and they kind of claim them as

their own. Underneath them is an early adopter, which is questionable exactly what their percentage is, but they kind of are the layer above mainstream, which is about 80 percent. And what they do is they take what the trendsetter is doing and they make it palatable for mass consumption. They take it, they tweak it, they make it more acceptable, and that's when the mass consumer picks up on it and runs with it and then it actually kills it.

This is a perfect description of the hierarchical diffusion of traits and trends in popular culture.

With these kinds of infrastructure behind the production of popular culture, we might expect popular culture to act as a blanket, evenly covering the globe. However, even as popular culture has diffused throughout the world, it has

> **Reterritorialization** With respect to popular culture, a process by which people start to produce an aspect of popular culture themselves, doing so in the context of their local culture, and making it their own.

not blanketed the world, hiding all existing local cultures underneath it. Rather, one aspect of popular culture (such as music or food) will take on new forms when it encounters a new locality and the people and local culture in that place. Geographers and anthropologists call this the **reterritorialization** of popular culture: a process by which people start to produce an aspect of popular culture themselves, doing so in the context of their local culture and place, and making it their own.

For example, hip hop music, which emerged as a subculture in New York City in the late 1970s, has become a global phenomenon. Incorporating MC-ing/rapping, DJ-ing, breakdancing, and graffiti writing, along with sampling and beatboxing, it quickly developed across the United States along an east-west divide. Its popularity increased during the 1980s, as Run-D.M.C., A Tribe Called West, Ice-T, and Notorious B.I.G. became well-known, and hip hop soon transformed from a subculture to popular culture. As it spread around the world, however, its sounds became unique to local cultures. Indonesian hip hop, for example, usually does not include swearing or references to drugs, sex, or violence, as the local radio stations and media outlets are very conservative. In Tanzania, hip hop has its own nickname, Bongo Flava, and incorporates Afrobeat, Tanzanian and English phrases, arabesque melodies, and dancehall and hip hop beats. Bongo Flava has spread to neighbouring countries, including Kenya, and there is even a Bongo Flava radio station that runs out of Chicago. This process of reterritorialization, in which local hip hop artists take a popular form and make it their own, reminds us of the importance of geography: where popular culture takes place is significant, because the local context will shape what is produced.

STEMMING THE TIDE OF POPULAR CULTURE— LOSING THE LOCAL?

The influence of western Europe, North America, and Japan in global popular culture makes many people feel threatened by cultural homogenization, especially as popular media such as music, television, and film now diffuse so quickly around the world. If you turn on the television in Harare, Zimbabwe, you can easily find reruns of a 10-year-old American television show or a contemporary CNN broadcast. If you walk down the street in Seoul, South Korea, you might hear a radio broadcasting a song recorded by the Beatles, Madonna, or Justin Timberlake. If you go to a cinema in Santiago, Chile, you can choose among several recently released American films.

The rapid diffusion of popular culture can cause consumers to lose track of the hearth of a good or idea. For example, the Nintendo Wii was, like most video game consoles and games, created in Japan, but the diffusion of the Wii into households and even retirement homes throughout North America was embraced by Americans and Canadians alike because it has not been seen as a threat to local culture.

However, when the diffusion of popular culture displaces or replaces local culture, it may be met with resistance. In response to the influx of American movies, the Canadian government heavily sponsors its domestic film industry. Ever since the National Film Board was founded in 1939, films have been seen as an important tool for the project of nation-building and cultural coherence in Canada. Both federal and provincial policy has supported not only the production and distribution of Canadian films, but also the making of U.S. films in Canada, thereby providing employment and creative opportunities for film workers in "Hollywood North." The largest source of financial support for Canadian film and television production is Telefilm Canada, a federal Crown corporation that oversees the Canadian Feature Film Fund. However, there are also a variety of provincial and private funds available, including the Bell Broadcast and New Media Fund, Bravo! Fact, Cogeco Program Development Fund, and Independent Production Fund, among others. Given that 90 percent of the feature films shown in Canadian theatres are American, financial support for the production, distribution, and exhibition of Canadian films is critical to the sustainability of the industry. Thanks to this support, Canadian films have received critical acclaim on the international stage, and Canadian filmmakers such as Denys Arcand, Atom Egoyan, David Cronenberg, and Deepa Mehta have become well-known globally (**Figure 8.22**).

Canada has also developed a series of Canadian content (Can Con) regulations for its music and television industries to ensure that Canadian content receives adequate exposure in the Canadian marketplace. The Canadian Radio-television and Telecommunications Commission (CRTC) oversees the implementation of Can Con regulations, which state, for example, that 35 percent of the music played on English pop music radio stations between 6:00 a.m. and 6:00 p.m. on weekdays must be Canadian. For French language radio, 55 percent of the music must be Canadian within the same parameters. A recording is deemed to be Canadian if it meets two of the following criteria (known as the MAPL system): the music is composed by a Canadian (M), the artist who performs music and/or lyrics is Canadian (A), the recording is produced in Canada (P), and the lyrics are written by a Canadian (L). Scholars such as Scott Henderson (2008) have argued that the presence of the quota system has led to the development of a "Canadian scene" that previously did not exist. It is important to mention, as well, that

FIGURE 8.22 Denys Arcand wins Academy Award. In 2004, Canadian filmmaker Denys Arcand won the Academy Award for Best Foreign Language Film for his 2003 release, *The Barbarian Invasions.*

digitization and the pervasiveness of the Internet have called into question the logic of the policy because it is nearly impossible to regulate music, television, and film downloading and file sharing.

Concern over the loss of local distinctiveness and identity is not limited to particular cultural or socio-economic settings. Such concern is also present among the dominant societies of wealthier countries, where it is reflected in everything from the rise of religious fundamentalism to the establishment of semi-autonomous communes in remote locations; among minorities (and their supporters) in wealthier countries, where it can be seen in efforts to promote local languages, religions, and customs by constructing barriers to the influx of cultural influences from the dominant society; among political elites in poorer countries, who promote a nationalist ideology that is explicitly opposed to cultural globalization; and among social minorities in poorer countries, who seek greater autonomy from regimes promoting acculturation or assimilation to a single national cultural norm.

Geographers realize that local cultures will interpret individual cultural productions in very different ways, depending on the cultural context in which they view them. What people choose to adopt from popular culture, how they reterritorialize it, and what they reject helps shape the character and culture of people, places, and landscapes.

Cultures are made up of a number of characteristics, from music and dress to religion and languages. Geographers can study one particular cultural trait or aspect of a complex cultural system of practices to understand how it has diffused geographically or been transformed. One fundamental cultural trait is language. Throughout the course of human history, languages have travelled the globe, creating connections and associations across vast networks of peoples and places. Understanding how language is diffused across a variety of scales helps us to understand the formation and transformation of these networks.

LANGUAGE AND CULTURAL DIFFUSION

A scene in Quentin Tarantino's cult classic movie *Pulp Fiction* shows Vincent and Jules in the front seat of a car, talking about France. Vincent, trying to demonstrate his knowledge of French culture, turns to Jules and says, "You know what they call a . . . a . . . a quarter pounder with cheese in Paris?" Jules replies, "They don't call it a quarter pounder with cheese?" Vincent, ever the expert, explains in a few choice words that France uses the metric system and that the French would not know what a quarter pounder is. Then he explains, "They call it a 'royale' with cheese." Jules, surprised, asks, "What do they call a Big Mac?" Vincent explains, "Well a Big Mac is a Big Mac, but they call it 'Le Big Mac.'"

This humorous exchange juxtaposes two opposing forces in our globalized world: globalization of culture and preservation of local and national culture. Are the two contradictory, or can we have globalization of restaurants, food, music, and culture while preserving local languages?

Language is an important trait at the heart of many cultures and is a fundamental element of local and national culture. The French government has worked diligently, even aggressively, to protect the French language, dating back to 1635 and the creation of the Académie française, an institution charged with standardizing and protecting the French language. In the last few decades, diffusion of globalized terms into France has posed a huge challenge for the Académie française. With the support of many citizens of France, the French government passed a law in 1975 that banned the use of foreign words in advertisements, television and radio broadcasts, and official documents unless no French equivalent could be found. In 1992, France amended its constitution to make French the official language. In 1994, the French government passed another law to stop the use of foreign (mainly English) words in France, with a hefty fine imposed for violations. The law mandates French translations for globalized words and requires that accepted French terms be used in official communications rather than anglicizations like "le meeting," "le weekend," "le drugstore," or "le hamburger." In 2013, when German president Joachim Gauck suggested that the European Union make English the working language of the EU as a cost-cutting measure, the French were up in arms, threatening boycotts among other things. The Internet, where more than 62 percent of all content is in English (Figure 8.23b), has posed another set of challenges. Some of the translations the Académie requires are somewhat cumbersome—for example, the official French term for e-mail is "courrier electronique," and the official term for hacker is "pirate informatique." In addition to demonstrating the conflicting forces of globalized language and local or national language, the French example reveals that language is much more than a set of sounds and symbols used to communicate. It is also an integral part of culture, reflecting and shaping it.

GUEST FIELD NOTE

Is the Internet Killing Language?

Today there are more than 7,700 languages spoken in the world. Of these, approximately 2,500 are considered "endangered"; that is, they are on the verge of falling out of use entirely. That languages change, appear, and disappear is not new. Language is social, and as societies ebb and flow, so too do their languages. But on the Internet, where a large portion of the Global North now does business, there is nowhere near this same level of diversity. According to linguist András Kornai, whose study *Digital Language Death* was published in 2014, less than 5 percent of the world's languages are being used on-line. Approximately 250 languages could be considered "well established" on-line, and 140 more are borderline. Other studies support the assertion that the Internet is filled with users who speak a relatively small number of languages (**Figure 8.23a**), and content that is, for the vast majority, English (**Figure 8.23b**). The spaces of the Internet, it would seem, have no room for the world's 7,000 languages; they are instead occupied by relatively very few voices.

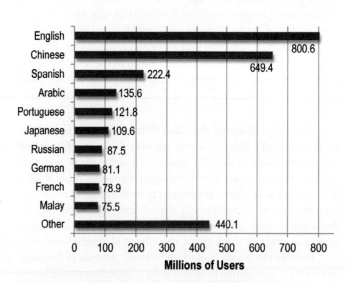

FIGURE 8.23 (a) Top ten languages by Internet user, **2013.** Source: Data from www.internetworldstats.com/stats7.htm.

FIGURE 8.23 (b) Percentage of languages used, by Internet content, 2013. Source: Data from www.factshunt.com/2014/01/world-wide-internet-usage-facts-and.html.

There are several reasons why experts are proclaiming the "death" of language on the Internet. A language is considered "dead" when its speakers cease to use it. According to UNESCO's Endangered Languages website, there are a variety of reasons why this might happen, some of them internal (such as a culture's turning away from its own language) and some external (including war; cultural violence; and economic, religious, or educational subjugation). The Internet, some experts claim, intensifies this process. Signs of a language's imminent death are threefold: (1) loss of function, as when an entire area of cultural practice, such as economics/commerce, is taken over by another language; (b) loss of prestige, as when young people lose interest in their cultural languages; and (c) loss of competence, when the younger generations can communicate with their elders, but cannot speak the language themselves. Over the course of 100 years, with these three factors in play, a language can disappear entirely.

However, while there is no doubt that the Internet plays a role in contemporary language shifts, we must remember that it affords opportunities at the same time. For example, National Geographic has launched its Enduring Voices Project, which aims to stem the death of languages by documenting endangered languages and trying to stop their extinction. Through the use of "Talking Dictionaries" and the Internet, videographers and linguists travel

the globe, seeking out and documenting as many of the world's languages as possible. For example, in Papua New Guinea, the National Geographic team created Talking Dictionaries for two languages, Yokoim and Panim. Yokoim is spoken by just 2,000 people in three small villages, and Panim is spoken by 400 people in one village. Local cultures preserve their languages, documenting their oral histories for new generations (**Figure 8.24**), and the Internet allows for these Talking Dictionaries to be shared, listened to, and talked about in ways that would not otherwise have been possible.

Is the Internet killing language? Time will tell, but the sense of acceleration that comes with constant and instantaneous communication suggests that, at least in digital spaces, languages are becoming fewer and fewer. However, the Internet is not ubiquitous; more than 60 percent of the world's population does not have access to the Internet. And whereas English may be the language of international business today, we must remain humbled by history, because it reminds us that language is a living tree—it grows, bends, and breaks over time.

Heather Maguire, York University

FIGURE 8.24 Preserving languages in Papua New Guinea. A village elder relates traditional tales to young men. Many of the languages of Papua New Guinea are in danger of disappearing. "Talking dictionaries" is one tool being used to try to preserve these languages.

This helps illustrate the claim that language is one of the cornerstones of culture; it shapes our very thoughts. We can use vast vocabularies to describe new experiences, ideas, and feelings, or we can create new words that represent these things. Who we are as a culture, as a people, is reinforced and redefined, moment by moment, through shared language. Language reflects where a culture has been, what a culture values, even how people in a culture think about, describe, and experience things.

Perhaps the easiest way to understand the role of language in culture is to examine people who have experienced the loss of language under pressure from others. During colonization, both abroad and within countries, colonizers commonly forced

the colonized people to speak the language of the colonizer. These language policies continued in many places until recently and were enforced primarily through public (government) and church (mission) schools.

American, Canadian, Australian, Russian, and New Zealand governments each had policies of forced assimilation during the 20th century, including rules that did not allow indigenous peoples to speak their native languages. For example, the United States forced American Indians to learn and speak English. Both mission schools and government schools enforced English-only policies in hopes of assimilating American Indians into the dominant culture. In an interview with the producers of the educational video *Alaska: The Last Frontier,* Clare Swan, an elder in the Kenaitze band of the Dena'ina Indians in Alaska, eloquently describes the role of language in culture:

> No one was allowed to speak the language—the Dena'ina language. They [the American government] didn't allow it in schools, and a lot of the women had married non-native men, and the men said, "You're American now so you can't speak the language." So, we became invisible in the community. Invisible to each other. And, then, because we couldn't speak the language—what happens when you can't speak your own language is you have to think with someone else's words, and that's a dreadful kind of isolation. [emphasis added]

A shared language helps to bind people together and helps to constitute a cultural identity. Language is also quite personal. We articulate our thoughts, expressions, and dreams in our language; if we lose that ability, we lose a lot of ourselves. Language can reveal much about the way people and cultures view reality. Some African languages have no word or term for the concept of a god. Some Asian languages have no tenses and no system for reporting chronological events, reflecting the lack of cultural distinction between then and now.

Language is so closely tied to culture that it is often found at the heart of cultural conflict and political strife. The province of Quebec has passed several laws that promote the use of the province's distinct version of the French language. In 1974, the Quebec National Assembly passed the *Official Language Act* (Bill 22), making French the sole language in the province. This was replaced in 1977 by the *Charter of the French Language* (Bill 101). The Charter made French the official language of education, business, legislation, and commercial signage in the province. It is important to remember, however, that Canada is officially bilingual, as stipulated in the federal *Official Languages Act* (established in 1969 and substantially amended in 1988), which reflects the colonial division of the country between France and Great Britain. This means that federal government documents, for example, are printed in both English and French. However, most of the country's French speakers live in the province of Quebec.

In recent history, the Québécois have periodically called for more independence for their province within Canada, even voting on secession twice, in the Quebec referendums of 1980 and 1995. Although a majority has never voted for secession, it continues to be a contentious issue within the province, and in Canada more broadly. As mentioned, Bill 101 compelled all businesses in the province to demonstrate that they functioned in French. When this law came into effect, many businesses and individuals moved out of the province of Quebec into neighbouring Ontario. In 1993, the Quebec government passed a law requiring the use of French in advertising. The law allowed the inclusion of both French and English (or another language) on signage, as long as the French letters were twice the size of the other language's letters.

Not all of Quebec's residents identify with the French language. Within the province, a small proportion of people

FIGURE 8.25 Street signs in Cree, English, and French in the Cree Nation of Mistissini, Quebec. Though French dominates in Quebec, other languages are also spoken.

speak English at home, others speak indigenous languages (**Figure 8.25**), and still others speak another language altogether—one associated with their country of origin. When the Quebec National Assembly passed laws promoting French during the 1980s and 1990s, members of Canada's First Nations, such as the Cree and Mohawk (who live in Quebec), expressed a desire to remain part of Canada should Quebec secede from the country. During the same period, Quebec experienced an influx of international migrants, many of whom seek residence in the province as a way to enter Canada and North America at large. Under Quebec law, these new immigrants must learn French.

Calls for independence in Quebec are waning, and the separatist political party has captured fewer seats in recent parliamentary elections for the province. Nonetheless, the Québécois still feel a connection to France (**Figure 8.26**), and the province even

FIGURE 8.26 A building displays the flags of France and Quebec in the historic district of Quebec City. The Québécois continue to strive to maintain their ties to France and their French language and culture.

has a presence in Paris in the *Maison du Québec* (House of Quebec), an embassy-like entity representing the province. As people, ideas, and power flow through the province, change will continue. Yet the province's laws, programs, and presence in France, and the desire of the Québécois to remain loyal to their French language, will at the very least keep the language alive as the province continues to experience change.

MAPPING LANGUAGES

One way we can understand how language is diffused is to examine where certain languages are spoken—by mapping languages. The first step in mapping the distribution of world languages is to classify languages. Linguists and linguistic geographers classify languages in terms that are also used in biology because, like species, some languages are related and others are not. At the global scale, we classify languages into **language families**. Members within a single language family have a shared but fairly distant origin. We break language families into sub-families (divisions within a language family), where the commonalities are more definite and the shared origin is more recent. Completing the categorization are individual languages, covering a smaller extent of territory, and dialects, covering the smallest extent of territory.

> **Language family** Group of languages with a shared but fairly distant origin.

The world map of languages in **Figure 8.27** maps 15 major language families. The Indo-European language family stretches across the greatest extent of territory and also claims the greatest number of speakers. Within the Indo-European language family, English is the most widely spoken language. Speakers of English encircle the world, with 300 million in

FIGURE 8.27 Language families of the world.
The swaths of yellow show the extent of speakers of Indo-European languages, including English, in the world. Although Chinese claims even more speakers than English, these speakers are concentrated in one area (coloured red). Adapted with permission from Hammond, Inc., 1977.

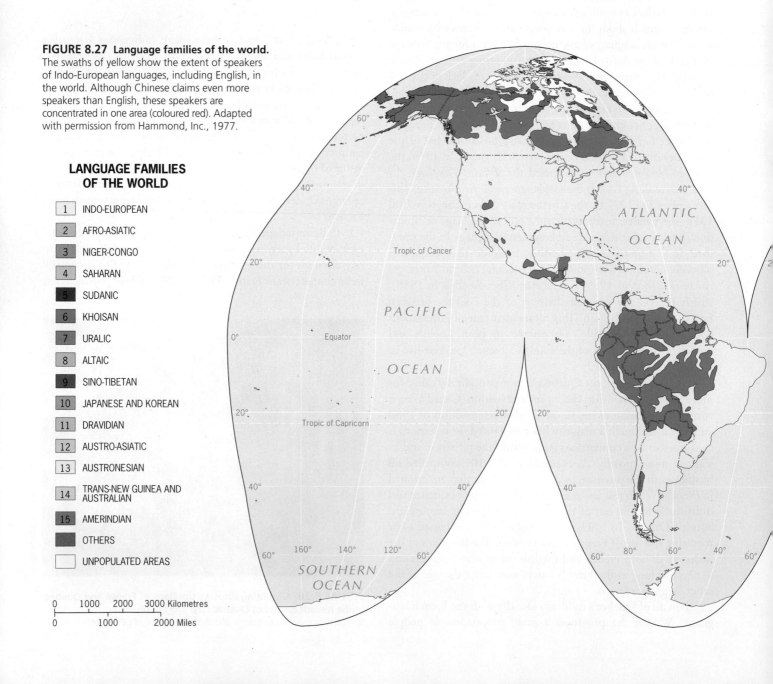

LANGUAGE FAMILIES OF THE WORLD

1. INDO-EUROPEAN
2. AFRO-ASIATIC
3. NIGER-CONGO
4. SAHARAN
5. SUDANIC
6. KHOISAN
7. URALIC
8. ALTAIC
9. SINO-TIBETAN
10. JAPANESE AND KOREAN
11. DRAVIDIAN
12. AUSTRO-ASIATIC
13. AUSTRONESIAN
14. TRANS-NEW GUINEA AND AUSTRALIAN
15. AMERINDIAN
   OTHERS
   UNPOPULATED AREAS

0   1000   2000   3000 Kilometres
0   1000   2000 Miles

North America, 64 million in Great Britain and Ireland, and 22 million in Australia and New Zealand. Hundreds of millions of people in India, Europe, and Africa use English as a second language.

The world map of language families shows several language families spoken by dwindling, often marginally located or isolated groups. The Indo-European languages of European colonizers surround the language families of Southeast Asia. Languages in the Austro-Asiatic language family survive in the interior of eastern India and in Cambodia and Laos. Languages in the Austronesian family are numerous and quite diverse, but many of the individual languages are spoken by fewer than 10 million people. Remoteness helps account for the surviving languages in the Amerindian language family. These languages remain strongest in areas of Middle America, the high Andes, and northern Canada.

Just a few thousand years ago, most habitable parts of the Earth were characterized by a tremendous diversity of languages. However, with the rise of empires under the rule of larger-scale, more technologically sophisticated and literate societies, some languages began to spread over larger areas. By 2,000 years ago, languages such as Chinese and Latin had successfully diffused over large regions. The Han Empire in China and the Roman Empire in Europe and North Africa knit together large swaths of territory, encouraging the diffusion of one language over these regions. The most powerful and wealthiest people were the first to learn Chinese and Latin in these empires, as they had the most to lose by not learning the languages. Local languages and illiteracy continued among the poor in the empires, and some blending of local with regional languages occurred. When the Roman Empire disintegrated, some places within the region discontinued interaction, prompting a round of linguistic divergence.

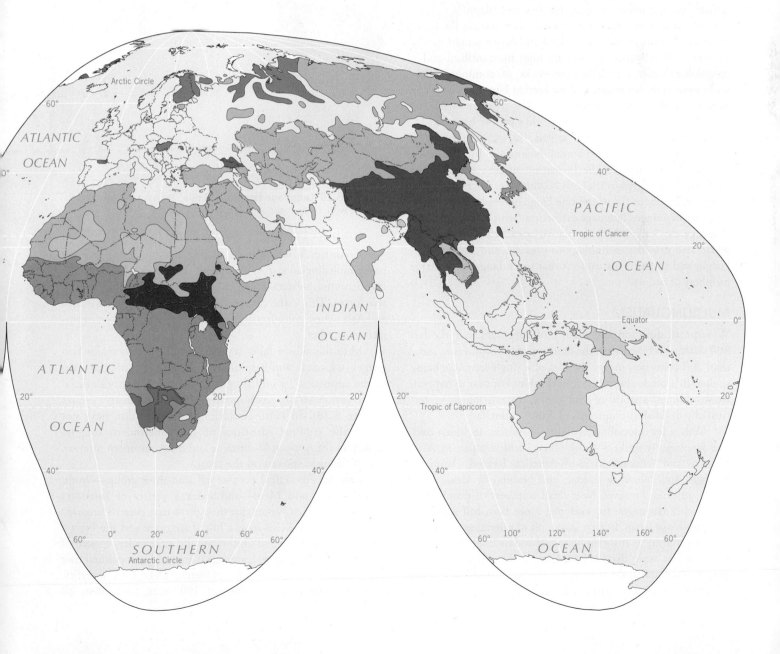

Johann Gutenberg perfected the movable-type printing press in Germany in 1440. Twelve years later he printed the first Gutenberg Bible (the sacred text for Christians), which brought the scriptures out of churches and monasteries. The Gutenberg press diffused quickly in the century following—throughout Europe and beyond—and allowed for unprecedented production of written texts in languages besides Latin. Gutenberg's press made it possible to print the Bible in one's own language, such as French or German, rather than Latin, which helped to standardize European languages and spread literacy.

The rise of relatively large nation-states was equally important (see Chapter 3), for these political entities had a strong interest in promoting a common culture, often through a common language (such as French or Dutch). Political elites, who were literate and had access to written texts, brought peoples together and played a key role in distributing printed texts. Moreover, as the leaders of countries such as England and Spain sought to expand their influence overseas through mercantilism and colonialism, they established networks of communication and interaction, helping to diffuse certain languages over vast portions of the Earth's surface.

Over the last 500 years, the world's people have had innumerable opportunities for spatial interaction and, as a result, contact between and among languages. The increasing contact has encouraged the formation of new languages to bridge linguistic gaps in trade and commerce, has spurred language replacement (in which one language replaces another), and has encouraged language extinction (which occurs when a language no longer has any native speakers). The modern world also provides technology to preserve and stabilize languages and supports institutions that teach languages to large numbers of people.

MULTILINGUALISM

Widespread diffusion and mixing of languages over the last 500 years, combined with the division of the world into more than 200 countries, means the idea of a single language being spoken in a single country is unrealizable. For that to happen, we would need a world of contiguous, discrete languages territorially divided into upwards of 3,000 countries.

Only a few monolingual states—countries in which only one language is spoken—exist. They include Japan in Asia; Uruguay and Venezuela in South America; Iceland, Denmark, Portugal, and Poland in Europe; and Lesotho in Africa. Even these countries, however, have small numbers of people who speak other languages; for example, more than half a million Koreans live in Japan. In fact, as a result of migration and diffusion, no country is truly monolingual today. English-speaking Australia has more than 180,000 speakers of Aboriginal languages. Predominantly Portuguese-speaking Brazil has some 1.5 million speakers of Amerindian languages.

LANGUAGE FAMILIES OF INDIA

- Indo-European Family (Indo-Aryan Group)
- Dravidian Family
- Sino-Tibetan Family
- Austro-Asiatic Family
- Andamanese

Adapted with permission from Hammond, Inc., 1977

FIGURE 8.28 Language families of India. India's states generally coincide with a major language family or language.

Countries in which more than one language is in use are called multilingual states. In some of these countries, linguistic fragmentation reflects strong cultural pluralism as well as divisive forces. This is the case in former colonial areas like Africa and Asia, where colonizers threw peoples speaking different languages together.

Multilingualism takes several forms. The two major languages in Canada and Belgium each dominate particular areas of the countries. In multilingual India, the country's official languages generally correspond with the country's states (**Figure 8.28**). In Peru, centuries of acculturation have not erased the regional identities of the Amerindian tongues spoken in the Andean Mountains and the Amazonian interior, and of Spanish, spoken on the coast.

Canada's Aboriginal peoples fall into three groups—Inuit, First Nations, and Métis—and speak a variety of languages (**Figure 8.29**). First Nations are thought to have over 10 language groups, while the Métis have a mixed language and the Inuit a single language. Cree and Ojibwe are the most widely spoken of the Aboriginal languages. Language is an important cultural trait and is central to the preservation of identity and cultural integrity. Some estimate that over the last 100 years, more than 10

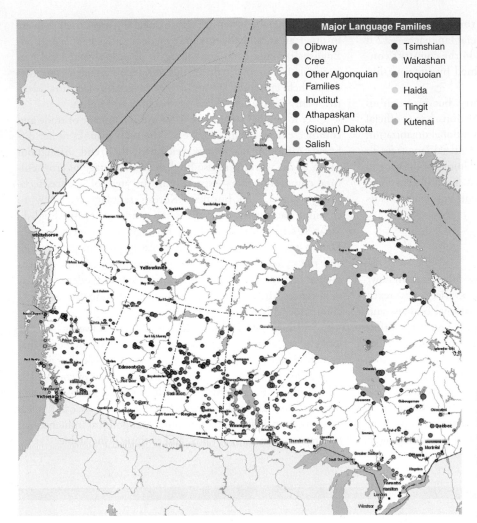

FIGURE 8.29 Languages of Canada's Aboriginal peoples. The main Aboriginal language families of Canada are distributed across the country. Aboriginal Languages by Community, 1996, http://atlas.nrcan.gc.ca/site/english/maps/peopleandsociety/lang/aboriginallanguages/by community. Reproduced with the permission of Natural Resources Canada 2011, courtesy of the Atlas of Canada.

Aboriginal languages in Canada have become extinct. The 2011 Census recorded over 60 Aboriginal languages (down from 70 a decade previously). Almost 213,500 people reported an Aboriginal mother tongue, and nearly 213,400 people reported speaking an Aboriginal language most often or regularly at home (a decline of 1.7 percent since the 2006 Census).

OFFICIAL LANGUAGES

Countries with linguistic fragmentation often adopt an official language (or languages) to draw people together. The hope is that one common language will promote communication and interaction among peoples who speak different local and regional languages. In former colonies, the official language is often one that binds them to their colonizer, as the colonizer's language is invariably already used by the educated and politically powerful elite. Reflecting its colonial heritage, Canada has two official languages. Many former African colonies have adopted English, French, or Portuguese as their official language, even though they have gained independence from former imperial powers. Thus, Portuguese is the official language of Angola, English is the official language of Nigeria and Ghana, and French is the official language of Côte d'Ivoire.

Such a policy is not without risks. In some countries, including India, citizens objected to using a language (English in India) that they associated with colonial repression. Some former colonies chose not just one but two official languages: the European colonial language plus one of the country's own major languages. English and Hindi are official languages of India. Similarly, English and Swahili are official languages of Tanzania. In Mauritania, French and Arabic are official languages. But this solution is not always enough. When India gave Hindi official status, riots and disorder broke out in non-Hindi areas of the country. Kenya, which at first made English and Swahili its official languages, decided to drop English in the face of public opposition to rules requiring candidates for public office to pass a test of their ability to use English.

The official languages in a country are a reflection of the country's history. In Peru, Spanish and the Amerindian language Quechuan have official status and are found in distinct regions. In the Philippines, English (spoken primarily in Manila) and a creolized Spanish called Pilipino are both official languages. Tiny Singapore, the city-state at the tip of the Malay Peninsula, has four official languages: English,

Chinese, Malay, and Tamil (an Indian tongue). India is the country with the largest number of official languages—22 if we include both official languages listed in the country's constitution and official languages proclaimed by states within India.

The European Union is not a country, but it recognizes 23 official languages, and the United Nations has 6 official languages. In each of these cases, the international organization offers simultaneous translation in all the official languages to any member of the parliament (European Union) or the general assembly (United Nations) who requests it. Each international organization also publishes paper documents and maintains its website in all official languages.

GLOBAL LANGUAGE

What will the global language map look like 50 years from now? More and more people are using English in a variety of contexts. It is now the standard language of international business and travel, much of contemporary popular culture bears its imprint, and the computer and telecommunications revolution relies heavily on the use of English terminology. Does this mean that English is on its way to becoming a global language?

If a global language is the principal language people use around the world in their day-to-day activities, the geographical processes we have examined so far emphatically do not point to the emergence of English as a global tongue. Population growth rates are generally lower in English-speaking areas than they are in other areas, and there is little evidence that people in non-English-speaking areas are willing to abandon their local language in favour of English. Indeed, since language embodies deeply held cultural views and is a basic feature of cultural identity, many people actively resist switching to English.

Yet if a global language is a common language of trade and commerce used around the world, the picture looks rather different. Although not always welcomed, the trend throughout much of the world is to use English as a language of cross-cultural communication—especially in the areas of science, technology, travel, and business. Korean scholars are likely to communicate with their Russian counterparts in English; Japanese scientific journals are increasingly published in English; Danish tourists visiting Italy may use English to get around; and the meetings of most international financial and governmental institutions are dominated by English. Under these circumstances, the role of English as an international language of commerce will grow.

We must be careful in this conclusion, however. Anyone looking at the world 200 years ago would have predicted that French would be the principal language of cross-cultural communication in the future. Times are different now, of course. The role of English in the computer revolution alone makes it hard to imagine a fundamental shift away from the dominance of English in international affairs. Yet economic and political influences on language use are always in flux, and nothing is inevitable.

MAIN POINTS 8.4 How Is Culture Diffused?

- Cultural traits can be diffused across a variety of scales, from the local to the global. This diffusion can occur through simple word of mouth and local circulation or through global transportation, marketing, and communication networks. Diffusion can occur quite rapidly or take place over many centuries.

- North America, Japan, and Europe dominate popular culture with the rapid diffusion of music, fashion, arts, television shows, literature, and games across the globe. For some local cultures, this raises concerns about cultural homogenization and the loss of particular local customs and traits. Diffusion may be so rapid and ubiquitous that knowledge of the original hearth may be lost.

- Loss of traditional cultures is also a concern for countries in the Global North that are experiencing rapid changes as a result of immigration and secularization. This is evident in the rise of some forms of religious fundamentalism and the implementation of restrictive immigration policies.

8.5 How Is Culture Reflected in the Landscape?

The tension between popular and local culture can be seen in the cultural landscape—the visible imprint of human activity on the physical environment. Cultural landscapes reflect the dominant values, norms, and aesthetics of a culture. Among the most important and visible cultural landscapes are those related to religion. Canadian cultural landscapes provide a

good example of this, given that Canada has historically been a Christian country, though this may be gradually changing. Statistics Canada captures information on religious affiliation in the nation every 10 years. Results from the 2001 Census indicate that Canada remains predominantly Roman Catholic and Protestant, with 7 out of 10 Canadians reporting one of these two affiliations (**Table 8.1**). In 2001, Roman Catholics composed 43 percent of those reporting religious affiliations; Protestants, 29 percent. Historically, Protestants outnumbered Roman Catholics in Canada. In 1901, for instance, Protestants

TABLE 8.1	Major Religious Denominations, Canada, 1991[1] and 2001				
	2001		1991		Percentage Change 1991 to 2001
	Number	%[3]	Number	%[3]	
Roman Catholic	12,793,125	43.2	12,203,625	45.2	4.8
Protestant	8,654,845	29.2	9,427,675	34.9	−8.2
Christian Orthodox	479,620	1.6	387,395	1.4	23.8
Christian, not included elsewhere[2]	780,450	2.6	353,040	1.3	121.1
Muslim	579,640	2.0	253,265	0.9	128.9
Jewish	329,995	1.1	318,185	1.2	3.7
Buddhist	300,345	1.0	163,415	0.6	83.8
Hindu	297,200	1.0	157,015	0.6	89.3
Sikh	278,415	0.9	147,440	0.5	88.8
No religion	4,796,325	16.2	3,333,245	12.3	43.9

[1] For comparability purposes, 1991 data are presented according to 2001 boundaries.
[2] Includes persons who report "Christian," as well as those who report "Apostolic," "Born-again Christian," and "Evangelical."
[3] Percentages do not add up to 100 due to rounding.
Source: Data from Statistics Canada.

accounted for well over half of all religious affiliations in Canada (56 percent). However, that changed in the 1971 Census, which reported Roman Catholic affiliation had surpassed Protestant (48 percent and 44 percent respectively). Part of the reason for the shift is immigration patterns. Since the 1960s, Roman Catholicism has been the predominant faith of new immigrants to Canada.

The predominance of particular religious affiliations in certain places is important as religion marks cultural landscapes with architecturally distinctive houses of worship (e.g., churches, mosques, synagogues, and temples), with cemeteries dotted with religious symbols and icons, with stores that sell religious goods, and even with services provided to religious adherents who travel to sacred sites—places or spaces people infuse with religious meaning. Members of a religious group may define a space or place as sacred out of either reverence or fear. If a sacred site is viewed with reverence, adherents may be encouraged to make a pilgrimage to the site for rejuvenation, reflection, healing, or fulfillment of a religious commitment.

Canada demonstrates considerable diversity in its religious cultural landscapes. Sacred places and spaces mark the Canadian landscape in particular ways, rendering visible the cultures of various belief systems. When we pass through cities and towns, we see a variety of churches, cathedrals, synagogues, mosques, and houses of assembly, and we "read" these architectures to get a sense of local populations (**Figure 8.30**).

Sacred places in Canada are sometimes spaces of controversy and even violence. First Nations land is particularly emblematic of the struggle over land and its cultural meaning. For example, a dispute over the lands of Ipperwash Provincial Park in Ontario goes back to 1942, when the Government of Canada implemented the *War Measures Act* and expropriated lands belonging to the Stony Point band to build a military base, Camp Ipperwash. The Stony Point band fought for years, claiming that the land contained a sacred burial ground destroyed during the making of the military base. In 1993, still with no resolution, Stony Point band members began moving back onto the land, and the military withdrew. However, in 1995, during a confrontation on these sacred lands with the Ontario government, Stony Point band member Dudley George was shot and killed by a member of the Ontario Provincial Police. The lands were returned to the Kettle and Stony Point First Nation in 1998, and a public inquiry into George's death was held in 2007. One of the inquiry reports discusses the difficulty in identifying Aboriginal burial grounds, stating that governments will not accept First Nations' identification of burial grounds, but, rather, require physical proof, which usually means uncovering remains. Moreover, as these sacred grounds are not marked in ways easily identifiable to non-First Nations people, they are often not discovered until the graves have been disturbed, usually for urban development, archaeological research, or road building. Efforts are being made to establish better connections between local First Nations groups and local and regional governments to ensure sacred places such as burial grounds are found before they are disturbed.

UBIQUITOUS LANDSCAPES

On major roadways in North American towns and suburbs, the landscape is a series of big box stores, gas stations, and restaurants that reflect popular culture (**Figure 8.31**). As you

> **Placelessness** The loss of uniqueness of place in the cultural landscape so that one place looks like the next, as defined by geographer Edward Relph.

drive down one of these roadways, one town or city looks like the next. You drive past Tim Hortons, KFC, Walmart, Boston Pizza, and McDonald's. Then, several miles down the road, you pass another conglomeration (clustering) of the same stores. Geographer Edward Relph (1976) coined the word **placelessness** to describe the loss of uniqueness of place in the cultural landscape to the point that one place looks like the next.

FIGURE 8.30 **Religious landscapes.** (a) Sainte-Anne-du-Beaupré Roman Catholic church, 30 kilometres east of Quebec City, receives more than half a million pilgrims each year. (b) Visitors to the Swaminarayan Mandir Hindu temple in Toronto marvel at its unique and intricately hand-carved marble structure. (c) Congregation Emanu-El in Victoria, British Columbia, is the oldest surviving synagogue in Canada, dating back to 1859.

FIGURE 8.31 **Tim Hortons, Napanee, Ontario.** This photograph was taken in Napanee, Ontario, but it could be anywhere in Canada.

Cultural landscapes can contain similar meanings and symbols across a variety of locations, places, and regions. This is usually the result of several factors, including (1) the broad diffusion of particular architectural forms and planning ideas; (2) the widespread visibility of individual businesses and products; and (3) the wholesale borrowing of idealized landscape images in ways that promote a blurring of place distinctiveness.

The global diffusion of the skyscraper provides a clear illustration of the first point—particular architectural forms and planning ideas have diffused around the world (**Figure 8.32**). In the second half of the 1800s, with advances in steel production and improved costs and efficiencies of steel use, architects and engineers created the first skyscrapers (the Home Insurance Building of Chicago, completed in 1885, is typically pointed to as the very first one). The fundamental difference between a skyscraper and another building is that the outside walls of the skyscraper do not bear the major load or weight of the building; rather, the internal steel structure or skeleton of the building bears most of the load. Once those first skyscrapers appeared in the United States, commercial centres of major cities began to be dominated by tall buildings, many of which were designed by the same architects and engineering firms.

Burj Khalifa, UAE
(2,717 ft, 828m)

Makkah Clock Royal Tower,
Saudia Arabia (1,971 ft, 608m)

One World Trade
Center, United States
(1,776 ft, 541m)

Taipei 101, Taiwan
(1,670 ft, 509m)

Shanghai World
Financial Center,
China (1,614 ft, 492m)

Xu Jian/Getty Images; Fayez Nureldine/AFP/Getty Images; vivalapenler/iStockphoto.com;
Patrick Donovan/Getty Images; Cuiphoto/Getty Images

FIGURE 8.32 The world's tallest buildings. Skyscrapers, buildings taller than 700 feet (213 metres), can be seen in all parts of the world, though this architectural form originated in the United States.

Geographer Mona Domosh (1988) argues that skyscrapers, as part of the built environment, are reflections of social and economic processes. She sees them as **cultural symbols** that "embody the intentions of the particular group of people who built them" (p. 322). Symbols, as part of a culture's language, convey social meaning—they are encoded with the norms, values, and beliefs of those who create them. Approaching the skyscraper as a cultural symbol allows geographers to "read" the landscape of the built environment in a particular way, so as to "decode" its meanings.

> **Cultural symbol** An artefact (e.g., building, image, article of clothing) encoded with the norms, values, and beliefs of the people who created it, which conveys social meaning that geographers can "read" and "decode."

For example, **Figure 8.33** shows the new headquarters of *The People's Daily*, China's state newspaper, in Beijing. At the end of 2013, as the building neared completion, it was being encased in

AFP/Getty Images

FIGURE 8.33 The new headquarters for *The People's Daily*, in Beijing, under construction.

gold. What might you "read" about this cultural landscape? What meanings might it raise? Whose symbols are dominating the landscape here? What does this text reveal to you about power relations in China? Beijing's gold-plated "penis tower" is not the only phallic-looking building to mark our cultural landscapes. There are many others, including the Palace of Culture and Science (aka "Stalin's Penis") in Warsaw, Poland; Torre Agbar in Spain, which marks the gateway to the new technological district of Barcelona; the Washington Monument in Washington, D.C.; the CN Tower in Toronto, called a "massive urban phallic symbol"; and, of course, winner of the 2003 Most Phallic Building Contest, the Ypsilanti Water Tower in Ypsilanti, Michigan. Phallic symbols embedded in our cultural landscape have a long history and can be traced back to Ancient Greeks and Romans. Yet today, they are ever present. Engaging with these icons of masculinity and power raises some fascinating questions about our cultural landscapes.

From Singapore to Johannesburg and from Caracas to Toronto, the cultural landscape of cities has been profoundly impacted. Skyscrapers require substantial land clearing in the vicinity of individual buildings; the construction of wide, straight streets to promote access; and the reworking of transportation systems around a highly centralized model. The proliferation of skyscrapers in Taiwan, Malaysia, and China in the 1990s marked the arrival of these economies as major players in the world economy. Today, the appearance of skyscrapers in Dubai, United Arab Emirates, signals the world city status of the place.

Reading commercial signs is an easy way to see the second dimension of cultural landscape convergence: the far-flung stamp of global businesses on the landscape. Walking down the streets of Rome, you will see signs for Blockbuster and Pizza Hut. The main tourist shopping street in Prague hosts Dunkin' Donuts and McDonald's. A tourist in Munich, Germany, will wind through streets looking for the famed beer garden, the Hofbrauhaus, and will happen upon the Hard Rock Cafe right next door. Marked landscape similarities such as these can be found everywhere from international airports to shopping centres. The global corporations that develop spaces of commerce have wide-reaching impacts on the cultural landscape. Architectural firms often specialize in building one kind of space—for example, performing arts centres, medical laboratories, or international airports. Property management companies have worldwide holdings and encourage the Gap, the Cheesecake Factory, Barnes and Noble, and other companies to lease space in all of their properties. As a result, all facilities, such as airports and college food courts, begin to look the same, even though they are separated by thousands of miles.

The third dimension of cultural landscape convergence is the wholesale borrowing of idealized landscape images across the world. As you study the cultural landscape, you may notice landscape features transplanted from one place to another, regardless of whether that feature even "fits." The Strip in Las Vegas, Nevada, represents an extreme case of this tendency, with various structures designed to evoke different parts of the planet. The popular Venetian Hotel and Casino, for example, replicates the Italian city of Venice, including canals. The Las Vegas Sands Corporation, a casino developer and

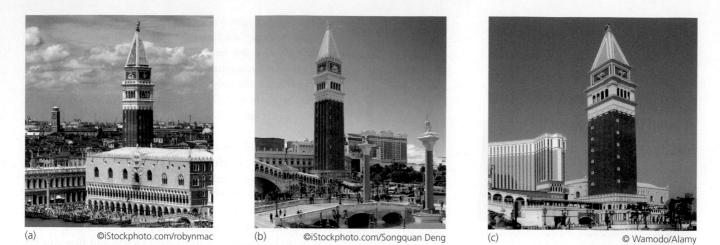

(a)   ©iStockphoto.com/robynmac   (b)   ©iStockphoto.com/Songquan Deng   (c)   © Wamodo/Alamy

FIGURE 8.34 Venice in Italy, Las Vegas, and Macao. (a) Venice, Italy, is an internationally renowned tourist destination. (b) The Venetian Hotel and Casino in Las Vegas is an attempt to create an "authentic" Venetian experience at a casino. (c) The Venetian Macao Resort is another example of cultural borrowing as the global city becomes a local attraction. The diffusion of popular culture through such media as film and television enables us to "read" the Las Vegas and Macao images as Venice, even if we have never actually been in Italy.

owner, recently built a new Venetian Hotel and Casino across the Pacific in Macao (formerly a Portuguese port that became part of China again in 1999). The Venetian Macao Resort cost $2.4 billion and is three times the size of the largest casino in Las Vegas (**Figure 8.34**). Gambling is illegal in mainland China, but Macao's special status has allowed gambling to grow on the small island.

In less obvious ways, cultural borrowing and mixing happens all around the world. This borrowing and mixing is behind the concept of the **global-local continuum**, a notion that emphasizes that what happens at one scale is not independent of what happens at other scales. Human geography is not simply about documenting the differences between places; it is also about understanding the processes unfolding at different scales that produce those differences. What happens in an individual place is the product of interaction across scales. People in a local place mediate and alter regional, national, and global processes, in a process called *"glocalization"* (described in Chapter 2). The character of place ultimately arises from a multitude of dynamic interactions between local distinctiveness and events and influences on a wider scale.

> **Global-local continuum** The notion that what happens at the global scale has a direct effect on what happens at the local scale, and vice versa. This idea posits that the world comprises an interconnected series of relationships that extend across space.

MAIN POINTS 8.5 How Is Culture Reflected in the Landscape?

- Cultural landscapes reflect the dominant values, norms, and aesthetics of a culture.

- Cultural landscapes can contain similar meanings and symbols across a variety of locations, places, and regions. This is usually a product of (1) the broad diffusion of particular architectural forms and planning ideas; (2) the widespread visibility of individual businesses and products; and/or (3) the wholesale borrowing of idealized landscape images in ways that promote a blurring of place distinctiveness.

- Cultural landscapes are the product of interaction across scales. People in a local place mediate and alter regional, national, and global processes, in a process called glocalization. The character of place ultimately arises from a multitude of dynamic interactions between local distinctiveness and events and influences on a wider scale.

SUMMARY

Cultural geographers study how culture—a set of shared belief systems, norms, and values practised by a particular group of people—is reflected in landscapes and the built environment. Some geographers regard culture as a "way of life" that becomes visible in building styles, music, food, fashion, and language.

Geographers have approached the study of culture in different ways. The work of Carl Sauer and the Berkeley School dominated cultural geographical enquiry until the 1960s. This intellectual approach saw culture as a unified active agent in creating or determining a cultural landscape that was in a constant state of transition. With the social and political upheavals in the Global North during the 1960s and 1970s, geographers began to focus on whether a culture was universally shared by all individuals in a particular place or region. Given that individuals experienced places differently based on race, gender, class, and sexual orientation, geographers began to argue that what was visible in the landscape was in fact the dominant cultural beliefs, norms, and values, and different cultural perspectives were rendered invisible. Geographers such as Don Mitchell went so far as to argue that there is no such thing as culture.

Geographers who accept the view that there is a discernible thing called "culture" that can be studied have traditionally described cultures as fitting along a continuum from local to popular. Local cultures are groups of people associated with particular locations, places, or regions who understand that they share experiences, customs, and traits, and who work to preserve those traits and customs in order to claim uniqueness and to distinguish themselves from others. Local cultures often have

to work hard to preserve their culture and avoid its commodification and appropriation. In contrast, popular culture is dominant and ubiquitous and often changes rapidly. This is particularly so now given the activities of the media and marketers who seek not only to manufacture hearths but also to direct and control cultural diffusion. Given that cultures can be subject to appropriation and rapid change, questions are raised about the authenticity of certain places and practices and the potential to "freeze" certain groups in both place and time.

Geographers can trace the diffusion of culture or particular cultural traits, such as language, from their hearths to all corners of the globe. Popular culture, particularly from the Global North, can diffuse rapidly around the world, and in some cases raise concerns about the preservation of local cultures. On the other hand, some traditional cultures in the Global North express concern about the apparent loss of their cultural values; in some places, we see the rise of religious fundamentalism and more stringent immigration policies in response.

DISCUSSION AND REVIEW QUESTIONS

1. Discuss the story of the Tata Corporation and what it reveals about (a) cultural geography in India and (b) the role of globalization in shaping the experiences of a local cultural group.

2. Though culture is a highly contested concept, geographers and academics recognize that cultural groups can be viewed as displaying varying aspects of folk culture and popular culture. Compare and contrast the aspects of folk culture with that of popular culture. How are both influenced by, and through, geographic scale? Can you think of any particular aspects of your cultural milieu that are rooted in folk customs or in popular culture?

3. Identify and explain the various means by which Canada has worked to preserve and maintain a distinctive, local,

Canadian culture. What have been some of the positive and negative results of the Canadian approach?

4. Who are the Anabaptists and what has been their experience in North America? What influence does geography have on such cultural groups?

5. Geographers accept that cultural landscapes reflect the tensions between popular and local culture. One of the results of the tension, combined with the globalizing forces of the capitalist world economy, is what Edward Relph called "placelessness." What is placelessness and what are the factors that lead to it? Can you think of examples in your own context that reflect this placelessness? Conversely, can you identity unique places and what it is about them that makes them "unique"?

GEOGRAPHIC CONCEPTS

assimilation 223
authenticity 227
commodification 227
cultural appropriation 226
cultural landscape 216
cultural symbol 243
cultural trait 220
culture 215

custom 223
discourse 217
folk culture 220
global-local continuum 244
hearth 222
hierarchical diffusion 222
language family 236
local culture 220

material culture 221
nonmaterial culture 221
placelessness 241
popular culture 220
reterritorialization 231
tourism commodification 229

ADDITIONAL RESOURCES ON-LINE

About the Hutterites: www.hutterites.org

National Geographic's Enduring Voices Project: http://travel.nationalgeographic.com/travel/enduring-voices/

Merchants of Cool: www.pbs.org/wgbh/pages/frontline/shows/cool

The Way the Music Died: www.pbs.org/wgbh/pages/frontline/shows/music

Last Call at the Gladstone Hotel: www.hotdocslibrary.ca/en/detail.cfm?filmId=11105

Alaska: The Last Frontier? www.learner.org/resources/series85.html

CHAPTER 9 AGRICULTURE

Winds of Change in Farming Communities

DRIVING THROUGH the Townships of Ashfield and Colborne in Ontario's Huron County on a sunny summer afternoon, one could clearly see the important role that agricultural activities play in the local economy. However, it is also evident that the individuals who own these farms have witnessed many significant changes in recent decades that have forced them to adapt their operations in order to remain competitive, both with their neighbours and with farm operators in other parts of the world. Indeed, the winds of change are blowing throughout Canada's agricultural sector. What was once the country's most prominent source of employment has become a relatively small part of the job market. There has been a trend to mechanization, replacing human labour with machine labour, along with a shift to industrialization and agribusiness (**Figure 9.1**). This has created challenges for the family farm, an important part of Canada's agricultural heritage.

Through an in-depth study of farming in Ashfield and Colborne, geographers John Smithers, Paul Johnson, and Alun Joseph found that farm families have adapted in a variety of ways to increasing global competition and other changes. Some have expanded and intensified their operations. By growing the size of their farms, purchasing the most up-to-date and efficient equipment, and specializing in only a few types of crops, these farmers are hoping to achieve the economies of scale needed to compete with large corporate-owned farms and with farmers in other countries, whose costs of production are often lower and are also often heavily subsidized by their governments. Other farmers have opted to diversify their operations by, for example, entering into the world of agri-tourism, in order to increase their incomes. Still others have found off-farm work, using the additional source of income to sustain the family farm through hard economic times, or have chosen to downsize their farms by selling or

renting land, reducing the size of their herds, or leaving some of their fields to sit idle for one or more growing seasons. Many farm families have been forced to make a much more painful decision—to exit farming completely, often bringing to an end a lifestyle that had been passed on from one generation to the next over a century or more.

A look at the data compiled through the Census of Agriculture—which, like the Census of Canada, is conducted every five years—reveals that family farm operators throughout Canada have been making decisions similar to those made by the farmers in Ashfield and Colborne Townships. Perhaps most telling about the precarious status of the family farm is the decline in the number of farms operating across the country over time. In 1941, there were 732,800 farms in Canada; in 2011,

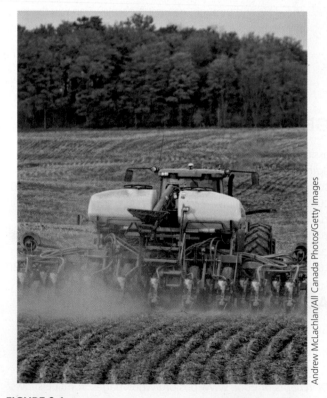

FIGURE 9.1 Agricultural activity in Huron County, Ontario.

Andrew McLachlan/All Canada Photos/Getty Images

this had fallen by more than half a million to 205,730. Those farms that remain, however, tend to be much larger than in the past; for example, the average farm size in Canada increased from 728 acres to 778 acres between 2006 and 2011 alone. Indeed, many farm families across the country have sought to adapt to increasing global competition and other economic challenges by expanding their operations through either the purchase or rental of additional land. Another notable statistic from the 2011 Census of Agriculture relates to the amount of land being used for farming in Canada. In 2011 it was 160.2 million acres, a decline of 4.1 percent from the 2006 figure. This decrease can be attributed to a number of factors, such as the encroachment of urban land uses onto agricultural land, and land being taken out of productive use due to farm closures or soil exhaustion. Thus, Canada has witnessed a decline in the number of farms and the amount of farmland being used, but also an increase in the average farm size. What this all means for farm operators, for the communities in which they live, for consumers, and for the natural environment are among the topics that we will explore in this chapter.

KEY QUESTIONS FOR CHAPTER 9

1. What is agriculture, and where did it begin?

2. How did agriculture change with industrialization?

3. What is the contemporary global pattern of agriculture and agribusiness?

4. How has agriculture influenced settlement patterns and the cultural landscape?

9.1 What Is Agriculture, and Where Did It Begin?

Where does our food come from? When we walk up and down the aisles in the grocery store, we see that some produce is grown in Canada, and some comes from faraway places. We hear about the "100 Mile Diet"—the challenge to eat only produce grown within 100 miles of where we live—while at the same time we can buy tender fruit from Chile or apples from New Zealand. Agriculture, then, can sometimes be very local and sometimes global in terms of both production and consumption. Bound up in these considerations is our spatial perspective—location, region, landscape, place, and movement—because where our food is grown, and how it moves from where it is produced to where it is consumed, are central to geographers' questions about agriculture.

Agriculture has long been a key topic of study for human geographers across Canada and around the world. It is one area of human activity that clearly illustrates the important but tenuous symbiotic relationship existing between humans and the natural environment. In fact, agriculture makes up one of the most significant human uses of land in the world, with pasture lands and croplands alone taking up more than one-third of the Earth's land area at the turn of the 21st century. Also, more than two-thirds of global water consumption by humans is for agricultural purposes. Thus, geographical variations in the availability and quality of agricultural lands, along with the availability of water, are among the central matters of concern to agricultural geographers and other human geographers.

Unfortunately, many of the agriculture-related issues examined by geographers today are related to the negative environmental and social consequences of contemporary farming practices. Nowhere in the world, including Canada, is immune to at least some of these challenges. For example, the methods and materials used to engage in the intensive forms of crop and livestock production practised in many countries have become a major source of water and air pollution, and they are also among the leading causes of biodiversity loss. They are also responsible for significant land degradation, water supply depletion, deforestation, and desertification in many world regions.

Agriculture is defined as the deliberate tending of crops and livestock to produce food, feed, and fibre. As evidenced in the opening field note, agriculture in Canada has changed enormously in the last 50 years, as it has in much of the rest of the world. However, this is just the latest episode in a human activity that has been going on for thousands of years.

> **Agriculture** The purposeful tending of crops and livestock in order to produce food, feed, and fibre.

In this chapter, we examine the origins of agriculture and trace the geography of change in agriculture across time to the latest movements in agricultural production, such as genetic modification, organic production, and the practice of sustainable agriculture. In the process, we describe the early hearths (source areas) of agriculture, the geography of technological changes in agriculture, global patterns of agricultural production, and the imprint of agriculture on the cultural landscape.

In this section of the chapter, we discuss how people lived before the origins of agriculture, and the circumstances that gave rise to the invention of agriculture many millennia ago.

HUNTING, GATHERING, AND FISHING

Before agriculture, people subsisted on food they obtained through hunting, gathering, and fishing. What people hunted or gathered depended on the region, and the size of hunting and gathering clans varied according to climate and resource availability. Areas of abundance could support larger populations. For example, people living on the margins of forests could gather food in the forest when hunting yielded poor results and then return to hunting when opportunities improved. In contrast, people living in areas with only one source of food were likely to starve—or would be forced to move—if that food source disappeared.

Over time, hunter-gatherers worked to perfect tools, control fire, and adapt environments to their needs. The first tools used in hunting were simple clubs—tree limbs that were thin at one end and thick and heavy at the other. When people began using bone and stone, and developing spears, their hunting technique became far more effective. Fashioning stone into hand axes and, later, handle axes was a crucial innovation that enabled hunters to skin their prey and cut the meat; it also made it possible to cut down trees and build better shelters and tools.

The controlled use of fire was another important early achievement of human communities. The first opportunities to control fire were offered by natural conditions (e.g., lightning strikes or spontaneous combustion of surface-heated coal). Archaeological finds at ancient settlement sites suggest that people would capture fire that was caused accidentally and would work to keep the fire burning continuously. Later, people learned they could generate fire by rapidly rotating a wooden stick in a small hole surrounded by dry tinder. Fire became the focal point of settlements, and the campfire became a symbol of the community. It was a means of making foods digestible and was also used to drive animals into traps or over cliffs.

In addition to hunting game on the land, humans harvested shellfish, trapped fish by cutting off small patches of standing water from the open sea, and invented tools such as harpoons for spearing large fish, hooks for catching fish, and baskets to capture fish in streams that had fish runs.

Using tools and fire, human communities altered their environments, establishing more reliable food supplies by combining hunting and fishing with some gathering. They also migrated to take advantage of cyclical movements of fish and animals and to avoid exhausting the supply of edible plants in any one area.

THE FIRST AGRICULTURAL REVOLUTION

Where did **plant domestication** begin? Carl Sauer (mentioned in Chapter 8), one of the first geographers to consider this question, believed that the experiments necessary to establish agriculture and settle in one place occurred in "lands of plenty"—that is, in places where there was substantial game and plants for sustenance.

> **Plant domestication** Genetic modification of a plant such that its reproductive success depends on human intervention.

Only in such places could people afford to experiment with raising plants or take the time to capture animals and breed them for domestication. As part of a lifetime spent studying cultural origins and diffusion, Sauer closely examined the geography of early agricultural practices, focusing particularly on the location of the agriculture hearths and on the kinds of agricultural innovations that took place in those hearths. He suggested that Southeast and South Asia may have been the location, more than 14,000 years ago, of the first domestication of tropical plants. There, Sauer believed, the combination of human settlements, forest margins, and freshwater streams may have given rise to the earliest planned cultivation of **root crops**—crops that are reproduced by cultivating either the roots or cuttings from the plants (such as tubers, including manioc or cassava, yams, and sweet potatoes in the tropics).

The planned cultivation of **seed crops**, plants that are reproduced by cultivating seeds, is a more complex process that involves seed selection, sowing, watering, and well-timed harvesting. This practice seems to have developed in more than one area at different times.

> **Root crops** Crops that are reproduced by cultivating the roots of or the cuttings from the plants.
>
> **Seed crops** Crops that are reproduced by cultivating the seeds of the plants.
>
> **First Agricultural Revolution** Dating back 10,000 years, the First Agricultural Revolution achieved plant domestication and animal domestication.

Some scholars believe that the first domestication of seed plants may have occurred in the Nile River Valley in North Africa, but the majority view is that this crucial development took place in a region of southwestern Asia (also called the Fertile Crescent) through which flow the two major rivers of present-day Iraq, the Tigris and the Euphrates (**Figure 9.2**). Regardless of where it actually began, this period marked the beginning of what has been called the **First Agricultural Revolution**.

Archaeologists note that, as part of the First Agricultural Revolution, a number of changes occurred in southwestern Asia along with plant domestication. First, the plants themselves changed because people chose seeds from the largest, heartiest plants to save for planting, yielding domesticated plants that grew larger over time than their counterparts in the wild. Archaeologists in southwestern Asia have found preserved seeds, which tell them what plants were being domesticated and when. Grain crops, such as wheat and barley, grew well in the warming Asian climate. People also discovered that the river-inundated plains of Mesopotamia provided yet another location suitable for farming. Agriculture provided a reliable food source, and grain surpluses enabled people to store grain for long-term distribution and use, making it possible to settle permanently in one place. With a reliable food source and a permanent base, the population of settlements began to increase, an event more fully explored in Chapter 10.

Figure 9.3 depicts the global distribution of plant domestication hearths. In Southeast Asia (Region 1), taro, yams, and bananas were the leading food plants. In southwestern Asia (Region 4), plant domestication centred on wheat, barley, and

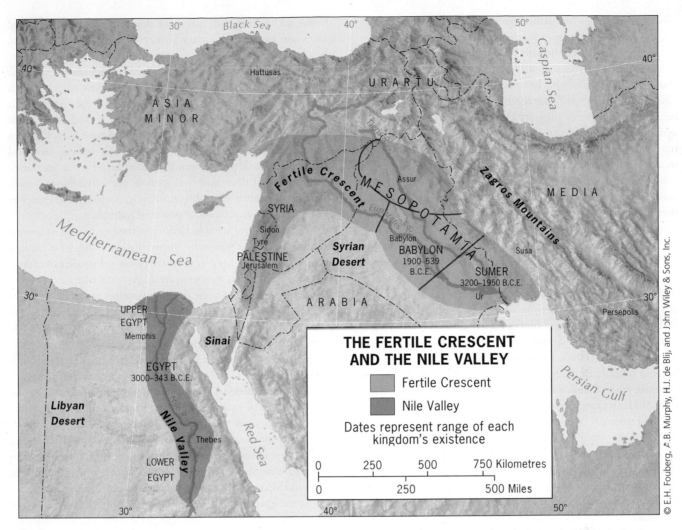

FIGURE 9.2 The Fertile Crescent. Archaeologists and geographers believe the first planned cultivation of seed crops took place in the Fertile Crescent of Mesopotamia (green), between the Tigris and Euphrates Rivers, or possibly in the Nile Valley (grey). Other ancient states and civilizations are shown in different colours. Modern political boundaries are shown for reference.

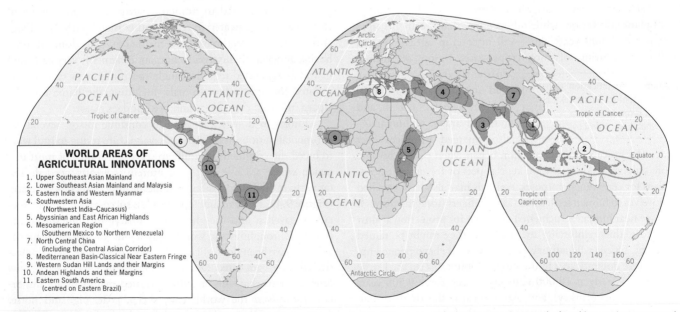

FIGURE 9.3 World areas of agricultural innovations. Cultural geographer Carl Sauer identified 11 areas where agricultural innovations occurred. Adapted with permission from C.O. Sauer, *Agricultural Origins and Dispersals*. New York: American Geographical Society, 1952, p. 24.

other grains. In the Mesoamerican region (Region 6), the basic plants were maize (corn), squashes, and several kinds of beans.

Archaeologists continually find new sites to excavate, and as these sites are analyzed, academics revise their assumptions about the timing of the hearths of agriculture. The central China hearth (Region 7) has recently attracted greater attention because new evidence suggests a much earlier development of agriculture in this region—so early, in fact, that Chinese farmers may have been among the world's first. Another agricultural source region lies in West Africa (Region 9). Archaeological research on agriculture in this area is relatively recent, and analysts are not certain whether agriculture developed independently there, but they are certain that secondary domestication took place in West Africa.

In many cases, what we now think of as centres of production of particular crops are not the places where those crops were originally domesticated. The corn (maize) we associate with the corn belts of southwestern Ontario and the midwestern United States, for example, diffused from Central America and southern Mexico into North America due to early migrations (Chapter 5) and colonization (Chapter 3). Later, the Portuguese took it back across the Atlantic to Europe, and corn became a staple in much of Africa. The white potato that we associate with Ireland, Prince Edward Island, and the American state of Idaho came originally from the Andean highlands along the western coast of South America but was carried to Europe in the 1600s, where it became a staple all the way from Ireland to the eastern expanses of the north European plain. The banana we associate with Central America came from Southeast Asia, as did a variety of yams. Diffusion of crops and seeds was greatly accelerated by worldwide trade and communications networks established by mercantilism and colonialism.

DOMESTICATION OF ANIMALS

Some scholars believe that animal domestication began earlier than plant cultivation, while others argue that it only began as recently as 8,000 years ago—well after crop agriculture. As with the growing of root crops, the notion of **animal domestication**—adapting wild animals to accept life in intimate association with, and to the advantage of, humans—also emerged in stages over time. The process of domestication began when people became more sedentary. Animals were kept as pets or for other reasons, such as for ceremonial purposes. Animals may also have attached themselves to human settlements as scavengers (foraging through garbage near human settlements) and even for protection against predators, thus reinforcing the idea that they might be tamed and kept. Docile wild animals could have easily been penned up. Goats were domesticated in the Zagros Mountains (in the Fertile Crescent) as early as 10,000 years ago, sheep some 9,500 years ago in Anatolia (Turkey), and pigs and cattle shortly thereafter. The advantages of domesticating animals for use as beasts of burden, companions/protectors, and providers of milk or meat

> **Animal domestication** Genetic modification of an animal such that it is rendered more amenable to control by humans.

stimulated the rapid diffusion of this idea among interlinked places and gave the sedentary farmers of southwestern Asia and elsewhere a new measure of security.

Once in captivity, animals changed considerably from their wild state. Archaeological research indicates that when animals such as wild cattle were penned in a corral, they underwent physical changes over time. The corral protected them from predators, which meant animals that would have been killed in the wild survived. Our domestic versions of goat, pig, cow, and horse differ considerably from those first kept by our ancestors. In early animal domestication, people chose the more docile, often smaller, animals to breed in order to protect themselves from the larger, fiercer, more powerful animals.

Archaeologists are able to discern the beginnings of animal domestication in a region by inspecting the bones of excavated animals. They look for places where bones get smaller over time as indicative of early domestication. As with plant domestication, archaeologists can use the combination of bone fragments and tools to identify general areas where the domestication of particular animals occurred. In southwestern Asia and adjacent parts of northeastern Africa, people domesticated the goat, sheep, and camel. Southeast Asians domesticated several kinds of pigs, the water buffalo, chickens, and some waterfowl (such as ducks and geese). In South Asia, people domesticated cattle, which then came to occupy an important place in the regional culture. In Central Asia, people domesticated the yak, horse, sheep, and some species of goats. In the Mesoamerican region (including the Andes from Peru northward and Central America north to central Mexico), early Americans domesticated the llama and alpaca, along with a species of pig and the turkey.

Some species of animals may have been domesticated almost simultaneously in different places. The water buffalo, for example, was probably domesticated in both Southeast and South Asia during the same period. Camels may have been domesticated in Central Asia as well as in southwestern Asia. The pig was domesticated in numerous areas. Different species of cattle were domesticated in regions other than South Asia. Dogs and cats may, in fact, have been the first animals domesticated, having attached themselves to human settlements very early and in widely separated regions. Single specific hearths can be pinpointed for only a few animals, including the llama and the alpaca, the yak, the turkey, and the reindeer.

Efforts to domesticate animals continue today. Several experimental stations in the African savannas are trying to find ways to breed the continent's wildlife to serve as a source of meat in a region where a stable supply of protein is greatly needed. The farms have had some success domesticating a species of eland (**Figure 9.4**), a type of antelope, but less success with various species of gazelles, and they have been unable to domesticate the buffalo. Throughout the world, only about 40 species of higher animals have been domesticated—and most of these were domesticated long ago. Jared Diamond, author of *Guns, Germs, and Steel*, explains that only five domesticated mammals are important *throughout* the world: cow, sheep, goat, pig, and horse. According to Diamond, if we select only the big (over 50 kilograms), herbivorous, terrestrial animals, we have 148 species that meet these criteria "in the wild." However, only 14 of these have been domesticated successfully, each of which was domesticated at least 4,500 years ago. Modern attempts at animal domestication, even those driven by knowledgeable geneticists, have failed because of problems with the particular animal's diet, growth rate, breeding patterns, disposition, or social structure. Thus, the process of animal domestication, set in motion more than 8,000 (and perhaps as long as 14,000) years ago, continues.

FIELD NOTE

Animal Domestication in Kenya

Attempts to tame wildlife started in ancient times, and still continue. At Hunter's Lodge in Kiboko, we met an agricultural officer who reported that an animal domestication experimental station was located not far into the bush, about 16 kilometres south. On his invitation, we spent the next day observing this work. In some herds, domestic animals (in this case, goats) were combined with wild gazelles, all penned together in a large enclosure. This was not working well; all day the gazelles sought to escape. By comparison, these eland were docile, manageable, and in good health. More important, they were also reproducing in captivity.

© H.J. de Blij

FIGURE 9.4 Eland domestication in Nairobi, Kenya.

SUBSISTENCE AGRICULTURE IN THE MODERN WORLD

> **Subsistence agriculture** Self-sufficient agriculture that is small in scale and low in technology, and that emphasizes food production for local consumption, not for trade.

Hundreds of millions of farmers around the world are involved in **subsistence agriculture**, a self-sufficient form of agriculture that is small in scale, uses little technology, and emphasizes food production for local consumption, not for trade. Subsistence farms usually consist of small landholdings of a few hectares and the cultivation of a diverse mix of traditional crops. Livestock are also often a key part of a subsistence farming unit, thus providing the owners with milk, meat, fuel, fertilizer, draft power, and transportation.

The term "subsistence" is often used in the strictest sense of the word—that is, to refer to farmers who grow food only to sustain themselves and their families, who find building materials and firewood in the natural environment, and who do not enter into the cash economy at all. This definition fits farmers in remote areas throughout South and Central America, Africa, and South and Southeast Asia (**Figure 9.5**). However, many farm families living at the subsistence level will occasionally sell a small quantity of produce (perhaps to pay taxes), and are therefore not subsistence farmers in the strict sense. Nonetheless, the description is surely applicable to societies where farmers with small plots sometimes sell a few kilos of grain on the market but where poverty, indebtedness, and tenancy are ways of life. This includes many indigenous peoples in the Amazon Basin, sedentary farmers in Africa's savannas, villagers throughout much of India, and peasants in Indonesia.

Subsistence farmers often hold land in common, and all the members of the community share surpluses. Accumulation of personal wealth is restricted, and individual advancement at the cost of the group as a whole is limited. Although much has changed for subsistence farmers in modern times, a strong sense of community remains important to the social fabric of these people.

Some subsistence farmers are sedentary, living in one place throughout the year, but many others move from place to place in search of better land. The latter engage in a form of agriculture known as **shifting cultivation**. This activity is found primarily in tropical and subtropical zones and is still widely practised. In fact, between 150 million and 200 million people sustain themselves today through shifting cultivation in Africa, Central America, tropical South America, and parts of Southeast Asia.

> **Shifting cultivation** Cultivation of crops in tropical forest clearings in which the forest vegetation has been removed by cutting and burning. These clearings are usually abandoned after one to several years in favour of newly cleared forest land.

This system of shifting cultivation is very similar to what has been practised for thousands of years. People usually live in a central village surrounded by parcels of land that are worked successively. The farmers first clear vegetation from a parcel of land. Then they plant crops that are native to the region: tubers in the humid, warm, tropical areas; grains in the more humid subtropics; vegetables and fruits in cooler zones. However, when soils in these regions are stripped of their natural vegetative cover and deprived of the constant input of nutrients from decaying vegetative matter on the forest floor, they can quickly lose their nutrients as rain water leaches out organic matter. Faced with these

WORLD REGIONS OF PRIMARY SUBSISTENCE AGRICULTURE
In the shaded areas, subsistence crop farming is the leading way of life. In an average year, little surplus can be sold on markets.

FIGURE 9.5 World regions of primarily subsistence agriculture. Definitions of subsistence farming vary. On this map, India and China are not shaded because farmers sell some produce at markets; in equatorial Africa and South America, subsistence farming allows little excess, and thus little produce is sold at markets.

circumstances, farmers move to another parcel of land, clear the vegetation, turn the soil, and try again. In tropical areas, a plot of cleared soil will carry a good crop at least once and perhaps two or three times. After that, the land is best left alone to regenerate its natural vegetative cover and replenish the soil with nutrients lost during cultivation. Several years later, the plot may yield a good harvest once again.

When the village grows too large and the distance to usable land becomes too great, part of the village's population may establish a new settlement some distance away. Shifting cultivation is possible only in areas where population densities are low and there is less competition for land. In cases where population densities have been increasing, the greater number of people in search of food leads to both more clearing of forests and more frequent use of the same land without giving it time for the nutrients to regenerate. With these actions come many environmental consequences, which are discussed later in this chapter.

MARGINALIZATION OF SUBSISTENCE FARMING

During the era of colonialism (ca. 1500 to 1950), European powers sought to "modernize" the economies of the colonies by ending subsistence farming practices and integrating farmers into colonial systems of production and exchange. One way they did this, described by Duckham and Masefield in *Farming Systems of the World* (1970), was by tempting farmers to want cash by making desirable consumer goods available. Often their methods were much harsher: by demanding that farmers pay taxes, colonizers forced subsistence farmers to begin selling some of their produce to raise the necessary cash. They also compelled many subsistence farmers to devote some land to a cash crop, such as cotton, thus bringing them into the commercial economy. The colonial powers encouraged commercial farming by conducting soil surveys, building irrigation systems, and establishing lending agencies that provided loans to farmers. In addition, the colonial powers sought to make profits, yet it was difficult to squeeze very much from subsistence-farming areas. Forced cropping schemes were designed to solve this problem. If farmers in a subsistence area cultivated a certain acreage of corn, they were required to grow a specified acreage of a cash crop, such as cotton, as well. Whether this crop would be grown on old land that was formerly used for grain or on newly cleared land was the farmers' decision. If no new lands were available, the farmers would have to give up food crops for the compulsory cash crops. In many areas, severe famines resulted, and local economies were disrupted.

MAIN POINTS 9.1 What Is Agriculture, and Where Did It Begin?

- Agriculture is the deliberate tending of crops and livestock to produce food, feed, and fibre.

- Geographer Carl Sauer suggested that Southeast and South Asia may have been the scene of the first domestication of tropical plants more than 14,000 years ago. The first domestication of seed plants, which marked the start of what is now referred to as the First Agricultural Revolution, is believed to have taken place in a region of southwestern

Asia known as the Fertile Crescent, although some have argued that this may have occurred in the Nile River Valley in northern Africa.

- The process of animal domestication began when people became more sedentary. The advantages of animal domestication stimulated the rapid diffusion of this idea among interlinked places and gave sedentary farmers a new measure of security.

- Hundreds of millions of farmers around the world are involved in subsistence agriculture, a self-sufficient form of agriculture that is small in scale, uses little technology, and emphasizes food production for local consumption rather than for trade. Many farm families living at the subsistence level are only able to grow enough food for their own use and survival; thus, they are only occasionally able to sell a small quantity of produce in order to generate some income.

- Some subsistence farmers are sedentary, living in one place throughout the year, but many others engage in shifting cultivation, moving from place to place in search of better land.

- During the colonial era, European powers sought to "modernize" the economies of their colonies by ending subsistence farming practices and integrating farmers into colonial systems of production and exchange. In some cases, they forced subsistence farmers to begin selling produce in order to raise the cash needed to pay their taxes, while in other instances they compelled subsistence farmers to move into the commercial economy by devoting land to a cash crop, such as cotton or rubber.

9.2 How Did Agriculture Change with Industrialization?

THE SECOND AGRICULTURAL REVOLUTION

As we will discuss in Chapter 10, for the Industrial Revolution to take root, a **Second Agricultural Revolution** had to take place—one that would move agriculture beyond subsistence to generate the kinds of surpluses needed to feed thousands of people working in factories instead of in agricultural fields. Like the Industrial Revolution, the Second Agricultural Revolution was composed of a series of innovations, improvements, and techniques, which in this case took place in Great Britain, the Netherlands, Denmark, and neighbouring countries.

> **Second Agricultural Revolution** Dovetailing with and benefiting from the Industrial Revolution, the Second Agricultural Revolution saw improved methods of cultivation, harvesting, and storage of farm produce.

By the 17th and 18th centuries, European farming had undergone significant changes. New crops, including corn and potatoes, came into Europe from trade with the Americas, after Christopher Columbus's 1492 arrival in the "New World." Several of the new crops were well suited for the climate and soils of western Europe, and new lands were brought into cultivation, including many that were previously defined as marginal. Farmers increased the size of their farms by consolidating fields that had been communally owned into large, single-owner holdings. Many also fenced in their land and instituted field rotation. New technologies improved production as well. For example, the seed drill enabled farmers to avoid wasting seeds and to plant in rows, which made it easier to distinguish weeds from crops.

Advances in breeding livestock allowed farmers to develop new breeds that were either strong milk producers or good for beef. By the 1830s, farmers were using new fertilizers on crops and giving artificial feeds to livestock. Increased agricultural output made it possible to feed much larger urban populations, permitting the growth of a secondary (industrial) economy.

Innovations in machinery, made possible by the Industrial Revolution in the late 1800s and early 1900s, helped sustain the Second Agricultural Revolution. The railroad moved agriculture into new regions, such as Canada's Prairie provinces and the United States' Great Plains. The railroad companies advertised in Europe (**Figure 9.6**) to attract immigrants to these regions, and the railroads took the migrants to their new homes, where they would transform prairie grasslands to agricultural fields. In Chapter 5, for example, we saw how the Canadian government attracted immigrants, including Ukrainians, Poles, Germans, Slavs, and Russians, in the late 1800s and early 1900s to farm the Canadian prairies. Later, the internal combustion engine made possible the invention of tractors, combines, and a multitude of large farm equipment. New banking and lending practices helped farmers afford the new equipment.

THE THIRD AGRICULTURAL REVOLUTION

The **Third Agricultural Revolution** dates as far back as the 1930s, when agricultural scientists in the midwestern United States began experimenting with technologically manipulated seed varieties to increase crop yields. In the 1940s, American philanthropists funded research on maize (corn) production in Mexico, trying to find a hybrid seed that would grow better. They were successful,

> **Third Agricultural Revolution** Currently in progress, the Third Agricultural Revolution has as its principal orientation the development of genetically modified organisms (GMOs).

FIGURE 9.6 Canadian Pacific Railway (CPR) advertisement, ca. 1893. The CPR played an essential role in bringing European immigrants into western Canada throughout the late 19th and early 20th centuries.

> **Green Revolution** The recently successful development of higher-yield, fast-growing varieties of rice and other cereals in certain developing countries, which led to increased production per unit area and a dramatic narrowing of the gap between population growth and food needs.

thus launching a period of significant global agricultural change commonly referred to as the **Green Revolution**, and by 1960 Mexico was no longer importing corn because production within the country was high enough to meet demand. In the 1960s, the focal point of the Green Revolution shifted to India, where farmers began growing a strain of rice developed by scientists at a research institution in the Philippines. These scientists crossed a variety of Chinese dwarf rice with an Indonesian variety and produced IR8, which, among other desirable properties, developed a bigger head of grain and had a stronger stem that did not collapse under the added weight of the bigger head.

IR8 produced much better yields than either of its parents, but the researchers were not satisfied. In 1982 they produced IR36, bred from 13 parents to achieve genetic resistance against 15 pests. IR36 had a growing cycle of 110 days under warm conditions, which made it possible to grow three crops per year in some places. By 1992, IR36 was the most widely grown crop on Earth, but two years later, scientists had developed a strain of rice that was even more productive. They

continue to work on improvements. Researchers at the International Rice Research Institute, for example, are working to breed a genetically modified "super rice" that can be seeded directly in the paddy soil, instead of having to be transplanted as a seedling. It may yield nearly twice as much rice per acre than the average for strains in current use. The charting of the rice genome (the 12 chromosomes that carry all of the plant's characteristics) is underway, which means it may soon be possible to transform rice genetically so that it will continuously acquire more desirable properties. Not only could yields improve; so could resistance to diseases and pests.

In addition to improving the production of rice, the Green Revolution brought new high-yield varieties of wheat and corn from the United States to other parts of the world, particularly South and Southeast Asia.

Coming at a time of growing concern about global hunger, the successes of the Green Revolution were truly extraordinary. Today, most famines result from political instability rather than production failure. India became self-sufficient in grain production by the 1980s, and Asia saw a two-thirds increase in rice production between 1970 and 1995. These drastic increases in production stemmed not only from new seed varieties but also, in some places, from the use of fertilizers, pesticides, and irrigation, as well as significant capital improvements.

The geographical impact of the Green Revolution has been highly variable. Its traditional focus on rice, wheat, and corn meant that it had only limited impact throughout much of Africa, where agriculture is based on different crops and where lower soil fertility makes agriculture less attractive to foreign investment. Increasingly, however, researchers are turning their attention to new agricultural products, and this could expand the geographical impact of the Green Revolution. Research has already led to methods for producing high-yield cassava and sorghum, both of which are grown in Africa. And beyond Africa, research on fattening livestock faster and improving the appearance of fruits is having an impact in North and South America.

The promise of increasing food production in a world in which almost a billion people are malnourished has led many people to support genetically engineered foods (see next section). However, many others question whether gene manipulation could create health risks and environmental hazards. For example, environmentalists have speculated about the impacts of pollen dispersal from genetically modified plants and the potential for disease-resistant plants to spur the evolution of superpests. Vandana Shiva, a vocal opponent of the Green Revolution in India, argues that

> *the Green Revolution has been a failure. It has led to reduced genetic diversity, increased vulnerability to pests, soil erosion, water shortages, reduced soil fertility, micro-nutrient deficiencies, soil contamination, reduced availability of nutritious food crops for the local population, the displacement of vast numbers of small farmers from their land,*

rural impoverishment and increased tensions and conflicts. The beneficiaries have been the agrochemical industry, large petrochemical companies, manufacturers of agricultural machinery, dam builders and large landowners. (Shiva, 1991)

One difficulty of assessing the present situation is that developments are occurring so fast that it is not easy to keep up with them. The Green Revolution today has a large number of detractors concerned that the higher inputs of chemical fertilizers and pesticides can lead to reduced organic matter in the soil and to groundwater pollution. Moreover, many small-scale farmers lack the resources to acquire genetically enhanced seeds and the necessary fertilizers and pesticides. In most of the world that is affected by the Green Revolution, farmers produce on very small acreages. In addition, as we saw in Chapter 1, critics argue that these changes increase the power of multinational corporations such as Monsanto, which copyright their genetically modified seeds and ban farmers from reusing seeds year after year, thereby reducing farmers' abilities to be self-sustaining (Figure 1.23). A 2005 report in *Scientific American* by Paul Polak explains that, in these cases, the Green Revolution has done little to alleviate poverty: "The supply-driven strategies of the Green Revolution . . . may not help subsistence farmers, who must play to their strengths to compete in the global marketplace. The average size of a family farm is less than four acres in India, 1.8 acres in Bangladesh and about half an acre in China." Small-scale farmers are in a poor competitive position, and some are being driven off their lands. In addition, the need for capital from the West to implement Green Revolution technologies has led to a shift away from production for local consumers toward export agriculture. In the process, local places become subject to the ups and downs of the global economy, where a downward fluctuation in the price of a given crop can create enormous problems for farmers dependent on the sale of that crop.

GENETICALLY MODIFIED FOODS

An entire field of biotechnology has sprung up in conjunction with the Third Agricultural Revolution, and the development of genetically engineered (GE) crops, or **genetically modified organisms (GMOs)**, is its principal orientation. Since the origin of agriculture, people have experimented with hybrid crops and crossbreeding animals. Today, some experts estimate that about 60 percent of processed foods and as many as 30,000 items on grocery store shelves in Canada contain genetically modified organisms. The GMO Compass, a website created with the financial support of the European Union to provide users with up-to-date information regarding genetically modified food quality and safety issues, noted that Canada was the world's fifth-highest producer of genetically engineered crops in 2013 (behind only the United States, Brazil, Argentina,

> **Genetically modified organisms (GMOs)** Crops that carry new traits that have been inserted through advanced genetic engineering methods.

FIGURE 9.7 "Not made with genetically modified ingredients." Cheerios announced its voluntary labelling program in early 2014.

and India). While most developed countries have strict guidelines for the labelling of GMOs, with some going so far as to ban GM food production and imports, Canada does not. Canadians are often unaware that the foods they purchase contain GM ingredients. A growing movement argues that Canadians have a right to know, and choose, whether or not to purchase GM foods. In what is considered to be a significant move in the United States, General Mills Corporation, which owns the breakfast cereal Cheerios, announced in January 2014 that Cheerios are now being manufactured using only GM-free ingredients, and will be labelled accordingly—the first major brand of packaged food to be so labelled (**Figure 9.7**).

Some regions have embraced genetically engineered crops; others have banned them. While many of the poorer countries of the world do not have access to the necessary capital and technology to obtain GM crops, some 46 percent of fields in which such crops are grown are found in developing nations. Moreover, ideological resistance to genetically engineered foods is strong in some places—particularly in western Europe. Agricultural officials in most western European countries have declared genetically modified foods to be safe, but the public has a strong reaction against them based on combined concerns about health and taste, as well as their possible effect on the environment. Such concerns have spread to less affluent parts of the world. In many poorer regions, seeds are a cultural commodity, reflecting agricultural lessons learned over generations. In these regions, many resist the invasion of foreign, genetically engineered crops.

MAIN POINTS 9.2 How Did Agriculture Change with Industrialization?

- Like the Industrial Revolution, the Second Agricultural Revolution was composed of a series of innovations, improvements, and techniques. The Second Agricultural Revolution moved agriculture beyond subsistence to generate the kinds of surpluses needed to feed thousands of people working in factories instead of in agricultural fields. This phase in the evolution of agriculture involved the introduction of new crops, the expansion of farm sizes, innovations in farm machinery, and improvements in methods of soil preparation, fertilization, crop care, and harvesting.

- The Third Agricultural Revolution, of which the Green Revolution has been a part, dates as far back as the 1930s. Over time, this phase has been marked by drastic increases in agricultural production that stemmed from the creation

of new seed varieties; the use of fertilizers, pesticides, and irrigation in some places; and significant capital improvements.

- The geographical impact of the Green Revolution has been highly variable. While countries such as Mexico and India have experienced large increases in productivity, Africa has thus far seen only a limited impact.

- One controversial element of the Third Agricultural Revolution has been the creation of genetically modified organisms, which prompted fears about food quality and safety. Moreover, small-scale farmers often have not benefited because they lack the resources to acquire genetically enhanced seeds and the necessary fertilizers and pesticides.

FIGURE 9.8 World agriculture. General areas where various kinds of agriculture are practised throughout the world are indicated with different colours on this map. Note, however, that the boundaries between agricultural regions are broad approximations. Adapted with permission from Hammond, Inc., 1977.

WORLD AGRICULTURE

1. Dairying
2. Fruit, Truck and Specialized Crops
3. Mixed Livestock and Crop Farming
4. Commercial Grain Farming
5. Subsistence Crop and Livestock Farming
6. Mediterranean Agriculture
7. Diversified Tropical Agriculture –chiefly plantation
8. Intensive Subsistence Farming –chiefly rice
9. Intensive Subsistence Farming –chiefly wheat and other crops
10. Rudimentry Sedentary Cultivation
11. Shifting Cultivation
12. Livestock Ranching
13. Nomadic and Semi-Nomadic Herding

☐ Nonagricultural Areas

0   1000   2000   3000 Kilometres

0   1000   2000 Miles

9.3 What Is the Contemporary Global Pattern of Agriculture and Agribusiness?

WORLD AGRICULTURE

When looking at general patterns of agriculture at the global scale (**Figure 9.8**), it is important to recognize the interplay of market location, land use, and transportation costs. We must also consider the effects of different climate and soil conditions, variations in farming methods and technology, involvement by governments, and the lasting impacts of history. For example, decisions made by colonial powers in Europe led to the establishment of plantations from Central America to Southeast Asia. The

plantations grew crops not for local markets but for consumers in Europe; similarly, U.S. companies founded huge plantations in the Americas. Over the past few centuries, the impact of this plantation system transformed the map of world agriculture. And the end of colonial rule did not signal the end of the agricultural practices and systems that had been imposed on the former colonial areas. Long-entrenched agricultural systems and patterns are not quickly or easily transformed, and even food-poor countries must continue to grow commercial crops for export on some of their best soils, where their own food should be harvested.

Commercial farming—the agriculture of large-scale grain producers and cattle ranches, mechanized equipment and factory-type labour forces, plantations, and profit—has come to dominate in the world's economic core, as well as in some places in the semi-periphery and periphery. As we will see, it is a world apart from the traditional farms of Asia and Africa.

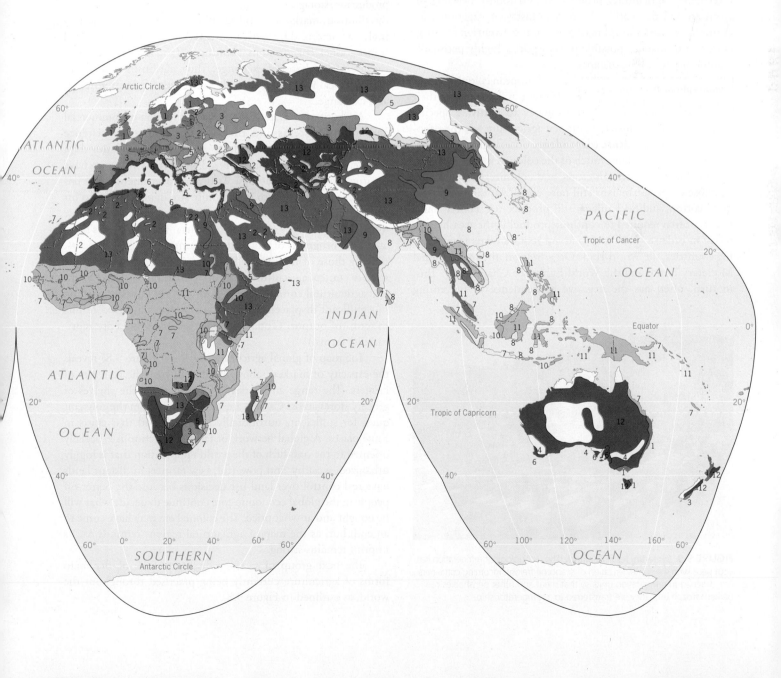

> **Commercial agriculture** Large-scale farming and ranching operations that employ vast land bases, large mechanized equipment, factory-type labour forces, and the latest technology.

The roots of modern **commercial agriculture** can be traced to the vast colonial empires established by European powers in the 18th and 19th centuries. Europe became a market for agricultural products from around the world, but with an added dimension: European countries manufactured and sold in their colonies the finished products made from imported raw materials. Thus, cotton grown in Egypt, Sudan, India, and other countries colonized by Europe was bought cheaply, imported to European factories, and made into clothes—many of which were then exported and sold, often in the very colonies where the cotton had been grown in the first place (see Chapter 2). Major changes in transportation and food storage, especially refrigeration and containerization (**Figure 9.9**), have further intertwined agricultural production and food-processing regions around the world. The beef industry of Argentina, for example, secured a world market when the invention of refrigerated ships made it possible to transport a highly perishable commodity over long distances.

> **Monoculture** Dependence on a single agricultural commodity.

European colonial powers also required farmers in their colonies to cultivate specific crops. One major impact of colonial agriculture was the establishment of **monoculture** (dependence on a single agricultural commodity) throughout much of the colonial world. Colonies became known for certain crops, and colonizers came to rely on those crops. Ghanaians still raise cacao, Mozambicans still grow cotton, and Sri Lankans still produce tea. Poorer countries are often required to continue producing these cash crops today in order to meet loan and aid requirements from lending countries, the World Trade Organization, the International Monetary Fund, and the World Bank (see Chapter 11). This, in turn, often has the negative consequence of preventing those countries from growing food for consumption by their own people.

AGRIBUSINESS AND THE CHANGING GEOGRAPHY OF AGRICULTURE

In more recent decades the commercialization of crop production and the associated development of new agricultural technologies have changed how agricultural goods are grown and have sparked the rapid growth of **agribusiness**—an encompassing term for the businesses that provide a vast array of goods and services to support the agricultural industry in the production of a final food product for consumption. This includes the manufacturing and distribution of farm supplies, on-farm production, storage, processing, distribution, marketing, and retailing. Agribusiness is increasingly characterized by vertical integration, whereby individual transnational corporations coordinate (and profit from) activities in all spheres of exchange. Thus, agribusiness serves to connect local farms to a spatially extensive web of production and exchange.

> **Agribusiness** The businesses that provide the vast array of goods and services that support the agriculture industry in the production of a final food product for consumption.

Agribusiness is shaping the world distribution of commercial agricultural systems and their relationship to subsistence agriculture. Many factors have affected that relationship. History and tradition have played important roles, as have environment and technology. At times, governments have encouraged their citizens to limit family size in an attempt to lift the population above the subsistence level. Some governments upheld the privileges of large landowners, whereas others initiated bold programs of land reform. Communist governments, notably those of the former Soviet Union and Maoist China, tried to control agricultural output by creating collective farms and agricultural communes—a giant experiment that resulted in significant displacement of rural peoples and mixed results in terms of output. (Today, both Russia and China are reprivatizing farms.)

The map of global agricultural regions (Figure 9.8) reveals the capacity of markets, above all, to influence the activities of farmers. The range and variety of products on the shelves of grocery stores across Canada are a world away from the constant quest for sufficient, nutritionally balanced food that exists in some places. A global network of farm production is especially oriented to the one-fifth of the world's population that is highly urbanized, wealthy, and powerful. Few farmers in distant lands have real control over land-use decisions because the better-off people in the global economic core continue to decide what will be bought and at what price. The colonial era may have come to an end, but, as the map of agricultural regions reminds us, its imprint remains strong.

The next group of sections discusses some of the main forms of agriculture currently being practised throughout the world, as outlined in Figure 9.8.

© H.J. de Blij

FIGURE 9.9 Dunedin, New Zealand. The technology of refrigeration has kept pace with the containerization of seaborne freight. Incoming containers are attached to refrigeration units so that meat and other perishables can be kept frozen until they are transferred to a refrigerator ship.

HUNTING AND GATHERING

In the modern world, hunter-gatherers live in the context of a globalized economy and are pressured to change their livelihoods. In many cases, the state tries to force hunter-gatherers to settle in one place and farm. Cyclical migration by hunter-gatherers does not mesh well with bounded, territorial states. Some nongovernmental organizations encourage settlement by digging wells or building medical buildings, permanent houses, or schools for hunter-gatherers. Even hunter-gatherers who continue to use their knowledge of seeds, roots, fruits, berries, insects, and animals to gather and trap the food they need for survival do so in the context of the world economy. For example, the San of southern Africa, the Aborigines of Australia, the indigenous peoples of Brazil, and several other groups in the Americas, Africa, and Asia have been studied, mapped, recorded, photographed, donated to, defended, and, in many cases, exploited.

SUBSISTENCE AGRICULTURE

As noted earlier, subsistence farming, traditionally practised throughout the entire world prior to industrial agriculture, still persists in many places, including Asia, sub-Saharan Africa, and Latin America. The map of world agriculture in Figure 9.8 labels three types of subsistence agriculture: subsistence crop and livestock farming, intensive subsistence farming (chiefly rice), and intensive subsistence farming (chiefly wheat and other crops). In some regions, the "subsistence" label does not tell the whole story. For example, most Southeast Asian farmers are subsistence grain farmers, but the area is also a source of significant rice exports, so subsistence and export production occur side by side. However, the rice is grown on small plots while the grain is grown on a much larger proportion of the land. Accordingly, Southeast Asia appears on the map as primarily a subsistence grain-growing area.

In the interests of "progress" and "modernization," subsistence farmers have been pushed away from their traditional modes of livelihood. Yet many aspects of subsistence farming may be worth preserving. Regions with shifting cultivation do not have neat rows of plants, carefully turned soil, or precisely laid-out fields. Nonetheless, shifting cultivation conserves both forest and soil, its harvests are substantial given the environmental limitations, and it requires better organization than one might assume. It also requires substantially less energy than more modern techniques of farming. Shifting cultivation has been a sustainable method of farming for thousands of years. It gave ancient farmers opportunities to experiment with various plants, learn the effects of weeding and crop care, cope with environmental vagaries, and discern the decreased fertility of soil after sustained farming.

Nevertheless, in many parts of the world, subsistence land use is giving way to more intensive farming and cash cropping—even to mechanized farming, in which equipment does much of the actual work. In the process, societies from South America to Southeast Asia are profoundly affected. Land that was once held communally is being parcelled out to individuals for cash cropping. As a result, the system that ensured an equitable distribution of resources for centuries is breaking down. Furthermore, the distribution of wealth has become stratified, with poor people at the bottom and rich landowners at the top.

CASH CROPS AND PLANTATION AGRICULTURE

Non-subsistence farming in many poorer countries is a leftover from colonial times. As noted earlier, colonial powers implemented particular agricultural systems to benefit their needs, a practice that has tended to lock poorer countries into production of one or two "cash" crops. Cash farming continues to provide badly needed money, even if the conditions of sale to the urban-industrial world are unfavourable.

In the Caribbean region, for example, whole national economies depend on the export of sugar, which was introduced by the European colonists in the 1600s. These island countries wish to sell the sugar at the highest possible price, but they are not in a position to dictate prices. Sugar is produced by many countries in various parts of the world, as well as by farmers in the core. Governments in the core regions place quotas on imports of agricultural products and subsidize domestic production of the same commodities. Occasionally, producing countries attempt to form a cartel in order to present a united front to the importing countries and gain a better price, as oil-producing states did during the 1970s. Such collective action is difficult, as the wealthy importing countries can buy products from countries that are not members of the cartel. Also, if exporting countries withhold their products, they might end up stimulating domestic production among importers. For example, although cane sugar accounts for more than 70 percent of the world's commercial sugar crop each year, farmers in countries such as France, Germany, the United States, and Russia produce sugar from sugar beets. In Europe and Russia, these beets currently yield 25 percent of the annual world sugar harvest. Collective action by countries producing sugar cane, such as Brazil, India, China, and Thailand, could easily cause that percentage to increase.

When cash crops are grown on large estates, we describe the production system as **plantation agriculture**. Plantations are colonial legacies that persist, along with subsistence farming, in poorer, primarily tropical, countries. Figure 9.8 shows that plantation agriculture (number 7 in the legend) continues in Central and South America, Africa, and South Asia. Established to produce bananas, sugar, coffee, and cocoa in Central and South America; rubber, cocoa, and tea in West and East Africa; tea in South Asia; and rubber in Southeast Asia, these

> **Plantation agriculture**
> Production system based on a large estate owned by an individual, family, or corporation and organized to produce a cash crop. Almost all plantations were established within the tropics; in recent decades, many have been divided into smaller holdings or reorganized as co-operatives.

© Xu Suhui/Xinhua Press/Corbis

FIGURE 9.10 A tea plantation in Kenya. The tea industry plays an important role in Kenya's economy. Much of the tea is grown on large and often foreign-owned plantations, while the rest is grown by small-scale growers.

plantations have outlasted the period of decolonization and continue to provide specialized crops to wealthier markets (**Figure 9.10**). Many of the most productive plantations are owned by European or American individuals or corporations.

COTTON AND RUBBER

Two of the most significant contemporary cash crops are cotton and rubber. Colonialism encouraged the plantation-scale production of cotton in many regions of the world. India, for example, began producing cotton on a large scale under British colonialism.

Cotton cultivation expanded greatly during the 19th century, when the Industrial Revolution led to the invention of machines for cotton ginning, spinning, and weaving that increased productive capacity, brought prices down, and put cotton goods within the reach of mass markets. As with sugar, the colonial powers laid out large-scale cotton plantations, sometimes under irrigation. Cotton cultivation was also promoted on a smaller scale in numerous other countries: in Egypt's Nile Delta, in the Punjab region shared by Pakistan and India, and in Sudan, Uganda, Mexico, and Brazil. The colonial producers received low prices for their cotton, and the European industries prospered as cheap raw materials were converted into large quantities of items for sale at home and abroad.

Wealthier countries continue to buy cotton, and cotton sales remain important for some former colonies. Today, however, they must also compete with cotton being grown in the United States, northeastern China, and Central Asia. Much of the cotton purchased by Japan, the United Kingdom, and western Europe, for example, comes from the United States. Cotton is now also in competition with synthetic fibres such as nylon and rayon.

Similarly, rubber is now in competition with synthetic rubber. Before the synthetic form was developed, rubber was collected from rubber-producing trees in equatorial rainforests,

mainly in the Amazon Basin of northern South America. Around 1900, for example, the town of Manaus on the Amazon River experienced a rubber boom. Rubber companies in the Congo Basin in Africa experienced a similar period of prosperity. The boom in wild rubber was short-lived, however. Rubber-tree plantations were created to make rubber collection easier and more efficient. Seedlings of Brazilian rubber trees were planted elsewhere, and they did especially well in Southeast Asia. Within two decades, nearly 90 percent of the world's rubber came from new plantations in colonial territories in Malaysia, the Netherlands East Indies (now Indonesia), and neighbouring colonies.

As time went on, manufacturers found more and more uses for rubber, and consumer demand grew continuously. The advent of the automobile was an enormous boost for the industry, and most of the rubber now produced is used to manufacture vehicle tires. World War II created a need for alternative sources of rubber, since Japan had occupied much of Southeast Asia. This stimulated the production of synthetic rubber. In 2013, world rubber production totalled approximately 27.5 million tonnes, more than 15.5 million tonnes of which was synthetic. Of the natural rubber produced that year, more than 70 percent came from the plantations of the Asia-Pacific region.

The development of rubber plantations in Southeast Asia, rather than in the Amazon Basin or the Congo Basin, is due less to environmental factors than to the availability of labour. The colonial powers were aware that Southeast Asia combined conditions of tropical environment and labour availability that neither the Amazon region nor Equatorial Africa could match. Eventually, a large-scale rubber industry developed in Liberia (West Africa), but in the 1990s it was destroyed during the country's disastrous civil war. Lately, efforts have been made to introduce the plantation system along the Amazon River in the heart of northern Brazil.

LUXURY CROPS

A combination of suitable environment and available labour led the European colonial powers to establish huge plan-

> **Luxury crops** Non-subsistence crops such as tea, cacao, coffee, and tobacco.

tations for the cultivation of **luxury crops** such as tea, cacao, coffee, and tobacco. Among these, palm oil, which is derived from the African oil palm tree, has become a staple of Western lifestyles. Palm oil accounts for more than 30 percent of the world's vegetable oil production, and vast quantities are used by fast food chains and confectionary companies. Palm oil is also found in shampoo, toothpaste, cosmetics, cleaning agents, and laundry detergent, making it a significant commodity in North America and Europe. Although African oil palm trees can be grown in many different regions of the world, 85 percent of the world's palm oil production comes from Malaysia and Indonesia, most of it produced unsustainably (**Figure 9.11**). Palm oil production is linked to several significant issues, including climate

Jason Isley/Scubazoo/Getty Images

FIGURE 9.11 Oil palms displace native plant and animal species, Sabah, Borneo, East Malaysia.

change, animal abuse, deforestation, environmental degradation, and indigenous rights abuses.

After petroleum, coffee is now the second-most-valuable traded commodity in the world. It is also one of the best examples of colonialism's impact on present-day agricultural practices. In the early 18th century, coffee was virtually unknown in most of the world. It was first domesticated in the region of present-day Ethiopia, but today it thrives in Central and South America, where approximately 70 percent of the world's annual production is harvested.

It is estimated that 400 billion cups of coffee are consumed each year, equivalent to about 12,000 cups per second. The United States buys more than half of all the coffee sold on world markets annually, and western Europe imports most of the rest. The most familiar image of coffee production in North America is probably that provided by Juan Valdez, who is portrayed as a simple yet proud Colombian peasant who handpicks beans by day and enjoys a cup of his own coffee by night. However, this image is far from the reality of much coffee production in Latin America or elsewhere. In many cases, coffee is produced on enormous, foreign-owned plantations, where it is picked by local labourers who are hired at very low wage rates. Most coffee is sent abroad; if the coffee pickers drink coffee themselves, it is probably of the imported and instant variety.

Coffee production is undergoing changes as more consumers demand fair trade coffee and more coffee producers seek fair trade certification. CNN reports that "retailers who are certified Fair Traders return up to 40 percent of the retail price of an item to the producer." Once a producer meets the requirements of organic coffee production and a few other criteria, that producer can be registered on the International Fair Trade Coffee Register. Coffee importers then purchase the fair trade coffee directly from the registered producers. Being registered guarantees coffee producers a base "fair trade price" of anywhere from $1.01 to $1.40 per pound of coffee (plus bonuses of $0.30 per pound for organic). Over 500,000 farmers

in 20 countries in the periphery and semi-periphery are on the fair trade register. The fair trade campaign pressured Starbucks into selling fair trade coffee, and the coffee chain now purchases more than 10 percent of the global production of fair trade coffee. Major Canadian supermarkets, such as western Canada's Co-op stores and those owned by the Loblaw Companies, also sell fair trade coffee.

Tea is a more recent addition to the Western diet. It was grown in China perhaps 2,000 years ago, but it became popular in Europe only during the 19th century. The colonial powers (mainly the British) established enormous tea plantations in Asia and thus began the full-scale flow of tea into European markets. Tea production, both the fair trade and traditionally traded varieties, is on the rise globally to meet the increasing consumption of the luxury crop. Compared with coffee, tea is consumed in greater quantities in areas where it is grown, including India, China, Sri Lanka, and Japan. Whereas coffee is cultivated and consumed mainly in the Americas, tea is the dominant beverage in significant parts of Eurasia. Tea goes from the Asian-producing areas to the United Kingdom and the rest of Europe and North America.

Today, fair trade production goes far beyond coffee and tea. Dozens of other commodities and products, ranging from bananas and fresh cut flowers to chocolate and soccer balls, can also be certified fair trade. According to Fairtrade Labelling Organizations International, consumers worldwide spent more than C$7billion on fair trade certified products in 2013.

COMMERCIAL LIVESTOCK, FRUIT, AND GRAIN AGRICULTURE

By far the largest areas of commercial agriculture (numbers 1 through 4 on Figure 9.8) lie outside the tropics. Dairying (1) is widespread at the northern margins of the mid-latitudes—particularly in southeastern Canada, the northeastern United States, and northwestern Europe. Fruit, truck, and specialized crops (2), which include crops grown on small farms that are transported to market by truck, are found in the eastern and southeastern United States and in widely dispersed small areas where environments are favourable. (Major oases can be seen in the Sahara and in Central Asia.)

Mixed livestock and crop farming (3) is widespread in the more humid parts of the mid-latitudes, including much of the eastern United States, western Europe, and western Russia, but it is also found in smaller areas in Uruguay, Brazil, and South Africa. Commercial grain farming (4) prevails in the drier parts of the mid-latitudes, including the southern portions of Canada's Prairie provinces and the Dakotas, Montana, Nebraska, Kansas, and adjacent areas in the United States. Spring wheat (planted in the spring and harvested in the summer) grows in the northern zone, and winter wheat (planted in the autumn and harvested in the spring of the following year) is primarily used in the southern area. An even larger belt of wheat farming extends from Ukraine through Russia into Kazakhstan. The Argentinean and Australian wheat zones are smaller in area, but their exports are an important component of world trade.

Even a cursory glance at Figure 9.8 reveals the wide distribution of **livestock ranching** (12), the raising of domesticated animals for meat and by-products, such as leather and wool.

> **Livestock ranching** The raising of domesticated animals for the production of meat and other by-products, such as leather and wool.

In addition to the large cattle-ranching areas in Canada, the United States, and Mexico, much of eastern Brazil and Argentina are devoted to ranching, along with large tracts of Australia, New Zealand, and South Africa. Commercial livestock farming has grown in conjunction with the higher levels of meat consumption worldwide, which has occurred largely as a result of households' increased purchasing power and changing diets. At the global scale, per capita meat consumption stands at about 41.9 kilograms per person each year. However, there are significant geographical variations between countries. In the developing world, individuals eat about 32 kilograms of meat a year on average, while those residing in the industrial world eat about 80 kilograms per person each year. To meet the demand for this growing level of consumption, worldwide meat production has tripled since the 1970s, with global production amounting to some 308.5 million tons in 2013. The most widely produced meat in the world is pork, followed by poultry, beef, and sheep. At the same time, as we read in Chapter 4, the world's population is growing, and western taste for diets rich in meat and dairy products continues to grow exponentially around the world.

Commercial livestock farming is not without controversy. Animal rights activists have long argued that the practice of industrial livestock farming is cruel to animals, and environmentalists assert that the continued conversion of rainforests and savannahs into pasture lands, together with the increased burden on the water supply, creates serious harm to the ecosystem (**Figure 9.12**). The environmental impacts of industrial farming more generally are discussed at greater length later in this chapter.

FIGURE 9.12 A rancher herds cattle in Belem, Brazil. The UN says agriculture is on par with fossil fuel consumption in terms of environmental impact because both rise rapidly with increased economic growth.

MEDITERRANEAN AGRICULTURE

Only one form of agriculture mentioned in the legend of Figure 9.8 refers to a particular climatic zone: **Mediterranean agriculture** (6). As the map shows, this kind of specialized

> **Mediterranean agriculture** Specialized farming that occurs only in areas where the Mediterranean dry summer climate prevails.

farming occurs only in areas where the Mediterranean dry summer climate prevails: along the shores of the Mediterranean Sea, in parts of California and Oregon in the United States, in central Chile, at South Africa's Cape, and in parts of southwestern and southern Australia. Farmers in these regions grow a special combination of crops: grapes, olives, citrus fruits, figs, certain vegetables, dates, and others. These areas also produce many wines, which, along with other commodities, are exported to distant markets because Mediterranean products tend to be popular and command high prices.

ILLEGAL DRUGS

Cash crops that are turned into illegal drugs cannot be easily mapped and do not appear in Figure 9.8. Globally, the United Nations Office on Drugs and Crime estimates that between 167 and 315 million people (3.6 to 6.9 percent of the world population aged 15 to 64) used illicit substances at least once in 2011. Because of the high demand for drugs, particularly in the core, farmers in the periphery often find it more profitable to cultivate opium poppies, coca, or marijuana than standard food crops. Cultivation of these plants increased steadily through the 1980s and 1990s. Although cultivation has levelled off in recent years, and even declined in some areas, these crops continue to make up an important source of revenue for parts of the global economic periphery. Coca, the source plant of cocaine, is grown widely in Colombia, Peru, and Bolivia. Over half of the world's cultivation of coca occurs in Colombia alone.

Heroin and opium are derived from opium poppies, grown predominantly in southeastern and southwestern areas of Asia, especially Afghanistan and Myanmar. In its 2012 *Afghanistan Opium Survey*, the United Nations reported that almost two-thirds of the world's opium production (65 percent) took place in Afghanistan that year (**Figure 9.13**). The United States-led overthrow of the Taliban in Afghanistan in 2001 created a power vacuum in the country and an opportunity for illegal drug production to quickly rebound (the austere Taliban government had virtually eradicated opium production in Afghanistan). Most opium production in Afghanistan occurs in nine unstable southern and western regions; many of the more stable northern provinces are poppy-free.

ENVIRONMENTAL IMPACTS OF COMMERCIAL AGRICULTURE

Commercial agriculture creates significant environmental change. If you travel to Mediterranean Europe today, for example, you will see a landscape that reflects the clearing of forests in ancient

© Benjamin Lowry/Getty Images

FIGURE 9.13 Opium poppy field in the Nangarhar province, Afghanistan. Afghan police and provincial security forces destroy poppy fields in the Nangarhar province of Afghanistan.

times to facilitate agriculture and trade. Look carefully at many hill slopes and you will see evidence of terraces cut into the hills many centuries ago (see Figure 6.30 in Chapter 6). The industrialization and commercialization of agriculture has accelerated the pace and extent of agriculture's impact on the environment. More land has been cleared, and the land that is under cultivation is used more and more intensively.

Significant changes in the natural environment go far beyond the simple clearing of land. They range from soil erosion to changes in the organic content of soils to the presence of chemicals (e.g., herbicides, pesticides, and even antibiotics and growth hormones from livestock feces) in soils and groundwater. In places where large commercial crop farms dominate, the greatest concern is the introduction of chemical (or inorganic) fertilizers and pesticides into the environment. The Worldwatch Institute has pointed out that inorganic fertilizers contain three major nutrients—nitrogen, phosphorous, and potash—but that they lack the organic matter and other ingredients that are found in organic fertilizers (such as manures) and that help to sustain soil health. Furthermore, chemical fertilizers also act as a water pollutant. Unfortunately, demand for these fertilizers has been growing significantly in conjunction with a higher demand for crops used as livestock feed and to produce biofuels.

DEFORESTATION

People have been degrading forests and converting them to other land uses since humans first evolved, but the extent of areas converted and degraded has accelerated continuously as agriculture was invented, populations grew, and the global economy expanded to incorporate even the most remote communities into its processes. Forest conversion and degradation rates increased dramatically as human societies shifted from hunting and gathering to fixed field farming, and then from feudal agriculture to industrial capitalism. Today, national policies, supported by global actors, drive deforestation by encouraging elites to harvest forest wealth through logging, to undertake large-scale forest clearing for ranching

and plantations, and to maintain highly concentrated land ownership patterns, thereby driving poor farmers into forests for survival.

From 1700 to 1980, the area of world croplands expanded almost fivefold from a small base to well over 1.2 billion hectares, while the world's large stock of forest lands decreased by 19 percent over the same time. Today, greater environmental awareness and the introduction of more sustainable management practices mean that forest area continues to decline in only 40 percent of the world's countries. However, most of these countries are in the biologically rich tropics. Over the last quarter-century alone, some 4 to 5 percent of tropical forests have been disappearing each decade. Tropical forest conversion and degradation are estimated to be contributing 20 percent of the carbon dioxide being released into the atmosphere each year. These processes also threaten mass extinctions at alarming rates.

Environmental impacts can be particularly severe when commercial agriculture expands into marginal environments. This has happened, for example, with the expansion of livestock herding into arid or semi-arid areas. The natural vegetation in these areas cannot always sustain the herds, especially during prolonged droughts. This can lead to ecological damage and, in some areas, to desertification (discussed further below).

In recent years, the popularity of fast-food chains that serve hamburgers has led to the deforestation of wooded areas in order to open up additional pastures for beef cattle, notably in Central and South America. Livestock ranching is an extremely land-, water-, and energy-intensive process. Significant amounts of land must be turned over to the cultivation of cattle feed, and the animals themselves need extensive grazing areas (**Figure 9.14**). By stripping away vegetation, the animals exacerbate the erosion of riverbanks, with implications for everything from water quality to wildlife habitat.

The consequences of deforestation are numerous and range from local and regional to national and global in their impacts. Forests provide a range of benefits, some or all of

Education Images/UIG via Getty Images

FIGURE 9.14 Cattle graze on pasture formed by cleared rainforest land. The growing global appetite for meat has resulted in the extensive deforestation of wooded areas around the world, particularly in Central and South America.

which are lost when deforestation occurs. First, intact forests can provide a steady supply of products—such as foods, construction materials, medicines, fuel, industrial raw materials, and fresh water. Second, forests and other ecosystems provide environmental services by regulating environmental processes. For example, they clean the air and water of pollutants, and they absorb and sequester greenhouse gases, especially carbon dioxide. Forests also provide habitat for insect, bird, and mammal pollinators of human crops. They reduce soil erosion and minimize runoff of nutrients and rainfall. Finally, they also perform important cultural and social roles in different world regions by providing the locale for spiritual, religious, and esthetic experiences, by providing people with habitats within which they develop their cultures, and by offering opportunities for recreation and ecotourism.

DESERTIFICATION

Land ownership patterns, the need for crops and protein sources (both for local consumption and for export), and power differences among groups of people lead some farmers and ranchers to turn marginal, semi-arid lands into farms and ranches. The impoverished farmers forced to work these lands can ill afford such luxuries as fertilizers, and educational levels are typically too low to achieve widespread soil conservation efforts. As a result, the decision to farm these semi-arid regions more intensively in order to increase agricultural production has the unintended consequence of eroding the land, causing migration flow and creating conflict. Although the expansion and contraction of deserts can occur naturally and cyclically, the process of **desertification** is more often caused by humans destroying vegetation and eroding soils through the overuse of lands for livestock grazing or crop production.

As much as 35 percent of the world's land surface is affected by desertification, and as much as one-fifth of the global population lives in regions at serious risk of this process (**Figure 9.15**). Desertification has been occurring in developed and developing countries, and in areas with low and high population densities. However, it has hit Africa harder than any other continent. More than half of Africa is arid or semi-arid, and many people farm the marginal, dry lands of the continent. In sub-Saharan Africa over the last 50 years, more than 700,000 square kilometres of farming and grazing land have become desert, extending the Sahara Desert to the south. Some cases of desertification may be caused by climatic fluctuations (such as changes in the amount of precipitation), but human-induced problems such as overgrazing, soil exhaustion, salinization (a buildup of salt in the soil), woodcutting and fuelwood collection, and bushfires have undoubtedly accelerated the process.

As with deforestation, desertification also has a number of negative impacts that are felt far beyond the areas actually suffering it. For example, the degraded soils sequester less carbon, helping to cause global warming. Also, silt running from damaged land may damage rivers, irrigation schemes, and lakes hundreds of kilometres away. Rivers draining affected regions may become more prone to flash floods and periodic drying up. Desertification is also frequently a cause of major dust storms, which sweep into surrounding regions, causing damage and disruption well outside the desertified area.

> **Desertification** The encroachment of desert conditions on moister zones along the desert margins, where plant cover and soils are threatened by desiccation—through overuse, in part by humans and their domestic animals, and, possibly, in part because of inexorable shifts in the Earth's environmental zones.

FIGURE 9.15 Areas at risk of human induced desertification. Deserts expand and contract cyclically, but nature's cycles can be distorted by human intervention. This map shows areas threatened or affected by human-induced desertification. Source: Global Desertification Vulnerability map, US Department of Agriculture, Natural Resources Conservation Service. Soil Survey Division and World Soil Resources, 1998. Accessed at www.nrcs.usda.gov/wps/portal/nrcs/detail/national/home/?cid=nrcs142p2_054004.

LOSS OF PRODUCTIVE FARMLAND

As cities expand outward and agricultural lands are converted into suburbs, some of the most fertile, productive farmlands are lost to housing and retail developments (**Figure 9.16**). Many cities were established amid productive farmlands that could supply the needs of their inhabitants. Now the cities are absorbing the productive farmlands as they expand. When this happens, farmers' rights, and ability, to use agricultural lands come into conflict more frequently with neighbouring non-farm uses—as when residential neighbours complain about farm odours and noise.

Concerns about the encroachment of cities onto farmland are made more pressing by the fact that only about 5 percent of Canada's

FIGURE 9.16 Calgary, Alberta, and surrounding area. Calgary's exponential population growth in the late 20th and early 21st centuries, driven largely by its important role as a headquarters for Alberta's prosperous oil and gas industry, has led to the city's outward growth onto surrounding agricultural lands. Between 1991 and 2001, for example, Calgary's population grew by 24 percent, but its urban land area grew by 43 percent. In other words, for every 100 new residents, Calgary added 6.3 hectares of urban land.

total land mass is considered to be dependable farmland. The largest of these areas are concentrated in Manitoba, Saskatchewan, and Alberta. Furthermore, much of Canada's

Image courtesy of Earth Sciences and Image Analysis Laboratory, NASA

most fertile ("Class 1") farmland is found in Ontario, with a large proportion of this located within the province's most heavily urbanized regions. In fact, a 1999 Statistics Canada report pointed out that on a clear day one could see about 37 percent of Canada's Class 1 farmland from the top of Toronto's CN Tower.

Urbanization rates for other countries in the richer parts of the world (such as Japan), as well as for less affluent countries (such as Egypt), prove that the loss of productive farmland is a global problem with serious implications for the future.

LAND ACQUISITION BY FOREIGN BUYERS

Another issue affecting agriculture in developing countries is the heightened number of land deals that have taken place in recent years. A "land deal" refers to the purchase of agricultural land by foreign investors. A document released in 2012 by researchers involved in the Land Matrix Project, a worldwide network of research and civil society organizations, shows that an estimated 70.2 million hectares of agricultural land around the world has been sold or leased to private and public investors in the form of land deals. As the authors note, this equates to 1.4 percent of the world's agricultural land and also represents a land mass roughly the size of the Democratic Republic of Congo. The researchers warn that these figures are conservative, as some governments are far more open and transparent than others about such deals taking place. The Land Matrix Project argues that monitoring large scale land acquisition at the global scale is significant; foreign investment can bring prosperity through agricultural production, conservation, and tourism to a region, but it can also bring exploitation of land and labour, and extraction of natural resources such as fossil fuels and timber.

MAIN POINTS 9.3 What Is the Contemporary Global Pattern of Agriculture and Agribusiness?

- Today's global agricultural patterns are influenced by a wide array of factors, including the location and accessibility of markets, land use and transportation costs, climate and soil conditions, variations in farming methods and technology, involvement by governments, and the lasting impacts of history (such as decisions made by colonial powers and historical trade patterns).

- Commercial farming dominates in the world's economic core, as well as in some regions of the semi-periphery and periphery. The roots of modern commercial agriculture can be traced to the vast colonial empires established by European powers in the 18th and 19th centuries.

- Colonial powers implemented particular agricultural systems to benefit their needs, a practice that has tended to lock poorer countries into production of one or two "cash"

crops. However, cash farming continues to provide badly needed money for some countries, even if the conditions of sale to the urban-industrial world are unfavourable.

- Commercial agriculture creates significant environmental change that goes beyond the simple clearing of land. Soil erosion, deforestation, desertification, and the infiltration of chemicals from fertilizers and pesticides into soils and groundwater are among the greatest concerns.

- Many cities in Canada and around the world were established amid productive farmlands that could supply the needs of their inhabitants. Today, the processes of urban growth and urban sprawl have resulted in the widespread absorption of productive farmlands. In the case of Canada, this is of particular concern, given that only about 5 percent of the country's total land area is made up of dependable farmland.

9.4 How Has Agriculture Influenced Settlement Patterns and the Cultural Landscape?

A pilot flying from the west coast of Canada to the east coast will see the imprint agriculture makes on Canada's cultural landscape. The green circles standing out in arid regions of the country, such as those around the town of Rolling Hills, Alberta (**Figure 9.17**), show where centre-pivot irrigation systems have been in place, providing irrigation to a circle of crops. In turn, the checkerboard pattern on the landscape reflects the cadastral system—the method of land survey by which land ownership and property lines are defined. Cadastral systems were adopted in places where settlement could be regulated by law, and land surveys were crucial to their implementation. The type of survey that prevails throughout much of Canada, and which appears as checkerboards across agricultural fields, is the **rectangular survey system**. The U.S. government adopted the rectangular survey system after the American Revolution as part of a cadastral system known as the **township-and-range system**. This was replicated throughout most of present-day Manitoba, Saskatchewan, and Alberta during the late 1800s and early 1900s. Designed to facilitate the movement of non-Aboriginals across the Canadian prairies, the system imposed a rigid grid-like pattern on the land (**Figure 9.18**). The basic unit was the one-square-mile "section"—land was bought and sold in whole, half, or quarter sections. The lines of each section were drawn without reference

> **Rectangular survey system** Also called the Public Land Survey, the system was used by the U.S. Land Office surveyors to parcel land west of the Appalachian Mountains. The system divides land into a series of rectangular parcels.
>
> **Township-and-range system** A rectangular land division scheme designed by Thomas Jefferson to disperse settlers evenly across farmlands of the U.S. interior.

© 2011 Google, Imagery © 2011 Terra Metrics

FIGURE 9.18 Regina, Saskatchewan, and surrounding agricultural area. The imprint of the township-and-range system that was used to survey and subdivide land throughout western North America is clearly evident in images of land taken from space. At the centre of this photo sits the city of Regina, one of the main service centres for Saskatchewan's agricultural industry.

to the terrain; as a result, they imposed a remarkable uniformity across the land.

Different cadastral patterns predominate in other parts of Canada and the United States. These patterns reflect particular notions of how land should be divided and used. Among the most significant are the **metes and bounds survey system**, adopted along the eastern seaboard, in which natural features are used to demarcate irregular parcels of land. One of the most distinct regional approaches to land division can be found in the Canadian Maritimes and in parts of Quebec, Louisiana, and Texas, where a **long-lot survey system** was implemented. This system divided land into narrow parcels stretching back from rivers, roads, or canals. It reflects a particular approach to surveying that was especially common in the French colonies of North America.

> **Metes and bounds survey system** A system of land surveying, used east of the Appalachian Mountains, that relies on descriptions of land ownership and natural features such as streams or trees. Because of the imprecise nature of metes and bounds surveying, the U.S. Land Office abandoned the technique in favour of the rectangular survey system.
>
> **Long-lot survey system** Distinct regional approach to land surveying found in the Canadian Maritimes, parts of Quebec, Louisiana, and Texas in which land is divided into narrow parcels stretching back from rivers, roads, or canals.

UNDERSTANDING THE SPATIAL LAYOUT OF AGRICULTURE

When commercial agriculture is geared to producing food for people who live in a nearby town or city, a clear geography based on perishability of products and cost of transportation emerges. In the 1800s, Johann Heinrich von Thünen (1783–1850) experienced the Second Agricultural Revolution first-hand: he farmed an estate not far from the town of Rostock, in northeastern

© 2011 Google, Imagery © 2011 Cnes/Spot Image, DigitalGlobe, GeoEye, M.D. of Taber

FIGURE 9.17 Centre-pivot irrigation, Rolling Hills, Alberta. These circles show the unique physical imprint of centre-pivot irrigation. This technique is commonly used where water scarcity or rough terrain necessitate creative approaches to agricultural activity.

Germany. Studying the spatial patterns of farming around towns such as Rostock, von Thünen noted that one commodity or crop generally gave way to another, in succession, as one moved away from the town. He also noted that this process occurred without any visible change in soil, climate, or terrain. When he mapped this pattern, he found that each town or market centre was surrounded by a set of more or less concentric rings within which particular commodities or crops dominated.

Nearest the town, farmers produced commodities that were perishable and commanded high prices, such as dairy products and strawberries. In this zone, von Thünen believed agriculture was practised with a high level of intensity, and much effort went into production, in part because of the value of the land closer to the city. In von Thünen's time, the town was still surrounded by a belt of forest that provided wood for fuel and building; however, immediately beyond the forest, the ring-like pattern of agriculture continued. In the next ring the crops were less perishable and bulkier, including wheat and other grains. Still farther out, livestock began to replace field crops.

Based on his observations, von Thünen built a model of the spatial distribution of agricultural activities. As with all models, he had to make certain assumptions. For example, he assumed that the terrain was flat, that soils and other environmental conditions were the same everywhere, and that there were no barriers to transportation to market. Under such circumstances, he reasoned, the costs of transportation would govern the use of land. He reasoned that the greater the distance to market, the higher the transport costs that had to be added to the cost of producing a crop or commodity. At a given distance to market, then, it would become unprofitable to produce high-cost, perishable commodities, and market gardens would give way to field crops such as grains and potatoes. Still farther away, livestock would replace field agriculture.

The **von Thünen model** (**Figure 9.19**) is often described as the first effort to analyze the spatial character of economic activity. The Thünian patterns discerned in many parts of the world are not solely the result of the forces modelled by von Thünen. Differences in climate type and soil quality heavily influence the kinds of goods produced in a place. However, even when agricultural production does not conform to the concentric rings of von Thünen's model, his underlying concern with the interplay of land use and transportation costs is frequently still determinative.

> **von Thünen model** A model that explains the location of agricultural activities in a commercial, profit-making economy. A process of spatial competition allocates various farming activities into rings around a central market city, with profit-earning capability the determining force in how far a crop locates from the market.

VILLAGES

Throughout this book we have taken note of various core-periphery contrasts that our world presents. Such contrasts are prominent in rural areas as well as urban settings. Traditional farm-village life is still common in India, sub-Saharan Africa, China, and Southeast Asia. In India, for example, farming, much of it subsistence farming, still occupies nearly 70 percent of the population. In the world's core areas, however, agriculture has taken on a very different form, and true farm villages—in which farming or providing services for farmers are the dominant activities—are disappearing. In Canada, where farming once was the leading economic activity, productivity remains high, but only about 2 percent of the labour force remains engaged in agriculture.

Traditionally, the people who lived in villages either farmed the surrounding land or provided services to those who did the farming. Thus, they were closely connected to the land, and most of their livelihoods depended, directly or indirectly, on the cultivation of nearby farmland. These villages tended to reflect historical and environmental conditions. Houses in Japanese farming villages, for example, were so tightly packed together that only the narrowest passageways remained between them. This reflected the need to allocate every possible square foot of land to farming; villages must not use land where crops could grow. On the Canadian prairies, on the other hand, individual farmhouses lay quite far apart in what we call a "dispersed settlement" pattern: the land was intensively cultivated, but by machine rather than by hand. On the populous Indonesian island of Java, villages are still located every kilometre or so along rural roads, and settlement there is defined as nucleated. Land use is just as intense, but the work is done by people and animals. Hence, when we consider the density of human settlement as it relates to the intensity of land use, we should keep in mind the way the land is cultivated. "Nucleated settlement" is by far the most prevalent rural residential pattern in agricultural areas (**Figure 9.20**). When houses are grouped together in tiny

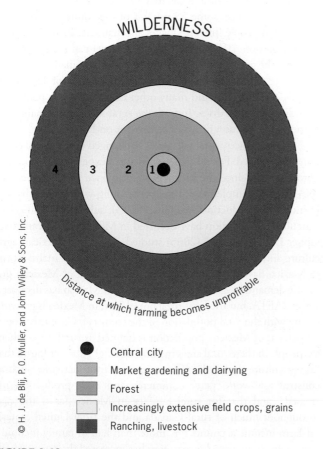

WILDERNESS

Distance at which farming becomes unprofitable

● Central city

Market gardening and dairying

Forest

Increasingly extensive field crops, grains

Ranching, livestock

© H. J. de Blij, P. O. Muller, and John Wiley & Sons, Inc.

FIGURE 9.19 Von Thünen's model.

© Concord Aerial Photo

FIGURE 9.20 Strathclair, Manitoba. The "nucleated settlement," such as that shown in this photo, is by far the most prevalent rural residential pattern in agricultural areas throughout the world.

FIGURE 9.21 Village forms. Examples of five different representative village layouts are shown here. Adapted with permission from J.E. Spencer and W.H. Thomas, *Introducing Cultural Geography.* New York: John Wiley & Sons, Inc., 1978, p. 154.

clusters or hamlets, or in slightly larger clusters we call villages, their spatial arrangement also has significance.

In the hilly regions of Europe, villages were frequently clustered on sloping hillsides, leaving the level land for farming. Often an old castle sat atop the hill, for in earlier times the site offered protection as well as land conservation. In the low-lying areas of western Europe, many villages were located on dikes and levees, so they often took on linear characteristics; the long-lot system used in Quebec fits this description as well (**Figure 9.21a**). Where there was space, a house and outbuildings would have been surrounded by a small garden; the farms and pasturelands lay just beyond. In other cases, a village took on the characteristics of a cluster (**Figure 9.21b**). It might have begun as a small hamlet at the intersection of two roads and then developed by accretion. The European version of the East African circular village, with its central cattle corral, was the round village or rundling (**Figure 9.21c**). This layout was first used by Slavic farmer-herdsmen in eastern Europe and was later modified by Germanic settlers.

In many parts of the world, farm villages were fortified to protect their inhabitants from marauders. Ten thousand years ago, the first farmers in the Fertile Crescent faced attacks from the horsemen of Asia's steppes and clustered together to ward off this danger. In Nigeria's Yorubaland, the farmers would go out into the surrounding fields by day but retreat to the protection of walled villages at night. Villages, as well as larger towns and cities in Europe, were frequently walled and surrounded by moats. When the population became so large that people had to build houses outside the original wall, a new wall would be built to protect them. Walled villages (**Figure 9.21d**) still exist in rural areas of many countries, reminders of a turbulent past.

More modern villages—notably, planned rural settlements—may be arranged on a grid pattern (**Figure 9.21e**). This is not, however, a 20th-century novelty. Centuries ago the Spanish invaders of Central America laid out grid villages and towns, as did other colonial powers elsewhere in the world. In urban Africa, such imprints of colonization are pervasive.

Although the 20th century has witnessed unprecedented urban growth throughout the world, approximately half of the world's people still reside in villages and rural areas. As total world population increases, total population in rural areas is also increasing in many parts of the world (even though the proportion of the total population in rural areas may be stagnant or declining). In China, for instance, some 58 percent of the country's more than 1.35 billion people inhabit villages and hamlets. In India, with a population over 1.15 billion, about 72 percent of the people live in places the government defines as non-urban. Small rural settlements are also home to most of the inhabitants of Indonesia, Bangladesh, Pakistan, and many other countries of the periphery, including those in Africa. Indeed, the agrarian village remains one of the most common forms of settlement on Earth.

In some places, rural villages have changed as the global economy has changed. For example, Mexico has experienced rapid economic change since the North American Free Trade Agreement (NAFTA) was implemented in 1994. Along with major changes in industrial production (see Chapter 13), substantial changes in agricultural production have occurred in Mexico. American geographer Daniel Klooster (2005) studied changes in Mexican agriculture and found that, since 1994, U.S. exports of maize (corn) to Mexico have tripled and "now supply a third of Mexican domestic demand." Agricultural production in Mexico has decreased since NAFTA, but the total rural population in Mexico is growing (along with the total population of the country). Currently, about 24 percent of Mexico's population is defined as rural. How, then, are people in these rural areas making a living? Klooster found that "as agriculture declined, off-farm income from activities such as construction work, petty commerce and craft production increased," and that for rural families in Mexico (as is the case throughout much of rural Canada and the rural United States), off-farm income accounts for "more than half of family income." Decreasing agricultural production has increased the rate at which

Mexicans are migrating to the United States, with many jobless people from rural areas moving to the United States to work and sending remittances home. At the same time, migration from Mexico to Canada has increased significantly since NAFTA came into force. Between 1981 and 2001, the number of Mexicans given permanent or temporary residency in Canada doubled. Interestingly, many of them have migrated in order to fill labour shortages in some parts of Canada's agricultural sector.

REGIONAL AND LOCAL CHANGE

Recent changes in agriculture, such as shifts from subsistence agriculture to commercial agriculture and the decline of the family farm, have had a dramatic impact on rural life throughout the world. Land-use patterns, land-ownership arrangements, agricultural labour conditions, and even intra-community relations have all changed as rural residents cope with shifting economic, political, and environmental conditions. In Latin America, huge increases in the production of export crops (cash crops like fruits and coffee) have occurred at the expense of crop production for local consumption. In the process, subsistence farming has been pushed to ever more marginal lands. In Asia, where the Green Revolution has had the greatest impact, the production of cereal crops (i.e., grains such as rice and wheat) has increased for both foreign and domestic markets. Agricultural production in this region remains relatively small in scale and depends on manual labour. In sub-Saharan Africa, total commercialized agriculture has increased, but overall agricultural exports have decreased. As in Asia, farm units in sub-Saharan Africa have remained relatively small and dependent on intensified manual labour.

What this regional-scale analysis does not tell us is how these changes have affected local rural communities. These changes can be environmental, economic, and social. For example, a study by Judith Carney in the small West African country of Gambia has shown how changing agricultural practices have altered not only the rural environment and economy but also relations between men and women (**Figure 9.22**). Over the last several decades, international developmental assistance in Gambia has funded ambitious projects designed to convert wetlands to irrigated agricultural lands, making possible the production of rice year-round. By the late 1980s, virtually all of the country's suitable wetlands had been converted to year-round rice production. This transformation created tensions within rural households by converting lands women traditionally used for family subsistence into commercialized farming plots. In addition, when rice production was turned into a year-round occupation, women found themselves with less time for other activities crucial for household maintenance.

This situation underscores the fact that in Africa, as in much of the rest of the less-industrialized world, agricultural work is overwhelmingly carried out by women. In fact, more than half of all food produced worldwide is produced by women farmers. Women also make up some 43 percent of the global agricultural labour force. In sub-Saharan Africa, over 85 percent of all women in the labour force work in agriculture; in China the number is close to 75 percent, and in India 70 percent. A geographical perspective that is sensitive to scale helps shed light on how changes in agricultural practices throughout the world not only alter rural landscapes but also affect family and community relationships.

GUEST FIELD NOTE

Gambia

I am interested in women and rural development in sub-Saharan Africa. In 1983, I went to Gambia to study an irrigated rice project that was being implemented to improve the availability of rice, the dietary staple. What grabbed my attention? The donors' assurance that the project would benefit women, the country's traditional rice growers. Imagine my surprise, a few months after the project was implemented, when I encountered hundreds of angry women refusing to work because they received nothing for their labour from the first harvest.

In registering women's traditional rice plots as "family" land, project officials effectively sabotaged the equity objectives of the donors. Male heads of households held control of "family" land, and they reaped the income produced by female labour. Contemporary economic strategies for Africa depend increasingly upon labour intensification. But whose labour? Human geography provides a way of seeing the significance of gender in the power relations that mediate culture, environment, and economic development.

Judith Carney, University of California, Los Angeles

FIGURE 9.22 Women cultivating rice in Gambia.

A 2014 study by the advocacy group One, and the World Bank, indicates that there is a significant gender gap in agricultural farming in Africa. Although women comprise more than 50 percent of the workforce, the study found that their production levels were significantly lower than those of men. Comparing the farming levels of men and women in similar-sized lots in Ethiopia, Malawi, Niger, Nigeria, Tanzania, and Uganda, the study found that women's production rates were anywhere from 23 percent to 66 percent lower. Researchers attribute this disparity to a variety of factors, including the fact that women have less access to extra labour than men; less access to, and use of, seeds and fertilizers; and less time in the day due to their domestic responsibilities. Cultural forces play a significant role here; the study pointed to political indifference and cultural constraints as the reasons for the gender gap in agricultural production. Among the recommendations of the report: strengthen women's land rights, provide childcare facilities, offer education to women, support women's access to markets, and increase their access to quality seeds and fertilizer. Advocates argue that policies that support women in agriculture through the above initiatives are the best way to directly address these issues.

GUEST FIELD NOTE

Gravelbourg, Saskatchewan

To many people, the town of Gravelbourg, Saskatchewan, appeared to be at serious risk of disappearing from Canada's prairie landscape in the early 1990s, a victim of changing demographics, a globalizing agricultural economy, and a preference for urban living. But an aggressive program of grassroots-based community development and activism, made possible by the town's rich stock of historical, social, and cultural resources, helped save this community. In recent years, Gravelbourg (population 1,200) has experienced economic and population growth at a time when many other prairie agricultural communities are turning into "ghost towns." Gravelbourg's success story has captured the attention of media outlets across Canada, as well as interested professionals, local community organizations, and politicians at all levels of government.

The community economic development approach emphasizes the pursuit of a variety of economic, social, cultural, and environmental objectives through the grassroots-based planning and implementation of projects. Gravelbourg's community economic development success story, which began in 1998, has been referred to as "hyperactive," with the town experiencing significant population and economic growth in the past few years. This itself is surprising, given its relatively remote location in the heart of the Canadian prairies and the fact that many other communities in the same region have shrunk considerably in size. These positive changes include: the retention of residents and the attraction of new ones (including over 250 newcomers between 2006 and 2008 alone); the purchase, expansion, and renovation of several existing businesses and the creation of several new ones; and significant growth in levels of tourism activity. In my interviews with over a dozen key informants in Gravelbourg between 2005 and 2010, many attribute the town's revitalization to the broad range of community-based initiatives implemented over the past decade. Various community economic development initiatives—beautification projects, a Main Street revitalization strategy, the enhancement of local tourism resources, and the hosting of numerous special events—created a high "quality-of-place" in Gravelbourg, which in turn heightened people's perceptions of the quality of life that the community had to offer.

Arguably, much of Gravelbourg's success can be attributed to the abundance of "social capital" found within the community. Gravelbourg is replete with citizens who are committed to their community, who are more than willing to volunteer their time and money for community projects and events, and who make efforts to ensure that all members of the community can participate if they wish. This strong cohesiveness and commitment to Gravelbourg has clearly influenced residents' desire and ability to ensure their community remains an attractive place to live.

One cannot assume that what works in one place will always work in another. In Gravelbourg's case, for example, the success of the town's community economic development efforts cannot be considered without also thinking about the multitude of local "place-based" resources that residents have been able to harness. For instance, tourism has boomed due to the presence of several national and provincially designated historic sites—many related to the town's former role as an important centre for the French-Canadian Roman Catholic Church (**Figure 9.23**)—and culturally themed

© Christopher Fullerton

FIGURE 9.23 Our Lady of the Assumption Cathedral, Gravelbourg. This majestic church, a National Historic Site, has played a central role in the development of a thriving tourism economy in Gravelbourg as it adjusts to its reduced role as an agricultural service centre.

community events building on Gravelbourg's multicultural diversity. The town's most significant business development, the creation of a new mustard milling and processing facility driven by local and regional financial investments, was a natural choice due to Gravelbourg's location at the centre of the world's largest mustard-growing region. Whether Gravelbourg's remarkable community revitalization story is exceptional, or if it is an approach that can be replicated in other rural places, remains to be seen.

Christopher Fullerton, Brock University

FOOD SECURITY

Despite the many advancements made in agriculture through the First, Second, and Third Agricultural Revolutions, a sizable proportion of the world's population still suffers from a lack of nutritious food. In fact, food security remains a major development concern in all countries, core and peripheral. According to the World Food Summit (FAO 1996), **food security** "exists when all people, at all times, have physical and economic access to sufficient, safe and nutritious food that meets their dietary needs and food preferences for an active and healthy life." There are several reasons why people might suffer from a lack of food security. Access to food can be seriously affected by factors such as their levels of access to agricultural lands, land tenure issues, post-harvest losses, the increasing cost of farm inputs, lack of proper transport infrastructure, violent conflict, rainfall variability, and a lack of available water for irrigation. However, food security is not just about the availability of food, but also depends on the ability of people to acquire enough food for a nutritious diet. Thus, poverty and lack of income-generating opportunities have also been identified as strong drivers of food insecurity.

> **Food security** Situation where all people, at all times, have physical and economic access to sufficient, safe, and nutritious food that meets their dietary needs and food preferences for an active and healthy life.

As noted above, food security issues prevail around the world. In fact, it has been estimated that about 7 percent of Canadian households and almost 13 percent of American households are food insecure (Nord & Hopwood, 2008), contributing to an increase in nutrition-related ailments such as obesity and compromised psychosocial functioning (Olson, 1999). However, the most extensive cases of food insecurity are typically found in peripheral regions. According to the Food and Agriculture Organization of the United Nations (FAO), approximately 900 million people suffered from hunger in 2010. The FAO identified 22 countries as being in "protracted crisis" for the period from 1996 to 2010, with 17 of these located in Africa. More recently, Kenya was hit by a major food crisis in August 2011, during which 3.75 million people were identified as being food insecure. Although the food crisis was initially triggered by extended drought conditions, political issues are what made the situation worse. Conflicts in Somalia impeded the migration of pastoralists to locations where they could graze their livestock, while a poor and disorganized government response prevented aid from being distributed to affected people in a timely and efficient manner.

ALTERNATIVE FOOD INITIATIVES

Growing concerns about the nature of today's commercial agricultural production methods and the widespread prevalence of food insecurity, as well as the social and environmental consequences of these issues, have prompted the adoption of community food initiatives and alternative food initiatives in many places. These include attempts to reconnect farmers and consumers (for example, through the operation of farmers' markets) and to increase marginalized urban eaters' access to healthy food (for example, through urban agriculture projects).

FARMERS' MARKETS

Geographers interested in agricultural issues have begun to focus on the growing number of farmers' markets across North America. These markets have been identified as part of a broader consumer trend in which people are actively seeking to engage in more local food consumption. They are also seen as bringing numerous benefits to communities, including creating a focal point that fosters social interaction between neighbours and between farmers and their customers, and helping to strengthen the local economy. Researchers have also noted that when a farmers' market is located in a low-income or minority neighbourhood, it can help local residents procure a healthy diet by improving access to nutritious foods that may otherwise not be available in nearby stores. In an economic sense, farmers' markets are seen as an important alternative to the widespread commercial agricultural systems that are dominated by agribusiness. More specifically, they provide opportunities for small family farms to remain profitable by enabling direct farmer-to-consumer sale of farm goods, thus eliminating steps between themselves as producers and the consumer.

URBAN AGRICULTURE

Urban agriculture is generally defined as the practice of growing crops and grazing livestock in urban, suburban, and peri-urban areas. By growing food in or near urban areas, farmers can more effectively deliver food to people and reduce the environmental costs of agriculture, especially the costs involved in transporting food. From subsistence backyard gardening in Harare to for-profit rooftop greenhouses in North America urban agriculture involves a wide range of people and practices. A widely cited 1996 survey estimated that about 800 million people (about 15 percent of the world population at that time) were involved in urban agriculture (UNDP 1996).

ORGANIC FOOD

Consumers have also sought to deal with concerns about contemporary agricultural practices by purchasing organic produce. Organic farming attempts to enhance the health and vitality of the soil, preserving biodiversity, promoting animal welfare, and preserving the ecological integrity of the natural environment. In order to achieve these goals, **organic products** are raised, grown, stored, and/or processed without the use of synthetic chemicals or fertilizers; herbicides, insecticides, fungicides, or any other pesticides; growth hormones; or growth regulators.

> **Organic products** Products that are raised, grown, stored, and/or processed without the use of synthetic chemicals or fertilizers; herbicides, insecticides, fungicides, or any other pesticides; growth hormones; or growth regulators.

The growing popularity of organic products has led to the establishment of international regulation for organic farming. In order to label their products as organic, farmers must produce their food according to a set of standards, undergo evaluation by other certified growers, and pass a yearly inspection by a trained independent inspector. According to the Worldwatch Institute, 84 countries had put formal organic regulations into place by 2010.

Organic farming is practised throughout the world. Data compiled by the Worldwatch Institute show that organic farming—including that which is certified, uncertified, or on lands in the midst of transitioning from non-organic to organic production—was conducted on 37.2 million hectares of land in 2009, a threefold increase since 1999. Over 1.8 million producers were involved in this activity, with India being home to over 677,000 of them. Uganda (188,000) and Mexico (129,000) had the second- and third-highest numbers of organic producers, respectively. Most operations in these three countries were uncertified; for the most part, *certified* organic agricultural activities are concentrated in the world's developed countries.

MAIN POINTS 9.4 How Has Agriculture Influenced Settlement Patterns and the Cultural Landscape?

- A society's norms for property ownership are reflected in the landscape. Property ownership is symbolized by landscapes in which parcels of land are divided into neat, clearly demarcated segments. The size and order of those parcels are heavily influenced by the cadastral system (the method of land survey by which land ownership and property lines are defined).

- Although the 20th century saw unprecedented urban growth throughout the world, approximately half of the world's people still reside in villages and rural areas. Indeed, the agrarian village remains one of the most common forms of settlement on Earth.

- Traditional farm-village life remains especially common in much of the world's periphery, where agriculture is often still the most prominent economic activity. In the world's core areas, on the other hand, true farm villages, in which farming or providing services for farmers are the dominant activities, are disappearing. This has forced many agricultural communities to find new development opportunities as they adjust to these changing circumstances.

- Growing concerns about the social, environmental, and economic costs of contemporary agricultural practices have prompted alternative food initiatives, such as farmers' markets and urban agriculture projects. These have helped to reduce the social and physical distance between farmers and consumers, while at the same time having numerous environmental benefits.

SUMMARY

Agricultural production has changed drastically since the First Agricultural Revolution, but not to the same extent in all places around the world. In many parts of the world, especially in peripheral regions, agricultural practices remain the same as they have been for hundreds of years. Hundreds of millions of farmers around the world are involved in subsistence agriculture, growing only enough food, on small plots of land and through heavily labour-intensive means, to sustain themselves and their families. In many other parts of the world, however, agriculture has become heavily industrialized and spurred the growth of agribusiness. Today, agricultural products, even perishable ones, are routinely shipped thousands of kilometres and from one continent to another. At the same time, however, agriculture in the globalized economy is complicated by concerns about new technologies, environmental degradation, genetically engineered crops, cultural change, government involvement, and the lasting impacts of history. This has prompted the adoption of alternative food initiatives that seek to reconnect farmers and consumers through the development of more local and personal relationships, such as those established at farmers' markets and by urban agriculture projects.

DISCUSSION AND REVIEW QUESTIONS

1. The most significant events in the history of humanity are arguably the agricultural and animal domestication revolutions. Where did the first revolutions take place and why did they occur in those locations? What were some of the specific impacts of the revolutions?

2. Since its inception, the agricultural revolution has evolved into a second and third phase. Compare and contrast the so-called Second Agricultural Revolution with the Third Agricultural Revolution. Further, how do the two evolutionary phases compare and contrast spatially?

3. Discuss whether or not the "green revolution" has been a success or a failure, and provide reasons for either case.

4. Commercial agriculture has come to dominate the world's economic core. Discuss how and where commercial agriculture developed, as well as its various forms. How has commercial agriculture impacted the environment?

5. Beginning with Johann Heinrich von Thünen, identify and discuss the various ways geographers have tried to understand the spatial layout of agricultural systems. Geographers are also interested in the cultural landscapes of agricultural systems. Explain the various systems that have profoundly shaped the North American landscape.

GEOGRAPHIC CONCEPTS

agribusiness   258
agriculture   247
animal domestication   250
commercial agriculture   258
First Agricultural Revolution   248
food security   271
genetically modified organisms (GMOs)   255
Green Revolution   254
livestock ranching   262
long-lot survey system   266
luxury crops   260
Mediterranean agriculture   262
metes and bounds survey system   266

monoculture   258
organic products   272
plant domestication   248
plantation agriculture   259
rectangular survey system   266
root crops   248
Second Agricultural Revolution   253
seed crops   248
shifting cultivation   251
subsistence agriculture   251
Third Agricultural Revolution   253
township-and-range system   266
von Thünen model   267

ADDITIONAL RESOURCES ON-LINE

Food and Agriculture Organization of the United Nations: www.fao.org

2011 Census of Agriculture, Statistics Canada: www.statcan.gc.ca/eng/ca2011/index

About genetically modified organisms: www.gmo-compass.org
United Nations Office on Drugs and Crime: www.unodc.org
Fairtrade Canada: www.transfair.ca
Canadian Water Network: www.cwn-rce.ca

CHAPTER
10 URBAN GEOGRAPHY

Rising from the Ruins

KNOWN AS THE "MOTOR CITY," Detroit is one of the United States' most iconic cities. It has been home to the "big three" automakers, General Motors, Ford, and Chrysler, and in its heyday, it was a bustling international urban centre (**Figure 10.1**). Its population grew quickly, from 285,000 in 1900, to over 1.5 million in 1950, and at one time it was the fourth-largest city in the United States. People flocked to Detroit as the auto industry grew and prospered, while labour unions improved working conditions, establishing the eight-hour workday and minimum wage. It had a thriving arts community, with the Detroit Opera House, and the Museum of Art, which opened in 1888. Buildings were grandiose, including luxury hotels where presidents and auto industry executives stayed, and parks were scenic and filled with people.

The population of Detroit has fallen from 1.5 million in 1950 to 700,000 in 2013, making it now approximately the same size as it was in 1920, before the city's automotive boom. In many ways, Detroit's population rose and fell with the automotive industry, and as the auto industry changed—with offshore "just in time" production, and technological changes including automation—so too did the need for assembly line labour. The city also experienced massive change in the 1950s, with the rise of the suburbs. People left urban centres, seeking opportunities for home ownership in suburban places outside Detroit proper.

In the last decade, Detroit has become iconic in a different way, as its population continues to decline. Some of the recent population loss has been attributed to middle-class African Americans leaving the city, looking for better schools and safer streets for their children. The mass exodus from the city by industry and people alike has resulted in swaths of abandoned buildings, increased poverty, and a new kind of tourism called "ruins porn." Photographers have flocked to the city, seeking to find beauty in urban decay.

These pictures depict haunting images of abandoned factories such as the Detroit Book Depository, Michigan Central Station, and the Packard Automotive Plant, a 3.5-million-square-foot car-manufacturing plant, built in 1911. With as many as 85,000 abandoned buildings, from grand hotels to simple bungalows, there is no lack of subject matter for these photographers. These abandoned spaces are also challenges to the residents of Detroit, policy-makers, and city planners as the city seeks to rebuild itself. In 2014 the administration of U.S. President Barack Obama issued a report recommending that Detroit spend $850 million to raze over 40,000 abandoned homes (**Figure 10.2**), which have, as local Detroit photographer James D. Griffioen puts it, gone "feral". These recommendations, if followed, would drastically change the face of the city.

Detroit Publishing Company collection, Prints & Photographs Division, Library of Congress

FIGURE 10.1 Downtown Detroit in the early 1900s.

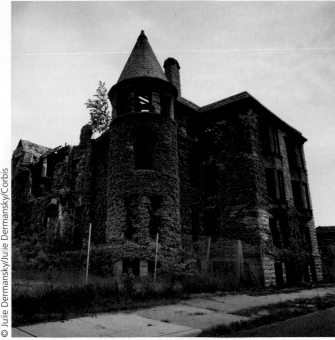

FIGURE 10.2 Detroit's abandoned homes.

Urban geographers study cities such as Detroit; they also study how governments work to build and rebuild cities, and they try to understand the interlinkages between political, social, and cultural geography and urban geography. We must remember that cities do not simply grow; sometimes they decline as well. How cities such as Detroit evolve is complex, involving economic, social, cultural, geographic, and political factors. Since it went bankrupt in 2013, Detroit has sought to reimagine itself as a smaller city than it once was. With beautiful historic buildings, some of the United States' most famous artworks and sculptures, a vibrant arts and cultural community, successful sports franchises, a growing tourist industry, and an active, engaged community, the spaces of the city will continue to evolve and change. As geographers, we are interested in tracing the evolution of urbanization in geographic context; in understanding how economic, cultural, and political factors influence the shaping of a city's form and function; and in studying how people live, work, and play in the cities they create.

Heather Maguire, doctoral candidate, York University

KEY QUESTIONS FOR CHAPTER 10

1. When and why did people start living in cities?

2. Where are cities located, and why?

3. How are cities organized, and how do they function?

4. How do cities evolve?

5. What is the connection between cities and globalization?

10.1 When and Why Did People Start Living in Cities?

Cities hold a prominent place in our imaginations. Perhaps you hope to travel to one or more of the world's most famous cities, such as Montreal, New York, Paris, or Beijing. You can probably recognize the more well-known city skylines in **Figure 10.3** even though you may never have been there. You may live in the suburbs or rural areas surrounding a major Canadian city, such as Ottawa or Calgary, and view a trip into the city centre for shopping or the theatre with a sense of adventure and excitement. Cities are centres of political and economic power, administration and government, technological innovation, and artistic achievement. They are the location of dominant economic markets, centres of specialization and interaction, sources of news and information, suppliers of services, and providers of sports and entertainment. Cities are the anchors of modern culture; urban systems and their spokes form the structural skeleton of society. Former Toronto mayor David Miller summed up the importance of Canadian cities in a 2010 editorial in the *Toronto Star*, stating, "As our large cities go, so goes the nation. When we succeed, the province and the country succeed." Geographical study of cities and urban areas straddles subdisciplinary boundaries, drawing on political and economic geography, social and cultural geographies, and other disciplinary work on humans and the built environment.

We can define a **city** as a conglomeration of people and buildings clustered together to serve as a centre of politics,

> **City** Conglomeration of people and buildings clustered together to serve as a centre of politics, culture, and economics.

©iStockphoto.com/IVYPHOTOS

(a)

©iStockphoto.com/Kokkai Ng

(b)

©iStockphoto.com/Adam Petto

(c)

FIGURE 10.3 Distinctive city skylines. (a) Toronto, Ontario; (b) Sydney, Australia; (c) London, England.

culture, and economics. As of 2011, 81 percent of Canadians lived in urban areas, with half of them living in Canada's four major cities. In this context, Statistics Canada defines "urban" as a combination of total population (at least 1,000) and density (at least 400 persons per square kilometre).

Virtually everywhere in the world we discover the same pattern as the one we see in Canada. People are moving from the countryside to urbanized areas—to towns, cities, and suburbs. Globally, more people live in towns and cities than in rural areas, making the global population predominantly **urban**, a term we use to describe the build-up of the central city and the **suburban realm**, which refers to the surrounding environs connected to the city. An urban place is distinctively non-rural and non-agricultural. The movement of people from rural to urban locations reflects the changing global economy (Chapter 2) and the increasing ease of movement in our globalized world (Chapter 5). Urbanization is happening everywhere; however, the distribution of urbanization across the globe is not even. **Figure 10.4** illustrates the population densities of urban areas in the six main regions of the world. The most densely populated urban areas in the world—those with over 10 million people—can be found in Latin America and the Caribbean (14 percent) and Asia (10 percent). The least densely populated urban areas, with fewer than 500,000 residents, can be found in Europe (68 percent) and Africa (58 percent). Oceania does not have any urban centres with more than 5 million people, which is somewhat similar to Canada, where only one urban area, the Greater Toronto Area, has a population of more than 5 million. Other major urban areas in Canada—Montreal, Vancouver, and Ottawa-Gatineau—each have a population between 1 and 5 million.

Despite our sense that much of the global population lives in cities, it is important to remember that over half of the world's population lives in cities of fewer than 500,000 people. On the other hand, some cities in the world are what we would now term **mega-cities**, having populations of over 10 million inhabitants. These are more properly understood as **urban agglomerations**, defined by the United Nations as those populations of 1 million or more people "within a contiguous territory inhabited at urban levels of residential density." In the past, urban agglomerations were centred in North America and Europe. However, there is a growing number of urban agglomerations in Latin America, Africa, and Asia, and this is expected to continue to increase in the future.

In this chapter, we focus on the processes of urbanization—how and why people began living in cities, and how cities change over time. We are interested in why cities are located where they are and the reasons for their internal form and function. We also consider how cities evolve and how their relationships with each other vary across a variety of scales—local, regional, national, and global. Urban geographers, with their spatial perspective, focus on the location of cities, their regional

> **Urban (area)** The entire built-up, non-rural area and its population, including the most recently constructed suburban appendages. Provides a better picture of the dimensions and population of such an area than the delimited municipality (central city) that forms its heart.
>
> **Suburban realm** The surrounding environs connected to the city.

> **Mega-city** A city having a population of more than 10 million inhabitants.
>
> **Urban agglomerations** Defined by the United Nations as those populations of 1 million or more people "within a contiguous territory inhabited at urban levels of residential density."

UN Department of Economic and Social Affairs

FIGURE 10.4 Distribution of urban populations by size of urban settlement, major areas, 2007. Source: From the United Nations, Department of Economic and Social Affairs, Population Division, Urban Agglomerations, 2007, www.un.org/esa/populatlon/publicatlons/wup2007/2007_urban_agglomerations_chart.pdf.

interconnections, movements between and within cities, and the sense of place people have about cities and the landscapes they inhabit.

THE HEARTHS OF URBANIZATION

The process of urbanization, which can happen so quickly today, originally took thousands of years to develop; indeed, the rise of the city is a very recent phenomenon in human history. While human communities have existed for over 100,000 years, more than 90,000 years of human existence passed before people began to cluster more densely in villages and towns. Archaeological evidence indicates that people established the first cities about 8,000 years ago. However, it is only in the last 200 years that cities began to assume their modern size and structure.

Scholars argue that there were essentially two urban revolutions. The first, beginning about 3500 BCE, was driven by shifts in technology associated with agricultural production and changing social relations. The second, occurring in the core region about 500 CE, resulted from rapid technological and scientific advances related to the Industrial Revolution. Before people could live in cities, they had to switch from a hunting and gathering society to an agricultural one. This switch was the result of improved technologies and new forms of social order and social relations. As we discussed in Chapter 9, agricultural advances, including the domestication of animals and the planting and harvesting of crops, began between 10,000 and 12,000 years ago, allowing people to become more sedentary, staying in one place to tend their fields. People clustered in small **agricultural villages** and towns, living there year round. The dwellings in

> **Agricultural village**
> A relatively small, egalitarian village, where most of the population was involved in agriculture. Starting over 10,000 years ago, people began to cluster in agricultural villages as they stayed in one place to tend their crops.

ancient agricultural villages were all about the same size and contained about the same number of possessions, reflecting the egalitarian nature of such societies, in which people shared goods in common and lived at near-subsistence levels.

Egalitarian societies persisted long after agriculture began. When urban areas of some size and population began to develop, however, the egalitarian social order began to change as well. In cities, people, mainly men, engaged in trade over long distances, pursued a diversity of economic activities—not just agriculture—and generated material wealth that was owned by the individual. This led to changing social and political structures, including the development of differing social classes and methods of governance. Archaeologists, anthropologists, and geographers studying the remains and records of the first cities have developed numerous theories on how cities came about. Most agree that some series of events led to the establishment of two main components that allowed early cities to form—**agricultural surplus** and **social stratification**—although which came first varies by theory. The series of events spurring these two components also varies according to the theory proposed.

One theory maintains that advances in technology, such as irrigation, generated an agricultural surplus; then a leadership class, largely made up of men, formed to control the surplus as well as the technology that produced it. Another theory holds that a king or priest-king centralized political power and then demanded more labour to generate an agricultural surplus, which would help the ruler retain political power.

> **Agricultural surplus** Agricultural production in excess of that which the producer needs for his or her own sustenance and that of his or her family and which is then sold for consumption by others. One of two components, together with social stratification, that enable the formation of cities.
>
> **Social stratification** The differentiation of society into classes based on wealth, power, production, and prestige. One of two components, together with agricultural surplus, that enables the formation of cities.

The **leadership class**, or urban elite, consisted of a group of male decision-makers and organizers who controlled the resources, and often the lives, of others. Generating an agricultural surplus allowed some to devote their efforts to pursuits besides agriculture, such as religion and philosophy, out of which came the concepts of writing and record keeping. Writing made possible the codification of laws, the keeping of accurate records of trade and commerce, and the preservation of traditions. Urban elites saw to the defence of the city (and the preservation and protection of trade, commerce, and wealth) by constructing walls, controlling access to the city, and maintaining a standing army. The leadership class was also able to collect taxes and tribute from people under their control beyond the city walls in order to pay for a growing administration.

> **Leadership class** Group of decision-makers and organizers in early cities who controlled the resources, and often the lives, of others.

THE FIRST URBAN REVOLUTION

> **First urban revolution** The innovation of the city, which occurred independently in as many as six separate hearths.

Some cities grew out of agricultural villages; others grew in places previously unoccupied by sedentary people. The innovation of the city is called the **first urban revolution**, and it occurred independently in as many as six separate hearths (**Figure 10.5**). It is important to note that scholars do not agree on the number of hearths. Those who argue that there are fewer than six hearths attribute more urbanization to diffusion. In each of the urbanization hearths, something triggered the establishment of a leadership class and

an agricultural surplus. People became engaged in economic activities beyond agriculture, including specialty crafts, the military, trade, and government.

Not surprisingly, the six urban hearths are tied closely to the hearths of agriculture. The first hearth of agriculture, the Fertile Crescent, is the first place we see cities, in about 3500 BCE. This urban hearth is called **Mesopotamia** and is the region of great cities, such as Ur and Babylon, located between the Tigris and Euphrates rivers (**Figure 10.6**). Studies of the cultural landscape of Mesopotamian cities have found signs of social inequality in the varying sizes and ornamentation of houses. Urban geographers use concepts like **urban morphology**, which refers to the layout (physical form and structure) of a city, when they study urban areas in order to understand how states build and rebuild cities, and to recognize the linkages between political geography and urban geography.

> **Mesopotamia** Region of great cities (e.g., Ur and Babylon) located between the Tigris and Euphrates Rivers; chronologically the first urban hearth, dating to 3500 BCE, which was founded in the Fertile Crescent.
>
> **Urban morphology** The study of the physical form and structure of urban places.

In Mesopotamia, male urban elites erected palaces, protected themselves with walls, and employed countless artisans to beautify their spaces. They also established a priest-king class and developed a religious-political ideology to support the priest-kings. The ancient Mesopotamian city was usually protected by a mud wall surrounding the entire community. Temples dominated the urban landscape, not only because they were the largest structures in town but also because they were built on artificial mounds that were often over 30 metres high. Male priests and other authorities resided in substantial

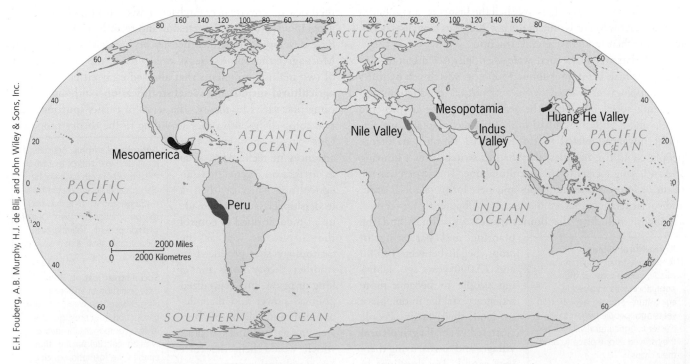

FIGURE 10.5 Six hearths of urbanization.

E.H. Fouberg, A.B. Murphy, H.J. de Blij, and John Wiley & Sons, Inc.

FIGURE 10.6 Babylon. (a) The city-state of Babylon was located approximately 85 kilometres south of Baghdad. This map shows the area as it was in the time of Hammurabi, king of Babylon from 1792 BCE to 1750 BCE. (b) In 1983, the ruler of Iraq, Saddam Hussein, began a reconstruction project on the grounds of the ruins of Babylon, visible in this aerial view from Google Earth in 2004.

buildings, many of which might be called palaces. Ordinary citizens lived in mud-walled houses packed closely together and separated only by narrow lanes. The poorest inhabitants lived in tiny huts, often with mud-smeared reed walls, on the outskirts of the city. The leadership class held slaves in prison-like accommodations that were sometimes outside the city wall. Lacking waste-disposal or sewage facilities, ancient cities were far from sanitary: Mesopotamians threw their garbage and waste into the streets and other open spaces, where it might accumulate to a depth of several metres. As a result, disease kept the populations of ancient cities small. Archaeologists have been able to sift through the garbage for clues to life in the ancient city.

The second hearth of urbanization, dating back to 3200 BCE, is the **Nile River Valley**. Some scholars contend that this region is not a hearth but, rather, a case of diffusion from Mesopotamia, although other evidence strongly supports the claim that there was independent invention of urbanization in the Nile River Valley. At the very least, the interrelationship between urbanization and irrigation in this region distinguishes it from other urban hearths. Unlike residents of other early cities, the people of the Nile River Valley did not build walls around their cities. From early on, power along the river was concentrated in the hands of the men who controlled the irrigation systems. The absence of walls around individual cities reflects the singular control of the region. The might of the rulers of the Nile River Valley is reflected in the feats of architecture such as the pyramids, tombs, and sphinx that were built by thousands of slaves.

The third urban hearth, dating to 2200 BCE, is the **Indus River Valley**, another place where agriculture likely

Nile River Valley Chronologically, the second urban hearth, dating to 3200 BCE.

Indus River Valley Chronologically, the third urban hearth, dating to 2200 BCE.

diffused from the Fertile Crescent. Unable to decipher ancient Indus writing, scholars are puzzled by the characteristics of Harappa and Mohenjo-Daro, the first cities of this hearth (**Figure 10.7**). The intricate planning of the cities points to the existence of a leadership class, but the houses continued to be equal in size, with no palaces or monuments appearing in the cities. In addition, all the dwellings in the cities had access to the same infrastructure—including wastewater drains and carefully maintained stone-lined wells. The cities had thick walls, and the discovery of coins from as far away as the Mediterranean at the gateways in these walls points to significant trade over long distances.

The fourth urban hearth arose around the confluence of the **Huang He (Yellow) River Valley** and **Wei (Yangtze) River Valley** of present-day China, dating to 1500 BCE. The Chinese purposefully planned their ancient cities to centre on a vertical structure in the middle of the city and then built an inner wall around it. Within the inner wall, the people of this hearth typically placed temples and palaces for the leadership class. The urban elite of the Huang He and Wei region, like the urban elite of the Nile River Valley, demonstrated their power by building enormous, elaborate structures. Around 200 BCE, the Emperor Qin Xi Huang directed the building of the Great Wall of China. Like the Egyptians, he also had an elaborate mausoleum built for himself (**Figure 10.8**).

Chronologically, the fifth urban hearth is **Mesoamerica**, dating to 200 BCE. The male urban elite in Mesoamerica

Huang He (Yellow) River Valley and **Wei (Yangtze) River Valley** Chronologically, the fourth urban hearth, established around 1500 BCE, at the confluence of the Huang He and Wei rivers of present-day China.

Mesoamerica Chronologically, the fifth urban hearth, dating to 200 BCE.

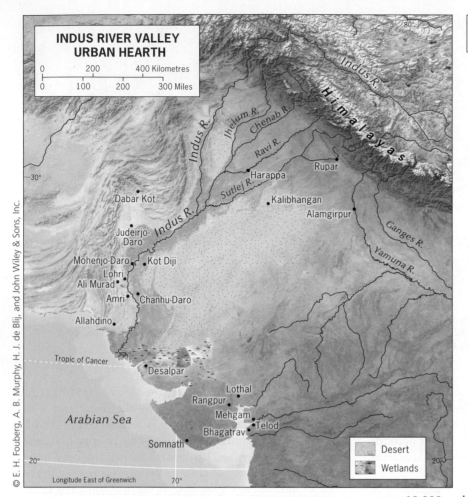

FIGURE 10.7 The urban hearth in the Indus River Valley.

FIGURE 10.8 Terracotta warriors guarding the tomb of the Chinese emperor Qin Xi Huang. An estimated 700,000 slaves worked for over 40 years, around 200 BCE, to craft more than 7,000 terracotta warriors who stand guard over the emperor's tomb.

Peru Chronologically, the sixth urban hearth, dating to 900 BCE.

augmented their authority with priests, temples, and shrines, and many ancient cities in the region were religious centres, where rulers were deemed to have divine authority and were, in effect, god-kings. Examples of these theocratic centres include the great structures of Yucatan, Guatemala, and Honduras (including Tikal, Chichén Itza, Uxmal, and Copán in **Figure 10.9**) built by the Maya Indians.

The most recent archaeological evidence establishes **Peru** as the sixth urban hearth, chronologically. The Chavín built cities in Peru dating to 900 BCE. The largest settlement, Chavín, was sited at an elevation of 10,530 feet (3,200 metres) in the Andean highlands.

How large were the ancient cities? We have only estimates, given that it is nearly impossible to judge the dimensions of a city at its height, or the number of people who might have occupied each residential unit, from excavated ruins. By modern standards, the ancient cities were not particularly large. The cities of Mesopotamia and the Nile River Valley are thought to have had between 10,000 and 15,000 inhabitants after nearly 2,000 years of growth and development. That number of people is thought to be about the maximum sustainable size based on existing systems of social organization and food production, gathering, and distribution. These urban places were geographical exceptions in an overwhelmingly rural world.

DIFFUSION OF URBANIZATION

Urbanization diffused from Mesopotamia in several directions. Populations in Mesopotamia grew with the steady food supply and a sedentary lifestyle. People migrated out from the hearth, diffusing their knowledge of agriculture and urbanization. Diffusion from Mesopotamia happened quite early in the process, and mainly before agriculture developed independently in some other hearths. In fact, urbanization diffused to the Mediterranean from Mesopotamia (and perhaps from the Nile River Valley) more than 3,500 years ago, at about the same time cities were developing in the hearth of the Huang He, and long before cities emerged in Mesoamerica.

GREEK CITIES

More than 3,500 years ago, the city of Knossos, on what is now the Greek island of Crete, was the cornerstone of a system of towns in the Minoan civilization. By 500 BCE, Greece had become one of the most highly urbanized areas on Earth, and the

FIGURE 10.9 Maya and Aztec domains Unlike the urban hearths of the eastern hemisphere, many of the earliest cities in the Americas were founded in the highlands.

urbanization of ancient Greece ushered in a new stage in the evolution of cities. At its height, ancient Greece encompassed a network of more than 500 cities and towns, not only on the mainland but also on the many Greek islands. Seafarers connected these urban places with trade routes and carried the notion of urban life throughout the Mediterranean region. Athens and Sparta soon became Greece's leading cities, often vying with each other for power. Athens may have been the largest city in the world at the time, with an estimated 250,000 inhabitants.

> **Agora** In ancient Greece, public spaces where citizens debated, lectured, judged each other, planned military campaigns, socialized, and traded.

In Ancient Greece, cities had public spaces designed to be more open and spacious. They were often in a low part of town, with steps leading down to them. On these steps, the men in Greek society debated, lectured, judged each other, planned military campaigns, and socialized. As time went on, this public space, called the **agora** (meaning "market"), also became the focus of commercial activity.

Although Greece was not a hearth of urbanization, the Greek city had global, rather than regional, impact. Urbanization diffused from Greece to the Roman Empire, which in turn diffused its urbanization and urban culture through western Europe. The city declined in Europe for a time after the fall of the Roman Empire, but Europeans eventually carried their notions of city life around the world through colonialism, imperialism, and capitalism. From Washington, DC, to Toronto,

FIGURE 10.10 Union Station, Toronto, Ontario. Opened In 1927, Toronto's Union Station is imprinted with Greco-Roman architectural styles, most noticeably its 12-metre columns, each weighing 75 tonnes, which mark the entrance to this grand building.

the urban landscape shows the imprints of Greco-Roman urban culture (**Figure 10.10**).

ROMAN CITIES

Most of Greece's cities and towns were located near the Mediterranean Sea on peninsulas and islands and linked by sea

FIGURE 10.11 Roman Empire ca. 117 CE. The Romans established a system of cities linked by a network of land and sea routes. Many of the Roman cities have grown into modern metropolises.

routes. When the Romans succeeded the Greeks (and Etruscans) as rulers of the region, their empire incorporated not only the Mediterranean shores but also a large part of interior Europe and North Africa (**Figure 10.11**). The Roman urban system was the largest yet—much larger than that in ancient Greece. The capital, Rome, served as the apex of a hierarchy of settlements ranging from small villages to large cities. The Romans linked these places with an extensive transportation network that included hundreds of kilometres of roads, well-established sea routes, and trading ports along the roads, sea, and rivers. Roman regional planners displayed a remarkable capacity for choosing the site of cities, identifying suitable locales based on their trade location, defensive advantages, or appropriateness as a religious location.

Romans were greatly influenced by the Greeks, as is evident in Roman mythology and most visibly in the cultural landscape and urban morphology of Roman cities. Greeks planned their colonial cities in a rectangular grid pattern, and Romans adopted this plan

> **Forum** The focal point of ancient Roman life, combining the functions of the ancient Greek acropolis and agora.

wherever surface conditions made it possible. Romans also took the Greek acropolis and agora and combined them into one zone, the **Forum**, the focal point of Roman public life (**Figure 10.12**). In Rome, the Forum included the world's first great stadium, the Colosseum, which was a much grander version of the Greek theatre. Before crowds of thousands of onlookers, Roman gladiators fought each other or killed wild animals imported from Africa. After Christianity diffused to Rome, but before the Roman Empire adopted Christianity as the state religion, Romans even forced Christians into the Colosseum, where hungry lions attacked and ate them. All Roman cities of any size had an arena like the Colosseum, where competitions, war games, ceremonies, and other public events took place.

URBAN GROWTH AFTER GREECE AND ROME

After the Roman Empire fell in 495 CE, Europe entered an era historians call the Middle Ages, which ran from about 1,300 to 500 years ago (or later in some parts of Europe). During the first two-thirds of this period, little urban growth occurred in Europe; in fact, urbanism went into sharp decline in some parts of the continent.

© Alexander B. Murphy

FIGURE 10.12 The Forum, Rome, Italy.

Urbanization continued vigorously outside Europe, particularly on the sites of oases and resting places along the Silk Route between Europe and Asia. Many of these settlements grew into towns, and some, such as Bukhara and Samarqand, became major cities. In Asia, Chinese styles of city building diffused into Korea and Japan, with Seoul becoming a full-fledged city by 1200 and Kyoto, Japan's historic capital, growing rapidly after the turn of the ninth century. In West Africa, trading cities developed along the southern margin of the Sahara.

By 1350, Timbuktu (part of Mali today) was a major city—a seat of government, a university town, a market, and a religious centre.

The Americas also experienced significant urban growth during Europe's Middle Ages, especially within the Mayan and Aztec empires (**Figure 10.13**). The largest pre-Columbian city in the Americas was the Aztec capital of Tenochtitlán, on the Mexican Plateau, which had nearly 100,000 inhabitants when many European cities lay in ruins.

H.J. de Blij

FIGURE 10.13 Altun Ha, Belize. Between 300 and 900 CE, Altun Ha served as a thriving trade and distribution centre for the Caribbean merchant canoe traffic. Some of the trails in Altun Ha led all the way to Teotihuacan.

THE SECOND URBAN REVOLUTION

During the last decades of the 18th century, the Industrial Revolution began in Great Britain and Europe. None of Europe's cities were prepared for what lay ahead: an avalanche of changes that ripped the fabric of urban life. Around 1800, western Europe was still overwhelmingly rural, but as thousands migrated to the cities as a result of industrialization, cities had to adapt to the mushrooming population, the proliferation of factories and supply facilities, the expansion of transportation systems, and the construction of tenements for the growing labour force.

The Industrial Revolution marks a moment in human history where rapid advances in technology and science radically altered society. As we noted in Chapter 4, Europe went through a demographic transition at this time. During the late 17th century and into the 18th century, Europeans experienced a series of important improvements in agriculture, including development of hybrid seeds, and improved breeding practices for livestock, which ensured an agricultural surplus. No longer needed in the fields, labourers were forced to migrate to cities in hopes of finding work. Scientific advancements in medicine ensured a steady decline in death rates for the young, higher survival rates for infants and

young children, and greater longevity for the population as a whole. These improvements in health and medicine contributed to a population explosion supported by improved food production techniques. Urban factories and the growing industrial sector drew workers to cities. Manufacturers tapped into this labour force for the burgeoning manufacturing and resource industries (for a further discussion of industrialization, see Chapter 13).

Not all mercantile cities—that is, those engaged in trade—turned into industrial cities. The primary determinant in the development of early industrial cities was proximity to a power source. For example, textile manufacturers had to be sited near fresh water sources that would power the water loom. In Great Britain, industrial cities involved in textile manufacturing were located in the Pennines, where vast quantities of fresh water rushed down the hillsides. Iron manufacturers were located around Birmingham and Coalbrookdale, which offered easy access to Great Britain's coal and iron ore fields. When industrialization diffused from Great Britain to the European mainland, those areas poised to industrialize had already undergone their own second agricultural revolution and had surplus capital from mercantilism and colonialism (**Figure 10.14**).

FIGURE 10.14 Industrialized regions of Europe, 1914.

With industrialization, cities became unregulated jumbles of activity. Factories engulfed private homes. Open spaces became garbage dumps. Urban dwellers converted elegant housing into overcrowded slums. Sanitation systems failed, and water supplies were inadequate and often polluted. By the late 1800s, the Industrial Revolution had changed transportation significantly. The steam engine, powered by coal, not only pumped water from mines for coal mining but also powered the railroad and steamship. The diffusion of the railroad gave cities that were not near coalfields the chance to industrialize. The central areas of cities like London, Paris, and Amsterdam retained their pre-industrial shape, but with the diffusion of the railroad, rail tracks knifed through long-stable neighbourhoods.

Living conditions were dreadful for workers in cities, and working conditions were shocking. Children worked 12-hour shifts in textile mills, typically six days a week. In industrial cities, health conditions were worse than they had been in medieval times; the air was polluted and the water contaminated. The grimy, soot-covered cities of the British Midlands were appropriately deemed the "black towns." Few if any safety mechanisms protected the labourers, and injuries were common.

In the mid-1800s, as Karl Marx and Friederich Engels (writing in Germany, Belgium, and England) encouraged "workers of the world" to unite, conditions in European manufacturing cities gradually improved. Industries began to recognize workers' rights, and governments intervened by legislating workers' rights and introducing city planning and zoning. Many manufacturing cities in North America emulated their European predecessors, with working conditions for factory workers (and "blue-collar" workers generally) largely similar to those found in European industrial cities. During the late 19th and early 20th centuries, the North American manufacturing cities grew rapidly, often with inadequate planning and rapid immigration leading to the development of slums.

During the second half of the 20th century, the nature of manufacturing changed, as did its location. Cities moved many factories away from congested, overcrowded, expensive urban areas. Some companies simply abandoned large manufacturing plants, making "rust belts" out of once-thriving industrial districts. Many of these plants still stand today, overgrown by weeds, with broken windows and cracking walls.

Although factories and factory jobs are not permanent, the urbanization that went along with industrialization is still apparent. Today, western Europe is about 80 percent urban. The statistics on urbanization vary by source, as some define urban areas as being over 2,500 people and others over 5,000 people; still others use employment (i.e., the percent that is not agricultural) as the major criterion. By whatever definition, urbanization has become a global phenomenon, with the majority of the world's people living in cities today.

MAIN POINTS 10.1 When and Why Did People Start Living in Cities?

- Canada is truly an urban nation with over 80 percent of the population living in urban centres. Globally, more people live in towns and cities than in rural areas, making the global population predominantly urban as well. The modern city is a centre for economic development, technological innovation, services, and entertainment.

- The first urban revolution began around 3500 BCE, driven by changing technologies that resulted in an agricultural surplus and social stratification, and sprang up in six known hearth regions—Mesopotamia, Nile River Valley, Indus River Valley, Huang He and Wei River Valleys,

- Mesoamerica, and Peru. The diffusion of urbanization occurred throughout the Mediterranean, Central America, and South Asia and is evidenced in the great Greek and Roman cities of the period.

- The second urban revolution began in the last decades of the 18th century as a result of the Industrial Revolution, colonialism, and rapid technological changes. Rapid urbanization occurred throughout Europe and European colonies, including North America. Many cities became increasingly crowded, unsanitary, and poorly planned.

10.2 Where Are Cities Located, and Why?

Site The internal physical attributes of a place, including its absolute location, spatial character, and physical setting.

Situation The external locational attributes of a place; its relative location or regional position with reference to other nonlocal places.

A map in an atlas of the United States or Canada, or a road map of a state or province, shows an array of places of different sizes, with varying distances between them. The map looks like a jumble, yet each place is where it is because of some decision, some perception of the site or its situation. **Site** and **situation** help explain why certain cities were planned and why cities thrive or fail. To understand why a conglomeration of cities is distributed across space the way it is, and why cities are different sizes, it is necessary to examine more than one city at a time and see how those cities fit together in the region, the state, and the globe as a whole—in other words, we need to look at urban systems.

CENTRAL PLACE THEORY

Walter Christaller wrote the classic urban geography study to explain where cities, towns, and villages are likely to be located. He argued that villages, towns, and cities worked together in interlocking and hierarchical urban systems that could be examined on a local, regional, national, or international basis. In his book *The Central Places in Southern Germany* (1933), Christaller laid the groundwork for **central place theory**. He

> **Central place theory** Theory proposed by Walter Christaller that explains how and where central places in the urban hierarchy should be functionally and spatially distributed with respect to one another.

attempted to develop a model to predict how and where central places in the urban hierarchy, as well as their connected hamlets, villages, towns, and cities, would be functionally and spatially distributed. Christaller based his theory on a set of assumptions: the surface of the ideal region would be flat and have no physical barriers; soil fertility would be the same everywhere; population and purchasing power would be evenly distributed; the region would have a uniform transportation network to permit direct travel from each settlement to the other; and, finally, from any given place, a good or service could be sold in all directions out to a certain distance.

Through his studies, Christaller calculated the ideal central place system, then compared his model to real-world situations and tried to explain the variations and exceptions. In the urban hierarchy, the central places would be nested, so the largest central place provided the greatest number of functions to most of the region (see **Figure 10.15**). Within

> **Trade area** Region adjacent to every town and city within which its influence is dominant.

the **trade area** of the largest central place, a series of large towns would provide functions to several smaller places. The smaller places would then provide fewer central functions to an even smaller service area. To determine the locations of each central place, Christaller needed to define the goods and services provided. He studied the sale of goods and services and calculated the distance people would willingly travel to acquire them. Cities, he postulated, would be regularly spaced, with central places where the same product was sold at the same price located a standard distance apart. Central places were those locations with a larger number of higher-order goods and services. Customers would be prepared to travel greater distances to obtain these consumer goods, which are usually more expensive and purchased less frequently, such as automobiles or household appliances.

Central place theory maintains that each central place has a surrounding complementary region, an exclusive trade area within which the town has a monopoly on the sale of certain goods because it alone can provide such goods at a given price and within a certain range of travel. These are usually goods needed more frequently but not things for which people want to travel very far, such as bread, milk, or newspapers. Farther down the hierarchy are those locations, such as villages or hamlets, that may contain a corner store and a gas station.

Christaller postulated that there was a relationship between urban areas based not only on functional interdependency but also on population size. He argued that there would be a statistical regularity in population, which could be predicted using the **rank-size rule**, which posits that the size of a city has a direct relationship to the size of the largest city. For example, if the largest city in an urban system has 100,000 people, then the nth-largest city would have 1/nth the number of people. In other words, the fifth-largest city would have one-fifth the population of the largest city, or 20,000 people. In some cases, due to particular historical, political, or cultural circumstances, the population distribution within an urban system is distorted so that the largest city has a disproportionately large number of people. In this urban system, such a city is called a **primate city**.

> **Rank-size rule** In a model urban hierarchy, the idea that the population of a city or town will be inversely proportional to its rank in the hierarchy.
>
> **Primate city** A country's largest city—ranking atop the urban hierarchy—which is most expressive of the national culture and usually (but not always) the capital city as well.

In the current global context, cities such as London and Buenos Aires are primate cities in that they are substantially larger than the next-largest city in the urban system. However, just because a city has a large population, it is not necessarily a primate city. Primate cities are not only large but also have a primary functional role within a larger urban system. For example, they might be the seat of government or a financial centre. Conversely, some cities may have a relatively small population within an urban system but be very important in terms of administrative, economic, or political significance.

> **Centrality** The strength of an urban centre in its capacity to attract producers and consumers to its facilities; a city's "reach" into the surrounding region.

This is called **centrality**. Bangkok is an example of such a city; with only 10 percent of Thailand's population, it dominates the economic and political life of the region.

HEXAGONAL HINTERLANDS

Based on this description of Christaller's theory, we might expect the shape of each central place's trade area to be circular (like a bull's eye, with concentric circles surrounding each place). However, circles either overlap or leave certain areas unserved. Hence, Christaller chose perfectly fitted hexagonal regions as the shape of each trade area (Figure 10.15).

Urban geographers were divided on the relevance or usefulness of Christaller's model. Some saw hexagonal systems everywhere while others saw none at all. Christaller received support from geographers who applied his ideas to regions in Europe, North America, and elsewhere. In China, both the North China Plain and the Sichuan Basin display the seemingly uninterrupted flatness assumed by Christaller's model. Studies in the U.S. Midwest suggested that while the square layout of the township-and-range system imposed a different kind of regularity on the landscape, the economic forces at work tended to confirm Christaller's theory. The Canadian urban system, discussed in the next section, follows a similar pattern.

Christaller recognized that not all his assumptions would be met in reality; physical barriers, uneven resource distributions, and other factors all modify his hexagons. Nonetheless,

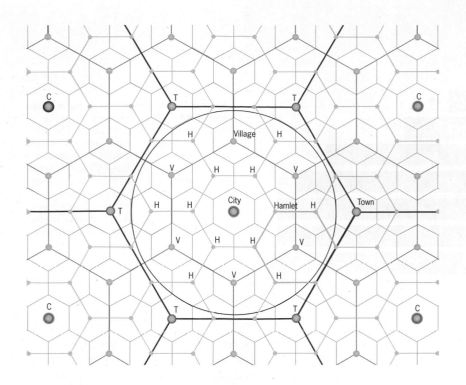

FIGURE 10.15 Christaller's hierarchy of settlements and their service areas. Christaller's interlocking model of a hierarchy of settlements and their service areas includes cities (indicated by C), towns (T), villages (V), and hamlets (H).

his model yielded a number of practical insights. His studies pointed to a hierarchy of urban places that are spatially balanced and also established that larger cities would be spaced farther from each other than smaller towns or villages. Although Christaller's model of perfectly fitting hexagons is not often realized, his studies confirm that the distribution of cities, towns, and villages in a region is not an accident but is tied to trade areas, population size, consumer buying patterns, and distance.

CANADA'S URBAN SYSTEM

Canada's urban system provides a good example of how urban areas are organized into a hierarchical and interlocking relationship. For much of the country's history, Montreal has vied with Toronto to be the largest city in our urban hierarchy, with Vancouver holding that position in the west. Each city is distinctive in its own way due to its specific demographic composition, social and economic history, and political organization, but all are interconnected on the regional, national, and international scale. In turn, each of these cities holds a central place within its region, surrounded by smaller towns, villages, and hamlets. In most cases, their size and location are in keeping with the essential principles of Christaller's model.

However, urban systems are vibrant and constantly in flux, influenced by changing political, social, and economic circumstances, both national and global, and by each city's own local planning and policy decisions. As a result, as geographers Larry Bourne and J. Simmons argue, although the situation has been relatively stable throughout much of Canada's history, it is currently in a state of transition.

The 2011 Census is telling in terms of this transition. Toronto, Montreal, and Vancouver, Canada's three largest

census metropolitan areas **(CMA)**, accounted for 35 percent of the nation's population. The number of people living in CMAs continues to grow at a rate surpassing the national average. In fact, as **Figure 10.16** shows, Canadians continue the trend toward urban centres. Between 2006 and 2011, census metropolitan areas grew at a rate of 7.4 percent, above the national average of 5.9 percent. In total, Canada has 33 CMAs (**Figure 10.17**), and as of July 2013, CMAs were home to 69.7 percent of Canadians (over 24.5 million people). The only two CMAs to see a population decline between 2006 and 2001 were Windsor and Thunder Bay. The 2011 Census also reports growth in **census agglomerations**. A census agglomeration is an urban area in which the core has at least 10,000 people and often many more in surrounding communities. Canada has 114 census agglomerations. Of the top 15 census agglomerations with the highest growth, nearly all were in western Canada, including Okotoks, AB (+42.9 percent), Wood Buffalo, AB (+27.1 percent), Steinbach, MB (+22.2 percent), and High River (+20.6 percent) and Strathmore, AB (+19.7 percent).

New figures released since the 2011 Census continue to show the trend toward urbanization. According to Statistics Canada, between July 1, 2012, and July 1, 2013, the population growth rate was higher for the CMAs (+1.5 percent) than for non-CMAs (+0.3 percent). In comparison, for Canada as a whole, the population growth rate was 1.2 percent during the same period. In other words, people continue to move to large

> **Census metropolitan area (CMA)** A group of cities with a population of 100 000 or more that cluster around an urban core of at least 50,000.
>
> **Census agglomeration** An urban area in which the core has at least 10,000 people and often many more in surrounding communities.

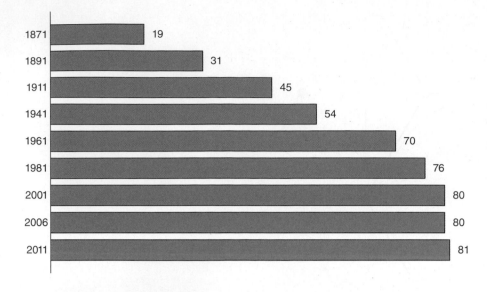

FIGURE 10.16 Population living in urban centres, 1871–2011 (percent). Note: For 1981 to 2011, "urban population" refers to persons living within centres with a population of 1,000 or more and within areas with at least 400 persons per square kilometre. Before 1981, "urban population" refers to populations within centres of 1,000 people or more. Source: Employment and Social Development Canada: For 1871 to 2001, Statistics Canada. Population urban and rural, by province and territory (Canada). Available from: Summary Tables; for 2006 and 2011, Population and Dwelling Count Highlight Tables, 2011 Census. Available from: 2011 Census.

urban areas. Moreover, for a second consecutive year, the four fastest-growing CMAs were in Alberta and Saskatchewan, with strong population growth rates in Calgary (+4.3 percent), Saskatoon (+3.9 percent), Edmonton (+3.8 percent), and Regina (+3.1 percent). On the other hand, Saint John (-0.5 percent), New Brunswick, was the only CMA in Canada to see its population decline in 2012–13.

Bourne and Simmons argue that Canada now has essentially two types of regions: those few dozen urban areas experiencing rapid growth and a large number of smaller places with declining populations. As a region's population and economic circumstances change, it finds itself occupying a different position within the urban system. Bourne and Simmons suggest several underlying factors for this uneven population growth. First, they argue that Canada no longer has a rate of natural increase that can sustain population growth, so the country relies on immigration to fill the gap. As we discussed in Chapter 5, nearly two-thirds of Canada's population growth is due to immigration, and more than 80 percent of all newcomers to Canada settle in Vancouver, Toronto, and Montreal, which is part of the explanation for the rapid growth of these regions.

FIGURE 10.17 Population growth of census metropolitan areas. This graphic shows the population growth (or decline) of CMAs in Canada, using 2011 Census data. Source: Rivait, J., "Census Canada 2011 infographic: How the new population stats break down by province and city." *National Post*, February 8, 2012.

Second, with economic change, employment opportunities have shifted away from manufacturing and resource industries toward the service sector and information technologies. Businesses in these sectors flourish in urban areas, which offer the concentrations of goods, services, and technologies such businesses need to be competitive. Therefore, these businesses are most likely to locate within one of Canada's five mega-regions (the Greater Toronto Area, the Greater Montreal Area, Alberta's central urban corridor of Edmonton-Red Deer-Calgary-Lethbridge, Vancouver-Victoria, and Ottawa-Gatineau).

Third, trade and commerce in Canada used to flow in an east-west direction, but with new trade agreements, including the North American Free Trade Agreement (NAFTA), Canadian trade has been reoriented toward the United States, consolidating the continental economy. This new orientation benefits some areas of Canada, such as Ontario and Alberta, but not others. With this change in orientation, a place such as Toronto, a gateway to the United States market, experiences an increase in population and economic growth, rising in importance in the urban hierarchy.

A number of implications arise from these changes in the Canadian urban system. Cities undergoing rapid growth also tend to exhibit an increase in congestion and pollution as well as a rise in costs for housing and social services, such as health care and schooling. Areas losing population or recording zero population growth lack the skilled workers needed to attract industry. Their tax base declines even as their aging population requires increased social services, such as health care. These uneven growth patterns may lead to inequalities in wealth and quality of life between regions, which can cause a weakening of the urban system and divisions between regions.

MAIN POINTS 10.2 Where Are Cities Located, and Why?

- Cities are interconnected in an urban system at a variety of scales, from the local and regional to the national, continental, and global. Urban geographers are interested in understanding the formation and operation of urban systems, their size, distribution, and organization.

- Central place theory is a model developed by Walter Christaller to predict where central places and their related urban areas would be located and how they would be connected. In the urban hierarchy, central places had the highest-order goods and services and were surrounded by lower-order places in a predictable way.

- Christaller's rank-size rule works out the statistical relationship between population size for various urban areas in an urban system. When the size of the largest city is distorted, in that it has a disproportionate population, it is called a primate city.

- The Canadian urban system continues to grow, with nearly 70 percent of the population living in CMAs.

- Growth in the mega-urban regions is important for economic competitiveness, but these areas also tend to have increasing congestion and pollution, and rising social service costs. Areas with declining populations have a declining tax base and an aging population that requires additional services. Policy-makers at all levels of government must consider how to address these issues.

10.3 How Are Cities Organized, and How Do They Function?

Within urban systems, each city is unique, with its own internal organization of land uses, transportation systems, and social life. Cities are not simply random collections of buildings and people. Rather, they exhibit functional structure, which means they are spatially organized to perform their functions as places of commerce, production, education, and much more. Certain spaces may be designated and developed as residential, industrial, commercial, or parkland. Needless to say, the internal form and function of a city depends on both its history and its geography. Cities in North America and Europe have evolved in a distinctly different way from cities in Latin America, Africa, or Asia. As urban geographers, we study, chart, and map cities to create models that describe how different parts of cities come together in different regions of the world. We are interested in the historical geography of the built environment; that is, we look at how the urban morphology of the city has changed over time and why those changes occurred.

MODELS OF THE CITY

Each model of the city, regardless of the region, is a study in **functional zonation**—the division of the city into certain **zones** for certain purposes (functions). For example, cities typically have residential zones, which are separate from industrial zones, which in turn are separate from garbage dumps. By studying the kinds of zones cities have, and by

> **Functional zonation** The division of a city into different regions or zones (e.g., residential or industrial) for certain purposes or functions (e.g., housing or manufacturing).
>
> **Zone** Area of a city with a relatively uniform land use (e.g., an industrial zone, or a residential zone).

examining where the zones are located with respect to one another, urban geographers draw models of cities. The organization of city spaces has a pattern that is stable but subject to change. Different cities may have similar patterns or land use organization, and these similarities allow us to develop general models describing, very broadly, how cities are laid out.

Before examining the models of urban spaces, we must define some terms commonly used in referring to parts of the city (especially cities in North America). Most models define the key economic zone of the city (if there is one) as the **central business district (CBD)**, where business and commerce are concentrated, usually in the city's downtown.

> **Central business district (CBD)** The downtown heart of a central city, marked by high land values, a concentration of business and commerce, and the clustering of the tallest buildings.

The Canadian CBD typically has high land values, tall buildings, busy traffic, converging highways, and mass-transit systems. One distinctive feature of the Canadian CBD in contrast to its American counterpart is the substantial residential population living and working in the downtown core and supporting a vibrant social and economic life. In Canadian cities such as Vancouver and Toronto, a number of high-density condominium developments have been built (**Figure 10.18**). While many people support the construction of condominiums and the residential population it brings downtown, others argue that, in Toronto, for example, some of these condominiums have cut the city off from its waterfront and increased traffic congestion even while they are available only for those with the money to afford such accommodation.

The term **central city** describes the urban area that is not suburban. In effect, the central city is the older city as opposed to the newer suburbs. A **suburb** is an outlying, functionally uniform part of an urban area that is often (but not always) adjacent to the central city. Most suburbs are residential, but some have other land uses, including schools, shopping malls, and office and industrial parks.

Suburbanization is the process by which lands that were previously outside the urban environment become urbanized, as people and businesses from the city and other areas move to these spaces. The process of suburbanization holds special interest for human geographers because it involves the transformation of large areas of land from rural to urban uses and affects large numbers of people who can afford to move to larger and more expensive suburban homes. The aesthetic of the suburb reveals the occupants' idealized living patterns because the suburban layout can be planned in response to choice and demand. Ideals of suburban living can also change. For example, in the 1970s and 1980s, many subdivision communities banned the use of clotheslines, arguing that hanging laundry was an "eyesore." However, as people became more concerned about the environment and conserving energy, the Ontario government passed legislation in 2008 that prohibited municipalities from implementing such bans. In Canada, the residential subdivision as we know it is largely a post–World War II phenomenon. As noted earlier, some 80 percent of Canadians now live in urban areas, but the vast majority of them live in suburban areas. All Canadian cities have suburbs, which have their own history and geography, influenced by changing demographics, economic and social phenomena, and the changing political landscape.

By using such terms as "residential area" and "central business district," people acknowledge the existence of a regional structure within cities. When we refer to the downtown, the airport, or the city zoo, we are in fact referring to urban regions where certain functions prevail (i.e., business activity, transportation, and recreation in the three just mentioned). One of the objectives of urban geographers is to develop a model of the zones of a city that can be recognized in every city along with a city's particular site, size, shape, and relief. Note that models do not explain how or why cities are organized the way they are. A model of a city shows us an end product, whether planned or not, and suggests the forces that created that end product.

> **Central city** The urban area that is not suburban; generally, the older or original city that is surrounded by newer suburbs.
>
> **Suburb** A subsidiary urban area surrounding and connected to the central city. Many are exclusively residential; others have their own commercial centres or shopping malls.
>
> **Suburbanization** The process by which lands that were previously outside the urban environment become urbanized, as people and businesses from the city and other areas move to these spaces.

(a)

(b)

FIGURE 10.18 Condominium developments in the central business district of (a) Toronto and (b) Vancouver.

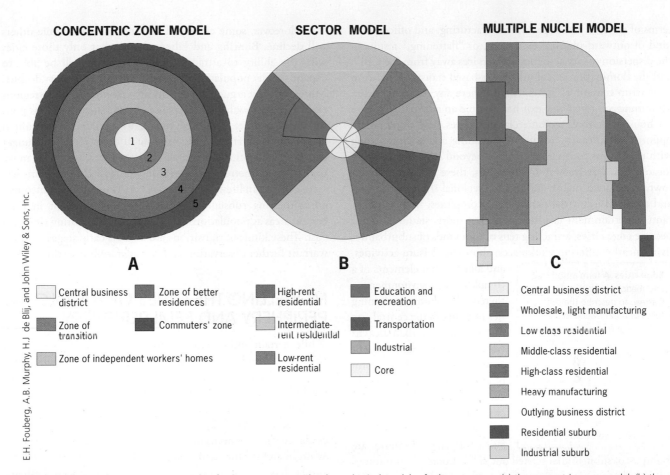

FIGURE 10.19 The three classical models of urban structure. The three classical models of urban structure: (a) the concentric zone model; (b) the sector model; and (c) the multiple nuclei model

MODELLING THE NORTH AMERICAN CITY

Urban geographers have constructed a succession of models that reflect change and growth in the geographic layout of North American cities. Figure 10.19 illustrates three different models reflecting various ideas of urban organization from the 1920s to the 1980s. The first is Ernest Burgess's **concentric zone model** of Chicago in the 1920s (**Figure 10.19a**). Second is Homer Hoyt's sector model of the 1930s (**Figure 10.19b**). Third is the multiple nuclei model (**Figure 10.19c**), which seemed to more clearly reflect the contemporary form of North American cities as they evolved in the 1970s. This model recognized that the CBD was losing its dominant position as the single nucleus of the urban area as several urban regions developed their own nuclei.

> **Concentric zone model**
> A structural model of the American central city that suggests the existence of five concentric land-use rings arranged around a common centre.

Although Canadian cities display great diversity in their form and function, certain commonalities or similarities exist. We can see the older inner-city core and its older residential subdivisions and areas of industry and manufacturing. Surrounding those districts are new subdivisions and newer town centres. Beyond that we can see the suburbanization of adjacent rural towns and villages within commuting distance of the city. Finally, there are rural residential developments for people who want a more rural lifestyle but want to be within commuting distance of the city.

Today, most urban geographers think these models are too simplistic to describe the modern city. Geographers Trudi Bunting and Pierre Filion have explored the changing nature of contemporary Canadian cities, marking three distinct periods: pre-1945 ("city development"), 1945–1975 ("metropolitan development"), and 1975 to the present ("suburban development"). The city development stage prior to World War II was marked by high levels of manufacturing as a main source of employment, high residential occupancy levels and overcrowding, a strong CBD due to reliance on public transportation, and a strong, centralized downtown. The metropolitan development period, from 1945 to 1975, saw the beginning of manufacturing's relocation to suburban industrial parks; the start of the "baby boom," which led to the spread of new suburban developments as demand for housing increased with population growth; the spreading out of services and activities due to the availability of cars and road networks; and the weakening of CBD as commuter roads and regional malls emerged outside the inner-city neighbourhoods.

The suburban development period, from 1975 to the present, is marked by suburbs surpassing central city areas in terms of population size, and becoming equal to central city areas in terms of services, retail spaces, manufacturing, and offices. This kind of outward physical expansion, or "flattening," results in the dispersion of city activities and services away from the CBD, and the domination of suburban, car-based transportation. An "exit ramp economy" has emerged, where any location within 15 minutes of a highway exit has become an adequate location for housing, schools, commercial properties, and employment opportunities, leading to further spreading out of cities, along with new access to rural regions just beyond these areas. Often located near key freeway intersections, these suburban downtowns developed mainly around big regional shopping centres and attracted industrial parks, office complexes, hotels, restaurants, entertainment facilities, and even sports stadiums. They became **edge cities**, attracting tens of thousands of suburbanites living nearby, offering workplaces, shopping, leisure activities,

> **Edge cities** A term introduced by American journalist Joel Garreau to describe the shifting focus of urbanization in the United States, away from the central business district (CBD) toward new loci of economic activity at the urban fringe. These cities are characterized by extensive amounts of office and retail space, few residential areas, and modern buildings (less than 30 years old).

and all the other elements of a complete urban environment—thereby loosening remaining ties not only to the central city but to other suburban areas as well. As a result, many suburbs have experienced their own form of urbanization and provide yet another example of the continuously changing city landscape. Richmond, British Columbia, and Mississauga, Ontario, are examples of suburbs that started out as "bedroom" communities but have become increasingly independent, with their own city centre, local economy, and community services.

What does the future of Canadian cities look like? The inequalities within and between Canadian urban areas are becoming increasingly evident. Impoverished inner-city neighbourhoods stand in stark contrast to the multitude of new condominium buildings being built in many large cities. Vancouver, for example, was dubbed the most expensive city in Canada in 2014, yet it is also known for its poverty-stricken Downtown Eastside. Comparing the skyline image of Vancouver (Figure 10.18b) to a scene from one of its downtown streets (**Figure 10.20**) is telling.

FIGURE 10.20 Vancouver's Downtown Eastside.

John Lehmann/The Globe and Mail/The Canadian Press

Moreover, some cities will continue to grow while others will decline. Bunting and Filion suggest that only those cities with the ability to attract immigrant groups will be able to expand their populations; others will stagnate or decline. Moreover, they argue that, historically, all metropolitan regions experienced growth at the expense of rural areas, whereas now, for the first time, we are beginning to see large metropolitan areas gain population at the expense of other cities as younger people (such as the Millennials, discussed in Chapter 4) move to the biggest metropolitan areas in search of employment, services, and urban lifestyles. Cities such as Toronto and Vancouver are witnessing substantial residential redevelopment in their central areas as populations seek to reduce commuting time and cost. These kinds of transitions are in their early stages and will warrant further observation and consideration over time.

MODELLING THE CITIES OF THE GLOBAL PERIPHERY AND SEMI-PERIPHERY

While certain models may help us understand how North American cities have evolved, these models are often not applicable elsewhere around the globe. Cities in other places, including Europe, can trace their function and internal organization to different historical and geographical circumstances. As we discussed in Chapter 2, "colonial" cities were structured in accordance with the needs of the colonizing country, using mainly Western architecture and styles. South American cities, for example, have been endowed with strong Iberian cultural imprints that define a certain common social-spatial geography.

Today, colonial cities defy any generalization. Mexico City, Mexico and São Paulo, Brazil, are examples of the kinds of megacities that are difficult to analyze and model. Even indigenous cities deep in continental interiors (such as those in West Africa's Sahel and in Central Asia) have been transformed by the processes of globalization and immigration. However, some former colonial cities in sub-Saharan Africa have retained the spatial components lost in enormous cities like Lagos, Nigeria, and Kinshasa, Democratic Republic of the Congo, and some middle-sized cities in Southeast Asia continue to exhibit a fairly consistent pattern.

THE LATIN AMERICAN CITY

Cities around the world developed in their own distinctive style as a result of local and national political, economic, and cultural forces as well as the city's position within global urban systems. Scholars studying Latin American cities argue that they reflect a blend of traditional Latin American culture and elements driven by the forces of globalization that have reshaped the urban scene.

A classic model of the Latin American city is the **Griffin-Ford model** (**Figure 10.21**). Such a city has a thriving CBD containing primary businesses, employment, and entertainment. The CBD is usually divided into a traditional

> **Griffin-Ford model** Developed by geographers Ernst Griffin and Larry Ford, a model of the Latin American city showing a blend of traditional elements of Latin American culture with the forces of globalization that are reshaping the urban scene.

Adapted with permission from L. Ford, "A New and Improved Model of Latin American City Structure," *The Geographical Review* 86 (1996), p. 438.

A NEW AND IMPROVED MODEL OF LATIN AMERICAN CITY STRUCTURE

- ■ Commercial
- ■ Market
- ■ Industrial
- ■ Zone of Maturity
- ■ Zone of In Situ Accretion
- ■ Zone of Peripheral Squatter Settlements
- ■ Elite Residential Sector
- ■ Gentrification
- ☐ Middle-Class Residential Tract

FIGURE 10.21 A model of the Latin American city structure. In a 1996 journal article, Larry Ford updated the model he originally developed with Ernst Griffin, adding a ring highway (*periférico*) around the outskirts of the city, dividing the downtown business district into a CBD and a market, adding a mall near the elite space, and leaving room for suburban industrial parks.

market sector and a more modern high-rise sector. The most successful cities have adequate public transit systems and nearby affluent residential areas that assure the continuing dominance of the CBD. Emanating outward from the urban core along the city's most prestigious axis is the commercial spine, which is surrounded by the elite residential sector. This widening corridor is essentially an extension of the CBD and features offices, shopping, high-quality housing for the upper and upper-middle classes, restaurants, theatres, and such amenities as parks, zoos, and golf courses.

At the end of this commercial/elite spine is an incipient edge city, shown as "mall" in Figure 10.21, and flanked by high-priced residences. This reflects the emergence of suburban nodes in South American cities. The remaining concentric zones are home to less well-off residents, who compose the great majority of the urban population. The zone of maturity in the inner city contains the best housing outside the spine sector and attracts the middle classes, who invest sufficiently to keep their solidly built but aging dwellings from deteriorating. The adjacent zone of in situ accretion is one of much more modest housing. Interspersed with the more modest areas are densely populated unkempt areas, which represent a transition from inner-ring affluence to outer-ring poverty. The outermost zone of peripheral squatter settlements is home to the impoverished and recent migrants. Although this ring consists mainly of teeming, high-density shantytowns, residents here are surprisingly optimistic about finding work and improving their living conditions.

FIGURE 10.22 The *favelas* of Rio de Janeiro.

A structural element of many Latin American cities is the **disamenity sector**, the very poorest sector, which in extreme cases is not connected to regular city services and is controlled by gangs and drug lords. The disamenity sectors in Latin American cities contain relatively unchanging slums known as barrios or favelas. In Rio de Janiero, 20 percent of the city's 6 million people live in favelas. These favelas, which have emerged in the city's hills, away from the wealthy oceanfront neighbourhoods, struggle with basic services including hydro and fresh water (**Figure 10.22**). The worst of these poverty-stricken areas are often inhabited by large numbers of people who are so poor they are forced to live in the streets. There is little in the way of regular law enforcement within such communities, and drug lords are often in control— or battle with other drug lords for dominance. Such conditions also prevail in places beyond the ring highway or periférico, which is now a feature of most South American cities.

> **Disamenity sector** The very poorest parts of cities, which in extreme cases are not even connected to regular city services and are controlled by gangs or drug lords.

The model reflects the enormous differences between the spaces of privilege and the spaces of abject poverty within the Latin American city. It also describes elements of sector development evident in many large South American cities, but the concentricity suggested by the model seems to be breaking down.

THE SOUTHEAST ASIAN CITY

Some of the most populated cities in the world are in Southeast Asia. The city of Kuala Lumpur, Malaysia, is a complex of high-rise development, including the 450-metre-tall Petronas Towers, which until recently was the world's tallest building. The city of Jakarta, Indonesia, called Jabotabek by the locals, is an enormous conurbation of Bogor, Tangerang, and Bekasi.

Scholars studying the medium-sized cities of Southeast Asia found that they exhibited similar land-use patterns, which could be modelled (**Figure 10.23**). The focal point of the city is the old colonial port zone, which combines with the largely commercial district that surrounds it. There is often no formal central business district, although elements of the CBD are

Adapted with permission from T.G. McGee, *The Southeast Asian City*, London: Bell, 1967, p. 128.

A GENERALIZED MODEL OF LAND USE AREAS IN THE LARGE SOUTHEAST ASIAN CITY

A	Squatter areas	AC	Alien commercial zone
B	Suburbs	WC	Western commercial zone

FIGURE 10.23 Model of the large Southeast Asian city. A model of land use in a Southeast Asian city includes sectors and zones within each sector.

present as separate clusters surrounding the old colonial port zone. There is a government zone; the Western commercial zone (practically a CBD by itself); an ethnic commercial zone, dominated by Chinese merchants whose residences are attached to their places of business; and the mixed-land-use zone that contains miscellaneous economic activities, including light industry. The other non-residential areas are the market-gardening zone at the outskirts of the urban area and, still farther from the city, a recently built industrial park or "estate."

The residential zones in these models are similar to those in the models of the Latin American city. Other similarities are the hybrid structure of sectors and zones, an elite residential sector that includes new suburbs, an inner-city zone of middle-income housing, and peripheral low-income squatter settlements. One main difference is that the Latin American model includes middle-income housing in a suburban zone, reflecting the larger middle class in these cities of the global semi-periphery and the small middle class in Latin American cities.

THE AFRICAN CITY

Farmers make up a majority of the population in the tropical region of Africa; as a result, most countries in the tropics remain under 40 percent urbanized. Outside the tropics, sub-Saharan Africa is about 57 percent urban. At the beginning of this century, some countries in sub-Saharan Africa recorded the world's lowest levels of urbanization. Despite these statistics, Africa now

has the world's fastest-growing cities, followed by those in South Asia, mainland East Asia, and South and Central America. In contrast, the cities of North America, southern South America, and Australia are growing more slowly, and those of western Europe are barely growing at all.

The imprint of European colonialism can be seen in many African cities. During colonialism, Europeans laid out prominent urban centres such as Kinshasa (Democratic Republic of the Congo), Nairobi (Kenya), and Harare (Zimbabwe) in the interior, and Dakar (Senegal), Abidjan (Ivory Coast), Luanda (Angola), Maputo (Mozambique), and other ports along the coast. Other African cities are neither traditional nor colonial. South Africa's major urban centres (Johannesburg, Cape Town, and Durban) are essentially Western, with elements of European as well as American models, including high-rise CBDs and sprawling suburbs.

As a result of this diversity, it is difficult to formulate a model African city. Studies of African cities indicate that the central city often consists of not one but three CBDs (**Figure 10.24**): a remnant of the colonial CBD, an informal and sometimes periodic market zone, and a transitional business centre where commerce is conducted from curbside stalls or storefronts. Vertical development occurs mainly in the former colonial CBD; the traditional business centre is usually a zone of single-storey buildings with some traditional architecture; and the market zone tends to be open-air, informal, yet still important. Sector development occurs in the encircling zone of ethnic and mixed neighbourhoods (often characterized by strong ethnic identities); manufacturing or mining operations are found next to some parts of this zone. Finally, many African cities are ringed by satellite townships that are squatter settlements.

A MODEL SUB-SAHARAN AFRICAN CITY

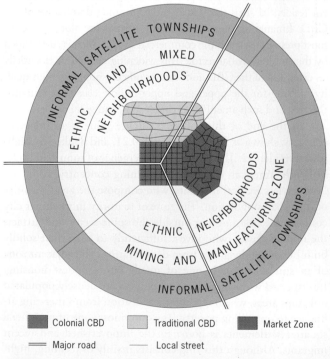

	Colonial CBD		Traditional CBD		Market Zone
	Major road		Local street		

E.H. Fouberg, A.B. Murphy, H.J. de Blij, and John Wiley & Sons, Inc.

FIGURE 10.24 Model of the sub-Saharan African city. One model of the African city includes a colonial CBD, traditional CBD, and market zone.

MAIN POINTS 10.3 How Are Cities Organized, and How Do They Function?

- All cities have their own internal structure, which arises as a result of their history and geography, and their functions, as well as city planning and policy.

- Urban geographers develop models of urban spaces to map out various functional zones. These zones include a central business district, inner-city residential and industrial/manufacturing areas, suburban zones, and rural countryside.

- There are three classic North American urban models—concentric zone model, sector model, and multiple nuclei model. While these are accurate to a point, the modern urban city is far more complicated than these early models suggest, particularly when we consider recent complex developments on the city's outer edge.

- Cities in the periphery and semi-periphery have developed very different internal structures. Colonial cities developed form and function for the benefit of the colonial or imperial power. Other cities around the globe, from South America to South Asia, develop their own distinctive style in response to national political and economic forces and their distinctive cultural and social development.

10.4 How Do Cities Evolve?

Numerous economic, social, political, technological, and cultural processes are at play in the ever-evolving form and function of cities. The roles individual people, governments, planners, corporations, developers, financial lenders, and realtors hold in the transformation of cities vary. In some parts of the world, governments pass strict laws limiting urban structures and enforce them; in other parts of the world, governments either do not pass laws or do not enforce them.

Powerful social and cultural preferences shape the character of particular parts of the city and influence who can choose to live where. As we can see in the opening field note and in chapters 7 and 8, indicators of these preferences and of historical processes are embedded in urban landscapes and are visible to passersby in various elements. These might include the presence of single-family or multi-family homes, particular styles of construction and building materials, the distance between houses, the nature and style of vegetation around houses, the distance between the houses and the streets, and even the amount of space devoted to automobile movement and storage. Cities take shape around their CBDs, and the form of the city is governed by planning and transportation decisions, immigration and settlement patterns, shifting economic circumstances, and the way these many factors play out within broader local, regional, national, and global processes.

CITIES IN THE GLOBAL CORE

Developers and governments are important actors in the making of cities, and they have had different goals over time. In the 1960s and 1970s, many North American and European cities experienced deindustrialization and a loss of manufacturing businesses as a result of changing global economic circumstances, as illustrated in the opening field note for this chapter. Many businesses deserted the downtown core, leaving behind abandoned buildings, factories, and warehouses as they moved into new industrial and residential subdivisions on the city's outskirts. In cities experiencing high levels of suburbanization, people left the central city for the suburbs for a number of reasons, including the need for work and the desire for single-family homes, yards, better schools, and safety. With suburbanization, city governments lost tax revenue as middle- and upper-class taxpayers left the central city and began paying taxes in the suburbs instead. In order to counter the suburbanization trend, city governments are encouraging commercialization of the central city and gentrification of the central city's neighbourhoods.

One way that people make cities is by remaking them, reinventing neighbourhoods or changing layouts to reflect current goals and aesthetics. The plans that city governments draft to revive central cities usually involve cleaning streets, sidewalks, and buildings; tearing down old, abandoned buildings; and building up commercial offerings and residences. In the CBD, city governments have often created programs to encourage **commercialization**, which entails transforming the central city into an area attractive to residents and tourists alike (**Figure 10.25**). Several cities—for example, Toronto and Halifax or Boston and New York—have created waterfront "theme" areas that include festival marketplaces, parks with exotic sculptures and play areas, and amusement zones occupying former industrial sites. Such ventures have been successful in attracting tourists and in generating business, but they cannot revive downtowns on their own because they cannot attract what the core of the city needs most: permanent residents with a stake in its future. The newly commercialized downtowns often stand apart from the rest of the central city.

> **Commercialization** The transformation of an area of a city into an area attractive to residents and tourists alike in terms of economic activity.
>
> **Gentrification** The rehabilitation of the deteriorated, often abandoned, housing of low-income inner-city residents for new middle- or upper-class residents.

Since the 1960s, some people have moved back into central cities—often in conjunction with a process known as **gentrification** (**Figure 10.26**). Gentrification occurs when individuals buy up and rehabilitate the houses in a previously abandoned or rundown neighbourhood, raising the housing value in the again, as governments encourage beautification programs and offer significant tax breaks to people who buy abandoned or dilapidated buildings and convert them to new residential and commercial uses. The growing interest in central city housing has resulted, in part, from the changing character of North American society: the proportion of childless couples and single people in the population is growing, and for these urbanites, the suburbs do not look very attractive. Living within walking distance of the workplace and being near cultural and recreational amenities attracts more residents to central city neighbourhoods every year.

However, there have been some negative consequences to these developments. Inner-city neighbourhoods are places where affordable housing can be found, and when these neighbourhoods go through the process of gentrification, the cost of living increases dramatically. Those who at one time could afford to live there, such as artists, single women, and low-income and immigrant families, are now forced to move out into other areas. Moreover, with gentrification comes commercialization, as brand name mega-developments set in, pushing out local cafes and small businesses in exchange for franchises. With the removal of the neighbourhood's often diverse populations and small businesses, the result is what geographer Neil Smith calls "a systematic class-remaking of city neighborhoods."

The suburb is not immune to gentrification. Rampant in many North American suburbs (especially those close to the city) is the tear-down phenomenon, in which individuals buy a house with the intention of tearing it down and building a much larger home. The new houses, sometimes referred to as "monster homes" because of their size, often stretch to the outer limits of the lot (**Figure 10.27**). Like gentrification, **tear-downs** change the landscape and increase the neighbourhood's average housing values and average household income. Unlike gentrification, tear-downs destroy the original houses instead of preserving them. Those in favour of tear-downs

> **Tear-downs** Homes bought in many North American suburbs with the intent of tearing them down and replacing them with much larger homes, often referred to as "monster homes."

FIGURE 10.25 Locke Street, Hamilton, Ontario. The Locke Street area of Hamilton, Ontario—a city known for its industrial sector and steel mills—is developing into a bustling area of festivals, boutiques, and upscale restaurants.

John Ellin CC SA BY

FIGURE 10.26 Osborne Village in Winnipeg, Manitoba. Osborne Village, previously known as one of Winnipeg's more poverty-stricken neighbourhoods, has recently been gentrified. The influx of stores such as American Apparel, along with an emerging "hipster" culture, has increased rents, pushing the poor out of the area.

Janelle Lagasse Photography

FIGURE 10.27 Monster home. Monster houses, such as this one, dwarf homes around them.

Karikaturka/Dreamstime.com/Getstock.com

neighbourhood and changing the neighbourhood itself. Gentrification began in cities with a tight housing market and defined central city neighbourhoods, such as Toronto, Chicago, and Paris. Gentrification slowed in the 1990s but is occurring argue that the phenomenon slows urban sprawl (see the next section) by replacing existing homes with new homes, rather than converting farmland to residential lots. Those opposed to tear-downs say the process destroys the character of a place by demolishing older homes and replacing them with houses that are too large for their lots and that dwarf the neighbouring houses.

URBAN SPRAWL AND NEW URBANISM

As populations have grown, urban areas in many parts of the world, including Canada, have experienced **urban sprawl**—the unrestricted growth of housing, commercial developments, and

> **Urban sprawl** Unrestricted growth of housing, commercial development, and roads over large expanses of land in many North American urban areas, with little concern for urban planning.

roads over large expanses of land, with little concern for urban planning. Urban sprawl, a phenomenon of the automobile era, is characterized by the razing of farmland and old industrial sites; the building or widening of roads; and the proliferation of strip malls, big-box stores, chain restaurants, huge intersections, and numerous housing developments, spread out over many acres along major roadways in any urbanized part of the country. Does population growth explain which cities experience the most urban sprawl? Scholars studying North American urbanized areas found that urban sprawl happened even in urban areas without significant population growth. It is important to note, as well, that concerns about the impact of urban living on the health and welfare of a city's inhabitants have existed from the outset, with early planning movements in North America focusing on the impact of industrialization, lack of proper sanitation, and overcrowded and ill-suited residential neighbourhoods.

> **New urbanism** A philosophy of urban design that calls for development, urban revitalization, and suburban reforms that create walkable neighbourhoods with a diversity of housing and jobs.

Among the ideas to counter urban sprawl, a group of architects, urban planners, and developers outlined an urban design vision they called **new urbanism**. The Congress for the New Urbanism, established in 1993, defines this as a philosophy of development, urban revitalization, and suburban reforms that create walkable neighbourhoods with a diversity of housing and jobs. The Congress for the New Urbanism website explains that "New Urbanists support regional planning for open space, appropriate architecture and planning, and the balanced development of jobs and housing. They believe these strategies are the best way to reduce how long people spend in traffic, to increase the supply of affordable housing, and to rein in urban sprawl." New urbanists want to create neighbourhoods that promote a sense of community and a sense of place, and they often use neo-traditional housing designs, with front porches, sidewalks, and mixed-use town centres.

New urbanism surfaced in Canadian planning policy in the 1980s, along with ideas of smart growth and sustainability.

Peter Power/GetStock.com

FIGURE 10.28 Cornell in Markham, Ontario. This subdivision is an example of new urbanism and neo-traditional design that encourages community interaction and sustainability.

According to Canadian urban planner Jill Grant, these ideas are now intertwined in Canadian planning policies at all levels of government. Sustainability, Grant argues, is concerned with ensuring "compact form, transportation options, healthy living environments, affordable housing, and environmental responsibility." The ideas behind smart growth developed in the United States in response to anti-growth movements; they sought to reduce the negative impacts of growth and encourage development and regional planning that struck a balance between jobs and housing. According to Canadian planners Andrejs Skaburskis and Diana Mok, the City of Markham is considered to have the highest concentration of "new-urbanist subdivisions in North America with Cornell as its flagship." As **Figure 10.28** illustrates, communities such as Cornell feature higher densities as well as sidewalks and more public transit, which encourage greater community interaction.

While many communities, planners, politicians, and developers may agree with the philosophy behind new urbanism, smart growth, and sustainability, researchers have found many of the ideas are not put into practice. Jill Grant asserts that political, economic, and social barriers operate to varying degrees to foil full implementation of these ideals. While planners may press for development that achieves the goals of new urbanism, smart growth, and sustainability, politicians may override their recommendations based on objections from developers, engineers, and traffic planners who find the new standards difficult to implement. Developers often claim that economic markets do not support innovative changes in community design, and that consumers are more interested in larger lots and privacy than in compact city living.

Canadian cities also attempt to regulate growth at the urban fringe through the use of "greenbelts," rural reserves, or urban growth boundaries that are meant to protect agricultural land, land with considerable environmental diversity, or land

Tony Bock/Toronto Star

FIGURE 10.29 Encroaching development on the Oak Ridges Moraine, 2004. Environmentalists, some urban planners, and local activists have lobbied for greater protection from development for greenbelt areas, such as the Oak Ridges Moraine and the Niagara Escarpment.

needed to preserve water (e.g., watersheds, lakes, and rivers). The province of Ontario implemented a greenbelt plan in 2005 to continue protecting environmentally sensitive areas, such as the Niagara Escarpment and the Oak Ridges Moraine (**Figure 10.29**). Central to this legislation was the creation of a greenbelt to contain and manage development around the Greater Toronto Area by ensuring varying degrees of protection depending on the nature, features, and functions of the natural landscape. Ontario's Greenbelt Plan has consistently been viewed as one of Ontario's most popular initiatives, protecting over 1.8 million acres of farmland, wetland, and forest. When Toronto's housing prices reached an all-time high in the summer of 2014, some commentators argued that the reduced access to development land due to the Greenbelt Plan had driven up housing prices, but researchers suggest that other factors, including low mortgage rates and demand for central location, are much more likely to increase housing costs. Greenbelt plans, together with other growth management strategies, are being implemented in a number of jurisdictions in Canada in order to regulate growth beyond various cities' current development areas and to encourage increasing densities in the built-up area.

Some geographers are critical of new urbanism because it seems to redefine certain kinds of urban spaces. For example, new urbanism's ideas often mean that public spaces become privatized for the enjoyment of the residents of the neighbourhood to the exclusion of others. Geographers Stuart Aitken, Don Mitchell, and Lynn Staeheli note that as new urbanism strives to turn neighbourhoods back in time, "spaces and social functions historically deemed public (such as parks, neighbourhood centres, shopping districts)" are privatized. The houses with porches that encourage neighbours to talk, and the parks that are within walking distance for the residents, create "mythic landscapes that are ingratiating for those who can afford them and exclusionary for those who cannot."

Noted geographer David Harvey offers one of the strongest critiques of new urbanism, explaining that most new urbanist designs are "greenfield" projects—that is, projects built on previously undeveloped land—designed for the affluent with the aim of making the suburbs more livable. Harvey argues that the new urbanism movement is a kind of "spatial determinism," which does not recognize that "the fundamental difficulty with modernism was its persistent habit of privileging spatial forms over social processes." Harvey, and others who critique new urbanism, claim that new urbanism does nothing to break down the social conditions that privilege some while disadvantaging others. The new urbanist projects arguably do take away much of the grittiness and character of the city, and they often create exclusionary communities that further the racial and class segregation of cities. Despite the critiques, however, developments in the new urbanist tradition are attracting a growing number of people, and when these developments are situated within cities, they can work against urban sprawl.

CITIES IN THE GLOBAL PERIPHERY AND SEMI-PERIPHERY

North America, with 82 percent living in urban areas in 2014, the Caribbean and Latin America (80 percent), and Europe (73 percent) are mostly urbanized areas. Africa (40 percent) and Asia (48 percent) remain mostly rural, but the United Nations predicts that these numbers will change quickly, becoming 56 percent and 64 percent urban respectively by 2050 (**Figure 10.30**). In other words, very shortly the world will be more urban than rural. Continuing population growth and urbanization are projected to add 2.5 billion people to the world's urban population by 2050, bringing the total world urban population to 6.4 billion (from the 2014 figure of 3.9 billion). Nearly 90 percent of the increase is concentrated in Asia and Africa. India, China, and Nigeria together are expected to account for 37 percent of the projected growth of the world's urban population between 2014 and 2050. India is projected to add 404 million urban dwellers, China 292 million, and Nigeria 212 million. China has the world's largest urban population, at 758 million, followed by India at 410 million.

Many of the world's most populous cities are located in the Global South. China alone has 6 mega-cities (greater than 10 million residents) and 10 cities with between 5 and 10 million inhabitants. Likewise, India has four cities (Ahmadabad, Bangalore, Chennai, and Hyderabad) with 5 to 10 million inhabitants presently; they are projected to become mega-cities in the coming years. Asia has seven other mega-cities and eleven other large cities in 2014. Africa has three mega-cities, Cairo, Kinshasa, and Lagos, but three more are expected to emerge by 2030, as Dar es Salaam in Tanzania; Johannesburg, South Africa; and Luanda, Angola, are each projected to surpass the 10 million mark.

Across the world, people continue to migrate to cities in response to "pull and push" factors of immigration (discussed in

FIGURE 10.30 Urban and rural population as proportion of total population, by major areas, 1950–2050. Source: *World Urbanization Prospects*, United Nations, Department of Economic and Social Affairs, Population Division, 2014.

Shantytown Unplanned slum development on the margins of a city, dominated by crude dwellings and shelters made mostly of scrap wood, iron, and even pieces of cardboard.

Chapter 5). Particularly in the economic periphery, new arrivals (as well as many long-term residents) are crowded together in overpopulated apartment buildings, dismal tenements, and teeming slums. New arrivals come from other cities and towns and from the rural countryside, often as large families, adding to the cities' rate of natural growth. Housing cannot keep up with this massive inflow. As a result, huge **shantytowns**—unplanned developments of crude dwellings and shelters made largely of scrap wood, iron, and pieces of cardboard—develop around these cities (Figure 10.22). The overcrowding and dismal conditions do not deter additional urban migration, and the result is that millions of people spend their entire lives in urban housing of wretched quality.

Cities in poorer parts of the world generally lack enforceable **zoning laws**, which evolved in most cities in North America over the last century. These laws are meant to ensure

Zoning laws Legal restrictions on land use that determine what types of building and economic activities are allowed to take place in certain areas. In North America, areas are most commonly divided into separate zones of residential, retail, or industrial use.

space is used in ways that the society at large would deem culturally and environmentally acceptable. If, for example, a city had zoned all the lots in a suburban block exclusively for single-family homes, a fast-food franchise could not occupy a corner lot in that block. Zoning laws do not exist, nor are they equally enforced, everywhere in the Global North. In Europe, for example, most cities have loose land-use plans but few have zoning laws. In the United States, Houston, Texas, is the only large city that does not have zoning laws on the books, and citizens in the city have voted against the creation of zoning laws three different times (most recently in 1993). All jurisdictions in Canada have some form of planning authority and legislation designed to guide development.

Without zoning laws, cities in the periphery will have mixed land use throughout the city. For example, in cities such as Chennai, India (and in other cities in India), open space between high-rise buildings is often occupied by squatter settlements (**Figure 10.31**). In Bangkok, Thailand, elementary schools and noisy, polluting factories stand side by side. In Nairobi, Kenya, hillside villas overlook some of Africa's worst slums. Over time, such incongruities may disappear, as is happening in many cities in East Asia, where rising land values and greater demand for enforced zoning regulations are transforming the central cities. But in South Asia, sub-Saharan Africa, Southwest Asia, North Africa, and Central and South America, unregulated growth continues.

Across the periphery and semi-periphery, one trait all major cities display is the stark contrast between the wealthy and the

Erin H. Fouberg

FIGURE 10.31 Squatter settlements, Hyderabad, India. Temporary shelters, built to withstand the summer monsoon, protect migrants who work on the construction in the background.

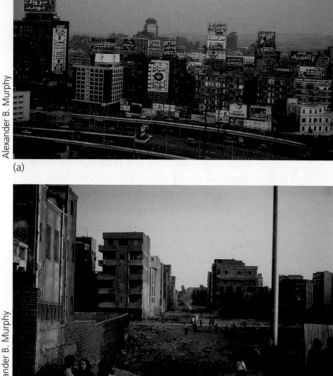

(a)

(b)

Alexander B. Murphy

FIGURE 10.32 Cairo, Egypt. (a) The modern high-rises and freeways of central Cairo are in stark contrast to (b) the rundown buildings and roadways outside the downtown core.

poor—for example, homeless people can be seen sleeping on heating grates half a block from the Parliament Buildings in Ottawa-Gatineau. Yet the intensity and scale of the contrast are greater in cities of the periphery. The central area of Cairo, Egypt, appears to be a modern, Mediterranean metropolis, but this impression fades as one nears the city's outskirts: paved streets give way to dusty alleys, apartment buildings to tenements, and sidewalk coffee shops to broken doors and windows (**Figure 10.32**). Traffic-choked, garbage-strewn, polluted Cairo is home to an estimated 12.5 million people, more than one-fifth of Egypt's population. The city is bursting at the seams, yet people continue to arrive, seeking the better life that pulls countless migrants from the countryside year after year.

IMMIGRANT NEIGHBOURHOODS IN THE GLOBAL PERIPHERY AND SEMI-PERIPHERY CITY

In cities of the periphery and semi-periphery, a sea of slum development typically begins where the permanent buildings end, in some cases engulfing and dwarfing the central city. From a hill outside Lima, Peru, or overlooking the Cape Flats near Cape Town, South Africa, one sees a conglomeration of makeshift shacks built of every conceivable material, vying for every metre of space, extending to the horizon. There are few trees, and narrow footpaths wind through the shacks, leading to a few unpaved streets that go into the central city.

Millions of migrants travel to such environments every year. The total number of people living in these places is unknown because government control is impossible and enumeration impractical. In Rio de Janeiro, Brazil, the migrants build their dwellings on dangerous, landslide-prone slopes; in Port Moresby, Papua New Guinea, the migrants sink stilts in the mud and build out over the water, risking wind and waves. In Kolkata, India, thousands of migrants do not even try to erect shelters; there and in many other cities they live in the streets, under bridges, even in storm drains. City governments do not have the resources to adequately educate, medicate, or police the burgeoning populations, let alone provide even minimal housing for most.

The vast slums of cities in poorer parts of the world are typically ethnically delineated, with new arrivals precariously accommodated. For example, Kibera, the large slum area in Nairobi, Kenya, with over 1 million dwellers, is one of the worst in sub-Saharan Africa in terms of amenities (**Figure 10.33**). Much of the land on which Kibera is situated is owned by Nubians, who are of Sudanese descent. They settled in the area during the colonial era, and many have become businesspeople in the city of Nairobi. The modern tenants of the shanty settlements in Kibera are largely Luo (from western Kenya) and Luhya (from northwestern Kenya). During the fall of 2001, some of the Kiberian tenants were unable to pay the latest increase in rents. The Nubian landowners came to evict them; in the fighting that followed, a number of people were killed. Groups of Luo, Luhya, and others even began fighting among themselves. The government intervened to stabilize the situation, and the rent increases were withdrawn, but the fundamental problems—crowding, unemployment, unsanitary conditions, hunger, and lack of education—remain, and the ethnic groups living in Kibera will likely experience fighting again.

©iStockphoto.com/master2

FIGURE 10.33 Kibera, Kenya. Kibera, located within 5 kilometres of Kenya's capital city, Nairobi, is considered one of the most crowded places on earth.

How do the many millions of urban immigrants living in the slum-ridden rings and pockets of the cities of the global periphery and semi-periphery survive? Extended families share the money they manage to earn; when one member of the family has a salaried job, his or her income supports a dozen or more relatives. When a family member (or several members of a larger community) emigrates to a core country or an island of development and makes good money there, part of that income is sent back home and becomes the mainstay for those left behind. Hundreds of millions of dollars are transferred this way every year; these "remittances" make a critical difference in the poorer countries of the world (see Chapter 5).

In the vast slums, barrios, and favelas, those who are jobless or unsalaried are not idle. They work inside or in front of their modest homes, fixing things, repairing broken items for sale, sorting through small piles of waste for salvageable items, trading and selling

> **Informal economy** Economic activity that is neither taxed nor monitored by a government and is not included in that government's gross national product (GNP); as opposed to a formal economy.

goods from makeshift stands. What prevails here is referred to as the **informal economy**—the economy that is not taxed and is not counted toward a country's gross national income. What is generated in the informal economy can add up to a huge total in unrecorded monetary value. This is of concern to governments, because no taxes are paid on this income. Similarly, remittances are usually delivered in cash, not via Western Union or a bank, and are also unrecorded and untaxed. Typically, a trusted community member (who might pay a comparatively small bribe at the airport when passing through immigration) carries remittances to family members.

Even as the informal economy thrives among the millions in the shantytowns, the new era of globalization is having a major impact in the major cities founded or fostered by the colonial powers. In 2002, geographers Richard Grant and Jan Nijman documented this transformation in former colonial port cities, including Mumbai, India (formerly Bombay), where colonial rule produced an urban landscape marked by strong segregation of foreign and local activities, commercial as well as residential (**Figure 10.34**), and high levels of

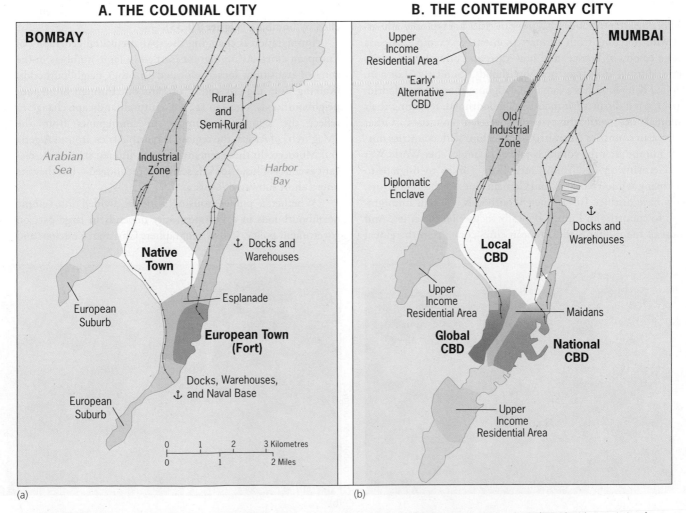

A. THE COLONIAL CITY

BOMBAY

Arabian Sea

Rural and Semi-Rural

Industrial Zone

Harbor Bay

⚓ Docks and Warehouses

Native Town

Esplanade

European Suburb

European Town (Fort)

Docks, Warehouses, ⚓ and Naval Base

European Suburb

| 0 | 1 | 2 | 3 Kilometres |
| 0 | | 1 | 2 Miles |

B. THE CONTEMPORARY CITY

MUMBAI

Upper Income Residential Area

"Early" Alternative CBD

Old Industrial Zone

Diplomatic Enclave

Local CBD

⚓ Docks and Warehouses

Upper Income Residential Area

Maidans

Global CBD

National CBD

Upper Income Residential Area

FIGURE 10.34 The changing character of Mumbai, India. (a) The colonial city and (b) the contemporary city. Adapted with permission from Richard Grant and Jan Nijman, "Globalization and the Corporate Geography of Cities in the Less-Developed World," *Annals of the Association of American Geographers*, 92, 2 (2002).

functional specialization and concentration. Adjacent to the port area was a well-demarcated European business district containing foreign (mostly British) companies. Economic activities in this European commercial area involved trade, transport, banking, distribution, and insurance. Zoning and building codes were strictly enforced. Physically separated from this European district were the traditional markets and bazaars of the so-called Native Town, a densely populated mix of commercial and residential land uses.

In the era of globalization, a new spatially demarcated foreign presence has arisen in Mumbai. The city now has a busy CBD at the heart of the original colonial city, housing mostly foreign corporations and multinational companies and linked mainly to the global economy. The former European Town has a large presence of big domestic companies and a pronounced orientation to the national (Indian) economy. The Native Town has a high concentration of small domestic company headquarters and the strongest orientation to the immediate urban area.

IMMIGRANT NEIGHBOURHOODS IN THE EUROPEAN CITY

Ethnic neighbourhoods in European cities are typically affiliated with migrants from former colonies. For example, Algeria was a colony of France, and now Paris and other French cities have distinct Algerian neighbourhoods. Similarly, London, United Kingdom, has a Jamaican neighbourhood, and Madrid, Spain, has a distinct Moroccan neighbourhood, reflecting their colonial ties with these now sovereign countries. Other European countries cultivated relationships with countries outside Europe after the colonial era. For example, after World War II, Germany invited young men from Turkey to migrate to Germany as guest workers, and German cities, such as Frankfurt, now have distinct Turkish neighbourhoods. Current immigration to countries in Europe typically focuses on the cities. And most of the migrants to European cities come from the global

periphery or from eastern Europe, not from other countries in western Europe.

Migration to Europe is constrained by government policies and laws. Many western European cities have public housing zones that were built following the devastation of World War II. Governments in Europe are typically very involved in the social rights of people, such as health care and housing. European cities are also much older than North American cities and were laid out for foot and horse traffic, not automobiles. Thus, European cities are generally more compact, densely populated, and pedestrian friendly. Much of the city's history took place in the city centre, which has been preserved and which attracts tourists today. While skyscrapers are typically the focal point of downtown in North American cities, a historic city centre is the focal point of downtown in European cities, and skyscrapers are reserved for developments on the outskirts of town. Housing in the European city is often combined with places of work, with work spaces on the bottom floors of buildings and housing above. Large zones of housing in Europe typically begin in a ring around the city centre, in what Ernest Burgess called the zone of transition. After the war, many European governments built public housing structures in the spaces around the city centre that had been levelled by bombing (**Figure 10.35**).

Immigration is changing the spatial-cultural geography of European cities. As immigrants settled in large numbers in the zone of transition, locals relocated to other neighbourhoods. Walking from the city centre of Paris out through immigrant neighbourhoods, one can see the cultural landscape change to reflect the significant number of immigrants from the "Maghreb" of Africa, the region of North Africa around Algeria and Morocco. In these tenement-lined, littered streets, the elegant avenues of historic Paris seem remote indeed—but they are only a short subway ride away.

Whether a public housing zone is divided into ethnic neighbourhoods in a European city depends in large part on government policy. Urban geographers Christian Kesteloot and

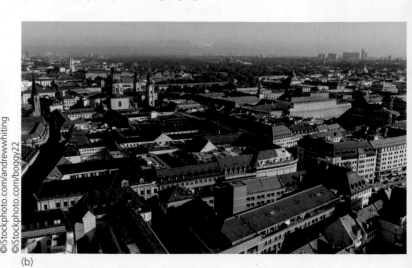

(a)   (b)

FIGURE 10.35 (a) Paris, France, and (b) Munich, Germany.

Cees Cortie studied housing policies and zones in Brussels, Belgium, and in Amsterdam, The Netherlands. They found that there is very little public housing in Brussels and that immigrants live in privately owned rentals throughout the city. Kesteloot and Cortie also found that immigrant groups in Brussels who came from a distinct region of their home country, especially rural regions, tended to cluster in ethnic neighbourhoods. In contrast, immigrant groups who came from cities chose rental units scattered throughout the city and, therefore, did not establish ethnic neighbourhoods in Brussels.

VISIBLE MINORITY NEIGHBOURHOODS IN CANADA

North American cities have varying degrees of segregated or concentrated minority communities in inner-city and suburban neighbourhoods. Certainly, it is difficult to compare the Canadian and American situation given each country's distinctive history and geography. American cities remain deeply divided along racial lines. In major Canadian cities there are some spatial concentrations of Aboriginal people, visible minorities, and newcomers, but most scholars conclude that Canadian cities do not have urban ghettos of the type generally associated with American cities.

Geographers Alan Walks and Lawrence Bourne argue that there has also been a change in how planners, sociologists, and others understand urban concentrations of visible minorities. In the 1960s and 1970s, scholars and policy makers regarded the formation of ethnic neighbourhoods as a "breakdown in the process of assimilation and integration" and as a form of social exclusion. Yet Canada, with its policy of multiculturalism, is among a number of countries that have come to regard visible minority concentrations in a more positive light. Such neighbourhoods are not only seen as contributing positively to the diversity and cosmopolitanism of a city (e.g., they ensure a diverse and interesting variety of foods, types of music, and fashions), but they are also seen as a necessary place for newcomers to find the support and community they need as they learn about Canadian society. Such neighbourhoods are seen as maintaining important cultural ties and group identities in an increasingly global world.

Given their research, Walks and Bourne argue that Canada's visible minority populations are not forming ghettos in the sense that term is usually understood—i.e., involuntarily segregated neighbourhoods that give residents little opportunity for advancement beyond those locations. As well, while there is some suggestion in a few cases of a link between visible minority neighbourhoods and a lower income level or poverty, there is no discernible connection between poverty and visible minority concentrations. As we noted in Chapter 5, most newcomers to Canada settle in the country's largest CMAs, including Toronto, Vancouver, Montreal, Edmonton-Calgary and Ottawa-Gatineau. The majority of Canadian cities do have some segregation and concentration of visible minorities, but at levels lower than are seen in countries such as Britain and Australia. However, in the four most segregated CMAs—Toronto, Vancouver, Winnipeg, and Montreal—levels of polarization are higher.

One example of a visible minority neighbourhood in Canada is Thorncliffe Park, in Toronto. Thorncliffe Park, in the east end of the city, consists of 34 high- and low-rise buildings spread over 2.2 square kilometres. Housing more than 26,000 people, this neighbourhood is a mix of post-war planning, strip malls, kebab houses, gas stations, and convenience stores. The average household income is $50,000, and 43 percent of the population is considered low income. The neighbourhood is a well-known immigrant community; the majority of its residents have roots in India and Pakistan, with others hailing from the Philippines, Afghanistan, Africa, Greece, and the Middle East. Doug Saunders, in his 2010 book *Arrival City: The Final Migration and Our Next World*, includes the neighbourhood in his profiles of those "always fascinating, bustling, unattractive, improvised, difficult places, full of new people and big plans" (**Figure 10.36**). Thorncliffe Park, since the 1980s, has been a place for newcomers to Canada. Originally, people stayed here until they were able to accumulate enough capital to move elsewhere; however, according to Toronto Community and Neighbourhood Services, this has changed over the last 15 years. Since 2000, more people are arriving at, and staying in, Thorncliffe Park.

Given Canada's social history, Walks and Bourne suggest that it is difficult to predict whether we are going to see greater spatial assimilation or more social exclusion. What we can say, they argue, is that "for certain groups a new pattern of cultural pluralism" is developing, "marked by the emergence of ethnic communities." How these new patterns develop in various cities will depend on numerous factors, including immigration policy, global and political economic processes, government policy, and the specific directions taken by different visible minority groups.

G. Brown

FIGURE 10.36 Thorncliffe Park, Toronto.

MAIN POINTS 10.4 How Do Cities Evolve?

- Cities are constantly changing as a result of economic, social, technological, political, and cultural processes at the local, regional, national, and global level.

- Cities in the core region have developed within the broader context of globalization and deindustrialization, which have influenced the development of downtown cores. Processes such as gentrification and redevelopment play a role in the changing shape of central city residential neighbourhoods, while shifting immigration policies influence the emergence of particularly racialized and ethnic neighbourhoods.

- In core regions, new planning and development policies—such as new urbanism, smart growth, and sustainability—attempt to ameliorate the negative impacts of rapid

urbanization, such as urban sprawl and the loss of agricultural land and environmentally sensitive ecosystems. These new concepts are only partially successful, given political and economic circumstances and consumer tastes.

- Cities in the periphery and semi-periphery often have fewer regulatory controls of development, which allow for makeshift communities to spring up at the city's edge. Suburban development in many cities reflects instances of formal and informal segregation and concentrations of various groups along ethnic and racial lines. While some may see these neighbourhoods as a failure of certain groups to assimilate, others argue they reflect the positive aspects of multiculturalism and diversity.

10.5 What Is the Connection between Cities and Globalization?

> **World city** Dominant city in terms of its role in the global political economy. Not one of the world's biggest cities in terms of population or industrial output, but rather a centre of strategic control of the world economy.

Globalization, as we defined the term in the second chapter, is a set of processes and outcomes that occur on the global scale, circumventing and leaping over state boundaries and making new connections between places. In the context of globalization, cities are playing an integral role that was not anticipated. Most statistics about economic activity at the global scale are gathered and disseminated by states. However, many of the most important processes occur among and between cities, not states as a whole. **World cities** function at the global scale, transcending state borders and functioning as the service centres of the world economy.

In this newly emerging system, models of cities and hierarchies of cities within states (such as we see in Christaller's model) no longer represent what is happening with the city. Geographers Taylor and Lang maintain that the city has become something other than a simple CBD tied in to a hierarchy of other cities within the state. The world city is a node in globalization—a place through which action and interaction occur. As a node, a world city is connected to other cities at the global level, and the forces shaping globalization pulse across these connections and through the cities—a phenomenon geographer Manuel Castells calls the "space of flows." Most lists of world cities provide a hierarchy of the most important world cities, then the next most important, and so forth. Virtually all agree that New York, London, and Tokyo (the world's largest city, with 38 million

inhabitants) are the most important world cities, but beyond that point the definition of what makes a world city, and the list of world cities, changes depending on the perspective of the researcher. For example, one of the most recent assessments of which cities can be considered "global," and the criteria for assessment, is from the Institute for Urban Strategies at the Mori Memorial Foundation in Tokyo. The institute has developed a Global Power City Index (GPCI) (**Figure 10.37**) that evaluates

FIGURE 10.37 Global Power City Index, top 10 cities in overall ranking, total score and rank by functions, 2014. Source: Institute for Urban Strategies, The Mori Memorial Foundation, Global Power City Index 2014. Available at www.mori-m-foundation.or.jp/gpci/index_e.html.

six main city functions to determine the strength of individual cities. The six functions are economy (purple), research and development (dark blue), cultural interaction (pink), livability (light blue), environment (green), and accessibility (orange).

Figure 10.37 illustrates the ranking of the top 10 world cities and a breakdown of where each city ranks for each of the functions. Note, for example, that New York and London top the list but rank poorly with respect to livability and environment. On the other hand, Paris is ranked third overall but is positioned at the top in terms of livability and is second in terms of accessibility. While such rankings are important in terms of understanding the characteristics of cities, their functions, and their position in the global urban system, there is some disagreement about which functions are the most important criteria for evaluating a world city. As the *Guest Field Note* from Robert Oliver suggests, cities vie for such high-profile events as the Olympics or the World University Games, although not everyone agrees that hosting such events is in a city's best interests.

World cities do not exist merely to service players in the global economy. Major world cities such as London and Paris are also capital cities. Even though London and Paris are a short distance apart, both function as world cities, in part because of the role they play within their respective states: each became a magnet for economic and political activity within its state and then the globe. States often focus development in one particular city, such as the capital city, and encourage interconnectedness between that city and the rest of the world, thereby bolstering that city above the rest of the cities in the state. As we noted earlier, a primate city is one that is disproportionately large within a regional or national urban system. Primate cities tend to be the largest and most economically influential within the state, with the next largest city in the state being much smaller and much less influential.

There are primate cities in many former colonies, as the colonial powers often ruled from a single dominant city, where economic and political activities were concentrated. In the noncolonial context, London and Paris each serve as examples of primate cities and world cities today, but some countries, such as the United States and Germany, have two or more world cities within their state borders. They thus do not have a single, distinct primate city. To understand the role of cities in globalization, we must also consider the services cities provide to places and peoples around the world, as well as the interconnectedness among cities. Geographers are now working to uncover the globalized flows and processes occurring across world cities, bringing them closer together.

GUEST FIELD NOTE

A Sporting Chance for Cities

More than a century ago, French nobleman Pierre Coubertin restored the Olympic Games as a mechanism to internationalize the benefits of sport. Coubertin believed that through participation or spectatorship, the Olympic spectacle had the capacity to reduce the social distance between various nations, regions, or societies of the world. As a researcher, and as someone with a lifelong passion for sports, I am interested in the role that sport plays in modern life.

One of the most visible opportunities to witness the symbolic power of sport is during the Olympic bidding process. Cities vie aggressively for what many see as the privilege of hosting the Olympic Games. Success means a city may gain recognition on the international stage and the construction of new sports and recreational facilities that enhance the quality of life for inhabitants while also contributing, many argue, to the overall economic, political, and social life of the city.

It is the interplay between the sporting spectacle and the socially educative potential that has made the Olympics a very powerful symbol, capable of catering to numerous agendas and interests across a range of spatial scales. Many cities competing in an economic climate characterized by globalization and deindustrialization have been forced to adopt more entrepreneurial models of urban growth. The competition for talented workers and wealthy tourists has produced fierce place wars, with numerous cities seeking to demonstrate their competitive advantages. With the capability of mixing sport, cultural consumption, and entertainment, the Olympic Games provide a seductive new form of urban development. The pursuit of the Olympic Games can be an occasion to leverage funds from senior levels of government, to address the city-building desires of the citizenry, and to trumpet the physical and social benefits of sport, physical education, and recreation across a range of skill levels and ages. At a time when cuts to physical education programs, the cancelling of after-school sports programs, increased municipal user fees for swimming pools and skating rinks, and skyrocketing rates of obesity dominate urban itineraries, winning the right to host the Olympics can offer a reprieve. Without question, sport and leisure, as budget items, simply do not rank as high as health and social services.

The Olympics offer city managers, corporate stakeholders, and local residents an occasion to address questions concerning both image and infrastructure. Thinking about the Olympics allows our imaginations to soar. It is exciting to imagine thousands of the world's fastest and strongest athletes convening in one place. At the same time, the construction of multiple sporting venues and their supporting infrastructure, the demands on the transportation network, and the refashioning of the city to meet the communicative and consumptive demands of tourists, often overshadows the fact that people actually live in the host city (**Figure 10.38**). Not surprisingly, residents' understanding of what an Olympic city is does not always mesh with those of growth-minded visionaries.

Residents work and play in the Olympic city long after the crowds have dissipated. While the Olympics are often presented as a politically saleable commodity, cities often struggle with very difficult questions about the benefits and drawbacks of hosting the Games. Concerns over massive operating and capital costs, exorbitant security expenses, corporate greed, and other local inconveniences and injustices make hosting seem a risky proposition. For local-area residents, concerns over inflation, housing prices, and increased policing are just as important as the issues of job creation, urban regeneration, and city image. Social justice groups argue that instead of sinking critical resources into new sport installations, we should invest in social programs.

Exploring how the various claims to urban space become visible during the Olympic planning and hosting process provides geographers with a prime opportunity to examine myriad social and political conflicts around urban space. What are the risks of trying to appease global markets, develop international contacts, and open our borders to the world? These and other questions continue to attract the interest of geographers seeking to understand the implications of the globe's premier sporting event on the fabric of our local communities. By examining the manner by which claims to urban space are negotiated and represented, we have a prime opportunity to examine the "conflicting geographies of democracy." Do the Olympics represent

FIGURE 10.38 Rio de Janeiro prepares to host the 2016 Olympic Games. From left, developer and builder Carlos Fernando Carvalho, Rio de Janeiro's mayor Eduardo Paes, International Olympic Committee president Jacques Rogge, head of the IOC Evaluation Commission Nawal El Moutawakel, and Brazil Olympic Committee president Carlos Arthur Nuzman view a model of Rio's Olympic village, December 29, 2010.

a modern version of bread and circuses—the subjugation of democracy—or can they be utilized to create an urban culture that is both socially and spatially accessible?

Robert Oliver, Virginia Polytechnic Institute and State University

CITIES AS SPACES OF CONSUMPTION

> **Spaces of consumption** Areas of a city, the main purpose of which is to encourage people to consume goods and services; driven primarily by the global media industry.

In addition to being nodes in globalization, cities are also products of globalization. Major changes in cities, such as the redevelopment of New York's Times Square and the remaking of Berlin's Potsdamer Platz, are the result of global processes. Frank Roost has found that "the global media industry is becoming the driving force in the reshaping of cities" such as New York and Berlin, transforming city centres into **spaces of consumption**. Media companies are investing heavily in urban centres in order to create major entertainment districts, places where tourists can go to consume their products.

For example, in New York City—ranked second on the 2014 GPCI—government entities began to redevelop Times Square in the early 1980s. At that time, this area of the city was known for its neon lights, pornographic movie houses, prostitution, and other illicit economic activities. The city sought to push these businesses out of Times Square and bring back the conglomeration of restaurants, hotels, bars, and entertainment spaces that had filled the business district

before World War II. Over the next decade the city closed hundreds of small businesses in Times Square, and in 1995, Mayor Rudolph Giuliani reached a deal with Michael Eisner, CEO of Walt Disney Company. The mayor promised to remove the remaining sex shops, and Eisner committed to renovating the New Amsterdam Theater, a focal point in Times Square (**Figure 10.39**). Secured with a $26-million low-interest loan from the state of New York, Disney set the course for a new family-friendly entertainment district in New York. The restored New Amsterdam Theater now hosts Disney musicals such as The Lion King and Beauty and the Beast (both based on Disney movies), and the area around Times Square has become a space of consumption and a variation on a theme park with themed restaurants (e.g., Hard Rock Cafe, ESPN Zone), cross-promoting themed stores (e.g., Warner Brothers Store, Disney Store), and retail stores that cater to families (for example, an enormous Toys R Us with a Ferris wheel inside).

Potsdamer Platz in Berlin is also becoming a new space of consumption in the city centre. Prior to the bombing of Berlin during World War II, Potsdamer Platz was a centre of entertainment for Berlin's middle class. After the war, little was left of the area. By the 1960s a 460-metre border zone and the Berlin Wall occupied the formerly vibrant area of the city. After

(b)

FIGURE 10.39 New Amsterdam Theater, Times Square, New York City. (a) The New Amsterdam Theater in Times Square as it appeared in 1947. Note the signs around the building advertising arcade games and a flea circus. (b) During the 1980s and 1990s, Times Square was "cleaned up" and reinvigorated. The Walt Disney Company renovated the New Amsterdam Theater and now shows productions of musicals such as *Beauty and the Beast* and *The Lion King*.

(a)

reunification, the city divided Potsdamer Platz and sold the land. The two largest owners are the German company Daimler-Benz and the Japanese company Sony. Sony built a huge entertainment structure called the Sony Center (**Figure 10.40**) for cross-promotion. According to Roost, much of the Daimler-Benz structure, known as Daimler City, is a space of consumption, with entertainment venues, restaurants, bars, and hotels.

Although tourists will be focused on the theme park atmosphere of these spaces of consumption, the renovations have also brought spaces of media production to both cities. Sony has placed its European headquarters in Berlin, Warner Brothers moved its offices to Times Square, and new office towers around Times Square house many other media companies.

FIGURE 10.40 The Sony Center, Potsdamer Platz, Berlin.

MAIN POINTS 10.5 What Is the Connection between Cities and Globalization?

- The processes of globalization have repositioned certain cities within economic and political contexts that are beyond the reach of the nation-state. Cities that function in this global context are called world cities.

- World cities operate within a global urban system, forming important nodes in the global flow of people, technologies, finances, and goods and services. New York, London, and Tokyo are the most important world cities.

- There are various ranking systems for determining where a city fits in the world system. The Institute for Urban Strategies at the Mori Memorial Foundation in Tokyo,

Japan, has developed a Global Cities Power Index (GCPI), which uses six main city functions to determine a city's strength. These functions are economy, research and development, cultural interaction, livability, environment, and accessibility.

- Cities are also spaces of consumption when they are marketed as places tourists can experience and consume as entertainment. World cities market themselves as unique locations with distinctive features—e.g., buildings and structures that everyone recognizes, even though they may never have been there.

SUMMARY

Today much of the world's population resides in cities; indeed, in Canada, 80 percent of the population resides in urban areas. Human beings initially began living in urban areas some 3,500 years ago, and the development of cities can be traced to six urban hearths. The modern city emerged at the time of the Industrial Revolution, during the era of colonialism and imperialism. With more efficient agricultural practices, a food surplus, and the development of mass manufacturing, rural people flocked to cities for the opportunities they offered. The growth of city planning and development helped organize the city into distinctive land uses, and various models were created to map the various areas of a city—the CBD, inner residential and industrial zones, suburban zones, and the rural hinterland. The form a city takes varies, and individual political, economic, and cultural histories determine the evolving structure of core, peripheral, and semi-peripheral cities. While models give us some sense of how cities are structured, each city is unique and must be studied for its own particularities.

Cities are also interconnected to each other, and models such as central place theory and the rank-size rule seek to make sense of the patterns found in various urban systems. Urban

systems develop at a variety of scales, from the local and the regional to the national. As a result of the processes of globalization, certain cities have become world cities, functioning as nodes for the global flow of people, technologies, finances, and goods and services.

The city is an ever-changing cultural landscape, its layers reflecting grand plans by governments, impassioned pursuits by individuals, economic decisions by corporations, and processes of globalization. In North America, planning concepts such as new urbanism, smart growth, and sustainability were developed to try to deal with some of the more negative aspects of city growth and development, including congestion, sprawl, loss of agricultural land, and environmental damage. Geographers who study cities have a multitude of topics to examine. From gentrification to tear-downs, from favelas to monster homes, from spaces of production to spaces of consumption, from ancient walls to gated communities, cities have so much in common, yet each has its own pulse, its own feel, its own spatial structure, its own set of realities. The pulse of the city is undoubtedly created by the peoples and cultures who live there.

DISCUSSION AND REVIEW QUESTIONS

1. The process of urbanization took thousands of years to develop. What were the key innovations and technologies that led to the first urban revolution? Where were the hearths of humanity's urban revolution, and when did they initially develop?

2. Similar to the agricultural revolution, the urban revolution occurred in phases. What precipitated the second urban

revolution, and what were the spatial changes associated with the second wave?

3. Urban geographers are interested in where cities form; how they develop (urban morphology), and how cities act as organizing centres for a collection of settlements. Walter Christaller was one of the first to develop models and a theory of city formation. Discuss Christaller's

contribution to our understanding of urban geography. What was his key theory?

4. Discuss the spatial characteristics of Canada's urban history and the evolution of a Canadian urban system. What are the primary factors that have led to its unique spatial pattern?

5. One of the major challenges in modern cities is urban sprawl. What is urban sprawl? What has caused it? What, if anything, is being done to counteract it? What has been your experience with urban sprawl?

6. Cities are very much caught up in the processes of globalization. How do world cities operate distinctly across a variety of scales, from the local to the global?

GEOGRAPHIC CONCEPTS

agora   281
agricultural surplus   277
agricultural village   277
census agglomeration   287
census metropolitan area (CMA)   287
central business district (CBD)   290
central city   290
central place theory   286
centrality   286
city   275
commercialization   295
concentric zone model   291
disamenity sector   293
edge cities   292
first urban revolution   278
Forum   282
functional zonation   289
gentrification   295
Griffin-Ford model   292
Huang He (Yellow) River Valley and Wei (Yangtze) River Valley   279
Indus River Valley   279
informal economy   301
leadership class   278
mega-city   276

Mesoamerica   279
Mesopotamia   278
new urbanism   297
Nile River Valley   279
Peru   280
primate city   286
rank-size rule   286
shantytowns   299
Site   285
situation   285
social stratification   277
spaces of consumption   306
suburb   290
suburban realm   276
suburbanization   290
tear-downs   296
trade area   286
urban (area)   276
urban agglomerations   276
urban morphology   278
urban sprawl   297
world city   304
zone   289
zoning laws   299

ADDITIONAL RESOURCES ON-LINE

Congress for the New Urbanism: www.cnu.org

Globalization and World Cities Research Network: www.lboro. ac.uk/gawc/index.html

Sierra Club Challenge to Sprawl Campaign: www.sierraclub. org/sprawl

About Berlin: www.learner.org/resources/series85.html

Click on Video On Demand for "Berlin: Changing Centre of a Changing Europe"

CHAPTER 11
DEVELOPMENT

Geography, Trade, and Development

WALKING DOWN ONE of the major streets of Timbuktu, Mali (**Figure 11.1**), one could hardly believe they were in the renowned intellectual, spiritual, and economic centre of the 13th to 16th centuries—a place with such a great reputation for wealth that it spurred the first European explorations along the African coast. What survives is a relatively impoverished town of some 15,000 people that functions as the central place for the surrounding area and seeks to attract some tourist business based on its legendary name.

What happened to Timbuktu? Many centuries ago the city derived its wealth from its ability to control the trans-Sahara trade in gold, salt, ivory, kola nuts, and slaves. However, when trade patterns shifted with the development of maritime routes along

the west coast of Africa, Timbuktu lost its strategic position, and a long period of decline set in. This has been made worse by ongoing droughts and desertification. More recently, in 2012 and 2013, the city was seized and occupied by secessionists and Islamists linked to al-Qaeda. Early in 2013, Mali's former colonial power, France, sent in its military to intervene. This was followed by the assignment of some 1,200 United Nations peacekeepers to Timbuktu, which is now only a shadow of its former self.

Timbuktu's story serves as a reminder that where a place is located, as well as its political and environmental context, can be as important as, or even more important than, the commodities found in that place. Indeed, there are many examples of places where the presence of a valuable commodity does not translate into an improved economy for those living nearby. The people working on the oil wells in Gabon or chopping down rare hardwood trees in Thailand, for example, are not the ones who most benefit from the wealth associated with demand for the goods they help produce. Instead, international corporations or the wealthiest families in a place, those who own the industry, tend to be the principal beneficiaries.

Such is the structure of the global economy today, which has benefitted a relatively few people and places far more than it has helped many others.

The concept of the commodity chain can help us understand how the production of an item creates wealth for some and not for others. A commodity chain is a series of links connecting the many places of production and distribution that produce a commodity, which is then exchanged on the market and, ultimately, consumed (see Chapter 2). Each link along the chain adds a certain value to the commodity, generating different levels of wealth for the places and the people where production occurs.

What Timbuktu had to offer was the ability to coordinate and facilitate an overland trade based on its geographic situation near the Niger River, the last major water source for those crossing

FIGURE 11.1 Timbuktu, Mali. The dirt streets found throughout much of the town reflect the impoverishment of this once celebrated place.

© Alexander B. Murphy

the Sahara from south to north across what is now Mali and Algeria. When the trade that was essential to the commodity chain shifted westward, Timbuktu's economic foundation crumbled. In modern times, commodity chains include miners and agriculturalists, manufacturers, exporters and importers, wholesalers and retailers, advertisers and designers, and, of course, consumers. Places positioned strategically along a commodity chain can benefit, but they benefit in different ways. Furthermore, the structure and geographical characteristics of a commodity chain can always shift in response to changing conditions, in many cases quite quickly. The amount of wealth generated at each link of the commodity chain depends on how production occurs at that particular point.

In Chapter 2, we introduced the concepts of core and periphery. Sophisticated technology, high skill levels, extensive research and development, and high salaries tend to be associated with segments of global commodity chains located in the core. The segments located in the periphery, by contrast, tend to be associated with basic technology, less education, little research and development, and lower wages. Since the people with the highest salaries own the businesses or work in advertising, and the people with the lowest salaries work in the mines or fields, global commodity chains often reinforce sharp divisions between core and peripheral regions.

As the 21st century unfolds, countless governments, academics, non-governmental organizations, and international financial institutions will offer ideas about how to improve conditions within the peripheral and semi-peripheral parts of the world. The theories, methods, and recommendations vary, but they are all focused on the elusive concept of development. For some, it is a matter of enabling the periphery and semi-periphery to achieve the same levels of productivity, consumption, and wealth as the core. Others argue that this is a Western-centric point of view that focuses far too heavily on wealth generation as a measure of progress. Furthermore, many critics of this perspective have pointed out that a world in which all countries followed such a path would be environmentally unsustainable. At the same time, many observers have argued that broader quality-of-life and human development considerations should take precedence over the long-standing pursuit of unfettered economic growth, not only in the periphery and semi-periphery, but in the world's core regions as well.

In this chapter, we review how development is defined and measured, and look at some of the theories of development. We examine how geography affects development, considering the structures of the world economy. We also look at the barriers to and costs of development within countries and consider reasons why uneven development occurs within the state.

KEY QUESTIONS FOR CHAPTER 11

1. How is development defined and measured?

2. How does geographical situation affect development?

3. What are the barriers to, and the costs of, development?

4. How do political and economic institutions influence uneven development within states?

11.1 How Is Development Defined and Measured?

In the modern world, the concept of development is typically discussed as "progress." In turn, progress implies some form of improvement or advancement in areas such as technology and material production, and in people's social and economic welfare. To say a country is **developing**, then, is to say that progress is being made in technology, production, and socio-economic welfare. This popular

> **Developing** With respect to a country, making progress in technology, production, and socio-economic welfare.

contemporary notion of development dates back to the time of the Industrial Revolution and the idea that technology can do much to improve people's lives. To be sure, advances in technology have given people the ability to produce more food, create new products, and accrue material wealth. At the same time, however, a near-exclusive focus on economic considerations has made the notion of development, as it is currently understood, a narrow and sometimes controversial indicator of the human condition. Indeed, in more recent years there has been growing recognition that these things do not necessarily bring happiness, social stability, or environmental sustainability—and, thus, that our conceptualization of what development *really* means, and how we pursue it, should be modified accordingly.

FIGURE 11.2 Practising traditional agriculture in Niger, Africa.

The economic and social geography of the contemporary world is a patchwork of almost inconceivable contrasts. On their shifting fields carved out of equatorial American and African forests, farmers grow root crops using ancient methods and rudimentary tools (**Figure 11.2**). On the Great Plains of North America, in the Ukraine, and in eastern Australia, farmers use expensive, modern machines to plough the land, seed the grain, and harvest the wheat. Tool-makers in the villages of Papua New Guinea still fashion their implements by hand, as they did many centuries ago, whereas factory workers in Ontario use cutting-edge robotics to produce automobiles by the shipload for distribution throughout the world (**Figure 11.3**).

FIGURE 11.3 Honda plant in Alliston, Ontario.

Between these extremes, the variety of productive activities and the means of production are virtually endless.

These contrasts point to a major issue in understanding development: wealth does not depend solely on what is produced but also depends in large part on how and where it is produced. People can grow agricultural commodities with rudimentary tools or with expensive combines. Is one or the other necessary for development to occur? Do both count as forms of development? What exactly are countries trying to achieve when they pursue development? The idea of development is everywhere, but rarely do we pause to ask exactly what development means, what it should do for people, or how we can measure it.

GROSS NATIONAL INCOME

Methods of measuring development typically fit into three major areas of concern: development in economic welfare, development in technology and production, and development in social welfare. Over the past six decades, the most common way to compare development in economic welfare was to use the index economists created to compare countries, the gross national product. **Gross national product (GNP)** is a measure of the total value of the officially recorded goods and services produced by the citizens and corporations of a country in a given year. It includes things produced both inside and outside the country's territory, and it is therefore broader than **gross domestic product (GDP)**, which measures only goods and services produced within a country's borders during a given year.

In recent years, economists have turned to **gross national income (GNI)** as a more accurate way of measuring a country's wealth in the context of a global economy. GNI measures the total value of all goods and services produced within a country plus income received from investments outside the country. In order to compare GNI across countries, however, economists must standardize the data. The most common way to standardize GNI data is to divide it by the population of the country, yielding the **per capita GNI**. For example, according to the World Bank, Norway's per capita gross national income in U.S. dollars in 2013 was $102,610. That same year, the per capita GNI of the United States was $53,470, and Canada's was $52,200. But in Pakistan, the

> **Gross national product (GNP)** The total value of all goods and services produced by a country's economy in a given year. It includes all goods and services produced by corporations and individuals of a country, whether or not they are located within the country.
>
> **Gross domestic product (GDP)** The total value of all goods and services produced within a country during a given year.
>
> **Gross national income (GNI)** The total value of all goods and services produced within a country plus income received from investments outside the country.

> **Per capita GNI** The total value of all goods and services produced within a country plus income received from investments outside the country, divided by the population of the country.

world's sixth most populous country, it was only $1,360; in Mali (where Timbuktu is located) it was $670; and in Togo, the per capita GNI in 2013 was a mere $530. This enormous range across the globe in per capita GNI reflects the often searing contrasts between rich and poor.

Although the table of per capita GNI in 2013 (**Table 11.1**) clearly shows the startling differences between rich and poor in the world, the use of this statistic as an indicator of development has several shortcomings. Most critically, GNI is a limited measure because it includes only transactions made in the **formal economy**, the legal economy that governments tax and monitor. Many of the countries have a per capita GNI of less than $1,000 per year—a figure so low it seems impossible that people could survive on it. However, a key component of survival in these countries is the **informal economy**, the illegal or uncounted economy that governments do not tax or keep track of, which can include everything from the black market to illegal drug trade to a garden plot in a yard to waste pickers salvaging recyclable materials (**Figure 11.4**). For example, the Swedish International Development Cooperation Agency reported in 2004 that the size of the informal labour force in Africa is almost 80 percent, and this sector accounts for over 90 percent of the new jobs that are created on that continent. The informal

> **Formal economy** The legal economy that is taxed and monitored by a government and is included in a government's gross national product (GNP); as opposed to an informal economy.
>
> **Informal economy** Economic activity that is neither taxed nor monitored by a government and is not included in that government's gross national product (GNP); as opposed to a formal economy.

Chandan Khanna/AFP/Getty Images

FIGURE 11.4 Waste pickers in Delhi, India sort through garbage for recyclable material. Waste pickers are part of the country's informal economy. A 2010 study in India estimated waste pickers in that country numbered 1.5 million people, primarily women and those from socially marginalized groups.

economy is clearly a significant element in the economies of many countries, but GNI statistics omit it entirely.

Another limitation of using per capita GNI as a development indicator is that it masks the extremes in the distribution of wealth within a country. The Middle Eastern oil countries of Kuwait and the United Arab Emirates (UAE) have per

TABLE 11.1	Per Capita World GNI, 2013		
Country	**GNI (U.S.$)**	**Country**	**GNI (U.S.$)**
Norway	102,610	Mali	670
Switzerland	90,760	Burkina Faso	670
Qatar	86,790	Sierra Leone	660
Luxembourg	69,900	Tanzania	630
Australia	65,390	Rwanda	630
Sweden	61,760	Mozambique	610
Denmark	61,680	Guinea-Bissau	590
Singapore	54,040	Uganda	550
United States	53,470	Togo	530
Canada	52,200	The Gambia	500
Netherlands	51,060	Eritrea	490
Austria	50,430	Ethiopia	470
Finland	48,820	Guinea	460
Germany	47,270	Madagascar	440
Iceland	46,400	Democratic Republic of Congo	430
Japan	46,330	Liberia	410
Belgium	46,290	Niger	400
France	43,460	Central African Republic	320
Ireland	43,110	Malawi	270
United Kingdom	41,680	Burundi	260

Source: Data from the World Bank, accessed at http://data.worldbank.org/indicator/NY.GNP.PCAP.CD/countries?display=default.

capita GNIs higher than that of several European countries. However, these figures give us no hint of the degree of overall participation in the country's economy, the average citizen's material standard of living, or the development gaps between genders or among regions. We know from other indicators that economic production and the wealth it generates are not distributed evenly across the seven emirates that make up the UAE. For example, Abu Dhabi, the emirate that dominates the petroleum industry, generated over half of the country's GNI in 2007. Dubai, the next largest emirate, generated about a quarter of the GNI. The Qaywayn emirate, on the other hand, generated less than 1 percent of the country's gross GNI.

Similarly, Canada's relatively high per capita GNI would also seem to indicate that it is a prosperous core country. Much like the UAE, however, significant developmental disparities exist across different regions of Canada and among the country's various population subgroups. Unemployment rates, for example, vary considerably across Canada. In August 2014, Newfoundland and Labrador's unemployment rate was 13.5 percent, while 10.5 percent of Prince Edward Island's active labour force was out of work. Alberta's unemployment rate, on the other hand, was only 4.9 percent, and Saskatchewan had the lowest provincial unemployment rate in the country, at 4.2 percent. Unemployment rates also vary among men and women in Canada and are sometimes much higher for particular age groups. In August 2014, for example, the national unemployment rate for women over the age of 25 was only 5.5 percent, while it was 6.2 percent for men aged 25 and over. However, for youth aged 15 to 24 years, the unemployment rate that month was more than twice as high, 13.4 percent. Unemployment rates must be used cautiously as indicators of economic development, as they only take into account people who are actively working or looking for work. Thus, they do not count discouraged workers, people who have lost their jobs and have had such difficulty finding new employment that they have simply withdrawn from the labour market, or people who are out of the labour force for other reasons, such as going to school for retraining after losing a previous job. They also do not count people who are underemployed, which refers to people who are working fewer hours than they would like due to a lack of adequate employment. Nonetheless, these interprovincial and demographic variations certainly confirm the need to consider geographical circumstances and differences within the country or region being analyzed when assessing levels of development.

Yet another limitation of the per capita GNI indicator is that it measures only the value of the outputs created in a particular place. That is, it does not account for the negative costs or consequences of production, such as when the natural environment is harmed by the depletion of resources or pollution of the air and water. Per capita GNI may even treat such externalities as a good thing. For example, the sale of cigarettes augments GNI by way of the value created through the growing and processing of tobacco. If the cigarettes cause sickness in smokers that requires their hospitalization, the GNI is boosted further by the money being spent on the patients' health care. Similarly, the use of energy-efficient devices can lower GNI, despite their environmental benefits, by reducing the number of times these devices must be purchased and by lowering the amount of money spent to pay for electricity.

Another useful example of how the per capita GNI indicator may fail to adequately consider the negative costs of production is provided by looking at Canada's Athabasca oil sands. Industrial development of these bituminous sands, which are found in three large areas across northeastern Alberta and are believed to be one of the world's largest oil reserves, began in the late 1960s and has accelerated dramatically since the late 1990s. In 2012 some 1.9 million barrels of oil were being produced each day, and this is projected to increase to as much as 3.8 million barrels of oil per day (or more) by 2022. The province of Alberta, the Canadian government, the various corporations doing business in the region, and the many individuals and families who have moved there in search of work have certainly enjoyed numerous economic benefits as a result of this growing production. Indeed, oil sands production contributes significantly to Canada's GNI each year. However, criticism of some of the practices associated with oil extraction and processing in the oil sands has been mounting in recent years. Areas of concern include the incredibly high levels of water consumption required to extract the oil from the sand (two to five barrels of water per barrel of oil), the toxicity of the waste water created by this extraction process, and the harm this water has done to fish and other aquatic life as it seeps into the area's water bodies. The extent to which these and other problems exist in the oil sands region, and the question of how long such practices can be sustained environmentally, are hotly debated topics. David Schindler of the University of Alberta has noted that "environmental groups and the handful of Aboriginal communities living in towns near the oil sands have repeatedly warned that the rapid development has come at too high a cost to the environment."

Together, the various deficiencies of the per capita GNI indicator underscore the importance of reading and interpreting development indicators with caution. The clear need to measure and compare levels of development more accurately has prompted many analysts to create indices based on the advancement and integration of technology, improvements in productivity, or improvements in social welfare as alternatives.

For example, to gain a sense of the role of technology in the economy, analysts can measure the occupational structure of the labour force, which is based on the percentage of workers employed in various sectors of the economy. A high percentage of labourers engaged in the production of food staples (i.e., agriculture) signals a low overall level of development, as conventionally defined, while a high percentage of workers involved in high-tech industries and services implies a high level of development. Productivity per worker is examined by summing production over the course of a year and dividing it by the total number of people in the labour force. A more productive workforce points to a higher level of mechanization in production. To measure access to technology, some analysts measure

FIGURE 11.5 Access to communications around the world. This map shows the number of phone calls made in different countries, illustrating the unevenness of access to, and use of, telecommunications equipment. Source: Pankaj, G. and Altman, S. A., *DHL Global Connectedness Index 2014*, p.106–107. Accessed at www.dhl.com/content/dam/Campaigns/gci2014/downloads/dhl_gci_2014_study_high.pdf.

transportation and communications facilities per person, which reduces railway, road, airline connections, telephone, radio, television, and so forth to a per capita index—and reflects the amount of infrastructure that exists to facilitate economic activity. **Figure 11.5** highlights some of the extraordinary disparities in access to communications around the world. By mapping telephone calls around the world, researchers are able to visualize the unevenness of access to, and use of, telecommunications equipment. Compare, for example, the larger circles in North America and Europe to the much smaller circles in Africa; we can see how much more access there is to telephone communication in the core regions of the world.

Other analysts focus on social welfare to measure development. One tool in this regard is the dependency ratio, a measure of the number of dependents, young and old, that each 100 employed people must support (**Figure 11.6**). A high dependency ratio can result in significant economic and social strain. Yet, as discussed in Chapter 4, the aging countries of Europe have high dependency ratios and also very high per capita GNIs.

We can employ countless other statistics to measure social welfare, including literacy rates, infant mortality, life expectancy, caloric intake per person, percentage of family income spent on food, and amount of savings per capita. Looking through all of these, we quickly gain a sense that many countries come out in approximately the same position no matter which measures are used. Each indicator shares one limit with per capita GNI, however, in that they do not capture differences in development within countries.

Although it is also focused on economic concerns, one measurement tool that is increasingly used to identify intranational differences in levels of development is the Gini

coefficient (or "Gini index"). This tool, developed by the Italian statistician and sociologist Corrado Gini in 1912, is used to measure the levels of income or wealth distribution. A Gini coefficient of zero means there is perfect equality across the population of a particular place when it comes to the distribution of incomes, while a Gini coefficient of one means the exact opposite: there is a major imbalance in income distribution. A coefficient of one means one person has all of the income. A 2012 article in *The Economist* pointed out that in most Latin American countries, the Gini coefficient dropped between 2000 and 2010 as a result of governments' and other agencies' development efforts. The Gini index for the entire Latin American region dropped from 0.54 to 0.50, which is lower than at any other time in the previous 30 years.

Another measure that is gaining attention because it takes a broader range of factors into account is the Gross National Happiness (GNH) Index (**Figure 11.7**). First introduced by Jigme Singye Wangchuck, the King of Bhutan, the GNH Index has been used in the small Asian country of Bhutan since 1971. In the five decades since, many detractors of the current economics-dominated approach to measuring and comparing development levels across countries have pointed to the GNH Index as a much more suitable development measure. It takes a more holistic approach to measuring progress and assigns equal value to economic and non-economic indicators of population well-being. This includes compiling data regarding the four "pillars" of happiness: good governance; sustainable socio-economic development; cultural preservation; and environmental conservation. The four pillars are then broken into nine domains, which include 33 different indicators. Based on these indicators, the GNH Index is calculated as a number between 0 and 1—an index figure closer to one is considered better. In 2010,

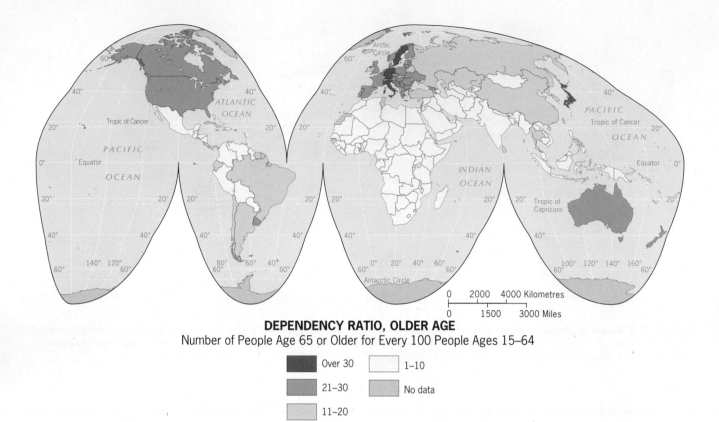

DEPENDENCY RATIO, OLDER AGE
Number of People Age 65 or Older for Every 100 People Ages 15–64

- Over 30
- 1–10
- 21–30
- No data
- 11–20

FIGURE 11.6 (a) Older person dependency ratio. The older person dependency ratio is a measure of the number of people 65 and older relative to 100 working-age adults, between 15 and 64. The working-age adults in the formal economy contribute to a country's tax base, thereby supporting the older population of a country. Data from: World Bank, 2014.

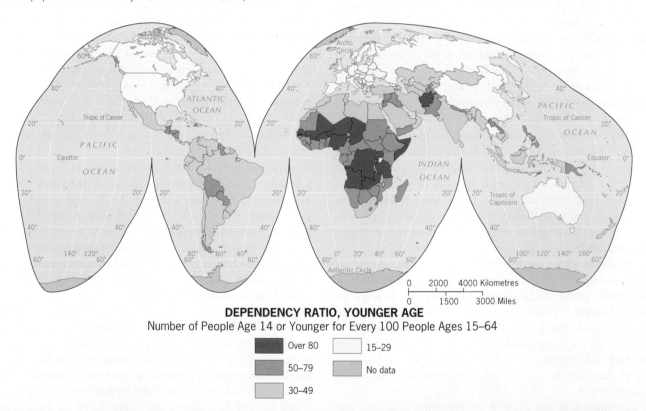

DEPENDENCY RATIO, YOUNGER AGE
Number of People Age 14 or Younger for Every 100 People Ages 15–64

- Over 80
- 15–29
- 50–79
- No data
- 30–49

FIGURE 11.6 (b) Younger person dependency ratio. The younger person dependency ratio is a measure of the number of people birth to age 14 relative to 100 working-age adults, between 15 and 64. The working-age adults in the formal economy contribute to a country's tax base, thereby supporting the younger population of a country. Data from: World Bank, 2014.

FIGURE 11.7 Gross National Happiness Index. Jigme Singye Wangchuck, the former King of Bhutan, created the Gross National Happiness Index in the 1970s. He stated, "GNH is more important than GDP. The understanding of what humans need to make them happy is vital to our society."

out from more commonly used indicators is that researchers can separate data for particular sub-populations, which provides a means to determine levels of equality across the country. For example, the 2010 GNH survey results showed that, on average, men were happier than women, urban people were happier than rural people, and unmarried and young people had a higher index value than married and older people. In 2012 the United Nations set up a panel that is now working to build a model that other countries can use to replicate this more holistic approach to the measurement of development around the world.

While indicator tools such as the Gini coefficient and Gross National Happiness Index are growing in popularity and credibility, one of the most widely influential measurements of development over the past three decades has been the Human Development Index, first employed by the United Nations in 1990. The Human Development Index was designed to go beyond economics by incorporating the "three basic dimensions of human development: a long and healthy life, knowledge and a decent standard of living." Several statistics—including life expectancy at birth, literacy rates and school enrolment rates, and per capita GDP—factor into the calculation of the Human Development Index. The 2014 Human Development Report, which presented the Human Development Index for countries based on 2013 and 2014 data, once again demonstrated the stark disparities that exist among world regions and, as part of this, between the core and periphery (see **Figure 11.8**).

Bhutan achieved a GNH figure of 0.743. The survey found that 41 percent of Bhutanese people had achieved sufficiency in six or more of the nine domains and could thus be considered happy. Another element of the GNH Index that makes it stand

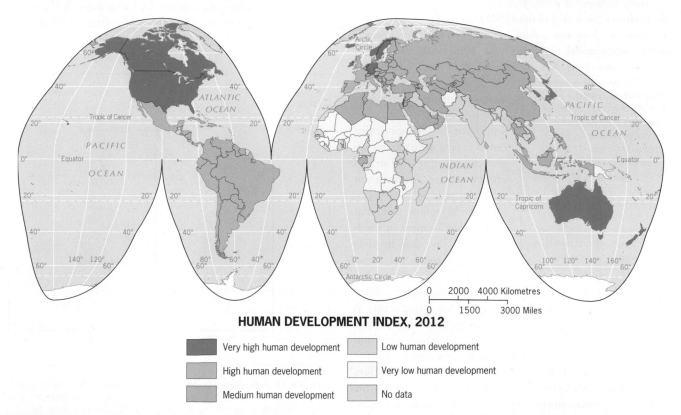

HUMAN DEVELOPMENT INDEX, 2012

- Very high human development
- High human development
- Medium human development
- Low human development
- Very low human development
- No data

FIGURE 11.8 Human Development Index, 2012. The Human Development Index incorporates three dimensions of human development: life expectancy, education and knowledge, and standard of living. Like other measures of development, it shows the disparities between world regions and between the core and periphery. Data from United Nations Human Development Report, http://hdr.undp.org/en/content/table-1-human-development-index-and-its-components.

DEVELOPMENT MODELS

This discussion of ways of measuring development takes us back to the problem with terminology. The word "developing" suggests that all countries are consistently making progress as it pertains to each of these indicators by, for example, increasing literacy, improving communications, or raising levels of worker productivity. The central concern here is that current conceptualizations of development suggest that all countries have moved or will move through the same process of development, as if travelling from the bottom to the top of a scale or ladder, but this does not take geographical differences seriously. Just because Japan moved from a rural, agrarian state to an urbanized, industrial one, for example, does not mean that Sudan will, or that it might do so in the same way. Another criticism is that today's prevailing conceptualization of development has a Western bias. Critics argue that some of the measures taken in poorer countries that the West views as progress, such as attracting industry and mechanizing agriculture, can actually lead to worsened social and environmental conditions for many people in the poorer countries. Still others criticize the development model because it treats countries as autonomous units moving through a process of development at different speeds. The model does not consider geography or interrelations across scales, and does not account for the fact that actions at one scale influence socio-economic changes at other scales.

Many theories of development grew out of the major de-colonization movements of the 1950s and 1960s. In this regard, the classic development model is economist Walter Rostow's **modernization model**, presented in his 1960 book *The Stages of Economic Growth: A Non-Communist Manifesto*. Economists

> **Modernization model**
> A model of economic development most closely associated with the work of economist Walter Rostow. The modernization model (sometimes referred to as modernization theory) maintains that all countries go through five interrelated stages of development, which culminate in an economic state of self-sustained economic growth and high levels of mass consumption.

like Rostow, questioning how dozens of newly independent countries in Africa and Asia would survive economically, looked to how the economically powerful countries had arrived where they were. The result was a model that assumed all countries would follow a similar path to development or modernization, one that involves advancing through five stages of growth.

The first stage is "traditional," in which the society's dominant activity is subsistence farming, its social structure is rigid, and technology is slow to change. The second stage brings "preconditions for takeoff," during which new and more active leadership deliberately pushes the country toward greater flexibility, openness, and economic diversification. This, in turn, leads to the third stage, "takeoff," in which the country experiences something akin to an industrial revolution. Breakthroughs in technology and mass-production occur, industrialization proceeds, urbanization increases, and

sustained growth takes hold. Next, the economy enters the fourth stage, the "drive to maturity," during which technologies diffuse, industrial specialization occurs, and international trade volumes expand. Modernization is evident in key areas of the country and population growth slows. In Rostow's model, some countries reach the final stage, "high mass consumption," which is marked by high incomes and widespread domestic production of many goods and services. During this stage, a majority of workers enter the service sector of the economy, and only much smaller proportions of workers are employed in the primary sector.

Another concept associated with Rostow's model (and other models derived from it) is the idea of a "Ladder of Development." Visually, we can see his five stages of development as rungs on a ladder (**Figure 11.9**), with each country climbing the ladder one rung at a time. In addition to the general criticisms of development models, the major problem with Rostow's model is that it provides no larger context to development. Is a country's climb up the ladder truly dependent only on what happens within that country? Or do we need to take into account the role of external factors? For example, how do all of the world's other countries, their relative positions on the ladder, and those countries' actions affect an individual country's movement on the ladder? These questions are especially pertinent in the context of contemporary economic globalization, which is characterized by the interdependence and interconnectedness of places. Modernization theory has also been criticized for ignoring the context *within* an individual country, leaving us to wonder where regional or cultural differences fit

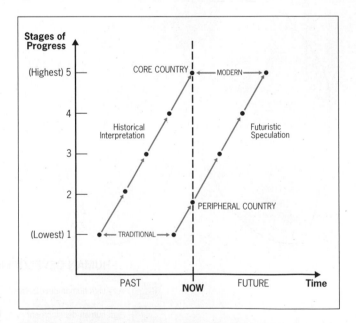

FIGURE 11.9 Rostow's Ladder of Development. Rostow's model assumes that all countries can reach the same level of development and that all will follow a similar path. Adapted with permission from P.J. Taylor, "Understanding Global Inequalities: A World-Systems Approach," *Geography* 77 (1992): 10–21.

into the picture. Even the notion of calling wealthy countries "industrialized" and poor countries "non-industrialized" implies that economic development can only be achieved by following the same trajectory as that taken by today's wealthy countries. Yet if a poor country quickly industrialized today

with the help of foreign investment, it might not reap much economic benefit and could experience severe environmental damage at the same time. Nonetheless, and despite all of these criticisms, Rostow's model has been influential because it describes the experiences of some countries.

MAIN POINTS 11.1 How Is Development Defined and Measured?

- A major issue in understanding development is that wealth does not depend solely on what is produced, but also depends in large part on how, where, and in what context (e.g., environmental, political, etc.) it is produced.

- A near-exclusive focus on economic considerations makes the notion of development, as it is currently understood, a narrow and sometimes controversial indicator of the human condition. To many observers, economic measures of development neglect to consider other elements that influence people's quality of life, such as their levels of health and well-being, feelings of safety and security, and overall sense of happiness with their life circumstances.

- Some development models, such as Walter Rostow's modernization model, have been criticized for their assumption that all countries will follow the same path to development as today's core countries did. Major weaknesses of such models are their assumption that countries throughout the world want to follow the same development trajectory as Western countries, their assumption that there are no suitable development approaches apart from the modernization model, and their failure to consider the internal and external contexts within which a country's development takes place.

11.2 How Does Geographical Situation Affect Development?

As noted earlier, a major and long-standing criticism of Rostow's modernization model is its failure to consider how development happens in **context**. That is, the type and level of development in a place reflects what is happening there as a result of multiple forces operating concurrently at multiple scales. It has been argued that, in order to understand why so many countries are poor with only a relatively few wealthy people, we need to consider the context not only at the state scale, but also at the local, regional, and global scales.

> **Context** The geographical situation in which something occurs; the combination of what is happening at a variety of scales concurrently.

Colonialism brought most countries into the capitalist world economy (see Chapters 2 and 3). As we discussed in Chapter 3, colonies exported raw materials to the colonizing countries, which then manufactured products using those commodities and exported the finished products for sale back in those same colonies. This trading relationship made the colonies dependent on the colonizers and brought immense wealth to the colonizers. Even after the end of colonization, the economic, political, and social interlinkages of the world economy persisted, and the flow of capital changed little after decolonization. In fact, many development scholars argue that the poor are

simply now experiencing **neo-colonialism**, which means the major world powers continue to control the economies of the poorer countries, as they did in the past, even though the poorer countries are now politically independent states. Thus, the achievement of political independence in these places has not necessarily translated into economic independence.

> **Neo-colonialism** The entrenchment of the colonial order, such as trade and investment, under a new guise.

Development scholars have produced a number of theories that take into account the context of neo-colonialism. One example of these **structuralist theories** holds that large-scale, difficult-to-change economic arrangements shape what can happen in fundamental ways. In Chapter 2, we considered how globalization and the emergence of the global economy firmly entrenched a set of structural circumstances—such as the concentration of wealth in certain areas and unequal relations among places—that make it very difficult for poorer regions to improve their economic situation. Structuralists argue that these countries face a much different set of development circumstances than those faced by the small number of western European countries on which Rostow based his modernization model. Accordingly, they assert, the success of today's

> **Structuralist theory** A model of economic development that treats economic disparities among countries or regions as the result of historically derived power relations within the global economic system.

core countries cannot be considered a realistic model for those in the periphery and semi-periphery.

DEPENDENCY THEORY

> **Dependency theory**
> A structuralist theory that offers a critique of the modernization model of development. Based on the idea that certain types of political and economic relations (especially colonialism) between countries and regions of the world have created arrangements that both control and limit the extent to which regions can develop.

Structuralists have developed a major body of development theory called **dependency theory**, many elements of which are attributed to Raul Prebisch, the director of the United Nations Economic Commission for Latin America in the late 1950s. Prebisch, whose ideas were further developed over time by scholars such as Andre Gunder Frank in the 1970s, suggested that the imbalanced political and economic relationships between countries and regions of the world have limited the economic development possibilities of poorer areas. Dependency theorists note, for example, that colonialism created political and economic structures that caused the colonies to become dependent on the colonial powers. They further argue that such dependency helped to sustain the prosperity of dominant regions and the poverty of other regions, even after decolonization occurred. Indeed, they claim, the ensuing international division of labour that sees peripheral countries dependent largely on primary-sector employment, while core countries have witnessed significant growth in the tertiary, quaternary, and quinary sectors, is responsible for much of the underdevelopment found throughout the world today.

Given this outlook, dependency theorists see little hope for economic prosperity in regions and countries that have traditionally been dominated by external powers. Instead, they see the persistent poverty of the world's peripheral countries as an intrinsic part of the contemporary global economy; that is, for the core to be wealthy and "developed," the periphery must remain poor and "underdeveloped." This aspect of dependency theory has been criticized, however, since some traditionally "dependent" regions have made economic gains. Indeed, as with modernization theory, dependency theory is based on generalizations about economic change that pay relatively little attention to geographical differences in culture, politics, and society. Although both models provide some insights into the development process, neither is adequately concerned with the spatial and cultural situation of places, both of which are central elements of geographical analysis.

GEOGRAPHY AND CONTEXT

As geographers, economists, and other social scientists came to realize that studying economic development without considering the political and social contexts within which it takes place does not reflect reality, geographers began to search for a development theory that did encompass geography, scale, place, and culture. For many, Immanuel Wallerstein's **world-systems theory**, first introduced in Chapter 2, has provided a useful framework.

> **World-systems theory** Theory originated by Immanuel Wallerstein and illuminated by his three-tier structure, which proposes that social change in the developing world is inextricably linked to the economic activities of the developed world.

World-systems theorists hold that to understand any levels of development within any state or region, we must also understand its spatial and functional relationships within the world economy. To simplify their research, we can study the three basic tenets of world-systems theory, as Wallerstein defines them:

1. The world economy has one market and a global division of labour.

2. Although the world has multiple states, almost everything takes place within the context of the world economy.

3. The world economy has a three-tiered structure.

> **Capitalism** Economic model wherein people, corporations, and states produce goods and exchange them on the world market, with the goal of achieving profit.
>
> **Commodification** The process through which something is given monetary value. Commodification occurs when a good or idea that previously was not regarded as an object to be bought and sold is turned into something that has a particular price and that can be traded in a market economy.

Regarding the first tenet, Wallerstein explains that the development of a world economy began with capitalist exchange around 1450 and encompassed the globe by 1900. Under the current system of **capitalism**, people, corporations, and states produce goods and exchange them on the world market, with the goal of achieving profit. To generate a profit, producers seek the cheapest labour from around the globe, which means a corporation can move production of a good from southern Ontario to Mexico and then to China, simply to take advantage of cheaper labour. In addition to the world labour supply, producers gain profit by commodifying whatever they can. As we first discussed in Chapter 8, **commodification** is the process of placing a price on a good and then buying, selling, and trading the good. Companies create new products, generate new twists on old products, and create demand for the products through marketing. When the authors of this book were children, none of them could have imagined buying a bottle of water; now we do it all the time, as water has been commodified.

According to Wallerstein's second tenet, despite the existence of approximately 200 states, everything takes place within the context of the world economy (and has done so since 1900). Colonialism set up this system, exporting the concept of the politically independent state and also constructing an interdependent global economy. During the first wave of colonialism (which happened during the period of mercantilism in the 16th to 18th centuries), colonizers extracted goods from the Americas and the Caribbean and exploited Africa for slave labour, amassing wealth from sugar, coffee, fruit, and cotton production.

During the second wave of colonialism (which happened after the Industrial Revolution), colonizers set their sights on cheap industrial labour, cheap raw materials, and large-scale agricultural plantations. Gaining the legal status of sovereign states was relatively easy for most colonies when they became independent; the United Nations Charter even set up a committee to help colonies gain legal independence after World War II. But gaining economic independence is proving to be a difficult task for many former colonies. The economies of the world are tied together, generating intended and unintended consequences that fundamentally change places.

Finally, as we first outlined in Chapter 2, a world-systems approach presents the world economy as a **three-tier structure** with a core, periphery, and semi-periphery. **Core** processes incorporate higher levels of education, higher salaries, and more technology; core processes generate more wealth in the world economy. **Periphery** processes incorporate lower levels of education, lower salaries, and less technology; peripheral processes generate less wealth in the world economy. Wallerstein defined the **semi-periphery** as places where core and periphery processes are occurring simultaneously—places that are exploited by the core but in turn exploit the periphery. By taking advantage of its cheap labour or lax environmental standards,

> **Three-tier structure** With reference to Immanuel Wallerstein's world-systems theory, the division of the world into the core, the periphery, and the semi-periphery as a means to help explain the interconnections between places in the global economy.
>
> **Core** Processes that incorporate higher levels of education, higher salaries, and more technology, and that generate more wealth than periphery processes in the world economy.
>
> **Periphery** Processes that incorporate lower levels of education, lower salaries, and less technology, and that generate less wealth than core processes in the world economy.
>
> **Semi-periphery** Places where core and periphery processes are both occurring; places that are exploited by the core but in turn exploit the periphery.

the core exploits the periphery. The semi-periphery acts as a buffer between the core and periphery, preventing the polarization of the world into two extremes.

The core and periphery are processes, but these processes happen in places. Some geographers stress the processes and try to avoid labelling places as core or periphery because processes in places are not static and are not confined by state borders. Other geographers, however, are drawn to the world-systems theory because it is sensitive to geographical differences and the relationships among development processes that occur in different places. As a result, some of these geographers have defined certain places as core and others as peripheral in the world economy (**Figure 11.10**).

Wallerstein's division of the world into a three-tier structure helps explain the interconnections between places in the global economy. As discussed in more detail in Chapter 2, core processes generate wealth in a place because they require higher levels of education, more sophisticated technologies, and higher wages and benefits. When core processes are embedded in a place (such as the Technology Triangle in southwestern Ontario's Waterloo region, for example), wealth is generated for the people in that place. Core regions are those that have achieved high levels of socio-economic prosperity and are dominant players in the global economic game. Peripheral processes, on the other hand, require little education, lower technologies, and lower wages and benefits. When peripheral processes are embedded in a place (such as the growing of bananas in Ecuador), the processes often generate little wealth for the people in that place. Peripheral regions are poor regions that are dependent in significant ways on the core and do not have as much control over their own affairs, economically or politically. The semi-periphery supports both core and peripheral processes, and semi-peripheral places serve as a buffer between core and periphery in the world economy. Countries of the semi-periphery exert more power than peripheral regions but nonetheless remain heavily influenced by core regions.

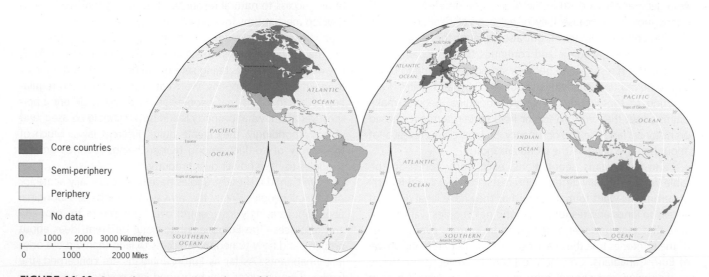

FIGURE 11.10 Countries' status within the world system, 2000. Data from Christopher Chase-Dunn, Yukio Kawano, and Benjamin D. Brewer (2000). "Trade globalization since 1795: Waves of integration in the world-system," *American Sociological Review* 65 (1), pp. 77–95, Table A2.

Dividing the world into cores, semi-peripheries, and peripheries might seem to do little more than replace "developed—developing—underdeveloped" with a new set of terms. But the core-periphery model is fundamentally different from the modernization model because it holds that not all places *can* be equally wealthy, given the structure of the contemporary capitalist world economy.

World-systems theory also makes the power relations among places explicit and does not assume that socio-economic change will occur in the same way in all places. It is thus more sensitive to geographical context than dependency theory and the modernization model, at least in economic terms. Geographer Peter J. Taylor uses the analogy of a school of tadpoles to demonstrate these ideas. He envisions different places in the world as tadpoles and explains that not all tadpoles can survive to develop into toads. Rather, those who dominate survive; the others perish. World-systems theorists see such domination (i.e., exploitation) as a function of the capitalist drive for profit in the global economy. Thus, capitalists can move production quickly from one place to another around the globe to enhance profits, but places that lose a production facility can suffer. Moreover, their coping capacity can be small if, as is often the case, they abandoned traditional ways and shifted to an export economy when external investment first came in.

Economic geographers, political geographers, and other academics continue to debate world-systems approaches.

Some argue that this approach overemphasizes economic factors in the development process (rather than cultural or technological factors, for example) and that it is very state-centric in that it does not focus enough attention on processes operating at micro or macro scales. Nonetheless, Wallerstein's work has encouraged many to see the world map as a system of interlinking parts that need to be understood in relation to one another, as well as a whole. As such, a world-systems approach has a considerable impact on human geography (particularly the economic and political aspects of human geography), and it is increasingly common for geographers to refer to the kinds of core-periphery distinctions suggested by world-systems approaches.

It is important to note that world-systems theory is also applicable at scales beyond the state. A core-periphery relationship can exist within a region, a state (country), or a local area. For example, the Johannesburg area can be described as the core of the South African state, the Greater Golden Horseshoe can be described as the core of the province of Ontario, and the Central Business District can be described as the core of São Paulo, Brazil. Yet another example of how the core-periphery relationship can exist within a country is provided in the following *Guest Field Note*, where geographer Nicole Gombay discusses the lasting legacy of, and challenges created by, the colonization of Canada's Arctic and sub-Arctic regions.

GUEST FIELD NOTE

Land Claims, Property, and Aboriginal Peoples in Canada

As a geographer working in the Arctic, I am interested in land claims, not only because they reveal a great deal about how peoples and lands intersect, but also because they help me to recognize how Canada is and continues to be fundamentally constructed in response to people's struggles to come to terms with differing understandings about land. By land claims, I am referring to those instances where Aboriginal peoples make claims about their right to use or hold certain territories based on historical land use and occupancy. So land claims reveal a lot about how we perceive the world around us.

In land claims negotiations, each party comes to the table with essentially different interests. Provincial and federal governments want to make sure that they have legal rights of access to lands and resources. Aboriginal peoples want to ensure that they preserve or regain some control over portions of the territories that they have occupied since before the arrival of Euro-Canadians. Common to both, however, is the desire to legitimize and control property rights. So why is having

access to property so important? The answer, at least in part, is economics.

All economic systems essentially seek to ensure we obtain the basic material requirements of life. We need clothing, a roof over our heads, and enough to eat and drink, which depends on having access to natural resources. This means that we have to develop mechanisms for ensuring that we have access to them. If people do not have rights to property, how are they going to get the things they need to survive? Thus all economic systems rely on property rights being set up and preserved, and in order to make sure this happens, we create various laws and regulations. The trouble is that people can have widely differing perspectives about what property is and how it should be used, and so correspondingly, they create quite different laws. Much of the history of conflict among human beings revolves around struggles to have power over property.

In Canada, these struggles have been especially acute for Aboriginal peoples. With the arrival of colonizers, Aboriginal peoples increasingly lost control over, and access to, property and resources. The Europeans had quite different ideas about property and how to negotiate access to land than did the original inhabitants. As far as Euro-Canadians are concerned, the land and its resources may be turned into private property, and the laws of the state are designed to protect that property. Land that is not privately owned is called "Crown land" and is commonly viewed as belonging to nobody. From the perspective of many of the Aboriginal peoples in Canada, the idea that land and resources can be privately owned makes no sense. Aboriginal peoples have their own complex laws that have traditionally governed people's access to land and resources. For Aboriginals, property is understood as owned commonly by a limited number of people via laws that control their access to, and use of, that land and its resources.

Because of these fundamentally different conceptions of property, the colonizers who came to the "New World" regarded the land as not owned by anyone, so they just occupied it. In other instances, after battles or prolonged negotiations, the new arrivals set up legal arrangements designed to set territorial boundaries and delineate resource use. Historical treaties and ongoing land claims are the outcomes of such negotiations.

Land claims in the Arctic have had an enormous impact on the lives of the people who live there. Since the mid-twentieth century, provincial, territorial, and federal governments have negotiated land claims agreements with Inuit across the Canadian Arctic (**Figure 11.11**). The first among them—the James Bay and Northern Quebec Agreement (JBNQA)—came about after the Government of Quebec announced that it planned to build large hydroelectric developments on James Bay. With limited time to negotiate the agreement, and knowing that parts of their lands would soon be flooded, Cree and Inuit consulted with people in far-flung settlements to try to identify what

territories they might control and what territories they had to cede to the provincial government. As a result of these consultations and negotiations, the JBNQA was hastily signed in 1975.

The agreement divided the area up into a Cree territory (called Eeyou Istchee) and an Inuit territory (called Nunavik). In turn, under the JBNQA the land was divided into three categories (**Figure 11.12**), each with designated property and access rights based on ethnicity. Under the agreement, Aboriginal residents are called "beneficiaries," while non-Aboriginals are "non-beneficiaries." Category I lands (shown in red in Figure 11.12) are exclusively for use by beneficiaries. Category II (in green) are Crown lands in which hunting, fishing, and trapping rights are reserved for beneficiaries, while activities such as forestry, mining, and tourism development are subject to shared authority with the state. Category III (in white) are Crown lands that are subject to a joint regulatory scheme, though non-beneficiaries may harvest resources from these lands as long as they respect provincial regulations.

Figure 11.12 might lead us to think that the categories of land and rights of resource use have been tidily sorted out. In fact, this is far from the case. The white spaces on the map make the land appear empty. All its cultural content is erased. The traditional laws of the Inuit, which up to the signing of the agreement had defined how the land was used, are simply invisible, and indigenous presence is instead neatly located and contained in small coloured pockets. So the map silently suppresses one set of laws and replaces them with another; in the process, state control of a huge area of property is legitimized. Yet a careful look at the map reveals two settlements—Puvirnituq and Ivujivik—whose residents refused to sign the agreement. They have come to be called "dissident communities" because they did not agree to relinquish their land and resources to the state.

Most people in Nunavik did sign the agreement, though, and as a result, they have essentially lost control over how their local resources are to be used. Instead, the state has taken over that power. This is a source of profound unease for many Inuit whose own rules governing people's access to resources are being challenged by Euro-Canadian laws. So, for example, Inuit are now being told that they are not allowed to harvest certain animals, like belugas, in the ways they had been accustomed to doing for millennia. This has caused great distress among many Inuit in Nunavik. As one person from one of the dissident settlements put it, "[The JBNQA] opened the door for the Qallunaat [non-Inuit] to do as they wished. The people were fooled. They were taken for a ride. They thought that they were given land to say, 'Hey, this is mine! Keep off! I'll do what I want.' When we already were *doing* that!" For many, it appears that rather than retaining control over the land and its resources, the Inuit lost that control and can no longer govern themselves according to their own laws of property and access to resources.

CANADIAN INUIT

LEGEND:
- ---- Nunavut Settlement Area
- ▰ Nunavut
- ---- Inuvialuit Settlement Region
- ▰ Inuvialuit Region
- Nunavik Marine Region
- ▰ Nunavik Region
- ········ Nunatsiavut Settlement Region
- ▰ Nunatsiavut Region
- —— Nunavik Inuit / Labrador Inuit Overlap

Makivik Corporation, Nunavik Research Centre-Cartographic Services

FIGURE 11.11 Inuit land claims settlement regions of Canada.

Nicole Gombay, University of Canterbury, New Zealand

Makivik Corporation, Nunavik Research Centre-Cartographic Services

FIGURE 11.12 Nunavik offshore claims and land regime. Valid as of 2003.

MAIN POINTS 11.2 How Does Geographical Situation Affect Development?

- Development happens in context. The type and level of development in a place reflects what is happening there as a result of forces operating concurrently at multiple scales, from the local to the regional, and from the national to global.

- Development scholars have produced a number of theories, referred to as structuralist theories, that take into account the context of neo-colonialism and its influences on the development prospects of peripheral regions. For example, one structuralist theory holds that large-scale, difficult-to-change economic arrangements shape what can happen in fundamental ways.

- Structuralists have developed a major body of development theory, called dependency theory, that sees little hope for economic prosperity in regions and countries that have traditionally been dominated by external powers. Like modernization theory, however, dependency theory

has been criticized for not considering the importance of context; indeed, it is based on generalizations about economic change that pay inadequate attention to geographical differences in culture, politics, and society.

- A world-systems approach, developed by Wallerstein, argues that states find themselves organized in a hierarchical relationship as core, periphery, or semi-peripheral participants in the global economy. This means that some states gain greater benefits through their position in the global economy than others.

- World-systems theory helps us understand the geography of development. It is sensitive to geographical differences and the relationships among development processes that occur in different places. World-systems theory divides the world into a three-tier structure, with a core, periphery, and semi-periphery, that helps explain the interconnections between places in the global economy.

11.3 What Are the Barriers to, and the Costs of, Development?

International organizations and governments measure individual countries' progress in development and then create programs that they hope will break down barriers to development and help improve the condition of people around the world, especially in the poorest countries.

In 2000, 189 world leaders at a high-profile United Nations summit adopted the UN Millennium Declaration, which stated their goal of improving conditions for people in countries with the lowest standards of human development. At the summit, leaders recognized the principal barriers to economic development and identified eight key development goals to be achieved by the year 2015, each of which would be realized by reaching a corresponding set of targets (**Table 11.2**). These **Millennium**

Development Goals (MDGs) represent a high degree of consensus about the conditions that must be changed if economic development is to be attained.

With the target date of 2015 close at hand, the *2014 Millennium Development Goals Report* opened by asserting that "the MDGs have made a profound difference in people's lives." It noted that, despite the many barriers to development in different parts of the world, pursuit of the MDGs has brought numerous benefits to the world. For instance, the number of people living in poverty was cut in half by 2010, 90 percent of primary-school-aged children in developing regions are now being educated, and death rates as a result of illnesses and diseases such as malaria and tuberculosis have declined greatly. Ban Ki-Moon, Secretary General of the United Nations, also noted

> **Millennium Development Goals** A set of eight human development–related goals for the world's most impoverished countries, which were adopted at the United Nations Millennium Summit in 2000 with the intention of achieving all of these goals by the year 2015.

TABLE 11.2 Millennium Development Goals and Corresponding Targets
Goal 1: Eradicate extreme poverty and hunger
Target 1.A: Halve, between 1990 and 2015, the proportion of people whose income is less than $1 a day
Target 1.B: Achieve full and productive employment and decent work for all, including women and young people
Target 1.C: Halve, between 1990 and 2015, the proportion of people who suffer from hunger
Goal 2: Achieve universal primary education
Target 2.A: Ensure that, by 2015, children everywhere, boys and girls alike, will be able to complete a full course of primary schooling
Goal 3: Promote gender equality and empower women
Target 3.A: Eliminate gender disparity in primary and secondary education, preferably by 2005, and in all levels of education no later than 2015
Goal 4: Reduce child mortality
Target 4.A: Reduce by two-thirds, between 1990 and 2015, the under-five mortality rate
Goal 5: Improve maternal health
Target 5.A: Reduce by three-quarters, between 1990 and 2015, the maternal mortality ratio
Target 5.B: Achieve, by 2015, universal access to reproductive health
Goal 6: Combat HIV/AIDS, malaria, and other diseases
Target 6.A: Have halted, by 2015, and begun to reverse the spread of HIV/AIDS
Target 6.B: Achieve, by 2010, universal access to treatment for HIV/AIDS for all those who need it
Target 6.C: Have halted, by 2015, and begun to reverse the incidence of malaria and other major diseases
Goal 7: Ensure environmental sustainability
Target 7.A: Integrate the principles of sustainable development into country policies and programs and reverse the loss of environmental resources
Target 7.B: Reduce biodiversity loss, achieving, by 2010, a significant reduction in the rate of loss
Target 7.C: Halve, by 2015, the proportion of people without sustainable access to safe drinking water and basic sanitation
Target 7.D: By 2020, achieve a significant improvement in the lives of at least 100 million slum dwellers
Goal 8: Develop a global partnership for development
Target 8.A: Develop further an open, rule-based, predictable, non-discriminatory trading and financial system
Target 8.B: Address the special needs of the least developed countries
Target 8.C: Address the special needs of landlocked developing countries and small island developing states
Target 8.D: Deal comprehensively with the debt problems of developing countries through national and international measures in order to make debt sustainable in the long term
Target 8.E: In co-operation with pharmaceutical companies, provide access to affordable, essential drugs in developing countries
Target 8.F: In co-operation with the private sector, make available the benefits of new technologies, especially information and communications

From Millenium Development Goals, United Nations Development Programme website at www.un.org/millenniumgoals.

in the report that the likelihood of children dying before the age of five has also been cut in half over the last 20 years, thus saving about 17,000 children every day, and that the proportion of people lacking access to improved sources of water was also cut by over 50 percent.

Given that there is still much work to be done in improving living conditions around the world (including in the core countries), the United Nations is now looking ahead to the creation of a new development agenda for the next 15 years. Thus, the Millennium Development Goals will be followed after 2015 by the Sustainable Development Goals (SDGs), which will be formally pursued with a target date of 2030. In 2014 the United Nations General Assembly's Open Working Group on Sustainable Development Goals submitted a proposed set of SDGs that was much more expansive than the MDGs. If approved, there would be 17 SDGs that focus on a broad range of objectives, such as eliminating poverty and hunger, improving health and education, making cities more sustainable, combating climate change, and protecting oceans and forests. Progress in achieving these objectives, and through them the 17 SDGs (more than twice as many goals as were set out in the Millennium Development Goals initiative), would be measured using 169 indicators.

BARRIERS TO ECONOMIC DEVELOPMENT

As described earlier in this chapter, the structures and geography of the world economy have created numerous obstacles and barriers that inhibit economic development in the periphery. In Chapter 4, we discussed the causes of malnutrition and examined how AIDS has ravaged sub-Saharan Africa. In Chapter 6, we discussed the natural hazards found in many peripheral countries and the lack of infrastructure to cope with those hazards. It is clear that the world economic system often works to the disadvantage of the periphery, but it is also clear that the system is not the only obstacle that peripheral countries face.

Conditions within the periphery, such as high population growth rates, lack of education, high foreign debt, political instability, and widespread disease, can seriously hamper development efforts. There is a conundrum here: did the structures of the world economy create these conditions or did these conditions help create the structures of the world economy? Many think that neither argument can stand alone, as it seems that both factors have combined to create a cycle that will be difficult to interrupt. Indeed, regardless of which came first, the fact remains that millions of people throughout the periphery are burdened with familial, economic, cultural, and political upheavals. In this section of the chapter, we will discuss several of the conditions that affect the economic development prospects of people in the poorest countries of the world, including many factors outlined in the UN Millennium Development Goals.

SOCIAL CONDITIONS

Countries in the periphery face numerous demographic, economic, and social problems. As noted in Chapter 4, most of the less well-off countries have high birth rates, along with a

relatively low life expectancy at birth. Across the global periphery, as much as half the population is 15 years old or younger, making the supply of adult, tax-paying labourers low relative to the number of dependents. Low life expectancies and high infant and child mortality rates stem largely from inadequate nutrition. For example, protein deficiency is a common problem in many places. Many in the global economic periphery also lack public sewage systems, clean drinking water, and access to health care, making economic development all the more difficult.

Lack of access to education is also a major problem in the periphery. In some places, even the poorest families must pay for their children to attend school. As a result, large numbers of school-age children do not go to school, and illiteracy rates are high. Moreover, access to education in the periphery is often gendered, with boys attending school longer than girls (**Figure 11.13**). Girls often stop attending school in order to work to earn the money needed to pay for their brothers' school fees.

Lack of education for girls is founded on, and compounded by, the widespread assumption (not just in the periphery, but in most of the world) that girls will leave their homes (and communities) when they marry, no longer bringing income to the family. In parts of the periphery, trafficking in children, especially girls, is common. Mike Dottridge, a modern anti-slavery activist, explains that **trafficking** happens when "adults and children fleeing poverty or seeking better prospects are manipulated, deceived, and bullied

> **Trafficking** When a family sends a child or an adult to a labour recruiter in hopes that the labour recruiter will send money, and the family member will earn money to send home.

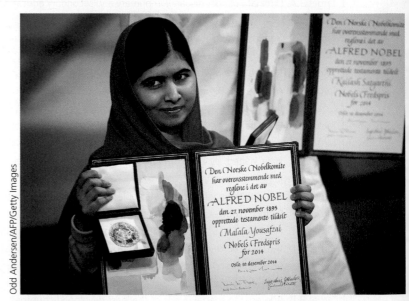

FIGURE 11.13 Malala Yousafzai receives the 2014 Nobel Peace Prize. Malala Yousafzai is a children's and women's rights activist from Pakistan. As a girl, she defied the Taliban in Pakistan, demanding that girls have access to education. In 2012, when she was 15 years old, Malala was shot in the head by a Taliban gunman on her way home from school. She survived the attack and continues to speak out internationally about the importance of education. In 2014, she became the youngest person to receive the Nobel Peace Prize.

Odd Andersen/AFP/Getty Images

into working in conditions that they would not choose." This phenomenon is not considered slavery because the family does not sell a child; instead, the child is sent away with a recruiter in the hopes that the recruiter will send money and the child will earn money to send home. The trafficked children are often taken to neighbouring or nearby countries that are wealthier and in need of domestic servants. Others are trafficked across the world, again typically to work as domestic servants. Dottridge explains that the majority of trafficked children are girls, and that the majority of girls are "employed as domestic servants or street vendors," although some girls are "trafficked into prostitution." The extent of this problem is well illustrated in statistics compiled by the International Labour Organization, which estimates that close to 21 million people around the world are victims of forced labour. Also, in its *Global Report on Trafficking in Persons 2012*, the United Nations has noted that women and girls account for about three-quarters of human trafficking victims, and that victims of 136 different nationalities were detected in 118 countries between 2007 and 2010.

Some countries are working to improve access to primary education in order to make education universally available. In 2000, the Millennium Development Report prompted the government of Rwanda to improve access to education. In 2003, fees for primary education were eliminated, and two years later, schools started receiving revenues based on the number of students they were educating. Rwanda set the goal of making primary education available to all by 2010. By 2009, more than 2 million children were enrolled in primary school, up significantly from about 1.4 million students in 1998–99. The country now has the highest primary school enrolment rates in Africa, and the primary school completion rate has risen from 53 percent in 2008 to 73 percent in 2012. At the same time, however, Rwandan students are often required to meet under trees and in overcrowded classrooms due to a lack of adequate funding for the infrastructure needs that come with a growing student population.

FOREIGN DEBT

Complicating the picture further is the foreign debt crisis that many peripheral and semi-peripheral countries face. Shortly after the decolonization wave of the 1960s, banks and other international financial institutions began lending large sums of money to the newly independent states, money earmarked for development projects. By the 1980s and 1990s, the World Bank and the International Monetary Fund (IMF) were lending massive amounts of money to peripheral and semi-peripheral countries, but with strings attached. To secure these **structural adjustment loans**, as they were known, countries had to agree to implement economic or governmental reforms, such as privatizing government entities, opening the country to foreign trade, reducing tariffs, and encouraging foreign direct investment. (These loans provide one example of how political independence has not translated into economic independence for many countries.)

> **Structural adjustment loans**
> Loans granted by international financial institutions such as the World Bank and the International Monetary Fund to countries in the periphery and the semi-periphery in exchange for certain economic and governmental reforms in that country (e.g., privatization of certain government entities and opening the country to foreign trade and investment).

The IMF, which is traditionally managed by a European, lends money to peripheral countries in an effort to head off major economic problems. Once peripheral countries owe money to the IMF, the World Bank, and private banks and lending institutions, they need to repay their debts. Spending a large part of the country's budget on debt repayment makes it difficult for that country to invest in more development projects. In many cases, the cost of servicing the debt (that is, the cost of repayments plus interest) has exceeded the country's revenues from the export of goods and services (**Figure 11.14**). Meanwhile, in many countries, the returns on development projects have been much lower than anticipated. These factors have created a global debt crisis for the poorest countries in the world.

Structural adjustment loans were part of a larger trend toward neo-liberalism in the late 20th century. Neo-liberalism derives from the neo-classical economic idea that government intervention in markets is inefficient and undesirable, and should be resisted wherever possible. These ideas were at the heart of the conditions that were attached to loans and refinancing programs, but neo-liberal ideas also spurred a general shift toward the transfer of economic control from states to the private sector. This, in turn, fostered economic globalization while shrinking the size of the public sector in a number of countries. The result was the expansion of corporate control and the erosion of the ability of regions and states to control their economic destinies. Hence, the "neo-liberal turn" has been highly contentious.

High debt obligations and related neo-liberal reforms arguably contributed to the economic and political crisis in Argentina at the end of 2001. This led to overreliance on a privatized export sector that left the country vulnerable when shifts in the global economy weakened the competitiveness of Argentinian exports. Government spending was also unsustainably high, and corruption was rampant. By 2005, internal economic growth and aid from Venezuela put Argentina in a position to work out a complex debt-restructuring plan that has pulled the country back from the brink. However, in other cases where countries are facing imminent economic, political, and social meltdown, the only alternative may be to default on loans. Defaulting countries then find themselves in a severely disadvantaged position when it comes to attracting future external investment. And if a substantial number of countries were to default at the same time, a global economic crisis could ensue that would work to the disadvantage of almost everyone. Moreover, as we saw in Chapter 2, nongovernmental organizations and other groups actively resist neoliberal economic policies, sometimes violently, arguing that international organizations such as the World Bank, IMF, and World Trade Organization are set up to benefit the countries of the global economic core.

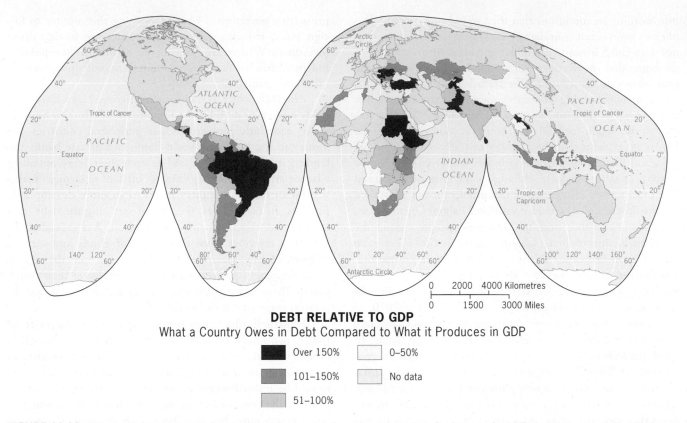

DEBT RELATIVE TO GDP
What a Country Owes in Debt Compared to What it Produces in GDP

- Over 150%
- 101–150%
- 51–100%
- 0–50%
- No data

FIGURE 11.14 External debt service as a percentage of exports of goods and services for low- and middle-income economies, 2012.
Data from http://data.worldbank.org/indicator/DT.DOD.DECT.EX.ZS

DISEASE

Those living in the global periphery experience comparatively high rates of disease and a corresponding lack of adequate health care. These circumstances directly affect economic development, making survival difficult for many people, orphaning children, and weakening the labour force.

As highlighted in Chapter 4, a number of **vectored diseases**—those spread by one host (person) to another by an intermediate host or vector—are a particular scourge in warm, humid parts of the periphery and semi-periphery. The warm, moist climates of tropical environments enhance biological activity. Vectors abound in such environments, and infectious diseases spread rapidly through host populations.

> **Vectored disease** A disease carried from one host to another by an intermediate host.
>
> **Malaria** Vectored disease, spread by mosquitoes that carry the malaria parasite in their saliva, which kills approximately 150,000 children in the global periphery each month.

Malaria is an infectious disease spread by mosquitoes that carry the parasite in their saliva. Scientists did not determine the role of mosquitoes in the diffusion of the disease until the late 18th century. Today, the sequence of the disease is well known. The mosquito stings an infected host and sucks up some of the disease agents. In the mosquito's stomach, the parasites reproduce and multiply, eventually reaching its saliva. When the mosquito stings the next person, some of the parasites are injected into that person's bloodstream. The person who has been stung develops malaria and becomes a host. The disease manifests itself through recurrent fever and chills, with associated symptoms such as anemia and an enlarged spleen.

Malaria is a major factor in infant and child mortality, as most of the victims are children age five or younger. If a person survives the disease, he or she will develop a certain degree of immunity. However, many infected by malaria are weak, lack energy, and face an increased risk of other diseases taking hold in their weakened body.

Malaria occurs throughout much of the world, particularly in regions between the Tropic of Cancer and the Tropic of Capricorn (**Figure 11.15**). People in the tropical portions of Africa suffer most from this disease, but malaria also prevails in India, Southeast Asia, China, and the tropical Americas. Several types of malaria spread throughout these regions, with some being more severe than others. In addition to humans, various species of monkeys, rats, birds, and even snakes can be affected by the disease. In sub-Saharan Africa, malaria's virulence results from the effectiveness of its vectors—three African mosquitoes (Anopheles gambiae, A. arabiensis, and A. funestus). Whole populations are afflicted, and entire regions have been abandoned because of the prevalence of the disease.

Development experts look at malaria as a "silent tsunami" in the periphery, comparing its death toll to the tsunami that ravaged South and Southeast Asia in late 2004. That tsunami

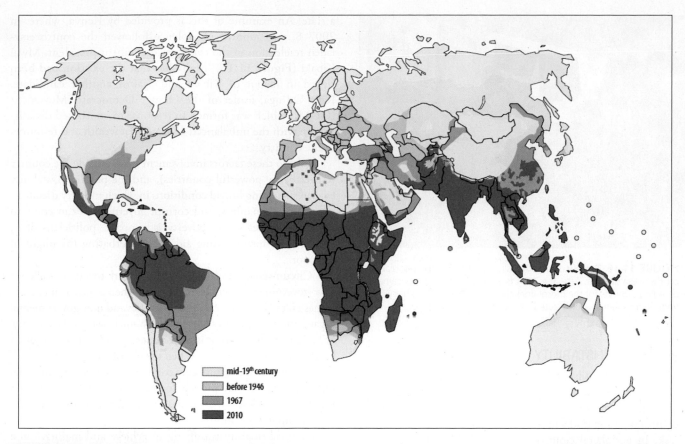

FIGURE 11.15 World distribution of malaria, mid-19th century to 2010. Source: from World Health Organization on behalf of Roll Back Malaria Partnership (2011), *Eliminating Malaria: Learning from the Past, Looking Ahead*, Figure E.1, p. 9.

killed some 300,000 people at one time. Malaria kills about 150,000 children in the global periphery each month. Antimalarial drugs exist, but to defeat malaria, afflicted regions must eliminate the vector: the mosquito. During the 1940s, the government of Sri Lanka (then Ceylon) launched a massive attack on the mosquito with the aid of a pesticide called dichlorodiphenyltrichloroethane (DDT). The results were dramatic. The mosquito was practically wiped out, and the rate of deaths attributable to malaria fell markedly. In 1945, Sri Lanka's overall death rate had been 22 per 1,000; in 1972, it reported a death rate of only 8 per 1,000. Furthermore, there has not been a single death attributed to malaria in Sri Lanka since 2007.

The conquest of malaria produced a new set of problems, however. DDT proved to be highly carcinogenic and to have negative health and environmental consequences of its own. Also, the death rate lowered by the eradication of malaria led to a substantial rise in the population growth rate, creating new problems for Sri Lanka. By the time the birth rate dropped (it was estimated at 16 per 1,000 in 2010), the island had experienced a population explosion.

Success in combating major vectored diseases is often only temporary. Following the Sri Lankan experiment, India initiated a massive assault against the malaria mosquito, and the number of new cases of malaria declined dramatically. But 10 years after the program was introduced, India reported that 60 million people were infected with malaria, more than half the number who had the disease before the anti-malarial campaign began. This example proved the mosquito population's ability to rebound quickly after even the most intensive application of pesticides.

Today the war against malaria is taking a new tack in the form of genetic interference with the mosquito so that its capacity to transmit the malaria parasite, Plasmodium, is destroyed. By introducing "engineered" mosquitoes into the general population, health experts hope that the number of non-virulent mosquitoes will rise significantly. A number of programs also focus on distributing insecticide-laden mosquito nets to surround sleeping quarters and protect people from the mosquitoes, which are most active at night (**Figure 11.16**). One such program, the "Spread the Net" campaign, was co-founded by two Canadians, television personality Rick Mercer and former Member of Parliament Belinda Stronach, in 2006 (**Figure 11.17**). The project's initial goal of raising enough money to buy 500,000 bed nets was achieved in 2010, with half of the nets being shipped to Liberia and the other half to Rwanda. Efforts such as this one are having some dramatic impacts in parts of Africa, but malaria remains a scourge of the poorer peoples of the world—and a major impediment to economic development.

Pallava Bagla/Corbis

FIGURE 11.16 Tamalu, India. Tamalu is on the Car Nicobar islands off the coast of India. After the 2004 tsunami, the wetlands became breeding grounds for the mosquitoes that carry malaria. This baby sleeps under a mosquito net distributed to villagers by United Nations Children's Fund (UNICEF) workers.

POLITICAL INSTABILITY

Although not addressed in the Millennium Development Goals, political instability can greatly impede economic development. Establishing a government that's able to maintain control over and lead a low-income country can be a daunting task. In peripheral countries, a wide divide often exists between the very wealthy and the poorest of the poor. In Kenya, for example, the wealthiest 10 percent of the population controls over 40 percent of the country's income. The disenfranchisement of the poor and the competition among the rich for control of the government (and the potential spoils that go along with that) can lead to extreme political instability within

a state. An example of this is provided by Kenya, where, in 2007–8, two months of violence followed the controversy-laden re-election of the country's incumbent president, Mwai Kibaki (**Figure 11.18**). Many felt that the election had been rigged in favour of Kibaki and against another candidate, Raila Odinga, leader of the Orange Democratic Movement (ODM), which was formed in response to continued dissatisfaction with the imbalanced allocation of wealth and resources in the country.

Add to these factors involvement from outside the country (especially by powerful countries), and the political instability escalates, yielding horrid conditions in which military dictators, selfish megalomaniacs, and corrupt governments can come to power. In places where poverty is rampant, politicians often become corrupt, misusing aid and exacerbating the plight of the poor.

Circumstances and timing need to work together to allow a new government to come to power. When a government becomes excessively corrupt, other countries and non-governmental organizations sometimes cut off development aid to the country. Yet when this happens, it is the ordinary people who most often bear the brunt of hardship. When the global community cuts off a corrupt government's aid, core countries and non-governmental organizations typically provide food aid to the people, although this is rarely sufficient to meet basic needs or reverse the trajectory of hardship in the country.

Political stability is difficult to achieve and maintain in a poorer country. Countries of the core have established liberal democracies for themselves; since World War II, all of them have held regularly scheduled democratic elections. But countries in the periphery and semi-periphery have had a much harder time establishing and maintaining democracies. In the process of decolonization, the colonizing countries typically left governments that reflected political and social hierarchies during the colonial period. Some failed, some were overthrown by military coups, and some saw the consolidation of power

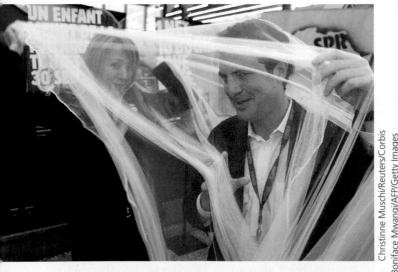

Christinne Muschi/Reuters/Corbis

FIGURE 11.17 Rick Mercer's "Spread the Net" campaign. Former Liberal Member of Parliament Belinda Stronach (left) and Canadian comedian Rick Mercer are part of the "Spread the Net" Campaign, an initiative designed to reduce malaria outbreaks by ensuring that bed netting is available to protect children when they are sleeping.

Boniface Mwangi/AFP/Getty Images

FIGURE 11.18 Civil unrest in Kenya following 2007 election. The controversial re-election of Kenya's incumbent president, Mwai Kibaki, led to mass violence throughout the country, leaving some 1,300 people dead.

around a dictatorial strongman. Many countries in the periphery and semi-periphery have alternated repeatedly between quasi-democratic and military governments.

The Central African Republic (CAR), a landlocked country of some 4.6 million people, provides a prime example of a place where political instability has mired its people in poverty. The current borders of the country were set by France, which ruled over the CAR from the late 1800s until it gained independence in 1960. The country's population is made up of over 80 different ethnic groups, each with its own language. This, in turn, has been the cause of a great deal of political instability, as different groups have wrestled with each other to take control of the country. There have been six different coups since 1960, much of this involving conflict between Christians and Muslim militias. A U.K.-based newspaper, *The Guardian*, referred to the CAR in 2013 as a "lawless" place, where there are only about 200 police to guard the country's 4.6 million people "from rebel gangs who attack women, kill men and recruit children at will." Today, the CAR is one of the poorest countries in the world and sits near the bottom of the United Nations' Human Development Index. This has happened despite the country having an abundance of natural resources—such as oil, gold, and diamonds—and an abundance of arable agricultural land that could otherwise provide a solid foundation for development.

Yet another cause of political instability in many peripheral and semi-peripheral countries has been what Jeffrey Herbst refers to as the "haphazard and arbitrary" way in which colonizing nations such as Great Britain, France, Belgium, and Germany subdivided their claims to African territories during the late 1800s and early 1900s. Indeed, the borders separating many present-day African countries were delineated without any consideration for the cultural or social characteristics or the needs of the people living there at the time. In this regard, John Ravenhill has noted, "The arbitrary division of the continent by the European powers, with little or no respect for pre-existing social and political groupings or even, sometimes, for 'natural' geographical features, has immensely complicated the tasks of nation and state building faced by African governments."

Opening the homepage of any major newspaper on any given day will reveal a story somewhere in the world that demonstrates the link between economic stability and political stability. In post-Taliban Afghanistan, for example, economic woes represent one of the greatest threats to the stability of the government in Kabul. More than half of the population is impoverished, and the government lacks the funds to invest in development. Foreign aid has provided some help, but the flow of aid has been variable and its amount insufficient to address the country's searing economic problems. Many analysts see this as a key impediment to achieving stability in Afghanistan. As *The Economist* put it in 2006, "poverty helps the Taliban."

COSTS OF ECONOMIC DEVELOPMENT

Economic development changes a place. In order to increase productivity, whether industrial or agricultural, people transform the environment. When a country goes through intensification of industrial production, air and surface water are often polluted. When a country goes through intensification of agricultural production, the introduction of pesticides and herbicides can have deleterious impacts on the soil and groundwater. Tourism can be just as hard on the environment and can tax the existing infrastructure beyond its capacities, often to the detriment of the country's permanent residents. The costs of tourism often stretch far beyond the environment, affecting ways of life and fundamentally altering the cultural landscape.

INDUSTRIALIZATION

In their efforts to attract new industries, the governments of many countries in the global periphery and semi-periphery have set up special manufacturing zones called **export processing zones (EPZs)**, which offer favourable tax, regulatory, and trade arrangements to foreign firms. According to the International Labour Organization there were more than 3,500 EPZs around the world in 2007, many of which have become major manufacturing centres (**Figure 11.19**). It is estimated that as many as 63 million people are employed in these areas, about 40 million of them in China alone. The vast majority of EPZs are located in peripheral regions, although they are increasingly used to stimulate development in core countries as well. For example, Canada now has two such zones—CentrePort Canada in Winnipeg, Manitoba, and the Gander Foreign Trade Zone in Newfoundland and Labrador.

> **Export processing zones (EPZs)** Zones established by many countries in the periphery and semi-periphery that offer favourable tax, regulatory, and trade arrangements to attract foreign trade and investment.

Two of the best-known EPZs are the **special economic zones** of China and Mexico's **maquiladoras**. Governments site such zones in places with easy access to export markets. Thus, the maquiladora zone in Mexico is located directly across the border from the United States, while the special economic zones of China are sited near major ports. These zones typically attract a mix of manufacturing operations, depending on the skill levels of the labour force and the available infrastructure.

> **Special economic zone** Specific area within a country in which tax incentives and less-stringent environmental regulations are implemented to attract foreign business and investment.
>
> **Maquiladoras** Zones in northern Mexico with factories supplying manufactured goods to the U.S. market. The low-wage workers in the primarily foreign-owned factories assemble imported components and/or raw materials and then export finished goods.

The maquiladoras started in 1965 when the Mexican government designated northern Mexico as a district where manufactured products could be sent to the United States free of import tariffs. In response, many U.S. corporations established manufacturing plants in the area, where Mexican workers assembled a collection of components and raw materials into finished industrial products, tax-free. The corporations then exported at least 80 percent of these goods to the United States.

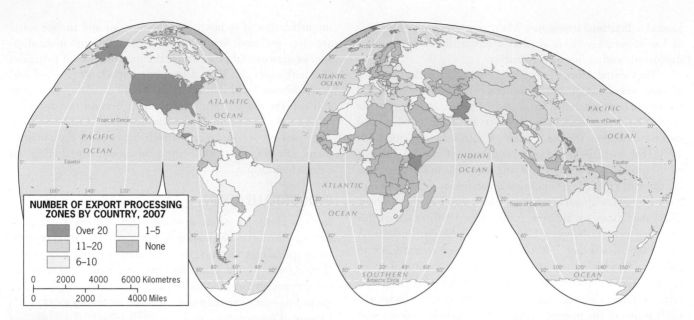

FIGURE 11.19 Export processing zones, 2007. Number of export processing zones by country. Data from International Labour Organization.

Although the maquiladora phenomenon started in the mid-1960s, it did not really take off until the 1980s. This was when American companies recognized the growing wage gap between U.S. and Mexican workers and began relocating to the maquiladora district. Although competition from other parts of the world has led to the closure of some plants, today some 3,000 maquiladoras continue to function, employing 1 million workers and accounting for 45 percent of Mexico's exports. The maquiladora plants produce such goods as electronic equipment, electrical appliances, automobiles, textiles, plastics, and furniture. The plants are controversial both in Mexico and the United States, as corporations that have relocated there avoid the employment and environmental regulations that are in force just a few kilometres to the north. Many maquiladora factories hire young women and men for low pay and few, if any, benefits, putting them to work in repetitive jobs, often in environmentally questionable conditions.

In 1992, Canada, the United States, and Mexico ratified the **North American Free Trade Agreement (NAFTA)**, which took effect January 1, 1994, and prompted further industrialization of the border region. In addition to manufacturing plants, NAFTA has facilitated the movement of service industries, including data-processing operations, from the United States to Mexico. Most of the new plants are located in two districts: Tijuana on the Pacific coast, linked to San Diego across the border, and Ciudad Juarez on the Rio Grande across from El Paso, Texas.

North American Free Trade Agreement (NAFTA)
Agreement entered into by Canada, Mexico, and the United States in December 1992 that took effect on January 1, 1994, to eliminate the barriers to trade in, and facilitate the cross-border movement of, goods and services between the countries.

AGRICULTURE

As discussed in Chapter 9, agricultural activities in peripheral countries typically focus on personal consumption (i.e., subsistence farming) or on production for a large agricultural conglomerate. Where zones of larger-scale, modernized agriculture have developed in the periphery, foodstuffs are produced for the foreign market and often have minimal impact on the impoverished conditions of the surrounding lands. Little is produced for the local marketplace because distribution systems are poorly organized and the local population is typically unable to pay for foodstuffs. If the local population owns land, their landholdings are usually fragmented, creating small plots of land that are difficult to farm in a manner that produces much income. Even if farmers have larger plots of land, they are generally equipped with outdated, inefficient tools and equipment. The main crops tend to be grains and roots; farmers produce little protein because high-protein crops typically have lower yields than grain crops. On the farms in the periphery, yields per unit area are low, subsistence modes of life prevail, and many families are constantly in debt.

TOURISM

All development strategies have pros and cons, something that is well illustrated by the case of tourism. Peripheral countries in the Caribbean region of Central America and in other parts of the world have become leading destinations for millions of tourists from richer states. Among the countries that earn substantial income from tourism are Thailand, Kenya, Barbados, and Fiji. Tourism brings some wealth and employment to these and other countries (see Chapter 13), but the industry's contributions are often narrow in scope and time. Tourism may also have serious negative effects on cultures and environments in the periphery.

FIGURE 11.20 Cruise ship, Labadee, Haiti. Vessels such as this one often dock in poor countries, but passengers are often strictly segregated from local residents and contribute little to the region's economy through their visits.

In economic terms, the "host" country must make a substantial investment to support tourism development. Sometimes imports of building materials and equipment strain the country's supply system, and funds are diverted to the construction of hotels, airports, cruise-ports, and other tourism-supportive infrastructure that could have been spent on internal needs, such as education or housing for citizens. Moreover, many hotels and other tourist facilities are owned not by the host country but by large multinational corporations. These corporations earn enormous profits, most of which are sent back to their headquarters in their home country. At the same time, tourism-generated income does not always benefit local economies (**Figure 11.20**). Tourism can create local jobs, but they are often low-paying and offer little job security. In tourist zones, many employees work two or three jobs in order to break even.

In social terms, tourism frequently strains the fabric of local communities as well. Wealthier visitors' invasion of poor communities can foster antipathy and resentment. Tourism can also debase local culture, which is adapted to suit the visitors' tastes. In many instances, tourism fosters a "demonstration effect" among locals, encouraging them to behave in ways that may please or interest the visitors but that is disdained by the larger local community. Some tourism workers consider employment in the tourist industry dehumanizing because it demands displays of friendliness and servitude that locals find insulting.

The idea of a flood of affluent tourists may be appealing to the government of a poor country (whose elite may have a financial stake in the hotels where they can share the pleasures of the wealthy), but local entrepreneurs often take a different view. Indeed, powerful multinational corporations and national governments may intervene to limit the opportunities of local, small-scale operators in favour of mass, prearranged tourist destinations (e.g., "exclusive" resorts) that isolate the tourist from local society. Overreliance on tourism can also leave an economy vulnerable if changing economic circumstances cause a sharp decline in the number of tourists or if natural disasters hit. Because many tourist destinations in poorer countries are beach attractions, natural hazards such as the 2004 tsunami in Southeast Asia can destroy the lynchpin of a country's economy. Locals must suffer the loss of thousands of people; deal with the after-effects of sewage, homelessness, orphans, and the destitute; and rebuild the tourist destinations, all while the flow of tourist-related income has stopped.

The cultural landscape of tourism is frequently a study in harsh contrasts: gleaming hotels tower over modest, often poor, housing; luxury liners glide past poverty-stricken villages; opulent meals are served in hotels, while children suffer from malnutrition just down the street. If the tourist industry offered real prospects for economic progress in low-income countries, such circumstances might be viewed as temporary, unfortunate by-products. However, the evidence too often indicates that tourism does not produce development.

MAIN POINTS 11.3 What Are the Barriers to, and the Costs of, Development?

- International organizations and governments have created a variety of programs and initiatives such as the Millennium Development Goals to help improve the condition of humans around the world especially in the periphery.

- The structures and geography of the world economy have created numerous obstacles and barriers that inhibit economic development in the periphery. Conditions within the periphery, such as high population growth rates, lack of education, foreign debt, political instability, and widespread disease, can seriously hamper development efforts. Indeed

people and places throughout the periphery are burdened with familial, economic, cultural, and political upheavals that prevent long-term progress in the improvement of people's quality of life.

- Regardless of whether it takes place in the core, the semi-periphery, or the periphery, economic development changes a place. These changes are not always for the better. Some negative consequences of development can include environmental degradation, alterations to the cultural landscape, and changes in people's ways of life.

11.4 How Do Political and Economic Institutions Influence Uneven Development Within States?

In our globalized world, poverty is not confined to the periphery. Core countries, including Canada, have regions and peoples that are markedly poorer than others, or regions where people's economic lives do not improve when the country's economy grows. In Europe, areas of isolation and stagnation persist—particularly in the east. At the same time, some places in peripheral countries are experiencing rapid economic growth. The local conditions in these places differ sharply from those prevailing in surrounding areas. Recent economic growth on the Pacific Rim of East Asia has created huge regional disparities in economic conditions between some coastal provinces of China and distant interior provinces. Such regional economic contrasts have significant political, as well as social, consequences.

As noted at the beginning of this chapter, regional contrasts in wealth are a reminder that per capita GNI does not accurately represent the economic development of individual places. Any statistic that is derived for an entire country hides the variety of economic situations within that country. Peripheral countries are notoriously marked by severe regional disparities. In Chapter 10, we discussed the stark contrasts between wealthy and poor citizens in Latin American and African cities. When viewed at the scale of the state, however, major cities (particularly capitals) and their surroundings often look like islands of prosperity, with modern buildings, factories on the outskirts, and modern farms nearby. In some cases, roads and rails lead to a bustling port, where luxury automobiles are unloaded for use by the privileged elite, and raw materials or agricultural products from the country are exported to points around the world. In these core areas of countries, the rush of "progress" may be evident. If you travel a few kilometres into the countryside or even into a different neighbourhood in the city, however, you will likely see a very different picture. In this section of the chapter, we discuss how government policy affects development, how governments collaborate with corporations to create islands of development, and how people try to generate growth in the periphery of the periphery (the poorest regions of peripheral countries).

THE ROLE OF GOVERNMENTS

Governments play a critical role in determining whether, how, and where wealth is produced. This is because the distribution of wealth is influenced by tariffs, trade agreements, taxation structures, land ownership rules, environmental regulations, and many other manifestations of governmental authority. Government policies play an important role at the international level, but they also shape patterns of development within states—not just between urban and rural areas, but also within each of these sectors.

Of course, governments alone do not determine patterns of wealth and poverty, but they are almost always part of the picture. Consider the case of the Lower Ninth Ward in New Orleans, which was devastated by Hurricane Katrina in 2005. On its surface, what happened to the Lower Ninth Ward was the result of a natural disaster. But the flooding of that part of New Orleans was also the result of government decisions, made decades earlier, to build levies and settle flood-prone areas. The concentration of people living there was also the product of innumerable policies affecting housing, the construction of businesses, and the like. Once the hurricane hit, many looked to government to rebuild this devastated section of the city. The limited nature of the governmental response, however, is clearly evident in the landscape today (**Figure 11.21**).

An examination of commodity chains can also help us understand the role of governments in uneven distribution of wealth and development, both within and between states. In her 2005 book *The Travels of a T-Shirt in the Global Economy*, economist

FIELD NOTE

New Orleans After Katrina

Walking through New Orleans' Lower Ninth Ward in late 2007, more than two years after Hurricane Katrina, it seemed as if the natural disaster had only just happened. Street after street of devastated, vacant buildings was all the eye could behold—many still bore the markings made by the emergency crews that had moved through the neighbourhood in the wake of the hurricane, showing whether anyone had died inside. It struck the observer that reconstruction of this primarily African-American, working-class community would require a public commitment on the order of what occurred in Europe after World War II, when cities reduced to rubble by bombing were rebuilt almost from scratch.

FIGURE 11.21 Destroyed house in the Lower Ninth Ward, New Orleans.

© Alexander B. Murphy

Today, it is fair to ask whether a comparable commitment has ever existed to rebuild the Lower Ninth Ward. Such a sentiment was expressed in a *Time* magazine headline on the five-year anniversary of Katrina: "New Orleans' Lower Ninth: Katrina's Forgotten Victim?" In the article, author Tim Padgett noted that "homeowners in predominantly black communities like the Lower Ninth Ward have received substantially lower house-

reconstruction grants from local, state and federal agencies than white Katrina victims have, even though it usually costs as much to rebuild a house in the Lower Ninth as it does in more upscale districts." At the same time, Padgett noted that many of the Lower Ninth's parks, schools, and community centres have also not yet been reestablished, despite the passage of five years since Katrina devastated New Orleans.

Pietra Rivoli described grabbing a T-shirt out of a bin at a Walgreens in Florida, buying it, and then tracing its production back through the commodity chain to see how it ended up in her hands. The cotton for her T-shirt was grown in West Texas, where the cotton lobby (the political arm of America's cotton producers) has effectively pressed for governmental labour programs and price supports that help the lobby grow cotton and sell it at predictable prices. From West Texas, the cotton bale travelled to China by ship. There, it was spun into thread and woven into fabric. Women from rural China worked in state-owned factories set up in regions slated for economic development; they cut and sewed T-shirts and kept the textile machines in good repair. The women were considered cheap labour at the global scale, earning about $100 per month. Rivoli reports that over 40,000 garment factories operate in China alone.

The T-shirts were then shipped to the United States for sale. In an attempt to protect T-shirts produced in America with higher labour costs from those produced in China, the U.S. government has established quotas on how many items from various clothing categories can be imported into the United States from China and other countries. An unintended consequence of the quota system has been a "quota market," in which countries buy and sell their U.S. quota numbers to producers in other countries (an illegal but rampant practice). Instead of trading in quotas, some production facilities have moved to places where quotas and cheap labour are available—places such as Sri Lanka, Poland, and Lesotho. Rivoli describes how one producer of cotton shirts has moved around the world:

> *The Esquel Corporation, today the world's largest producer of cotton shirts, started in Hong Kong in the late 1970s, but, unable to obtain quota to sell to the United States, shifted production to mainland China. When the United States tightened Chinese shirt quotas in the early 1980s, Esquel moved production to Malaysia. When Malaysian quota also became difficult to obtain, Esquel moved yet again, this time to Sri Lanka. The globe hopping continued, with the Chinese shirt producer setting up operations in Mauritius and Maldives.*

The point is that quota laws, like other policies made by governments, regional trade organizations, and international political regimes (such as the World Trade Organization and the

International Labour Organization), affect whether and how regions can produce and exchange goods on the world market.

ISLANDS OF DEVELOPMENT

In both core and periphery, governments often prioritize the creation of wealth in the capital city, which is the seat of governmental authority. In most states, the capital city is the political nerve centre of the country, home to government buildings and jobs, and often to universities, museums, heritage centres, convention centres, and the headquarters of large corporations as well. After gaining independence, many former colonial states spent lavishly on their capitals during the 1950s and 1960s. This was not because this was essential to political or economic success but because the states wanted to showcase their independence and their futures, and create a national treasure. They were following the example of their European colonizers, who focused their wealth and treasures on such capital cities as Great Britain's London, France's Paris, and Spain's Madrid.

In many countries of the global economic periphery, the capital cities are by far the largest and most economically influential cities in the state (i.e., primate cities). Some newly independent states have built new capital cities, away from the colonial headquarters, in order to either separate themselves from their colonizers, bring together diverse groups into one state with a city built to reflect their common culture, or extend economic development into the interior of the state.

Nigeria, for example, moved its capital from Yoruba-dominated Lagos, on the coast, to Abuja, an ethnically neutral territory in the centre of the state. Malawi moved its capital from Zomba, deep in the south, to a more central location, Lilongwe. Pakistan moved the capital from the colonial headquarters of Karachi to Islamabad in the far north to symbolize the country's reorientation toward its historically important interior and north. Brazil moved its capital from coastal Rio de Janeiro to centrally located Brasilia in order to direct attention to the huge, sparsely populated, yet poorly integrated, interior. More recently, Malaysia has moved its capital from the colonial capital of Kuala Lumpur to a completely new centre called Putrajaya, about 40 kilometres to the south. In this case, the Malaysian government decided to build a new, ultramodern seat of government to symbolize the country's rapid economic growth (**Figure 11.22**).

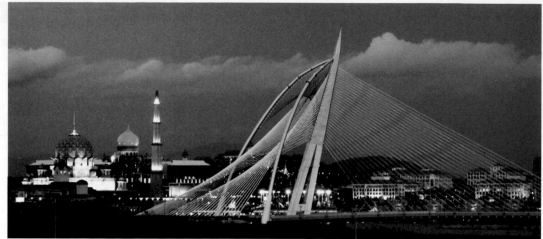

FIGURE 11.22 Putrajaya, Malaysia. Putrajaya is the capital of Malaysia, replacing Kuala Lumpur.

Bazuki Muhammad/Reuters/Corbis

Corporations can also make cities focal points of development by concentrating corporate activities in a particular place. Often, corporations build up the cities near the resources they are extracting or near manufacturing centres they have built. Multinational oil companies create subsidiaries in peripheral and semi-peripheral countries, creating or expanding cities near oil reserves. For example, in the African country of Gabon, Elf and Shell, two oil companies based in Europe, run Elf Gabon and Shell Gabon. The oil companies took the small colonial town of Port Gentil in Gabon and turned it into a city that the locals call "oil city." The oil companies built housing, roads, and stores and provide much of the employment in the town (**Figure 11.23**).

FIELD NOTE

Economic Growth in Gabon

Before the 1970s, Gabon's principal exports were manganese, hardwoods, and uranium ores. The discovery of oil off the Gabonese coast changed all that. This oil storage tank at the edge of Port Gentil is but one reminder of a development that has transformed Gabon's major port city—and the economy of the country as a whole. Oil now accounts for 80 percent of Gabon's export earnings, and that figure is climbing as oil prices rise and new discoveries are made. But how much the average citizen of Gabon is benefitting from the oil economy remains an open question. Even as health care and infrastructure needs remain unmet, the French publication *L'Autre Afrique* lists Gabon's ruler as the African leader with the largest real estate holdings in Paris.

FIGURE 11.23 Port Gentil, Gabon.

© Alexander B. Murphy

When a government or corporation builds up and concentrates economic development in a certain city or small region, geographers call that place an **island of development**. In Chapter 5, we identified islands of development in the periphery and semi-periphery and discussed why people migrate to these cities from rural areas and other poorer cities. The hope for a job drives many migrants to move to these islands of comparative prosperity.

> **Island of development** Place built up by a government or corporation to attract foreign investment and that has relatively high concentrations of paying jobs and infrastructure.

CREATING GROWTH IN THE PERIPHERY OF THE PERIPHERY

One of the greatest challenges is creating opportunities outside the islands of development. In the most rural, impoverished regions of developing countries, some non-governmental organizations try to improve the plight of residents. **Non-governmental organizations (NGOs)** are not run by state or local governments. Rather, NGOs operate independently, and the term is usually reserved for entities that operate as non-profits. Thousands of NGOs operate in the world today, from churches to charities such as the Red Cross, Doctors without Borders, Greenpeace, the World Wildlife Fund, Oxfam, the Aga Khan Foundation, and World Vision. Each NGO has its own set of goals, depending on the primary concerns outlined by its founders. The World Bank distinguishes between two broad groups of NGOs: operational NGOs focus on development projects, while advocacy NGOs promote particular causes.

> **Non-governmental organizations (NGOs)** International organizations that operate outside the formal political arena but that are nevertheless influential in spearheading international initiatives on social, economic, and environmental issues.
>
> **Microcredit program** Program that provides small loans to poor people, especially women, to encourage development of small businesses.

In some countries, so many NGOs are operating that they serve as what *The Economist* calls "a parallel state, financed by foreigners and accountable to nobody."

For example, more than 20,000 NGOs operate within the country of Bangladesh at any time, focusing mainly on the rural areas and villages of the state. One particular kind of NGO venture that has been successful in South Asia and South America is the **microcredit program**. The idea behind these programs is simple: give loans to poor people, particularly women, to encourage them to develop small businesses. Finance the program by having borrowers in the village guarantee each other's credit, or make future lending to others contingent on repayment by the first borrowers. With repayment rates hovering at 98 percent, microcredit programs can be self-sufficient, and many NGOs offer them (**Figure 11.24**). One of the best-known examples of such a program is the Grameen Bank, which started in 1976 as a research project carried out by Professor Muhammad Yunus from Chittagong University in Bangladesh, who aimed to provide small loans to the rural poor in order to help recipients engage in entrepreneurial activities. Today, 95 percent of the Grameen Bank is owned by its 8.4 million borrowers, most of whom are poor rural women. The other 5 percent is owned by the Bangladesh government.

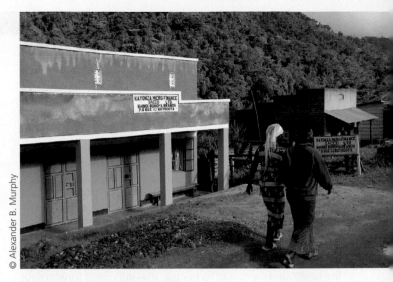

FIGURE 11.24 Bwindi, Uganda. Women walk by a microcredit agency that has facilitated economic development in the town.

By providing microcredit to women, NGOs can alter the gender balance in a region, giving more fiscal power to women who are otherwise often left out of economic development activities. Some microcredit programs are believed to have helped lower birth rates in parts of developing countries, and some have altered the social fabric of cultures by diminishing men's positions of power. Successful microcredit programs also help alleviate malnourishment, as women with income can feed themselves and their children.

Microcredit programs have been less successful in regions with high mortality rates from diseases such as AIDS. If borrowers are unable to work, or if their families have medical and funeral bills, borrowers are much more likely to default on the microcredit loan. When people in the periphery of the periphery experience a multitude of problems, such as disease, corrupt governments, high mortality rates, high fertility rates, and disruptions from natural hazards, the goal of economic development takes a back seat to daily survival.

MAIN POINTS 11.4 How Do Political and Economic Institutions Influence Uneven Development Within States?

- The distribution of wealth is greatly influenced by tariffs, quotas, trade agreements, taxation structures, land ownership rules, and environmental regulations. Accordingly, the actions of governments, regional trade organizations, and international political regimes play a critical role in determining whether, how, and where wealth is produced.

- In both core and periphery, governments often prioritize the creation of wealth in the seat of governmental authority, the capital city. Corporations can also make cities focal points of development by concentrating corporate

- activities in a particular place. When a government or corporation builds up and concentrates economic development in a certain city or small region, geographers call that place an island of development.

- In the most rural, impoverished regions of developing countries, some non-governmental organizations (NGOs) try to improve the plight of the people. Non-governmental organizations are not run by state or local governments, but instead operate independently and usually as non-profit agencies.

SUMMARY

The commonly held conceptualization of economic development, which first took hold in the wake of the Industrial Revolution, implies a sense of progressively improving a country's economic situation. Geographers focus on the spatial structure of the economy, assessing how that structure influences the ability of states and regions to reach the same level of economic development. Geographers also recognize that economic development in a single place is based on a multitude of factors, including its historical ties to other countries, its situation within the contemporary global economy, its place in commodity chains, the efficacy of its government and the success or failure of its policies, the health and welfare of its people, the amount of foreign debt it owes, and the influence of non-governmental programs. Geographers realize that all of these processes operate concurrently across scales, making a country's journey toward economic development much more complicated than climbing a metaphorical ladder.

Geographers have argued for a broader, more multifaceted conceptualization of development that goes beyond solely economic concerns. While it is widely agreed that economic growth is necessary in order to enable people to procure needed goods and services, there is a growing argument that development is also about ensuring social equity, environmental sustainability, and other non-economic concerns. Thus, the question of how to measure development has been a contentious one, with more recent measurement systems attempting to go beyond the economic in their assessment of people's living conditions.

Finally, geographers are also active in building our understanding of barriers to development, as well as the impacts of development on people and places.

DISCUSSION AND REVIEW QUESTIONS

1. What happened to Timbuktu? What does its story reveal about the fickle nature of geography, trade, and development?

2. Development is not a straightforward or uncontested process. What are some of the issues and critiques of how development is conceptualized and measured?

3. What is the world-systems theory and how does it assist economic geographers to contextualize development? How is it different from the modernization model?

4. Much attention, effort, and resources have been devoted to promoting development across the globe. The UN Millennium Development goals represent a high degree of consensus about the conditions that must be changed if progress is to be attained. However, there still exist many barriers to development. Identify and briefly explain these barriers. In your view, which barrier is the most challenging to overcome?

5. What are NGOs? What role do they play in development? Can you think of a specific example of how an NGO acted as a positive force for development? Are NGOs an inherently positive force in the promotion of development?

GEOGRAPHIC CONCEPTS

capitalism   320
commodification   320
context   319
core   321
dependency theory   320
developing   311
export processing zone (EPZ)   331
formal economy   313
gross domestic product (GDP)   312
gross national income (GNI)   312
gross national product (GNP)   312
informal economy   313
island of development   336
malaria   328
maquiladoras   331
microcredit program   337

Millennium Development Goals   325
modernization model   318
neo-colonialism   319
non-governmental organizations (NGOs)   337
North American Free Trade Agreement (NAFTA)   332
per capita GNI   312
periphery   321
semi-periphery   321
special economic zone   331
structural adjustment loans   327
structuralist theory   319
three-tier structure   321
trafficking   326
vectored diseases   328
world-systems theory   320

ADDITIONAL RESOURCES ON-LINE

Millennium Development Goals: www.un.org/millenniumgoals; http://mdgs.un.org/unsd/mdg/Default.aspx www.mdgmonitor.org/index.cfm

Sustainable Development Goals: http://sustainabledevelopment. un.org/

United Nations Development Programme: Human Development Reports and Human Development Index: http://hdr.undp.org/en

Human Trafficking: www.unodc.org/unodc/en/human-trafficking/ what-is-human-trafficking.html

Global Poverty: http://data.worldbank.org/topic/poverty

"Spread the Net" Program: http://plancanada.ca/spreadthenet

International Monetary Fund (IMF): www.imf.org/external/ index.htm

World Bank: www.worldbank.org

Grameen Bank: http://grameenfoundation.org/

Foreign Affairs, Trade and Development Canada: www. international.gc.ca/international/index.aspx?lang=eng

Maquila Solidarity Network: http://en.maquilasolidarity.org

World Tourism Organization: www2.unwto.org/

CHAPTER
12 TRANSPORTATION

Get on the Bus

IT WAS FOUR O'CLOCK on a Tuesday afternoon and I was standing at a bus stop at Brock University in St. Catharines, Ontario. I couldn't help but notice that each of the many bus stops was teeming with undergraduate and graduate students, and that as a steady flow of buses pulled up to their designated stops, a steady flow of students boarded each one (**Figure 12.1**). Almost every bus leaving the campus was filled with as many students as could be safely accommodated. "How much things have changed," I thought to myself. When I first started commuting to Brock University a few years earlier, only a very small proportion of students travelled by public transit. Instead, the poor availability of transit service, marked by long waits between buses and limited hours of operation, prompted most students to commute to the school's isolated suburban location atop the Niagara Escarpment by car.

As a strong proponent of sustainable transportation, I was pleased to witness this growth in the popularity of public transit among Brock's student population. I knew this change in transportation behaviour was largely an outcome of the introduction of a universal bus pass (or "U-Pass") program by the school's undergraduate student union in September 2003. I also knew that this program, in exchange for a modest ancillary fee added to their tuition, allowed most of Brock's 17,000 students to ride public transit for free simply by showing their student card to the driver. As a transportation geographer, I couldn't help asking a number of questions as I watched the flurry of activity at the bus stop that day. First, just how many Brock students were actually commuting by public transit and how did this compare to the proportion travelling by car? Second, what were some of the benefits of public transit's relatively new popularity at Brock University? Also, was this U-Pass program something that students wanted to see continued beyond its initial three-year trial period?

I set out to answer my questions by conducting a survey of Brock students and interviewing representatives of the three public transit agencies serving the university as part of the U-Pass program. Some of the results amazed me. Data from over 400 completed survey questionnaires showed that over half the students (56.0 percent) regularly commuted to and from Brock by public transit, while only 36.1 percent travelled as car drivers and 5.0 percent rode as car passengers. When considering only those students who lived in St. Catharines or Thorold, the two cities on whose border Brock is located, the proportion of students travelling by public transit rose to 72.6 percent. No wonder the buses were so busy!

I was also curious about the types of benefits that came from Brock University's implementation of the U-Pass program. From

FIGURE 12.1 Brock University, St. Catharines, Ontario. Transit ridership among students skyrocketed following the introduction of a universal bus pass program at the school in 2003.

St. Catharines Transit Commission

the students' perspective, some of these included an overall lower cost of attending university due to the lower transportation costs, and greatly enhanced levels of accessibility to affordable student housing, employment opportunities, and shopping and recreational facilities. For the participating transit agencies— St. Catharines Transit, Welland Transit, and Niagara Falls Transit— benefits included the additional revenue brought in through the program, ridership increases that qualified each agency for extra provincial government funding, and, more generally, a higher profile for public transit in each city. Research participants also identified broader environmental, social, and economic benefits, such as reductions in air pollution and fuel consumption, better transit service on some routes and the creation of entirely new routes, improved transit service for the broader community, as well as more students travelling off-campus to shop at local businesses.

In asking the participants if they felt the U-Pass program should continue beyond its initial three-year trial period, I assumed that transit riders would be in favour of such a move. But I also predicted that students who continued to travel by car after the program's introduction would be opposed to extending the program, given that they were required (with few exceptions) to pay for something they didn't use. I was wrong. Both groups—a total of 82 percent of those surveyed—turned out to be in favour of continuing the program. Why this surprising result? Beyond all the positive outcomes noted earlier, I also learned that even those who drove to school were benefitting from the program. For example, they had less trouble finding parking spaces on campus and could also use public transit for free when their cars weren't available or when they were going out on the town with friends and didn't want to drive.

Today, U-Pass programs are in place at dozens of post-secondary institutions throughout Canada and the United States. In every case, they offer students a low-cost alternative to travelling by car while also providing affordable transportation to those who do not have the option to drive. U-Pass programs have captured the interest of transportation researchers, including transportation geographers, because they serve as an effective example of how people's transportation behaviour can adapt to changing conditions. Before the U-Pass program was introduced at Brock University, public transit service was both expensive and inadequate in the eyes of most students. As a result, most travelled to school by car. By reducing the cost of using public transit and enhancing the level of service, a dramatic shift took place that saw public transit become the most used mode of travel to school among the university's students. The success of U-Pass programs like Brock University's also demonstrates that there is an important place for non-automobile modes of transportation within cities, despite the high and growing levels of automobile use that we currently see throughout many of the world's core regions.

Transportation issues, including the effort to promote public transit use on university campuses, are described by geographer David Keeling as being "quintessentially geographic" (2007, p. 218). In this chapter, we begin by reviewing why transportation issues matter in the study of human geography. We then review the roles that transportation has played in the long-standing but rapidly accelerating globalization process (Chapter 2), the transportation circumstances of peripheral regions, and the important roles that transportation must play in helping to improve the quality of life for people living in those places. The next section explores the enormous influence that transportation innovations have had on the growth and morphology of cities in Canada and other core countries. We also consider the ways in which automobile-dependent transportation patterns found in many places today have become matters of serious concern due to their negative consequences for people and places. We conclude by looking at some of the ways these issues might be resolved over the short and long term.

KEY QUESTIONS FOR CHAPTER 12

1. What is transportation geography, and why does it matter?

2. What has been the contemporary role of transportation in globalization?

3. Why is transportation an important concern in the development of peripheral regions?

4. How has transportation helped to shape the growth of Canadian cities?

5. What are some consequences of contemporary urban transportation patterns?

6. What are some ways by which urban transportation systems might be made more sustainable?

12.1 What Is Transportation Geography, and Why Does It Matter?

Transportation geography is defined in *The Dictionary of Human Geography* (2009, p. 773) as the study of "the movement of people and goods, the transportation systems designed to facilitate such movement, and the relationship of transportation to other facets of human geography such as economic development, energy, land use, sprawl, environmental degradation, values and culture." This means that transportation geographers are interested in building our understanding of everything from who and what is travelling from point A to point B; where, how, and why they are moving between these locations; and what are the implications of such patterns of movement.

> **Transportation geography**
> The study of the movement of people and goods, the transportation systems designed to facilitate such movement, and the relationship of transportation to other facets of human geography, such as economic development, energy, land use, sprawl, environmental degradation, values, and culture.

Transportation is first and foremost about movement, and movement is one of the five major themes of this textbook that draw on our spatial perspective. Humans have always been on the move, whether they are migrants moving to find a more prosperous life (Chapter 5), commuters travelling from the suburbs to the central business district for daily work, or people travelling to visit family and friends. At the same time, globalization, facilitated by new transportation systems, involves the movement of goods, information, people, and capital at the global scale, with local implications (Chapter 2). In other words, transportation geography matters on a multiplicity of scales, from the local to the global. Given geographers' inherent interest in such processes as spatial interaction and economic development, and in such issues as human-environment relations and quality-of-life differences among world regions, transportation constitutes a logical and important focus of concern within the study of human geography. Indeed, as transportation geographer Richard Knowles has stated, "The significance of transport and travel in geographical inquiry is undiminished" (2009, p. 449).

Until recently, transportation has been largely neglected by geographers. This is primarily because transportation was regarded as a relatively insignificant or taken-for-granted aspect of most geographical phenomena or processes, such as the spatial relationship between home and work or the expansion of the global economy. Transportation systems were often positioned as part of the "black box" of infrastructure, to the point that they might be understood as apolitical and asocial. Over time, geographers have come to appreciate the significance of transportation as a critical factor in shaping the structure of cities, globalization, and other geographical concerns. They also recognize that transportation patterns, such as levels of public or private transportation use or the patterns of spatial interaction created by the availability and accessibility of different modes, are influenced by a wide range of geographical factors. For instance, not everyone experiences transportation the same way. As we read in Chapters 7 and 8, aspects of our identity, such as race, gender, class, able-bodiedness, and sexuality all play a role in how we experience the spaces we move through in our everyday lives. Transportation geographers are becoming increasingly aware of the socio-cultural aspects of movement that lead to this unevenness. As a result, the work of contemporary transportation geographers increases our understanding of many issues that have historically been of interest within the discipline of human geography.

Transportation systems greatly influence the character of places, whether through their aesthetic qualities, the levels of noise they generate, or the routes they offer users. The degree to which different modes of transportation are available also plays a crucial role in shaping the connectedness of people and places, whether it is between different parts of the city, between rural and urban areas, across regions, or even across continents. The existence of an effective transportation system is essential for numerous ends: for example, it provides access to natural resources or sources of energy, enables the establishment of industry, provides people with the ability to move between their homes and necessary facilities and services, and makes leisure travel possible, among many other uses. The availability of **transport networks** and the levels of accessibility they provide can also greatly influence the locational distribution of people or things. Patterns of retail activity in the modern-day urban environment are shaped by a number of factors, for instance, but one of the most significant is the accessibility of local and regional road networks. Big-box stores and power centres are typically located at interchanges along major highways or arterial roadways so they are easy for car drivers to access from numerous directions, but are also often difficult to reach on foot or by bicycle.

> **Transport networks** The complete system of the routes pertaining to all means of transport available in a particular area.

The scales of analysis at which transportation geographers work vary considerably. Some focus on the movement of people or goods at the international level (i.e., between countries), while others examine movement between regions (i.e., interregional analyses, such as urban-to-rural flows or vice versa), between urban areas (inter-urban movements), or within urban areas (intra-urban movements). Similarly, transportation geography uses both aggregate and disaggregate data to study particular phenomena (Hanson, 2004). Aggregate-level data are used especially to examine large groups of travellers and the trips they are making; researchers using this data are more interested in the origins and destinations of these trips than in who exactly is travelling. On the other hand, disaggregate (or individual-level) data allow for the analysis of travel flows at a much smaller scale (i.e., the individual or household level). By using disaggregate data, transportation geographers have also come to understand that many issues affect different groups of people in different ways, and that some groups are more greatly affected by particular transportation problems than others. Accordingly, many current studies conducted by transportation geographers focus on specific population subgroups, such as seniors, persons with disabilities, low-income earners, or children and youth.

MAIN POINTS 12.1 What Is Transportation Geography, and Why Does It Matter?

- Transportation geography is the study of the movement of people and goods, the transportation systems designed to facilitate such movement, and the relationship of transportation to other facets of human geography.

- Whether it is to provide access to natural resources or sources of energy, to enable the establishment of industry, to provide people with the ability to move between their homes and necessary facilities and services, or to make leisure travel possible, the presence of an effective transportation system is essential.

- The scales of analysis at which transportation geographers work vary considerably. Some focus on the movement of people or goods at the international level (i.e., between countries), while others examine movement between regions (i.e., interregional analyses, such as urban-to-rural flows or vice versa), between urban areas (inter-urban movements), or within urban areas (intra-urban movements).

12.2 What Has Been the Contemporary Role of Transportation in Globalization?

As we argued in Chapter 2, globalization refers to "an accelerating set of processes involving flows that encompass ever-greater numbers of the world spaces and that lead to increasing integration and interconnectivity among those spaces" (Ritzer, 2007, p. 1). Most of this increasing integration and interconnectivity would not have become possible without innovations in transportation and communication technologies.

In some parts of the world today, primarily within core regions, transportation systems are well developed and provide unprecedented levels of access to people and places. Numerous innovations in transportation technology over the past century have dramatically increased the ease and speed of passenger and freight travel over both short and long distances, as many places have witnessed a shift from the era of the steamship, steam locomotive, and horse and buggy to that of the automobile, airplane, high-speed train, and container ship (**Figure 12.2**). This "time-space compression," as David Harvey calls it (discussed in Chapter 2), is further intensified by digital communication technologies such as the Internet and mobile communications. Indeed, the high levels of mobility enjoyed by many people in the world's core regions have become so firmly entrenched that they are often taken for granted.

Transportation technologies have not diffused evenly across the entire globe. In many parts of the world, particularly within peripheral regions, transport systems are far less technologically advanced, or are tightly regulated for political ends (e.g., the lack of shipping lanes in North Korea, shown in Figure 2.4b). In many places, walking is still the only mode of transport people can rely on every day. This limitation, combined with the lack of proximity to necessary goods and services, such as safe drinking water and educational facilities, often has the effect of stifling development because it forces people to devote a great deal of their time to walking long distances just to meet their most basic daily needs, or it prevents them from making such trips and satisfying their needs at all.

MARINE TRAVEL

As we saw in Chapter 2, perhaps the single most important transportation mode in the globalization of the world economy is the ship. As Marc Levinson, author of *The Box: How the Shipping Container Made the World Smaller and the World Economy Bigger,* states, "Attributing the vast changes in the world economy to a single cause would be foolhardy, but the possibility should not be dismissed that the sharp drop in freight costs from the introduction of container shipping played a major role in increasing the integration of the global economy" (2006, p. 12). Over the past few decades, innovations in the construction of ships have enabled the building of much larger bulk carriers and container ships than ever before (Figure 12.2).

FIGURE 12.2 Container ship. Marine vessels such as this one carry most of the manufactured products that move between continents.

These larger vessels, combined with the enhancement of port facilities that make it quicker and easier to transfer containers directly from ships onto trains, airplanes, and trucks, greatly increase the attractiveness of international trade for many firms. The availability of large bulk carriers enables the global sourcing of raw materials, while the availability of massive container ships makes it more cost-effective to situate manufacturing operations in peripheral and semi-peripheral regions, where dramatically lower wage rates prevail.

> **Containerization** The use of containers to unitize cargo for transportation, supply, and storage.
>
> **Break-of-bulk point**
> A location along a transport route where goods must be transferred from one carrier to another. In a port, the cargoes of oceangoing ships are unloaded and put on trains, trucks, or perhaps smaller riverboats for inland distribution.

Transportation geographers Robert McCalla, Brian Slack, and Claude Comtois study the growth of **containerization** in Canada and at the global scale. They observe that the location of, and level of traffic at, the world's largest container ports serve as excellent indicators of the spread of economic globalization. Historically, the world's biggest ports were generally located within core regions, such as the United States and Europe. Ports such as those in New York and London once served as major **break-of-bulk points**, places where cargo is transferred from one mode of transportation (for example, a ship) to another mode of transportation (e.g., a truck or train). By 2012, the geographic distribution of major world ports had changed considerably, with China having seven of the world's 10 largest ports (**Figure 12.3**). China's importance in global container shipping patterns is a testament to its emergence as one of the world's main manufacturing export countries and also highlights the critical role that

FIGURE 12.4 Beijing Capital International Airport, Beijing, China. Almost 84 million passengers travelled through Beijing Capital International Airport in 2013, making it one of the world's busiest airports. To keep up with the increase in air travel, the Chinese government has announced plans to build another airport by 2018.

its special economic zones (discussed in Chapter 11) play in China's integration into the global economy.

AIR TRAVEL

A close counterpart to shipping in the globalization process is air travel. According to Timothy Vowles, a transportation geographer specializing in air travel, aircraft carry goods worth about 40 percent of the value of all products traded in the world today. Vowles points out that the air travel industry is an important source of economic development benefits for many places, as it employs over 4 million people around the world and generates over $400 billion in economic output. As is often the case, there are huge discrepancies between core and peripheral regions when it comes to the importance and accessibility of air travel. The vast majority of air passenger and cargo traffic moves within or between three regions: North America, Europe, and East Asia (**Figure 12.4**). The world's leading airlines are also headquartered in these regions. Air travel is particularly significant in the United States; for example, the U.S. domestic market makes up about one-third of all passenger air travel in the world.

The important roles that marine and air transport modes play in shaping globalization processes also make these industries vulnerable to outside forces. During the economic crisis of 2009, for example, world container traffic fell by 26 percent, and world air freight tonnage fell by 10 percent (International Transport Forum, 2010). This led to widespread job losses and problems of overcapacity.

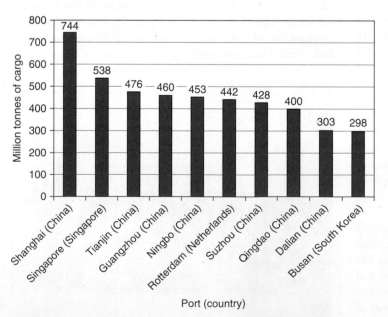

FIGURE 12.3 World's largest shipping ports, 2012. This chart shows the 10 largest shipping ports in the world, based on volume of cargo (measured in million tonnes). Data from ship-technology.com.

(a)

(b)

Andre Forget/The Canadian Press

© Marmaduke St. John/Alamy

FIGURE 12.5 Intermodal transportation. Intermodal shipment of containers accounts for a large portion of business for railway companies such as CN. (a) A crane loads a container onto a train at CN's Montreal intermodal terminal at Taschereau. (b) A crane lifts a maritime cargo container from a truck to load it onto a cargo ship at a container facility.

LAND TRAVEL

While marine and air travel clearly play key roles in globalization processes, particularly at the inter-continental scale, they are far from the only important forms of transportation influencing the geographical characteristics of these processes. Rail- and truck-based modes of transportation have also enabled the expansion of global, international, and regional trade over the past several decades. This is particularly the case in North America, where growth in the use of rail and road transport coincides with the growing use of containerized shipping to move goods. According to American geographer Andrew Goetz (2009), the transformation of these industries began in the 1980s, when many North American railroads began to carry double-stacked containers from coastal ports, particularly along the Pacific coast, to inland terminals, where the containers were often transferred directly onto trucks for the trip to their final destination. Goetz notes that the use of railroads to move containers for this purpose creates a form of "land bridge" between Asia and the east coast of North America. Finally, he points out that this **intermodal transportation** of containers accounts for a large segment of business for each of the five North American railroads, including Canadian National Railway (CN), and also for some of the continent's largest trucking firms (**Figure 12.5**).

> **Intermodal transportation**
> The transportation of a person or a load from its origin to its destination by a sequence of at least two transportation modes, the transfer from one mode to the next being performed at an intermodal terminal.

MAIN POINTS 12.2 What Has Been the Contemporary Role of Transportation in Globalization?

- Many of the interactions, relationships, and interdependencies between places that have been created as part of globalization would not be possible were it not for the transportation innovations that the world has witnessed over the past several decades.

- Perhaps the single most important transportation mode in the globalization of the world economy is the ship. Over the past few decades, innovations in the construction of ships have enabled the building of much larger bulk carriers and container ships than ever before.

- The vast majority of air passenger and cargo traffic moves within or between three regions: North America, Europe, and East Asia.

- Rail and road transport provide important means of conveying containers between ocean ports and the final destination of the goods being shipped, particularly in North America.

12.3 Why Is Transportation an Important Concern in the Development of Peripheral Regions?

Given the pervasiveness of globalization processes, it is easy to assume that transportation innovations have diffused evenly throughout the world, providing a fairly universal level of access to modern means of transportation. The availability of transportation infrastructure is widely viewed as a critical factor in the economic development of a country. Ports, railways, and roads all contribute to the economy by ensuring access to raw materials and providing a means of exporting products to their ultimate markets. In his modernization theory (discussed in Chapter 11), Walter Rostow recognizes the development of transportation networks as an important part of a country's movement along the "ladder of development." Nevertheless, many countries today suffer from a lack of such infrastructure, which, in turn, seriously hampers their economic development efforts and limits their integration into the global economy. Further, a large proportion of the world's population suffers from inadequate access to even the most basic daily needs due to transportation constraints.

For example, the country of Laos, located in southeastern Asia, is one place where a lack of good transportation infrastructure limits economic development. The country is already somewhat isolated from global trade activity due to its status as a landlocked nation. Much of Laos's road network is rather primitive, a problem that is exacerbated by the country's mountainous terrain. Almost half of Laos's roads are rural roads, and only a fraction of these are in decent condition. Many of the roads are impassable during the rainy season, effectively cutting some communities off from the outside world for extended periods each year.

Governments and international development organizations have invested heavily to provide transportation infrastructure in many countries over the past several decades (**Figure 12.6**). For example, improving the national transportation network has been a high priority in the African country of Malawi; in some years, transportation has received over 30 percent of public sector investment. One of the problems with such investment is that it tends to be focused primarily on urban areas and often neglects to serve the needs of those residing in peripheral regions of the country, thus inhibiting rural development. In Malawi, most road investments support the construction and maintenance of primary highways, despite the fact that over 80 percent of the country's rural population relies more heavily on footpaths, tracks, and bridges than on any formal road network.

Throughout much of the world, especially in Africa and parts of Asia and South America, the automobile is a luxury beyond the reach of most people. The primary means of travel is walking. If one can afford it, transport may sometimes include a bicycle or public transportation, if it is available locally. Thus, most transportation investments do little to improve accessibility for rural dwellers in many peripheral countries. This results in serious quality-of-life concerns. The majority of people

FIGURE 12.6 Highway construction in Sri Lanka, 2009. Projects such as this can stimulate economic development in countries of the periphery by improving accessibility. However, for those in rural areas, new roads do little to improve access to basic needs, such as clean water, food, employment, or schools. In those areas, infrastructure enhancements that enable the use of non-motorized transportation modes, such as walking or cycling, can do far more good.

living in rural areas spend much of their time walking to access such things as health care, education, and even clean drinking water, which are often taken for granted or which do not even require travel in core countries. They must also walk to procure firewood for cooking and to access grinding mills. Like Malawi, the country of Zimbabwe suffers from an acute shortage of rural transportation infrastructure. In the late 1990s, Zimbabwe's government examined the travel needs of its rural citizens. It found that an average rural household spent between 60 and 70 hours per week gaining access to water, firewood, grinding mills, markets, clinics, and schools. Significantly, it was women who did most of this walking (about 77 percent), often carrying loads on their heads (a technique called "headloading," illustrated in **Figure 12.7**). An important conclusion of this study

FIGURE 12.7 Headloading. These women in India, like those in many peripheral and semi-peripheral countries, bear much of the burden when it comes to walking with heavy loads, a consequence of inadequate transportation alternatives.

was that improving the proximity of necessary services would be a much more significant development initiative than building new roads. The inconvenient location of services is most problematic, but is something easily remedied through the provision of local services, or by ensuring that footpaths, bridges, and other necessary walking infrastructure are in place and well

maintained. Similar studies in other parts of Africa and other peripheral regions come to comparable conclusions (Riley et al., 2000; Wynd, 1995). One study showed that children in rural Zambia often missed school during the rainy season because they could not safely cross bridges along their walking route (Musonda, 2006).

MAIN POINTS 12.3 Why Is Transportation an Important Concern in the Development of Peripheral Regions?

- A different set of transportation-related problems prevails in peripheral countries. First, the economic development of many places is limited by a lack of adequate transportation infrastructure. Second, a large proportion of the world's population suffers from inadequate access to even the most basic daily needs due to transportation constraints.

- Transportation-related development efforts in many peripheral countries focus primarily on the provision of road infrastructure in metropolitan regions. Little attention has been paid to the enhancement of accessibility in rural settings. This is particularly problematic because a high proportion of rural dwellers must walk to fulfill even their most basic needs.

12.4 How Has Transportation Helped to Shape the Growth of Canadian Cities?

> **Automobile dependence**
> A situation in which a city develops on the assumption that automobile use will predominate so that it is given priority in infrastructure and in the form of urban development.

Transportation and urban geography (Chapter 10) are closely connected. Transportation systems have always had a strong influence on urban morphology, which refers to the physical form and structure of the city. Numerous transportation innovations have been introduced in cities over the past two centuries. Each time this happens, the increased speed of travel typically associated with these innovations dramatically affects the urban morphology by expanding the area of development. As transportation technologies evolve, they require vast amounts of land to accommodate their related infrastructures. In the cities of many core countries, including Canada, and increasingly in many cities of the periphery, we are witnessing the creation of automobile-dependent landscapes. Urban transportation researchers Peter Newman and Jeff Kenworthy have defined **automobile dependence** as "a situation in which a city develops on the assumption that automobile use will predominate so that it is given priority in infrastructure and in the form of urban development" (1999, p. 60).

Up to the late 19th century, walking was the predominant mode of travel in Canadian cities. This necessitated the efficient distribution and mixing of different land use activities and resulted in a compact city, laid out in a roughly circular shape. The advent of public transportation in the latter half of the 19th century led to significant outward expansion of cities along streetcar lines. The size and shape of the city continued to evolve

with the introduction of the private automobile in the first half of the 20th century. Over the past 70 years the car has become the most dominant mode of transportation in cities, to a point where most urban areas in Canada, the United States, Australia, and a growing number of other countries can accurately be described as "automobile dependent."

In their book *Sustainability and Cities: Overcoming Automobile Dependence*, Newman and Kenworthy suggest that automobile-dependent cities share three interrelated characteristics. First, they have automobile-oriented land use patterns, including an abundance of road infrastructure and parking facilities, low development densities, and rigidly segregated land use activities. Second, automobile-dependent cities often have poor non-automobile transportation choices, meaning that modes such as walking, cycling, and public transit are not always viable due to a lack of appropriate infrastructure or inadequate levels of service. This, in turn, often makes it inconvenient, or even impossible, for a person to travel without a car. The third characteristic of an automobile-dependent city is a high level of per capita automobile travel, meaning that the number of trips taken by car is fairly high when averaged across the city's population. These high rates of automobile usage typically prompt governments to invest further in the provision of automobile-oriented transportation infrastructure and to make fewer investments in non-automobile modes.

Over the years, automobile dependence has created numerous environmental, economic, and social consequences, many of them negative. These have prompted a growing number of transportation geographers and other researchers to advocate a transition toward the development of more sustainable transportation systems. While this may seem an impossible task, it is important to remember that automobile dependence, as pervasive as it is in so many places today, is a relatively recent phenomenon. Most cities have at one time or another in their history been more "walkable" and more transit-friendly. Given that urban areas have not always been automobile dependent, it is conceivable that one day the automobile will again play a less dominant role. Certainly, many believe that walking, cycling, and public transit can return to their former levels of importance within the urban transportation system. Researchers and activists holding this perspective suggest that the alternatives simply require greater priority, and less discrimination, in urban transportation policy-making and planning processes.

THE "WALKING CITY" AND THE INTRODUCTION OF PUBLIC TRANSPORTATION

Up to the latter half of the 19th century, city dwellers relied primarily on walking for any intra-urban travel. At the same time, industrial firms relied heavily on railways and waterways to acquire raw materials and ship their finished products to market. Commercial and retail enterprises also obtained most of their goods by train or boat. These transportation networks led to the development of a compact urban form in which industrial, commercial, and residential land uses were, out of necessity, located in close proximity to one another and heavily interspersed. A reliance on walking also restricted the outward expansion of Canadian cities. As Newman and Kenworthy note, "One characteristic people have shown that has been important in shaping the nature of our cities is that they do not like to commute, on average, more than half an hour to major urban destinations" (1999, p. 27). Thus, with walking being the predominant mode of travel throughout the 19th century, most Canadian cities tended not to grow beyond a radius of about two kilometres.

The first form of public transportation widely introduced in Canadian cities and elsewhere was the horse-drawn omnibus, a wheel-based conveyance that held about seven to 10 passengers (**Figure 12.8**). This innovation did little to enhance the mobility of urban dwellers and had a minimal influence on urban expansion, due primarily to two factors. First, most city streets in the mid-1800s were composed of dirt, and rainy weather often created muddy conditions in which the horse-drawn vehicles would get stuck. Similar problems emerged in many places during winter months, when heavy snowfalls hampered the efficient movement of the omnibus along its route. Second, the omnibus only reached a maximum speed of about eight kilometres per hour, even in the most favourable weather conditions. As a result, riding the omnibus was often more time-consuming than travelling on foot.

The deficiencies of the horse-drawn omnibus were largely absent from the electric streetcar, introduced in the late 1880s. These vehicles had a much higher passenger capacity, ran along steel rails instead of on wheels, and could travel at much higher speeds than the omnibus, up to 25 kilometres per hour. This allowed individuals to remain within a reasonable commuting time (i.e., no more than 30 minutes) and distance even while living much farther away from the city's centre than they had done in

FIGURE 12.8 Horse-drawn omnibus in Ottawa, Ontario, ca. 1877. The introduction of this vehicle marked the start of public transportation in many cities, but its effectiveness was greatly limited by its slow travel speed and poor road conditions.

City of Ottawa Archives

the past. Middle- and upper-class families were attracted to the idea of residing farther from the central city and its problems of overcrowding and industrial pollution. The ensuing impact on urban morphology was a sizeable outward expansion, with streetcar lines in some cases stretching 10 kilometres or more from the city's centre. Public transit operators simply extended their lines out from the city centre and through the "streetcar suburbs" that were constructed adjacent to these routes.

As with all public spaces, these streetcars were a site of contested gender relations. Early public transportation systems were largely the domain of men who travelled to and from the central business district for work. Women's experiences on these systems were vastly different. Canadian researchers Donald Davis and Barbara Lorenzkowski argue that for women, public transportation in Canada in the pre-World War II period consisted of battling issues such as sexual harassment and the rights of (male) smokers and (female) shoppers, in addition to women's attempts to become employed as conductors and drivers. They argue, "Always at issue was the place of women in a country that generally regarded women as intruders whenever they ventured into the public, male sphere of travel and commerce" (1998, p. 432). Often, women accessed public transit at different periods of the day than men did, but when the space needed to be shared, women experienced stark reminders that streetcars, by their very design, were the domain of men (**Figure 12.9**). "Climbing onto streetcars, women met the first reminder that they were entering a man's world; the steps were often too high for those short of limb, encumbered by small children, or dressed in long

FIGURE 12.9 Passengers line up to board a streetcar in Winnipeg circa 1940s.

FIGURE 12.10 A streetcar travels along Portage Avenue, Winnipeg, Manitoba, 1904. By the turn of the 20th century, electric streetcars were a prominent part of Canada's urban transportation landscape. The development of "streetcar suburbs" around this time also represented the first major phase of suburbanization across the country.

skirts" (Davis and Lorenzkowski, 1998, p. 435). In fact, a 1941 Canadian Transit Association study revealed that 90 percent of injuries sustained getting on and off the streetcar were suffered by women, the result of handle heights, women's restrictive clothing, and the fact they were often balancing small children and parcels. In the early 1940s, women fought to work on the electric streetcars as conductors (called "conductorettes") and drivers, gaining access to these positions as men left to fight in World War II. In 1943, for example, the B.C. Electric Railway, which had nearly doubled its ridership from 150,000 in 1938 to 270,000 in 1943, began hiring women as conductors as it expanded its services to meet growing demand. Early advertisements called for women between the ages of 25 and 35, who would be considered "on the basis of good appearance and general intelligence." At a period in history when women were doing many non-traditional jobs, the conductorettes became a mainstay, but were limited to the city of Vancouver. Routes to the suburbs remained the domain of male conductors. Even today, public transportation remains a key site of contestation over who has the right to occupy these spaces, and under what conditions. Controversy erupted in Toronto in 2013 when there was public discussion about banning strollers (which are predominantly used by women transporting small children) from the Toronto Transit Commission buses and streetcars at certain times of day, such as rush hour. After public outcry, the motion was dropped, but it stands as a stark reminder that these battles are ongoing.

While the creation of the electric streetcar and the streetcar suburbs encouraged considerable urban growth on the city's periphery, it was a relatively efficient form of development compared to much of the low-density sprawl evident in many places today. These older neighbourhoods were generally built at medium-to-high densities and with an efficient grid-pattern road layout, because individuals residing in streetcar suburbs wanted only a short walk to the streetcar stop and because the

higher development densities enabled developers to maximize the return on their investments. Moreover, many businesses selling goods and services were located in commercial areas near the streetcar stops. As a result, people could satisfy many of their daily needs by walking to a store near where they lived, while any needs requiring access to the city centre could be fulfilled by taking the electric streetcar, which followed direct routes and often operated frequently throughout the day.

By the turn of the 20th century, most Canadian cities had electric streetcar services, and public transit had become the dominant mode of travel for local residents (**Figure 12.10**). Around the same time, the automobile began to appear on city streets. Due to its high cost, the automobile started off primarily as a "toy" for the wealthy through the first few decades of the century and was most commonly used for recreational purposes, such as weekend drives in the countryside, rather than for more utilitarian purposes such as commuting to work or shopping. Throughout the 1920s, automobile ownership became increasingly common among wealthier segments of Canadian society, but there was little increase in this regard through the lean years of the Great Depression and World War II.

URBAN TRANSPORTATION AFTER WORLD WAR II

Although there were numerous technological innovations in transportation during the period from the mid-1800s to the mid-1900s, urban morphology generally remained compact and efficient in places like Canada and the United States throughout this period. A diverse mix of land uses, combined with pedestrian- and transit-oriented streetscapes, enabled most urban dwellers to reach their destinations on foot or by using public transportation. The second half of the 20th century was marked by two interrelated trends—dramatic growth in automobile ownership and increasing suburbanization—that prompted considerable change not only in the spatial relationship between different land use activities, but also in terms of the priority accorded to various modes of transportation in the urban planning process.

After World War II ended in 1945, several trends produced a dramatic increase in private automobile ownership. These included unprecedented levels of economic prosperity, low unemployment, lower car prices resulting from innovations in mass-production technologies (discussed in Chapter 13), and lower fuel costs. The cumulative impact of these trends was to increase significantly the proportion of households that could afford to purchase an automobile.

This increasing demand for automobiles was accompanied by an unprecedented demand for new housing. The poor economic conditions of the Great Depression, and the economic restraint accompanying World War II, had prevented many families from buying a new home, which created a pent-up demand for housing throughout the 1930s and early 1940s. The post-war baby boom (which, as discussed in Chapter 4, lasted from the mid-1940s to the mid-1960s) and massive waves of immigration from Europe to Canadian cities increased the demand for housing even further. Most families searching for new housing were the same ones who could now also afford the purchase of an automobile. This stimulated a massive outflow of households from the central city and streetcar suburbs to more distant and newly constructed suburbs that were often only accessible by car. This shift had drastic effects on the lives of women, as they found themselves confined to these new suburban spaces. Having spent the better part of a decade labouring in factories and other non-traditional employment during the war, women were pushed back into the domestic sphere to ensure men could have the manufacturing jobs. But the domestic sphere was no longer located in highly dense urban areas; instead, it was in the suburban developments that emerged during the post-war boom. These largely middle- and upper-middle-class women, unable to access public transportation and no longer within walking distance of the city centre, found themselves dealing with a growing sense of isolation in the subdivisions of the 1950s.

Before World War II, development activities were largely governed by the market forces of supply and demand, with little in the way of formal planning or government intervention. After 1945, the incredibly fast pace of suburban growth (**Figure 12.11**), and the subsequent increase in demand for community services and infrastructure, prompted governments to take a much more active role in the urban development process. Most post-war suburban housing developments were still designed and built primarily by private developers. As discussed in Chapter 10, developers were now more often required to adhere to municipal master plans and zoning by-laws that regulated what land uses were allowed in a given area and at what densities such development could occur. Of utmost importance to planners and politicians in formulating their policies was the desire to avoid two perceived shortcomings of the pre-World War II city: overcrowding and the mixing of incompatible land use activities, such as housing and industry. In response to these concerns, master plans and zoning regulations typically sought to impose low-density, functionally segregated land use patterns on the urban landscape.

TRANSPORTATION IN POST-WORLD WAR II NEIGHBOURHOOD DESIGN

One important difference between pre-war and post-war urban development was the influence of the automobile in shaping the physical design of residential communities after 1945. Most designers of post-war suburban housing developments in Canada and the United States adopted principles first articulated in the

(a)   (b)

Courtesy Scarborough Archive   Courtesy Scarborough Archive

FIGURE 12.11 Scarborough, Ontario, in (a) 1954 and (b) 1969. Canadian cities grew quickly after World War II, thanks largely to the widespread adoption of automobiles as the primary means of intra-urban travel. The influence of the neighbourhood unit model is also evident in the street layout of the residential areas in the 1969 photo. From Donald Boyce Kirkup, *Boomtown: Metropolitan Toronto. A Photographic Record of Two Decades of Growth.* Toronto: Lockwood Survey Corporation, 1969.

Neighbourhood unit
A planning concept developed by Clarence Perry as a means of reconciling the problems of automobile traffic with public safety objectives, most notably those aimed at the safety of children.

Radburn Idea A highly influential community planning concept incorporating a hierarchy of roadways, the deliberate segregation of pedestrian and automobile traffic, and the residential "superblock."

neighbourhood unit concept and the **Radburn Idea**, two planning innovations introduced in the United States during the late 1920s. The neighbourhood unit was conceived by American planner Clarence Perry as an attempt to adapt residential areas to the increasing presence of the automobile (**Figure 12.12**). Alarmed by the number of people, especially young children, being killed or injured by motor vehicles driving through residential districts, Perry sought to design a neighbourhood in which "the automobile menace" could be reconciled with public safety objectives (Perry, 1929, p. 31). A distinguishing feature of the neighbourhood unit concept was abandonment of the grid-pattern street layout typical of the pre-war city. In its place, Perry's design located main thoroughfares on the neighbourhood's perimeter, while internal roadways took the form of winding crescents and cul-de-sacs. This latter feature was intended to prevent vehicles from using neighbourhood streets as through-routes and also to discourage drivers from travelling at excessive speeds. Furthermore, vehicular access into the neighbourhood was limited to only a few streets. As yet another way of promoting residential safety, Perry's model also situated public facilities, such as libraries and elementary schools, at the centre of the neighbourhood unit. This was meant to ensure that no children living within the neighbourhood would have to walk more than half a kilometre to these destinations and that they could get to these destinations without having to cross any busy streets along the way. The

FIGURE 12.13 Plan of Radburn, New Jersey, 1929. Although the community was never fully built, Clarence Stein and Henry Wright's "Radburn Idea" stands to this day as one of history's most influential planning ideas. The principles embodied in the original plan for Radburn have been incorporated into the design of suburban communities around the world, including Canada. From Clarence S. Stein, *Toward New Towns for America* (Cambridge, MA: MIT Press, 1969), Figure 21, p. 43.

central location of these facilities was intended to provide a focal point for neighbourhood life, with the aim of building a strong sense of community among local residents.

Another important and significant influence on the design of post-war suburban housing developments was the Radburn Idea (**Figure 12.13**), devised by Americans Clarence Stein and Henry Wright. The planned community of Radburn, New Jersey, was built in a rural setting just outside New York City between 1926 and 1929. The initial plan for Radburn was to create a community composed of three distinct yet interconnected neighbourhoods (Stein, 1969). As for its precursor, the neighbourhood unit, the intention was to accommodate the private automobile while at the same time ensuring public safety. The end result, the Radburn Idea, included three especially innovative elements: the incorporation of a hierarchy of roadways, the deliberate segregation of pedestrian and automobile traffic, and the creation of the residential "superblock."

Stein and Wright's solution to mitigate the negative impacts of automobile traffic on residential streets was to further refine Clarence Perry's ideas by physically isolating the community from the rest of the city and introducing a hierarchy of specialized

Bettmann/Corbis

FIGURE 12.12 The "automobile menace," New York, ca. 1924. The growing presence of the automobile and the number of people being killed or injured by motor vehicles in residential areas prompted American planner Clarence Perry to design a "neighbourhood unit" plan in which "the automobile menace" could be reconciled with public safety.

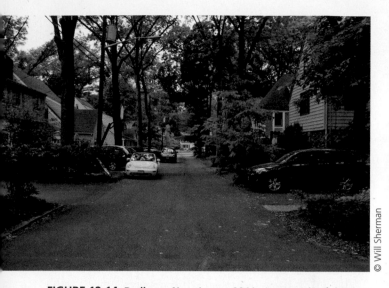

FIGURE 12.14 Radburn, New Jersey, 2011. An example of the smaller roads that limited traffic in front of houses to vehicles that were destined for those addresses.

FIGURE 12.15 Gardiner Expressway under construction, Toronto, 1962. The mass wave of suburban expansion that began after World War II was accompanied by the construction of new highways in several Canadian cities. The Gardiner Expressway was built to carry people between Toronto's western suburbs and its central business district.

roads and pathways within its boundaries. Smaller roads, including service lanes and cul-de-sacs, were built for specialized uses, such as providing automobile and delivery access to houses (**Figure 12.14**). As a result, the only vehicles passing directly in front of houses were those destined specifically for those dwellings. The small roads led to secondary collector roads, which in turn led to main thoroughfares that served two purposes: linking adjoining neighbourhoods and providing access to the expressways that connected Radburn to the outside world.

Although the entire community plan for Radburn was never fully implemented due to the onset of the Great Depression in 1929, the underlying ideas of the Radburn Idea and the neighbourhood unit concepts had considerable influence on the design of post-war suburban developments throughout the United States and Canada. As urban planning scholar Gerald Hodge has stated in his book *Planning Canadian Communities*, "The neighbourhood unit became probably one of the strongest physical organizing principles in modern community plans. Its outcome is readily seen when one flies over almost any Canadian city" (2003, p. 53).

Along with the increasing suburbanization of households after 1945 came a substantial amount of road and highway building on the part of local and provincial governments. Although this did not occur in Canada to anywhere near the same extent as it did in the United States, several expressways were built in Canadian cities to help move suburban residents between their homes and their jobs, which were typically found in the core of the central city. For example, the Gardiner Expressway in Toronto (**Figure 12.15**) was Canada's first urban expressway, followed soon after by the Décarie Expressway in Montreal and Ottawa's Queensway.

Suburban development in the immediate post-war period was primarily residential in nature. However, employment functions soon began to decentralize as well, with retailing and manufacturing activities leading the way. Prior to World War II,

most retail businesses were found in the central business district (or CBD, as described in detail in Chapter 10) and along streetcar lines. After 1945, people running shops and services found a growing proportion of their clientele moving to suburban neighbourhoods, so it was logical for them to decide to locate closer to these residential developments. The movement of retailing and other commercial functions to suburban areas generally led to the construction of small neighbourhood shopping plazas in the 1950s. This gave shoppers easy access to stores, and allowed retail employees to reside close to their workplaces.

As suburban development and growth in automobile ownership accelerated through the 1960s, developers also began to build much larger community shopping centres replete with massive parking lots. This was followed in the 1980s and early 1990s by the development of regional-scale shopping centres intended to serve huge market areas. These were typically located near freeway interchanges in order to provide high levels of accessibility for car drivers. Today, suburban retail activities tend to be concentrated in "big-box" stores and "power centres" (i.e., planned agglomerations of big-box stores), which are also commonly located along arterial roads or adjacent to highway interchanges. According to Brian Lorch, a Canadian geographer who specializes in the changing geography of urban retail activities, "the power centre format has all but replaced the enclosed shopping centre as the preferred choice of developers" since the early 1990s (2004, p.1). At the same time, he notes, "power centres are more conveniently accessed by automobile" than by non-automobile modes, such as walking, cycling, or public transit (2004, p. 2).

Manufacturers also began to locate in the suburbs after World War II. As noted earlier in this chapter, manufacturing

FIGURE 12.16 **Suburban industrial park.** Aerial view of an industrial park and suburban houses, London, England.

industries in the 19th and early 20th centuries relied heavily on railways and waterways for the receipt of raw materials and the shipment of finished products. Furthermore, their workforce's primary mode of commuting was walking. As a result, the manufacturers' location within the city was largely dictated by the distribution of railway lines and waterways, and by the need to be located within a reasonable walking distance of their mostly male workforce. Since these facilities and households tended to be located at or near the centre of the city, the pre-World War II urban core was characterized by the presence of not only commercial activities but also industrial activity. Growing use of transport trucks in the second half of the 20th century greatly diminished manufacturers' dependence on rail- and water-based modes of transportation. Just as the automobile freed households from transport-related locational constraints, the transport truck did the same for manufacturing firms. So long as a given tract of land was accessible by road and connected to the inter-urban highway network, virtually any location within or outside the city was suitable for the location of a factory.

Yet another important innovation that influenced the suburbanization of manufacturing industries was the horizontal assembly line. Before World War II, many manufacturing enterprises were located in multi-storey buildings, but the adoption of the assembly line frequently compelled their relocation to a more appropriate facility. This need for horizontal space also made suburban settings more attractive to manufacturing firms, because the cost of land there tended to be far lower than it was in the CBD and the central city. As a result, firms were able to buy large tracts of land at relatively low cost on the urban periphery. In response to these trends, many suburban municipalities that were hungry to increase the size of their commercial tax base began to zone large tracts of land exclusively for industrial uses. They also frequently built industrial parks that contained various forms of supporting infrastructure, such as roads, electricity, and water supplies, in the hopes of making their communities more attractive to manufacturing firms. These industrial parks were usually

segregated from other sites of urban activity, often by considerable distance, under the assumption that anyone working there would have access to an automobile. Over the past several decades, suburban industrial parks and other settings on the urban periphery have become the location of choice for most urban manufacturing activities (**Figure 12.16**).

Institutional land uses also began to decentralize in the post-World War II period as universities, hospitals, and other community facilities were drawn to suburban areas, due primarily to the availability of large and relatively inexpensive tracts of land in such settings. For example, in Canada during the 1950s and 1960s, several newly established post-secondary institutions, such as Simon Fraser University (Burnaby, British Columbia), University of Calgary (Alberta), Brock University (St. Catharines, Ontario), Trent University (Peterborough, Ontario), Nipissing University (North Bay, Ontario), and York University (Toronto, Ontario), were built on suburban sites (**Figure 12.17**). This was

(a)

(b)

FIGURE 12.17 **Two examples of suburban universities.** (a) Simon Fraser University in Burnaby, British Columbia, was built on a mountaintop in the suburban community in the late 1960s. (b) Brock University was established in St. Catharines, Ontario, in 1964. The first buildings on its current campus, located atop the Niagara Escarpment, opened in 1966.

in contrast to the location of longer-standing post-secondary institutions, such as the University of Toronto (Ontario), Queen's University (Kingston, Ontario), and the University of British Columbia (Vancouver), which were mostly located in the centre of their respective cities.

More recently, a great deal of office employment has relocated from the central city to suburban settings. In many cases this has involved the relocation of "back-office" functions, activities that do not require face-to-face contact with clients, from high-cost CBD locations to suburban office parks (**Figure 12.18**). There are several primary reasons for such moves, including the fact that land is less expensive and allows for large parking lots for workers and visitors; information and communication technologies (ICTs), including Internet access and mobile computing, allow for high-speed connections with less need for "face to face" communication; and the suburbs provide easy access to the "pink collar ghetto," the large, inexpensive, part-time, female workforce.

FIGURE 12.18 Suburban office parks. This building represents a typical example of a suburban office location in the contemporary Canadian city.

MAIN POINTS 12.4 How Has Transportation Helped to Shape the Growth of Canadian Cities?

- Transportation systems have always had a strong influence on urban morphology, the physical form and structure of the city.

- In the mid-to-late 1800s, Canadian cities were small and densely developed. Mixed land use patterns also provided people with easy access to necessary facilities and services.

- The introduction of the electric streetcar in the late 1800s brought about the first major wave of suburbanization in Canadian cities, but this growth was accompanied by the provision of high-quality public transit service that connected new suburbs with the central city. These services were not experienced evenly and became a contested terrain for gender relations.

- The massive increase in automobile ownership after World War II led to rapid and unprecedented levels of suburbanization. In many places, urban planning policies at this time began to devote more attention to accommodating the car and increasingly less attention to serving the needs of pedestrians, cyclists, and public transit users.

- The car has come to be by far the most dominant mode of transportation in cities over the past 60 years, to a point where most urban areas in Canada, the United States, Australia, and a growing number of other countries can accurately be described as being "automobile dependent."

12.5 What Are Some Consequences of Contemporary Urban Transportation Patterns?

Transportation plays an integral role in our daily lives, and the increasingly high levels of automobile dependence in many countries today, including Canada, have resulted in a number of environmental, economic, and social consequences ranging from the local to the global in their impact.

ENVIRONMENTAL CONSEQUENCES

Transportation contributes to all types of pollution and also consumes non-renewable resources and agricultural land. As a result, current patterns of urban transportation place considerable strain on the carrying capacities of ecosystems.

POLLUTION

As Chapter 6 argues, the environmental impact of each innovation in transportation technology has been greater and greater. This is particularly true with the generation of pollution, especially as it relates to automobile dependence in urban areas. Indeed, the automobile is a major contributor to air, water, and noise pollution, each of which is discussed in turn below.

Air Pollution.   **Air pollution** is perhaps the biggest problem emanating from dependence on the automobile, as its effects range from local to global in scale. These airborne emissions

> **Air pollution** Pollution of the atmosphere.

include a wide range of environmentally harmful chemicals and compounds, such as carbon monoxide, particulates, nitrogen oxides, volatile organic compounds, sulphur oxides, carbon dioxide, methane, road dust, and toxic gases such as benzene. While many of these pollutants may degrade relatively quickly, others penetrate and remain within the atmosphere for hundreds of years, thus presenting long-term environmental threats. This is why there is growing concern about the negative long-term global impact of automobile emissions. Carbon dioxide (CO_2) is one of the main emissions from fossil fuel combustion in road vehicles (**Figure 12.19**), and while CO_2 itself is not a pollutant, it is identified as the primary contributor to recent global warming and climate change trends. This is especially true in core countries and, increasingly, in semi-peripheral countries like China and India.

As the automobile became increasingly important in developed countries, automobile manufacturers modified their car designs and their sales and marketing practices to reflect consumer preferences and government policies in different places. In Japan and Europe, for example, the high cost of heavily taxed fuel and the low amount of road space available in cities have resulted in a marked consumer preference for small and mid-sized vehicles. In the United States, on the other hand, the lower cost of fuel and an abundance of road space have resulted in much higher sales of

larger vehicles, such as SUVs, minivans, and pickup trucks, which emit relatively high amounts of carbon dioxide.

When considering the ways in which motor vehicles add to global carbon dioxide emissions, it is also important to note that these contributions extend far beyond those generated during the actual use of the vehicle. In fact, carbon dioxide emissions are released throughout the life of a motor vehicle, from the initial extraction of raw materials to be used in the manufacture of the vehicle and thousands of automotive parts, through to the vehicle's distribution to dealerships that can be thousands of kilometres away from the location where it was assembled.

Motor vehicle traffic is also a substantial contributor to the formation of **smog**, a combination of ground-level

> **Smog** A combination of ground-level ozone, airborne particles, and other air pollutants.

ozone, airborne particles, and other air pollutants (**Figure 12.20**). Smog's impact on humans ranges from the simple irritation of one's eyes, nose, and throat through to the reduction of lung capacity and the aggravation of respiratory diseases. On a global scale, smog accounts for 7 million deaths each year, according to 2014 World Health Organization statistics, making it the single largest environmental health risk. Importantly, approximately 90 percent of these deaths are in developing countries. While smog comes from many sources, researchers cite the high increase in car use as being a key cause. A study published in the British medical journal, *The Lancet*, noted that more than 2.1 million people in Asia died prematurely from air pollution in 2010, most of which consisted of the tiny particles of diesel soot and gasses emitted from cars and trucks. Smog can also have economic and environmental impacts, such as inhibiting plant and forest growth and reducing crop yields.

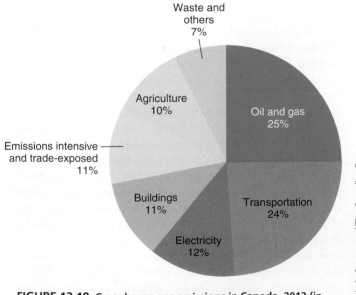

FIGURE 12.19 Greenhouse gas emissions in Canada, 2012 (in metric tonnes). Carbon dioxide emissions from transportation make up a large proportion of all greenhouse gas emissions, second only to emissions from the oil and gas industry. Data from Environment Canada.

Mario Beauregard/The Canadian Press

FIGURE 12.20 Smog in Montreal, Quebec, July 2010. Smog, a combination of ground-level ozone, airborne particles, and other air pollutants, is largely caused by motor vehicle emissions.

Acid rain is another environmental consequence of a heavy dependence on motorized vehicles, particularly the use of automobiles in urban areas, although the biggest culprit in the formation of acid rain is industrial activity. Acid rain is caused by the emission of pollutants such as sulphur dioxide and nitrogen oxide as a by-product of fuel combustion. These are converted to sulphuric and nitric acids that, when mixed with falling precipitation, can acidify soils and water bodies, erode building materials, and contribute to human respiratory problems. In Canada, approximately 60 percent of all nitrous oxide emissions come from transportation, as do about 4 percent of sulphur dioxide emissions.

Water Pollution.

Contemporary transportation patterns are responsible for a great deal of the world's problems with **water pollution**. Automobile-oriented cities devote large proportions of their land to road transportation infrastructure, such as highways and parking lots. In the cities of core nations, it is not uncommon for road transportation infrastructure to occupy 30 to 60 percent of developed land. In the extreme case of Los Angeles, this figure is closer to 75 percent. This infrastructure prevents rainwater from reaching the subsoil, and the resulting runoff carries various surface pollutants—such as motor oil and other automotive fluids, road salt and sand, and litter—into nearby streams and rivers. This leads to a greater volume of stormwater pollution than would be found in higher-density areas, where less land is paved and more land remains in its natural state.

> **Water pollution** Pollution caused when discharges of energy or materials degrade water for other users.

The extraction of oil from underwater wells and the transport of oil using ships have both created significant water pollution problems. For example, the massive oil spill in the Gulf of Mexico in 2010, which lasted for close to three months before finally being contained, and the *Exxon Valdez* disaster in Alaska in 1989 (both of which are discussed in Chapter 6) serve as blunt reminders of the dangers associated with a heavy dependence on oil. These two incidents were highly publicized due to the amount of oil that contaminated water bodies, but there are many other oil spills that do not receive the same amount of attention. In fact, the U.S. Environmental Protection Agency has noted that there are approximately 20,000 reported oil spills around the world every year (EPA, 2014).

Noise Pollution.

Noise pollution is yet another negative environmental consequence of excessive automobile transportation. According to a 2010 World Health Organization (WHO) study, noise pollution, especially that coming from road traffic, railways, and airports, has become a critical public health problem. It is the second-biggest environmental problem affecting health after air pollution. The WHO estimates that one in three people experiences disruptions to daily routines, including sleep, due to noise pollution. Noise pollution has been shown to have a variety of

> **Noise pollution** A type of pollution in which distracting, irritating, or damaging sounds are freely audible.

Windsor Border Initiatives Implementation Group, Ontario Ministry of Transportation

FIGURE 12.21 Construction of noise barrier in Windsor, Ontario, 2010. This two-kilometre-long, five-metre-tall noise barrier was installed at the request of local residents alongside the new Windsor-Essex Parkway. The parkway was constructed to accommodate heavy volumes of traffic expected to travel between Highway 401, Canada's busiest freeway, and a proposed new international bridge that will connect Windsor with Detroit, Michigan.

negative impacts: it reduces residential property values (especially near urban expressways), contributes to hearing loss, increases stress caused by lack of sleep, increases the risk of cardiovascular diseases and high blood pressure, and disrupts wildlife habitats. Constructing noise barriers along busy highways is one method being used to minimize noise pollution in urban and suburban areas (**Figure 12.21**).

CONSUMPTION OF NON-RENEWABLE ENERGY RESOURCES

In their report "Energy and Transport Futures" (2005), Canadian transportation researchers Richard Gilbert and Anthony Perl note that oil products fuel more than 97 percent of all motorized transport activity in Canada, and that road transportation is responsible for almost 80 percent of this consumption. At the same time, about 71 percent of all oil consumption in Canada is used for transportation purposes, while most of the remainder is used by industry and for electricity generation. Such high levels of fossil fuel consumption, which many see as egregiously wasteful, have concerned researchers and governments for decades. For example, the energy crisis of the early 1970s brought to the public's notice the finite nature of the world's fossil fuel reserves. Since that time, governments have encouraged and supported research and development activities that sought to increase the efficiency of the internal combustion engine. They have also created various promotional campaigns to encourage urban dwellers to purchase more fuel-efficient vehicles and/or to use alternative and renewable transportation fuels, such as electricity, natural gas, hydrogen, propane, or solar power. Despite these efforts, the consumption of non-renewable energy resources by core nations continues to rise, primarily because of the increasing numbers of cars on the road.

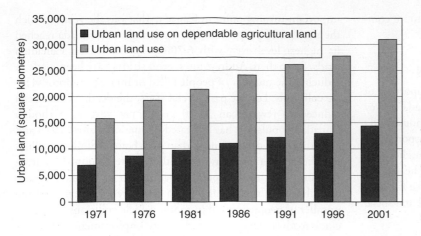

FIGURE 12.22 Urban land use on dependable agricultural land in Canada, 1971–2001. The amount of land converted from agricultural use to urban development during this 30-year period was equivalent to the size of Prince Edward Island. Adapted from "The Loss of Dependable Agricultural Land in Canada," *Rural and Small Town Canada Analysis Bulletin*, vol. 6, no. 1 (January 2005), Figure 3, p. 7, Catalogue 21-006-XIE2005001, www.statcan.gc.ca/pub/21-006-x/21-006-x2005001-eng.pdf.

CONSUMPTION OF AGRICULTURAL LAND

As noted in Chapter 9, the patterns of urban sprawl associated with automobile dependence are also responsible for the widespread consumption of agricultural lands on the edges of cities in Canada, the United States, and other countries. Most of Canada's major urban areas are located amid the country's very small stock of prime agricultural land. For example, on a clear day, over one-third of Canada's best agricultural land can be seen from the top of Toronto's CN Tower (Statistics Canada, 1999). According to a study released by Statistics Canada in 2005, some 12,000 square kilometres of these lands were converted to urban uses between 1971 and 2001 alone (**Figure 12.22**). This represents an area equivalent to the size of Prince Edward Island. This issue is made all the more alarming when one considers that over 18 percent of Ontario's Class 1 farmland—some of Canada's most fertile farmland—was removed from agricultural production between 1996 and 2006 in order to accommodate urban development. Similarly, when geographers Federico Martellozzo and Navin Ramankutty of McGill University and their research colleagues used satellite imagery to examine the consumption of agricultural land in Alberta, they found that 60 percent of new urban and peri-urban growth that occurred in the Edmonton-Calgary corridor between 1988 and 2010 took place on good-quality agricultural land. This area, which is already home to over 2.7 million people (nearly three-quarters of Alberta's total population), is expected to house as many as 4 million people by 2036, an increase of some 48 percent. Martellozzo, Ramankutty, and their associates argue that this projected increase in population highlights the need to develop and implement effective land use planning policies in order to prevent further loss of high-quality agricultural land.

ECONOMIC CONSEQUENCES

The economic costs that individuals, firms, and governments incur in supporting automobile-oriented development have become a matter of concern and debate in recent years. Transportation places considerable strain on financial resources as roads and highways are built and maintained, individuals buy and maintain their automobiles, and businesses cope with the effects of traffic congestion on their employees.

COST OF BUILDING AND MAINTAINING ROADS AND HIGHWAYS

The massive expense of building and maintaining highways is a major economic concern (**Figure 12.23**). The cost of building a new highway can vary considerably from place to place, and depends in part on the type of terrain over which the road will pass, the type of road to be built, and whether it is to be located in a rural or urban area. The Government of Nova Scotia has noted that in 2009 the cost of building a new two-lane highway, including bridges, was approximately $3.5 million per kilometre, while a new four-lane highway cost about $6 million per kilometre. Ontario's Ministry of Transportation has stated that, on average, it costs about $10 million per kilometre, plus an additional $8 million to $12 million per interchange, to build a four-lane highway in northern Ontario, where the rocky terrain

Peter A. Lusztyk/First Light/Getty Images

FIGURE 12.23 Highway 404/407 interchange, Toronto, Ontario. While engineering projects such as this do much to reduce traffic congestion and maintain the flow of traffic, at least temporarily (i.e., until traffic volumes increase beyond the road's capacity), their financial cost can be enormous.

of the Canadian Shield makes road construction a more complicated process.

HOUSEHOLD COST OF TRANSPORTATION

Transportation costs also make up a significant proportion of many household budgets. A 2012 Statistics Canada survey found that 20 percent of the average Canadian household's spending on goods and services goes toward transportation. This is second only to shelter costs as the biggest household expense. Later in this chapter we will discuss how the cost of transportation in many cities is especially prohibitive for low-income earners and can create a number of financial and social hardships for these individuals.

COSTS TO BUSINESSES

Transportation geographers and other researchers pay attention to several additional economic consequences as automobiles have come to dominate personal travel, and trucks have done the same for shipping and commercial purposes. In places where traffic congestion has become a routine part of daily life, research shows that businesses incur costs of millions of dollars each year—sometimes even billions of dollars—as a result of reduced productivity due to employees' late arrival at work or lost production time when necessary components are late reaching factories by truck because of traffic jams. The Toronto Board of Trade has estimated the combined total of such costs to be around $6 billion per year in the Greater Toronto and Hamilton areas alone.

Researchers identify further consequences of traffic congestion and automobile dependence on businesses and their workers. For example, Richard Wener, Gary Evans, and their colleagues (2006) found that workers who engage in longer and more traffic-filled commutes tend to suffer greater levels of stress and job dissatisfaction, which in turn lead to greater levels of employee turnover, as workers seek out more commuter-friendly places of employment. Some businesses also appear to have difficulty hiring employees for similar reasons or because prospective employees cannot reach the workplace without the use of a car.

SOCIAL CONSEQUENCES

Since the late 1960s, transportation geographers and other researchers have worked to build a better understanding of the social consequences of automobile dependence. They have focused on such issues as road safety, the effects of different modes of transportation on levels of public health and fitness, the ways in which traffic volumes affect neighbourhood interaction, and the consequences of automobile dependence for those who do not have access to a car.

TRANSPORT-RELATED DEATHS AND INJURIES

Road safety has been a prominent topic of concern for almost as long as cars have been on the road. According to transportation geographer Jean Andrey (2010, p. 248), 1973 marked an important turning point in Canada. That was the year in which the number of people killed in road crashes in Canada reached its highest level ever, with 6,706 people killed on Canadian roads. Since then, Andrey notes, great strides have been made in reducing the number of people killed or injured in motor vehicle collisions. For the past several years, the death toll has been reduced to fewer than 3,000 people per year, even though Canada's population has increased dramatically since 1973 and Canadians are driving more than ever before. Similar declines have been experienced in many other Western countries during the same time. Andrey points to a number of factors that have contributed to this decline and a concurrent reduction in the number of people injured in motor vehicle collisions. These include roadway and automobile safety improvements, improvements in emergency medicine, socio-demographic shifts, and evolving driving norms (e.g., higher rates of seat belt use and a greater social stigma associated with impaired driving).

As with so many other aspects of people's lives, there are notable geographical differences within and between places. Much of this has to do with place-based differences in transportation policy, such as the minimum driving ages and differences in vehicle types discussed earlier in this chapter. Another important variation is the way in which deaths and injuries from motor vehicle collisions vary demographically—that is, by age group.

In terms of place-based differences, collision rates can vary due to a number of factors, such as the climate of a region or the level of car use in a place. With respect to the latter, it has been shown that most motor vehicle collisions in Canada take place within urban areas, a fact that is not surprising given that, as noted in Chapter 10, in 2011, nearly seven of every ten Canadians lived in the country's 33 census metropolitan areas. Researchers have also found that the motor vehicle collisions most likely to result in death or injury are those that take place in low-density suburban environments. It is in these settings that automobiles tend especially to dominate the transportation landscape, and the needs of pedestrians, cyclists, and transit users are far less likely to be adequately served by the provision of infrastructure, such as safe road crossings, sidewalks, and bike lanes.

Although, in general, countries like Canada have seen substantial road safety improvements, motor vehicle collisions remain a leading cause of death and injury for users of all major transport modes. In 1999 and 2000, 48 percent of all reported severe injuries in Canada were caused by motor vehicle collisions. Furthermore, over 2,000 people were killed in motor vehicle collisions across Canada in 2011 (**Table 12.1**). The continued danger of today's busy transportation environment is particularly evident among two demographic cohorts: children and young adults. Indeed, motor vehicle collisions remain the most common cause of injury-related deaths among Canadian children aged 1 to 14, while they are also the most common cause of death overall among people aged 15 to 24.

The dangers of contemporary urban transportation were made especially apparent in the Greater Toronto Area, Canada's most populated metropolitan region, during the month of January 2010 (**Figure 12.24**). Fourteen people were killed by

TABLE 12.1	Fatalities by Road User Class, 2007–2011					
Road User Class		**2007**	**2008**	**2009**	**2010**	**2011**
Drivers	#	1,415ʳ	1,306ʳ	1,159ʳ	1,132ʳ	1,033
	%	51.4ʳ	53.6ʳ	52.1ʳ	50.6ʳ	51.5
Passengers	#	613ʳ	501ʳ	446ʳ	491ʳ	387
	%	22.3ʳ	20.6ʳ	20.1ʳ	21.9ʳ	19.3
Pedestrians	#	379ʳ	308ʳ	316ʳ	305ʳ	315ʳ
	%	13.8ʳ	12.6ʳ	14.2	13.6ʳ	15.7
Bicyclists	#	67ʳ	44ʳ	45ʳ	62ʳ	52
	%	2.4	1.8	2.0	2.8ʳ	2.6
Motorcyclists*	#	226ʳ	224ʳ	199ʳ	192ʳ	168
	%	8.2ʳ	9.2ʳ	9.0ʳ	8.6ʳ	8.4
Not stated/other	#	53ʳ	53	58ʳ	55ʳ	51
	%	1.9ʳ	2.2	2.6	2.5ʳ	2.5
Total	#	**2,753ʳ**	**2,436ʳ**	**2,223ʳ**	**2,237ʳ**	**2,006**
	%	**100.0**	**100.0**	**100.0**	**100.0**	**100.0**

*Includes moped riders.
r Revised.
Canada has witnessed substantial road safety improvements since the 1970s; however, motor vehicle collisions remain a leading cause of death and injury for users of all major transport modes. For example, almost one out of every six people killed in incidents involving motor vehicles in 2011 was a pedestrian. Source: Data from *2011 Canadian Motor Vehicle Traffic Collision Statistics*, Ottawa: Transport Canada.

motor vehicles while walking in the City of Toronto or one of its surrounding municipalities during the first 25 days of that month, with three such incidents happening on the same day. After the tenth fatality in a span of nine days, a headline in the *Toronto Star* asked "Why So Many Pedestrian Deaths?" Mathematicians were quick to point to this frightening trend as a statistical anomaly, but people also wondered if there were any commonalities among the incidents that could offer further explanation. There were few. The victims ranged from teenagers and young adults to the middle-aged and senior citizens, while the motor vehicles involved were cars, trucks, buses, streetcars, and passenger trains. Several of the incidents occurred in densely developed inner-city and downtown neighbourhoods, while others occurred in sprawling suburban settings. In some cases the accidents were attributed to driver error, while in others it was the pedestrian who was seen to be at fault.

Critics argue that these urban transportation systems are not neutral, apolitical entities; they are imbued with, and shaped by, the politics and practices of those who design, develop, and implement them. For example, some would argue that racism is sometimes designed *into* transportation networks. Two key examples illustrate this argument. First, cultural critic Langdon Winner uses the example of Robert Moses, an American urban planner, to demonstrate the politics of the development of freeway overpasses on Long Island, New York. Winner argues that 204 overpasses were built too low to allow buses and trucks to pass through, thereby limiting the movement of poor, mostly Black, inner-city New Yorkers who relied on public transportation to get to the beaches of Long Island. While Winner's argument has been contested, it seems that, whether intended or unintended, the design of transportation infrastructure has uneven and sometimes inequitable consequences.

In a second example, Cynthia Wiggins, a 17-year-old Black woman from inner-city Buffalo, NY, was struck and killed by a dump truck in December 1995 as she attempted to run across six lanes of traffic to get to her job at the upscale Walden Galleria Mall, located in the suburbs outside Buffalo. While the developers of the Walden Galleria Mall allowed charter buses onto the property, bringing Canadian tourists for day-long shopping trips, it refused to allow city buses, which linked Buffalo's

Rick Eglinton/Toronto Star

FIGURE 12.24 Mixed traffic at Queen's Quay, Toronto. Over time, as cities have grown and new transportation modes have been introduced into urban environments, there has been a growing competition for space among users of different modes. The priority accorded to the car and other motorized vehicles in these settings has often created dangerous travel environments for pedestrians, cyclists, and transit users, as evidenced by a spate of deaths in the Greater Toronto Area in January 2010, when 14 pedestrians were killed over the course of only 25 days.

inner-city minority neighbourhoods to the suburbs, onto the grounds. Although many people who worked in the stores, fast food restaurants, and maintenance areas of the mall came from these neighbourhoods, they had no safe route to access their place of employment. In this example, transportation policies not only worked to separate the rich from the poor and the Black from the White; they also further reinforced cultural segregation by making it extremely dangerous for impoverished, inner-city minorities to gain access to employment that would help improve their situations. In both of these examples, we can see the tremendous unevenness between those who design the transportation infrastructure, and those who use it.

Social Costs of Motor Vehicle Collisions.

As noted earlier in this textbook, policy-makers have a predilection for quantitative (especially economic) indicators when dealing with public interest issues. Accordingly, experts have attempted over the years to build further evidence of the negative consequences of automobile dependence by estimating the social cost of motor vehicle collisions. One such study, prepared for Ontario's Ministry of Transportation (Vodden et al., 2007), concluded that motor vehicle collisions generated $18 billion in social costs in 2004. Of this, fatalities and injuries were estimated to cost about $15 billion (e.g., through life insurance claims and lost earnings potential), and damage to public and private property was estimated to cost $2 billion; the remaining $1 billion was attributed to the cost of hospital and health care; tow trucks; and police, fire, and ambulance services, as well as productivity losses resulting from post-accident traffic jams. The study also calculated the average social cost of a single collision in 2004 to be $74,000.

IMPACTS ON PUBLIC HEALTH AND WELL-BEING

Beyond the heavy toll of transportation-related deaths and injuries, another social cost that has been attributed to our dependence on the automobile is the detrimental effect on physical health and fitness. One Statistics Canada study found that close to one-half of Canadians were physically inactive, and another one-quarter were only moderately active in 2005, thus putting these groups at greater risk of long-term negative health repercussions. Although television, the Internet, and other technological tools have also been blamed for reducing the amount of time people devote to physical activity, transportation geographers and other researchers have identified automobile-dependent landscapes and automobile-dependent lifestyles as further contributors. Evidence of the growing dependence on automobiles is seen in the findings of the *Transportation Tomorrow Survey*, a comprehensive travel survey conducted in the Greater Toronto Area and the City of Hamilton every five years. Transportation geographer Reihane Marzoughi's 2011 analysis of the survey found that teenagers travelled more frequently as automobile passengers in 2006 than they did in 1986, usually at the expense of using public transit. In a similar study, geographers Ron Buliung and Raktim Mitra, along with their University of Toronto colleague Guy Faulkner (2009), discovered a sizeable decrease in the proportion of teenagers travelling to school on foot or by bicycle in the Greater Toronto Area between 1986 and 2006, particularly within the more suburban reaches of this metropolitan region.

IMPACTS ON NEIGHBOURHOOD INTERACTION

Just as automobile-oriented streetscapes have been shown to reduce people's willingness to walk, cycle, or use public transit, researchers have found that heavier volumes of motor vehicle traffic can decrease levels of neighbourhood interaction. What is perhaps the best-known study of this type was conducted several decades ago by Donald Appleyard in San Francisco, California, and chronicled in his book *Livable Streets* (Appleyard, 1981). Like many researchers, Appleyard is interested in the ways that traffic in urban areas affects the lives of local residents. In the late 1960s, Appleyard identified three streets with differing traffic volumes, which he labelled Light Street (on which 2,000 vehicles travelled per day), Medium Street (8,000 vehicles per day), and Heavy Street (16,000 vehicles per day). He found that people living on Light Street demonstrated much greater levels of interaction with their neighbours and a much stronger sense of community than those living on Heavy Street. In fact, compared to those on Heavy Street, the residents of Light Street had three more friends and twice as many acquaintances on their street. Appleyard also found that the amount of space people considered part of their "community" shrank as traffic volumes increased. This study served as an important reminder of the social implications of automobile-oriented transportation policies. It also prompted planners to take into account more than just engineering-related concerns when dealing with traffic and transportation issues.

SOCIAL EXCLUSION

Over the past several decades, researchers have sought to better understand the various accessibility constraints that automobile-oriented development has imposed on those people—such as persons with disabilities and low-income earners—who do not have automobile access to employment, shopping, childcare, and other required facilities and services. By seeking primarily to accommodate demands for automobile transportation, transportation planners and policy-makers have failed to adequately serve the accessibility needs of individuals who do not have the use of an automobile, contributing to the **social exclusion** of these individuals. Social exclusion can be defined as "the loss in the ability (by people or households) to fully participate in activities and society and connect with many of the jobs, services, and facilities" (Hine, 2009, p. 429). Todd Litman of the Victoria

> **Social exclusion** The inability of people or households to fully participate in society, engage in activities, or access jobs, services, and facilities.

Transport Policy Institute has estimated that about 20 percent of Canadian households do not own an automobile, and that about a third or more of households have at least one member who has been disadvantaged by the creation of automobile-oriented transportation systems (Litman, 2003).

In their study of transportation-related social exclusion in Edmonton, geographers Joseph Mensah and Geoff Ironside (1993) found that many inner-city residents suffered from limited job opportunities due to a lack of adequate public transit service to job sites, especially as more employment was moving from Edmonton's central city to its outer suburbs. They argued that in order to promote social equity, it was necessary to modify routes, schedules, and fares to make transit more accessible to low-income earners. Mensah and Ironside stated, "The need to restructure the city's transportation system to cater for the shopping and employment needs of the city's poor cannot be overemphasized."

Social exclusion intersects with the various aspects of our identity (discussed in Chapter 7), such as gender, ethnicity, class, sexuality, age, and able-bodiedness. Throughout this chapter we have considered several examples of how transportation is experienced unevenly, with disparate outcomes. Lack of accessible transport, whether it be car or public transportation, directly affects how people are able to attend school, get to work, access public services, go to the doctor, vote, and take part in many other civic activities. People with disabilities experience social exclusion for a variety of reasons, including lack of economic resources, the obstacles presented by the layout of infrastructure, and even the design of cars and other forms of transit. In Toronto, for example, Metrolinx, an agency of the Government of Ontario that operates GO Transit, has pledged to be completely accessible by 2025, as required by the *Accessibility for Ontarians with Disabilities Act, 2005* (AODA) (**Figure 12.25**). Likewise, people whose first language is not

© GO Transit

FIGURE 12.25 Accessible public transit. Metrolinx, which operates GO Transit, has pledged to be completely accessible by 2025.

English, but who are living in English-speaking parts of Canada, often struggle with access to public transportation. Age is also a factor; both the very young, in strollers, and the elderly are limited in their ability to access public transportation. In its accessibility platform, Metrolinx recognizes the special needs of many people, not just those with disabilities.

MAIN POINTS 12.5 What Are Some Consequences of Contemporary Urban Transportation Patterns?

- The increasingly high levels of automobile dependence seen in many countries today have resulted in a number of environmental, economic, and social consequences that range from the local to the global in their impact.

- Environmental consequences include air, water, and noise pollution, as well as the excessive consumption of non-renewable energy resources and agricultural land.

- Economic costs of automobile dependence include the high cost of building and maintaining roads, the drain on household expenses, and the impacts on the cost of doing business in urban areas.

- Social consequences of automobile dependence range from the social cost of motor vehicle collisions to the social exclusion of people who cannot drive or do not have access to a car.

12.6 What Are Some Ways by Which Urban Transportation Systems Might Be Made More Sustainable?

In light of the enormous consequences associated with growing levels of automobile dependence in developed countries, as well as the fears that these trends will expand into the world's

developing nations, geographers have become more active in calling for the adoption of sustainable transportation policies. The idea of sustainable transportation, which is derived directly from the concept of sustainable development, represents a much more holistic approach to urban transportation planning and investment than what is seen in many cities today. Most importantly, building sustainable transportation systems involves simultaneous consideration of environmental, economic, and social objectives in the provision of transportation infrastructure and services. People and organizations working for sustainable transportation recognize that land use patterns influence transportation behaviour, and that the transportation infrastructure in place has a strong influence on decisions about land use. Canada's Centre for Sustainable Transportation (CST) plays a leading role in the global effort to promote sustainable transportation. In fact, CST's definition of the concept and its components has been adopted throughout the world since its formulation in the year 2000. Here is how the CST defines sustainable transportation:

A sustainable transportation system is one that . . .

- *allows the basic access needs of individuals and societies to be met safely, and in a manner consistent with human and eco-system health, and with equity within and between generations.*
- *is affordable, operates efficiently, offers choice of transport mode, and supports a vibrant economy.*
- *limits emissions and waste within the planet's ability to absorb them, minimizes consumption of non-renewable resources, re-uses and recycles its components, minimizes the use of land, and minimizes the production of noise (CST, 1998).*

Clearly, within the CST's conceptualization, **sustainable transportation** seeks to tackle the multitude of problems associated with automobile dependence described earlier in this chapter. While many of these can be dealt with through a reallocation of

Sustainable transportation
An approach to the provision of transportation infrastructure and services that involves simultaneous consideration of environmental, economic, and social objectives.

government funding and through the provision of better non-automobile transportation infrastructure, it is important to note that there are also a number of psychological obstacles to overcome in the pursuit of sustainable transportation systems. Researchers have come to understand that many people have more than simply utilitarian motives for using particular modes of transportation, especially the private motor car (Hiscock, et al., 2002). For example, driving a car has been shown to have symbolic value for many individuals. In this case, the vehicle they drive serves an important role in expressing their identity or communicating their social position. Transportation researchers Jillian Anable, Birgitta Gatersleben, and Linda Steg, among others, have also found that people display what are referred to as "affective motives" for using, or not using, certain modes of transportation (Anable and Gatersleben, 2005; Steg, 2005). In these cases, the emotions evoked when travelling are important to the individual's choice of transport mode. For example, driving a car might make one feel powerful, excited, independent, or relaxed, while using public transport may make one feel inferior, powerless, and stressed. It is important to note that driving a car does not always produce positive emotions, and using a non-automobile mode is not always a negative experience. For instance, a car driver caught in a traffic jam can feel frustrated and powerless, or commuter train users might find their mode of travel relaxing if they are able to read a book or listen to music during their journey. This latter point is exemplified in Katie Hemsworth's *Guest Field Note* below, which also demonstrates how transportation has become a topic of interest in other subdisciplines of human geography, such as cultural geography.

GUEST FIELD NOTE

Sonic Geography

Our world is saturated with music. Headphones are ubiquitous across cityscapes; recorded music fills shops, arenas, and waiting rooms; and live performances pipe through concert halls and streets. We even experience non-musical sounds as music, such as birdsong or the rhythmic chugging of trains. In recent years, we have seen the emergence of musical geography, a subfield of cultural geography that explores connections between music, place, and identity. Overlapping with sonic geography, which emphasizes the role of sound in the experience of everyday life, musical geography recognizes music as a creative realm through which social, cultural, and political contexts are expressed and actively shaped. Perhaps less obvious, but equally fascinating, are the connections between musical geography and transportation geography: we cherish music for its capacity to transport us to different times and places. The fluidity of sound allows music to mobilize ideas, to connect people and place, and to act

as a metaphorical vehicle that offers emotional escape from daily routines.

My musical influences have largely been tied to my own cultural and historical geographies connected to my hometown of Thunder Bay, a remote city in northwestern Ontario. Situated on the rocky shores of Lake Superior, the city has historically served as a major hub along fur trading and shipping routes. Migration across Canada brought many different people through the area and, along with them, their cultural practices, including music. An eight-hour drive from any other major city in Canada, and situated on the Trans-Canada Highway, musical artists typically include Thunder Bay as a tour stop between larger urban centres. As a result, locals have picked up musical ideas from travellers, while many of the touring artists have been inspired by northwestern Ontario's stunning and unforgiving terrain, incorporating it into their songs. These cultural exchanges through music have actively shaped my own "sense of place" regarding Thunder Bay, as they do for other people and other places. I use this example to show that music is sometimes an extension of transportation geography—it is tied to migration and movement, and because sounds themselves travel, music *moves*, and we are moved by it. The transformative capacity of music is taken for granted in our daily lives, but it holds exciting potential for political and social change.

For my master's research, I was interested in how people use music on public transportation as a way to reshape their experiences of space, time, and social interaction. I rode the bus to university daily and became aware of the number of people, myself included, listening to music through headphones. I wanted to learn more about how people selected their personal playlist and for what reasons, how their music shaped their experience of the bus ride, and how the surrounding environment in turn affected the way they heard the music.

I learned that a bus's soundscape can be very noisy, and people use music to filter or drown out unwanted noise. Not only is the bus full of people who make sound, but it also takes a lot of energy to operate the vehicle—energy that we can *hear* if we listen carefully. Brakes squeal, the engine roars, and doors flap open and shut, all while the surrounding outdoor soundscape also permeates the interior of the bus. In addition to physical confinement in a moving vehicle, overcrowding is also perceived to be a sonic issue because sound is one way people define personal space. Sounds overlap and move through the bus, creating a unique "urban symphony" for some, but more often perceived as "cacophony" by riders who simply use the bus as a way to get from one place to another. Unlike sight, which can be blocked by shutting our eyes, we cannot turn off our ears in the same way and are forced to hear the multiplicity of sounds in confined spaces. One way people try to mediate this, or to regain some form of control, is through personal listening devices that carve out a private soundworld in public. Music, research participants explained, is a very useful tool for passing time on a routine commute, and many use a selected soundtrack to enhance their mood. Songs might be used to add new meaning to the landscape outside the bus window; conversely, the surrounding environment along a bus journey might change the way listeners appreciate their music. Participants also relish the opportunity headphones provide to exist in multiple places at once, which have both enabling and constraining effects.

These findings point to the opportunity for transportation and musical geographers to enter into closer dialogue with one another. Transportation geographers might consider the role music might play in encouraging alternative and more sustainable modes of transportation. Likewise, musical geographers' work would surely benefit from transportation themes of movement, migration, and flows.

Katie Hemsworth, Queen's University

TRENDS AND PATTERNS AROUND THE WORLD: INTERNATIONAL COMPARISONS

The pursuit of sustainable transportation will no doubt be a long and difficult process; however, it will not be impossible. Earlier in this chapter we saw that, in the past, Canadian cities were quite pedestrian-, bicycle-, and transit-friendly. We also know there are many parts of the world we can look to for inspiration and ideas about how to reduce automobile dependence. Indeed, there are very clear geographical variations in the levels of automobile dependence in cities around the world, even among countries that share similar socio-economic and demographic characteristics. Jeff Kenworthy and Felix Laube (1999) have compiled and compared an extensive body of transportation data from different urban regions. Their findings show that the most automobile-dependent cities are found in the United States, Australia, and Canada, while European cities tend more often to convey the characteristics of sustainable transportation. Thus, by looking to European cities, we can identify various means by which Canadian and other Western cities can create more sustainable transportation systems. Several of these ideas are discussed in the sections below.

SUPPORT FOR PUBLIC TRANSIT

According to Todd Litman of the Victoria Transport Policy Institute (Litman, 2011), **public transit** includes various services that provide mobility to the general public in shared vehicles, ranging from shared taxis and shuttle vans, to local

> **Public transit** Various services that provide mobility to the general public in shared vehicles, ranging from shared taxis and shuttle vans, to local and intercity buses and passenger rail.

and intercity buses and passenger rail. The cost of providing public transit services is subsidized by governments just about everywhere. An important difference between and within countries is the *extent* to which such services are subsidized. Transit systems in European cities have been subsidized for much longer than those in North American cities, for example—a reality that transportation scholars David Banister, John Pucher, and Martin Lee-Gosselin (2007) attribute to international differences regarding how the citizens of each country value public transit. Based on their comparative research of Canada, the United States, and several European countries, they argue that people in European cities tend to place a greater value on the societal benefits of public transit than do people in North American cities, and they are therefore more willing to support

FIGURE 12.26 Cycling and walking percent of daily trips in Europe, North America, and Australia. The dramatic international differences in levels of walking and bicycle usage are largely a result of differences in urban development densities and in the provision of pedestrian- and bicycle-friendly transportation infrastructure. In countries such as Denmark and the Netherlands, for example, bicycles are an integral part of daily travel and are planned for accordingly. In automobile-dependent places like Canada, the United States, and Australia, a lack of attention to the needs of cyclists makes the bicycle a much less attractive mode of transportation. Data from R. Buehler and J. Pucher, "Walking and Cycling in Western Europe and the United States: Trends, Policies and Lessons," *TR News* 280 (May-June, 2012): pp. 35. Dissimilarities in data collection methods, timing, and variable definitions limit the comparability of the modal shares shown.

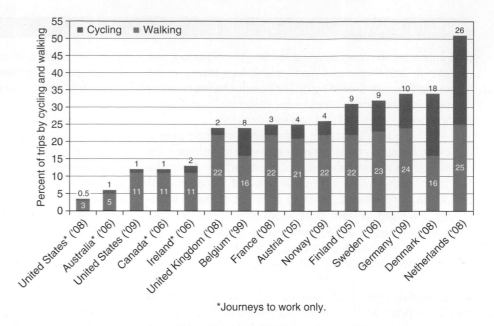

*Journeys to work only.

government expenditures on such services. As a result, there has been significant public investment in the construction of extensive public transit systems that often also serve as the framework around which urban development takes place.

POLICIES FOR CYCLING AND WALKING

Levels of automobile dependence within cities also vary considerably from country to country due to differences in the extent to which walking and cycling are promoted (**Figure 12.26**). In many, but certainly not all, European countries, far more attention is devoted to the provision and maintenance of pedestrian and cycling infrastructure. For example, several cities are crisscrossed by extensive and coordinated bicycle networks that provide cyclists with convenient access to popular destinations (Pucher and Buehler, 2012). Many such networks include bicycle

lanes that are separated from vehicular and pedestrian traffic and that are given traffic priority over automobiles. In Canada, cities including Montreal and Vancouver have implemented separated bicycle lanes in their downtown cores (**Figure 12.27**).

Byron Miller, a geographer at the University of Calgary, has studied European cities with the aim of understanding why some urban areas are more pedestrian- and bicycle-friendly than others. He found, for example, that the city of Groningen in the Netherlands has the highest rate of bicycle usage in Europe, with 57 percent of all trips there being made by bicycle. He attributes this to planning and policy decisions that included the creation of zones within the city centre that were open to pedestrians and cyclists only (**Figure 12.28**), and the construction

FIGURE 12.27 Bike lanes in downtown Montreal.

FIGURE 12.28 Car-free zone in Groningen, the Netherlands. This city's incredibly high rate of bicycle use has been nurtured through a series of proactive planning measures, such as closing off particular areas to automobile traffic and providing cyclists with separate off-street pathways.

of bicycle lanes that are separated from motor vehicle traffic, often with raised curbs or lines of trees serving as a buffer to protect cyclists. As Miller has argued, "If you plan a city so the only easy way to get around is by car, bicycling won't be a viable option. Successful promotion of bicycling depends on the extent to which infrastructure investment makes bicycling convenient and safe" (quoted in Myers, 2010).

The increased attention to issues of pedestrian and bicycle traffic, along with public transit, have led to the creation of new services that help people measure the walkability of any address in any city. For example, Walk Score compiles data on population density and road metrics (drawn from Google, the census, Open Street Map, transit routes, and city planning departments), measures the distance to amenities in a variety of categories, and then publishes data and scores on local addresses (available on real estate board listings such as MLS) and on global cities. Rankings range from Car Dependent (0–24) to Walker's Paradise (90–100). For Canadian cities with more than 200,000 people, Vancouver scored highest at 78.0, followed by Toronto at 71.4, and Montreal at 70.4 (**Figure 12.29**).

FIGURE 12.29 Pedestrians walking in Old Montreal, Quebec. Montreal's Walk Score is 70.4.

AUTOMOBILE TAXATION

Governments in Europe have also maintained relatively low levels of automobile use by imposing heavy taxes on the two main costs associated with driving a car. First, the cost of buying an automobile is made more expensive by the addition of a sales or registration tax that in some cases can amount to more than the cost of the vehicle itself. For example, the sales tax on the purchase of a car in Ireland is as much as 30 percent, while in Denmark the registration tax can be up to 180 percent, depending on the vehicle's purchase price and its fuel efficiency. Bigger and more expensive cars are charged higher registration taxes. The tax on fuel is also much higher in European countries than it is in automobile-dependent countries like Canada and the United States—in many cases up to eight times higher (**Figure 12.30**).

PARKING AND DRIVER LICENSING POLICIES

The limited availability of parking in most European cities, caused mainly by the relatively high development densities found there, makes it very expensive to park. This, in turn, creates a disincentive to drive and encourages people to walk, cycle, or use public transit instead. Those wishing to become drivers in European countries must also wait longer than most prospective Canadian and American drivers. The minimum driving age in most European countries is 18 years, while in most of Canada and the United States it is 16 years.

Furthermore, it is much more difficult to obtain a driver's licence in Europe, and it costs a lot more. In Denmark, for example, teens cannot get a learner's permit until they are 17 and a half. At 18 they can obtain a probationary licence, but all restrictions are not lifted until they are 21. Driver education

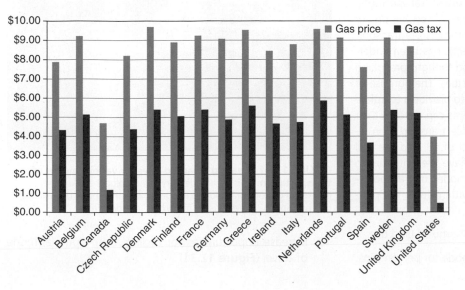

FIGURE 12.30 Vehicle fuel retail prices, 2011. This chart compares the gas prices in U.S. dollars/gallon (Y-axis) in Europe and North America. Gas prices are in green and total taxes (both excise and consumption levies) are in red. As this chart reveals, almost every European country charges more in fuel taxes alone than what North Americans pay for a gallon of gasoline. Data from D. Thompson, "Gas Prices around the World: Cheaper Than Water *and* $10 a Gallon." *The Atlantic*, May 3, 2011.

includes training in defensive driving, hazard perception, and driving manoeuvres. German teens must also wait until they are 18 before they can learn to drive at driving schools, which are rigorous and expensive. After training is completed, they earn a two-year probationary licence that can be extended for two more years or revoked if they are caught in a driving infraction, such as running a red light. These restrictions encourage young people to use non-automobile modes more often at a time in their lives when they are beginning to build the travel habits they will carry with them into adulthood. Delaying their ability to drive a car is seen as one way to encourage young adults to adopt less automobile-dependent transportation behaviours.

LAND USE POLICIES

Other government policies that seem to have little to do with transportation can also have a strong influence on levels of automobile dependence. Land use policies, for example, can affect how much people travel in cars, as opposed to using other modes of transportation. Such policies dictate how far apart different activity sites will be (e.g., the distance between homes and workplaces or shopping areas) and at what densities development may take place. As noted earlier in this chapter, suburban planning in Canada and the United States since the end of World War II has typically involved the extensive segregation of land uses and the low-density development of activity sites. This has done much to encourage automobile use—because of the resulting long travel distances—for even the most routine or basic trip, such as travelling to work or going to a grocery or convenience store. In many European countries, on the other hand, more rigid land use planning policies have been in place over the past several decades. This has limited sprawl and enabled patterns of development that are conducive to walking, cycling, and public transit use. Sweden and Denmark are often cited as good examples of countries where land use planning policies have effectively controlled automobile usage. In both cases, governments have adopted and adhered to policies that promote compact and well-coordinated urban development. They also use public transportation networks as the root of their community planning exercises by focusing the bulk of urban development along rail lines and near transit stations (Pucher and Buehler, 2008).

Susan Hanson and Genevieve Giuliano, two prominent transportation geographers, have rightly pointed out that "it is important to recognize that the urban transportation system we now experience is the result of choices made by individuals and institutions; it is not the outcome of some relentless natural or necessary process" (2004, p. 383). These decisions were made over several decades and will therefore not be reversed easily, and certainly not overnight. As the work of transportation geographers and other transportation researchers continues to further our understanding of the benefits and costs associated with different modes of travel, there are opportunities to mitigate some of the negative consequences described earlier in this chapter. The example of the universal bus pass program introduced at Brock University, discussed at the beginning of this chapter, shows that it is sometimes just a matter of creating conditions that favour the use of non-automobile modes where they previously did not exist.

FIELD NOTE

A New Vision for Urban Transportation

The elements necessary for a sustainable urban transportation system "on the ground" are presented in *A New Vision for Urban Transportation*. This document, written by the Transportation Association of Canada (TAC) (1993), has been widely cited as an innovative, comprehensive, and thought-provoking agenda for the role of transportation in cities. The purpose of *A New Vision for Urban Transportation* is to provide a template upon which local and regional governments can develop their own unique and place-specific sustainable transportation visions, plans, and policies. It includes a set of 13 land use and transportation planning principles that have the potential to create more balanced roles for various modes of transportation, including the private automobile, within cities. The principles are as follows:

1. Plan for increased densities and more mixed land use.

2. Promote walking as the preferred mode for person trips.

FIGURE 12.31 **Creating balanced roles for various modes of transportation.** This parked delivery vehicle blocks a bike lane. Increasing opportunities for cycling as an optional mode of travel is one principle of *A New Vision for Urban Transportation*.

Vince Talotta/Toronto Star

3. Increase opportunities for cycling as an optional mode of travel (**Figure 12.31**).

4. Provide higher-quality transit service to increase its attractiveness relative to the private automobile.

5. Create an environment in which automobiles can play a more balanced role.

6. Plan parking supply and price to be in balance with walking, cycling, transit, and auto priorities.

7. Improve the efficiency of the urban goods distribution system.

8. Promote inter modal and inter-line connections.

9. Promote new technologies that improve urban mobility and help protect the environment.

10. Optimize the use of existing transportation systems to move people and goods.

11. Design and operate transportation systems that can be used by the physically challenged.

12. Ensure that urban transportation decisions protect and enhance the environment.

13. Create better ways to pay for future urban transportation systems.

In the time since *A New Vision for Urban Transportation* was created, the TAC has turned its attention to monitoring progress toward achieving the vision. Using a set of indicators, the TAC's Urban Transportation Council has conducted several surveys of land use and transportation conditions in Canadian cities since 1994. Through its fourth and most recent survey, which looked at data for the country's 33 largest census metropolitan areas, the council found several encouraging signs of positive change. For example, it found that urban sprawl has been slowing down around most cities, urban development densities have been increasing (which promotes the viability of walking, cycling, and using transit), and the use of both public transit and cycling as modes of commuting to work has gone up in many places. At the same time, the firm entrenchment of automobile travel in many Canadians' daily lives was illustrated by survey results that showed increasing automobile ownership, longer travel distances to work, and higher levels of fuel consumption over time in many CMAs. While it is important to note that the council also found the levels of increase in these areas to be slowing down, it is also clear that much more needs to be done to achieve fully sustainable transportation. Given the success of many European cities in building places where pedestrians, cyclists, and transit riders enjoy high levels of accessibility, there is little reason to believe that the same cannot be achieved over time in Canada's urban settings. As Susan Hanson and Genevieve Giuliano are quoted as saying elsewhere in this chapter, urban transportation systems represent the cumulative outcome of choices made by individuals and institutions in deciding matters such as where to live, how to get around, and at what densities to build. Documents like *A New Vision for Urban Transportation* go a long way to inform those decisions.

MAIN POINTS 12.6 What Are Some Ways by Which Urban Transportation Systems Might Be Made More Sustainable?

- There are very clear geographical variations in the levels of automobile dependence in cities around the world. Most automobile-dependent cities are in the United States, followed (in order) by Australia, Canada, and Europe.

- Transportation geographers have become more active in calling for the adoption of sustainable transportation policies.

- Building sustainable transportation systems involves simultaneous consideration of environmental, economic, and social objectives in the provision of transportation infrastructure and services.

- The elements necessary for a sustainable urban transportation system "on the ground" are nicely consolidated in *A New Vision for Urban Transportation*, which includes a set of 13 land use and transportation planning principles that have the potential to create more balanced roles for various modes of transportation—including the private automobile—within cities.

- Decisions that have led to the creation of automobile-dependent cities were made over the course of several decades. Therefore, they will not be reversed easily, and certainly not overnight. However, ongoing monitoring of Canadian cities has shown slow, incremental progress being made in building more sustainable transportation systems.

SUMMARY

Transportation is an inherently geographical subject, bringing together geography's focus on spatial interaction, regional differences, human-environment relations, and economic development. In light of their overriding interest in helping to improve people's quality of life, transportation geographers have actively worked to identify transport-related problems, within both the core and the periphery, and to propose solutions for these problems. The solutions are often rooted in the notion of sustainable development, and frequently the same remedy may be applied to different problems. For example, a common initiative advocated by transportation geographers and others has been to bring destinations closer together so that they can be reached more easily on foot. This is effective whether the aim is to enable those in peripheral regions to meet their daily needs with less time devoted to travel, thus advancing the social sustainability agenda, or to enable those in core regions to reduce their levels of automobile dependence by making walking more attractive relative to travelling by car, thus helping achieve environmental sustainability objectives. Given its impact on so many aspects of our lives and on the places we live, transportation is clearly an important issue and growing even more so in our globalized world. It is becoming increasingly evident that transportation issues are worthy of much more detailed examination and, as we have shown throughout this chapter, transportation geographers are leading the way in identifying and addressing these issues.

DISCUSSION AND REVIEW QUESTIONS

1. What is the situation at Brock University with transportation? Does Brock University have a successful sustainable transportation program? Why? Think about your own university or college: would you consider its student transportation system adequate?

2. Until recently, transportation had been neglected by geographers. What is transportation geography and why has it recently emerged as an important subdiscipline of geography?

3. Discuss the themes and arguments presented by Peter Newman and Jeff Kenworthy in their book *Sustainability and Cities: Overcoming Automobile Dependence*. Does the city you live in reflect the ideas presented in their book? Identify any specific things your city is doing to address its transportation situation as it relates to the 13 principles laid out in *A New Vision for Urban Transportation*, published by the Transportation Association of Canada.

4. There are clear geographical variations in transportation systems across the globe—with some dominated by the automobile and others with high rates of non-motorized modes, such as walking and cycling. The most automobile-dependent cities in the world are found in the United States, Australia, and Canada. Describe the factors that explain these variations in transportation systems.

5. Transportation is an integral part of any place, and there are inevitable consequences based on the type of transportation systems that predominate. Identify and briefly explain the major consequences of contemporary transportation patterns. Which consequence most aptly fits your city or town?

GEOGRAPHIC CONCEPTS

ADDITIONAL RESOURCES ON-LINE

International Air Transport Association: www.iata.org

Air Transport Association of Canada: www.atac.ca

International Union of Railways: www.uic.org

Railway Association of Canada: www.railcan.ca

World Shipping Council: www.worldshipping.org

Shipping Federation of Canada: www.shipfed.ca/new

About automobile dependence: www.vtpi.org/tdm/tdm100.htm

Transportation Association of Canada: www.tac-atc.ca

Transport Canada: www.tc.gc.ca

Canadian Urban Transit Association: www.cutaactu.ca/en/index.asp

Campus transportation management programs: www.vtpi.org/tdm/tdm5.htm

About transportation issues in peripheral regions: www.worldbank.org/projects/sector?lang=en

CHAPTER
13 INDUSTRY AND SERVICES

Building a Logistics City

LOGISTICS IS A business framework for the coordination and management of the movement of goods, information, people, and capital at the global scale; in other words, logistics is the moving of boxes, the driving of trucks, the getting things onto the shelves "just in time." It occupies the space between production and consumption, and seems quite straightforward and uncomplicated to many of us. In the grand scheme of things, logistics might be considered "the easy part." Historically, logistics was one of the three arts of Napoleonic warfare, along with strategy and tactics, and it became a central organizing principle in military exercises; getting troops, fuel, ammunition, and technologies to the warfront became increasingly important by World War I. However, as Canadian geographer Deborah Cowen argues, logistics has quietly moved from military art to business science, such that "logistics has gradually become the *how that shapes the what*" (Cowen, 2010). What Cowen means is that logistics is no longer only practised in the military; it has gradually, since the 1960s, revolutionized the management practices of large industrial economies.

Logistics has become so crucial to contemporary industrial relations that there are now cities named in its honour. Dubai Logistics City (**Figure 13.1**) is one of these. Uniquely positioned between South Asia and Europe, Dubai has become known as the "gateway" between the East and West. It is the most populous city and emirate in the United Arab Emirates, and has fast positioned itself as an international trade hub with a geographic location that yields access to Africa, India, and China. It is the third-largest export region in the world, following Hong Kong and Singapore, and it has one of the largest and fastest-growing sea ports in the world. As Cowen's research shows, Dubai World Central, the world's largest planned settlement, began the Logistics City project in 2007, aiming to be "the world's first truly integrated logistics platform, with all transport modes, logistics and value added services, including light manufacturing and assembly, in a single customs bonded and Free Zone envi-

ronment" (Cowen, 2010, p. 69). Strategically positioned to join the Port of Jebel Ali (the world's largest harbour), and the Dubai World Central–Al Maktoum International Airport, as well as, more broadly, Asia and Europe, Logistics City exists *because of* location.

There are many reasons why Dubai Logistics City might attract the attention of industrial geographers. Some, like Cowen, are interested in the securitization aspects of industrial lands and ports in a post-9/11 world, where military arts and business practices seem more intertwined at a global scale than ever before. Others might be interested in the location—why Dubai? Why now? Still others would consider Logistics City within the broader spectrum of Dubai World Central (DWC), a strategic initiative of the Government of Dubai, which in 2011 facilitated foreign trade in Dubai of upwards of $190 billion. Even more significant, DWC's position as the "gateway" to the Middle East, North Africa, and South Asia (MENASA)—a region where a quarter of the world's population lives, and with a total cumulative gross domestic product (GDP) over $3.6 trillion—makes it one of the most powerful locations in the world. DWC's master plan lays out eight districts: logistics, aviation, residential, commercial, humanitarian, exhibition, golf, and the airport (**Figure 13.2**).

© Jorge Ferrari/epa/Corbis

FIGURE 13.1 Dubai Logistics City. It has been noted that the city's design looks like a computer's logic board.

What this master plan reveals is a strategically planned urban and industrial space, where labour is readily available and tightly controlled through a combination of on-site living quarters and rigid security measures, including biometric screening; where the flows of commodities are facilitated; and where "transportation infrastructure is giving rise to new forms of urban space—the logistics city" (Cowen, 2010, p. 71). Industrial geography considers this complex relationship between industrial practices and the built environment, questions the significance of location in industrial practices, and critically engages with the power relations that shape these contemporary forms. It asks us to look at landscapes—such as the landscape of Dubai Logistics City—and see in it the logic of economic life. That the design and layout of Dubai Logistics City eerily resembles the design and layout of a computer's logic board is no accident. What does this industrial landscape reveal about who we are? What we value? These compelling questions, among many others, are central concerns of industrial geography.

FIGURE 13.2 Visitors view a scale model of Dubai World Central (DWC). DWC has positioned itself as an unparalleled commercial, trade, and transportation hub. When completed, the 140-square-kilometre self-contained economic zone will support 12 million tonnes of cargo and 160 million passengers annually.

KEY QUESTIONS FOR CHAPTER 13

1. What are industrial and service economies?

2. Where did the Industrial Revolution begin, and how did it diffuse?

3. How do location theories explain historical patterns of industrialization?

4. What are the spatial implications of changes in industrial production?

5. What is the service economy, and where are services concentrated?

13.1 What Are Industrial and Service Economies?

When we look closely at the landscapes around us, we see people engaged in numerous and diverse economic activities. In our own neighbourhood, we drop into the local convenience store to buy gas, pick up milk, or take a chance on a lottery ticket. The nearby neighbourhood strip mall might have a drycleaners, a liquor store, a barber shop and hair salon, or a veterinarian, providing us with the services we use on a regular basis. As we make our daily commute to work, we travel past offices and industrial parks, manufacturing plants, and local factories employing neighbours and friends. From the hotdog vendor in the city park to the high-tech manufacturer, the industrial, manufacturing, and service sectors are major contributors to local and global economies. Driven by the processes of globalization detailed in Chapter 2, these economic activities are fully integrated into continental and worldwide networks and flows of knowledge, goods, services, and technologies. As geographers, we are interested in the spatial organization of industrial and service economies as well as questions of location, regional organization, and movement of goods, services, and labour. In this chapter we will consider the locational aspects of economic activities—more specifically, the locational characteristics of industrial and service-sector entities.

The types of employment associated with different economic activities are illustrated in **Table 13.1. Primary activities**, such as agriculture, logging, and mining, involve the extraction or production of raw materials. **Secondary activities** make something

> **Primary activities** Economic activities that involve the extraction or production of raw materials, such as agriculture, logging, and mining.
>
> **Secondary activities** Economic activities that involve making something from raw materials, such as food processing, the production of lumber or furniture, or building construction.

TABLE 13.1	Employment by Industry, Canada 2010–2014				
	2010	2011	2012	2013	2014
			Thousands		
All industries	16,964.3	17,221.0	17,438.0	17,691.1	17,802.2
Goods-producing sector	3,725.0	3,801.3	3,873.9	3,910.1	3,897.1
Agriculture	306.6	307.9	305.7	314.0	305.1
Forestry, fishing, mining, quarrying, oil and gas[1]	324.5	339.9	365.5	368.1	372.6
Utilities	141.3	137.1	133.4	135.0	136.9
Construction	1,241.9	1,294.6	1,322.8	1,369.8	1,371.5
Manufacturing	1,710.7	1,721.8	1,746.5	1,723.1	1,711.0
Services-producing sector	13,239.2	13,419.8	13,564.1	13,781.0	13,905.1
Trade	2,683.4	2,677.9	2,660.9	2,710.7	2,729.3
Transportation and warehousing	814.1	849.5	857.4	882.9	896.8
Finance, insurance, real estate and leasing	1,073.9	1,076.0	1,061.7	1,078.8	1,083.8
Professional, scientific and technical services	1,216.1	1,264.6	1,270.7	1,310.9	1,333.3
Business, building and other support services[2]	691.5	694.3	704.3	740.9	734.8
Educational services	1,166.3	1,170.2	1,209.6	1,226.5	1,236.9
Health care and social assistance	2,041.6	2,084.1	2,141.0	2,189.9	2,219.7
Information, culture and recreation	762.8	771.9	759.1	756.7	757.2
Accommodation and food services	1,097.6	1,141.1	1,170.1	1,169.6	1,207.5
Other services	771.4	769.5	804.9	795.3	795.1
Public administration	920.5	920.4	924.3	918.9	910.7

1. Also referred to as Natural resources.
2. Formerly Management of companies, administrative and other support services.
Source: Data from Statistics Canada, CANSIM, table 282-0008. Accessed at www.statcan.gc.ca/tables-tableaux/sum-som/l01/cst01/econ40-eng.htm.

from those raw materials and include such activities as food processing (e.g., cheese, soups, or pasta), the production of lumber or furniture, the manufacturing of granite countertops, building construction, or the making of diamond rings. Note that in Table 13.1, primary and secondary activities are grouped together under the heading "Goods-producing sector."

Tertiary activities are those service industries connecting the manufacturing and industrial processes to consumers, as well as services that facilitate trade and commerce. Businesses rely on services provided by bankers, salespeople, insurance brokers, lawyers, accountants, and secretaries. Workers need services that sustain them, including restaurants, clothing stores, doctors, and dentists. In the 21st century, services have become more complicated. We can divide the service-producing sector into a **tertiary sector** that includes trade, transportation, and warehousing; a **quaternary sector**, which includes individuals working with the exchange of information or money; and a **quinary**

> **Tertiary activities** Service industries connecting the manufacturing and industrial processes to consumers as well as services that facilitate trade and commerce.
>
> **Tertiary sector** The sector of tertiary economic activities that includes trade, transportation, and warehousing.
>
> **Quaternary sector** The sector of tertiary economic activities that includes individuals working with the exchange of information or money.
>
> **Quinary sector** The sector of tertiary economic activities that includes individuals involved in research or higher education.

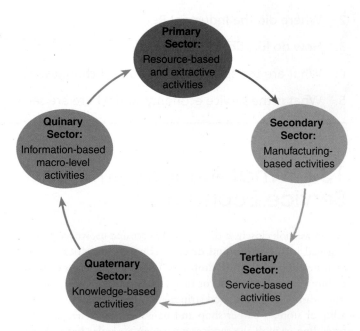

FIGURE 13.3 Sectors of the economy.

sector, with individuals involved in research or higher education. Universities and colleges educate individuals to use technologies (quinary) or to broker financial transactions and provide information (quaternary) that, in turn, are integral to the operation of strong agricultural, manufacturing, and service sectors (**Figure 13.3**).

Geographers and others use the term "stages of development" to describe how an economy might evolve. Regions are described as going through three stages of industrial development as emerging technologies diffuse across landscapes. The first stage is the pre-industrial stage, when primary activities form the backbone of an economy. They mostly take the form of agriculture but may also include lumber production, fishing, and some resource extraction, such as quarrying stone and gravel. A region is understood to have reached the second, or industrial, stage

> **Post-industrial economy** An economy in which most of a country's labour force is engaged in tertiary, quaternary, and quinary sectors. The world's core countries are all post-industrial economies.

when it develops a manufacturing economy with an output greater than that of the primary sector. In an industrial economy, a substantial portion of the labour force is engaged in secondary activities, which include processing raw materials and producing new goods. The third and last stage is the **post-industrial economy**, in which most of the labour force is engaged in tertiary, quaternary, and quinary sectors. The world's core countries have entered the post-industrial stage.

Canada is a country with bountiful natural resources. From its colonial past to its contemporary present, the Canadian economy has relied on the primary activities of logging, resource extraction, fishing, and, later, agriculture. This continued into the 1950s and 1960s with the expansion of American branch plants into Canada, most notably in the automobile sector. At the same time, oil and gas became an increasingly important staple, particularly in Alberta, with the seemingly insatiable demand for petroleum products from both Canada and the United States. Asian development in the 1980s and 1990s increased the demand for Canadian resources, such as copper and coal, especially on the west coast. Today, demand for Canadian natural resources from countries such as China has reinvigorated natural resource extraction and production. Increased demand for uranium and the discovery of diamonds in Nunavut and the Northwest Territories sparked the opening of a number of uranium and diamond mines (**Figure 13.4**).

As Table 13.1 illustrates, in 2014, approximately 22 percent of the Canadian workforce was involved in the goods-producing sector, which is composed of both primary and secondary

Diavik Diamond Mine

FIGURE 13.4 Diavik Diamond Mine, Northwest Territories. Contained within a 20-square-kilometre island at Lac de Gras, roughly 300 kilometres north of Yellowknife, Diavik Diamond Mine, a joint venture between Rio Tinto and Harry Winston, has been mining diamonds in the remote Canadian north since 2003.

activities. Only about 4 percent of the Canadian workforce was employed in primary activities such as agriculture, forestry, fishing, mining, oil, and gas. The remainder of the labour force in this sector was involved in secondary activities, including construction and manufacturing. The service-producing sector, which encompasses the tertiary, quaternary, and quinary sectors, employs the remainder of the Canadian workforce, or about 78 percent. By definition, this makes Canada a post-industrial economy. When we look at the service-producing sector, we can see that some 12.5 percent of the workforce is engaged in providing health care and social assistance. Taken together with those involved in public administration (5.1 percent) and educational services (6.9 percent), governments (federal, provincial, and local) employ about 25 percent of the labour force. By contrast, Canada has quite modest employment in manufacturing and construction, which employs only about 17.3 percent of the total workforce. Again, by definition, this means Canada is a post-industrial economy.

MAIN POINTS 13.1 What Are Industrial and Service Economies?

- Economies are classified by what is produced. Primary activities involve the extraction and production of resources. Secondary activities involve manufacturing goods from those raw materials. Tertiary activities are service industries connecting the manufacturing and industrial processes to consumers, while quaternary and quinary sectors involve knowledge and higher education, respectively.

- Economies go through three stages of development, from pre-industrial to manufacturing to post-industrial, where

the majority of the workforce is engaged in tertiary, quaternary, and quinary activities. The world's core countries have entered the post-industrial stage.

- Canada is a post-industrial country. Nevertheless, with the increasing demand for raw materials from countries such as China, Canadian resource-based industries extracting coal, lumber, uranium, and diamonds have shown considerable growth in the last decade.

13.2 Where Did the Industrial Revolution Begin, and How Did It Diffuse?

The **Industrial Revolution**, beginning in the 1700s and 1800s, was clearly a watershed event in human history. Technological

> **Industrial Revolution** The social and economic changes in agriculture, commerce, and manufacturing that resulted from technological innovations and specialization in late-18th-century Europe.

changes in agriculture led to the second agricultural revolution, with its improved farming techniques and resulting food surplus (see Chapter 9). Advances in medicine and in the sciences greatly improved human health, resulting in a rise in birth rates, a decline in death rates, and overall greater life expectancy, leading to a population explosion (see Chapter 4). Urban areas expanded as these growing populations sought employment in the manufacturing and industrial sectors developing in and around urban areas and transportation centres (Chapter 10). With improved technologies in ship construction and the growth in knowledge about navigation, European countries entered the age of exploration, colonialism, and imperialism, and the discoveries they made—from spices and precious metals to new civilizations and technologies—in turn fed the development of new ideas and technologies (Chapter 3).

What we think of as "industrial production" began long before the Industrial Revolution. Europeans travelled the "Silk Routes" between India, China, and the Mediterranean for some 3,000 years, ensuring an exchange of goods and technologies (**Figure 13.5**). China and Japan possessed a substantial industrial base long before the European Industrial Revolution. From the 11th century, cottage industries and community workshops were located throughout the world, and trade in the goods produced was widespread even before colonial and imperial

exploration. In the towns and villages of India, workshops produced items made from iron, gold, silver, and brass. India's carpenters were artists as well as artisans, and their work was in demand wherever it could be bought. India's textiles, made on individual spinning wheels and hand looms, were considered the best in the world. These industries were sustained both by local aristocrats and by international trade, and some European producers thought the Indian manufacturers had an unfair advantage. In Great Britain, textiles were produced by residents of rural villages within their individual homes where, during the winter months, they would spin thread or weave fabric. The quality of production varied according to place but was generally inferior to India's textiles. As a result, British textile makers rioted in 1721, demanding legislative protection against imports from India.

At the same time, pre-industrial technologies were changing the textile industry in Great Britain and Europe, which further increased tensions in the industry. The "Spinning Jenny" was one such technology (**Figure 13.6**). Developed in 1764 by James Hargreaves, a cotton weaver from Lancashire, England, the Spinning Jenny solved a serious problem in pre-industrial textile technology. Weaving had become increasingly efficient, and it took three spinners to keep up with one weaver. Hargreaves invented a new machine that could spin eight threads of cotton yarn, instead of a spinning wheel's one. While the Spinning Jenny made textile production more efficient, the spinners became increasingly angry at the threat to their livelihood. They broke into Hargreaves's house, sabotaged his equipment, and forced him to flee the region.

THE INDUSTRIAL REVOLUTION

In the era of colonial exploration and colonization, European countries such as England, Spain, and France travelled the globe, claiming "discovered" lands and peoples as their own.

FIGURE 13.5 The Silk Road and related trade routes. The historical Silk Road, which gets its name from the Chinese silk trade and is some 6,400 kilometres in length, is composed of a series of land and sea trade routes that crisscrossed Eurasia from the first millennium BCE through to the middle of the second millennium CE. (NASA Goddard Space Flight Center Image by Reto Stöckli (land surface, shallow water, clouds). Enhancements by Robert Simmon (ocean colour, compositing, 3D globes, animation). Data and technical support: MODIS Land Group; MODIS Science Data Support Team; MODIS Atmosphere Group; MODIS Ocean Group Additional data: USGS EROS Data Center (topography); USGS Terrestrial Remote Sensing Flagstaff Field Center (Antarctica); Defense Meteorological Satellite Program (city lights).)

FIGURE 13.6 Spinning Jenny. The Spinning Jenny was invented in 1764 by James Hargreaves, a cotton weaver.

Newly established commercial enterprises, such as the Dutch and British East India Companies in Asia and the Hudson's Bay Company in North America, laid the groundwork for Europe's colonial expansion. The companies' traders made contact with previously unknown peoples and slowly gained control over local industries in India, Indonesia, and elsewhere. Goods from this far-flung colonial empire flowed back to the home countries, providing local communities with the opportunity to purchase a hitherto unknown assortment of exotic and unfamiliar spices, foods, art, and fabrics. By the 18th century, the imported raw materials were being refined and turned into furniture, clothing, and household goods that were increasingly in demand in the colonies, leading to the invention of new machinery and the development of larger workforces to service this new market. New networks and flows of goods and people established new connections and relationships between previously unconnected places, facilitating the exchange of knowledge about peoples and places never before experienced. These networks and locations are the foundation for the current world economic system discussed in chapters 2 and 3.

During the 18th century, a series of inventions and discoveries created new uses for known energy sources, such as coal, and prompted the rapid development of communication technologies, such as the telegraph, to help manage and control the colonies. New machines to improve efficiencies, such as steam engines, enabled other new inventions from water pumps to railroads. Funding inventions and supporting inventors required money, and the 18th century was marked by a flow of capital from the colonies and global trade to Western Europe (**Figure 13.7**).

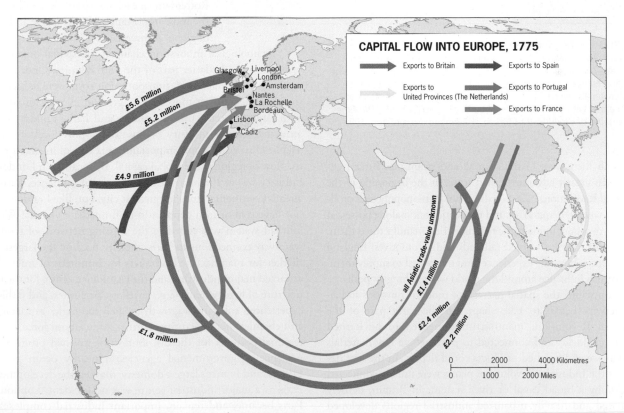

FIGURE 13.7 Capital flows into Europe during the era of colonialism. Major flows of capital entered Europe from European colonies. The capital helped fuel Europe's Industrial Revolution at the end of the 1700s and into the 1800s. Adapted with permission from Geoffrey Barraclough, ed., *The Times Concise Atlas of World History,* 5th ed., Hammond Incorporated, 1998.

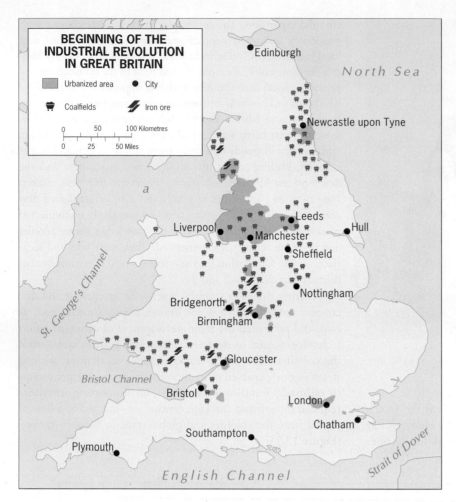

FIGURE 13.8 The origins of the Industrial Revolution. The areas of Great Britain that industrialized earliest were those closest to the resources—coal, iron ore, and capital—needed for industrialization. Large areas of urbanization grew near industrial zones and in the port cities where materials came in and from which industrialized products went out. Adapted with permission from Geoffrey Barraclough, ed., *The Times Concise Atlas of World History,* 5th ed., Hammond Incorporated, 1998.

With the advent of the railroad and steamship, Britain enjoyed even greater advantages than it did at the beginning of the Industrial Revolution. Not only did it hold a monopoly over products that were in demand around the world, but it alone possessed the skills necessary to make the machines that manufactured them. Europe and America wanted railroads and locomotives; England had the know-how, the experience, and the capital to supply them. Soon British influence around the world was reaching its peak.

Meanwhile, the spatial pattern of modern Europe's industrial activity began to take shape. In the early part of the Industrial ·Revolution, manufacturing needed to be located close to coalfields and connected to ports where raw materials could arrive and finished products could depart. In the first decades of the Industrial Revolution, plants were usually connected to ports by a broad canal or river system. In Britain, densely populated and heavily urbanized industrial regions developed near the coalfields (**Figure 13.8**). The largest such region was the Midlands of north-central England.

DIFFUSION TO MAINLAND EUROPE

In the early 1800s, as the innovations of Britain's Industrial Revolution diffused into mainland Europe, the same set of locational criteria for industrial zones applied: proximity to coalfields and connection via water to a port. A belt of major coalfields extends from west to east through mainland Europe, roughly along the southern margins of the North European Lowland—across northern France and southern Belgium, the Netherlands, the German Ruhr, western Bohemia in the Czech Republic, and Silesia in Poland. Iron ore is dispersed along a similar belt, and the map showing the pattern of diffusion of the Industrial Revolution into Europe reflects the resulting concentrations of economic activity (**Figure 13.9**). Industrial developments in one area, such as the Ruhr area of present-day Germany (Germany was not consolidated into a single country until the 1870s), changed the port cities to which they are linked—in this case Rotterdam in the Netherlands. The Rhine River flows through the Ruhr area and enters the sea at Rotterdam. Over the last 200 years, the Dutch radically altered the port of Rotterdam to ease transportation and make it the most important port in Europe and a hub of global commerce.

Technological innovation changed the spatial organization of industry in the latter part of the 18th century. Once the railroad was well established, transportation costs were reduced and some manufacturing moved to or grew in existing urban areas with large markets, such as London and Paris. London was an attractive site for industry because of its port location on the Thames River and, more importantly, because of its major role in the flow of regional and global capital. By locating in London, an industry was at the heart of Britain's global influence. Paris was already continental Europe's greatest city, but, like London, it did not have coal or iron deposits in its immediate vicinity. When a railroad system was added to the existing network of road and waterway connections to Paris, the city became the largest local market for manufactured products for hundreds of miles. Paris attracted major industries, and the city, long a centre for the manufacture of luxury items (e.g., jewellery, perfumes, and fashions), experienced substantial growth in such industries as metallurgy and chemical manufacturing. With a ready labour force, an ideal regional position for the distribution of finished products, the presence of governmental agencies, a nearby ocean port (Le Havre), and France's largest domestic market, the development of Paris as a major industrial centre was no accident. London and Paris became, and remain, important industrial complexes not because of their coalfields but because of their commercial and political connectivity to the rest of the world.

FIGURE 13.9 **Diffusion of the Industrial Revolution.** The eastward diffusion of the Industrial Revolution occurred during the second half of the 19th century.

In the 1700s and 1800s, the North American colonies of France and Britain were pre-industrial economies, providing raw materials to the home countries—predominantly tobacco, cotton, lumber, animal pelts, and fish—and serving as major markets for finished goods. The imports from North America provided the necessary inputs for the growing industrial regions of Europe and structured the spatial layout and organization of North American hamlets, towns, villages, cities, and ports (**Figure 13.10**). As in most colonial settlements, transportation systems were established to ensure the smooth flow of goods and materials. Initially, transportation was mainly by the major navigable waterways, and later it was by railways, as goods were conveyed from the centre of the continent to the eastern coast and the major ports of Montreal, Quebec City, Halifax, and Saint John as well as New York and Boston. Raw materials were processed in the major centres in Europe and imported by the North American colonies as finished goods such as clothing, textiles, books, and furniture. Local manufacturing in North America was modest and included saw and grist mills, blacksmithing, and shipbuilding designed mainly to support the export trade.

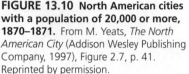

FIGURE 13.10 North American cities with a population of 20,000 or more, 1870–1871. From M. Yeats, *The North American City* (Addison Wesley Publishing Company, 1997), Figure 2.7, p. 41. Reprinted by permission.

1870–1871
.... 1,500,000
.... 750,000
.... 250,000
.... 100,000
.... 50,000
.... 20,000

By and large, those who benefited most from industrialization were countries that had access to land, labour, and financial resources, usually supported by government. Nations such as India were unsuccessful in developing jute and steel industries because, even though they had the natural resources and labour, early entrepreneurs lacked financial and government support. Globally, then, a division of labour happened, with industrialized nations producing manufactured goods, and less industrialized nations producing the raw materials necessary for that production. Through the process of colonization, countries such as England were able to access raw materials such as cotton from Egypt and India, thereby increasing the power and reach of the British Empire. Other countries in Latin America, sub-Saharan Africa, and Asia became dependent on single cash crops such as sugar, cotton, or rubber. Known as "banana republics" because of their reliance on one crop, like bananas, and the accompanying exploitation of plantation agriculture, these countries were susceptible to market changes at the global scale due to heavy foreign ownership, with the majority of profit leaving the country and very little profit going to local workers or communities.

MAIN POINTS 13.2 Where Did the Industrial Revolution Begin, and How Did It Diffuse?

- The Industrial Revolution of the 18th and 19th centuries produced a profound shift in human history from agricultural and resource-based economies to manufacturing economies. It was marked by rapid technological change, increased urbanization, population growth, and global exploration and colonization.

- Colonial and imperial exploration increased trade around the globe and ensured increasing exchanges of goods, information, and technologies among far-flung regions. This established new networks of communication and trade and set the stage for the current interrelationships between different nations.

- Major inventions in Europe, such as improved communications (telegraph) and the steam engine (rail transportation and manufacturing), accelerated the rate of change. Innovations from Britain diffused to mainland Europe in the early 1800s, and industry developed near the major coalfields in northern France, southern Belgium, the Netherlands, the German Ruhr, western Bohemia in the Czech Republic, and Silesia in Poland.

- North America at this time had little industrial development as its main task was to provide raw materials to home countries. North American urban centres developed as transportation nodes began moving raw goods and materials from the centre of the continent to the east coast.

13.3 How Do Location Theories Explain Historical Patterns of Industrialization?

Economic activities have a particular spatial organization that depends on a number of factors as well as historical and cultural circumstances. Primary economic activities are usually located where resources are found—near forests, mineral deposits, or good soils. Secondary industrial and manufacturing activities also depend on obtaining the raw materials they need, and location decisions are often made based on access to those resources as well as the availability of skilled workers and transportation systems that can move their final product to market. However, technological improvements in transportation and communications have created time-space compression (see Chapter 2) in our globalized world, and these secondary industries are much less dependent on resource location than they used to be. Raw materials can be transported to distant locations to be converted into manufactured products—if the resulting profits outweigh the costs. A large body of work in economic geography focuses on **location theory**, which attempts to predict where businesses will or should be located. Clearly this is a very important undertaking given the economic and social advantages that come from having industrial and service businesses located in an area. Urban centres compete to attract companies by offering serviced industrial parks and tax incentives. New companies can offer employment, which, in turn, provides labourers with a wage to spend in the local economy.

> **Location theory** A logical attempt to explain the locational pattern of an economic activity and the manner in which its producing areas are interrelated.

Any attempt to establish a model for the location of secondary industries runs into complications much greater than those confronting J.H. von Thünen (discussed in Chapter 9), who dealt only with primary industries. The location of secondary industries depends to a large extent on human behaviour and decision-making; on cultural, political, and economic factors; and even on intuition or whim. Since models must be based on assumptions, geographers have to assume that decision-makers are trying to maximize their advantages over competitors and that they want to make as much profit as possible. Decision-makers should also take into account the **variable costs** of establishing a manufacturing enterprise in one location over another, such as energy supply, transport expenses, and labour costs.

> **Variable costs** Costs that change directly with the amount of production (e.g., energy supply and labour costs).
>
> **Friction of distance** The increase in time and cost that usually comes with increasing distance.

In making calculations that are designed to maximize advantages, a key issue is the **friction of distance**, which is defined as the increase in time and cost that usually comes with increasing distance. If a raw material has to be shipped hundreds of miles to a factory, rather than being manufactured right next door, the friction of distance increases. A corollary to the concept of the friction of distance is what geographers call **distance decay**, which assumes that the impact of a function or an activity will decline as one moves away from its point of origin. Distance decay suggests that manufacturing plants will be more concerned with serving the markets of nearby places than more distant places. This basic principle is important in efforts to understand the locational dynamics of a variety of phenomena, including manufacturing. In this section, we consider the location theories or models of Alfred Weber, whose work is prominent in examining the spatial organization of various industries and services at a variety of scales.

> **Distance decay** The effects of distance on interaction; generally, the greater the distance, the less interaction takes place.

WEBER'S MODEL

The German economic geographer Alfred Weber (1868–1958) (**Figure 13.11**) developed a basic model designed to predict the location of manufacturing plants within a region. Weber was thinking about why a manufacturing plant would pick one place over another to set up shop. He drew from the research of other economic geographers and began with a set of assumptions that enabled him to create his model. In *Theory of the Location of Industries* (1909), Weber calculated the "pulls" exerted on each point of manufacturing in his hypothetical region of analysis. Weber's **least cost theory** accounted for the location (P) of a manufacturing plant in terms of the desire to minimize three categories of costs.

> **Least cost theory** Model developed by Alfred Weber according to which the location of manufacturing establishments is determined by the minimization of three critical expenses: labour, transportation, and agglomeration.

Photo by ullstein bild via Getty Image

FIGURE 13.11 Alfred Weber. Weber's theory about the location of industries was that the site chosen must entail the lowest possible cost of moving raw materials to the factory and finished products to the market. The problem resides in finding an optimal factory location within respective distances of raw materials and the market.

The first and most important of these categories was transportation: the site chosen must entail the lowest possible cost of moving raw materials to the factory and finished products to the market. For example, if we are making furniture, we will need to bring wood (lumber) to the factory. We will need other materials, such as screws, glue, paint, and varnish perhaps, although clearly wood is going to be our greatest cost. It could be very expensive to transport these raw materials to our factory if we are located some distance away from the source of wood. The second concern is where we sell our finished tables and chairs. If we have to ship these products great distances to furniture stores and shopping malls, we may not make any money (profit). Weber suggested that the site where transportation costs are lowest is the place where it would be least expensive to bring raw materials to the point of production and distribute finished products to consumers.

The second category of cost was labour. Higher labour costs reduce the margin of profit, so a factory might do better farther from raw materials and markets if cheap labour made up for the added transport costs. We might want to establish our furniture factory nearer to our raw materials and perhaps in an area with higher unemployment, ensuring we have an inexpensive labour pool to draw on.

The third factor in Weber's model was what he called **agglomeration**. When a substantial number of enterprises cluster in the same area, as happens in a large industrial city, they can provide assistance to each other through shared talents, services, and facilities. All manufacturers need office furniture and equipment; the presence of one or more producers in a large city satisfies this need for all. Thus, agglomeration makes a big-city location more attractive, perhaps overcoming some increase in transport and labour costs. Excessive agglomeration, however, leads to high rents, rising wages, circulation problems (resulting in increased transport costs and loss of efficiency), and other problems that may eventually negate the advantages of agglomeration. Such factors have led many industries to leave the crowded urban centres and move to other locations—a process known as **deagglomeration**.

> **Agglomeration** A process involving the clustering or concentrating of people or activities. The term often refers to manufacturing plants and businesses that benefit from close proximity because they share pools of skilled labour and technological and financial amenities.
>
> **Deagglomeration** The process of industrial deconcentration in response to technological advances and/or increasing costs due to congestion and competition.

MAJOR INDUSTRIAL REGIONS OF THE WORLD BEFORE 1950

Considering Weber's model helps explain where industries might choose to locate and why. Before 1950, the main locational costs for industries were transportation of raw materials and shipping of finished products. Thus, the first manufacturing belts (i.e., regions of major manufacturing concentration) tended to be close to raw materials and accessible to transportation routes. Yet, at the global scale, several major areas that were sources of raw materials did not industrialize early. The map of major regional-industrial development before 1950 reveals that only a small minority of countries were major industrial economies. Many factors help explain this pattern, including relative location in relation to flows of goods and capital, political circumstances, economic leadership, labour costs, and levels of education and training. The four **primary industrial regions** that stand out on the world map are western and central Europe, eastern North America, Russia and Ukraine, and eastern Asia. Each of these regions consists of one or more core areas of industrial development with subsidiary clusters.

> **Primary industrial regions** Western and central Europe; eastern North America; Russia and Ukraine; and eastern Asia, each of which consists of one or more core areas of industrial development with subsidiary clusters.

WESTERN AND CENTRAL EUROPE

The manufacturing regions of western Europe are largely the regions that experienced industrialization between the late 18th and early 20th centuries. From this region of Europe came the European Coal and Steel Community (ECSC), which initiated the experiment with the integration of Europe's principal coal deposits, lying in a belt across northern France, Belgium, north-central Germany, the northwestern Czech Republic, and southern Poland—and it was along this zone that industrialization expanded in mainland Europe (**Figure 13.12**). Colonial empires gave France, Britain, Belgium, and the Netherlands, and later Germany, access to the capital necessary to fuel industrialization and, in some cases, the raw materials necessary for production. Three manufacturing districts lay in Germany: the Ruhr, based on the Westphalian coalfield; the Saxony district, near the border of the former Czechoslovakia; and Silesia, now part of Poland. Even though these areas were seriously damaged in World War II, Germany still ranks among the world's leading producers of both coal and steel and remains Europe's leading industrial power (**Table 13.2**). By the early 20th century, industry began to diffuse far from the original European hearth to such places as northern Italy (now one of Europe's major industrial regions), Catalonia (anchored by Barcelona) and northern Spain, southern Sweden, and southern Finland.

THE MANUFACTURING BELTS OF GERMANY

The Ruhr, named after a small tributary of the Rhine River in Germany, became Europe's greatest industrial complex (**Figure 13.13**) because it had the combined advantages of high-quality resources, good accessibility, and proximity to large markets. It emerged as a key region during the Industrial Revolution, with an industrial base in coal mines and steel mills. When local iron ore reserves became depleted, ores could be brought in from overseas. The Ruhr was already undergoing industrialization in the closing decades of the 19th century, and by the 1930s the river basin had become one of the most important industrial regions in the world, pouring forth the products of heavy industry, including tanks and other weapons for Hitler's armies.

FIGURE 13.12 Major industrial regions of Europe. Western and central Europe was one of the primary industrial regions before 1950, and the major industrial regions of Europe are shown here.

E.H. Fouberg, A.B. Murphy, H.J. de Blij, and John Wiley & Sons, Inc.

TABLE 13.2	Major Steel-Producing Countries, 2012				
	Country	**Metric Tonnes**		**Country**	**Metric Tonnes**
1	China	716.5	6	South Korea	69.1
2	Japan	107.2	7	Germany	42.7
3	United States	88.7	8	Turkey	35.9
4	India	77.6	9	Brazil	34.5
5	Russia	70.4	10	Ukraine	33.0

These leading steel-producing countries accounted for over 80 percent of the world's steel production in 2010. Data from World Steel Association website, www.worldsteel.org/media-centre/press-releases/2013/World-Steel-Figures-2013.html.

AP Photo/Frank Augstein

FIGURE 13.13 Ruhr District, Germany. An aerial view of the snow-covered Ruhr district, with the steel company ThyssenKrupp of Duisburg, western Germany, seen in the foreground.

Saxony (also in present-day Germany), on the other hand, was always oriented toward specialized lighter manufactures. Anchored by Leipzig and Dresden, it became known for such products as optical equipment and cameras, refined textiles, and ceramics. Farther east, the industrial district of Silesia was originally part of Germany but now lies in Poland and extends into the Czech Republic. The development of the Silesian district was based on high-quality coal resources and lesser iron ores that were later supplemented by imports from Ukraine.

The sophistication of European industry ensured that World War II would be the most destructive conflict ever fought, but the war ended up destroying much of the continent's industrial infrastructure in the process. This outcome created considerable challenges in the decade following the war, but from an industrial standpoint it was not altogether a minus. German industry had been reduced to rubble, but with Allied aid, new factories sprang up that incorporated the latest technology. In time, such factories had a competitive edge over older industrial establishments in North America and the parts of Europe that had been hit less hard by the war.

NORTH AMERICA

By the beginning of the 20th century, the only serious rival to Europe was North America, a realm heavily settled by Europeans with particularly close links to Britain, and with links to the capital and innovations that fuelled industrialization there. Manufacturing in North America began in New England as early as late colonial times, but the northeastern states are not especially rich in mineral resources.

Canada, as a colonial country, first developed its primary resources and a strong agrarian base. As the Canadian industrial economy developed in the late 19th century, much of the manufacturing was located in urban areas, contributing to the unique regional organization of the Canadian economy between its rural resource base and its urban manufacturing and service base. In the late 1800s, Canada's nascent manufacturing

base was protected from foreign competition by a series of tariffs and duties. The policies favoured central Canada—more specifically, Ontario (**Figure 13.14**)—and established the heartland-hinterland relationship between central Canada and the periphery. The Maritimes had difficulty sending raw materials to the central region due to the friction of distance. Construction of the Canadian Pacific Railway helped to overcome some of the problems and unite the country, but regional

Canada Science and Technology Museum

FIGURE 13.14 Massey-Harris Company Farm Implements, Brantford, Ontario. In 1847, Daniel Massey purchased a foundry in Newcastle, Ontario, and opened the Newcastle Foundry and Machine Manufactory, CW. By 1870, with an expanding farm implement export business to Europe, Massey Manufacturing Company was established. In 1891, Massey merged with A. Harris, forming the largest company of its kind in the British Empire, opening plants in the U.S., France, Germany, and Australia.

disparities continue to this day. Ontario still has the largest labour force engaged in industrial and service-sector employment.

Both Canada and the United States have benefited from the capacity of their companies to acquire needed raw materials from overseas sources. They did not have to go overseas for the raw materials to produce energy, however. Coal was the chief fuel for industries at the time, and there was never any threat of a coal shortage. North American coal reserves are among the world's largest and are widely distributed—from Appalachian Pennsylvania to the northwestern Great Plains through Alberta and Saskatchewan (**Figure 13.15**). North America still vies with China as the world's largest coal producer.

Steel played a pivotal role in the emergence of Canada as a player in the global economy in the 1950s and 1960s. From the mid-1700s, Upper Canada had relied on iron technology to provide the axes, ploughs, and other iron tools used in harvesting raw materials for export. Rapid technological innovations in smelting iron led to the production of steel between the 1850s and the 1890s. However, the Canadian iron industry was largely unable to compete with the advances made by British and American steelmakers. The industry lacked access to capital and was hampered by the long distance to market. A series of tariffs and bounties in the late 1800s held the fragile industry in place, and the secondary manufacture of nails, screws, and other

FIGURE 13.15 Major deposits of fossil fuels in North America. North America is the world's largest energy consumer, and the realm is also endowed with substantial energy sources.

products emerged in urban areas in Ontario, Quebec, New Brunswick, and Nova Scotia. The Ontario steel industry remained fragile without easily accessible iron ore.

It was not until the early 1900s that provincial and municipal governments began promoting local iron and steel production. The provincial government of Ontario sponsored the exploration of the vast resources of northern Ontario and subsidized transportation, such as the Temiskaming and Northern Ontario Railway, to link the resources to the southern communities. By the end of the 1800s, investment in infrastructure, including rail and roads and extraction technologies, began to bear fruit. Mining increased, scattered from Calabogie and Madoc in the east to mines along the Seine and Matawin rivers in the north. Algoma Steel was established in 1901 in Sault Ste. Marie to process ore from northern mines, such as the Helen mine near Boyer Lake. Much of central Canada's iron and steel industry continued to struggle well into the 20th century despite government intervention and financial support at all levels.

By World War II, fortunes in the industry began to change. The pressure of wartime production prompted a restructuring of the iron and steel industry, and the federal government introduced a new set of regulatory frameworks addressing labour, production, distribution, and profits that survived the end of the war and into peace. Post-war prosperity and reconstruction contributed to the growing health of the industry and its competitiveness on the global stage.

The 1970s marked a shift in the steel industry in both Canada and the United States. Several factors precipitated these changes. After an industry-wide strike in 1946, the United Steelworkers of America successfully established a union presence in major mills, thus ending decades of 12-hour workdays and seven-day workweeks under harsh conditions for low pay. Unions established better working conditions for steelworkers, higher pay, and stability. While Dofasco in Hamilton, Ontario, resisted unionization, it nevertheless matched the wages and benefits won by, and paid to, unionized employees at other mills (**Figure 13.16**). In the 1970s,

FIGURE 13.17 Canadian steel shipments by market classification, percentage of total shipments, 2012. A variety of products use Canadian steel. On average, Canadians own approximately 900 kilograms of steel in a wide array of products. Data from Canadian Steel Producers Association and Statistics Canada.

FIGURE 13.16 Steel mills, Hamilton Ontario. The landscape of Hamilton Harbour/Burlington Bay features an array of steel fabrication facilities, including U.S. Steel Canada and Dofasco.

competition from low-wage foreign producers began to pose a serious threat to the local industry. Technological innovations and specialized "mini-mills" also led to the shrinking of large mill market share. Moreover, the economic downturn in the 1980s, and the signing of the North American Free Trade Agreement (NAFTA) in 1994, led to more uncertainty in the industry. Through the 1980s and 1990s, companies responded to these pressures by drastically reducing their workforce, introducing flexible work plans, and investing in new technologies to drive industrial change. Today, the steel industry still plays a formidable role in the Canadian economy. In 2012, Canada ranked 17th in the world in steel production, with an output of 12.4 million metric tonnes and sales of $12 billion. Exports accounted for 33.7 percent of the Canadian industry's production (**Figure 13.17**), and over 20,000 Canadians were employed directly within the industry.

In the decades after World War I, the United States emerged as the world's pre-eminent industrial power, and both the Canadian and American economies thrived as they became increasingly integrated. Having escaped the destruction that the war brought to much of western Europe, the United States capitalized on its newfound global political stature, its developed infrastructure, and its highly trained workforce to build an industrial economy that was second to none. The Great Depression that began in 1929 was an enormous setback, of course, but only in absolute terms. The effects of the Depression were felt worldwide, and the United States came out of it with an expanded industrial dominance. That dominance grew even greater after World War II, when once again the United States avoided destruction within its own boundaries, yet received a major industrial boost from the wartime effort. Canada was also in a strong position, and a

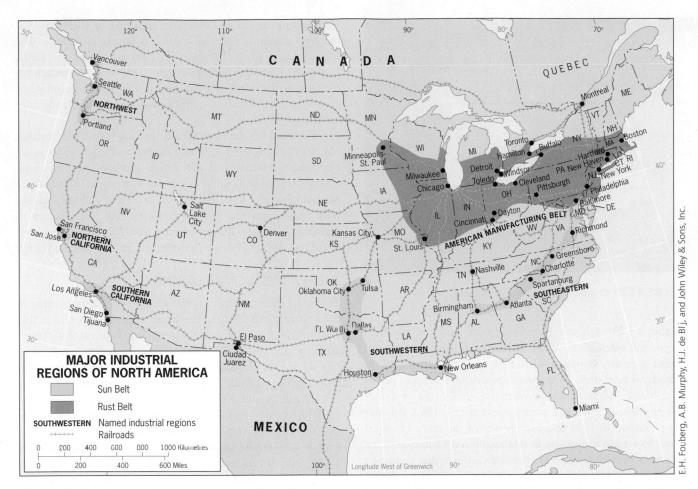

FIGURE 13.18 Major manufacturing regions of North America. North American manufacturing has dispersed westward and southward, but the eastern core area remains dominant.

major North American manufacturing belt emerged in the rectangular region shown in **Figure 13.18**.

The North American Manufacturing Belt.

The North American Manufacturing Belt extends from the northeastern seaboard to Iowa and from the St. Lawrence Valley and southern Ontario to the confluence of the Ohio and Mississippi rivers. At the belt's northeastern edge, the light industries of southern Ontario and Quebec and New England and New York give way to heavier manufacturing in the southeast Pennsylvania district (**Figure 13.19**), centred on metropolitan Philadelphia and encompassing the Baltimore area. Throughout much of the 20th century, iron ores were smelted right on the waterfront in tidewater steel mills. Major chemical industries (notably in northern Delaware), pharmaceutical industries, and lighter manufacturing plants were established there as well.

As part of the North American manufacturing belt, Lambton County, which includes the city of Sarnia, Ontario, its surrounding district, and the adjacent Aamjiwnaang First Nation reserve, has become known as "Chemical Valley"

FIGURE 13.19 Bethlehem Steel, Bethlehem, Pennsylvania. Bethlehem Steel, in operation for over 140 years, closed its doors in 1995. Now a "modern ruin," the buildings are a haunting reminder not only of the size, scale, and significance of industrial development, but also of its impact on the environment and landscape.

imac/Alamy

FIGURE 13.20 Chemical Valley, Sarnia, Ontario.

(**Figure 13.20**). Oil was discovered in the region in the mid-1850s, and when World War II led to the disruption of natural rubber supplies, Sarnia was selected by the Government of Canada to be the site of the development of synthetic, petroleum-based rubbers. Dow Chemical built the Polymer Corporation, a Canadian Crown corporation, in 1942. Polymer was privatized in 1988 and became one of the many chemical plants located in the region. In total, Lambton County is home to a large petrochemical and chemical complex that composes 40 percent of Canada's total chemical industry. There are 62 industrial facilities within a 25-kilometre radius, including oil refineries (e.g., Shell Oil, Imperial Oil, Suncor Energy) and chemical plants (e.g., Nova Chemicals, Bayer, Royal Group). Chemical Valley has been under criticism since the mid-1980s for the environmental effects of heavy industrialization, including a strange blob at the bottom of the St. Clair River. The "blob," discovered in 1985, was the size of a basketball court and turned out to contain at least 18 hazardous wastes, including dioxins and perchloroethylene. Dow Chemical was fined $16,000 for the blob. According to Ecojustice, a Canadian environmental law organization, Lambton County raises serious concerns about greenhouse gas emissions; air contaminants associated with acid rain, smog, and respiratory diseases; and toxic pollutants associated with environmental contamination and reproductive disorders.

Canada's southern Ontario district extends from the western end of Lake Ontario to the industrial zone at the western end of Lake Erie. This district links two parts of the U.S. manufacturing belt anchored by Buffalo and Detroit; the most direct route between these two industrial cities is through Ontario (Figure 13.18). Canadian and U.S. manufacturing complexes meet in two great horseshoe-shaped zones around the western ends of Lakes Ontario and Erie. In the northeast is a horseshoe-shaped cluster of industries that curls from Oshawa through Toronto and Hamilton to Buffalo. Westward, around the western end of Lake Erie, is another horseshoe-shaped cluster of industries, which extends from Windsor in Ontario through

Detroit and Toledo to Cleveland. The first of these zones is mainly Canadian, and the second is largely American. The Montreal area along the upper St. Lawrence River also forms part of the Canadian industrial zone. This area is no match for the Ontario district, but it has one big advantage: cheap hydroelectric power. Aluminum-refining and papermaking industries are located there.

Westward lies the remainder of the U.S. industrial heartland, comprising the interior industrial district, with such nodes as the Pittsburgh–Cleveland area, the Detroit–southeast Michigan area, Chicago–Gary–Milwaukee, and smaller areas centred on Minneapolis, St. Louis, and Cincinnati. Here, industrial power truly transformed the landscape during the 20th century as Appalachian coal and Mesabi iron ore (from Minnesota) were converted into autos, bulldozers, harvesters, armoured cars, and tanks.

THE FORMER SOVIET UNION

The Soviet effort to industrialize focused on manufacturing in the western part of Russia, the region of the Soviet Union that was the base of the Russian culture and the location of the country's capital, Moscow. In Moscow, the city and its surrounding area offered an important local market, converging transport routes, a large labour force, and strong centrality—just like Paris, London, and New York. Light manufacturing could already be found in this district during Tsarist times; under communist rule; heavy industries were added. One of the most famous automobile manufacturers in Russia is Lada (**Figure 13.21**), and its cars, manufactured since 1970, can be found on every continent on Earth. The success of Lada, whose exports totalled 60 percent of total sales, helped bring much-needed capital to the cash-strapped Soviet Union in the 1980s, in spite of the cars' sometimes suspect reputation. Renault purchased a

Peter Forsberg/Alamy

FIGURE 13.21 The Lada. The Russian Lada 2107, known as the "Classic," was a staple of the Russian economy and a common sight in urban centres around the world from the 1970s through to the 1990s. While other model lines were introduced, the Classic remained relatively unchanged for over 40 years. In July 2011, the manufacturer announced that it would cease production of the iconic vehicle.

FIGURE 13.22 Major manufacturing regions of Russia. The major manufacturing regions of Russia reflect the dominance of the west in the country's economic geography.

25 percent stake in Lada in 2008, and Lada continues to be a prominent manufacturer in Russia.

The Soviet Union had an enormous expanse of resources and raw materials within its borders (**Figure 13.22**). East of Moscow, the Ural Mountains yield an incredible variety of metallic ores, including iron, copper, nickel, chromite, and bauxite. In the first decades of the 1900s, Russia tapped a large supply of coal and iron ore in Siberia. The country's eastern region afforded a great deal of resources and raw materials for the industrialization of Russia's west. Between the Kuzbas and Lake Baykal lies the Krasnoyarsk–Baykal Corridors. Served by the Trans-Siberian Railroad and several important rivers, this 1,600-kilometre-long region contains impressive resources, including coal, timber, and water.

The St. Petersburg area is one of Russia's oldest manufacturing centres. Tsar Peter the Great chose it to serve not only as Russia's capital but also as the country's modern industrial focus. The skills and specializations that Peter the Great nurtured, with the help of western European artisans, still mark the area's key industries: high-quality machine building, optical products, and medical equipment. Industries such as shipbuilding, chemical production, food processing, and textile making were also located there.

The Volga experienced major development beginning in the mid-1930s, when the combination of accessible raw materials and ease of transport facilitated its development. When the Ukraine and Moscow areas were threatened by the German armies in World War II, whole industrial plants were dismantled and reassembled in Volga cities—protected from the war by distance. Samara (formerly Kuibyshev) even served as the Soviet capital for a time during World War II. This was part of a more general eastward shift of industry that occurred during the war, when Russia was invaded from the west.

After the war, the industrialization program continued. A series of dams on the Volga River made electrical power plentiful. Known oil and natural gas reserves were larger there than anywhere else in the former USSR. Canals linked the Volga to both Moscow and the Don River, making it easy to import raw materials. The cities lining the Volga, spaced at remarkably regular intervals, were assigned particular industrial functions in the state-planned economy of the Soviet Union. Samara became an oil refinery centre, Saratov acquired a chemical industry, and Volgograd became known for its metallurgical industries. The Volga was set on a course that has allowed it to remain one of Russia's dominant industrial regions to this day.

EASTERN ASIA

Japan and China were the most significant areas of eastern Asia that avoided direct European colonization—and these are the Asian countries where large-scale industrialization first took

FIGURE 13.23 Major manufacturing regions of East Asia. In China, the Northeast district was the first to take off. The Chang district followed, and most recently the Guangdong district has been growing.

root (**Figure 13.23**). Of the two, Japan was clearly the early dominant player. Less than a century after the beginning of the Industrial Revolution, Japan became one of the world's leading industrial countries. This accomplishment is all the more remarkable when one realizes that Japan has limited natural resources. Much of what Japan manufactures is made from raw materials imported from all over the world. Its transformation into the world's second-largest economy has often been described as a miracle.

Yet Japan's economic development was not a miracle. The country's modern economy was built on capital from

colonization and on government policies that had the specific goal of industrialization. Its economic development began during the second half of the 19th century, when it embarked on a campaign of industrialization and colonization. Between 1866 and 1869, under the banner of the Meiji Restoration, reformers mechanized Japan's domestic industries, moved the capital from the interior to the coast, organized its armed forces, and obtained advice from British experts on issues ranging from education to transportation (which is why the Japanese drive on the left side of the road). The Japanese also established colonies, and soon raw materials and capital were

E.H. Fouberg, A.B. Murphy, H.J. de Blij, and John Wiley & Sons, Inc.

flowing to Japan from an expanding colonial empire in Korea, Taiwan, and mainland China.

The 1930s and early 1940s brought triumph and disaster—triumph in the form of a military campaign that included vast conquests in the Pacific, East Asia, and Southeast Asia and a surprise attack on Pearl Harbor in Hawaii, and disaster when Japanese forces were driven back with great loss of life. The war ended with the utter destruction of two Japanese cities, Hiroshima and Nagasaki, by American atomic bombs. When U.S. forces took control of Japan in 1945, the nation's economy was in shambles. Yet a few decades later Japan had not only recovered but had become a global economic power.

The Japanese Manufacturing Belt.

Japan's dominant region of industrialization and urbanization is the Kanto Plain (see Figure 13.23), which contains about one-third of the nation's population and includes the Tokyo–Yokohama–Kawasaki metropolitan area. The Kanto Plain possesses a fine natural harbour at Yokohama and is centrally located with respect to the country as a whole. It has also benefited from Tokyo's designation as the country's capital. When Japan embarked on its planned course of economic development, many industries and businesses chose Tokyo as their headquarters in order to be near government decision-makers. During the mid-20th century, the Tokyo–Yokohama–Kawasaki metropolitan area became Japan's leading manufacturing complex, producing more than 20 percent of the country's annual output.

Japan's second-largest industrial complex extends from the eastern end of the Seto Inland Sea, Japan's pivotal waterway, to the Nagoya area and includes the Kobe–Kyoto–Osaka triangle. This, the Kansai district, comes close to rivalling the Kanto area: it is a vast industrial region with steel mills, a major chemical industry, automobile manufacturing, shipbuilding, textile factories, and many other types of production.

Even after Japan lost its colonial empire with the end of World War II, its industries continued to be sustained by a large, highly skilled labour force (which, before recent wage increases, was relatively cheap). Japanese products dominated markets around the world and allowed Japanese industries to purchase needed raw materials virtually anywhere. Australia, for example, became one of Japan's leading suppliers. The availability of cheap semi-skilled labour has had an immense impact on regional industrial development. Even in an era of automated assembly lines and computerized processing, the prospect of a large, low-wage, trainable labour force continues to attract manufacturers. Japan's post-war success was based in large measure on the skills and the low wages of its labour force, which allowed manufacturers to flood foreign markets with low-priced goods. Into the 1950s, Japanese goods had little reputation for quality but were known for their affordability. However, Japan's factories then began to excel in quality as well. This development in turn led to higher prices, higher wages, and, inevitably, competition from countries where cheaper labour could be found.

EASTERN CHINA

Although some industrial growth occurred in China during the period of European colonial influence, and later during the Japanese occupation, China's major industrial expansion occurred during the communist period. When the communist planners took over in 1949, one of their first priorities was to develop China's resources and industries as rapidly as possible. China is a vast country and has a substantial resource base. The quality of its coal is good, the quantity enormous, and many of the deposits are near the surface and easily extracted. China's iron ores are not as productive and are generally of rather low grade, but new finds are regularly being made.

Until the early 1960s, Soviet planners helped promote China's communist-era industrial development. China was spatially constrained by the location of raw materials, the developments that had taken place before the 1949 communist takeover, the pattern of long-term urbanization in the country, the existing transportation network, and the eastern clustering of the population. In a manner similar to their erstwhile Soviet allies, China's rulers were determined to speed up the industrialization of the economy, and their decisions created several major and lesser industrial districts.

Under state-planning rules, the Northeast district (formerly known as Manchuria and called Dongbei in China today) became China's industrial heartland, a complex of heavy industries based on the region's coal and iron deposits located in the basin of the Liao River. Shenyang became the "Chinese Pittsburgh," with metallurgical, machine-making, engineering, and other large factories. Anshan, to the south, emerged as China's leading iron- and steel-producing centre. Harbin, China's northernmost large city, with more than 5.4 million inhabitants, produced textiles, farm equipment, and other light manufacturing of many kinds.

The second-largest industrial region in China, the Shanghai and Chang Jiang district, developed in and around the country's biggest city, Shanghai. The communist planners never allowed Shanghai to attain its full potential, often favouring the Beijing-Tianjin complex, but the Chang Jiang district, containing both Shanghai and Wuhan, rose to prominence and, by some measures, exceeded the Northeast as a contributor to the national economy. As **Figure 13.24** shows, still another industrial complex developed farther upstream along the Chang Jiang (Yangtze) River, focused on the city of Chongqing. Whether we view the Chang Jiang district as one industrial zone or more, it became a pacesetter for Chinese industrial growth, if not in terms of iron and steel production, then in terms of its diversified production and local specializations. Railroad cars, ships, books, foods, chemicals—an endless variety of products—come from the thriving Chang Jiang district.

China's enormous labour force and the country's low daily wage have persuaded thousands of companies to move their manufacturing to China, although rather than move the entire company, most typically shift production of component parts to China to lower the cost of the product (**Figure 13.25**). Thousands of companies take advantage of the lower wages and

FIGURE 13.24 Chang Jiang district, China. A major industrial belt grew along the Chang Jiang (Yangtze) River, from the Chang Jiang district and Shanghai to Chongqing. Adapted from *The World Factbook 2009* (Washington, DC: Central Intelligence Agency, 2009).

World Factbook/Central Intelligence Agency

Jianan Yu/Reuters/Landov

FIGURE 13.25 Made in China. An employee works on circuit boards at an electronic component factory in Hefei, Anhui province, China.

favourable tax regulations, which have transformed cities and towns in the region.

At the same time, the Northeast has become China's rust belt. Many of its state-run factories have been sold or closed, or are operating below capacity. Unemployment is high, and economic growth has stopped. Eventually, the Northeast is likely to recover because of its resources and its favourable geographic site. But under the new economic policies, the dynamic eastern and southern provinces have grown into major manufacturing belts and have changed the map of this part of the Pacific Rim. We must remember, as well, that such massive industrialization is not without social and environment consequences. As we read in Chapter 6, the Three Gorges Dam project, which was completed in 2011, displaced millions of people whose lands were flooded or appropriated. At the same time, 75 percent of China's energy production is still dependent on coal, and the automobile industry is booming. The resulting air pollution is staggering, and Western media is replete with images of the thick smog hanging over many of China's main cities.

GUEST FIELD NOTE

Shipbuilding in Penglai

Penglai, located at the northernmost tip of the Shandong peninsula, is known as the "Water Fortress" because of its fortified harbour, one of China's oldest military ports, built in 1376 under the Ming Dynasty. It has long been a popular tourist destination because of the beautiful Penglai Pavilion, which stands high above the sea (**Figure 13.26**). Built approximately 1,000 years ago, Penglai Pavilion is referred to as "a place of the gods" in Chinese mythology, and the legend of Eight Immortals Crossing the Sea is said to have taken place here. In this legend, eight immortals got drunk at the castle and crossed the sea using magic, without ships.

It is ironic, therefore, that when I arrived in Penglai in the late spring of 2009, it was because of the ships. To be specific,

© TAO Images Limited/Alamy

FIGURE 13.26 Penglai Pavilion.

I had flown to Penglai from Canada, a journey of more than 22 hours, because I am a sailor, and I was sent to bring a ship being built at the Penglai Bohai Shipyard Company across the Pacific to her future home on the Great Lakes. Shandong Province, where Penglai is located on the east coast of China, is fast becoming known for its shipbuilding industry. With a coastline of over 3,000 km, and 1,150 km of inland navigable waterways, the province has the highest concentration of seaports in China, with 473 seaport berths. Between 2006 and 2010, the provincial government invested nearly U.S.$7.2 billion to expand the shipbuilding industry, developing synchronous industries including shipbuilding, ship repair, ocean equipment manufacturing, yacht manufacturing, and other supporting industries. By 2010, 127 shipbuilders were active in the province (**Figure 13.27**).

Although Canada has a long and proud history of ship-building, from wooden sailing ships in 1606 to steel shipbuilding yards on the Great Lakes in the early 1900s, its scale has been greatly reduced since the end of World War II. Today, Canadian shipping companies are seeking opportunities to acquire new vessels in the most cost-efficient way possible; for many, this means turning to nations like China, where the availability of raw materials, proximity to the ocean, and lower labour costs make it ideal. In fact, Canada's largest shipping companies, including Canada Steamship Lines (CSL) and Algoma Central

FIGURE 13.27 **Shipbuilding in Shandong Province, China.**

© Guo Xulei/Xinhua Press/Corbis

Corporation, are opting to do business in China, with CSL's nine Trillium Class vessels and Algoma's eight Equinox vessels being built as of 2014. Other nations, such as the Netherlands, Germany, Singapore, Japan, and Pakistan, are also doing their shipbuilding business in Penglai province.

Sean Jowsey, Canadian ship captain

SOUTH AMERICA AND AFRICA

In other regions of the world, including South America and Africa, industrialization came much later. By World War II, Brazil had a strong textile industry, with nearly 3 million cotton spindles that supplied the textile manufacturing demands of that country as well as several others. However, it was not until the post-war boom that South America's industrial development became global in context, in large part thanks to the financial and technological support of the United States. Examples of South American industry are Volta Redonda steel works in Brazil; rayon and nylon production in Argentina; tire factories in Chile, Peru, Cuba, Colombia, Uruguay, and Venezuela; glass plants in various countries; and paper production in Mexico.

The less-developed nations of South America and Africa attempted to break out of the global division of labour, outlined earlier in this chapter (in which nations relying on the export of raw materials and the import of manufactured goods are particularly susceptible to market trends), and achieve modernization and economic growth by adopting some form of Import Substitution Industrialization (ISI). ISI consists of establishing domestic manufacturing facilities, facilitated by the support of governments, to produce substitutes for formerly imported manufactured goods. Through a series of policy instruments—including protective tariffs, preferential import exchange rates for imported raw materials, cheap loans, and infrastructure programs—ISI gave local industries the opportunity to grow in

what would otherwise be an increasingly global market. In Argentina, Brazil, Mexico, and Chile, the result was the growth of industrialization in agriculture, manufacturing, and construction, in part because the large populations of these countries could support high levels of consumption. Critics argue that ISI policies produced a massive debt crisis in many Latin American countries, as most of these countries turned to foreign loans and investments to fund industrialization. These problems persist today.

Africa, rich in natural resources, has been acutely implicated in the global division of labour between primary and secondary industrial practices. Today, Africa remains largely a primary industrial zone, with mineral and oil extraction being some of the most significant contributors to its economy. A well-known example of the cost of primary industrial practices in Africa is the diamond industry. Controversy erupted in the late 1990s when Global Witness (an international NGO, established in 1993, that works to break the links between natural resource exploitation, conflict, poverty, corruption, and human rights abuses worldwide) traced the role of diamonds in funding the civil war in Angola. Known as "blood diamonds" or "conflict diamonds" because they are used to fund violent human rights abuses and conflicts, the sale of these gems has been shown to have funded wars in Liberia, Sierra Leone, Democratic Republic of Congo, and Côte d'Ivoire. Work in the diamond mines is backbreaking and incredibly dangerous, but, driven by poverty and necessity, workers continue to toil in hazardous

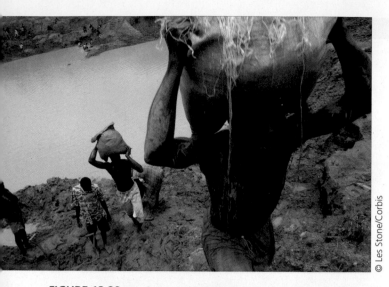

FIGURE 13.28 **Workers toil in diamond mines in Sierra Leone.**

conditions to produce diamonds for consumption in the Global North (**Figure 13.28**).

Only South Africa is considered a newly industrialized country (NIC) by global standards, with its GDP growth rate of 2.5 percent as of 2013. In the late 19th century, South Africa was a largely agricultural society, but with the discovery of diamond and gold deposits, it soon moved towards industrialization, fuelled by the British colonial control and development of diamond mines. Though there have been attempts at further industrial growth in South Africa, most of the country's economy remains dependent on primary industrial relations. China became South Africa's largest trading partner in 2009, with most of this trade involving raw materials exported from South Africa to China. Though both countries recognize that such a trade imbalance is not sustainable, and have pledged to correct the situation, as of 2014, their relationship remains one of raw material exportation.

MAIN POINTS 13.3 How Do Location Theories Explain Historical Patterns of Industrialization?

- Location theories, such as those put forward by Weber, attempt to explain the spatial organization of economic activities and the various factors influencing locational choices, such as transportation and labour costs, distance to market, and access to raw materials.

- Canadian manufacturing was initially a protected industrial base located in southern Ontario, although distinctly regional variations are evident in the organization of Canada's urban structure. Canadian manufacturing and industrial development is interwoven with the United States in a North American manufacturing belt that runs up the eastern seaboard of the United States and Canada. A variety of industries, from steel to chemicals and appliances to cars, make up this manufacturing belt.

- Prior to 1950, the major locational costs were those associated with transportation of raw materials and shipping goods to market. The four primary industrial regions—western and central Europe, eastern North America, Russia, and eastern Asia— reflect decisions related to these costs as well as the particular social, political, and historical circumstances of each region.

- The manufacturing regions of western Europe are largely the regions that experienced industrialization between the late 18th and early 20th centuries.

- Manufacturing and industrialization in eastern North America is grounded in the region's role as a colonial producer of raw materials for export to the "home" country. Urban patterns and transportation systems reflect this initial responsibility.

- In Russia, industrialization focused on manufacturing in the western part of Russia because this was home to the country's capital, Moscow. That city and its surrounding area offered an important local market, converging transport routes, a large labour force, and strong centrality.

- In eastern Asia, industrialization took root most strongly in Japan and China. While Japan is considered the dominant country in terms of industrialization, with its strong manufacturing belt and industrial development policies, China has also developed a strong industrial base since the communist party took power in 1949.

- In South America, industrialization occurred after World War II, through strategic domestic policy initiatives. In Africa, industrialization remains centred around the production and export of primary raw materials.

13.4 What Are the Spatial Implications of Changes in Industrial Production?

After World War II and the boom times of the 1950s, industrial production was restructured on both the local and global scale. Today, the world's major industrial regions still bear the marks of the transportation and communications technologies and skilled labour forces that were in place at that time. When methods of production change (e.g., become more efficient) or transportation improves (e.g., shift from water to rail), industries are able to make different locational choices, such as the growth of *maquiladora* or branch plant operations along the Mexican border with the United States. This means that companies such as General Motors, Fisher Price, and Acer Peripherals

FIGURE 13.29 Ford Model Ts ready for delivery. Henry Ford's assembly line system took hold worldwide and symbolizes the era of mass production. Ford became well known for his production and marketing technologies, as well as for his belief that workers should be paid enough to be able to afford the products they make.

can take advantage of lower labour costs, fewer environmental regulations, and lower taxes and import–export duties.

The manufacturing boom of the 20th century can be traced to early innovations in the production process. Perhaps the most significant of these innovations was the mass-production assembly line pioneered by Henry Ford, which allowed for the inexpensive production of consumer goods at a single site on a previously unknown scale (**Figure 13.29**). So significant was Ford's philosophy that the dominant mode of mass production that endured for much of the past century is known as **Fordist**.

> **Fordist** A highly organized and specialized system for organizing industrial production and labour. Named after automobile producer Henry Ford, Fordist production features assembly-line production of standardized components for mass production.

Economic geographers also see the Fordist system as including a set of political-economic structures. By this we mean the government ensures that the laws governing commercial enterprise support the economic system, and the structure of the financial system supports mass production by corporations. For example, the Bretton Woods agreement, put in place as part of the rebuilding effort after World War II, saw core countries adopt the gold standard and agree to peg the values of their currency to gold. This ensured these countries were working within the same monetary and financial systems, which supported their economic development and stability. Central to the Fordist system are economic theories developed by John Maynard Keynes, which advocated government intervention through the use of budget deficits to stimulate business activity and increase employment. Increased employment led to increased demand for consumer products, as well as social stability. At the same time, labour unions also experienced rapid growth from the 1930s to the 1950s, fighting for workers' rights to fair wages, benefits, and working conditions. During the height of Fordism, labour unions were very strong, which further contributed to economic stability and demand for consumer products. Both government policy and labour unions together strengthened the economy, balancing mass production with mass consumption.

Given the rapid changes brought about by the processes of globalization (see Chapter 2), the world economy has transitioned to what most economists and others call a **post-Fordist** system. Under the Fordist system, goods were mass-produced in one place. Raw materials were brought to the factory and the "good" (be it a car, television, or refrigerator) was assembled there. Post-Fordist processes are more flexible: the components of goods are made in different places around the globe and then brought together at different sites as needed to meet local market demand, "just in time."

Multinational companies play a major role in this system and are in a position to shift production to new sites when a given production site becomes uncompetitive. Post-Fordist production brings places closer together in time and space than would have been imaginable at the beginning of the 20th century.

Geographically, the easiest way to comprehend the dramatic changes in the way we think about time and space in the global economy is through the concept of time-space compression, which suggests that some places in the world are more connected through communication and transportation technologies than ever before (see Chapter 2). Fluctuations in the Tokyo stock market affect New York just hours, if not minutes, later. Overnight, marketing campaigns can turn a product innovation into a fad in far-flung corners of the globe. Kiwi fruit picked in New Zealand yesterday can be in the lunch boxes of boys and girls in Canada tomorrow. And decisions made in London can make or break a fast-developing deal over a transport link between Kenya and Tanzania.

Time-space compression has fundamentally altered the division of labour. When the world was less interconnected, most goods were produced close to the point of consumption. Thus, the major industrial belt in the United States was in the northeast, because coal and other raw materials were readily available there, and also because of the major concentration of the North American population in that region. Now, due to improved transportation and communications technologies, **just-in-time delivery** allows companies to keep just what they need for short-term production, and additional parts are shipped quickly when needed. The company no longer has to maintain a large inventory of components or products on-site in large warehouses. Corporations can draw from labour around the globe for different components of

> **Post-Fordist** World economic system characterized by a more flexible set of production practices in which goods are not mass-produced; in one place, instead, production has been accelerated and dispersed around the globe by multinational companies that shift production, outsourcing it around the world and bringing places closer together in time and space than would have been imaginable at the beginning of the 20th century.

> **Just-in-time delivery** Method of inventory management made possible by efficient transportation and communication systems, whereby companies keep on hand just what they need for near-term production, planning that what they need for longer-term production will arrive when needed.

Bettman/Corbis

> **Global division of labour**
> Phenomenon whereby corporations and others can draw from labour markets around the world, made possible by the compression of time and space through innovation in communication and transportation systems.

production, creating a **global division of labour**. For example, Kanban is an inventory and replenishment system used in "just in time" production, in which the manufacturing process does not begin until a customer order is in place. Drawing upon only the individual parts needed to make the finished product, inventory levels of individual parts are aligned with actual consumption, rather than production. Each individual piece is inspected for quality, so that the final product has been inspected at the level of its component parts, rather than just the end result. Toyota began applying the Kanban method in 1953 and, following its strict rules, has maintained high levels of quality within a "just in time" production model.

The major global economic players, such as General Motors, Philips, Union Carbide, and ExxonMobil, take advantage of low transportation costs, favourable governmental regulations, and expanding information technology to construct vast economic networks in which different facets of production are carried out in different places, allowing the company to benefit from the advantages of specific locations. This is substantially different from the spatial and structural organization of industries that located near their raw materials and their market and produced all components of the product in one place. Publicly traded companies (companies whose stock you can buy or sell on the stock exchange) are pressured by shareholders to grow their profits annually. One way to grow profits is to cut costs, and labour (i.e., wages, benefits, insurance) makes up a sizable proportion of production costs.

Multinational corporations such as Nike have moved the labour-intensive manufacturing aspects of their business, particularly assembly activities, to countries in the periphery, where labour is relatively inexpensive, regulations are few, and tax rates are low. The manufacturing that remains in the core is usually highly mechanized. Technologically sophisticated manufacturing also tends to be sited in the core, which has both the skilled labour supply and the supporting infrastructure. Research and development activities tend to be concentrated in the core, where high levels of education and access to technology are the norm.

The global division of labour has reshaped the role different economic sectors play within countries. With mechanized, highly efficient agriculture (see Chapter 9) and with the move of manufacturing jobs to the semi-periphery and periphery, core countries now have large labour forces employed in the tertiary sector of the economy. Supporting the global division of labour are elaborate trading networks and financial relations. Trade itself is a tertiary economic activity of considerable importance to the global economy. Regardless of where goods and their components are produced, consumption still takes place in the core and, increasingly, among the wealthy and middle classes of the semi-periphery. The newly industrializing countries of the semi-periphery send manufactured goods to the core (thus the "made in China" labels found on goods throughout North America). Trade flows among countries in the periphery are typically low because, for peripheral countries, the profitable flow is to the core. As the *Guest Field Note* by Heather Maguire suggests, companies that were not able to, or did not wish to, shift their operational organization in light of changing global forces, often were forced out of business, which was the case for Canada's Clairtone Sound Corporation.

GUEST FIELD NOTE

Clairtone Sound Corporation

Walking through the Design Exchange exhibit in Toronto in 2008, I came face to face with one of Canada's most successful, yet almost entirely forgotten, consumer electronics manufacturers. Clairtone Sound Corporation, founded in 1958 by Peter Münk and David Gilmour, was a Canadian-based manufacturer of consumer electronics, well known for innovative design and high quality. Munk's background in electronics and Gilmour's background in design led to the development of stereo consoles that reflected a European sensibility—Scandinavian-style teak and walnut consoles combined with high-quality sound equipment. Its award-winning design, Project G (**Figure 13.30**), attained international critical praise and became famous for its globe speakers and sleek image. Project G was also a Hollywood sensation, featured in such films as *The Graduate* and *Marriage on the Rocks*. Frank Sinatra and Hugh Hefner both owned a Clairtone. Oscar Peterson stated that his music sounded as good on a

clairtone.ca/photo DC Hillier

FIGURE 13.30 Clairtone Sound Corporation's Project G.

Clairtone as it did in a concert hall. Globally respected, Clairtone quickly became a sign of the times: sleek, modern, sophisticated. In 1966, sales topped $15 million, Clairtone employed nearly 1,000 people, and operations had moved from Toronto to a new plant in Stellarton, Nova Scotia, which produced both stereo units and televisions. The next year, Münk and Gilmour lost control of Clairtone, pushed out by Industrial Estates Limited, an economic development agency of the government of Nova Scotia. Within three years, Clairtone had effectively collapsed, and in 1971 the government of Nova Scotia permanently closed the doors of Clairtone and liquidated the assets. While there are myriad political and economic circumstances that led to the demise of Clairtone, central to its struggle was its made-in-Canada approach. While other manufacturers of consumer electronics, such as RCA, were by the mid-1960s seeking cheaper offshore manufacturing sites, Clairtone remained steadfast in its Canadian manufacturing philosophy.

Heather Maguire, York University

NEW INFLUENCES ON THE GEOGRAPHY OF MANUFACTURING

Over the last 30 years or so, new influences have been at work reshaping the locational choices of industries and manufacturing. All multinational companies (whether they produce televisions or anything else) are involved in designing products and finding buyers for the products. Many multinationals hire out the other steps in manufacturing, including extraction of raw materials, manufacturing, marketing, and distribution, to outside companies or subsidiaries. In the post-Fordist era, the major influences on industrial location include the low wages we have already discussed, intermodal transportation, regional and world trade agreements, and availability of energy.

IMPORTANCE OF TRANSPORTATION IN INDUSTRIAL LOCATION

Intermodal connections
Places where two or more modes of transportation meet (including air, road, rail, barge, and ship).

One factor we can map is transportation. Efficient transportation systems allow manufacturers to purchase raw materials from distant sources and distribute finished products to a widely dispersed population of consumers. Manufacturers desire maximum transport effectiveness at the lowest possible cost. They will also consider the availability of alternative systems in the event of emergencies (e.g., truck routes when rail service is interrupted). Since World War II, major developments in transportation have focused on improving **intermodal connections**, places where two or more modes of transportation (including air, road, rail, barge, and ship) meet, in order to ease the flow of goods and reduce the costs of transportation (see Chapter 12).

The current volume of resources and goods shipped around the globe daily could not be supported without the invention of the container shipping system, in which goods are packed in containers that are picked up by special mechanized cranes from a container ship at an intermodal connection and placed on the back of a semi-trailer truck, on a barge, or on a railroad car. This innovation lowered costs and increased flexibility, permitting many manufacturers to pay less attention to transportation in their location decisions. Refrigerated containers also facilitate the shipment of perishable goods around the globe.

In Canada, one of the most significant systems of transportation that is vital to industrial endeavours is the Great Lakes–St. Lawrence Seaway system (**Figure 13.31**). The history of this system dates back thousands of years, to First Nations trading routes. Spanning over 3,700 kilometres, Hwy H$_2$O, as

Air Photo Max Aerial Photography, www.airphotomax.com

FIGURE 13.31 Great Lakes–St. Lawrence Seaway system.
A westbound ship goes through the St-Lambert Lock, with the city of Montreal in the background. This lock is the gateway to the Great Lakes–St. Lawrence Seaway system.

it is known, comprises the St. Lawrence Seaway, the St. Lawrence River, and the Great Lakes and is a vital link between international shipping routes and the U.S. and Canadian industrial and agricultural heartlands, reaching approximately 25 percent of both countries' populations. The St. Lawrence Seaway opened in 1959 and moves such products as iron ore, coke, grain, coal, aggregate, and various chemicals, to name but a few. The efficiency of the system cannot be understated. One cargo ship can carry as much as 870 tractor-trailers and requires about 10 to 20 percent of the energy that trucks require.

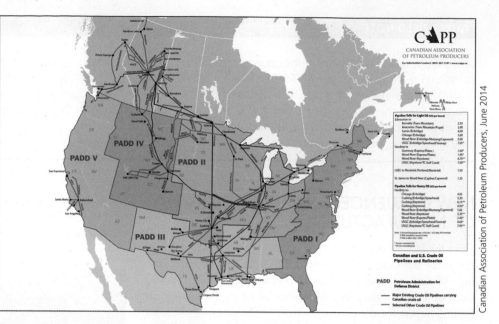

FIGURE 13.32 North American pipelines, June 2014. This map shows pipelines that carry crude oil between Canada and the United States.

Canadian Association of Petroleum Producers, June 2014

IMPORTANCE OF ENERGY IN INDUSTRIAL LOCATION

The role of energy supply as a factor in industrial location decisions has changed over time, in part because sources of energy have changed, but also because of changes in the infrastructure for transporting energy supplies. As discussed earlier in the chapter, during the Industrial Revolution, manufacturing plants were often established on or near coalfields because coal was the major source of energy. Through the 20th century, coal increasingly gave way to oil and gas as an energy source for industry, but major industrial complexes are not found near oil fields. Instead, a huge system of pipelines and tankers delivers oil and natural gas to manufacturing regions throughout the world. For some time during and after the global oil supply crises of the 1970s, fears of future increases in oil costs led some industries that require large amounts of electricity to move to sites where the climate is moderate and heating and air-conditioning costs are low. When the crisis waned, national energy-conservation goals were modified, and in the early 2000s the core countries' reliance on foreign energy resources was even greater than it had been in the 1970s.

Energy supply has become a less significant factor in industrial location, but securing an energy supply is an increasingly important national priority. Nowhere is this more true than in the United States. U.S. consumption of petroleum and natural gas today is about 27 percent and 37 percent, respectively, of the annual world total. By 2007, the United States required more than 20.6 million barrels of petroleum per day to keep its power plants, machinery, vehicles, aircraft, and ships functioning. However, U.S. production of oil in recent years has averaged about 10 percent of the world total. Even taking into account the known Alaskan potential, U.S. oil reserves are estimated to be only about 4 percent of the world total. In 2012, the country was the second-largest oil producer in the world (**Table 13.3**), but even with this level of production the United States remains heavily dependent on foreign oil supplies—including Canada's (**Figure 13.32**)—with all the uncertainties that involves.

Dependence on external fuel supplies affects three of the four principal regions of industrial development: the United States; Europe, which, despite discoveries of oil and gas in the North Sea, still depends on foreign shipments of petroleum; and Japan, which is almost totally dependent on oil from distant sources.

On the other side of the coin, countries with large reserves of oil and natural gas—Saudi Arabia, Kuwait, Iraq, Russia, and others—occupy a special position in the global economy. Of these countries, only Russia is a major industrial power, but they all played a key role in the industrial boom of the 20th century. And while oil has brought wealth to some in the Middle East, it has also ensured that outside powers, such as

TABLE 13.3	World Oil Production, 2012	
Country	Rank	Total Oil Production (in thousands of barrels per day)
Saudi Arabia	1	11,726
United States	2	11,117
Russia	3	10,397
China	4	4,372
Canada	5	3,856
Iran	6	3,518
United Arab Emirates	7	3,213
Iraq	8	2,987
Mexico	9	2,936
Kuwait	10	2,797
Brazil	11	2,652
Nigeria	12	2,524
Venezuela	13	2,489
Qatar	14	2,033
Norway	15	1,902

Data from U.S. Energy Information Administration.

the United States and Great Britain, are involved and invested in what happens in the region. This has often produced an uneasy relationship, at best, between countries in the Middle East and the major industrial powers of the West.

IMPORTANCE OF REGIONAL AND GLOBAL TRADE AGREEMENTS

The world economic structure and regional and national markets are affected by the movement of goods, services, labour, and money, which could not occur without the negotiation of trade agreements. In the years immediately following World War II, for example, many countries entered into the General Agreement on Tariffs and Trade (GATT), which worked to reduce barriers to

trade, starting in 1947. This liberalized the world economy and allowed for the free flow of goods among signatories. Regional trade agreements, such as NAFTA, influence where imported goods (and components of goods) are produced and sold.

In Canada, the Auto Pact, which the country signed with the United States in 1965, served to create a North American market for cars and trucks. At the time, the three major automobile companies had branch plants in Canada where they manufactured automobiles for the Canadian market. The Auto Pact allowed these companies to create a North American market and to compete more effectively with foreign producers. While the Auto Pact came to an end in 2001, it marked the beginning of the integration of the Canadian and American automobile markets. As **Figure 13.33** shows, we can understand

FIGURE 13.33 The North American auto plant corridor. The first auto manufacturing plants in North America were established in the northeast and spread north, south, and west from there. Adapted from Richard D. Vogel, *Monthly Review, 2007.*

Eric Thayer/Reuters/Landov

FIGURE 13.34 The abandoned Packard Motors plant, Detroit. The "Ruins of Detroit" are stark reminders of the effects of global capital movement, and examples of post-industrial landscapes and urban decay.

the development of the automobile manufacturing industry in North America in terms of three distinct periods. The first period, pre-1950, saw the establishment of the Big 3 automakers—Ford, General Motors, and Chrysler—in the United States. In the second period, from 1950 to 1989, the U.S. auto industry expanded into Canada and Mexico. The third period, from 1990 to 2006, saw the adoption of NAFTA, the extension of *maquiladora* manufacturing in Mexico, and the development of a globalized "corridor" running from north to south. Since 2006, we have witnessed the collapse and subsequent rebuilding of the North American automobile industry. Cities such as Detroit, once famous for its economic power and home to the major auto manufacturers in North America, are now being recast as part of the rust belt of America (**Figure 13.34**). Windsor, Ontario, known as the Automotive Capital of Canada, has been one of the hardest hit Canadian cities. In 2010, GM closed its last manufacturing plant in Windsor, thereby ending a 90-year relationship between Windsor and Detroit.

With the Free Trade Agreement of 1988, Canada and the United States agreed to develop an integrated North American economy. This agreement was replaced by NAFTA in 1994, which incorporated Mexico into the North American trading block. These agreements had a major impact on the structure and organization of the Canadian economy, including making Canada far more dependent on the United States. Canada is therefore much more susceptible to instability in the American economy, as has been the case in recent years. Canadian trade is increasingly oriented in a north-south direction rather than flowing east-west as it has done historically.

Similarly, governments have individual agreements with each other about production and imports, and most governments (153 states in 2008) are part of the World Trade Organization (WTO), which works to negotiate rules of trade among the member states. The WTO promotes freer trade by negotiating agreements among member states that, typically, dismantle import quota systems and discourage individual countries' protection of their domestically produced goods.

Agreements negotiated under the WTO are typically enacted in steps in order to avoid causing a major shock to any state's economy. In 2001, when the European Union (EU) and the United States agreed to allow China to become a member of the WTO, they also agreed to remove the quota system that restricts the importation of Chinese goods into Europe and the United States. Soon after these quotas were eliminated, both the United States and the EU issued "safeguard quotas" against Chinese imports. The safeguard quotas were part of the agreement that permitted China's admission to the WTO and were phased out in 2013 (12 years after accession). These safeguards slowed Chinese imports once again, buffering their impact on domestic producers.

In addition to the growth of the purview of the WTO, the proliferation of regional trade associations in the last two decades is unprecedented, as illustrated by the growing list of acronyms for regional trade associations: EU, NAFTA, MERCOSUR, SAFTA, CARICOM, ANDEAN AFTA, COMESA, to name but a few. The World Trade Organization estimates that there are close to 300 regional trade organizations, which are similar to bilateral agreements on trade between two countries, although they involve more than two countries. Most regional trade agreements encourage movement of production within the trade region and promote trade by diminishing or deleting trade quotas and tariffs among member countries. A regional trade agreement sets up a special free trade agreement among parties to the association, leaving non-member countries to trade through the rules of the WTO or an existing bilateral agreement. Whether regional or global, trade agreements directly affect the location of production and even what is produced in a place.

Canada's economy experienced considerable restructuring as a result of the various trade agreements and the Auto Pact in the 1980s and 1990s. Canada opened its borders to competition from American firms, and Canadian industry and manufacturing, particularly in central Canada, underwent a difficult transition. Canadian companies were forced to reduce the size of their labour force and to move some of their operations offshore to other countries where labour and other costs were lower. Canadian and American relations have been strained as a result of trade disputes over softwood lumber pricing and offshore fishing. Nevertheless, Canada has benefited from access to U.S. markets and from greater participation in the global economy.

TIME-SPACE COMPRESSION AND DEINDUSTRIALIZATION

The sensation that the world is shrinking is so strong that some commentators have proposed that we are entering an era characterized by the "end of geography," alluding to the idea that distance is no longer an important consideration in terms of the spatial organization of economic systems Some scholars argue that a combination of technological changes and developments in the global economy have reduced the significance of location and place to the point where they matter little. Geographers who study industrial production recognize that the nature and meaning of location and place have changed greatly in recent times, but they also note that these changes do not create an undifferentiated world. New production methods have reshaped the economic geography of the planet profoundly and rapidly. We need a greater understanding of how places have changed as a result of these new production methods and new corporate structures, as well as an examination of the networks and flows between global processes and local places.

Over the last 20 years, many manufacturing regions have experienced **deindustrialization**, a process by which companies move industrial jobs to other regions with relatively inexpensive labour, leaving the newly deindustrialized region to work through a period of high unemployment and, if possible, develop a service economy. At the same time, the places with lower labour costs and the right mix of laws attractive to businesses (often weak environmental laws and pro-free trade laws) become newly industrial regions. The new industrial regions emerge as shifts in politics, laws, capital flow, and labour availability occur.

> **Deindustrialization** Process by which companies move industrial jobs to other regions with cheaper labour, leaving the newly deindustrialized region to switch to a service economy and to work through a period of high unemployment.

Both Europe and the United States have large deindustrialized regions. In the United Kingdom, for example, the major industrial zones of Newcastle, Liverpool, and Manchester lost much of their industrial bases during the 1960s and 1970s. Similarly, the industrial zone of northeastern North America (around the Great Lakes) saw much of its industrial base disappear in the same time period as it lost steel-manufacturing jobs to areas of the world with lower wages. This region of North America, predominantly in the United States, which used to be called the Manufacturing Belt, is now commonly called the Rust Belt, evoking the image of long-abandoned, rusted-out steel factories (see the images of Bethlehem Steel and Detroit in this chapter).

The economic processes leading to deindustrialization in some parts of the world have led to industrialization in other parts of the world. More than two centuries after the onset of the Industrial Revolution, East Asia has become the cauldron of industrialization. Some of the economic policies we discussed in Chapter 11, such as structural adjustments and import quotas, encourage foreign direct investment in a country, and many draw industrial developers seeking to take advantage of economic breaks and inexpensive labour. From Japan to Guangdong and from South Korea to Singapore, the islands, countries, provinces, and cities fronting the Pacific Ocean are caught up in a frenzy of industrialization that has made the geographic term "Pacific Rim" synonymous with manufacturing.

Over the past decade, China has been pushing industrialization into the interior of the country. Economists have highlighted the growth of China's industrial economy and the drive to spread the wealth into the interior of the country as well as the coastal export-oriented zones. On the coast, Shanghai recently trumped the Netherlands' Rotterdam as the world's busiest port, but the Chinese government's new focus is on generating greater economic activity in the interior.

China is a major recipient of industrial work that is **outsourced** or moved **offshore**. Each of the steps in commodity production that used to take place within the confines of a single factory is now often outsourced to suppliers, which focus their production and offer cost savings. When outsourced work is located outside the originating country, it has gone "offshore." The movement of industry into China's interior will likely occur through the outsourcing of production from China's coasts to the interior.

> **Outsource** With reference to production, to turn over in part or in total to a third party.
>
> **Offshore** With reference to production, to outsource to a third party located outside of the country.

MAIN POINTS 13.4 What Are the Spatial Implications of Changes in Industrial Production?

- After World War II and the boom years of the 1950s, changes in transportation and communication technologies altered methods of production as the world's manufacturing industries shifted from Fordist to post-Fordist techniques, changing industries' locational choices.

- Due to time-space compression, industries do not need to be close to their raw materials or their marketplace and can draw on labour from around the globe, resulting in a global division of labour. Developments in transportation systems, from container transport to mechanization, have not only increased the flow of goods and services but also altered the location patterns of industry and manufacturing.

- Major industries now tend to locate labour-intensive manufacturing to peripheral countries, where labour is relatively inexpensive—a practice known as outsourcing—and

taxes and costly environmental regulations are relatively low. Conversely, research and development activities remain in core countries, where there are high levels of education and access to technology. Major consumption still remains in the core, although the growing middle class in the semi-periphery is increasing consumption there.

- While technological innovation has been key to changing locational choices for industry and manufacturing, new regional and global trade agreements and organizations such as NAFTA, the EU, and the World Trade Organization have also had an impact. Reducing trade barriers changes the direction, volume, and flow of goods, to the benefit of some regions over others. Further, access to inexpensive energy in the form of oil, gas, coal, and electricity is also becoming a major factor in manufacturing and industrial locational choices.

13.5 What Is the Service Economy, and Where Are Services Concentrated?

By the end of World War II, the increasing saturation of consumer markets, the tremendous growth in governmental activity, rising labour activism, and declines in the cost of transportation and communication began to challenge the Fordist economic structure. The challenge shifted into high gear in the early 1970s, when a sharp rise in oil prices during a period of international financial instability and inflation produced a dramatic downturn in the global economy. Under these circumstances, it became increasingly difficult for the core industrial regions to sustain their competitive advantage without significant readjustment. That readjustment took the form of mechanization and the development of service and information industries. These changes, along with the need for new markets and the growth of multinational concerns, brought about a post-industrial or post-Fordist economic order in many of the core economies.

Service industries (tertiary industries) do not generate an actual, tangible product; instead, they encompass the range of services that are found in modern societies. So many different types of activities can be thought of as service activities that, as we discussed at the beginning of this chapter, specialized aspects of the service economy are given their own designations: quaternary industries collect, process, and manipulate information and capital (e.g., financial, administrative, insurance, legal, and computer services) and quinary industries facilitate complex decision-making and the advancement of human capacities (e.g., scientific research, higher education, high-level management).

Distinguishing among types of services is useful, given the extraordinary growth in the size and complexity of the service sector. In the global economic core, service industries employ more workers than the primary and secondary industries combined, yet these service industries range from small-scale retailing to tourism services to research on the causes of cancer. Placing all these activities in a single category doesn't seem helpful. Specificity in terminology is also useful in highlighting different phases in the development of the service sector. In the early decades of the 20th century, the domestic and quasi-domestic tertiary industries were experiencing rapid growth in the industrialized world. With the approach of World War II, the quaternary sector began expanding rapidly, and this expansion continued after the war. During the last three decades, both the quaternary and quinary sectors have experienced very rapid growth, giving greater meaning to the term "post-industrial."

The expanding service sector in the core economies is only one aspect of the changing global economy. Accompanying, and in some cases driving, this expansion are several other developments that have already been mentioned: the increasing mechanization of production, particularly in manufacturing enterprises operating in the core; the growth of large multinational corporations; and the dispersal of the production process, with components for complex products such as automobiles and consumer electronics coming from factories in many different countries.

GUEST FIELD NOTE

Women's Work

In the post-industrial North American landscape, the broad umbrella of "service sector work" can be understood in many ways. Work in the so-called information society produces no tangible good; yet in our current economy, this work dominates the employment statistics. In Canada, 78 percent of all work is service-sector-based, and the statistics are even higher in the United States, at 86 percent. While images of post-industrial landscapes are dotted with abandoned factories and hard-hit factory towns, there seems to be far less imagery of the people whose jobs are lost as a result of deindustrialization and the rise of service-sector work. One example of the brute reality of service work is documented in the PBS *Frontline* series *Is Walmart Good For America?* Tracing the relationship between job losses in the United States and the growing demand for cheap consumer products, the series explores the shift in power, whereby for the first time in U.S. history, retailers are more powerful than manufacturers.

Walmart is the largest employer in the United States, employing upwards of 1.4 million people, two-thirds of whom are women (**Figure 13.35**). The average "associate" earns $11.75 per hour, or $20,744 per year, well under the poverty line of $22,000. While this hourly rate is above the minimum

FIGURE 13.35 Walmart associates.

wage, it nevertheless is reflective of a troubling trend in service-based sectors: service work generally pays less than manufacturing jobs, and more women tend to be employed in service work. Other service-related fields reveal similar "pink collar ghettos"— personal support work, call centres, clerical work, and bank tellers are all examples of often low-wage, service-sector work that is largely done by women. Gender imbalances in service-sector work are important to consider, because broad economic shifts restructure work and home life as women leave the home to take up these service-sector jobs. As geographers Kate Boyer and Kim England have argued in their studies on gender in the workplace, we must remember that women are not one monolithic group. The experiences of service-sector work are uneven not only in terms of gender, but also in terms of race, ethnicity, age, ability, and sexuality.

GEOGRAPHICAL DIMENSIONS OF THE SERVICE ECONOMY

Deindustrialization and the growth of the service economy unfolded in the context of a world economy that was already characterized by wide socio-economic disparities. Only areas that have industry can deindustrialize, of course, and at the global scale, the wealthier industrial regions were the most successful in establishing a post-industrial service economy. Deindustrialization describes a sustained decline in industrial activities, including manufacturing, which has a negative impact on output and employment. What is often left behind are the physical plants and infrastructure such as factories, warehouses, and industrial offices and buildings that are difficult to redevelop. We should not be surprised that deindustrialization did little to change the basic disparities between core and periphery that have long characterized the global economy. Indeed, even in the manufacturing realm, mechanization and innovative production strategies have allowed the core industrial regions to retain their dominance. In the first decade of the 21st century, eastern Asia, western Russia and Ukraine, western Europe, and North America still account for well over 75 percent of the world's total output of manufactured goods.

Despite its continued dominance in the manufacturing arena, the core has experienced some wrenching changes associated with the economic shifts of the past three decades. Anyone who has ever spent time in northern Indiana, the British Midlands, or Silesia (southern Poland and northeastern Czech Republic) knows that there are pockets of significant hardship within the core. These examples serve to remind us that not all deindustrialized regions, not even those in the core, are finding their way into the tertiary sector. Location, albeit often defined in new ways, affects where and what kinds of service economies are developed.

Some secondary industrial regions have made the transition to a service economy while retaining their manufacturing base. The **Sunbelt** is the southern region of the United States, stretching from Florida and Georgia through California. The population and economy of the Sunbelt have grown over the last few decades as companies from the service sector choose to locate in areas such as Atlanta and Phoenix, where

> **Sunbelt** The southern and southwestern regions of the United States.

the climate is warm and the local laws welcome their presence. The eastern part of the Sunbelt served as a secondary industrial region, with Birmingham, Alabama, developing an iron and steel economy, and Atlanta an industrial economy around cotton, tobacco, and furniture. In recent decades, high-tech and financial industries changed the economy and landscape of the Sunbelt, as can be seen in the toponyms of stadiums in the region, such as Alltel Stadium in Jacksonville, Florida; Bank of America Stadium in Charlotte, North Carolina; and Bank One Ballpark in Phoenix, Arizona.

NEW INFLUENCES ON SERVICE INDUSTRY LOCATION

With the striking growth of the service sector and information technologies, new factors have come into play that affect patterns of economic activity. Most service industries are not tied to raw materials and do not need large amounts of energy. Hence, those factors of production are markedly less important for service industries than for traditional manufacturing concerns. Market accessibility is more relevant for the service sector, but advances in telecommunications have rendered even that factor less important for some types of service industries.

To understand the new influences on the location of services, it is useful to go back to our distinction between tertiary, quaternary, and quinary industries. Tertiary services related to transportation and communication are closely tied to population patterns and to the location of primary and secondary industries. As the basic facilitators of interaction, they are strongly linked to the basic geography of production and consumption. Other tertiary services—restaurants, hotels, and retail establishments—are influenced mainly by market considerations. If they are located far from their consumers, they are unlikely to succeed.

Employing technologies such as geographic information systems (GIS) and remote sensing (see Chapter 1), economic geographers working for corporations use this understanding to model the best locations for new businesses, office complexes, government centres, or transportation connections. Major retailers not only shape the landscapes of the places where they choose to put stores, but they also change the landscapes of their hometowns, the location of their headquarters. An extreme example of this is Walmart's headquarters in Bentonville, Arkansas. If producers of consumer products want to sell their goods in

Walmart stores, they must travel to Bentonville, Arkansas, to negotiate deals with Walmart. In order to provide low prices to consumers, Walmart negotiates very low prices with major producers. To create lower-priced products, companies have moved production abroad, and to create good relationships with the world's number one retailer (with sales of $475.29 billion in fiscal year 2014), companies have moved into Bentonville, Arkansas.

The locational influences on quaternary services—high-level services that collect, process, and manipulate information and capital—are more diverse. Some of these services are strongly tied to a particular geographical locus of economic activity. Retail banking and various types of administrative services require a high level of interpersonal contact and therefore tend to be located near the businesses they are serving. Other types of quaternary services, however, can operate almost anywhere as long as they have access to digital processing equipment and telecommunications. When you send in your credit card bill, it is unlikely to go to the city where the headquarters of the issuing bank is located. Instead, it will go to North Dakota, South Dakota, Nebraska, or Colorado. Similarly, many "back-office" tasks related to insurance are performed in places such as Des Moines, Iowa, rather than Chicago or Hartford. Many of the call centres for technical help for computers and related industries (e.g., software, hardware) are located in India and the Philippines. With relatively high levels of college attainment, vast numbers of English speakers, and phones routed through the Internet, "help desks" need not be located down the hall or even down the street. These location curiosities occur because technological advances in the telecommunications sector have made it possible for all sorts of quaternary industries to be located far away from either producers or consumers. What matters most is infrastructure, a workforce that is sufficiently skilled but not too expensive, and favourable tax rates.

Those who work in the quinary sector tend to be concentrated around nodes of quinary activity—seats of government, universities, and corporate headquarters. Corporate headquarters tend to be located in large metropolitan areas, whereas seats of government and universities can be found in places that were chosen long ago as appropriate sites for administrative or educational activities based on cultural values or political compromises. The American ideal of the university town (which originated in Germany) led to the establishment of many universities at a distance from major commercial and population centres, in such towns as Champaign–Urbana, Illinois; Norman, Oklahoma; and Eugene, Oregon. Political compromises led to the establishment of major seats of government in small towns. Ottawa and Canberra (in Australia) are examples of this phenomenon. The point is that historical location decisions influence the geography of the quinary sector, and university professors and government officials are not the only ones affected. All sorts of high-level research and development activities are located on the fringes of universities, and a host of specialized consultants are concentrated around governmental centres. These then become major nodes of quinary activity.

HIGH-TECHNOLOGY CORRIDORS

A high-technology corridor is an area designated by local or state government to benefit from lower taxes and high-technology infrastructure with the goal of providing high-technology jobs to the local population. The goal of a high-technology corridor is to attract designers of computers, semiconductors, telecommunications, sophisticated medical equipment, and the like.

California's Silicon Valley is a well-known example of a high-technology corridor. Several decades ago, a number of innovative technology companies located their research and development activities in the area around the University of California, Berkeley, and Stanford University near San Francisco, California. The companies were attracted by the prospect of developing links with existing research communities and the availability of a highly educated workforce. Once some high-technology businesses located in the Silicon Valley, others were attracted as well. Today, Silicon Valley is home to dozens of computer companies, many of which are familiar to the computer literate (such as Cisco Systems, Adobe, Hewlett-Packard, Intel, and IBM) (**Figure 13.36**). The resulting collection of high-technology industries produced what Manuel Castells,

Silicon Valley Map

FIGURE 13.36 Silicon Valley, California. This map illustrates the concentration of high technology industries in the Silicon Valley region of California.

Technopole Centres or nodes of high-technology research and activity around which a high-technology corridor is sometimes established.

Peter Hall, and John Hutriyk call a **technopole**. These are locations planned for high technology, where agglomeration built on a synergy among technological companies occurs. A similar sort of technopole developed outside Boston, where the concentration of technology-based businesses close to Harvard and the Massachusetts Institute of Technology gave rise to what is called the Route 128 high-technology corridor. The Route 128 corridor has largely been supported by the federal government rather than the local government, which supports many other technopoles.

Technopoles can be found in a number of countries in western Europe and eastern Asia, as well as in North America and Australia. Few are on the scale of Silicon Valley, but they are noticeable elements of the economic landscape. Many of them have sprung up on the edges of good-sized cities, particularly near airports. In Brussels, Belgium, for example, the route into the city from the airport passes an array of buildings occupied by computer, communication, and electronics firms. In Washington, D.C., the route from Dulles International Airport (located in the Virginia suburbs) to the city passes the headquarters of such companies as AOL, MCI, and Orbital Sciences. It's known as the Dulles Corridor. In the Telecom Corridor of Plano-Richardson, just outside Dallas, Texas, telecom companies such as Nortel and Ericsson have taken root, but so too have numerous high-technology companies that are not telecom related. In each of these technopoles, the presence of the major multinational companies attracts other start up companies hoping to become major companies, provide services to major companies, or be bought by major companies. In Canada,

Research In Motion (RIM) Technologies, maker of the BlackBerry, was established in Waterloo, Ontario, in 1984. Since then, the region, comprising the cities of Kitchener–Waterloo, Cambridge, and London, and containing three universities (University of Waterloo, Wilfrid Laurier University, and University of Western Ontario), has become a technology hub, attracting other high-tech companies and related industries.

Many of the technology firms are multinationals. Like their counterparts in other countries, they function in an information environment and market their products all over the world. Being near raw materials or even a particular market is unimportant for these firms; what matters to them is proximity to major networks of transportation and communication. High-technology industries have become such an important symbol of the post-industrial world that local, regional, and national governments often implement aggressive policies to attract firms in this sector. These industries are thought to be pollution free and to offer positive benefits for the communities in which they are located. Bidding wars sometimes develop between localities seeking to attract such industries. Although high-technology industries do indeed bring a variety of economic benefits, they have some drawbacks as well. Communities that have attracted production facilities find that the manufacture of computer chips, semiconductors, and the like requires toxic chemicals and large quantities of water. Even research-oriented establishments sometimes have negative environmental impacts in that land must be cleared and buildings constructed to house them. Despite these drawbacks, the high technology sector is clearly here to stay, and areas that can tap into it are likely to find themselves in an advantageous economic position in the coming years.

MAIN POINTS 13.5 What Is the Service Economy, and Where Are Services Concentrated?

- Tertiary or service industries experienced substantial changes in the last 30 years. They now encompass a wide variety of activities (outlined in Table 13.1). As deindustrialization—a decline in industrial activities—has taken place in core countries, many of these economies, including Canada's, are now considered post-industrial. This has meant a substantial loss in manufacturing jobs and a need to develop a service economy as manufacturing processes relocated to peripheral and semi-peripheral nations.

- Service industries include secondary, tertiary, quaternary, and quinary industries. It is important to look at the specifics of each type of industry to understand the factors influencing locational choices.

- Core countries have experienced striking growth in service-sector and information technologies, and there are new

factors in play in terms of locational choices. Service industries are not tied to raw materials and do not need large amounts of energy. These industries are more closely tied to the basic geography of production and consumption; that is, they need to be located near their consumers and are strongly influenced by market forces.

- With advanced technologies, not all aspects of service-sector industries need to be located near their customers. Many companies place their "back office" activities (e.g., bookkeeping, accounting, and human resources) in the suburbs, where office space, transportation, and parking are less expensive. Further, service-sector communications services can be located anywhere in the world.

SUMMARY

Economic activities are classified by what is produced and are generally divided into primary, secondary, tertiary, quaternary, and quinary. Economies are categorized by their stages of development. Pre-industrial economies are largely composed of primary activities, while second-stage economies develop a manufacturing sector that has a greater output than the primary sector. The tertiary or post-industrial stage is an economy with most of the labour force engaged in tertiary, quaternary, and quinary activities. The world's core countries are largely post-industrial.

The Industrial Revolution took place in the 18th and 19th centuries and fundamentally transformed the world geographically, economically, politically, and socially. Industrial production began some 3,000 years before the Industrial Revolution, with trade along the Silk Routes. Rapid technological innovation led to advances in medicine, science, and new energy sources. Colonial and imperial exploration created new networks and flows between people and places and established the foundation of the current world economy. Advances in iron and coal production, and the invention of the steam engine, electricity, and modern manufacturing techniques, created manufacturing economies in England and at several sites in Europe and North America. Locational choices in this period were largely based on accessibility to raw materials and transportation systems.

Geographers, economists, and others have been particularly interested in developing models that can accurately forecast the spatial organization of manufacturing and industry. Weber's model takes into account a variety of factors influencing locational choices, such as labour costs, profitability, distance to market, agglomerations, and competitors' locations. Models such as these were useful for understanding the locational choices of the world's major industrial regions before 1950.

After the end of World War II and the boom years of the 1950s, manufacturing industries underwent substantial changes worldwide. Methods of production evolved from Fordist to post-Fordist as a result of rapid changes in technologies, communications, and transportation. These changes have resulted in time-space compression, which means that some places are more connected, changing the relationship between people,

businesses, and places. This has fundamentally altered the global division of labour so that companies can now locate any aspect of their production process in any part of the world with the least-expensive labour and production costs. Many labour-intensive industries have located to peripheral and semi-peripheral countries, with research and development remaining in core countries. Advances in transportation (e.g., air transport and container shipping), as well as energy needs, also influence locational choices.

These changing industrial location choices mean that many of the places where industrialization first took hold have since become deindustrialized, through the relocation of manufacturing plants, the outsourcing of steps of the production process domestically and offshore, or both. With changing economies, places change. Some urban centres now look like ghost towns, serving merely as a reminder that industrialization took place there. Others have booming economies and are thriving, having retained industry or successfully cultivated a service economy. Other places are still redefining themselves. (In Chapter 6, we considered another lasting effect of industrialization and deindustrialization: environmental change.)

The service economy has also changed in the post-World War II period. With the shock of the oil crisis in the 1970s and deindustrialization, economic redevelopment fostered growth in the service and information sectors, which encompass a range of employment from part-time retailing and restaurant staff to accounting, engineering, and high technology. In considering the locational choices of the service sector, it is important to focus on the particularities of the business under consideration. Most service industries are not tied to raw materials and do not need large amounts of energy. Accessibility to customers is often more relevant for the service sector, but advances in telecommunications mean that even these businesses can choose to locate aspects of their operations far from the actual marketplace, with back offices in the suburbs and call and help centres located offshore. The spatial organization of economic activities not only varies from place to place and industry to industry, but also has a distinctive historical organization across a variety of scales.

DISCUSSION AND REVIEW QUESTIONS

1. To understand the geography of economic activities, scholars have organized them into a variety of sectors. What are these sectors and with what type of economic activities are they associated? How does this framework apply to Canada's economic organization? Which particular set of economic activities predominate where you live?

2. Alfred Weber's theories and models provided an important means for studying industrial location. Discuss the primary factors of his model and provide a specific regional example that can be explained through Weber's theory.

3. Compare and contrast the Fordist with the post-Fordist industrial model. How have each shaped the processes and geography of industrialization in the last 100 years?

4. What are the "new influences" that are changing the scope and geography of manufacturing? Discuss how each has specifically affected the geography of manufacturing in Canada.

5. The expanding service sector in the core economy is one aspect of the changing global economy. What are the factors that have driven this change? How has the shift to a service economy affected the geography of the core?

GEOGRAPHIC CONCEPTS

agglomeration   380
deagglomeration   380
deindustrialization   399
distance decay   379
Fordist   393
friction of distance   379
global division of labour   394
Industrial Revolution   374
intermodal connections   395
just-in-time delivery   393
least cost theory   379
location theory   379
offshore   399

outsource   399
post-Fordist   393
post-industrial economy   373
primary activities   371
primary industrial regions   380
quaternary sector   372
quinary sector   372
Sunbelt   401
secondary activities   371
technopole   403
tertiary activities   372
tertiary sector   372
variable costs   379

ADDITIONAL RESOURCES ON-LINE

Ecojustice Canada: www.ecojustice.ca

About the port of Rotterdam: www.portofrotterdam.com

About Walmart's influence on Bentonville, Arkansas: www.pbs.org/wgbh/pages/frontline/shows/walmart

Canadian Steel Producers Association (CSPA): http://canadiansteel.ca

World Steel Association: www.worldsteel.org

Clairtone Sound Corporation: www.clairtone.ca

About Silicon Valley: www.siliconvalley.com

European Union: http://europa.eu

About the North American Free Trade Agreement: www.international.gc.ca/trade-agreements-accords-commerciaux/agr-acc/nafta-alena/index.aspx?view=d&lang=eng

APPENDIX A

MAPS

The geographer's greatest ally is the map. Maps can present enormous amounts of information very effectively, and can be used to establish theories and solve problems. Furthermore, maps often are fascinating, revealing things no other medium can. It has been said that if a picture is worth a thousand words, a map is worth a million.

Maps can be fascinating, but they often do not get the attention they deserve. You may spend 20 minutes carefully reading a page of text, but how often have you spent 20 minutes with a page-size map, studying what it reveals? No caption and no paragraph of text can begin to summarize what a map may show; it is up to the reader to make the best use of it. For example, in Chapter 4 on population issues, we study several maps that depict the human condition by country, in terms of birth rate, infant mortality, and life expectancy. In the text, we can refer only to highlights (and low points) on those maps. But make a point of looking beyond the main issue to get a sense of the global distributions these maps represent. It is part of an intangible but important process: to enhance your mental map of this world.

While on the topic of maps, we should remind ourselves that a map—any map—is an incomplete representation of reality. In the first place, the map is smaller than the real world it represents. Second, it must depict the curved surface of our world on a flat plane; for example, a page of this book. And third, it must contain symbols to convey the information that must be transmitted to the reader. These are the three fundamental properties of all maps: scale, projection, and symbols.

Understanding these basics helps us interpret maps while avoiding their pitfalls. Some maps look so convincing that we may not question them as we would a paragraph of text. Yet maps, by their very nature, to some extent distort reality. At the very least, we should be aware that maps are imperfect representations and are often created by entities with particular interests or purposes (see the field note by Jason Grek Martin in Chapter 3). Most of the time, such distortion is necessary and does not invalidate the map's message. But some maps are drawn deliberately to mislead. Propaganda maps, for example, may exaggerate or distort reality to promote political aims (**Figure A.1**). We should also be alert to cartographic mistakes when we read maps. The proper use of scale, projection, and symbolization ensures that a map is as accurate as it can be made.

FIGURE A.1 Propaganda map. Hark! Hark! The Dogs Do Bark! Serio-Comique Map of Europe at War (London, 1914).

Map Scale

The scale of a map reveals how much the real world has been reduced to fit on the page or screen on which it appears. It is the ratio between an actual distance on the ground and the length given to that distance on the map, using the same units of measurement. This ratio is often represented as a fraction (e.g., 1:10,000 or 1/10,000). This means that one unit on the map represents 10,000 such units in the real world. One centimetre on the map would actually represent 10,000 cm or 100 m. Such a scale would be useful when mapping a city's downtown area, but it would be much too large for the map of an entire province. As the real-world area we want to map gets larger, we must make our map scale smaller. As small as the fraction 1/10,000 seems in terms of distance, it still is 10 times as large as 1/100,000, and 100 times as large as 1/1,000,000. If the world maps in this book had fractional scales, they would be even smaller. A large-scale map can contain much more detail and be far more representative of the real world than a small-scale map. Look at it this way: when we devote almost a full page of this book to a map of a major city (**Figure A.2**), we are able to represent the layout of that city in considerable detail. But if the entire continental realm in which that city is located must be represented on a single page, the city becomes just a large dot on that small-scale map, and the detail is lost in favour of larger-area coverage (**Figure A.3**). So the selection of scale depends on the objective of the map.

But when you examine the maps in this book, you will note that most, if not all, of them have scales that are not given as ratios or fractions, but in graphic form. This method of representing map scale is convenient from several viewpoints. Using the edge of a piece of paper and marking the scale bar's length, the map reader can quickly—without calculation—determine approximate distances. And if a map is enlarged or reduced in reproduction, the scale bar is enlarged or reduced with it and remains accurate. That, of course, is not true of a ratio or fractional scale. Graphic scales, therefore, are preferred in this book.

FIGURE A.2 Large-scale map. The layout of a major city can be shown in considerable detail at this large scale.

FIGURE A.3 Small-scale map. This type of map allows display of a larger area, but with less local detail.

Map Projections

For centuries cartographers have faced the challenge of map projection—the representation of the spherical Earth, or part of it, on a flat surface. To get the job done, there had to be a frame of reference on the globe itself, a grid system that could be transferred to the flat page. Any modern globe shows that system: a set of horizontal lines, usually at 10-degree intervals

north and south from the equator, called parallels, and another set of vertical lines, converging on the poles, often shown at 15-degree intervals and called meridians (see *Numbering the Grid Lines*). On the spherical globe, parallels and meridians intersect at right angles (**Figure A.4**).

But what happens when these lines of latitude (parallels) and longitude (meridians) are drawn to intersect at right angles on a flat piece of paper? At the equator, the representation of the real world is relatively accurate. But go toward the poles,

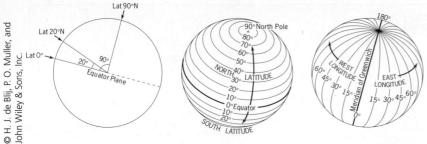

FIGURE A.4 Numbering of grid lines.

and distortion grows with every degree until, in the northern and southern higher latitudes, the continents appear not only stretched out but also misshapen (**Figure A.5**). Because the meridians cannot be made to converge in the polar areas, this projection makes Antarctica look like a giant, globe-girdling landmass.

Looking at this representation of the world, you might believe that it could serve no useful purpose. But in fact, the Mercator projection, invented in 1569 by Gerardus Mercator, a Flemish cartographer, had (and has) a very particular function. Because parallels and meridians cross (as they do on the spherical globe's grid) at right angles, direction is true everywhere on this map. Thus the Mercator projection enabled navigators to maintain an accurate course at sea simply by adhering to compass directions and plotting straight lines. It is used for that purpose to this day.

The spatial distortion of the Mercator projection serves to remind us that scale and projection are interconnected. What scale fraction or graphic scale bar could be used here? A scale

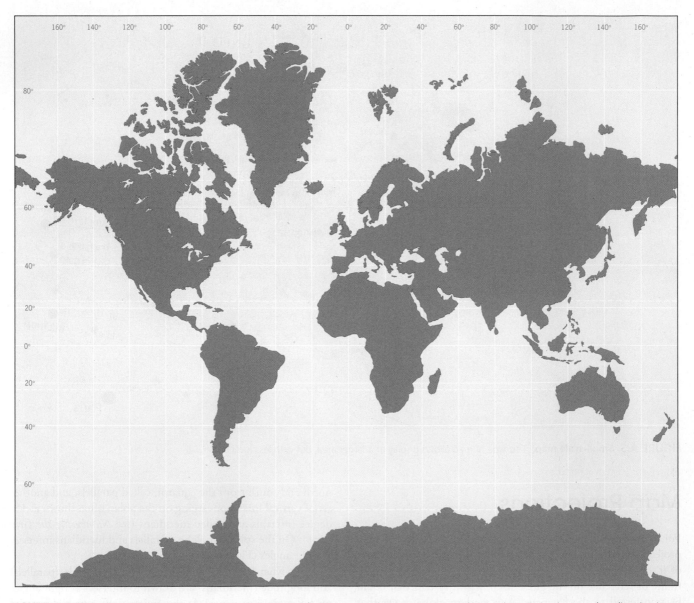

FIGURE A.5 Mercator's projection. Mercator's projection greatly exaggerates the size and shape of higher-latitude landmasses, but direction is true everywhere on this map.

Numbering the Grid Lines

When cartographers girdled the globe with their imaginary grid lines, they had to identify each line by number; that is, by degree. For the (horizontal) latitude lines, that was easy: the equator, which bisects the Earth midway between the poles, was designated as 0° (zero degree) Latitude, and all parallels north and south of the equator were designated by their angular position (see Figure A.4). The parallel midway between the equator and the pole, thus, is 45° North Latitude in the Northern Hemisphere and 45° South Latitude in the Southern Hemisphere.

But the (vertical) longitude lines presented no such easy solution. Among the parallels, the equator is the only one to divide the Earth into equal halves, but all meridians do this. During the second half of the nineteenth century, maps with conflicting numbers multiplied, and it was clear that a solution was needed. The most powerful country at the time was Britain, and in 1884, an international agreement was reached whereby the meridian drawn through the Royal Observatory in Greenwich, England, would be the prime meridian, 0° (zero degree) Longitude. All meridians east and west of the prime meridian could

now be designated by number, from 0° to 180° East and West Longitude. If you go to Greenwich, you can walk up the steep hill to the Observatory, and stand with one foot on either side of the prime meridian, a solid red line just like you would see on most maps (**Figure A.6**).

FIGURE A.6. **The prime meridian, Greenwich, England.**

that would be accurate at the equator on a Mercator map would be quite inaccurate at higher latitudes. So the distortion that is an inevitable by-product of any map projection also affects map scales.

One might imagine that the spatial (areal) distortion of the Mercator projection is so obvious that no one would use it to represent the world's countries. But in fact, many popular atlas maps (Mercator also introduced the term "atlas" to describe a collection of maps) and wall maps still use a Mercator for such purposes. The American National Geographic Society published its world maps on a Mercator projection until 1988, when it finally abandoned the practice in favour of a projection developed by the American cartographer Arthur Robinson (**Figure A.7**). During the news conference at which the change was announced, a questioner rose to pursue a point: Why had the Society waited so long to make this change? Was it because the distortion inherent in the Mercator projection made American and European middle-latitude countries large, compared to tropical countries in Africa and elsewhere? Although that was not the goal of the National Geographic Society, the questioner clearly understood the misleading subtleties inherent even in so apparently neutral a device as a map projection.

The Mercator projection is one of a group of projections called cylindrical projections. Imagine the globe's lines of latitude and longitude represented by a wire grid, at the centre of which we place a bright light. Wrap a piece of photographic paper around the wire grid, extending it well

beyond the north and south poles, flash the bulb, and the photographic image will be that of a Mercator projection (**Figure A.8**). We could do the same after placing a cone-shaped piece of paper over each hemisphere, touching the grid, say, at the 40th parallel north and south; the result would be a conic projection (**Figure A.9**). If we wanted a map of North America or Europe, a form of conic projection would be appropriate. Now the meridians do approach each other toward the poles (unlike the Mercator projection), and there is much less shape and size distortion. And if we needed a map of Arctic and Antarctic regions, we would place the photographic paper as a flat sheet against the North and South Poles. Now the photographic image would show a set of diverging lines, as the meridians do from each pole, and the parallels would appear as circles (**Figure A.10**). Such a planar projection is a good choice for a map of the Arctic Ocean or the Antarctic continent.

Projections are chosen for various purposes. Just as the Mercator is appropriate for navigation because direction is true, other projections are designed to preserve areal size, keep distances real, or maintain the outlines (shapes) of landmasses and countries. Projections can be manipulated for many needs. In this book, we examine global distributions of various phenomena. The world map that forms the base for these displays is one that is designed to give prominence to land areas at the expense of the oceans. This is achieved by "interrupting" the projection where loss of territory (in this case water area) is not problematic.

When a map is planned, therefore, the choice of projection is an important part of the process. An inappropriate selection may weaken the effectiveness of a map and may lead to erroneous interpretations. Of course, the problem diminishes when the area to be mapped is smaller and the scale larger. We may consider various alternatives when it comes to a map of all of North America, but a map of a single province presents far fewer potential problems of distortion. And for a city map—even of a large city such as Toronto—the projection problem virtually disappears.

The old problem of how to represent the round Earth on a flat surface has been attacked for centuries, and there is no single best solution. What has been learned in the process, however, will be useful in fields of endeavour other than

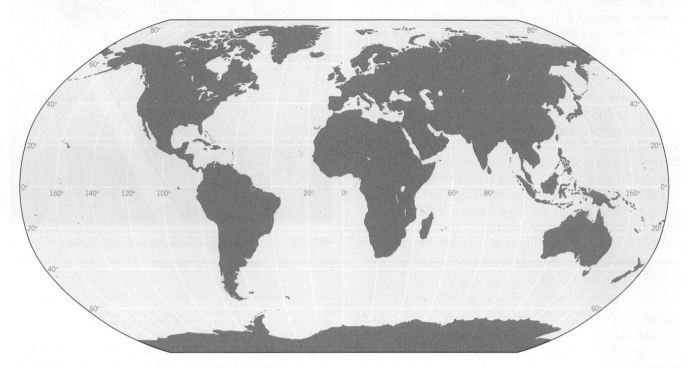

FIGURE A.7 The Robinson projection. The Robinson projection substantially reduces the exaggerated size of polar landmasses. It better approximates shape, but it lacks the directional utility of the Mercator projection.

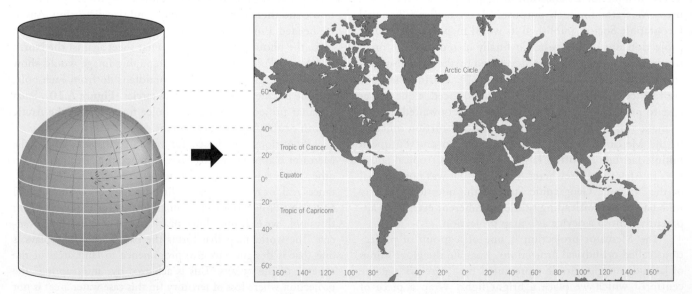

FIGURE A.8 Cylindrical projection. Shadows of the globe's grid lines on wraparound paper: a cylindrical projection results.

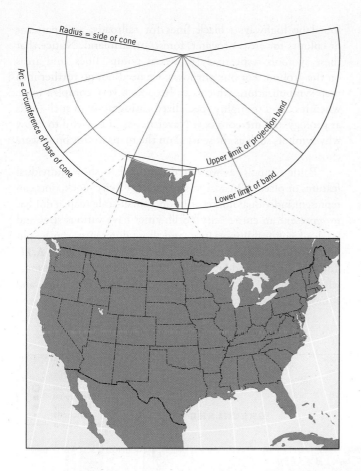

FIGURE A.9 Conic projection. Construction of a conic projection.

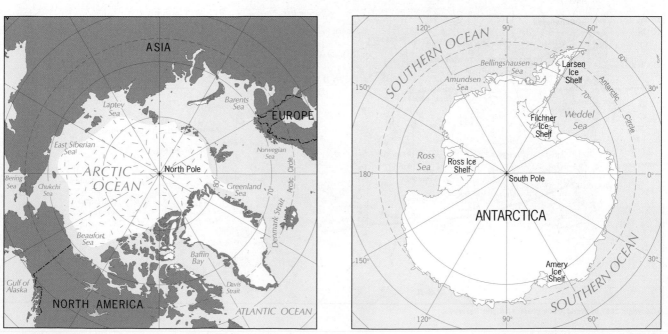

FIGURE A.10 Planar projection. The light at the centre of the globe projects diverging longitude lines on a flat sheet of paper placed over the North Pole (left) and the South Pole (right).

Earthly geography. As the age of planetary exploration dawns, and our space probes send back images of the surfaces of the Moon, Mars, Jupiter, and other components of our solar system, we will have to agree once again on grids, equators, and prime meridians. What we have learned in our efforts to map and represent the Earth will be useful in depicting the universe beyond.

Symbols on Maps

The third fundamental property of a map is its symbolization. Maps represent the real world, and this can be done only through the use of symbols. Anyone who has used an atlas map is familiar with some of these symbols: prominent dots (perhaps black or red) for cities; a large dot with a circle around it, or a star, for capitals; red lines for roads (double lines for

four-lane highways); black lines for railroads; and patterns or colours for areas of water, forest, or farmland. Notice that these symbols respectively represent points, lines, and areas on the ground. For our purposes, we need not go further into map symbolization, which can become a very complex topic when it comes to highly specialized cartography in such fields as geology and meteorology. Nevertheless, it is useful to know why symbols such as those used on the maps in this book were chosen.

Point symbols, as we noted, are used to show individual features or places. On a large-scale map of a city block, dots can represent individual houses. But on a small-scale map, a dot has to represent an entire "city." Still, cities have various sizes and levels of political importance, and those differences can be put into categories and mapped accordingly. Thus, in **Figure A.11**, Toronto, Regina, and Fredericton appear as squares on the map, whereas smaller cities, such as Medicine Hat, Flin Flon, and Rimouski, are illustrated with dots.

FIGURE A.11 Population map of Canada. This map uses a series of symbols to denote city size and importance. A circle with a star indicates country capital, a red square indicates administrative capital, a circle with a ring around it indicates a large city, and a circle on its own indicates a smaller city.

NASA/JPL/University of Arizona/University of Colorado

Hannah Sizemore, University of Colorado

FIGURE A.12 Contour lines. Contour map of Mars surface.

Line symbols include not only roads and railroads, but also political and administrative boundaries, rivers, and other linear features. Again, scale plays its crucial role: on a large-scale map, it is possible to represent the fenced boundaries of a single farm, but on a small-scale map, such detail cannot be shown.

Some lines on maps do not actually exist on the ground. When physical geographers do their field work they use contour maps, lines that represent a certain consistent height above mean sea level (**Figure A.12**). All points on such a contour line are at the same elevation. The spacing between contour lines immediately reveals the nature of the local topography (the natural land surface). When the contour lines at a given interval (e.g., 100 feet) are spaced closely together, the slope of the ground is steep. When they are widely separated, the land surface slopes gently. Of course contour lines cannot be found in the real world, and neither can the lines drawn on the weather maps in our daily newspaper. These lines connect points of equal pressure (isobars) and temperature (isotherms) and show the development of weather systems. Note that the letters "iso" (meaning "the same") appear in these terms. Invisible lines of this kind are collectively known as isolines, lines of equal or constant value. These are abstract constructions, but they can be of great value in geographic research and representation.

Area symbols take many forms, and we will see some of them on the maps in this book. Area symbols are used in various ways to represent distributions and magnitudes. Maps showing distributions (of such phenomena as regionally dominant languages or religions in human geography, and climates or soils in physical geography) show the world, or parts of it, divided into areas shaded or coloured in contrasting hues. But be careful: those sharp dividing lines are likely to be transition zones in the real world, and a dominant language or religion does not imply the exclusion of all others. So distribution maps, and there are many in this book, tend to be small-scale

generalizations of much more complex patterns than they can reveal. Again, maps showing magnitudes also must be read with care. Here the objective is to reveal how much of a phenomenon prevails in one unit (e.g., country) on the map, compared to others. The maps on population in Chapter 4 are examples of such maps. The important cartographic decision has to do with colour (or black and white, grey tones). Darker should mean more, and lighter implies less. That is relatively easily done when the dominant colour is the same. But on a multicoloured map, the use of reds, greens, and yellows can be confusing, and first impressions may have to be revised upon examination of the key.

Symbols are powerful, and sometimes mapmakers use symbols to convey particular ideas about places (as in the propaganda map in Figure A.1). In medieval times, mapmakers used dragons and sea monsters, with the legend *hic sunt dracone* (Here be dragons), to illustrate unexplored territories and unknown areas. Chet Van Duzer, who studies the history of cartography, has written extensively about the use of symbols on maps, focusing on dragons and sea monsters. In his book *Sea Monsters on Medieval and Renaissance Maps* (2013), Van Duzer writes:

> From dragons and serpents to many-armed beasts that preyed on ships and sailors alike, sea monsters have terrified mariners across all ages and cultures and have become the subject of many tall tales from the sea. Accounts of these creatures have also inspired cartographers and mapmakers, many of whom began decorating their maps with them to indicate unexplored areas or areas about which little was known.

In a map of Iceland that first appeared in 1590 (**Figure A.13**), sea monsters writhe in the uncharted waters beyond Iceland, probably placed there after the mapmaker had consulted shipping logs and mariners' sketches.

Geographers are always aware of the political nature of maps, recognizing that the symbols, including sea monsters and dragons,

FIGURE A.13 Sea monsters surrounding Iceland. A rich collection of sea monsters swarm on Abraham Ortelius's map of Iceland in the 1598 Antwerp edition of his *Theatrum orbis terrarum.*

and the place names (the study of which is called toponymy) are not neutral markers, but instead are infused with power relations and shaped by the culture out of which they are produced.

Some students who are first drawn to the discipline of geography go on to become professional cartographers, and their work is seen in atlases, foldout magazine maps, books, and many other venues. Although cartographic technology is changing, the world's great atlases and maps are still designed and produced by researchers, compilers, drafts people, and other specialists.

APPENDIX B

AREA AND DEMOGRAPHIC DATA FOR THE WORLD'S STATES

This data table is a valuable resource, and should be consulted throughout your reading. Like all else in this book, this table is subject to continuous revision and modification. Compared to previous U.S. editions, we have deleted some indices, elaborated others, and introduced new ones. For example, in a world with ever-slower population growth, the so-called Doubling Time index—the number of years it will take for a population to double in size based on its current rate of natural increase—has lost most of its utility. On the other hand, when it comes to Life Expectancy and Literacy, general averages conceal significant differences between male and female rates, which in turn reflect conditions in individual countries, so we report these by gender. Also in this edition, we continue to use the Corruption Index, not available for all countries but an important reflection of a global problem. The Big Mac Price index, a measure introduced by the journal *The Economist,* tells you much more than what a hamburger with all the trimmings would cost in real dollars in various countries of the world—it also reflects whether those countries' currencies are overvalued or undervalued. And the final column, which we formerly used to report the per-capita GNP (Gross National Product), now reveals the GNI; that is, the Gross National Income per person and what this would buy in each country. In the language of economic geographers, this is called the GNI-PPP, the per-capita Gross National Income in terms of its Purchasing Power Parity.

Indexes that may not be immediately obvious to you include Arithmetic Population Density, the number of people per square kilometre in each country; Physiologic Population Density, the number of people per square kilometre of agriculturally productive land; Birth and Death Rates per thousand in the population, resulting in the national population's rate of Natural Increase; a population's Infant Mortality, the number of deaths per thousand in the first year of life, thus largely reflecting the number of deaths at birth; Child Mortality, the deaths per thousand of children in their first five years, the Corruption Index, based on Transparency International data in which 10.0 is perfect and 0.1 is the worst; the Big Mac Price index, which tells you why Argentina in 2011 was the best place to buy a hamburger in U.S. dollars; and the Per Capita GNI (U.S.$), the GNI-PPP index referred to above, which tells you how spendable income varies around the globe.

Appendix B   Area and Demographic Data for the World's States (Categories explained on page 417)

| | Land Area | | Population | | Population Density | | Birth Rate | Death Rate | Natural Increase % | Infant Mortality per 1,000 | Child Mortality per 1,000 | Life Expectancy | | Percent Urban Pop. | Literacy | | Corruption Index | Big Mac Price (U.S.$) | Per Capita GNI (U.S.$) |
	Sq. km.	Sq. mi.	2010 (Millions)	2025 (Millions)	Arithmetic	Physiologic						Male (years)	Female (years)		Male %	Female %			
WORLD	134,134,451	51,789,601	6,879.9	8,104.4	51	443	20	8	1.2	33	45	67	71	51	84.0	70.8			$10,030
REALM	5,930,511	2,289,783	594.9	607.1	26	204	11	11	0.0	5	6	72	80	71	99.4	98.4			$25,580
EUROPE																			
Albania	28,749	11,100	3.2	3.3	113	451	10	5	0.5	14	15	72	79	49	95.5	88.0	3.3		$7,950
Austria	83,859	32,378	8.4	8.9	100	556	9	9	0.0	3	4	78	83	67	100.0	100.0	7.9		$37,680
Belarus	207,598	80,154	9.6	9.1	46	150	12	14	-0.3	11	12	65	76	74	99.7	99.2	2.5		$12,150
Belgium	30,528	11,787	10.7	11.8	352	1,408	11	9	0.2	4	5	77	82	99	100.0	100.0	7.1		$34,760
Bosnia	51,129	19,741	3.8	3.7	74	572	9	9	0.0	13	14	72	77	46	96.5	76.6	3.2		$8,620
Bulgaria	110,908	42,822	7.5	6.9	68	165	11	14	-0.4	8	10	70	77	71	99.1	98.0	3.6		$11,950
Croatia	56,539	21,830	4.4	4.3	77	298	10	12	-0.2	5	5	72	79	56	99.4	97.3	4.1		$18,420
Cyprus	9,249	3,571	1.1	1.1	120	751	13	7	0.6	3	4	77	80	62	98.7	95.0	6.3		$24,040
Czech Republic	78,860	30,448	10.4	10.9	132	307	11	10	0.1	3	4	74	80	74	100.0	100.0	4.6	3.43	$22,790
Denmark	43,090	16,637	5.5	5.8	128	229	11	10	0.1	3	4	76	81	72	100.0	100.0	9.3	4.90	$37,280
Estonia	45,099	17,413	1.3	1.3	29	107	12	12	0.0	4	6	69	79	69	99.9	99.6	6.5	2.62	$19,280
Finland	338,149	130,560	5.3	5.8	16	225	11	9	0.2	3	3	77	83	65	100.0	100.0	9.2		$35,660
France	551,497	212,934	62.6	66.1	114	324	13	9	0.4	3	4	78	85	77	98.9	98.7	6.8		$34,400
Germany	356,978	137,830	81.9	79.7	229	655	8	10	-0.2	4	4	77	82	73	100.0	100.0	7.9		$35,940
Greece	131,960	50,950	11.2	11.7	85	283	11	10	0.1	3	3	77	82	73	98.6	96.0	3.5		$28,470
Hungary	93,030	35,919	9.9	9.8	107	194	10	13	-0.3	5	6	70	78	67	99.5	99.3	4.7	3.33	$17,790
Iceland	102,999	39,768	0.3	0.4	3	297	15	6	0.9	2	3	80	83	93	100.0	100.0	8.5		$25,220
Ireland	70,279	27,135	4.6	5.7	65	327	17	6	1.0	4	4	77	82	60	100.0	100.0	8.0		$37,350
Italy	301,267	116,320	59.8	61.9	198	536	10	10	0.0	3	4	79	84	68	98.9	98.1	3.9		$30,250
Kosovo	10,887	4,203	2.3	2.7	208		21	7	1.4	5		67	71	—	96.6	87.5	2.8		—
Latvia	64,599	24,942	2.3	2.1	35	122	10	13	-0.4	7	8	67	78	68	99.8	99.6	4.3	2.80	$16,740
Liechtenstein	161	62	0.1	0.1	874	3,495	10	6	0.4	2	2	79	82	15	100.0	100.0			—
Lithuania	65,200	25,174	3.4	3.1	52	112	11	12	-0.1	5	6	66	78	67	99.7	99.4	5.0	2.71	$18,210
Luxembourg	2,587	999	0.5	0.6	194	778	11	7	0.4	2	3	78	83	83	100.0	100.0	8.5		$64,320
Macedonia	25,711	9,927	2.0	2.0	78	300	12	9	0.2	10	11	71	76	65	94.2	83.8	4.1		$9,950
Malta	321	124	0.4	0.4	1,250	3,678	10	8	0.2	6	7	77	82	94	91.4	92.8	5.6		$22,460
Moldova	33,701	13,012	4.1	4.0	121	184	11	12	0.0	15	17	66	73	41	99.6	98.3	2.9		$3,210
Montenegro	13,812	5,333	0.6	0.6	44	156	13	9	0.4	8	9	71	76	64	100.0	100.0	3.7		$13,920
Netherlands	40,839	15,768	16.5	17.2	404	1,496	11	8	0.3	4	4	78	82	90	100.0	100.0	8.8		$41,670
Norway	323,878	125,050	4.8	5.6	15	497	13	9	0.4	3	3	79	83	80	100.0	100.0	8.6	7.20	$58,500
Poland	323,249	124,807	38.1	37.4	118	251	11	10	0.1	6	7	71	80	61	99.8	99.8	5.3	2.60	$17,310
Portugal	91,981	35,514	10.6	10.9	115	397	9	10	-0.1	3	4	75	82	55	94.8	90.0	6.0		$22,080
Romania	238,388	92,042	21.4	20.6	90	204	10	12	-0.2	10	12	69	76	55	99.1	97.3	3.7		$13,500
Serbia	88,357	34,115	7.3	6.8	83	219	9	14	-0.5	6	7	71	76	58	100.0	100.0	3.5		$11,150
Slovakia	49,010	18,923	5.4	5.4	110	324	11	10	0.2	6	7	71	79	55	100.0	100.0	4.3		$21,300

Continued

	Land Area		Population		Population Density		Birth Rate	Death Rate	Natural Increase %	Infant Mortality per 1,000	Child Mortality per 1,000	Life Expectancy		Percent Urban Pop.	Literacy		Corruption Index	Big Mac Price (U.S.$)	Per Capita GNI (U.S.$)
	Sq. km.	Sq. mi.	2010 (Millions)	2025 (Millions)	Arithmetic	Physiologic						Male (years)	Female (years)		Male %	Female %			
Slovenia	20,251	7,819	2.0	2.0	99	707	11	9	0.2	2	3	75	82	50	98.6	96.8	6.4		$26,910
Spain	505,988	195,363	46.7	48.4	92	237	11	8	0.3	4	4	78	84	77	100.0	100.0	6.1		$31,130
Sweden	449,959	173,730	9.2	10.2	21	293	12	10	0.2	2	3	79	83	84	100.0	100.0	9.2	6.56	$38,180
Switzerland	41,290	15,942	7.6	8.3	185	1,540	10	8	0.2	4	4	80	84	73	99.5	97.4	8.7	6.19	$46,460
Ukraine	603,698	233,089	45.6	41.9	76	128	11	15	−0.4	13	15	63	74	69	100.0	100.0	2.4	1.84	$7,210
United Kingdom	244,878	94,548	61.8	68.6	252	971	13	9	0.4	5	6	77	82	80	97.6	89.2	7.6	3.48	$36,130
							RUSSIAN REALM												
REALM	**17,261,421**	**6,664,672**	**157.7**	**158.7**	**9**	**123**	**12**	**14**	**20.2**	**13**	**14**	**62**	**74**	**73**	**99.7**	**99.1**	**2.1**		**$15,531**
Russia	17,075,323	6,592,819	141.0	140.8	8	138	12	14	−0.2	11	12	62	74	73	99.8	99.2	2.1	2.33	$15,630
Armenia	29,800	11,506	3.1	3.3	105	526	15	10	0.6	20	22	68	75	64	99.4	98.1	2.6		$6,310
Azerbaijan	86,599	33,436	8.9	10.3	103	468	17	6	1.1	30	34	70	75	54	98.9	95.9	2.4		$7,770
Georgia	69,699	26,911	4.6	4.3	66	441	13	10	0.3	26	29	69	79	53	99.7	99.4	3.8		$4,850
							NORTH AMERICA												
REALM	**19,941,634**	**7,699,508**	**341.9**	**391.1**	**17**	**139**	**13**	**8**	**0.6**	**7**	**8**	**76**	**81**	**79**	**97.6**	**97.4**			**$45,890**
Canada	9,970,600	3,849,670	33.6	39.7	3	67	11	7	0.4	5	6	78	83	80	95.7	95.3	8.9	4.00	$36,220
United States	9,629,047	3,717,796	308.2	351.4	32	160	14	8	0.6	7	8	75	80	79	99.0	99.0	7.1	3.73	$46,970
							MIDDLE AMERICA												
REALM	**2,714,579**	**1,048,105**	**196.3**	**223.3**	**72**	**447**	**21**	**5**	**1.6**	**19**	**23**	**72**	**78**	**71**	**90.3**	**87.1**			**$11,910**
Antigua and Barbuda	440	170	0.1	0.1	232	1,287	14	6	0.9	11	12	73	77	31					$20,570
Bahamas	13,880	5,359	0.3	0.4	22	2,209	15	6	0.9	9	12	71	77	83	95.4	96.8	3.6		—
Barbados	430	166	0.3	0.3	706	1811	13	8	0.5	10	11	71	76	38	98.0	96.8	7.8		—
Belize	22,960	8,865	0.3	0.4	14	342	27	4	2.3	16	18	71	74	51					$6,040
Costa Rica	51,100	19,730	4.6	5.3	90	1,002	17	4	1.3	10	11	77	82	59	95.5	95.7	5.3	3.83	$10,950
Cuba	110,859	42,803	11.3	11.1	102	248	11	8	0.3	4	6	76	80	75	99.8	99.8	3.7		—
Dominica	751	290	0.1	0.1	135	675	15	8	0.7	8	10	72	78	73			5.2		$8,300
Dominican Republic	48,731	18,815	10.3	11.6	211	679	23	6	1.7	27	32	69	75	67	84.0	83.7	3.0		$7,890
El Salvador	21,041	8,124	7.5	6.9	355	909	20	7	1.4	15	17	67	76	63	81.6	76.1	3.6		$6,670
Grenada	339	131	0.1	0.1	302	943	17	9	0.8	13	15	68	72	31					$8,060
Guadeloupe	1,709	660	0.4	0.5	238	1,585	14	7	0.7	7		78	83	100	89.7	90.5			—
Guatemala	108,888	42,042	14.5	20.0	133	739	34	6	2.8	33	40	66	73	47	76.2	61.1	3.2		$4,690
Haiti	27,749	10,714	9.4	12.2	340	1,030	28	9	1.8	64	87	58	62	48	51.0	46.5	2.2		$1,180
Honduras	112,090	43,278	7.6	9.8	68	378	28	5	2.3	25	30	70	75	50	72.5	72.0	2.4		$3,870
Jamaica	10,989	4,243	2.8	2.9	25	1,005	20	7	1.2	26	31	68	75	52	82.5	90.7	3.3		$7,360
Martinique	1,101	425	0.4	0.4	368	1,839	13	7	0.6	8		77	83	89	96.0	97.1			—
Mexico	1,958,192	756,062	111.0	123.4	57	405	19	5	1.4	15	17	74	79	77	93.1	89.1	3.1	2.50	$14,270
Netherlands Antilles	800	309	0.2	0.2	253	2,534	14	7	0.7	11		73	80	92	96.6	96.6			—
Nicaragua	129,999	50,193	5.9	7.5	46	208	23	4	1.8	22	26	69	73	56	64.2	64.4	2.5		$2,620
Panama	75,519	29,158	3.5	4.3	46	516	20	5	1.6	16	23	73	78	64	92.6	91.3	3.6		$11,650

Continued

	Land Area Sq. km.	Land Area Sq. mi.	Population 2010 (Millions)	Population 2025 (Millions)	Population Density Arithmetic	Population Density Physiologic	Birth Rate	Death Rate	Natural Increase %	Infant Mortality per 1,000	Child Mortality per 1,000	Life Expectancy Male (years)	Life Expectancy Female (years)	Percent Urban Pop.	Literacy Male %	Literacy Female %	Corruption Index	Big Mac Price (U.S.$)	Per Capita GNI (U.S.$)
Puerto Rico	8,951	3,456	4.0	4.1	450	5,005	12	7	0.4	9		75	82	94	93.7	94.0	5.8		—
Saint Lucia	619	239	0.2	0.2	328	1,172	14	7	0.7	19	20	71	76	28					$9,190
St. Vincent & the Grenadines	391	151	0.1	0.1	260	930	17	8	0.9	18	12	70	74	40	96.0	96.0			$8,770
Trinidad and Tobago	5,131	1,981	1.3	1.4	256	1,068	14	8	0.6	31	35	66	73	12	99.0	97.5	3.6		$23,950
SOUTH AMERICA																			
REALM	**17,867,238**	**6,898,579**	**397.5**	**444.0**	**22**	**356**	**18**	**6**	**1.2**	**17**	**20**	**70**	**77**	**82**	**90.1**	**89.0**			**$10,150**
Argentina	2,780,388	1,073,514	40.6	46.2	15	146	18	8	1.0	13	14	72	79	91	96.9	96.9	2.9	1.78	$14,020
Bolivia	1,098,575	424,162	10.4	13.3	9	474	27	7	2.0	40	51	64	68	65	92.1	79.4	2.8		$4,140
Brazil	8,547,360	3,300,154	200.6	212.4	23	335	17	6	1.0	17	21	69	77	84	85.5	85.4	3.7	4.91	$10,070
Chile	756,626	292,135	17.1	19.1	23	754	15	6	0.9	7	9	76	82	87	95.9	95.5	7.2	3.34	$13,270
Colombia	1,138,906	439,734	45.7	53.5	40	1,002	20	6	1.4	16	19	71	78	75	91.8	91.8	3.5	4.39	$8,510
Ecuador	283,560	109,483	14.4	16.6	51	460	21	5	1.6	20	24	72	78	65	93.6	90.2	2.5		$7,760
French Guiana	89,999	34,749	0.2	0.3	2	235	28	3	2.4	14		75	81	81	83.6	82.3			—
Guyana	214,969	83,000	0.8	0.8	4	191	23	7	1.6	29	35	62	70	28	99.0	98.1	2.7		$2,510
Paraguay	406,747	157,046	6.5	8.1	16	265	25	6	1.9	19	23	70	74	58	94.4	92.2	2.2		$4,820
Peru	1,285,214	496,224	28.7	34.5	22	745	21	6	1.6	19	21	71	76	76	94.7	85.4	3.5	3.54	$7,980
Suriname	163,270	63,039	0.5	0.6	3	312	19	7	1.3	24	26	65	73	67	95.9	92.6			$7,130
Uruguay	177,409	68,498	3.3	3.5	19	268	14	9	0.5	11	13	72	80	94	97.4	98.2	6.9	3.74	$12,540
Venezuela	912,046	352,143	29.1	35.1	32	797	21	5	1.6	15	18	71	77	88	93.3	92.7	2.0		$12,830
SUBSAHARAN AFRICA																			
REALM	**24,292,983**	**9,379,573**	**769.5**	**1,150.7**	**32**	**421**	**40**	**14**	**2.6**	**79**	**127**	**51**	**53**	**34**	**73.1**	**59.9**			**$1,974**
Angola	1,246,693	481,351	17.7	27.4	14	473	42	17	2.5	98	161	45	49	57	55.6	28.5	1.9		$5,020
Benin	112,620	43,483	9.9	13.6	88	548	40	10	3.0	75	118	57	60	41	47.8	23.6	2.8		$1,460
Botswana	581,727	224,606	1.8	2.2	3	316	30	11	1.9	43	57	55	55	60	74.4	79.8	5.8		$13,100
Burkina Faso	274,000	105,792	16.1	25.4	59	490	46	12	3.4	91	166	51	54	23	31.2	13.1	3.1		$1,160
Burundi	27,829	10,745	9.4	11.6	339	789	36	15	2.1	101	166	49	52	10	56.3	40.5	1.8		$380
Cameroon	475,439	183,568	19.4	26.5	41	255	37	14	2.3	95	154	50	52	53	81.8	69.2	2.2		$2,180
Cape Verde	4,030	1,556	0.5	0.7	130	1,185	25	6	2.0	23	28	69	76	61	84.3	65.3	5.1		$3,450
Central African Rep.	622,978	240,533	4.6	6.6	7	244	38	16	2.2	112	171	47	50	38	59.6	34.5	2.1		$730
Chad	1,283,994	495,753	10.7	16.9	8	277	46	17	2.9	124	209	47	50	27	66.9	40.8	1.7		$1,160
Comoros	2,230	861	0.7	0.9	332	626	33	7	2.6	75	104	62	66	28	63.5	49.1	2.1		$1,170
Congo	341,998	132,046	4.0	5.5	12	1,165	38	13	2.5	81	128	52	54	60	87.5	74.4	2.1		$3,090
Congo, The	2,344,848	905,351	70.7	101.4	30	754	47	17	2.9	126	199	46	49	33	86.6	67.7	2.0		$290
Djibouti	23,201	8,958	0.8	1.1	36	3,573	29	11	1.8	75	94	54	57	76	65.0	38.4	3.2		$2,330
Equatorial Guinea	28,050	10,830	0.6	1.0	23	252	39	16	2.3	88	145	48	51	39	92.5	74.5	1.9		$21,700
Eritrea	117,598	45,405	5.3	7.4	45	1,128	37	9	2.9	39	55	57	62	21	43.9	33.4	2.6		$630
Ethiopia	1,104,296	426,371	83.1	119.8	75	684	39	12	2.7	67	104	54	57	16	83.7	70.0	2.7		$870

Continued

	Land Area Sq. km.	Land Area Sq. mi.	Population 2010 (Millions)	Population 2025 (Millions)	Pop. Density Arithmetic	Pop. Density Physiologic	Birth Rate	Death Rate	Natural Increase %	Infant Mortality per 1,000	Child Mortality per 1,000	Life Expectancy Male (years)	Life Expectancy Female (years)	Percent Urban Pop.	Literacy Male %	Literacy Female %	Corruption Index	Big Mac Price (U.S.$)	Per Capita GNI (U.S.$)
Gabon	267,668	103,347	14	2.0	5	269	29	10	1.9	52	69	58	61	84	79.8	62.2	2.8		$12,270
Gambia	11,300	4,363	17	2.5	149	711	38	12	2.7	78	103	54	57	54	43.8	29.6	3.2		$1,280
Ghana	238,538	92,100	25.0	31.8	105	455	31	9	2.2	47	69	58	61	48	79.5	61.2	4.1		$1,430
Guinea	245,860	94,927	10.9	15.9	44	738	41	11	3.0	88	142	55	58	28	55.1	27.0	2.0		$1,190
Guinea–Bissau	36,120	13,946	1.8	2.3	50	385	43	18	2.4	115	193	45	48	30	53.0	21.4	2.1		$530
Ivory Coast	322,459	124,502	21.7	30.8	67	293	37	14	2.4	83	119	51	54	50	54.6	38.5	2.2		$1,580
Kenya	580,367	224,081	40.2	51.3	69	865	37	10	2.7	55	84	56	57	18	89.0	76.0	2.1		$1,580
Lesotho	30,349	11,718	1.8	2.0	60	541	28	19	0.9	61	84	40	43	23	73.6	93.6	3.5		$2,000
Liberia	111,369	43,000	4.2	6.1	37	932	43	11	3.3	80	112	54	57	58	69.9	36.8	3.3		$300
Madagascar	587,036	226,656	20.0	28.6	34	680	37	9	2.7	41	58	59	62	31	87.7	72.9	2.6		$1,040
Malawi	118,479	45,745	14.5	22.9	122	582	44	15	2.9	69	110	48	50	14	74.5	46.7	3.4		$830
Mali	1,240,185	478,838	13.6	22.3	11	273	46	15	3.1	101	191	50	53	33	47.9	33.2	2.7		$1,090
Mauritania	1,025,516	395,954	3.4	4.4	3	328	34	11	2.3	74	117	55	59	40	50.6	29.5	2.3		$2,000
Mauritius	2,041	788	1.3	1.4	646	1,242	12	7	0.5	15	17	69	76	42	87.7	81.0	5.4		$12,480
Mozambique	801,586	309,494	21.3	31.2	27	663	40	16	2.3	96	142	47	49	31	59.9	28.4	2.7		$770
Namibia	824,287	318,259	2.1	2.8	3	260	28	9	1.9	34	48	60	62	35	82.9	81.2	4.4		$6,270
Niger	1,266,994	489,189	15.6	27.4	12	308	52	17	3.5	76	160	47	49	20	23.5	8.3	2.6		$680
Nigeria	923,766	356,668	155.6	217.4	168	495	42	17	2.4	86	138	47	48	47	72.3	56.2	2.4		$1,940
Réunion	2,510	969	0.8	1.0	328	2,185	18	5	1.3			75	82	92	84.8	89.2			—
Rwanda	26,340	10,170	10.1	15.8	384	915	42	14	2.9	70	111	50	53	17	73.7	60.6	4.0		$1,010
São Tomé and Príncipe	961	371	0.2	0.2	220	511	37	7	2.9	52	78	64	69	58	70.2	39.1	3.0		$1,780
Senegal	196,720	75,954	13.4	17.4	68	570	39	11	2.8	51	93	54	57	41	47.2	27.6	2.9		$1,760
Seychelles	451	174	0.1	0.1	227	1,512	18	7	1.0	11	12	68	78	53	82.9	85.7	4.8		$19,770
Sierra Leone	71,740	27,699	5.8	8.1	81	1,007	40	16	2.4	123	192	46	49	36	50.7	22.6	2.4		$750
Somalia	637,658	246,201	9.5	13.9	15	744	46	16	3.0	109	180	48	51	34	85.5	84.5	1.1		—
South Africa	1,221,034	471,444	49.1	54.4	40	309	21	12	0.9	43	62	54	57	52	68.3	46.0	4.5	2.45	$9,780
South Sudan	628,755	242,763	8.5		13.5		45	20	2.5			45	46	12	21.0	11.0			$490
Swaziland	17,361	6,703	1.1	1.5	63	576	31	16	1.5	52	73	46	45	22	80.9	78.7	3.2		$5,010
Tanzania	945,087	364,900	42.1	67.4	45	890	42	12	3.0	68	108	54	56	25	84.1	66.6	2.7		$1,230
Togo	56,791	21,927	7.2	9.3	127	294	33	8	2.5	64	98	60	63	40	72.2	42.6	2.4		$820
Uganda	241,040	93,066	31.1	53.4	129	379	47	13	3.4	79	128	52	53	17	77.7	57.1	2.5		$1,140
Zambia	752,607	290,583	12.7	20.3	17	241	45	20	2.5	86	141	42	42	37	85.2	71.2	3.0		$1,230
Zimbabwe	390,759	150,873	13.8	16.8	35	392	30	17	1.3	56	90	42	44	37	95.5	89.9	2.4		—
REALM	**19,318,887**	**7,459,064**	**592.4**	**739.2**	**63**	**687**	**25**	**7**	**1.9**	**33**	**43**	**67**	**71**	**57**	**83.1**	**64.5**			**$8,387**
NORTH AFRICA/SOUTHWEST ASIA																			
Afghanistan	652,086	251,772	34.4	39.4	53	440	39	18	2.1	134	199	44	44	22	51.0	20.8	1.4		—
Algeria	2,381,730	919,591	36.0	43.6	15	503	23	5	1.8	29	32	74	74	63	75.1	51.3	2.9		$7,940
Bahrain	689	266	0.8	1.6	1,201	13,345	15	2	1.3	10	12	76	77	100	91.0	82.7	4.9		—

Continued

	Land Area		Population		Population Density		Birth Rate	Death Rate	Natural Increase %	Infant Mortality per 1,000	Child Mortality per 1,000	Life Expectancy		Percent Urban Pop.	Literacy		Corruption Index	Big Mac Price (U.S.$)	Per Capita GNI (U.S.$)
	Sq. km.	Sq. mi.	2010 (Millions)	2025 (Millions)	Arithmetic	Physiologic						Male (years)	Female (years)		Male %	Female %			
Egypt	1,001,445	386,660	78.1	103.6	78	2,599	27	6	2.1	18	21	69	75	43	66.6	43.7	3.1	2.28	$5,460
Iran	1,633,182	630,575	74.4	87.1	46	414	19	6	1.3	26	31	70	73	69			2.2		$10,840
Iraq	438,319	169,236	30.9	44.7	71	543	32	6	2.6	35	44	64	72	67	70.7	45.0	1.5		—
Israel	21,059	8,131	7.7	9.4	368	1,751	22	5	1.6	3	4	79	83	92	97.9	94.3	6.1	3.86	$27,450
Jordan	89,210	34,444	6.1	8.5	68	1,363	31	4	2.6	22	25	72	74	83	94.9	84.4	4.7		$5,530
Kazakhstan	2,717,289	1,049,151	16.0	18.4	6	49	23	9	1.4	26	29	63	74	54	99.1	96.1	2.9		$9,690
Kuwait	17,819	6,880	2.8	4.1	157	15,734	22	2	2.0	8	10	76	80	98	84.3	79.9	4.5		$52,610
Kyrgyzstan	198,499	76,641	5.4	6.5	27	387	24	7	1.6	32	37	64	72	35	98.6	95.5	2.0		$2,130
Lebanon	10,399	4,015	4.1	4.7	396	1,276	20	5	1.5	11	12	70	74	87	92.3	80.4	2.5		$10,880
Libya	1,759,532	679,359	6.6	8.1	4	373	23	4	1.9	17	19	72	77	77	90.9	67.6	2.2		$15,630
Morocco	446,548	172,413	32.1	36.6	72	327	21	6	1.5	33	38	69	73	57	61.9	36.0	3.4		$4,330
Oman	212,459	82,031	2.8	4.2	13	1,325	20	3	1.8	9	12	70	74	72	80.4	61.7	5.3		$20,650
Palestinian Territories	6,260	2,417	4.5	6.0	716	35,797	33	4	2.8	25	30	70	73	83	96.3	87.4			—
Qatar	11,000	4,247	0.9	2.1	84	8,429	9	1	0.8	10	11	75	77	100	80.5	83.2	7.7		—
Saudi Arabia	2,149,680	829,996	29.6	35.7	14	688	28	2	2.6	18	21	74	78	81	84.1	67.2	4.7	2.67	$22,950
Sudan (North)	1,877,063	724,735	41.1	44.7	16	234	31	10	2.1	69	115	57	60	46	44.0	18.0	1.5		$2,145
Syria	185,179	71,498	20.9	28.6	113	376	28	3	2.5	14	16	72	76	54	88.3	60.4	2.5		$4,350
Tajikistan	143,099	55,251	7.6	9.8	53	761	28	4	2.4	52	61	64	69	26	99.6	98.9	2.1		$1,860
Tunisia	163,610	63,170	10.5	12.1	64	201	18	6	1.2	18	21	72	76	66	81.4	60.1	4.3		$7,070
Turkey	774,816	299,158	76.8	85.0	99	261	18	6	1.2	19	20	69	74	76	93.6	76.7	4.4	3.89	$13,770
Turkmenistan	488,099	188,456	5.4	6.1	11	276	22	8	1.4	42	45	61	69	47	98.8	96.6	1.6		$6,210
United Arab Emirates	83,600	32,278	4.6	7.0	55	5,524	15	2	1.4	7	7	77	79	83	75.5	79.5	6.3	2.99	—
Uzbekistan	447,397	172,741	28.1	34.4	63	524	23	5	1.8	32	36	65	71	36	98.5	96.0	1.6		$2,660
Western Sahara	252,120	97,344	0.5	0.7	2	5	34	9	2.5			58	62	81					—
Yemen	527,966	203,849	23.6	34.5	45	1,493	38	8	3.0	51	66	62	64	29	67.4	25.0	2.2		$2,210
SOUTH ASIA																			
REALM	**4,487,762**	**1,732,734**	**1,569.5**	**1,946.0**	**146**	**291**	**24**	**7**	**1.7**	**51**	**66**	**64**	**66**	**29**	**66.1**	**39.9**			**$2,882**
Bangladesh	143,998	55,598	152.4	195.0	1,058	1,679	22	7	1.5	41	52	65	67	25	51.7	29.5	2.4		$1,440
Bhutan	47,001	18,147	0.7	0.9	16	520	25	8	1.7	52	79	67	68	32	61.1	33.6	5.7		$4,880
India	3,287,576	1,269,340	1,186.4	1,444.5	361	633	23	7	1.5	50	66	63	65	29	68.6	42.1	3.3		$2,960
Maldives	300	116	0.3	0.4	1,029	10,287	22	3	1.9	11	13	72	74	35	96.3	96.4	2.3		$5,280
Nepal	147,179	56,826	28.1	35.7	191	909	28	8	1.9	39	48	64	65	17	59.1	21.8	2.2		$1,120
Pakistan	796,098	307,375	180.8	246.3	227	783	30	7	2.3	71	87	66	67	35	57.6	27.8	2.3	2.46	$2,700
Sri Lanka	65,610	25,332	20.8	23.2	317	1,093	19	7	1.2	13	15	72	76	15	94.5	88.9	3.2	1.86	$4,480
EAST ASIA																			
REALM	**11,774,215**	**4,546,050**	**1,573.4**	**1,703.9**	**134**	**1,083**	**12**	**7**	**0.5**	**16**	**17**	**73**	**77**	**52**	**94.9**	**84.7**			**$9,447**
China	9,572,855	3,696,100	1,338.0	1,484.7	140	998	12	7	0.5	17	19	72	76	47	92.3	77.4	3.5	1.95	$6,020
Japan	377,799	145,869	127.7	119.3	338	2,600	9	9	0.0	2	3	79	86	86	100.0	100.0	7.8	3.67	$35,220

Continued

	Land Area		Population		Population Density		Birth Rate	Death Rate	Natural Increase %	Infant Mortality per 1,000	Child Mortality per 1,000	Life Expectancy		Percent Urban Pop.	Literacy		Corruption Index	Big Mac Price (U.S.$)	Per Capita GNI (U.S.$)
	Sq. km.	Sq. mi.	2010 (Millions)	2025 (Millions)	Arithmetic	Physiologic						Male (years)	Female (years)		Male %	Female %			
Korea, North	120,541	46,541	23.9	23.6	198	1,240	15	10	0.5	26	33	61	66	60	99.0	99.0		—	—
Korea, South	99,259	38,324	49.1	49.1	495	2,603	9	5	0.4	5	5	77	83	82	99.2	96.4	5.4	2.82	$28,120
Mongolia	1,566,492	604,826	2.8	3.3	2	178	25	6	1.9	24	29	63	70	61	99.2	99.3	2.7		$3,480
Taiwan	36,180	13,969	23.1	23.9	640	2,558	8	6	0.2			75	82	78	97.6	90.2	5.8	2.34	—
REALM	**4,494,790**	**1,735,448**	**601.8**	**698.6**	**134**	**642**	**20**	**7**	**1.3**	**28**	**35**	**68**	**72**	**42**	**93.0**	**86.1**			**$4,510**
SOUTHEAST ASIA																			
Brunei	5,770	2,228	0.4	0.5	72	3,578	16	3	1.3	5	7	75	80	72	94.7	88.2	5.5		$50,200
Cambodia	181,040	69,900	15.2	19.0	84	382	25	8	1.6	68	88	59	63	20	79.7	53.4	2.1		$1,820
East Timor	14,869	5,741	1.2	1.9	79	655	41	10	3.1	48	56	60	62	22			2.5		$4,690
Indonesia	1,904,561	735,355	247.2	273.2	130	763	20	6	1.4	30	39	69	73	43	91.9	82.1	2.8	2.51	$3,830
Laos	236,800	91,429	6.2	8.3	26	871	28	7	2.1	46	59	63	66	27	73.6	50.5	2.1		$2,060
Malaysia	329,750	127,317	28.6	34.9	87	361	21	5	1.6	6	6	72	77	63	91.5	83.6	4.4	2.19	$13,740
Myanmar (Burma)	676,577	261,228	50.1	61.7	74	463	20	11	0.9	54	71	56	60	31	89.0	80.6	1.4		$1,290
Philippines	299,998	115,830	94.3	117.6	314	953	26	5	2.1	26	33	70	74	63	95.5	95.2	2.4	2.19	$3,900
Singapore	619	239	4.9	5.7	7,848	392,384	10	4	0.6	2	3	79	84	100	96.4	88.5	9.3	3.08	$47,940
Thailand	513,118	198,116	66.8	72.6	130	325	15	9	0.6	12	14	66	72	31	97.2	94.0	3.5	2.17	$5,990
Vietnam	331,689	128,066	88.3	103.2	266	1,210	17	5	1.2	20	24	72	76	28	95.7	91.0	2.7		$2,700
AUSTRAL REALM																			
REALM	**8,012,942**	**3,093,814**	**26.0**	**31.9**	**3**	**45**	**14**	**6**	**0.8**	**4**	**5**	**79**	**84**	**83**	**100.0**	**100.0**			**$32,850**
Australia	7,741,184	2,988,888	21.6	26.9	3	40	14	6	0.7	4	5	79	84	82	100.0	100.0	8.7	3.84	$34,040
New Zealand	270,529	104,452	4.4	5.0	16	135	14	7	0.8	5	6	78	82	86	100.0	100.0	9.3	3.59	$25,090
PACIFIC REALM																			
REALM	**975,341**	**376,804**	**9.6**	**13.1**	**17**	**806**	**29**	**9**	**2.0**	**42**	**55**	**60**	**65**	**22**	**65.9**	**52.1**			**$2,114**
Federated States of Micronesia	699	270	0.1	0.1	149	286	25	6	1.9	32	39	67	68	22	67.0	87.2			$3,000
Fiji	18,270	7,054	0.9	0.9	51	317	24	7	1.7	15	18	66	71	51	95.0	90.9			$4,270
French Polynesia	3,999	1,544	0.3	0.3	77	964	18	5	1.3			72	77	53	94.9	95.0			—
Guam	549	212	0.2	0.2	375	1,706	19	4	1.5			76	82	93	99.0	99.0			—
Marshall Islands	179	69	0.1	0.1	596	3,506	34	6	2.8	29	35	64	67	68	92.4	90.0			—
New Caledonia	18,581	7,174	0.2	0.3	11	1,105	16	5	1.2			72	80	58	57.4	58.3			—
Papua New Guinea	462,839	178,703	6.8	9.1	15	1,464	31	10	2.2	52	68	57	62	13	63.4	50.9	2.1		$2,000
Samoa	2,841	1,097	0.2	0.2	74	171	26	5	2.0	21	25	72	74	22	100.0	100.0	4.1		$4,340
Solomon Islands	28,899	11,158	0.5	0.8	18	607	33	8	2.5	30	36	62	63	17	62.4	44.9	2.8		$2,580
Vanuatu	12,191	4,707	0.2	0.3	17	172	31	6	2.5	14	16	66	69	24	57.3	47.8	3.6		$3,940

GLOSSARY

Absolute location   The position or place of a certain item on the surface of the Earth as expressed in degrees, minutes, and seconds of latitude, 0° to 90° north or south of the equator, and longitude, 0° to 180° east or west of the Prime Meridian passing through Greenwich, England (a suburb of London).

Accessibility   The degree of ease with which it is possible to reach a certain location from other locations. Accessibility varies from place to place and can be measured.

Acid rain   An environmental peril whereby acidified rainwater severely damages plant and animal life; caused by the oxides of sulphur and nitrogen that are released into the atmosphere when coal, oil, and natural gas are burned, especially in major manufacturing zones.

Acropolis   Literally "high point of the city." The upper fortified part of an ancient Greek city, usually devoted to religious purposes.

Agglomeration   A process involving the clustering or concentrating of people or activities. The term often refers to manufacturing plants and businesses that benefit from close proximity because they share pools of skilled labour pools and technological and financial amenities.

Agora   In ancient Greece, public spaces where citizens debated, lectured, judged each other, planned military campaigns, socialized, and traded.

Agribusiness   The businesses that provide the vast array of goods and services that support the agriculture industry in the production of a final food product for consumption.

Agricultural surplus   Agricultural production in excess of that which the producer needs for his or her own sustenance and that of his or her family and which is then sold for consumption by others. One of two components, together with social stratification, that enable the formation of cities.

Agricultural village   A relatively small, egalitarian village, where most of the population was involved in agriculture. Starting over 10,000 years ago, people began to cluster in agricultural villages as they stayed in one place to tend their crops.

Agriculture   The purposeful tending of crops and livestock in order to produce food, feed, and fibre.

AIDS (acquired immune deficiency syndrome)   Immune system disease, caused by the human immunodeficiency virus (HIV), which over a period of years weakens the capacity of the immune system to fight off infection. Weight loss and weakness set in and other afflictions, such as cancer or pneumonia, may hasten an infected person's death.

Air pollution   Pollution of the atmosphere.

Animal domestication   Genetic modification of an animal such that it is rendered more amenable to human control.

Anthropocentric view   A view in which human interests and perspectives are highlighted.

Aquifers   Subterranean, porous, water-holding rocks that provide millions of wells with steady flows of water.

Arithmetic population density   The population of a country or region expressed as an average per unit area. The figure is derived by dividing the population of the areal unit by the number of square kilometres or miles that make up the unit.

Assimilation   The process through which people lose originally differentiating traits, such as dress, speech particularities, or mannerisms, when they come into contact with another society or culture. Often used to describe immigrant adaptation to new places of residence.

Asylum   Shelter and protection in one state for refugees from another state.

Atmosphere   Blanket of gases surrounding the Earth and located some 600 kilometres above the Earth's surface.

Authenticity   In the context of local cultures or customs, the accuracy with which a single stereotypical or typecast image or experience conveys an otherwise dynamic and complex local culture or its customs.

Automobile dependence   A situation in which a city develops on the assumption that automobile use will predominate so that it is given priority in infrastructure and in the form of urban development.

Barrioization   Defined by geographer James Curtis as the dramatic increase in Hispanic population in a given neighbourhood; referring to *barrio*, the Spanish word for neighbourhood.

Behavioural geography   An approach that seeks to understand and model human behaviour and the decision-making processes implicated in human relationships with place.

Biodiversity   The total variety of plant and animal species in a particular place, as well as the diversity of all aspects of life found on Earth from genes to ecosystems.

Boundary   Vertical plane between states that cuts through the rocks below (called the subsoil) and the airspace above the surface, dividing one state territory from another.

Break-of-bulk point   A location along a transport route where goods must be transferred from one carrier to another. A port, for example, is a break-of-bulk point where the cargoes of ocean-going ships are unloaded and put on trains, trucks, or perhaps smaller riverboats for inland distribution.

Capitalism   Economic model wherein people, corporations, and states produce goods and exchange them on the world market, with the goal of achieving profit.

Cartography   The art and science of making maps, including data compilation, layout, and design. Also concerned with the interpretation of mapped patterns.

Caste system   The strict social segregation of people—specifically in India's Hindu society—on the basis of ancestry and occupation.

Census   A periodic and official count of a country's population.

Census agglomeration   A census agglomeration is an urban area in which the core has at least 10,000 people and often many more in surrounding communities.

Census metropolitan area (CMA)   A census metropolitan area is a group of cities with a population of 100,000 or more that cluster around an urban core of at least 50,000.

Central business district (CBD)   The downtown heart of a central city, marked by high land values, a concentration of business and commerce, and the clustering of the tallest buildings.

Central city   The urban area that is not suburban; generally, the older or original city that is surrounded by newer suburbs.

Central place theory   Theory proposed by Walter Christaller that explains how and where central places in the urban hierarchy should be functionally and spatially distributed with respect to one another.

Centrality   The strength of an urban centre in its capacity to attract producers and consumers to its facilities; a city's "reach" into the surrounding region.

Centrifugal   Forces that tend to divide a country—such as internal religious, linguistic, ethnic, or ideological differences.

Centripetal   Forces that tend to unify a country—such as widespread commitment to a national culture, shared ideological objectives, and a common faith.

Chain migration   Pattern of migration that develops when migrants move along and through kinship links (i.e., one migrant settles in a place and then writes, calls, or communicates through others to describe this place to family and friends, who in turn then migrate there).

Child mortality rate   A figure that describes the number of children who die between the first and fifth years of their lives in a given population.

Chlorofluorocarbons (CFCs)   Synthetic organic compounds first created in the 1950s and used primarily as refrigerants and as propellants. The role of CFCs in the destruction of the ozone layer led to the signing of an international agreement (the Montreal Protocol).

Chronic or degenerative diseases Generally, long-lasting afflictions that are now more common because of higher life expectancies.

City Conglomeration of people and buildings clustered together to serve as a centre of politics, culture, and economics.

Colonialism Rule by an autonomous power over a subordinate and alien people and place. Although often established and maintained through political structures, colonialism also creates unequal cultural and economic relations. Because of the magnitude and impact of the European colonial project of the last few centuries, the term is generally understood to refer to that particular colonial endeavour.

Colonization Physical process whereby the colonizer takes over another place, putting its own government in charge and either moving its own people into the place or bringing in indentured outsiders to gain control of the people and the land.

Commercial agriculture Large-scale farming and ranching operations that employ vast land bases, large mechanized equipment, factory-type labour forces, and the latest technology.

Commercialization The transformation of an area of a city into an area attractive to residents and tourists alike in terms of economic activity.

Commodification The process through which something is given monetary value. Commodification occurs when a good or an idea that previously was not regarded as an object to be bought and sold is turned into something that has a particular price and that can be traded in a market economy.

Commodity chain Series of links connecting the many places of production and distribution that result in a commodity, which is then exchanged on the world market.

Complementarity A condition that exists when two regions, through an exchange of raw materials and/or finished products, can specifically satisfy each other's demands.

Concentric zone model A structural model of the American central city that suggests the existence of five concentric land-use rings arranged around a common centre.

Connectivity The degree of direct linkage between one particular location and other locations in a transport network.

Conservationism A human-centred view of nature that advocates for conservation of resources for future human use.

Contagious diffusion The distance-controlled spreading of an idea, innovation, or some other item through a local population by person-to-person contact—analogous to the communication of a contagious illness.

Containerization The use of containers to unitize cargo for transportation, supply, and storage.

Context The geographical situation in which something occurs; the combination of what is happening at a variety of scales concurrently.

Core Processes that incorporate higher levels of education, higher salaries, and more technology, and that generate more wealth than periphery processes in the world economy.

Critical geopolitics Process by which geopoliticians deconstruct and focus on explaining the underlying spatial assumptions and territorial perspectives of politicians.

Crude birth rate (CBR) The number of live births yearly per thousand people in a population.

Crude death rate (CDR) The number of deaths yearly per thousand people in a population.

Cultural appropriation The process by which cultures adopt customs and knowledge from other cultures and use them for their own benefit.

Cultural barrier Prevailing cultural attitude rendering certain innovations, ideas, or practices unacceptable or unadoptable in that particular culture.

Cultural diffusion The expansion and adoption of a cultural element, from its place of origin to a wider area.

Cultural landscape The visible imprint of human activity and culture on the landscape. The layers of buildings, forms, and artefacts sequentially imprinted on the landscape by the activities of various human occupants.

Cultural symbol An artefact (e.g., building, image, article of clothing) encoded with the norms, values, and beliefs of the people who created it, which conveys social meaning that geographers can "read" and "decode."

Cultural trait A single element of normal practice in a culture, such as the wearing of a turban.

Culture A set of shared belief systems, norms, and values practised by a particular group of people. According to cultural theorist Raymond Williams, culture is both "ordinary" and a "whole way of life."

Custom Practice routinely followed by a group of people.

Deforestation The clearing and destruction of forests to harvest wood for consumption, clear land for agricultural uses, and make way for expanding settlement frontiers.

Deagglomeration The process of industrial deconcentration in response to technological advances and/or increasing costs due to congestion and competition.

Deindustrialization Process by which companies move industrial jobs to other regions with cheaper labour, leaving the newly deindustrialized region to switch to a service economy and to work through a period of high unemployment.

Demographic transition Multistage model, based on Western Europe's experience, of changes in population growth exhibited by countries undergoing industrialization. High birth rates and death rates are followed by plunging death rates, producing a huge net population gain; this is followed by the convergence of birth rates and death rates at a low overall level.

Demography The study of the characteristics of a population, such as race, age, sex, and ethnicity.

Dependency theory A structuralist theory that offers a critique of the modernization model of development. Based on the idea that certain types of political and economic relations (especially colonialism) between countries and regions of the world have created arrangements that both control and limit the extent to which regions can develop.

Deportation The act of a government sending a migrant out of its country and back to the migrant's home country.

Desertification The encroachment of desert conditions on moister zones along the desert margins, where plant cover and soils are threatened by desiccation—through overuse, in part by humans and their domestic animals, and, possibly, in part because of inexorable shifts in the Earth's environmental zones.

Developing With respect to a country, making progress in technology, production, and socio-economic welfare.

Devolution The process whereby regions within a state demand and gain political strength and growing autonomy at the expense of the central government.

Diaspora From the Greek "to disperse," a term describing forceful or voluntary dispersal of a people from their homeland to a new place. Originally denoting the dispersal of Jews, it is increasingly applied to other population dispersals, such as the involuntary relocation of Black peoples during the slave trade or Chinese peoples outside of Mainland China, Taiwan, and Hong Kong.

Diffusion The spatial spreading or dissemination of a culture element (such as a technological innovation) or some other phenomenon (such as a disease outbreak). See also *contagious*, *expansion*, *hierarchical*, *relocation*, and *stimulus diffusion*.

Disamenity sector The very poorest parts of cities that in extreme cases are not even connected to regular city services and are controlled by gangs or drug lords.

Discourse The representative codes and conventions of language that produce culturally specific meanings.

Distance Measurement of the physical space between two places.

Distance decay The effects of distance on interaction; generally the greater the distance, the less interaction takes place.

Dot maps Maps where one dot represents a certain number of a phenomenon, such as a population.

Doubling time The time required for a population to double in size.

Dowry death   In the context of arranged marriages in India, the death of a bride arising from a dispute over the price (the dowry) to be paid by the family of the bride to the father of the groom.

Edge cities   A term introduced by American journalist Joel Garreau in order to describe the shifting focus of urbanization in the United States, away from the central business district (CBD) toward new loci of economic activity at the urban fringe. These cities are characterized by extensive amounts of office and retail space, few residential areas, and modern buildings (less than 30 years old).

Emigration   The act of leaving one location or place for another, from the perspective of the beginning location.

Endemic   When disease prevails throughout a particular locality or region.

Environmental determinism   The view that the natural environment has a controlling influence over various aspects of human life, including cultural development.

Environmental stress   The threat to environmental security by human activity such as atmospheric and groundwater pollution, deforestation, oil spills, and ocean dumping.

Epidemic   Regional outbreak of a disease. See also *pandemic*.

Ethnicity   Affiliation or identity within a group of people bound by common ancestry and culture.

Eugenic population policies   Government policies designed to favour one racial or cultural sector over others.

Expansion diffusion   The spread of an innovation or an idea through a population in an area in such a way that the number of those influenced grows continuously larger, resulting in an expanding area of dissemination.

Expansive population policies   Government policies that encourage large families and raise the rate of population growth.

Explorer   A person examining a region that is unknown to them.

Export processing zones (EPZs)   Zones established by many countries in the periphery and semi-periphery that offer favourable tax, regulatory, and trade arrangements to attract foreign trade and investment.

Federal (state)   A political-territorial system in which a central government represents the various entities within a nation-state where they have common interests—defence, foreign affairs, and the like—but allows these various entities to retain their own identities and to have their own laws, policies, and customs in certain spheres.

First Agricultural Revolution   Dating back 10,000 years, the First Agricultural Revolution achieved plant domestication and animal domestication.

First Urban Revolution   The innovation of the city, which occurred independently in as many as six separate hearths.

Five themes (of geography)   The five themes derived from the spatial perspective of geography are location, region, place, landscape, and movement.

Folk culture   The cultural traits, such as dress modes, dwellings, traditions, and institutions, of usually small, traditional communities.

Food security   A situation where all people, at all times, have physical and economic access to sufficient, safe, and nutritious food that meets their dietary needs and food preferences for an active and healthy life.

Forced migration   Human migration flows in which the movers have no choice but to relocate.

Fordist   A highly organized and specialized system for organizing industrial production and labour. Named after automobile producer Henry Ford, Fordist production features assembly-line production of standardized components for mass production.

Formal economy   The legal economy that is taxed and monitored by a government and is included in a government's gross national product (GNP); as opposed to an informal economy.

Formal region   A type of region marked by a certain degree of homogeneity in one or more phenomena; also called uniform region or homogeneous region.

Forum   The focal point of ancient Roman life, combining the functions of the ancient Greek acropolis and agora.

Free trade zones   Areas set aside within countries to make foreign investment and trade easier by reducing or eliminating trade barriers and providing inexpensive labour and raw materials.

Friction of distance   The increase in time and cost that usually comes with increasing distance.

Functional region   A region defined by the particular set of activities or interactions that occur within it.

Functional zonation   The division of a city into different regions or zones (e.g., residential or industrial) for certain purposes or functions (e.g., housing or manufacturing).

Gender   Social differences between men and women, rather than the anatomical, biological differences between the sexes. Notions of gender differences—that is, what is considered "feminine" or "masculine"—vary greatly over time and space.

Gendered   In terms of a place, whether the place is designed for or claimed by men or women.

Genetic or inherited diseases   Diseases caused by variation or mutation of a gene or group of genes in a human.

Genetically modified organisms (GMOs)   Crops that carry new traits that have been inserted through advanced genetic engineering methods.

Genocide   The deliberate and systematic destruction, in whole or in part, of an ethnic, racial, religious, or national group.

Gentrification   The rehabilitation of the deteriorated, often abandoned, housing of low-income inner-city residents for new middle- or upper-class residents.

Geocaching   A hunt for a cache, the Global Positioning System (GPS) coordinates of which are posted on the Internet by other geocachers.

Geographic information system (GIS)   A collection of computer hardware and software that permits spatial data to be collected, recorded, stored, retrieved, manipulated, analyzed, and displayed to the user.

Geomatics technologies   Those processes and tools used in the collection and analysis of spatial data, including remote sensing (RS), geographic information systems (GIS), global positioning systems (GPS), and related forms of earth mapping.

Geometric boundary   Political boundary defined and delimited (and occasionally demarcated) as a straight line or an arc.

Global division of labour   Phenomenon whereby corporations and others can draw from labour markets around the world, made possible by the compression of time and space through innovations in communication and transportation systems.

Global positioning system (GPS)   Satellite-based system for determining the absolute location of places or geographic features.

Global warming   Theory that the Earth is gradually warming as a result of an enhanced greenhouse effect in the Earth's atmosphere caused by ever-increasing amounts of carbon dioxide and other gases produced by various human activities.

Global-local continuum   The notion that what happens at the global scale has a direct effect on what happens at the local scale, and vice versa. This idea posits that the world is comprised of an interconnected series of relationships that extend across space.

Globalization   "An accelerating set of processes involving flows that encompass ever-greater numbers of the world spaces and that lead to increasing integration and interconnectivity among those spaces" (Ritzer, 2007, p. 1).

Glocalization   The process by which people in a local place mediate and alter regional, national, and global processes.

Gravity model   A mathematical prediction of the interaction of places, the interaction being a function of population size of the respective places and the distance between them.

Green Revolution   The recently successful development of higher-yield, fast-growing varieties of rice and other cereals in certain developing countries, which led to increased production per unit area and a dramatic narrowing of the gap between population growth and food needs.

Griffin-Ford model   Developed by geographers Ernst Griffin and Larry Ford, this model of the Latin American city shows a blend of traditional elements of Latin American culture with the forces of globalization that are reshaping the urban scene.

Gross domestic product (GDP)   The total value of all goods and services produced within a country during a given year.

Gross national income (GNI)   The total value of all goods and services produced within a country plus income received from investments outside the country.

Gross national product (GNP)   The total value of all goods and services produced by a country's economy in a given year. It includes all goods and services produced by corporations and individuals of a country, whether or not they are located within the country.

Guest worker   Legal immigrant who has a work visa, usually short term.

Hearth   The area where an idea or cultural trait originates.

Heartland theory   A geopolitical hypothesis, proposed by British geographer Halford Mackinder during the first two decades of the 20th century, that any political power based in the heart of Eurasia could gain sufficient strength to eventually dominate the world. Mackinder further proposed that since eastern Europe controlled access to the Eurasian interior, its ruler would command the vast "heartland" to the east.

Heteronormative   A term used to describe a belief system that assumes heterosexuality to be the norm and includes assumptions about biologically based male and female and normative gendered behaviours of "masculine" and "feminine." Other forms of sexuality, gender, and embodied physicality are excluded or marginalized.

Hierarchical diffusion   A form of diffusion in which an idea or innovation spreads by passing first among the most connected places or peoples. An urban hierarchy is usually involved, encouraging the leapfrogging of innovations over wide areas, with geographic distance a less important influence.

Horizontal integration   Ownership by the same firm of a number of companies that exist at the same point on a commodity chain.

Huang He (Yellow) and Wei (Yangtze) river valleys   Chronologically, the fourth urban hearth, established around 1500 BCE, at the confluence of the Huang He and Wei rivers of present-day China.

Human geography   One of the two major divisions of geography; the spatial analysis of human population, its cultures, activities, and landscapes.

Human-environment   The second theme of geography as defined by the Geography Educational National Implementation Project; reciprocal relationship between humans and environment.

Humanistic geography   An approach that focuses on the human aspects of place, including human emotions, values, and desires.

Identifying against   Constructing an identity by first defining the "other" and then defining ourselves as "not the other."

Identity   Defined by geographer Gillian Rose as "how we make sense of ourselves"; how people see themselves at different scales.

Ideology   A set of shared ideas or beliefs that serve to justify the interests of dominant groups. In political geography, often understood as a world view about how societies do and should work.

Immigration   The act of migrating into a new country or area, from the perspective of the destination.

Immigration wave   Phenomenon whereby different patterns of chain migration build upon one another to create a swell in migration from one origin to the same destination.

Indus River Valley   Chronologically, the third urban hearth, dating to 2200 BCE.

Industrial Revolution   The term applied to the social and economic changes in agriculture, commerce, and manufacturing that resulted from technological innovations and specialization in late-18th-century Europe.

Infant mortality rate (IMR)   A figure that describes the number of babies that die within the first year of their lives in a given population.

Infectious diseases   Diseases that are spread by bacteria, viruses, or parasites. Infectious diseases diffuse directly or indirectly from human to human.

Informal economy   Economic activity that is neither taxed nor monitored by a government and is not included in that government's gross national product (GNP); as opposed to a formal economy.

Intermodal (connections)   Places where two or more modes of transportation meet (including air, road, rail, barge, and ship).

Intermodal transportation   The transportation of a person or a load from its origin to its destination by a sequence of at least two transportation modes, the transfer from one mode to the next being performed at an intermodal terminal.

Internal migration   Human movement within a nation-state, such as ongoing westward and southward movements in Canada.

Internally displaced persons (IDPs)   People who have been displaced within their own countries and who do not cross international borders as they flee.

International migration   Human movement involving movement across international boundaries.

Intersectionality   The complex connections and relationships between various social categories such as race, class, gender, and sexuality.

Intervening opportunity   The presence of a nearer opportunity that greatly diminishes the attractiveness of sites farther away.

Island of development   Place built up by a government or corporation to attract foreign investment, which has relatively high concentrations of paying jobs and infrastructure.

Just-in-time delivery   Method of inventory management made possible by efficient transportation and communication systems, whereby companies keep on hand just what they need for near-term production, planning that what they need for longer-term production will arrive when needed.

Kinship links   Types of push factors or pull factors that influence a migrant's decision to go where family or friends have already found success.

Landscape   The fourth theme of geography; the overall appearance of an area. Most landscapes are comprised of a combination of natural and human-induced influences.

Language family   Group of languages with a shared but fairly distant origin.

Laws of migration   Laws developed by British demographer Ernst Ravenstein, that predict the flow of migrants.

Leadership class   Group of decision makers and organizers in early cities who controlled the resources, and often the lives, of others.

Least Cost Theory   Model developed by Alfred Weber according to which the location of manufacturing establishments is determined by the minimization of three critical expenses: labour, transportation, and agglomeration.

Life expectancy   A figure indicating how long, on average, a person may be expected to live. Normally expressed in the context of a particular state.

Livestock ranching   The raising of domesticated animals for the production of meat and other by-products such as leather and wool.

Local culture   Group of people in a particular place who see themselves as a collective or a community, who share experiences, customs, and traits, and who work to preserve those traits and customs in order to claim uniqueness and to distinguish themselves from others.

Local Exchange Trading System (LETS)   A barter system whereby a local currency is created through which members trade services or goods in a local network separated from the formal economy.

Location   The first theme of geography; the geographical situation of people and things.

Location theory   A logical attempt to explain the locational pattern of an economic activity and the manner in which its producing areas are interrelated. The agricultural location theory contained in the von Thünen model is a leading example.

Long-lot survey system   Distinct regional approach to land surveying found in the Canadian Maritimes, parts of Quebec, Louisiana, and Texas in which land is divided into narrow parcels stretching back from rivers, roads, or canals.

Luxury crops   Non-subsistence crops such as tea, cacao, coffee, and tobacco.

Malaria   Vectored disease, spread by mosquitoes that carry the malaria parasite in their saliva, which kills approximately 150,000 children in the global periphery each month.

Maquiladora   Zones in northern Mexico where factories are established to supply manufactured goods to the U.S. market. The low-wage workers in the primarily foreign-owned factories assemble imported components and/or raw materials and then export finished goods.

Material culture   The art, housing, clothing, sports, dances, foods, and other similar items constructed or created by a group of people.

Mediterranean agriculture   Specialized farming that occurs only in areas where the dry Mediterranean summer climate prevails.

Mega-city   A city having a population of more than 10 million inhabitants.

Megalopolis   Large coalescing supercities that are forming in diverse parts of the world; the term was formerly used specifically with an uppercase "M" to refer to locations such as the Boston–Washington multi-metropolitan corridor on the northeastern seaboard of the United States.

Mental map   Image or picture of the way space is organized as determined by an individual's perception, impression, and knowledge of that space.

Mercantilism   In a general sense, associated with the promotion of commercialism and trade. More specifically, a protectionist policy of European states during the 16th to the 18th centuries that promoted a state's economic position in the contest with other countries. The acquisition of gold and silver and the maintenance of a favourable trade balance (more exports than imports) were central to the policy.

Mesoamerica   Chronologically, the fifth urban hearth, dating to 200 BCE.

Mesopotamia   Region of great cities (e.g., Ur and Babylon) located between the Tigris and Euphrates Rivers; chronologically, the first urban hearth, dating to 3500 BCE, which was founded in the Fertile Crescent.

Metes and bounds system   A system of land surveying east of the Appalachian Mountains that relies on descriptions of land ownership and natural features such as streams or trees. Because of the imprecise nature of metes and bounds surveying, the U.S. Land Office abandoned the technique in favour of the rectangular survey system.

Microcredit program   Program that provides small loans to poor people, especially women, to encourage development of small businesses.

Migrant labour   A common type of periodic movement involving millions of workers in the United States and tens of millions of workers worldwide who cross international borders in search of employment and, in many instances, become immigrants.

Migration   A change in residence intended to be permanent. See also *chain, forced, internal, international, step,* and *voluntary migration*.

Millennium Development Goals   A set of eight human development-related goals for the world's most impoverished countries, which were adopted at the United Nations Millennium Summit in 2000 with the intention of achieving all of these goals by the year 2015.

Modernization model   A model of economic development most closely associated with the work of economist Walter Rostow. The modernization model (sometimes referred to as modernization theory) maintains that all countries go through five interrelated stages of development, which culminate in an economic state of self-sustained economic growth and high levels of mass consumption.

Monoculture   Dependence on a single agricultural commodity.

Montreal Protocol   An international agreement signed in 1987 by 105 countries and the European Community (now European Union). The protocol called for a 50 percent reduction in the production and consumption of chlorofluorocarbons (CFCs) by 2000. Subsequent meetings in London (1990) and Copenhagen (1992) accelerated the timing of CFC phase-out, and a complete worldwide ban has been in effect since 1996.

Movement   The fifth theme of geography; the mobility of people, goods, and ideas across the surface of the planet.

Multinational state   A state with more than one nation within its borders.

Multistate nation   A nation that stretches across borders and across states.

Nation   A tightly knit group of people possessing bonds of language, ethnicity, religion, and other shared cultural attributes. Such homogeneity actually prevails within very few states.

Nation-state   Theoretically, a recognized member of the modern state system possessing formal sovereignty and occupied by a people who see themselves as a single, united nation. Most nations and states aspire to this form, but it is realized almost nowhere. Nonetheless, in common parlance, nation-state is used as a synonym for country or state.

Nationalism   Both an ideology and a political practice that says all nations need their own sovereign government and territory.

Neighbourhood unit   A planning concept developed by Clarence Perry as a means of reconciling the problems of automobile traffic with public safety objectives, most notably those aimed at the safety of children.

Neo-colonialism   The entrenchment of the colonial order, such as trade and investment, under a new guise.

Neo-liberalism   An ideology that emphasizes self-regulating markets, minimal state intervention, and individual choice, as a means of ensuring economic and social well-being.

Networks   A set of interconnected nodes without a centre, as defined by Manuel Castells.

New urbanism   A philosophy of urban design that calls for development, urban revitalization, and suburban reforms that create walkable neighbourhoods with a diversity of housing and jobs.

Nile River Valley   Chronologically, the second urban hearth, dating to 3200 BCE.

Noise pollution   A type of pollution in which distracting, irritating, or damaging sounds are freely audible.

Nomadism   Movement among a definite set of places—often cyclic movement.

Non-governmental organizations (NGOs)   International organizations that operate outside the formal political arena but are nevertheless influential in spearheading international initiatives on social, economic, and environmental issues.

Nonmaterial culture   The beliefs, practices, aesthetics, and values of a group of people.

Non-renewable resources   Resources that cannot regenerate as they are exploited.

North American Free Trade Agreement (NAFTA)   Agreement entered into by Canada, Mexico, and the United States to eliminate the barriers to trade in, and facilitate the cross-border movement of, goods and services between the countries.

Offshore   With reference to production, to outsource to a third party located outside the country.

One-child policy   A program established by the Chinese government in 1979 to slow population growth in China. Under the policy, families having more than one child were penalized financially and denied educational opportunities and housing privileges.

Organic products   Products that are raised, grown, stored, and/or processed without the use of synthetic chemicals or fertilizers; herbicides, insecticides, fungicides, or any other pesticides; growth hormones; or growth regulators.

Outsource   With reference to production, to turn over in part or in total to a third party.

Oxygen cycle   Cycle in which natural processes and human activity consume atmospheric oxygen and produce carbon dioxide and the Earth's forests and other flora, through photosynthesis, consume carbon dioxide and produce oxygen.

Ozone layer   The layer in the upper atmosphere, located between 30 and 45 kilometres above the Earth's surface, where stratospheric ozone is most densely concentrated. The ozone layer acts as a filter for the Sun's harmful ultraviolet rays.

Pandemic An outbreak of a disease that spreads worldwide. See also *epidemic*.

Participatory development The notion that locals should be engaged in deciding what development means for them and how it should be achieved.

Pattern The design of a spatial distribution (e.g., scattered or concentrated).

Peace of Westphalia Peace negotiated in 1648 to end the Thirty Years' War, Europe's most destructive internal struggle over religion. The treaties contained new language recognizing statehood and nationhood, clearly defined borders, and guarantees of security.

Per capita GNI The gross national income (GNI) of a given country (that is, the total value of all goods and services produced within a country, plus income received from investments outside the country) divided by the population of the country.

Perceptual region A region that exists only as a conceptualization or an idea and not as a physically demarcated entity. For example, the North or the Maritimes.

Periphery Processes that incorporate lower levels of education, lower salaries, and less technology, and that generate less wealth than core processes in the world economy.

Peru Chronologically, the sixth urban hearth, dating to 900 BCE.

Physical geography One of the two major divisions of systematic geography; the spatial analysis of the structure, processes, and location of the Earth's natural phenomena such as climate, soil, plants, animals, and topography.

Physical-political (natural-political) boundary A political boundary defined and delimited (and occasionally demarcated) by a prominent physical feature in the natural landscape—such as a river or the crest ridges of a mountain range.

Physiologic population density The number of people per unit area of arable land.

Place The uniqueness of human experience, including sights, smells, emotions, and experiences of a specific area or location on Earth.

Placelessness The loss of uniqueness of place in the cultural landscape so that one place looks like the next, as defined by geographer Edward Relph.

Plant domestication Genetic modification of a plant such that its reproductive success depends on human intervention.

Plantation agriculture Production system based on a large estate owned by an individual, family, or corporation and organized to produce a cash crop. Almost all plantations were established within the tropics; in recent decades, many have been divided into smaller holdings or reorganized as cooperatives.

Political geography A subdivision of human geography focused on the nature and implications of the evolving spatial organization of political governance and formal political practice on the Earth's surface. It is concerned with why political spaces emerge in the places that they do and with how the character of those spaces affects social, political, economic, and environmental understandings and practices.

Popular culture Cultural traits, such as dress, diet, and music, that identify and are part of today's changeable, urban-based, media-influenced western societies.

Population composition Structure of a population in terms of age, sex, and other characteristics such as marital status and education.

Population density A measurement of the number of people per given unit of land.

Population distribution Description of locations on the Earth's surface where populations live.

Population explosion The rapid growth of the world's human population during the past century, attended by ever-shorter doubling times and accelerating rates of increase.

Population geography The study of why populations have certain characteristics and why they distribute themselves across space in particular ways.

Population pyramids A tool used to visually represent of the age and sex composition of a population, in which the percentage of each age group (generally divided in five-year increments) is represented by a horizontal bar, the length of which indicates its relationship to the total population. The males in each age group are represented to the left of the centre line of each horizontal bar; the females in each age group are represented to the right of the centre line.

Possibilism Geographic viewpoint—a response to environmental determinism—that holds that human decision making, not the environment, is the crucial factor in cultural development. Nonetheless, possibilists view the environment as providing a set of broad constraints that limit the possibilities of human choice.

Post-Fordist World economic system characterized by a more flexible set of production practices in which goods are not mass-produced; instead, production has been accelerated and dispersed around the globe by multinational companies that shift production, outsourcing it around the world and bringing places closer together in time and space than would have been imaginable at the beginning of the 20th century.

Post-industrial economy An economy in which most of a country's labour force is engaged in tertiary, quaternary, and quinary sectors. The world's core countries are all post-industrial economies.

Preservationism A view asserting that nature should be preserved for its own sake, rather than for human use.

Primary activities Economic activities that involve the extraction or production of raw materials, such as agriculture, logging, and mining.

Primary industrial regions Western and central Europe; eastern North America; Russia and Ukraine; and eastern Asia, each of which consists of one or more core areas of industrial development, with subsidiary clusters.

Primate city A country's largest city—ranking atop the urban hierarchy—which is most expressive of the national culture and usually (but not always) the capital city as well.

Primogeniture System in which the eldest son—or, in exceptional cases, the eldest daughter—in a family inherits all of a dying parent's land.

Public transit Various services that provide mobility to the general public in shared vehicles, ranging from shared taxis and shuttle vans, to local and intercity buses and passenger rail.

Pull factor Positive conditions and perceptions that effectively attract people to new locales from other areas.

Push factor Negative conditions and perceptions that induce people to leave their abode and migrate to a new locale.

Quaternary sector The sector of tertiary economic activities that includes individuals working with the exchange of information or money.

Quinary sector The sector of tertiary economic activities that includes individuals involved in research or higher education.

Quotas Established limits by governments on the number of immigrants who can enter a country each year.

Race A categorization of humans based on skin colour and other physical characteristics. Racial categories are social and political constructions because they are based on ideas that some biological differences (especially skin colour) are more important than others (e.g., height, etc.), even though the latter might have more significance in terms of human activity. With its roots in 16th-century England, the term is closely associated with European colonialism because of the impact of that development on global understandings of racial differences.

Racism An ideology that ascribes (predominantly negative) significance and meaning to culturally, socially, and politically constructed ideas based on visible differences in individuals.

Radburn Idea A highly influential community planning concept incorporating a hierarchy of roadways, the deliberate segregation of pedestrian and automobile traffic, and the residential "superblock."

Radioactive waste Hazardous waste emitting radiation from nuclear power plants, nuclear weapons factories, and nuclear equipment in hospitals and industry.

Rank-size rule In a model urban hierarchy, the idea that the population of a city or town will be inversely proportional to its rank in the hierarchy.

Rate of natural increase An indicator of population change, calculated by subtracting the crude death rate from the crude birth rate.

Rectangular survey system Also called the Public Land Survey, the system was used by the U.S. Land Office to parcel land west of the Appalachian Mountains. The system divides land into a series of rectangular parcels.

Reference maps Maps that show the absolute location of places and geographic features determined by a frame of reference, typically latitude and longitude.

Refugees People who have fled their country because of political persecution and seek asylum in another country.

Region The second theme of geography; an area on the Earth's surface marked by a degree of formal, functional, or perceptual homogeneity of some phenomenon.

Regional geography The study of a region's unique characteristics, including its natural and human characteristics, in order to understand how areas differ from each other.

Regional scale Interactions occurring within a region, in a regional setting.

Relative location The regional position or situation of a place relative to the position of other places. Distance, accessibility, and connectivity affect relative location.

Relocation diffusion Sequential diffusion process in which the items being diffused are transmitted by their carrier agents as they evacuate the old areas and relocate to new ones. The most common form of relocation diffusion involves the spreading of innovations by a migrating population.

Remittances Money migrants send back to family and friends in their home countries, often in cash, forming an important part of the economy in many poorer countries.

Remote sensing A method of collecting data or information through the use of instruments (e.g., satellites) that are physically distant from the area or object of study.

Renewable resources Resources that can regenerate as they are exploited.

Repatriation The process of returning a refugee or group of refugees to their home country, usually with the assistance of a government or a nongovernmental organization.

Rescale Involvement of players at other scales to generate support for a position or an initiative (e.g., use of the Internet to generate interest on a national or global scale for a local position or initiative).

Restrictive population policies Government policies designed to reduce the rate of natural increase.

Reterritorialization With respect to popular culture, a process by which people start to produce an aspect of popular culture themselves, doing so in the context of their local culture, and making it their own.

Root crop Crops that are reproduced by cultivating the roots of or the cuttings from the plants.

Sanitary landfills Disposal sites for non-hazardous solid waste that is spread in layers and compacted to the smallest practical volume. The sites are typically designed with floors made of materials to treat seeping liquids and are covered by soil as the wastes are compacted and deposited in the landfill.

Scale (1) Representation of a real-world phenomenon at a certain level of reduction or generalization. In cartography, the ratio of map distance to ground distance; indicated on a map as a bar graph, representative fraction, and/or verbal statement. (2) The territorial extent of something. When we refer to scale throughout this book, we are generally using the second of these definitions.

Second Agricultural Revolution Dovetailing with and benefiting from the Industrial Revolution, the Second Agricultural Revolution saw improved methods of cultivation, harvesting, and storage of farm produce.

Secondary activities Economic activities that involve making something from raw materials, such as food processing, the production of lumber or furniture, or building construction.

Seed crops Crops that are reproduced by cultivating the seeds of the plants.

Semi-periphery Places where core and periphery processes are both occurring; places that are exploited by the core but in turn exploit the periphery.

Sense of place State of mind derived when we infuse a place with meaning and emotion by remembering important events that occurred in that place or by labelling a place with a certain character.

Sex/gender/sexuality matrix The expectation that a person is only one of two biological sexes (male or female); that the proper gender characteristics (masculinity or femininity) will be exhibited by that body; and that the normative sexuality is heterosexuality.

Shantytown Unplanned slum development on the margins of a city, dominated by crude dwellings and shelters made mostly of scrap wood, iron, and even pieces of cardboard.

Shifting cultivation Cultivation of crops in tropical forest clearings in which the forest vegetation has been removed by cutting and burning. These clearings are usually abandoned after one to several years in favour of newly cleared forestland. See also *slash-and-burn agriculture*.

Site The internal physical attributes of a place, including its absolute location, spatial character, and physical setting.

Situation The external locational attributes of a place; its relative location or regional position with reference to other non-local places.

Slash-and-burn agriculture The technique in which tools (e.g., machetes and knives) are used to slash down trees and tall vegetation, which are then burned on the ground, forming a layer of ash that contributes to the soil's fertility. See also *shifting cultivation*.

Smog A combination of ground-level ozone, airborne particles, and other air pollutants.

Social construction A perspective that argues that there are not essentialist, biologically based, and "natural" social categories of identity, but, rather, that human perceptions and activities generate particular knowledges about particular groups of people of individuals. These knowledges may vary historically, culturally, and geographically.

Social exclusion The inability of individuals or households to fully participate in society, engage in activities, or access jobs, services, and facilities.

Social stratification The differentiation of society into classes based on wealth, power, production, and prestige. One of two components, together with agricultural surplus, that enables the formation of cities.

Soil erosion The wearing away of the land surface by wind and moving water.

Solid waste Non-liquid, non-soluble materials ranging from municipal garbage to sewage sludge, agricultural refuse, and mining residues.

Sovereignty A principle of international relations that holds that final authority over social, economic, and political matters should rest with the legitimate rulers of independent states.

Space Defined by Doreen Massey and Pat Jess as "social relations stretched out."

Spaces of consumption Areas of a city, the main purpose of which is to encourage people to consume goods and services; driven primarily by the global media industry.

Spatial Pertaining to space on the Earth's surface; sometimes used as a synonym for "geographic."

Spatial analysis Quantitative procedures used to understand the spatial arrangement of phenomena and the related patterns of connections and flows.

Spatial distribution Physical location of geographic phenomena across space.

Spatial interaction The nature and extent of interconnections and linkages. This depends on the distance between places, the accessibility of places, and the transportation and communication connectivity among places.

Spatial perspective Observing variations in geographic phenomena across space.

Special economic zone Specific area within a country in which tax incentives and less stringent environmental regulations are implemented to attract foreign business and investment.

Staples thesis The theory that Canada's economy developed through the export of raw resources to Europe and that, as a result, Canada did not develop a strong manufacturing base, preferring to import finished goods.

State A politically organized entity that is administered by a sovereign government and is recognized by a significant portion of the international community. A state has a defined territory, a permanent population, and a government and is recognized by other states.

Stateless nation A nation that does not have a state.

Stationary population level The level at which a national population ceases to grow.

Step migration Migration to a distant destination that occurs in stages—for example, from farm to nearby village and later to town and city.

Stimulus diffusion A form of diffusion in which a cultural adaptation is created as a result of the introduction of a cultural trait from another place.

Structural adjustment loans Loans granted by international financial institutions, such as the World Bank and the International Monetary Fund, to countries in the periphery and the semi-periphery in exchange for certain economic and governmental reforms in that country (e.g., privatization of certain government entities and opening the country to foreign trade and investment).

Structuralist theory A model of economic development that treats economic disparities among countries or regions as the result of historically derived power relations within the global economic system.

Subsistence agriculture Self-sufficient agriculture that is small in scale and low in technology and that emphasizes food production for local consumption, not for trade.

Suburb A subsidiary urban area surrounding and connected to the central city. Many suburbs are exclusively residential; others have their own commercial centres or shopping malls.

Suburban realm The surrounding environs connected to the city.

Suburbanization The process by which lands that were previously outside the urban environment become urbanized, as people and businesses from the city and other areas move to these spaces.

Succession Process by which new immigrants to a city move to and dominate or take over areas or neighbourhoods occupied by older immigrant groups. For example, in the early 20th century, Puerto Ricans "invaded" the immigrant Jewish neighbourhood of East Harlem and successfully took over the neighbourhood or "succeeded" the immigrant Jewish population as the dominant immigrant group in the neighbourhood.

Sunbelt The southern and southwestern regions of the United States.

Supranational organization A venture involving three or more nation-states that agree to formal political, economic, and/or cultural cooperation to promote shared objectives. The European Union is one such organization.

Sustainability Defined by Castree et al., 2013, as "the property of a system or process that allows for both its use and long-term regeneration."

Sustainable transportation An approach to the provision of transportation infrastructure and services that involves simultaneous consideration of environmental, economic, and social objectives.

Synergy The cross-promotion of vertically integrated goods.

Tear-downs Homes bought in many North American suburbs with the intent of tearing them down and replacing them with much larger homes, often referred to as "monster homes."

Technopole Centres or nodes of high-technology research and activity around which a high-technology corridor is sometimes established.

Territorial integrity The right of a state to defend sovereign territory against incursion from other states.

Territoriality In political geography, a country's or more local community's sense of property and attachment toward its territory, as expressed by its determination to keep it inviolable and strongly defended.

Tertiary activities Service industries connecting the manufacturing and industrial processes to consumers as well as services that facilitate trade and commerce.

Tertiary sector The sector of tertiary economic activities that includes trade, transportation, and warehousing.

Thematic maps Maps that tell stories, typically showing the degree of some attribute or the movement of a geographic phenomenon.

Third Agricultural Revolution Currently in progress, the Third Agricultural Revolution has as its principal orientation the development of genetically modified organisms (GMOs).

Three-tier structure With reference to Immanuel Wallerstein's world-systems theory, the division of the world into the core, the periphery, and the semi-periphery as a means to help explain the interconnections between places in the global economy.

Time-space compression The process by which global markets seem to reorganize the perception of time so as to reduce the constraints of space on their activities; associated with the work of David Harvey.

Total fertility rate The average number of births per woman of childbearing age, usually considered between 15 and 49 years of age.

Township-and-range system A rectangular land-division scheme designed by Thomas Jefferson to disperse settlers evenly across farmlands of the U.S. interior. See also *rectangular survey system*.

Toxic waste Hazardous waste containing chemicals and infectious materials.

Trade area A region adjacent to every town and city within which its influence is dominant.

Trafficking When a family sends a child or an adult to a labour recruiter in hopes that the labour recruiter will send money, and the family member will earn money to send home.

Transport networks The complete system of the routes pertaining to all means of transport available in a particular area.

Transportation geography The study of the movement of people and goods, the transportation systems designed to facilitate such movement, and the relationship of transportation to other facets of human geography, such as economic development, energy, land use, sprawl, environmental degradation, values, and culture.

Unilateralism World order in which one state is in a position of dominance, with allies following rather than joining the political decision-making process.

Unitary (state) A nation-state that has a centralized government and administration that exercises power equally over all parts of the state.

Urban (area) The entire built-up, non-rural area and its population, including the most recently constructed suburban appendages. Provides a better picture of the dimensions and population of such an area than the delimited municipality (central city) that forms its heart.

Urban agglomerations Defined by the United Nations as those populations of 1 million or more people "within a contiguous territory inhabited at urban levels of residential density."

Urban morphology The study of the physical form and structure of urban places.

Urban sprawl Unrestricted growth of housing, commercial development, and roads over large expanses of land in many North American urban areas, with little concern for urban planning.

Variable costs Costs that change directly with the amount of production (e.g., energy supply and labour costs).

Vectored disease A disease carried from one host to another by an intermediate host.

Vertical integration Ownership by the same firm of a number of companies that exist along a variety of points on a commodity chain.

Vienna Convention for the Protection of the Ozone Layer The first international convention aimed at addressing the issue of ozone depletion. Held in 1985, the Vienna Convention was the predecessor to the Montreal Protocol.

Voluntary migration Movement in which people relocate in response to perceived opportunity, not because they are forced to move.

Von Thünen model   A model that explains the location of agricultural activities in a commercial, profit-making economy. A process of spatial competition allocates various farming activities into rings around a central market city, with profit-earning capability the determining force in how far a crop locates from the market.

Water pollution   Pollution caused when discharges of energy or materials degrade water for other users.

World city   Dominant city in terms of its role in the global political economy. Not one of the world's biggest cities in terms of population or industrial output, but rather a centre of strategic control of the world economy.

World-systems theory   Theory originated by Immanuel Wallerstein and illuminated by his three-tier structure, which proposes that social change in the developing world is inextricably linked to the economic activities of the developed world.

Zone   Area of a city with a relatively uniform land use (e.g., an industrial zone or a residential zone).

Zoning laws   Legal restrictions on land use that determine what types of building and economic activities are allowed to take place in certain areas. In the United States, areas are most commonly divided into separate zones of residential, retail, or industrial use.

REFERENCES

Chapter 1 Introduction to Human Geography

Cresswell, T., & Merriman, P. 2011. *Geographies of mobilities: Practices, spaces, subjects.* Farnham and Burlington, VT. Ashgate.

Entrikin, J. N. 1976. Contemporary humanism in geography. *Annals of the Association of American Geographers*, 66.

Franklin, U. 1999. *The real world of technology.* Toronto: House of Anansi Press.

Hägerstrand, T. 1970. *What about people in regional science?* Papers, Regional Science Association, 24, 7–21.

Hartshorne, R. 1939. *The nature of geography.* Washington, DC: Association of American Geographers.

Huntington, E., & Cushing, S. W. 1940. *Principles of human geography,* 5th ed. New York: John Wiley & Sons.

Johnston, R. J. 1986. *On human geography.* Oxford, New York: Blackwell.

Lawson, V. 2004. *The geographical advantage in development studies.* Keynote Address. Annual Meeting of the Great Plains/Rocky Mountains Division of the Association of American Geographers.

Lewis, P. 1979. Axioms for reading the landscape: Some guides to the American scene. In *The interpretation of ordinary landscapes: Geographical essays,* D. W. Meinig, ed. New York: Oxford University Press, 11–32.

Michener, J. 1970. The mature social studies teacher. *Social Education*, November, 760–766.

Peet, R. 1998. *Modern geographical thought.* Oxford, Malden, MA: Blackwell Publishers.

Relph, E. 1997. Sense of place. In *Ten geographic ideas that changed the world,* S. Hanson, ed. New Brunswick, NJ: Rutgers University Press.

Sauer, C. 1927. Recent developments in cultural geography. In *Recent developments in the social sciences,* C. A. Elwood, C. Wissler, and R. H. Gault, eds. Philadelphia: J. B. Lippincott, 154–212.

Sauer, C. 1952. *Agricultural origins and dispersals.* American Geographical Society.

Schaefer, F. K. 1953. Exceptionalism in geography: A methodological examination. *Annals of the Association of American Geographers*, 43, 226–245.

Tuan, Y. F. 1976. Humanistic geography. *Annals of the Association of American Geographers*, 66, 266–276.

Chapter 2 Globalization and Geographies

Anderson, B. 1991. Imagined communities: reflections on the origin and spread of nationalism (Revised and extended ed.). London: Verso.

Burger, J. 1990. *The Gaia atlas of first peoples.* London: Gaia Books Ltd.

Castells, M. 2000. Materials for an exploratory theory of the network society. *British Journal of Sociology*, 51(1), 5–24.

Corbridge, S. 1988. The asymmetry of interdependence: The United States and the geopolitics of international financial relations. *Studies in Comparative International Development*, Spring, 3–29.

Dicken, P. 2011. *Global shift: Reshaping the global economic map in the 21st century,* 6th ed. London: Guilford Press.

Friedman, T. H. 2005. *The world is flat.* New York: Farrar, Straus and Giroux.

Giddens, A. 1990. *The consequences of modernity.* Stanford: Stanford University Press.

Goodman, D. J., & Cohen, M. 2004. *Consumer culture: A reference handbook.* Santa Barbara, CA: ABC–CLIO.

Harvey, D. 1989. *The condition of postmodernity.* Oxford and Cambridge, MA: Basil Blackwell.

Harvey, D. 2005. *A brief history of neoliberalism.* Oxford: Oxford University Press.

Kirby, A. 2004. The global culture factory. In *Globalizaton and its outcomes,* J. O'Loughlin, L. Stacheli, and E. Grcenbcrg, eds. New York: Guilford Press, 133–158.

Kumar, S., & Corbridge, S. 2002. Programmed to fail? Development projects and the politics of participation. *Journal of Development Studies,* 39(2), 73–103.

Maskus, K. E. 2004. A system on the brink: Pitfalls in international trade rules on the road to globalization. In *Globalizaton and its outcomes,* J. O'Loughlin, L. Staeheli, and E. Greenberg, eds. New York: Guilford Press, 98–116.

Norcliffe, G. 2001. Canada in a global economy. *Canadian Geographer*, 45, 14–30.

O'Brien, R. 1992. *Global financial integration: The end of geography.* New York: Council on Foreign Relations Press.

O'Loughlin, J., Staeheli, L., & Greenberg, E., eds. 2004. *Globalization and its outcomes.* New York: Guilford Press.

Pacione, M. 1997. Local exchange trading systems as a response to the globalization of capitalism. *Urban Studies,* 34(8), 1179–1199.

Pereira, M., & Mendes, M. 2002. EU competition law, convergence, and the media industry. European Commission, Media and Music Publishing Unit.

Ritzer, G. 2007. Introduction. In *The Blackwell companion to globalization,* G. Ritzer, ed. Malden, MA: Blackwell Publishing, 1–13.

Wallerstein, I. 1983. *Historical capitalism.* London: Verso.

Wallerstein, I. 2001. *The essential Wallerstein.* New York: New Press.

Williams College Museum of Art. 2011. *Julie Mehretu: City sitings.* http://wcma.williams.edu/exhibit/julie-mehretu-city-sitings/. Last accessed March 31, 2015.

Wrigley, N., Coe, N. M., & Currah, A. 2005. Globalizing retail: Conceptualizing the distribution-based transnational corporation (TNC). *Progress in Human Geography,* 29(4), 437–457.

Chapter 3 Political Geography

Anderson, B. 1991. *Imagined communities: Reflections on the origin and spread of nationalism.* London: Verso.

Bush, G. W. 2005. *Address to the Joint Session of Congress.* September 20, 2001. http://www.september11news.com/PresidentBush-Speech.htm. Last accessed October 2005.

Castells, M. 2000. *The rise of the network society,* 2nd ed. Malden, MA: Blackwell Publishing.

Clinton, W. J. 1998. *Oval Office remarks.* http://news.bbc.co.uk/2/hi/americas/155412.stm. Last accessed March 31, 2015.

Flint, C., & Taylor, J. P. 2007. *Political geography: World economy, nation-state and locality,* 5th ed. Harlow, UK: Longman, Scientific and Technical.

Hartshorne, R. 1950. The functional approach in political geography. *Annals of the Association of American Geographers,* 40(2), 95–130.

Jackson, R. H. 1990. *Quasi-states: sovereignty, international relations, and the third world.* New York: Cambridge University Press.

Johnston, R. J., Gregory, D., Pratt, G., & Watts, M., eds. 2000. *Dictionary of human geography,* 4th ed. Malden, MA: Blackwell Publishing Co.

Mackinder, H. J. 1904. The geographical pivot of history. *Geographical Journal,* 23, 421–444.

Mackinder, H. J. 1919. *Democratic ideals and reality: A study in the politics of reconstruction.* New York: H. Holt & Company.

Mackinder, H. J. 1943. The round world and the winning of the peace. *Foreign Affairs.*

Minghi, J. V. 1963. Boundary studies in political geography. *Annals of the Association of American Geographers,* 53(3), 407–428.

O'Tuathail, G., & Agnew, J. 1992. Geopolitics and discourse: Practical geopolitical reasoning and American foreign policy. *Political Geography,* 11, 155–175.

Paasi, A. 2009. Political boundaries. *International Encyclopedia of Human Geography.* Linninmaa, Finland: Elsevier.

Ratzel, F. 1969. Laws of the spatial growth of states. In R. E. Kasperson & J. Minghi, eds., *The structure of political geography,* trans. R. L. Bolin. Chicago: Aldine.

Ritzer, G. 2007. *The Blackwell companion to globalization.* Malden, MA: Blackwell Publishing.

Sack, R. D. 1986. *Human territoriality: Its theory and history.* Cambridge: Cambridge University Press.

White, G. 2000. *Nationalism and territory: Constructing group identity in southeastern Europe.* Lanham, MD: Rowman & Littlefield.

Chapter 4 Population

Boserup, E. 1966. *The conditions of agricultural growth: The economics of agrarian change under population pressure.* Chicago: Aldine Publishing Co.

Ehrlich, P. 1983. *The population bomb.* New York: Ballantine Books.

Gould, P. 1993. *The slow plague: A geography of the AIDS pandemic.* New York: Blackwell.

Keil, R., & Ali, S. H. 2006. The avian flu: Some lessons learned from the 2003 SARS outbreak in Toronto. *AREA,* 38(3), 107–109.

Malthus, T. R. 1976. *An essay on the principle of population.* A. Appelman, ed. New York: W.W. Norton.

Paddock, W., & Paddock, P. 1967. *Famine 1975! America's decision, who will survive?* Boston: Little, Brown & Co.

Population Reference Bureau. *1997 World Population Data Sheet.* Washington, DC: Author.

Robson, E. 2004. Hidden child workers: Young carers in Zimbabwe. *Antipode,* 36(5), 227–248.

Sibley, D. 1995. *Geographies of exclusion: Society and difference in the west.* London: Routledge.

Chapter 5 Migration

Bissoondath, N. 1994. *Selling illusions: The cult of multiculturalism in Canada.* Toronto: Penguin.

Blaut, J. 1993. *A colonizer's model of the world: Geographical diffusionism and Eurocentric history.* New York: Guilford Press.

Boyle, P. 2002. Population geography: Transnational women on the move. *Progress in Human Geography,* 26(4), 531–543.

Cresswell, T. 2006. *On the move: Mobility in the modern western world.* London and New York: Routledge.

Dallaire, R. 2003. *Shake hands with the devil: The failure of humanity in Rwanda.* Toronto: Random House Canada.

Dittmer, J. 2004. The Soufrière hills volcano and the postmodern landscapes of Mont-Serrat. *FOCUS on Geography,* 1–7.

Gilbert, M. 1974. *Atlas of the Arab-Israeli conflict.* New York: Macmillan.

Hill, L. 2007. *Book of negroes.* Toronto: Harper Collins.

Kobayashi, A. 1993. Multiculturalism: Representing a Canadian institution. In *Place/culture/representation,* J. Duncan and D. Ley, eds. London/New York: Routledge.

Lawson, V. 1998. Hierarchical households and gendered migration in Latin America: Feminist extensions to migration research. *Progress in Human Geography,* 22, 39–53.

Mountz, A. 2004. Embodying the nation state: Canada's response to human smuggling. *Political Geography,* 23, 323–345.

National Commission on Terrorism. 2004. *9/11 commission report.* www.911commission.gov/report/911Report.pdf. Last accessed March 31, 2015.

Office of the United Nations High Commissioner for Human Rights. 1951. *United Nations Convention relating to the Status of Refugees.* http://www.ohchr.org/EN/ProfessionalInterest/Pages/StatusOfRefugees.aspx. Last accessed March 29, 2015.

Ravenstein, E. 1885. The laws of migration. *Journal of the Statistical Society,* 48, 167–235.

Schama, S. 2006. *Rough crossings: Britain, the slaves, and the American Revolution.* New York: Ecco.

Stein, J. G. (1993). The political economy of security agreements: The linked costs of failure at Camp David. In *Double-edged diplomacy,* P. B. Evans et al., eds., 77–103. Berkeley: University of California Press.

Stiell, B., & England, K. 1997. Domestic distinctions: constructing difference among paid domestic workers in Toronto. *Gender, Place and Culture,* 4(3), 339–359.

Taylor, P. J., & Flint, C. 2007. *Political geography: World-economy, nation-state and locality,* 5th ed. Upper Saddle River, NJ: Pearson Education, 2007.

Toronto Star. 2009. Canadians not interested in 'home children' apology: Minister. http://www.thestar.com/news/canada/2009/11/16/canadians_not_interested_in_home_children_apology_minister.html. Last accessed March 29, 2015.

United Nations High Commissioner for Refugees. 2013. *The state of the world's refugees.* New York: Oxford.

Weiner, E. 2007. *Debunking global migration myths.* National Public Radio. http://www.npr.org/templates/story/story.php?storyId=10768751. Last accessed March 29, 2015.

Chapter 6 Human-Environment Relations

Blaikie, P. M., & Brookfield, H. 1987. *Land degradation and society.* London: Methuen.

Brown, L., & Wolf, E. 1984. *Soil erosion: Quiet crisis in the world economy.* Washington, DC, Paper No. 60.

Castree, N. 2005. *Nature.* London: Routledge.

Castree, N., Kitchen, R., & Rodgers, A. 2013. Sustainability. In *A dictionary of human geography.* Oxford: Oxford University Press.

Cosgrove, D., & Daniels, S. 1988. *The iconography of landscape: Essays on the symbolic representation, design, and use of past environment.* Cambridge: Cambridge University Press.

Crosby, A. 1972. *The Columbian Exchange: Biological and cultural consequences of 1492.* Westport, CT: Greenwich Publishing Co.

Harper, C. L. 2008. Religion and environmentalism, *The Kripke Center Supplement Series.* http://moses.creighton.edu/jrs/toc/SS03.html. Last accessed March 31, 2015.

Houghton, J. T., ed. 2001. Appendix I—Glossary. In *Climate change 2001: The scientific basis. Contribution of working group I to the third assessment report of the Intergovernmental Panel on Climate Change.* Cambridge: Cambridge University Press.

Intergovernmental Panel on Climate Change. 2007. *Climate change 2007: synthesis report. Contribution of working Groups I, II and III to the fourth assessment report of the Intergovernmental Panel on Climate Change* [Core Writing Team, Pachauri, R.K and Reisinger, A., eds.]. Geneva: Author. http://www.ipcc.ch/publications_and_data/publications_and_data_reports.shtml. Last accessed March 31, 2015.

Kates, R. W. 1994. Sustaining life on the earth. *Scientific American,* 271, 114–122.

Micklin, P., & Aladin, N. 2008. Reclaiming the Aral Sea. *Scientific American Magazine,* April.

Pimm, S., & Jenkins, C. 2005. Sustaining the variety of life. *Scientific American*, September, 66–73.

Simmons, I. G. 1996. Humanity's resources. In *The companion encyclopedia of geography: The environment and humankind*, I. Douglas, R. Huggett, & M. Robinson, eds. New York: Routledge.

Smith, N. 1984. *Uneven development: Nature, capital and the production of space*. New York: Blackwell.

United Nations Framework Convention on Climate Change. 1992. *Article 1, Definitions*. https://unfccc.int/files/essential_background/background_publications_htmlpdf/application/pdf/conveng.pdf. Last accessed March 31, 2015.

Williams, R. 1988. *Keywords: A vocabulary of culture and society.* Glasgow: Fortana Press.

Chapter 7 Social Geographies—Identities and Place

Anderson, B. 1991. *Imagined communities*. New York: Verso.

Bauder, H., & Sharpe, B. 2002. Residential segregation of visible minorities in Canada's gateway cities. *Canadian Geographer/Le Géographe Canadien*, 46(3), 204–222.

Blaut, J. 1993. *The colonizer's model of the world: Geographical diffusionism and Eurocentric history.* New York: Guilford Press.

Boyd, M., Goldmann, G., & White, P. 2000. Race in the Canadian census. In *Race and racism: Canada's challenge*, L. Driedger & S. S. Halli, eds. Montreal & Kingston, ON: McGill-Queen's University Press, 33–54.

Castree, N., Kitchen, R., & Rodgers, A. 2013. Race. In *Oxford dictionary of human geography*. Oxford: Oxford University Press.

Crang, M. 2011. Virtual life. In *A companion to social geography*, V. J. Del Casino, M. Thomas, P. Cloke, R. Panelli, eds. Malden, MA: Wiley-Blackwell.

Curtis, A., Warren Mills, J., & Leitner, M. 2007. Katrina and vulnerability: The geography of stress. *Journal of Health Care for the Poor and Underserved*, 18, 315–330.

Curtis, J. R. 2004. Barrio space and place in southeast Los Angeles, California. In *Hispanic spaces, Latino places: Community and cultural diversity in contemporary America*, Daniel D. Arreola, ed. Austin: University of Texas Press.

Domosh, M., & Seager, J. 2001. *Putting women in place: Feminist geographers make sense of the world*. New York: Guilford Press.

Elder, G., Knopp, L., & Nast, H. 2003. Sexuality and space. In *Geography in America at the dawn of the 21st century*, G. L. Gaile and C. J. Willmott, eds. New York: Oxford University Press.

Florida, R. 2002. *The rise of the creative class: And how it's transforming work, leisure, community and everyday life.* New York: Basic Books.

Forest, B. 2002. A new geography of identity? Race, ethnicity and American citizenship. In *American space/American place: Geographies of the United States on the threshold of a new century*, J. Agnew and J. Smith, eds. Edinburgh: University of Edinburgh Press, 231–263.

Gates, G., & J. Ost. 2004. *The gay and lesbian atlas*. Washington, DC: Urban Institute Press.

Gotham, K. F. 2002. Marketing Mardi Gras: commodification, spectacle and the political economy of tourism in New Orleans. *Urban Studies,* 39(10), 1735–1756.

Hall, S. 1995. New cultures for old. In *A Place in the world? Places, cultures, and globalization*, D. Massey and P. Jess, eds. New York: Oxford University Press.

Hancock, P. 2000. The lived experience of female factory workers in rural West Java. *Labour and Management in Development Journal,* 1(1), 1–18.

Holloway, S. L., & Valentine, G. 2000. *Children's geographies. Playing, living, learning.* London: Routledge.

Johnson Jr., J. H., Jones, C. K., Farrell, W. C., & Oliver, M. L. 1992. The Los Angeles rebellion: A retrospective in view. *Economic Development Quarterly,* 6(4), 356–372.

Lee, H. L. 2007. Speech to Parliament on reading of Penal Code (Amendment) Bill. Singapore, 22 October.

Massey, D., & Jess, P. 1995. Places and cultures in an uneven world. In *A place in the world? Places, cultures, and globalization*, D. Massey and P. Jess, eds. New York: Oxford University Press.

Nash, C. J. 2006. Toronto's gay village (1969 to 1982). Plotting the politics of gay identity. *Canadian Geographer* (March) 50(1), 1–16.

Native Women's Association of Canada. 2010. Sisters in spirit: 2010 research findings. http://www.nwac.ca/files/reports/2010_NWAC_SIS_Report_EN.pdf. Last accessed March 31, 2015.

Oberhauser, A. M., Rubinoff, D., De Bres, K., Mains, S., & Pope, C. 2003. Geographic perspectives on women. In *Geography in America at the dawn of the 21st century*, G. L. Gaile and C. J. Willmott, eds. New York: Oxford University Press.

Oppong, J. R. 1998. A vulnerability interpretation of the geography of HIV/AIDS in Ghana, 1986–1995. *The Professional Geographer,* 50, 437–448.

Oswin, N. 2008. Critical geographies and the uses of sexuality: Deconstructing queer space. *Progress in Human Geography*, 32(1), 89–103.

Peake, L., & Ray, B. 2001. Racializing the Canadian landscape: Whiteness, uneven geographies and social justice. *Canadian Geographer/Le Géographe Canadien*, 45(1), 180–186.

Rose, G. 1995. Place and identity: A sense of place. In *A place in the world? Places, cultures, and globalization*, D. Massey and P. Jess, eds. New York: Oxford University Press.

Rose, H. M., & McClain, P. D. 1990. *Race, place and risk: Black homicide in urban america*. Albany: State University of New York Press.

Said, E. 1978. *Orientalism*. London: Routledge.

Smith, S. J., Pain, R., Marston, S. A., & Jones III, J. P. 2009. *The SAGE handbook of social geographies*. London: SAGE.

Turkle, S. 1995. *Life on the screen : identity in the age of the Internet*. New York: Simon & Schuster.

Winchester, H., Kong, L., & Dunn, K. 2003. *Landscapes: Ways of imagining the world*. New York: Prentice Hall.

Winders, J. 2009. Race. In *International Encyclopedia of Human Geography*, Elsevier (online).

Chapter 8 Local Culture, Popular Culture, and Cultural Landscapes

Bowen, D. 1997. Lookin' for Margaritaville: Place and imagination in Jimmy Buffett's songs. *Journal of Cultural Geography*, 16(2), 99–109.

Bowen, D. 2002. Agricultural expansion in northern Alberta. *Geographical Review*, 92, 503–526.

Domosh, M. 1988. The symbolism of the skyscraper. *Journal of Urban History*, 14(3), 321–345.

Harrison, S. 1999. Cultural boundaries. *Anthropology Today*, 15(5), 10–13.

Harvey, D. 1989. *The condition of postmodernity: An enquiry into the origins of cultural change*. Cambridge, MA: Blackwell.

Henderson, S. 2008. Canadian content regulations and the formation of a national scene. *Popular Music*, 27, 307–315.

Kraybill, D., & Bowman, C. 2001. *On the backroad to heaven: Old order Hutterites, Mennonites, Amish, and brethren*. Baltimore: Johns Hopkins University Press.

Merchants of Cool. 2001. www.pbs.org/wgbh/pages/frontline/shows/cool/. Last accessed March 31, 2015.

Mitchell, D. 1995. There's no such thing as culture: Towards a reconceptualization of the idea of culture in geography. *Transactions of the Institute of British Geographers*, 20, 102–116.

Relph, E. C. 1976. *Place and placelessness*. New York: Routledge, Kegan and Paul.

Rosati, C. 2005. The image factory: MTV, geography, and the industrial production of culture. Syracuse University, Ph.D. dissertation.

Rosati, C. 2007. MTV: 360 degrees of the industrial production of culture. *Transactions of the Institute of British Geographers*, 32, 556–575.

Sauer, C. 1925. The morphology of landscape. *University of California Publications in Geography*, 2(2).

Williams, R. 1983. *Keywords: A vocabulary of culture and society*, revised edition. New York: Oxford University Press.

Williams, R. 1989. Culture is ordinary. In *Resources of hope: Culture, democracy, socialism*, R. Gale, ed. New York: Verso.

Chapter 9 Agriculture

Carney, J. A. 1996. Converting the wetlands, engendering the environment: The intersection of gender with agrarian change in Gambia. In *Liberation ecologies*, R. Peet & M. J. Watts, eds. London: Routledge.

Diamond, J. 1997. *Guns, germs and steel: The fates of human societies*. New York: W.W. Norton & Company.

Duckham, A. N., & Masefield, G. B. 2005. *Farming systems of the world*. New York: Praeger.

Klooster, D. J. 2005. Producing social nature in the Mexican countryside. *Cultural Geographies*, 12, 321–344.

Nord, M., & Hopwood, H. 2008. A comparison of household food security in Canada and the United States. *Economic Research Report 56488*, United States Department of Agriculture, Economic Research Service.

Olson, C. M. 1999. Nutrition and health outcomes associated with food insecurity and hunger. *The Journal of Nutrition Online*, 129(2), 521S–524S.

Polak, P. 2005. The big potential of small farms. *Scientific American*, September, 84–91.

Sauer, C. O. 1969. *Agricultural origins and dispersals*, 2nd rev. ed. Cambridge, MA: MIT Press.

Shiva, V. 1991. The violence of the green revolution: Ecological degradation and political conflict in Punjab. *The Ecologist*, 21(2), 57–60.

Smithers, J., Johnson, P., & Joseph, A. 2004. The dynamics of family farming in North Huron County; Part II: farm–community interactions. *The Canadian Geographer*, 48(2), 209–224.

Spencer, J. E., & Thomas, W. H. 1969. *Cultural geography: Introduction to our humanized earth*. Cartography by R. E. Winter. New York: Wiley.

United Nations Office on Drugs and Crime. 2002. United Nations calls for greater assistance to Afghans in fight against opium cultivation. http://www. unodc.org/unodc/press_release_2002-10-24_1.html. Last accessed November 2005.

Von Thünen, J. H. 1966. *Der isolierte staat.* Trans. C. M. Wartenberg. In *Von Thünen's isolated state*, P. Hall, ed. Elmsford, NY: Pergamon.

Chapter 10 Urban Geography

Aiken, S., Mitchell, D., & Staeheli, L. 2004. Urban geography. In *Geography in America at the dawn of the 21st century*, G. L. Gaile and C. J. Willmott, eds. New York: Oxford University Press.

Bourne, L., & Simmons, J. 2002. The dynamics of the Canadian urban system. In *International handbook of urban systems*, H. S. Geyer, ed. Cheltenham UK: E. Elgar, 391–418.

Bunting, T., & Filion, P. 2010. Canadian cities in transition: New directions in the 21st century (fully revised 4th ed.). Toronto: Oxford University Press.

Burgess, E. 1925. The growth of the city. In *The city*, R. Park et al., eds. Chicago: University of Chicago Press, 47–62.

Castells, M. 2000. *The rise of the network society*, 2nd ed. Malden, MA: Blackwell Publishing.

Christaller, W. 1950. The foundations of spatial organization in Europe. *Frankfurter Geographische Hefte*, 25.

Christaller, W. 1966 [orig. 1933]. *The central places in southern Germany.* Trans. C. Baskin. Englewood Cliffs, NJ: Prentice-Hall.

Congress for New Urbanism. *Charter of the New Urbanism.* http://www.cnu.org/charter. Last accessed March 31, 2015.

Ford, L. R. 1994. *Cities and buildings: Skyscrapers, skid rows, and suburbs.* Baltimore, MD: Johns Hopkins University Press.

Grant, J. 2009. Theory and practice in planning the suburbs: Challenges to implementing new urbanism, smart growth, and sustainability principles. *Planning Theory and Practice*, 10(1), 11–33.

Grant, R., & Nijman, J. 2002. Globalization and the corporate geography of cities in the less-developed world. *Annals of the Association of American Geographers*, 92(2), 320–341.

Griffin, E., & Ford, L. 1980. A model of Latin American city structure. *Geographical Review*, 70(4), 397–422.

Harvey, D. 1997. The new urbanism and the communitarian trap. *Harvard Design Magazine*, 1–3.

Hoyt, H. 1939. *The structure and growth of residential neighborhoods in American cities.* Washington, DC: U.S. Federal Housing Administration.

Kesteloot, C., & Cortie, C. 1988. Housing Turks and Moroccans in Brussels and Amsterdam: The difference between private and public markets. *Urban Studies*, 35(10), 1835–1853.

McGee, T. G. 1967. *The Southeast Asian city: A social geography of the primate cities of Southeast Asia.* New York: Praeger.

Roost, F. 1998. Recreating the city as entertainment center: The media industry's role in transforming Potsdamer Platz and Times Square. *Journal of Urban Technology*, 5(3), 1–21.

Saunders, D. 2012. *Arrival city: How the largest migration in history is reshaping our world.* New York: Pantheon Books.

Skaburskis, A., & Mok, D. 2006. Cities as land markets. In *Canadian cities in transition*, 3rd ed., T. Bunting and P. Filion, eds. Don Mills, ON: Oxford University Press.

Taylor, P. J., & Lang, R. E. 2004. The shock of the new: 100 concepts describing recent urban change. *Environment and Planning A*, 36(6), 951–958.

Walks, R. A., & Bourne, L. S. 2006. Ghettos in Canada's cities? Racial segregation, ethnic enclaves and poverty concentration in Canadian urban areas. *Canadian Geographer*, 50(3), 273–297.

Chapter 11 Development

Dottridge, M. 2002. Trafficking in children in West and Central Africa. *Gender and Development*, 10(1), 38–42.

The Economist. 2002. With the wolf at the door. May 30.

Herbst, J. 1989. The creation and maintenance of national boundaries in Africa. *International Organization*, 43(4), 673–692.

Padgett, T. 2010. New Orleans' lower ninth: forgotten victim? *Time*, August 27.

Pankaj, G., & Altman, S. A. 2014. *DHL Global Connectedness Index.* Accessed at www.dhl.com/content/dam/Campaigns/gci2014/downloads/dhl_gci_2014_study_high.pdf.

Ravenhill, J. 1988. Redrawing the map of Africa. In *The precarious balance: State and society in Africa*, D. Rothchild and N. Chazan, eds. Boulder, CO: Westview Press.

Rivoli, P. 2005. *The travels of a t-shirt in the global economy: An economist examines the markets, power, and politics of world trade.* New York: John Wiley & Sons.

Rostow, W. W. 1971. *The stages of economic growth*, 2nd ed. New York: Cambridge University Press.

Schindler, D. 2010. Tar sands need solid science. *Nature*, 468, 499–501.

Taylor, P. J. 1992. Understanding global inequalities: A world-systems approach. *Geography*, 77, 10–21.

Wallerstein, I. 1983. *Historical capitalism.* London: Verso.

Chapter 12 Transportation

Anable, J., & Gatersleben, B. 2005. All work and no play? The role of instrumental and affective factors in work and leisure journeys by different travel modes. *Transportation Research Part A*, 39, 163–181.

Andrey, J. 2010. Long-term trends in weather-related crash risks. *Journal of Transport Geography*, 18(2), 247–258.

Appleyard, D. 1981. *Livable streets*. Berkeley, CA: University of California Press.

Banister, D., Pucher, J., & Lee-Gosselin, M. 2007. Making sustainable transport politically and publicly acceptable. In *Institutions and sustainable transport: Regulatory reform in advanced economies*, P. Rietveld and R. Stough, eds. Cheltenham, England: Edward Elgar Publishing, 17–50.

Buliung, R., Mitra, R., & Faulkner, G. 2009. Active school transportation in the Greater Toronto Area, Canada: An exploration of trends in space and time (1986–2006). *Preventive Medicine*, 48(6), 507–512.

Centre for Sustainable Transportation (CST). 1998. *Definition and vision of sustainable transportation*. Toronto: Author.

Davis, D. F., & Lorenzkowski, B. 1998. A platform for gender tensions: Women working and riding on Canadian urban public transit in the 1940s. *Canadian Historical Review*, 79(3), 431–465.

Gilbert, R., & Perl, A. 2005. *Energy and transport futures*. Report prepared for the National Round Table on the Environment and the Economy. http://www.gttconline.com/files/nrtee_rpt_10.pdf. Last accessed March 31, 2015.

Goetz, A. 2009. Intermodality. In *International encyclopaedia of human geography*, R. Kitchin and N. Thrift, eds. Oxford, UK: Elsevier, 529–535.

Gregory, D., ed. 2009. *The dictionary of human geography*. Malden, MA: Blackwell.

Hanson, S., & Giuliano, G. 2004. *The geography of urban transportation*, 3rd ed. New York: Guilford Press.

Hine, J. 2009. Transport and social exclusion. In *International encyclopedia of human geography*, R. Kitchin and N. Thrift, eds. Oxford, UK: Elsevier, 429–434.

Hiscock, R., Macintyre, S., Kearns, A., & Ellaway, A. 2002. Means of transport and ontological security: Do cars provide psycho-social benefits to their users? *Transportation Research Part D*, 7, 119–135.

Hodge, G. 2003. *Planning Canadian communities: An introduction to the principles, practice and participants*. Toronto: Nelson Thomson Learning.

International Transport Forum (ITF). 2010. New data on major trends in the transport sector. (Press Release), Paris, France, May 19, 2010. http://www.internationaltransportforum.org. Last accessed March 31, 2015.

Keeling, D. J. 2007. Transportation geography: New directions on well-worn trails. *Progress in Human Geography*, 31(2), 217–225.

Kenworthy, J. R., & Laube, F. B. 1999. Patterns of automobile dependence in cities: an international overview of key physical and economic dimensions with some implications for urban policy. *Transportation research part A: policy and practice*, 33(7–8), 691–723.

Knowles, R. D. 2009. Transport geography. In *International encyclopedia of human geography*, R. Kitchin and N. Thrift, eds. Oxford, UK: Elsevier, 441–451.

Levinson, M. 2006. *The box: How the shipping container made the world smaller and the world economy bigger*. Princeton: Princeton University Press.

Litman, T. 2003. Social inclusion as a transport planning issue in Canada. *Contribution to the FIA Foundation G7 Comparison Paper*, presented at the European Transport Conference held in Strassbourg in June, 2003.

Litman, T. 2011. *Evaluating public transit benefits and costs: Best practices guidebook*. Victoria, BC: Victoria Transport Policy Institute. http://www.vtpi.org/tranben.pdf.

Lorch, B. J. 2004. Big boxes, power centres and the evolving retail landscape of Winnipeg: A geographical perspective. *Research and Working Paper #43*. Winnipeg: University of Winnipeg, Institute of Urban Studies.

Martellozzo, F., Ramankutty, N., Hall, R. J., Price, D. T., Purdy, B., & Friedl, M. A. 2014. Urbanization and the loss of prime farmland: a case study in the Calgary-Edmonton corridor of Alberta. *Regional Environmental Change*, 1–13.

Marzoughi, R. 2011. Teen travel in the Greater Toronto Area: A descriptive analysis of trends from 1986 to 2006 and the policy implications. *Transport Policy*, 18(4), 623–630.

McCalla, R. J., Slack, B., & Comtois, C. 2004. Dealing with globalisation at the regional and local level: the case of contemporary containerization. *The Canadian Geographer*, 48(4), 473–487.

Mensah, J., & Ironside, R. G. 1993. Employment opportunities of the urban poor: An assessment of spatial constraints and the mismatch hypothesis. In *Public issues: A geographical perspective*, J. Andrey and J. G. Nelson, eds. Waterloo, ON: University of Waterloo, Faculty of Environmental Studies, Department of Geography, 111–131.

Musonda, H. M. 2006. *The rapid assessment of rural transport services in Luapula Province, Zambia: Draft report.* Report prepared for the World Bank's Sub Saharan Africa Transport Policy Program.

Myers, J. n.d. Pedalling to a sustainable future. *U Magazine,* accessed at http://arts.ucalgary.ca/artsnow/pedalling-sustainable-future on March 31, 2015.

Newman, P., & Kenworthy, J. 1999. *Sustainability and cities: Overcoming automobile dependence.* Washington, DC: Island Press.

Perry, C. A. 1929. The neighborhood unit: A scheme of arrangement for the family-life community. In *Regional study of New York and its environs*, Volume VII. New York: Port of New York Authority, 2–140.

Pucher, J., & Buehler, R. 2008. Making cycling irresistible: Lessons from The Netherlands, Denmark and Germany. *Transport reviews*, 28(4), 495–528.

Riley, K., Craig, H., Poston, M., Saunders, L., & Flynn, A. 2000. *Effective schooling in rural Africa* (Project report 1). UK: Authors.

Ritzer, G. 2007. Introduction. In *The Blackwell companion to globalization*, G. Ritzer, ed. Malden, MA: Blackwell Publishing, 1–13.

Steg, L. 2005. Car use: lust and must. Instrumental, symbolic and affective motives for car use. *Transportation Research Part A*, 39, 147–162.

Stein, C. 1969. *Toward new towns for America.* Cambridge, MA: MIT Press.

Toronto Board of Trade, 2003. *A strategy for rail-based transit.* Central Ontario Smart Growth Panel Report.

Transport Canada. 2011. *Canadian motor vehicle collision statistics.* Ottawa: Author. http://www.tc.gc.ca/media/documents/roadsafety/TrafficCollisionStatisitcs_2011.pdf. Last accessed March 18, 2015.

Transportation Association of Canada (TAC). 1993. *A new vision for urban transportation.* Ottawa. http://tac-atc.ca/sites/tac-atc.ca/files/site/doc/resources/briefing-newvisionurban.pdf.

Victoria Transport Policy Institute. 2011. *Fuel taxes: Increasing fuel taxes and fees.* Victoria, BC. http://www.vtpi.org/tdm/tdm17.htm. Last accessed March 31, 2015.

Vodden, K., Smith, D., Eaton, F., & Mayhew, D. 2007. *Analysis and estimation of the social cost of motor vehicle collisions in Ontario.* Report prepared for Ministry of Transportation. http://www.tc.gc.ca/media/documents/roadsafety/TP14800E.pdf. Last accessed March 31, 2015.

Vowles, T. M. 2009. Aviation. In *International encyclopedia of human geography*, R. Kitchin and N. Thrift, eds. Oxford, UK: Elsevier, 257–264.

Wener, R., Evans, G. W., & Boately, P. 2005. Commuting stress: Psychophysiological effects of the trip and spillover into the workplace. *Transportation Research Record 1924*, TRB, 112–117.

Winner, L. 1980. Do artifacts have politics? *Daedalus*, 109(1), 121–136.

Wynd, S. 1999. Education, schooling and fertility in Niger. In C. Heward and S. Bunwaree, eds. *Gender, education and development: Beyond access to empowerment.* London: Zed Books Ltd, 101–116.

Chapter 13 Industry and Services

Boyer, K. & England, K. 2009. Women's work: The feminization and shifting meanings of clerical work. *Journal of Social History*, 43(2), Winter 2009, 307–340.

Castells, M., Hall, P., & Hutriyk, J. 1996. Technopoles of the world: The making of 21st century industrial complexes. *The Sociological Review*, 43(4), 895–900.

Cowen, D. 2010. Containing insecurity: US port cities and the "War on Terror." In S. Graham, ed., *Disrupted cities: When infrastructure fails.* New York and London: Routledge, 69–84.

Weber, A. 1929 [1909]. *Theory of the location of industries.* Trans. C. Friedrich. Chicago: University of Chicago Press.

INDEX